1993

YALE UNIVERSITY PRESS
PELICAN HISTORY OF ART

Founding Editor: Nikolaus Pevsner

Henry-Russell Hitchcock

ARCHITECTURE: NINETEENTH AND TWENTIETH CENTURIES

Henry-Russell Hitchcock, born in Boston, Massachusetts, in 1903, was educated at Harvard University. A professor of the history of art at Smith College in Northampton, Massachusetts, from 1949 to 1968, he was for six years also Director of the Smith College Museum of Art, and later Adjunct Professor at the Institute of Fine Arts of New York University. He taught in addition at Wesleyan University, the Massachusetts Institute of Technology, Yale University, Harvard University, and Cambridge University. He was a president of the Society of Architectural Historians and of the Victorian Society in America. He published books on many of the subjects with which this book deals: among other things, full monographs on Frank Lloyd Wright and on H. H. Richardson; shorter studies of J. J. P. Oud and of Gaudí; a two-volume work on Early Victorian architecture in Britain; and a short book on the International Style. Thus, in his writings as well as his extensive travels, he dealt at first hand with most of the aspects of the story recounted here. Professor Hitchcock died in 1987, soon after his final revision of this work.

ARCHITECTURE:

NINETEENTH AND TWENTIETH CENTURIES

Henry-Russell Hitchcock

Yale University Press · New Haven and London

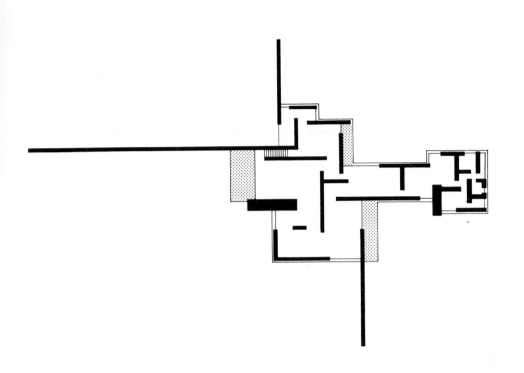

First published 1958 by Penguin Books Ltd
Fourth edition 1977
Bibliography revised 1987
20 19 18 17 16 15 14 13 12 11 10 9 8 7 6 5 4

Set in Monophoto Ehrhardt, and printed in Hong Kong through World Print Ltd

Designed by Gerald Cinamon

ISBN 0-300-05320-7
Library of Congress catalog card number 75-128606

To the memory of A.C. O'M.-W.

CONTENTS

PREFACE TO THE FIRST INTEGRATED EDITION

Despite its considerably modified physical form, this is not a 'new edition', such as may well one day be prepared to succeed the third (hardback) edition, but effectively, if not technically, a re-issue of that third edition of 1968. The very different handling of the illustrations has led to a few substitutions of new copy for old, and even some additions. The death-dates since 1958 of a good many architects have been added, thanks to Adolf Placzek and the staff of the Avery Library. As regards the Bibliography, it should be noted that it is intended to cover only books published by 1967, as is also true of many references, first added in the Notes of the third edition, that are included here.

The first (hardback) edition of 1958 carried acknowledgements running to a full page. Further brief acknowledgements for later assistance were made in the Prefaces of the second edition of 1963 and of the third. To all those thus mentioned I am naturally still most grateful. Perhaps they may, however, after so many years in most cases, forgive the omission here of any renewed expression of individual thanks. There are no new debts of gratitude in connexion with this paperback edition that need mention beyond an expression of my gratification that the editors of the Pelican History of Art selected this book as one of the first in the series to be issued in this format.

H.R.H.
New York, March 1970

PREFACE TO THE SECOND INTEGRATED EDITION

The 1976 edition offers various additions and emendations. The most considerable are in the Bibliography. Very many books that have appeared since 1967 are included, down to the spring of 1976. There are, for example, some seventy individual architects, and a few men who were not architects, newly represented in the Monographs section; and further additions of books on individual countries and some general works. Many other references have been included in the Notes, some of which have been extended, while others are quite new. On the other hand, there has been little substantial revision of the main text, and no actual rewriting

beyond a sentence or two here and there. Minor changes – modified tenses, or modulated emphases affecting some critical or historical implications – from the original writing of the 1950s have been made, this to a rather greater degree than in the first integrated edition of 1971, now superseded.

In the preparation of this edition I had the able assistance of Mosette Broderick. The extension of the Bibliography was largely her work. It will be evident how important that contribution was in updating the book. The emendations of the text are all mine.

H.R.H.
New York, March 1976

The 1987 reprint incorporates one or two emendations to the text, and considerable additional bibliography, covering the years

from 1976 to spring 1986, prepared once again by Mosette Broderick.

ARCHITECTURE:
NINETEENTH AND TWENTIETH CENTURIES

INTRODUCTION

The round numbers of chronology have no necessary significance historically. Centuries as cultural entities often begin and end decades before or after the hundred-year mark. The years around 1800, however, do provide a significant break in the history of architecture, not so much because of any major shift in style at that precise point as because the Napoleonic Wars caused a general hiatus in building production. The last major European style, the Baroque, had been all but dissolved away in most of Europe. The beginnings of several differing kinds of reaction against it – Academic in Italy, Rococo in France, Palladian in England – go back as far as the first quarter of the century; shortly after the mid century there came a more concerted stylistic revolution.

In the forty years between 1750 and 1790 the new style that is called 'Romantic Classicism'[1] took form, producing by the eighties its most remarkable projects, and even before that some executed work of consequence in France and in England. Thus the early nineteenth century inherited the tradition of a completed architectural revolution, and at its very outset was in possession of a style that had been fully mature for more than a decade. The most effective reaction against the Baroque in the second, and even to some extent the third, quarter of the eighteenth century had taken place in England; the later architectural revolution that actually initiated Romantic Classicism centred in France.

Yet Paris was not the original locus of the new style's gestation but rather Rome.[2] From the early sixteenth century Rome had provided the international headquarters from which new ideas in the arts, by no means necessarily originated there, were distributed to the Western world. To Rome came generation after generation of young artists, connoisseurs, and collectors to form their taste and to formulate their aesthetic ideals. Some even settled there for life. From the time of Colbert the French State maintained an academic establishment in Rome for the post-graduate training of artists. Thus French hegemony in the arts of the late seventeenth and early eighteenth centuries was based on a tradition maintained and renewed at Rome. The nationals of other countries came to Rome more informally, and were for the most part supported by their own funds or by private patrons; only in the seventies were young English architects of promise first awarded travelling studentships by George III. In the fifties the number of northern architects studying in Rome notably increased; some of them, beginning with the Scot Robert Mylne (1734–1811) in 1758, won prizes in the competitions held by the Roman Academy of St Luke.[2a]

The initiation of Romantic Classicism was by no means solely in the hands of architects. In the mid-century period of Roman gestation, Winckelmann, Gavin Hamilton, and Piranesi – a German archaeologist, a Scottish painter, and a Venetian etcher – played significant roles, as well as various architects, some *pensionnaires* of the French Academy, others Britons studying on their own. Certain aspects of Romantic Classicism are already boldly presaged in the etchings of G. B. Piranesi (1720–78), not the projects in his *Prima parte di architettura* of 1743 or the plates of ruins in his *Antichità romane* of 1748 but his fanciful *Carceri* dating from the mid 1740s.[2b] On the theoretical side the *Essai sur l'architecture* of M.-A. Laugier (1713–70), which first appeared anonymously in 1752 with further French editions in 1753 and 1755, had something of real consequence to contribute as a basic critique of the dying Baroque style. In simple terms Laugier may be called both a Neo-Classicist and a Functionalist. The bolder functionalist ideas of an Italian Franciscan, Carlo Lodoli (1690–1761), as presented by Francesco Algarotti in his *Lettere sopra l'architettura*, beginning in 1742, and in his *Saggio sopra l'architettura* of 1756 were also influential.[2c] However, despite all the new archaeological treatises inspired by the Roman milieu, of which the first was the *Ruins of Palmyra* published in 1753 by Robert Wood (1717–71), and all the excavations undertaken at Herculaneum over the years 1738–65 and those at Pompeii beginning a decade later, the first architectural manifestations of Romantic Classicism did not occur on Italian soil.

Two buildings begun in the late 1750s, one a very large church in France completed only in 1790, the other a mere garden pavilion in England, may be considered to announce the architectural revolution: Sainte-Geneviève [1] in Paris, desecrated and made a secular Panthéon in 1791 immediately after its completion, was designed by J.-G. Soufflot (1713–80);[3] the Grecian Doric Temple at Hagley Park in Worcestershire is by his contemporary James Stuart (1713–88). The Panthéon remains one of the most conspicuous eighteenth-century monuments of Paris; the Hagley temple is familiar today only to specialists. Yet, historically, Stuart's importance is rather greater than Soufflot's, even though his production was almost negligible in quantity. Born and partly trained in Lyons, Soufflot studied early in Rome and returned to Italy again in the middle of the century. Like several of the French theorists of the day, he had had a lively interest in Gothic construction from his Lyons days. He owed his selection to design Sainte-Geneviève in 1755 to his friendship with Louis XV's Directeur Général des Bâtiments, the Marquis de

Marigny, brother of Mme de Pompadour, whom he had accompanied to Italy in 1749 along with the influential critics C.-N. Cochin and the Abbé Leblanc.

The Scottish architect James Stuart had also gone to Rome, and formed there as early as 1748 the project of visiting Athens; by 1751 he was on his way, accompanied by Nicholas Revett (c. 1721–1804), with whom he proposed to produce an archaeological work on the *Antiquities of Athens*. The publication of the first volume of this epoch-making book was delayed until 1762. In the meantime, in 1758, the year Stuart designed his Hagley temple, J.-D. Leroy (1724–1803) got ahead of him by publishing *Les Ruines des plus beaux monuments de la Grèce*; but the very pictorial and inaccurate plates in this had little practical effect on architecture.

The significance of Stuart's temple may be readily guessed; small though it is, this fabrick was the first example of the re-use of the Greek Doric order[4] – so barbarous, or at least so primitive, in appearance to mid-eighteenth-century eyes – and the first edifice to attempt an archaeological reconstruction of a Greek temple. By the fifties many architects and critics were ready to accept the primacy of Greek over Roman art, if not the necessity for imitating its monuments so closely. With little or no knowledge of Greek architecture several French writers before Laugier had praised it. J. J. Winckelmann also recommended Greek rather than Roman models in his *Gedanken über die Nachahmung der griechischen Werke* (Dresden, 1755) published just before he settled in Rome.[5]

Out of Italian chauvinism Piranesi attacked the theory of Grecian primacy in the arts; yet before his death he had prepared an impressive and influential set of etchings of the Greek temples at Paestum which his son Francesco published. In 1760, moreover, Piranesi decorated the Caffè Inglese in Rome in an Egyptian mode. Eventually Greek precedent in detail all

1. J.-G. Soufflot and others: Paris, Panthéon (Sainte-Geneviève), 1757-90

but superseded Roman for over a generation; yet a real Greek Revival, at best but one aspect of Romantic Classicism, did not mature until after 1800. There was never a widespread Egyptian Revival,[6] but Egyptian inspiration did play a part in crystallizing the aesthetic ideals of Romantic Classicism; it also provided certain characteristic architectural forms, such as the pyramid and the obelisk, and occasional decorative details.

Soufflot's vast cruciform Panthéon provides no such simple paradigm as Stuart's temple. No longer really Baroque, it is by no means thoroughly Romantic Classical. Like most of the work of the leading British architect of Soufflot's generation, Robert Adam (1728-92),[7] the Panthéon must rather be considered stylistically transitional. For example, the purity of the temple portico at the front, in any case Roman not Grecian, is diminished by the breaks at its corners. The tall, hemispherical dome[8] over the crossing is even less antique in character, owing its form to Wren's St Paul's rather than to the Roman Panthéon, which was the favourite domical model for later Romantic Classicists. In the interior, up to the entablatures, the columniation is Classical enough and the structure entirely trabeated[9] – at least in appearance [1]. Above, the domes in the four arms are perhaps Roman, but hardly the pendentives that carry them; these are, of course, a Byzantine structural device revived in the fifteenth century by Brunelleschi. Over the aisles the cutting away of the masonry and the general statical approach, while not producing anything that *looks* very Gothic, illustrate the results of Soufflot's long-pursued study of Gothic vaulting. Many aspects of nineteenth-century architectural development were thus presaged by Soufflot here, as will become very evident later (see Chapters 1-3, 6, and 7).[9a]

The Panthéon was finally finished in the decade after Soufflot's death by his own pupil Maximilien Brébion (1716-c. 1792), J.-B.

Rondelet (1743-1829), a pupil of J.-F. Blondel, and Soufflot's nephew (François, ? - c. 1802). Well before that, a whole generation of French architects had developed a mode, similar to Adam's in England, which is usually called, despite its initiation long before Louis XV's death in 1774, the *style Louis XVI*. Whether or not this mode in its inception owed much to English inspiration is still controversial. In any case it was widely influential outside France from the seventies to the nineties, and in those decades both French-born and French-trained designers were in great demand all over Europe, except in England; and even in England French craftsmen were employed.[9b] With that completely eighteenth-century phase of architectural history this book cannot deal, even though most of the architects who designed for Napoleon the chief public monuments of Paris just after 1800 had first made their reputation under Louis XVI, or even earlier under Louis XV. The *style Louis XVI* and the English 'Adam Style' were over, except in remote provinces and colonial dependencies, by 1800.

In various executed works of the decades preceding the French Revolution it is possible to trace the gradual emergence of mature Romantic Classicism in France, as also to some extent in the executed buildings and, above all, the projects of the younger George Dance (1741-1825)[10] in England. But it is in the extraordinary designs, dating from the eighties, by two French architects a good deal younger than Soufflot that the new ideals were most boldly and completely visualized. In the last thirty-five years these two men, L.-E. Boullée (1728-99) and C.-N. Ledoux (1736-1806), have increasingly been recognized as the first great masters of Romantic Classical *design* if not, in the fullest sense, the first great Romantic Classical *architects*. Boullée built little and few of his projects and none of the manuscript of his book on architecture, both now preserved at the Bibliothèque Nationale, were published – or at least not until modern times.[11] Yet they must have been well known to his many pupils – including J.-N.-L. Durand, who was the author of the most influential architectural treatise of the Empire period – and doubtless to others as well (see Chapters 2 and 3).

Ledoux was from the first a very successful architect, working with assurance and considerable versatility in the *style Louis XVI* from the late sixties, particularly for Mme du Barry. He became an academician and *architecte du roi* in 1773 and spent the next few years at Cassel in Germany. His major executed works are in France, however, and belong to the late seventies and eighties. These are the Besançon Theatre of 1775–84, the buildings of the Royal Saltworks at Arc-Senans near there built in 1775–9 – he had been made *inspecteur* of the establishment in 1771 – and the *barrières* or toll-houses of Paris, which were built in 1784–9

just before the Revolution [2]. In this later work most of the major qualities of his personal style, qualities carried to much greater extremes in his projects, are readily recognizable; his earlier work was of rather transitional character and not at all unlike what many other French architects of his generation were producing.

The massive cube of the exterior of Ledoux's Besançon Theatre, against which an unpedimented Ionic portico is set, can already be found, however, at his Château de Benouville begun in 1768; the later edifice is nevertheless much more rigidly cubical and much plainer in the treatment of the rare openings. In the interior Ledoux substituted for a Baroque horseshoe with tiers of boxes a hemicycle[12] with rising banks of seats and a continuous Greek Doric colonnade around the rear fronting the gallery. The extant constructions at Arc-Senans are less geometrical; instead of the Greek orders

2. C.-N. Ledoux: Paris, Barrière de la Villette, 1784–9

there is much rustication and also various Piranesian touches of visual drama. It was this commission which set Ledoux to designing his 'Ville idéale de Chaux'; that was his greatest achievement, even though it never came even to partial execution, nor could perhaps have been expected to do so, so cosmic was the basic concept.

The *barrières* varied very widely in character; some were very Classical, others in a modest Italianate vernacular; some were rather Piranesian in their bold rustication, others as plain and flat in their forms as the cubic block of the Besançon Theatre. The most significant, however, were notable for the crisp and rigid geometry of their flat-surfaced masses. The extant Barrière de St Martin in the Place de Stalingrad in the La Villette district of Paris consists of a tall cylinder that rises out of a low square block; this is intersected by a T-shaped element projecting as three pedimented porticoes beyond the edges of the square [2]. Although the range of Ledoux's restricted detail here is not very great, it is varied to the point of inconsistency all the same. The rather heavy piers of the porticoes are square, with capitals simplified from the Grecian Doric; yet around the cylinder extends an open arcade of Italian character carried on delicate coupled columns.

Had Ledoux's ideas been known only from his executed work, he would probably not have been especially influential; certainly he would not have attained with posterity the very high reputation that is his today. Inactive at building after the Revolution – he was even imprisoned for a while in the nineties – he concentrated on the publication of his designs both executed and projected. His book *L'Architecture considérée sous le rapport de l'art, des mœurs et de la législation* appeared in 1804, and a second edition was published by Daniel Ramée (1806–87) in 1846–7.[12a] This book has a long and fascinating text which is sociological as much as it is architectural; but it is in its plates, both of

executed work and projects, that Ledoux's originality can best be appreciated. By no means all of his ideas, known before the Revolution to his pupils and undoubtedly to many others as well, passed into the general repertory of Romantic Classicism; some of the most extreme were hardly buildable. The 'House for Rural Guards' is a free-standing sphere, a form that he utilized as space rather than mass in the interior of a project for a Columbarium. For the 'Coopery', the coopers' products dictated the target-like shape [3]. The 'House for the Directors of the Loue River' is also a cylinder set horizontally, but a much more massive one, through which the whole flood of the river was to pour to the thorough discomfort, one would imagine, of the inhabitants. Even where the forms are more conventional, as in the project for the church of his 'Ville idéale' of Chaux – a purified version of Soufflot's Panthéon: cruciform, temple-porticoed, and with a Roman saucer dome – or for the bank there – a peristylar rectangle with high, plain attic, flanked at the corners by detached cubic lodges – the clarity and originality of his formal thinking is very evident, and was evidently influential well before his book actually appeared in 1804. Masses are of simple geometrical shapes, discrete and boldly juxtaposed; walls are flat and as little broken as possible, the few necessary openings mere rectangular holes. Minor features are repeated without variation of rhythm in regular reiterative patterns; the top surfaces of the masses, whether flat, sloping, or rounded, are considered as bounding planes, not modelled plastically in the Baroque way.[13]

Much of this is common to the projects of Boullée, more widely known than Ledoux's in the eighties because of his many pupils. The simple geometrical forms, the plain surfaces, the reiterative handling of minor features, all are even more conspicuous in his designs and generally presented at a scale so grand as to

3. C.-N. Ledoux: Project for Coopery, c. 1785

approach the megalomaniac [4]. Boullée could be, and often was, more conventionally the Classical Revivalist than Ledoux; he was also perhaps somewhat less bold in using such shapes as the sphere and the cylinder, if rather more addicted than Ledoux to the cube and the pyramid. His inspiration was on occasion actually medieval of a very special South European 'Castellated' order, and he thereby laid the foundations for that more widely eclectic use of the forms of the past which makes the Romantic Classical an eclectic style, not a mere revival of Roman or Greek architecture. Vari-

ous projects of the eighties by younger men, such as Bernard Poyet (1742–1824) and L.-J. Desprez (1743–1804), of whom we will hear again later, were of very similar character.

Both Boullée and Ledoux, but particularly Ledoux, were interested in symbolism. In that sense their architecture was not essentially abstract, despite the extreme geometrical simplicity of their forms, but in their own term *parlante* or expressive and meaningful. So special and personal is most of their symbolism, however, that even when quite obvious, as with the 'Coopery', it was hardly viable for other

4. L.-E. Boullée: Project for City Hall, c. 1785

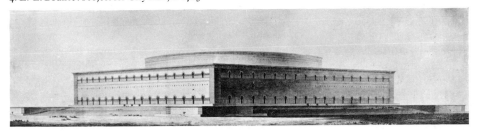

architects. When Ledoux gave to his *Oikema* or 'House of Sexual Education' an actual *plan* of phallic outline (which would be wholly unnoticeable except from the air) he epitomized the hermetic quality of much of his architectural speech. It is understandable that, of the many who accepted his architectural syntax, very few really attempted to speak his language. Such symbolism belonged on the whole to an early stage of Romantic Classicism; after 1800 architectural speech was generally of a rather less recondite order. Yet to each of the different vocabularies employed by Romantic Classicists – Grecian, Egyptian, Italian, Castellated, etc. – some sort of allusive meaning was commonly attached. Thus a restricted and codified eclecticism provided, as it were, the equivalent of a system of musical keys that could be chosen according to a conventional rule when designing different types of buildings.

One cannot properly say that international Romantic Classicism derives to any major degree from Ledoux and Boullée; one can only say that their projects of the eighties epitomized most dramatically the final ending of the Baroque and the crystallization of the style that succeeded it. Many French architects of the generation of Poyet and Desprez, however, such as J.-J. Ramée, Pompon, A.-L.-T. Vaudoyer, L.-P. Baltard, Belanger, Grandjean de Montigny, Damesme, and Durand (to mention only those whose names will recur later) came close to rivalling even the grandest visions of Ledoux and Boullée in projects prepared in the nineties.[14] After such exalted work on paper, the buildings actually executed by this generation of Romantic Classicists often seem rather tame. So also were the glorious social schemes of the political revolutionaries much diluted by the functioning governments of Consulate and Empire before and after 1800.

Only in England did the decades preceding the French Revolution produce any development in architecture at all comparable in significance to what was taking place then in France. But there also it is the projects rather than the executed work of Dance – of which very little remains except his early London church of All Hallows, London Wall, of 1765-7 – that modern scholars have now come to realize led most definitely away from the transitional 'Adam Style' towards Romantic Classicism. His Piranesian Newgate Prison, begun in 1769, was demolished in 1902. By 1790, both in France and in England, the new ideas had taken firm root, however, and other countries had not been slow to essay the mature style once it had been fully adumbrated.

The fact that the nineteenth century began with much of Europe under the hegemony of a a French Empire does not quite justify calling the particular phase of Romantic Classicism with which the nineteenth century opens *Empire*, although this is common usage in most European countries. Yet the prestige of Napoleon's rule, and indeed its actual extent, ensured around 1800 the continuance of that French leadership in architecture which began over a century earlier under Louis XIV. Beyond the boundaries of Napoleon's realm and the lands of his nominees and his allies, moreover, French émigrés carried the new architectural ideas of the last years of the monarchy – for many of them were revolutionaries in the arts, although like Ledoux politically unacceptable to the leaders of the Revolution in France. Even in the homeland of Napoleon's principal opponents, the English, the prestige of French taste, high in the eighties, hardly declined with the Napoleonic wars. The mature Romantic Classicism of England in the last decade of the old century and the first of the new is certainly full of French ideas, even though it is not always clear exactly how they were transmitted across the Channel in war-time.

If Romantic Classicism, the nearly universal style with which nineteenth-century architecture began, was predominantly French in origin and in its continuing ideals and standards, the same decades that saw it reach maturity also saw the rise of another major movement in the arts that was definitely English. The 'Picturesque', a critical concept that had been increasing in authority for two generations in England, received the dignity of a capital P in the 1790s. The term Romantic Classicism is a twentieth-century historian's invention, attempting by its own contradictoriness to express the ambiguity of the dominant mode of this period in the arts; the term Picturesque, on the other hand, was most widely used and the concept most thoroughly examined just before and just after 1800 (see Chapters 1 and 6).

To the twentieth century, on the whole, the aesthetic standards of Romantic Classicism – or perhaps one should rather say the visual results – have been widely acceptable. The results of the application of Picturesque principles in architecture, on the other hand, have not been so generally admired; indeed, until lately the more clearly and unmistakably buildings realized Picturesque ideals, the less was usually the esteem in which they were held by posterity. On the whole, in architecture if not in landscape design, the twentieth century has preferred to see the manifestations of the Picturesque around 1800 as aberrations from a norm considered primarily to have been a 'Classical Revival'. As the adjectival aspect of the term Romantic Classicism makes evident, however, the Classicism of the end of the eighteenth century and the beginning of the nineteenth was not at all the same as that of the High Renaissance, nor even that of the Academic Reaction of the early and middle decades of the eighteenth century. Romantic Classicism aimed not so much towards the 'Beautiful', in the sense of Aristotle and the eighteenth-century aestheticians, as towards what had been distinguished by Edmund Burke in 1756 as the 'Sublime'.

Posterity has admired in the production of the first decades of the nineteenth century a homogeneity of style which is in fact even more illusory than that of earlier periods. Horrified by the chaos of later nineteenth-century eclecticism, two twentieth-century generations, opposed in almost every other aspect of taste, often praised architects and patrons of the years before and after 1800 for a consistency that was by no means really theirs. In some ways, and not unimportant ways, the history of architecture within the period covered by this volume seemed to have come full circle so that the art historian Emil Kaufmann in 1933 actually wrote a book entitled *Von Ledoux bis Le Corbusier*. Kaufmann did not live quite long enough to realize how far from the spheres and cubes of the Ledolcian ideal the revolutionary twentieth-century architect would move in his later years (see Chapter 23); for Le Corbusier's church at Ronchamp [324], completed in 1955 after Kaufmann's death, seemed more in accord with extreme eighteenth-century illustrations of the Picturesque than with characteristic monuments of Romantic Classicism. Yet in the early works of the American Frank Lloyd Wright in the 1890s and those of the German Mies van der Rohe twenty years later a filiation to early nineteenth-century Classicism can be readily traced; that tradition informed almost the entire production of the French Perret, a good deal of that of the German Behrens, and even some of the work of the Austrians Wagner and Loos (see Chapters 18–21).

Forgetting for the moment the Picturesque, one may profitably set down here some of the characteristics that the aspirations and the achievements of the architects of 1800 share, or seem to share, with those of the architects of over a century later. The preference for simple geometrical forms and for smooth, plain surfaces is common to both, though the earlier men aimed at effects of unbroken mass and the later ones rather at an expression of hollow volume. The protestations of devotion to the 'functional' were similar, if as frequently sophistical in the one case as in the other. The preferred isolation of buildings in space is as evident in the ubiquitous temples of the early nineteenth century as in the towering slabs of the mid twentieth. Monochromy and even monotony in the use of homogeneous wall-surfacing materials and the avoidance of detail in relief was balanced in both periods by an emphasis on direct structural expression, whether the structure be the posts and lintels of a masonry colonnade or the steel or ferro-concrete members of a continuous space-cage. Finally, impersonality and, perhaps even more notably, 'internationality' of expression provided around 1800 a universalized sense of period rather than the flavours of particular nations or regions, just as they did again, up at least to the middle of the present century.

The full flood of Romantic Classicism came late, having been dammed so long by the political and economic turmoil of the last years of the eighteenth century and the first of the nineteenth; it also continued late, in some areas even beyond 1850. But dissatisfaction and revolt also started early; it is not a unique stylistic paradox that the greatest masters of Romantic Classicism were often those who were also most ready to explore the alternative possibilities of the Picturesque (see Chapter 6). The architectural production of the first half of the nineteenth century cannot therefore be presented with any clarity in a single chronological sequence. Parallel architectural events, even strictly contemporary works by the same architect, must be set in their proper places in at least two different sequences of development.

The building production of the early decades of the century has been divided only too readily under various stylistic headings. A Greek Revival, a Gothic Revival, etc., have often been assumed, indeed, to possess individual vitality; in fact, these and other 'revivals' were but aspects either of the dominant Romantic Classical tide or of the Picturesque counter-current (see Chapters 1-5 and Chapter 6, respectively). Only the story of the increasing exploitation of new materials, notably iron and glass, reaching some sort of a culmination around 1850, lay outside, though never quite isolated from, the realm of the revivalistic modes (see Chapter 7).

PART ONE

1800–1850

CHAPTER I

ROMANTIC CLASSICISM AROUND 1800

Despite the drastically reduced production of the years just before and after 1800, between the outbreak of the French Revolution and the termination of Napoleon's imperial career, there are prominent buildings in many countries that provide fine examples of Romantic Classicism in its early maturity; others, generally more modest in size, give evidence of the vitality of the Picturesque at this time. Since England and America were least directly affected by the French Revolution, however much they were drawn into the wars that were its aftermath, they produced more than their share, so to say, of executed work. French architects before 1806 were mostly reduced to designing monuments destined never to be built or to adapting old structures to new uses.

The greatest architect in active practice in the 1790s was Sir John Soane (1753–1837), from 1788 Architect of the Bank of England. The career of his master, the younger Dance, was in decline; he had made what were perhaps his greatest contributions a good quarter of a century earlier. Whatever Soane owed to Dance, and he evidently owed him a great deal, the Bank[1] offered greater opportunities than the older man had ever had. His interiors of the early nineties at the Bank leave the world of academic Classicism completely behind [6]. His extant Lothbury façade of 1795, with the contiguous 'Tivoli Corner' of a decade later –

now modified almost beyond recognition – and even more the demolished Waiting Room Court [5] showed that his innovations in this period were by no means restricted to interiors.

5. Sir John Soane: London, Bank of England, Waiting Room Court, 1804

Soane's style, consonant though it was in many ways with the general ideals of Romantic Classicism, is a highly personal one. At the

6. Sir John Soane: London, Bank of England, Consols Office, 1794

Bank, however, he was not creating *de novo* but committed to the piecemeal reconstruction of an existing complex of buildings, and controlled as well by very stringent technical requirements. Thus the grouping of the offices about the Rotunda, like the plan of the Rotunda itself, goes back to the work done by his predecessor Sir Robert Taylor (1714–88) twenty years earlier; while the special need of the Bank for several kinds of security made necessary both the avoidance of openings on the exterior and a fireproof structural system within. The architectural expression that Soane gave to his complex spaces in the offices which he designed in 1791 and built in 1792–4 had very much the same abstract qualities as those to which older masters of Romantic Classicism, such as Ledoux and Dance, had already aspired in the preceding decades [6]. The novel treatment of

as the frank revelation of the delicate cast-iron framework of his glazed lanterns (see Chapter 7). These interiors particularly appealed to mid-twentieth-century taste, while Soane's columnar confections of this period generally appear somewhat pompous and banal.

The Rotunda of 1794–5 was grander and more Piranesian in effect; thus it shared in the international tendency of this period towards megalomania. So also the contemporary Lothbury façade, with its rare accents of crisply profiled antae and its vast unbroken expanses of flat rustication, is less personal to Soane and more in a mode that was common to many Romantic Classical architects all over the Western world. The original Tivoli Corner of 1805, however, was almost Baroque in its plasticity, with a Roman not a Greek order, and a most remarkable piling up of flat elements

7. Sir John Soane: Tyringham, Buckinghamshire, Entrance Gate, 1792–7

the smooth plaster surfaces of the light vaults made of hollow terracotta pots, where he substituted linear striations for the conventional membering of Classical design, was as notable

organized in three dimensions at the skyline that could only be Soane's.

On the other hand, the reduction of relief and the linear stylization of the constituent elements of the Loggia in the Waiting Room Court of 1804, equally personal to Soane, illustrated an anti-Baroque tendency to reduce to a minimum the sculptural aspect of architecture [5]. Planes were emphasized rather than masses, and the character of the detail was thoroughly renewed as well as the basic formulas of Classical design that Soane had inherited. This was even more apparent in the New Bank Buildings, a terrace of houses, begun in 1807, that once stood across Prince's Street. Except for the paired Ionic columns at the ends, conventional Classical forms were avoided almost as completely as in the Bank offices of the previous decade, and the smooth plane of the stucco wall was broken only by incised linear detail.

Perhaps the most masterly example of this characteristically Soanic treatment is still to be seen in the gateway and lodge of the country house that he built at Tyringham in Buckinghamshire in 1792-7 [7]. There the simple mass is defined by flat surfaces bounded by plain incised lines. The house itself is both less drastically novel and less successful; various other Soane houses of these decades have more character.

Summerson has claimed that Soane introduced all his important innovations before 1800. However that may be, there is no major break in his work at the end of the first decade of the century, nor did his production then notably increase. It is therefore rather arbitrary to cut off an account of his architecture at this point; but it is necessary to do so if the importance of the Picturesque countercurrent in these same years, not as yet of great consequence as an aspect of Soane's major works, is to be adequately emphasized. His concern with varied lighting effects, however, if not necessarily Picturesque technically, gave evidence of an intense Romanticism; more indubitably Picturesque was his exaggerated interest in broken skylines.

While Soane's work at the Bank was proceeding, in these years before and after 1800, James Wyatt (1746-1813), capable of producing at Dodington House in 1798-1808 a quite conventional example of Romantic Classicism, was building in the years between 1796 and his death in 1813 for that great Romantic William Beckford the largest of 'Gothick' garden fabricks, Fonthill Abbey in Wiltshire.[2] This was a landmark in the rise of the Gothic Revival. In 1803 S. P. Cockerell (1754-1827), otherwise far more consistently Classical than Wyatt, was erecting for his brother, the Indian nabob Sir Charles Cockerell, a vast mansion in Gloucestershire in an Indian mode. The design of Sezincote was based on early sketches made by the landscape gardener Humphry Repton (1752-1818) and all its details were derived from the drawings Thomas Daniell (1749-1840) had made in India fifteen years before and published in *The Antiquities of India* in 1800. The 'Indian Revival' (so to call it) had little success; in these years only the stables built in 1805 by William Porden (*c.* 1755-1822) for the Royal Pavilion at Brighton followed Sezincote's lead.

The Neo-Gothic of Fonthill, however, a mode that had roots extending back into the second quarter of the eighteenth century, is illustrated in a profusion of examples by Wyatt, Porden, and many others. None, however, seems to have succeeded as well as Beckford and Wyatt at Fonthill in achieving the 'Sublime' by mere dimensions. The characteristic Gothic country houses of this period were likely to be elaborately Tudor, like Wyatt's Ashridge begun in 1808 and Porden's Eaton Hall of 1803-12, or lumpily Castellated like Hawarden of 1804-9 by Thomas Cundy I (1765-1825) and Eastnor of 1808-15 by Sir Robert Smirke (1781-1867). The last, moreover, differs very little from Adam's Culzean of 1777-90.

Some Gothic churches were built in these decades, too, as others had been ever since the 1750s. Such an example as Porden's church at Eccleston of 1809-13, while more recognizably Perpendicular, lacked the brittle charm of the earlier 'Gothick' churches of the eighteenth century.

The virtuoso of the Picturesque mode and, after Soane, the greatest architectural figure of these years in England, was John Nash (1752-1835). Working in partnership with Repton for several years at the turn of the century, he turned out a spate of Picturesque houses, many of them rather small, with various sorts of medieval detail: Killy Moon in Ireland, built in 1803, is Norman; more usually they are Tudor or at least Tudoresque: his own East Cowes Castle on the Isle of Wight, which was begun in 1798, for example, or Luscombe in Devonshire, begun the following year. The medieval detail was probably designed by the French émigré Augustus (Auguste) Charles Pugin (1762-1832), whom Nash employed at this time (see Chapter 6). It is rather for their asymmetrical silhouettes and for the free plans that this asymmetry encouraged, however, than for the stylistic plausibility of their detailing that these houses are notable.

Finer than such 'castles' is Cronkhill, which Nash built in 1802 at Atcham, Salop. Here the varied forms are all more or less Italianate, and the whole was evidently inspired by the fabrics in the paintings of Claude and the Poussins – literally an example of 'picturesque' architecture. Actually more characteristic of the Picturesque at this time, however, is the Hamlet at Blaise Castle. There Nash repeated in 1811 a variety of cottage types that he had already used individually elsewhere, arranging them in an irregular cluster [87].

The Rustic Cottage mode, like so many aspects of the Picturesque in architecture, had its origins in the fabrics designed to ornament eighteenth-century gardens. But the mode had by now attained considerable prestige thanks to the writings of the chief theorists of the Picturesque,[3] Richard Payne Knight (1750-1824) and Uvedale Price (1747-1829). Their support was responsible also for the rising prestige of the asymmetrical Castellated Mansion and the Italian Villa; indeed, Payne Knight's own Downton Castle in Shropshire of 1774-8 is both Castellated and Italianate. The appearance of several prettily illustrated books on cottages[4] in the nineties provided a variety of modes for emulation, and from the beginning of the new century the Cottage mode was well established for gate lodges, dairies, and all sorts of other minor constructions in the country.

For larger buildings a definite Greek Revival was now beginning to take form within the general frame of Romantic Classicism. More young architects were visiting Greece and, for those who could not, two further volumes of Stuart and Revett's *Antiquities of Athens*, appearing in 1787 and in 1794, and the parallel *Ionian Antiquities*, which began to be issued in 1769, provided many more models for imitation than had been available earlier. The Greek Doric order had first been introduced into England by Stuart himself in 1758 in the Hagley Park temple, as has been mentioned earlier; a little later, in 1763, he used the Greek Ionic on Lichfield House which still stands at 15 St James's Square in London. From the nineties, the Greek orders were in fairly common use, as such a splendid group as the buildings of Chester Castle, of 1793-1820 by Thomas Harrison (1744-1829), handsomely illustrates. However, the handling of them was not as yet very archaeological.

Summerson credits the attack made by the connoisseur Thomas Hope (1770?-1831) in 1804 on Wyatt's designs for Downing College, Cambridge, with helping to establish a more rigid standard of correctness. However that may be, the winning and partly executed design of 1806-11 for this college by William Wilkins (1778-1839) well illustrates the new ideals. Wilkins had made his own studies of Greek originals in Sicily and Southern Italy, and was publishing them in the *Antiquities of Magna Graecia* at this very time (1807). The inherited concepts of medieval college architecture, largely maintained through the earlier Georgian period, were all but forgotten at Downing. The group was broken down into free-standing blocks, each as much like a temple as was feasible, and repeated Ionic porticoes provided almost the only architectural features. There was no Soanic originality here, no Picturesque eclecticism; perhaps unfortunately, however, this provided a codified Grecian mode which almost anyone using handbooks of the Greek orders could apply.

Wilkins was also responsible for the first[5] British example of a giant columnar monument, the Nelson Pillar of 1808-9 in Dublin. This 134-foot Greek Doric column in Sackville (later O'Connell) Street, of which the construction was supervised by Francis Johnston (1760-1829), initiated a favourite theme of the period usually, and not incorrectly, associated with Napoleon (see Chapter 3).

The Covent Garden Theatre in London was rebuilt in 1808-9 by Smirke. This pupil of Soane had, like Wilkins, seen ancient Greek buildings with his own eyes and generally aimed to imitate them very closely. His theatre was somewhat less correct than the Cambridge college, but despite the castles he had built it was Smirke rather than Wilkins who carried forward the Grecian mode at its most rigid through four more decades (see Chapter 4). Wilkins, however, at Grange Park in Hampshire in 1809 had shown, as C.-E. de Beaumont (1757-1811) had done earlier in a house called 'Le Temple de Silence' built before the Revolution in France, how the accommodations of a fair-sized mansion could be squeezed inside the temple form (admittedly with some violence to the latter). Grange Park provided an early paradigm of a Grecian domestic mode destined to be curiously popular at the fringes of the western world in America, in Sweden, and in Russia, but very rarely employed in more sophisticated regions (see Chapter 5). The house was much modified by later enlargements of 1823-5 by S. P. Cockerell and of 1852 by his grandson F. P. Cockerell. It is now demolished.

Grecian design descended slowly to the world of the builders. The relatively restricted urban house-building of the two decades before Waterloo maintained a close resemblance to that of the 1780s. Russell Square in London, built up by James Burton (1761-1837) in the first decade of the new century, does not differ notably from Bedford Square of twenty years earlier – probably by Thomas Leverton (1743-1824) – except that the façades are smoother and plainer. But a still greater crispness of finish could be, and increasingly was, obtained by covering terrace houses – as for that matter most suburban villas also by this time – with stucco. In this respect the work of some unknown designer in Euston Square in London, which was built up at the same time as Russell Square, could long be contrasted with Burton's (which has in any case been much corrupted by the introduction in the 1880s of terracotta door and window casings), but has now been destroyed.

In industrial construction, such as the warehouses by William Jessop at the West India Docks, begun in 1799, and those by D. A. Alexander (1768-1846) at the London Docks, begun in 1802, the grandeur and simplicity characteristic of Romantic Classicism could be seen at their best.[6] These warehouses also presage the importance of commercial building in a world increasingly concerned with business (see Chapter 14).

During the years of the American Revolutionary War, 1776-83, years in which Romantic Classicism was maturing in France and in England, North Americans were not entirely cut off from the Old World. Not only did many earlier cultural ties remain unbroken – while a surprising reverse emigration of good painters from the New World to the Old occurred – but new cultural ties with the French ally were established, and these were maintained and reinforced by several émigrés of ability who arrived in the 1790s. Thomas Jefferson (1743–1826), hitherto as confirmed a Palladian as any English landowner of the mid eighteenth century, was much assisted in Paris by C. L. Clérisseau when he based his Virginia State Capitol[7] of 1785–96 at Richmond very closely on the best preserved ancient Roman structure that he had seen in France, the Maison Carrée at Nîmes, even though for the portico an Ionic instead of a Corinthian order was used. In this first major public monument initiated in the new republic Jefferson's drastic aim of forcing all the requirements of a fairly complex modern building inside the rigid mould of a Roman temple was more consonant with the absolutism of the French in this period than with the rather looser formal ideals of the English.

Jefferson was not able to impose so rigid a Classicism on the new Federal capital of Washington at its start, despite the efforts of various French and British engineers, architects, and amateurs who participated in the competitions of 1792 for the President's House (White House) and for the Capitol and who worked on the latter during its first decade of construction. The White House[8] as designed by the Irish architect James Hoban (c. 1762–1831) was still quite in the earlier eighteenth-century Anglo-Palladian manner, and Jefferson's own project was based on Palladio's Villa Rotonda. Neither the English amateur William Thornton (1759–1828) and his professional assistant who was also English, George Hadfield (c. 1764–1826), nor their French associate É.-S. Hallet succeeded in giving the Capitol[9] a very up-to-date character [147]. Yet it is these major edifices that still occupy two of the focal points in the Washington city plan,[10] which

was prepared by the French engineer P.-C. L'Enfant (1754–1825) before his dismissal from public service in 1792.

It was Benjamin H. Latrobe (1764–1820), an English-born architect of German and English connexions, who finally brought to America just before 1800, and shortly to Washington, the highest professional standards of the day and a complete Romantic Classical programme. Indeed, he almost succeeded in making Romantic Classicism the official style in the United States for all time; at least it remained so down to the Civil War in the sixties, and a later revival lasted, as regards public architecture in Washington, from the 1900s to the 1930s (see Chapter 24). A pupil of S. P. Cockerell, Latrobe emigrated in 1796 and was soon assisting Jefferson on the final completion of the Virginia State Capitol as well as undertaking the construction of canals as an engineer. Not inappropriately Latrobe's first important American building, the Bank of Pennsylvania begun in 1798, was also an Ionic temple, but with an order that aspired to be Greek. This Philadelphia bank included a great central hall whose saucer dome, visible externally, made it a more complex and architectonic composition than the Richmond Capitol. The flat lantern crowning the dome recalled, and may derive from, those over Soane's offices at the Bank of England. Characteristically, Latrobe at this very same time was also building a country house, Sedgley, outside Philadelphia, with 'Gothick' detailing. By 1803 he had taken charge of the construction of the Capitol, nominally under Thornton, with whom he had continual rows. Most of the early interiors there were his, notably those in the south wing, fine examples of Romantic Classicism with French as well as English overtones; moreover he was still in charge of rebuilding them after the burning of the Capitol in 1814 down to his forced resignation in 1817.

In 1805 Latrobe submitted alternative designs for the Catholic cathedral in Baltimore.

8. Benjamin H. Latrobe:
Baltimore, Catholic Cathedral, 1805-18

The Gothic design is one of the finest projects of the 'Sublime' or 'High Romantic' stage of the Gothic Revival; yet in its vast bare walls, carefully ordered geometry, and dry detail it is also consonant with some of the basic ideals of Romantic Classicism. The Classical design that was preferred and eventually built is perhaps less original; but internally, at least, this is one of the finest ecclesiastical monuments of Romantic Classicism, combining a rather Panthéon-like plan with segmental vaults of somewhat Soanic character[10a] [8]. The cathedral was largely completed by 1818. The portico, though intended from the first, was added only in 1863,

but the present bulbous terminations of the western towers are not of Latrobe's design.

Near by in Baltimore the Unitarian Church of 1817-18 is by a Frenchman, Maximilien Godefroy (1765-c. 1840), who was also responsible for the first Neo-Gothic ecclesiastical structure of any consequence in North America, the chapel of St Mary's Seminary there, built in 1807. The Unitarian Church is a monument which might well have risen in the Paris of the 1790s had the French Deists been addicted to building churches. The triple arch in the plain stuccoed front below the pediment comes straight from Ledoux's *barrières*; the interior, unhappily remodelled in 1916, was originally a dome on pendentives of the purest geometrical order. So Godefroy's Battle Monument of 1815-25, also in Baltimore, with its Egyptian base might easily have been erected in Paris to honour some general prominent in Napoleon's campaign on the Nile.[11] Another Frenchman, J.-J. Ramée (1764-1842), active since the Revolution in Hamburg and in Denmark, also came briefly to America. In 1813 he laid out Union College[12] in Schenectady, N.Y., on a rather Ledolcian plan and began its construction before he returned to Europe. His ranges of buildings long crowned the hill – although two only now survive[12a] – and Ramée here initiated a tradition of college architecture as remote from that of earlier American colleges, with their free-standing buildings set around a 'campus', as Wilkins's Downing at Cambridge was from earlier English colleges.

The French eventually departed leaving no line of descent; but Latrobe had a pupil, the first professionally trained American in the field and, like Latrobe, almost as much an engineer as an architect. By 1808 Robert Mills (1781-1855) was supervising for Latrobe the new Bank of Philadelphia, Gothic (or at least 'Gothick') where his earlier Bank of Pennsylvania had been Grecian, and also building on his own the Sansom Street Baptist Church, a competent but not distinguished essay in Romantic Classicism. In the same year another Latrobe pupil, William Strickland (1788-1854), designed for Philadelphia a Gothick Masonic Hall; this was built in 1809-11, and later rebuilt, but according to the original design, after a fire in 1819-20.

Far more successful than either of them, if now overshadowed by the megalomaniac Classicism of the twentieth-century Philadelphia Museum of Art by Horace Trumbauer and others on the hill above, are the waterworks begun in 1811 on the banks of the Schuylkill. These are probably but not certainly by Mills rather than by the engineer Frederick Graff, whose name is signed to the drawings. These very utilitarian structures are most characteristic of the beginnings of Romantic Classicism in America, where Latrobe, Mills, and also Strickland were all three engineers as well as architects. Moreover, it is evident that engineering considerations often influenced their approach to architecture, just as architectural considerations gave visual distinction to much of their engineering. Thus they may be compared with engineers like Telford and Rennie in England as well as with the English architects of their day.

In this so-called 'Federal' period, when Romantic Classicism centred in the Middle Atlantic states thanks to Latrobe, Godefroy, Mills, and Strickland, the leading architect outside this area, the Bostonian Charles Bulfinch (1763-1844), was a late-comer to Romantic Classicism. His great public monument of the 1790s, the Massachusetts State House in Boston, had been designed originally as early as 1787, and even as executed in 1795-8 it derived principally from the Somerset House in London of Sir William Chambers (1726-96) and in the interiors from Wyatt. His Boston Court House of 1810 first showed evidence of a change in his style, notably in its smooth ashlar walls of cold grey granite. That was a local material destined to lend particular distinction to the principal Romantic Classical buildings of Boston from this time forward (see Chapter 5).

The Frenchmen who came to America at the end of the eighteenth century or in the early 1800s (and shortly left again) could hardly import the French architecture of those decades; on the one hand, they had all been trained before the Revolution, from which most of them were in flight; on the other hand – and more consequently – there was almost no later architecture for them to reflect. Between 1789 and 1806 French building was at a standstill. Architects were mostly busy, if at all, with the decoration of various revolutionary fêtes and the accommodation of new political agencies in old structures.

One major example of the accommodation of an older structure to a new purpose deserves particular mention. In the years 1795-7 J.-P. de Gisors (1755-1828), E.-C. Leconte (1762-1818), and the former's brother A.-J.-B.-G. de Gisors (1762-1835) built within the old Palais Bourbon the Salle des Cinq Cents, the legislative chamber of the First Republic. This hemicycle, at least as rebuilt along much the original lines by Joly in 1828-33, still serves as the Chamber of Deputies of the Fifth Republic. Such a chamber, so different in plan from the college-chapel arrangement of the British House of Commons with facing benches for Government and Opposition, is characteristically Romantic Classical in its form, but this form unfortunately proved to be conducive to an indefinite shading of multiple parties from right to left. The British model, suited to two-party rule only, was rarely imitated; the French one has been rather frequently, beginning with Latrobe's House of Representatives in the Washington Capitol. Leaving aside the apparent political effect of the plan – not so notable in Washington as elsewhere – Gisors's chamber seems to have been respectable if not especially distinguished. Covered with a segmental half dome and a barrel vault, both top-lighted, the smooth though rather richly decorated surfaces of the walls and the vaults made clear the interesting geometrical form of the enclosed space. The prototype was the lecture theatre of the École de Médecine in Paris erected in 1769-76 by Jacques Gondoin (1737-1818), one of the most advanced interiors of its day.

There was some private building in the Paris of the 1790s and early 1800s before public building eventually revived at Napoleon's fiat. Typical and partly extant is the Rue des Colonnes, most probably by N.-A.-J. Vestier (1765-1816), although sometimes attributed to Poyet, who may have had some urbanistic

control. This has an open arcade at the base carried on Greek Doric columns, here very modestly scaled, and cold flat walls above that are almost without any detailing whatsoever. This Paris street, as much as the arcaded ones of medieval and Renaissance Italy, may well have been the prototype for Napoleon's first and greatest urbanistic project, the work of his favourite architects Charles Percier (1764-1838) and P.-F.-L. Fontaine (1762-1853). From his acquisition of La Malmaison in 1799 he kept them busy remodelling the interiors of his successive residences as First Consul and Emperor but rarely gave them new buildings to erect. This extensive planning scheme includes the Rue de Castiglione, running south out of the Place Vendôme, the Rue and Place des Pyramides, and the Rue de Rivoli facing the Tuileries Gardens. This last street was eventually extended to the east well beyond the Louvre by Napoleon III. The opening of the Rue de Castiglione was ordered in 1801; construction began the next year, and the execution of the rest went on, with long interruptions, for more than half a century.

Percier and Fontaine's façades are characteristic of Romantic Classicism in their coldness of detailing and their infinite repetition of the same formula; but their Italianism, thin and dry as it is, recalls many of the plates in *Maisons et palais de Rome moderne*, which the two architects had published in 1798 before their professional star had risen very high [9]. With Nash's Cronkhill, although in a very different and even opposed spirit, this scheme presages the international 'Renaissance Revival' of the second quarter of the century. The very effective high curved roofs, filling out completely the 'envelope' allowed by the Paris building code, were added in 1855; lower two-pitched mansards were provided originally.

But the Empire mode, particularly as elaborated by Percier and Fontaine in the service of the Emperor, was primarily a fashionable style

9. Percier and Fontaine: Paris, Rue de Rivoli, 1802–55

for interiors, and found perhaps its most characteristic expression in furniture, usually of dark mahogany with much ornate decoration of a character resembling gold embroidery on uniforms. Such flat decorative work is also found carved on exteriors, not only in France but wherever Napoleonic influence penetrated. Indeed, in furniture and interior design generally, non-French work is often of the highest quality, especially when executed for such clients as Napoleon's sister Caroline Murat at Naples.

Yet the character of French leadership in the arts had changed since the 1780s. The architects at the end of the *ancien régime* had been truly revolutionary in their aesthetic and their social ideals. Napoleon's designers, almost like Mussolini's and Stalin's and Hitler's[12b] in our century, were flatterers and time-servers. Emulation of their work abroad was chiefly a matter of following well-publicized fashion; creative

French influence still flowed, however, from men of the older generation now so largely forgotten at home. Thus it was at this point that Ledoux's projects became generally available to others, thanks to his book published in 1804 and dedicated to Napoleon's Russian ally of the moment, Alexander I.

Extensive building activity in Paris under Napoleon's aegis began only in 1806, but once it started there came a positive flood of projects in conscious emulation of Louis XIV's architectural campaigns. There was also the expectation that this activity would absorb unemployment in the building trades. But Napoleon, like later dictators who have initiated vast building projects, actually bit off a great deal more than he could chew. He was, however, more fortunate than Mussolini and Hitler in that the regimes which succeeded his in the decades between the First Empire and the Second were surprisingly willing to carry his unfinished monuments to completion. Still later, his nephew Napoleon III emulated him in an even more concerted programme of urbanism and monumental construction carried out over nearly two decades in a very different style – indeed in several (see Chapter 8).

The Colonne de la Grande Armée,[12c] replacing the statue of Louis XV at the centre of the Place Vendôme, is a properly symbolic monument of its epoch – first to be designed of the many giant columns that would arise all across the Western world from Baltimore to Petersburg within the next quarter century. Wilkins's Nelson Pillar in Dublin, actually completed before the Paris example, has already been mentioned. The column in Paris is Trajanesque not Grecian, however, and was entirely executed with the bronze of captured guns. It well represents the Imperial Roman megalomania already evident in many projected memorials of the 1790s. Gondoin, its architect, with whom was associated J.-B. Lepère (1761-1844), provides a real link with the past, since his already-mentioned École de Médecine was one of the earliest major edifices in which Romantic Classical ideals were carried beyond the transitional stage of Soufflot's Panthéon.

Even before the Colonne Vendôme was finished in 1810, a smaller and somewhat less typical monument, but equally Roman and also the first of a considerable line, had been completed by Percier and Fontaine. The Arc du Carrousel of 1806-8 – once a gate to the Tuileries from the Place du Carrousel, now unhappily floating in unconfined space – has much of the daintiness and, in the use of coloured marbles, the polychromy of its architects' contemporary palace interiors. Indeed, the richness of the detailing is far less characteristic of Empire taste in architecture than are their façades near by in the Rue de Rivoli [9]; the Arc du Carrousel must have provided a rather fussy pedestal for the superb Grecian horses stolen from St Mark's in Venice that were originally mounted upon it.

Far more satisfactorily symbolic of imperial aspiration is the enormous Arc de Triomphe de l'Étoile [10], which looks down the entire length of the Champs Élysées today to overwhelm its brother arch even at that great distance. J.-A. Raymond (1742-1811), a pupil of Leroy, first received the commission;[12d] but with him was associated J.-F.-T. Chalgrin (1739-1811), the master of the younger Gisors, who soon took over and imposed his own astylar design. Chalgrin, like Gondoin, was an architect already well established under the *ancien régime*. His major innovation had been the reintroduction of the basilican plan[13] at Saint-Philippe-du-Roule in Paris in the 1760s, henceforth one of the favourite models for Romantic Classical churches in France and elsewhere on the Continent. Like many of the monuments of that earlier period by Chalgrin's contemporaries, his Arc de l'Étoile reverts less to Roman antiquity than to certain aspects of the architecture of Louis XIV. Even its megalomaniac grandeur can be matched, relatively at least, in the Porte St Denis in Paris built in the 1680s by François Blondel, and it follows almost line for line the square proportions of that masterpiece. The arch was slowly brought to completion after Chalgrin's death, first by his pupil L. Goust from 1811 to 1813 and from 1823 to 1830; then by Goust's assistant, J.-N. Huyot (1780-1840), advised by a commission that included François Debret (1777-1850), Fontaine, and the younger Gisors; and finally from 1832 to 1837 by G.-A. Blouet (1795-1853). It owes its unmistakably nineteenth-century character partly to the crisp, hard quality of its imposts and entablatures and partly to the great Romantic figural reliefs executed in 1833 by Rude, Etex, and Cortot. These take the place on the piers of the more conventional trophy-hung obelisks on Blondel's seventeenth-century arch. A certain post-Empire quality derives from the plastic complexity of Blouet's attic; but on the whole the Arc de l'Étoile, if less original and less influential

10. J.-F.-T. Chalgrin and others:
Paris, Arc de Triomphe de l'Étoile, 1806-37

than Saint-Philippe-du-Roule, is Chalgrin's masterpiece and Napoleon's finest memorial.

The Place de la Concorde, projected by A.-J. Gabriel (1692-1782) at the end of the Baroque Age, continued to lack, even after a half century and more, appropriate monuments to terminate the cross axis. The project for a big church at the head of the Rue Royale to close the vista between Gabriel's two colonnaded ranges on the north side of the square had bogged down well before the Revolution; across the river the much earlier Palais Bourbon, set at an angle, was even more awkward than earlier, now that the roof of the Salle des Cinq Cents rose above it. Since the amelioration of this southern terminal required only a tall masking façade at right angles to Gabriel's axis, this was promptly provided. Poyet in 1806-8 used the most obvious Romantic Classical solution for such a problem, a high blank wall with a ten-columned temple portico at its centre. The result is certainly an urbanistic success, if without any particular intrinsic interest; the raising of the portico above a high range of steps ensured, for example, its visibility from the square across the bridge. The form of the pediment was slightly modified and the sculpture by Cortot added in 1837-41.

In 1761 Pierre Contant d'Ivry (1698-1777) and, after his death, G.-M. Couture (1732-99) had made successive designs for a church dedicated to the Magdalen at the head of the Rue Royale, the latter already proposing that it be surrounded by a Classical peristyle. This structure, which was as yet barely begun, Napoleon now decided should be not a church but a Temple de la Gloire – he reversed his decision in 1813 after the Battle of Leipzig and the loss of Spain. For such a temple he understandably preferred, in the competition held in 1806, neither the first nor the second premiated design, both of church-like character, but one by Pierre Vignon (1763-1828) that proposed the erection of an enormous Corinthian temple on a high Roman podium. Inside, a series of square bays covered with domes on pendentives sup-

ported by giant Corinthian columns provided a structural solution technically Byzantine but as imperially Roman in scale and detailing as the exterior.

Construction of the Madeleine, begun in 1807, dragged on interminably. J.-J.-M. Huvé (1783-1852) succeeded Vignon as architect in 1828 and, like the Arc de l'Étoile, the edifice was finally finished only under Louis Philippe in 1845. The interior has a somewhat funereal solemnity, more characteristic of the post-Napoleonic regimes than of the period of its initiation. The conventional temple form of the exterior is redeemed by the superb siting, the really grand scale, and the rich pedimental sculpture by Lemaire. Like Chalgrin's arch, Vignon's Madeleine has continued to provide a major monumental nexus in the urbanism of Paris ever since.

Also proposed in 1806 but not initiated until 1808 was the Bourse[13a] by A.-T. Brongniart (1739-1813), another architect who had, like

11. A.-T. Brongniart and others:
Paris, Bourse, 1808-15

Gondoin and Chalgrin, made his mark long before the Revolution [11]. Again a free-standing peripteral structure like the Madeleine, the Bourse has suffered somewhat from its enlargement in 1902-3 by J.-B.-F. Cavel (c. 1844-1905) and H.-T.-E. Eustache (1861-?). Nearly square originally and unpedimented – and also set much closer to the ground – it must always have lacked the monumental presence of the Madeleine. But the interior with its ranges of arcades, derived almost as directly from a Louis XIV monument – in this case the court of the Invalides by Libéral Bruant – as Chalgrin's arch was from that of Blondel, is very characteristic of the sort of reiterative composition generally favoured by Romantic Classicists. L.-H. Lebas (1782-1867) was associated with the elderly Brongniart from the start, and after Brongniart's death the building was finished in 1815 by E.-E. de Labarre (1764-1833). Labarre was responsible also for the Colonne de la Grande Armée at Boulogne; this was proposed in 1804 and begun in 1810, but, like so many Napoleonic monuments, not finished until Louis Philippe took up its construction again in 1833. It was finally completed by Marquise in 1844.

In 1799 a fire made it necessary to rebuild the Théâtre de l'Odéon; but the original design of M.-J. Peyre (1730-88) and Charles de Wailly (1729-98), dating back to 1779, was repeated in 1807 with little change, as was also the case in 1819 when it was rebuilt again after another fire. This provides excellent evidence of the continuity of Romantic Classical style in France before and after the Revolution (see Chapter 3).

Napoleon had in mind the erection of various less monumental and more utilitarian structures than the Bourse and the Odéon; some of these were started, and one or two even finished, before the Empire came to an end. Behind one section of the façades in the Rue de Rivoli an enormous and rather dull General Post Office was begun in 1810 and eventually completed

under Charles X to serve as the Ministry of Finance in 1827. Another ministry (Foreign Affairs) on the Quai d'Orsay was designed in 1810 by J.-C. Bonnard (1765-1818) and even begun in 1814; this was eventually carried to completion by Bonnard's pupil Jacques Lacornée (1779-1856) in 1821-35. With its rich ordonnance of columns and arches, Bonnard's façade had an almost High Renaissance air, or so it would appear from extant views of a structure long since destroyed.

The Marché St Martin of 1811-16 by A.-M. Peyre (1770-1843), the Marché des Carmes of 1813 by A.-L.-T. Vaudoyer (1756-1846), and the Marché St Germain of 1816-25 by J.-B. Blondel (1764-1825), with their clerestory lighting and open timber roofs, are typical of the more practical side of Romantic Classicism.[13b] The simple masonry vocabulary of these Parisian markets, so straightforward and without Antique pretension, was considered to be Italian (see Chapter 2).

The Napoleonic building flurry barely reached the provinces before its short course was over. The theatre in Dijon, begun about 1805 by Jacques Célérier (1742-1814), may be mentioned; but such plain square blocks with frontal porticoes could have been, and were, built in almost precisely the same form thirty years before – for example Ledoux's theatre at Besançon of 1775-84. At Pontivy in Brittany, then called Napoléonville, the younger Gisors built a Préfecture in 1809 and a Palace of Justice with associated prisons two years later. A rather dull church, Saint-Vincent at Mâcon, repeating a model that had been new at Saint-Philippe-du-Roule forty years earlier, was also erected by him in 1810. The pair of front towers was a novelty suggested by an earlier project of Lebas.

It is quite characteristic of this period, so ready (as the French have been ever since) to employ elderly architects and so content with stylistic innovations that dated from before the Revolution, that Mathurin Crucy (1749-1826) rebuilt in 1808-12 the theatre in Nantes – very like that at Dijon – in exactly the same form as it had originally been designed by him in 1784-8; while he also finished in 1809-12 the Bourse and Tribunal de Commerce there which he had begun in 1791, just after the Revolution started, with no change in the original design. The setting of his theatre in the Place Graslin provided by continuous ranges of five-storey houses is presumably contemporary; despite the rather high roofs, the façades are notably crisp and smooth. The rusticated arcuation of the lower storeys might make plausible a date in the 1780s, but the rather thin and geometrically detailed iron balcony railings suggest the first or second decade of the new century, when the theatre was rebuilt.

If the imperial effort in France barely extended outside Paris except for the interior alterations that Percier and Fontaine carried out in the royal châteaux at Versailles, Compiègne, Saint-Cloud, and Fontainebleau – major examples of Empire decoration but not of architecture – the emperor and his nominees left their mark on most of the great cities of continental Europe. The Palazzo Serbelloni in the Corso Venezia, where Napoleon stayed in Milan, was built by Simone Cantoni (1736-1818) in 1780-94. Similar to French work of the period, it would probably have impressed the Emperor as still quite up-to-date. He ordered in 1806 the laying out in Milan of the Foro Bonaparte, according to the designs of Giannantonio Antolini (1754-1842), and the erection of a conventionally Roman triumphal arch, the work of Luigi Cagnola (1762-1833), which was finally completed in 1838.[13c]

In Rome the development of the Piazza del Popolo, like the Foro Bonaparte a work of urbanism rather than of architecture, was based by Giuseppe Valadier (1762-1859), an Italian despite his French name and ancestry, on a project he had made as early as 1794. This project was modified by him under the Empire to incorporate 'corrections' by the younger Gisors and L.-M. Berthault (1771?-1823). Execution of the project actually began only in 1813 after Pope Pius VII returned from his Napoleonic captivity; Valadier carried it forward to ultimate completion in 1831. Valadier's Roman church work, such as his new façade for San Pantaleone of 1806, just off the present-day Corso Vittorio Emanuele, is mostly too dull to mention; his domestic work was somewhat more interesting, but with little personal or even Italian flavour.

In Naples Leconte, who had worked with the two Gisors on the Salle des Cinq Cents in Paris, remodelled the San Carlo opera house in 1809[13d] for Murat – it was, however, refronted in 1810-12 and rebuilt in 1816-17 by Antonio Niccolini (1772-1850). With Antonio de Simone, Leconte also decorated rooms in the Bourbon palace at Caserta,[14] originally built by Vanvitelli in 1752-74, for this Napoleonic brother-in-law. But the finest Empire things in the area were the Sala di Marte and the Sala di Astrea there, which de Simone, working alone, had begun to decorate slightly earlier in 1807 for Napoleon's brother Joseph Bonaparte [12]. As with so many architectural projects of the brief period of the Empire, it was left to a returning legitimate sovereign, in this case Ferdinand I of the Two Sicilies, to finish the job. Unlike the greater part of Percier and Fontaine's work in the French palaces, these rooms at Caserta are interior architecture, not just interior decoration, and fully worthy in their scale and their sumptuous materials of the magnificent spaces, created almost half a century earlier by Vanvitelli, which they occupy. This is the more remarkable as de Simone was really a decorator not an architect.

The Napoleonic emendation of the Piazza San Marco in Venice calls for little comment. There Sansovino's church of San Zimignan at the end was removed in 1807 and replaced in 1810 with a structure by G. M. Soli (1745-1822)

12. A. de Simone: Caserta, Royal Palace,
Sala di Marte, 1807

consonant with the early- and late-sixteenth-century Procurazie by Buon and by Scamozzi along the sides. Soli's emendation finally completed, and not unworthily, this most magnificent piece of urbanism in the form we now know it. La Fenice, the Venice opera-house, had been rebuilt by Giannantonio Selva (1753–1819) in 1790–2; of his work, however, only the rather dull façade remains. The exquisite Neo-Rococo interior is, rather surprisingly, of the second quarter of the nineteenth century, being by the brothers Tommaso and G. B. Meduna (1810–?), who restored the theatre after a fire in 1836.

Ever since the late fifteenth century Italian architects had worked much abroad, generally bringing with them the latest stylistic developments. Now that day was largely over: France, England, and very soon Germany were exporting taste as Italy had done for so many previous centuries. It was only after the Second World War that her position as architectural mentor revived for a few years again (see Chapter 25).

The employment of foreign architects by Russian Tsars was a well-established tradition by the late eighteenth century;[15] most of them had been Italians, but one, Charles Cameron (c. 1714–1812), who represents like Adam the transition from Academic to Romantic Classicism, was Scottish.[15a] There had also been a French designer of the most original order working in Russia early in the eighteenth century, Nicholas Pineau (1684-1754); he even formed his mature style there, initiating the 'Pittoresque' phase of the Rococo well before he returned to France. Half a century later Catherine the Great acquired the greater part of the drawings of Clérisseau, friend and mentor of Adam and also of Jefferson. Catherine's grandson, Alexander I, was so esteemed as a liberal ruler in what had earlier been the most advanced French architectural circle that Ledoux, long left behind as a builder by Revolution and Empire, dedicated to him his book on architecture in 1804, as has already been noted.

Soon after Alexander's accession in 1801 he called on a rather less original French architect, Thomas de Thomon (1754-1813), to design the Petersburg Bourse[16] for him; yet this structure, built in 1804-16, not Brongniart's slightly later Bourse in Paris, is the great, indeed almost the prime, monument of Romantic Classicism around 1800 [13]. The blank pediment, rising from behind a colonnade, the great segmental lunette lighting the interior, the flanking rostral columns, the smooth stucco so crisply painted, all establish this as a perfect exemplar of this period, even though every idea in it can be found in projects, if not in executed work, by Ledoux and Boullée dating from before the Revolution. An even more precise prototype is provided by a project for a 'Bourse Maritime' by Pompon that won a second Grand Prix de Rome in 1798; this was not published until 1806, after Thomon had begun his Bourse, but he was probably familiar with it all the same. Not only is the Bourse exemplary in itself; Petersburg – already a century old and with many vast Baroque palaces to its credit – rather than the newly founded city of Washington on the other side of the western world, offers the finest urban entity of this brief period and of the following decades during which Alexander and his brother Nicholas I continued for some thirty years major campaigns of construction along Romantic Classical lines.[16a]

Thomon's chief Russian rival, Nikiforovich Voronikhin (1760-1814), was French-trained,

13. Thomas de Thomon:
Petersburg, Bourse, 1804-16

a pupil of de Wailly. His Kazan Cathedral at Petersburg of 1801–11 is still rather Baroque in its obvious reminiscences of St Peter's in Rome. But the Academy of Mines, which he began ten years later, although somewhat heavy-handed in the way Romantic Classicism tended to be even in the great cultural centres, is almost as exemplary as Thomon's Bourse. More characteristically Russian in its incredible extension and the great variety of its silhouette is the Admiralty[17] of 1806–15 by Adrian Dimitrievich Zakharov (1761–1811). But the end façades successfully enlarged to monumental scale the theme of the arched entrance to the pre-revolutionary Hôtel de Salm in Paris by Pierre Rousseau (1751–1810). Altogether the Admiralty exceeds in quality as well as in scale almost everything that Napoleon commanded to be built in France, except perhaps the Arc de l'Étoile as finally completed.

Thus Romantic Classicism before Waterloo had major representatives all the way from Latrobe and Mills in America, the one a foreigner, the other a native, to Thomon and his two native rivals in Russia; while the work of Leconte in Naples could once be matched by that done by Ramée in Hamburg and Denmark before he went to America and by that of Desprez in Sweden and Finland (see below). Other Frenchmen were working throughout Napoleon's realm and outside it as well; but the most distinguished architect of this period hitherto unmentioned was a Dane, C. F. Hansen (1756–1845). The design of his Palace of Justice of 1805–15 in the Nytorv in Copenhagen, with its associated gaol, derives from the most advanced projects made by Frenchmen in the earlier years of Romantic Classicism before 1800. The gaol and the arches of its courtyard are more definitely Romantic than anything executed in France under Louis XVI, for they specifically recall the 'Prisons' of Piranesi, those strange architectural dreams in which the Baroque seems to become the Romantic before

one's very eyes. The gaol also resembles a prison designed for Aix by Ledoux and owes a slightly castellated flavour, one must presume, to Hansen's first- or second-hand knowledge of the projects of Boullée.

Still finer, because more homogeneous in conception if less pictorially Romantic, is the principal church in Copenhagen, the Vor Frue Kirke in the Nørregade, projected in 1808–10 by Hansen and built over the years 1811–29. The severely plain tower above the Greek Doric portico at the front illustrates the more primitivistic[17a] and Italianate aspects of Romantic Classical design – more precisely it might seem to derive from the tower of a scheme for a slaughter-house by F.-J. Belanger (1744–1818),[18] a pupil of Leroy. The interior, eventually furnished with statues of Christ and the Twelve Apostles by one of the greatest Romantic Classical sculptors, the Danish Thorwaldsen, raises its ranges of Greek Doric columns to gallery level above a smooth arcuated base [14]. These carry a coffered Roman barrel

14. C. F. Hansen:
Copenhagen, Vor Frue Kirke, 1811–29

vault in a way that follows quite closely, although with some change in the proportions, Boullée's project for the Bibliothèque Royale. Not the least successful and original feature of the exterior is the plain demi-cylinder of the half-domed apse broken only by a portal of almost Egyptian simplicity. But in Copenhagen, with its old tradition of building in brick, the characteristic Romantic Classical surfaces of smooth stucco seem alien and the curious pinky-brown that Hansen's buildings are painted is certainly a little gloomy today.

In Sweden the Rome-trained French architect Desprez, whose projects of the 1780s have been mentioned, was largely occupied not with building but with theatre settings; however, there is at least the excellent Botanical Institute that he built in Uppsala, designed in 1791 and completed in 1807, with its characteristic Greek Doric portico and plain wall surfaces. More notable was his grandiose project, also of 1791, for the Haga Slott in the form of a very long peripteral temple with an octastyle pedimented portico projecting in the middle of the side. His church of 1798, with tower of 1837, at Harmeenlinna in Finland is most impressive. Typical of Swedish production is the country house at Stjarnsund built in 1801 by C. F. Sundahl (1754-1831); this is more English than French in character, indeed with its plain rectangular mass and central portico almost literally Anglo-Palladian.

Harassed and recurrently conquered or *gleichgeschaltet* though most of the German states were in the Napoleonic Wars (while Sweden eventually received a Napoleonic marshal as sovereign through the testament of her legitimate ruler) there was much more building altogether in these years of the turn of the century in Germany than in Sweden, or indeed in France, much of it of high quality. The frontispiece to Romantic Classicism in Germany is the Brandenburg Gate[18a] in Berlin, built in 1789-93 by K. G. Langhans (1733-1808). Still

somewhat attenuated and un-Grecian in its proportions this is the first of the Doric ceremonial gateways that were to be so characteristic of Romantic Classicism everywhere and also one of the most complex and original in composition. More ponderous and provincial is Langhans's Potsdam theatre of 1795; but the Stadttheater at Danzig of 1798-1801 by Held, the City Architect, a cube with a Doric temple portico and a low saucer dome, actually followed a Ledolcian paradigm.

David Gilly (1748-1808) was a more advanced Berlin architect than the elderly Langhans; but his best work of these years is the Viewegsches Haus in Brunswick of 1801-5 with its smooth stucco wall-planes, boldly incised ornament, and Greek Doric porch. More elegantly French is another Brunswick house of this period, the free-standing Villa Holland of 1805 by P. J. Krahe (1758-1840).

Gilly would have been overshadowed by his son Friedrich (1771-1800) had the latter lived, or so one must judge, not from his modest Moller house in the Tiergartenstrasse in Berlin of 1799, but from certain major projects. One, of 1797, is for a monument to Frederick the Great which was widely and deeply influential for many years to come; another, of 1800, is for a Prussian National Theatre, improving upon Ledoux's at Besançon as regards the interior and very original in its external massing. The monument raised a Greek Doric temple on a tremendous substructure of the most abstract geometrical character, surrounded it with obelisks, and set the whole in a vast open space, unconfined but – as it were – defined by subsidiary structures of very fresh and varied design [15]. The handsome gateway to the square seems to provide evidence of Gilly's familiarity with such a highly personal work of Soane as his entrance arch at Tyringham [7]; however, the general tone of somewhat funereal grandeur recalls rather the monumental projects of Ledoux, Boullée, and the younger men of France

15. Friedrich Gilly:
Project for monument to Frederick the Great, 1797

who designed so much and built so little in this decade. Other contemporary Berlin architects, such as Heinrich Gentz (1766-1801) who built the old Mint in 1798-1800, and Friedrich Becherer (1746-1823) who built the Exchange in 1801, while up-to-date stylistically, were much less accomplished than Friedrich Gilly. His artistic heir was his fellow-pupil Schinkel, whose architectural career really began in 1816 (see Chapter 2).

The Baden architect Friedrich Weinbrenner (1766-1826) was already active in Strasbourg in the 1790s, and his monument of 1800 to General Desaix on the Île des Épis, Bas-Rhin, is so French in every way that it properly finds a place in the official publication by Gourlier and others of the public works of France in these years. Returning to Karlsruhe, Weinbrenner began perhaps the most productive architectural career of any German of his generation, transforming the Baden capital into a Romantic Classical city somewhat less monumental, but more coherently exemplary, than Petersburg. His own house there dated from 1801 and his Ettlinger Gate from 1803. In 1804 he began work on the central Marktplatz, basing himself,

however, on earlier projects that he had made in 1790 and in 1797 [16]. A Baroque scheme exists on paper for this square, closing it in with continuous façades and curving them round the ends. Weinbrenner's characteristically Romantic Classical approach to the design of a square is quite different, similar to if somewhat less open than Friedrich Gilly's intended setting for the Frederick the Great Monument [17]. Two balancing but not identical buildings, each more or less isolated, face each other across the centre of the oblong space. The other less important structures appear as separate blocks. Their relative geometrical purity is underlined by the even purer form of the plain pyramidal monument erected in the centre in 1823. Such had for some time provided favourite decorations in Romantic gardens, but this was the first to be used as a focal accent in place of an arch, a column, or an obelisk. The City Hall on one side, with the associated Lyceum, was begun in 1804 and completed some twenty years later. The temple-like Evangelical Church which faces the City Hall was built in 1807-16. Something of the grand scale of the Corinthian portico on the front of the church is carried over into the

16 and 17. Friedrich Weinbrenner:
Karlsruhe, Marktplatz, 1804–24

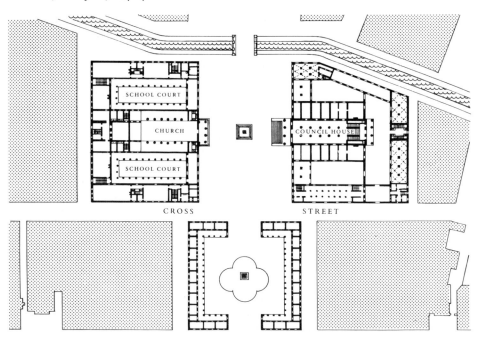

interior, where two tiers of galleries run along the sides behind giant Corinthian nave colonnades. In the circular Rondellplatz, punctuated eventually by an obelisk in the centre, there rose in 1805-13 Weinbrenner's Markgräfliches Palais, its portico set against the concave quadrant of the front. His domed Catholic church of 1808-17 was unfortunately entirely rebuilt in 1880-3.

Similar to Weinbrenner's Rondellplatz is the Karolinenplatz in Munich, laid out by Karl von Fischer (1782-1820) in 1808. But this was originally even more Romantic Classical in disposition, since the individual houses were all discrete blocks set in the segments between the entering streets. The 106-foot obelisk in the centre here was erected in 1833 by Leo von Klenze (1784-1864). Fischer's National Theatre[18b] in the Max-Josephplatz in Munich, projected in 1810 and built in 1811-18 – and later rebuilt by Klenze according to the original design after a fire in 1823 – is a quite conventional monument of its day dominated by a great temple portico. Though not very happy in its proportions, this theatre has real presence, particularly in relation to the less boldly scaled Renaissance Revival buildings by Klenze, the Königsbau of 1826 and the Hauptpostamt of ten years later, which flank it on the sides of the square. It was restored in the 1960s.

Not to extend unduly this catalogue of German work of the very opening years of the nineteenth century, one may conclude with mention of the Women's Prison in Würzburg by Peter Speeth (1772-1831) built in 1809-10. In this, much of the boldness of design of the French prison projects of Ledoux and Boullée is happily realized, if at a rather modest scale [18]. Speeth later proceeded to Russia, but what he did there is a mystery.

Austrian production was rather limited and on the whole undistinguished in this period. The extant façade by Franz Jäger (1743-1809) of the Theater an der Wien of 1797-1801 off the

18. Peter Speeth: Würzburg, Frauenzuchthaus, 1809-10

Linke Wienzeile in Vienna has a delicacy that is more *style Louis XVI* than Romantic Classical. Neither the Palais Rasumofsky at 23-25 Rasumofskygasse in Vienna of 1806-7, built by Louis Joseph von Montoyer (c. 1749-1811) for Beethoven's patron, nor his Albertina of 1800-4 on the Augustinerbastei has much character. There is equally little to be said for the Palais Palffy of 1809 at 3 Wallnerstrasse by the other leading Viennese architect of the day, Karl von Moreau (1758-1841). Despite his French name, Montoyer was a Habsburg subject from the Walloon provinces; Moreau's origin is uncertain, but he is reputed to have been trained, if not born, in France. If he was not French, Austria would be one of the few countries where no French architect worked in this period.

A certain sort of primacy must certainly be given to France in this period, although less definitely than in the decades 1750-90, because the French became the educators of the world in architecture and codifiers of taste once a new post-Baroque style had been created. Among Napoleon's new institutional establishments was the École Polytechnique. Here architecture was taught by Durand, a pupil of Boullée, under the Empire and the following Restoration. In Germany, the instruction of Durand provided the link between the innovations of the creative decades before the Revolution in France and a new generation of architects who matured just in time to take over the building activities of the kingdoms which rose from the ruins of Napoleon's empire. We may well precede any description of the achievements of Romantic Classicism after the year 1810 with some consideration of Durand's treatise.

CHAPTER 2

THE DOCTRINE OF J.-N.-L. DURAND

AND ITS APPLICATION IN NORTHERN EUROPE

From the time of Colbert France had been unique in possessing a highly organized system of architectural education. Under the aegis of the Académie, students were prepared for professional practice in a way all but unknown elsewhere. To crown their formal training came the opportunity, determined by competition, for the ablest to spend several years of further study as *pensionnaires* in Rome. The revolutionary years of the 1790s disrupted temporarily the French pattern of architectural education and recurrent wars cut off access to Rome. The Empire, however, early re-established the pattern of higher professional education with only slight and nominal differences. From 1806 on, moreover, the competition projects for the Prix de Rome, including those from as far back as 1791, were handsomely published in a series of volumes.[1] Thus the whole international world of architecture could henceforth have ready access to the visual results of official French training in architecture, if not to the actual discipline of the Parisian ateliers.

Napoleon, as an ex-ordnance officer, felt more sympathy with engineers than with architects; hence he established a new École Polytechnique, where architecture was included in the curriculum along with various sciences and technics. J.-N.-L. Durand (1760–1834), the new school's professor of architecture, published his *Précis des leçons d'architecture données à l'École Polytechnique* in two volumes in 1802–5, thus making a fairly complete presentation of the content of French architectural education generally available.[2]

Recurrent issues of this work down to 1840, of which at least one appeared outside France – in Belgium – allowed this popular treatise to become a sort of bible of Romantic Classicism that retained international authority for a generation and more.

Durand was a pupil of Boullée; but both the text and the plates of his book indicate his capacity for synthesizing and systematizing the diverse strands of theory and practice that had developed in France in the previous forty years. Because of his temperament and background, and *a fortiori* because he was teaching not in an art academy but in a technical school, Durand is doubtless to be classed within his generation as a proponent of structural rationalism. But he was a much more eclectic one than Soufflot's disciple Rondelet, from 1795 professor at the École Centrale des Travaux Publics and author of the major treatise on building construction of the period.[3] Durand's lessons incorporated many other aspects of Romantic Classicism, from the pure Classical Revivalism of one wing of the academic world to an eclectic interest in Renaissance and even, like his master Boullée, in earlier modes; only the recondite symbolism of earlier Ledoux is absent. In general, one feels in Durand's case, as always with the second generation of an artistic movement, some loss of intensity at various points where the awkward edges of opposed sources of inspiration were clipped to allow their coherent codification.

After a theoretical introduction concerning the goals of architecture, its structural means, and the general principles to be derived therefrom, Durand deals as a convinced 'constructor' with various materials and their proper employment before treating of specific forms and their combination. Only in the second part of his work, concerned with ways of combining architectural elements, do the visual results of his theories become fully evident. There he presents in plan and in elevation various structural systems from trabeated colonnades of Greek and Roman inspiration to arcuated and vaulted forms of Renaissance or even round-arched medieval character. Among his specific examples, 'vertical combinations' of fifteenth- or sixteenth-century elements outnumber the strictly Classical paradigms [19]; whole plates,

minority, although colonnades are frequent enough in his presentation of such specific features as porches, vestibules, halls, galleries, and central spaces. Here are to be found most of the detailed formulas – almost all derived from Boullée and from the Grand Prix projects of the previous decade – which the next generation of architects would follow again and again throughout most of the western world.[3a]

In his second volume Durand turns from a consideration of architecture in terms of structural elements to a notably systematic presentation of buildings in terms of their varying functions. First he deals with urbanistic features, including not only bridges, streets, and squares,

19. J.-N.-L. Durand: 'Vertical Combinations'

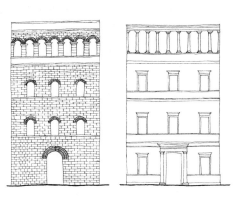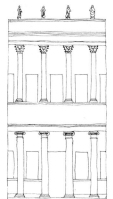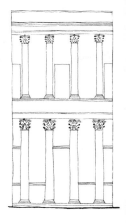

moreover, are given to schemes that are not only generically Italianate, but of Early Christian, Romanesque, or even Gothic, rather than Renaissance, inspiration. Common to most of his examples is the insistent repetition of elements, both horizontally and vertically, and most characteristic is his interest in the varied skylines that central and corner towers can provide, as also in the incorporation of voids in architectural compositions in the form of loggias and pergolas. More monumental façades fronted by temple porticoes are in a

but also such supposedly essential elements of the ideal classicizing city as triumphal arches and tombs. A second section considers temples (not churches, it is amusing to note), palaces, treasuries, law courts, town halls, colleges, libraries, museums, observatories, lighthouses, markets, exchanges, custom houses, exhibition buildings, theatres, baths, hospitals, prisons, and barracks. Here were all the individual structures of the model Napoleonic city, of which Napoleon had time to build so few but of which the next decades in France and abroad were to see so many executed by Durand's pupils and other emulators of his ideals.

For less representational edifices, from town halls and markets to prisons and barracks, Durand's utilitarianism led him to substitute for colonnades and domes plain walls broken by ranges of arcuated openings, sometimes of *quattrocento* or Roman-aqueduct character but as often of vaguely medieval inspiration. For nearly a half century such paradigms were frequently followed, not only in France but even more in other countries, as Classicism continued to grow more Romantic.

Nor were the designs for houses that Durand provided in the final section of his book entirely uninfluential.[4] However, there were fewer of these, and the inspiration of far more executed work of the next forty or fifty years can be traced to his paradigms for public monuments than to his prescriptions for private dwellings. Indeed, Romantic Classicism is a predominantly public style, and its utilitarianism is of the State rather than of the private individual. However, the opposing current of the Picturesque, reflected in Durand's book only in his concern for the 'employment of the objects of nature in the composition of edifices' (by which he meant hardly more than Italianate fountains and even more Italianate vine-hung loggias), provided amply for the individual (see Chapter 6).

It might seem natural to continue after this discussion of Durand's treatise with some account of the executed architecture of France during the final years of the Empire after 1810, under the last Bourbons, and under Louis Philippe. Actually, however, the most concrete examples of Durand's influence, and certainly the finest Durandesque monuments, are to be found not in France but in Germany and Denmark.

By the time of Napoleon, French influence on German architecture was a very old story. More and more French architects were employed by German princes as the eighteenth century proceeded, and by 1800 there were few German centres without examples of their work. As we have seen in the previous chapter, moreover, the work of various German architects in the 1790s and the early 1800s, whether or not they had actually studied or even travelled in France, showed their devotion to the early ideals of Romantic Classicism. Such men as K. G. Langhans and David Gilly in Berlin, Fischer in Munich, or Weinbrenner in Karlsruhe had no Napoleon to employ them; but they were happier than his architects in seeing their major works brought to relatively early completion. At Karlsruhe Weinbrenner's comprehensive projects for the new quarters of the town continued to go forward down to his death in 1826. By that time his City Hall had finally been finished, and street after street of modest houses filled out the pattern of a coherent Romantic Classical city.

The Karlsruhe Marktplatz stands as one of the happiest ensembles of the early nineteenth century, happy not alone because Weinbrenner, who first conceived it, was able to carry it to final completion before architectural fashions had begun to change, but even more because that first conception dated back to the most vigorous period of the architectural revolution in Germany and was notably undiluted by the more pedestrian standards of later days [16]. In detail, perhaps, the original designs for the individual buildings were bolder; but the ideal of a public square, not walled in in the Baroque way but defined by discrete blocks, balanced but not identical, and focused by the eye-catching diagonals of the central pyramid, a geometric shape as pure as the cube or the sphere yet also an established formal symbol and a subtle memory of the Egyptian past, was fully realized [17]. Outside the Marktplatz, except perhaps in the Rondellplatz with its central obelisk, Weinbrenner's work is more provincial, though in a very distinguished way. Here and there, moreover, a pointed arch or a touch of asymmetry showed his early response to the contemporary currents of the Picturesque.

Weinbrenner's death in 1826 and the succession as State architect of Baden of his pupil Heinrich Hübsch (1795-1863) provides a natural break in the Romantic Classical story at just that point when the rise of new ideals began to make the more Classical side of Romantic Classicism out of date – in 1828 Hübsch himself published a characteristic essay, *In welchem Styl sollen wir bauen?*, a question to which the answers were increasingly various, and rarely the Classical style. Elsewhere in Germany, and notably in Bavaria, where the Wittelsbachs, raised to kingship while in alliance with Napoleon, were also the most culturally ambitious rulers of a post-

Napoleonic state, there is no such sharp break. Leo von Klenze, born in 1784 in Hildesheim, lived until 1864; his Munich Propylaeon, completed only the year before his death and begun as late as 1846, is by no means the least Grecian of his works. Klenze (he was ennobled by his royal patron) had studied in Paris during the Empire not only under Durand at the École Polytechnique but also with Percier. In 1805 he had visited the other two main sources of up-to-date architectural inspiration: Italy with its Classical ruins and its Renaissance palaces, and England with its own early version of Romantic Classicism and its various illustrations of the Picturesque. In 1808 Napoleon's brother Gérome, then King of Westphalia, who was already employing A.-H.-V. Grandjean de

Montigny (1776–1850), had made the twenty-four-year-old Paris-trained German his court architect; in 1814 Maximilian I called him to Munich.

In 1816 Klenze began his first major construction, the Munich Glyptothek, a characteristic and externally somewhat dull sculpture gallery. This is dominated in the established French way by a tall temple portico in the centre, and the blank walls at either side are relieved, none too happily, by aedicular niches. But if the exterior (which survived the blitz) is conventional enough the interiors, completed in 1830 and filled – among various other magnificent antiquities – with the sculpture from the temple at Aegina as repaired and installed by Thorwaldsen, made it one of the finest

productions of the great early age of museum-building as long as they were intact [20]. The plan, with a range of vaulted galleries around a court, was generically Durandesque in its square modularity; the sections followed almost line for line one of Durand's paradigms for art galleries [21]. The sumptuous decoration of the vaults and the superb sculpture so handsomely arranged by Thorwaldsen provided a mixture of periods – real fifth-century Greek and Empire – distressing to purists but wonderfully symptomatic of the ideals of the age. It has now been very simply rebuilt internally.

The Glyptothek was the first building erected in the Königsplatz, a very typical Romantic Classical urbanistic entity. Faced by an even more completely columniated picture gallery,

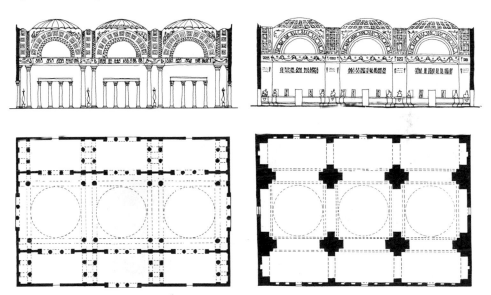

20 *(left)*. Leo von Klenze: Munich, Glyptothek, 1816–30

21 *(above)*. J.-N.-L. Durand: 'Galleries'

built by G. F. Ziebland (1800-73) in 1838-48, with Klenze's Propylaeon of 1846-63 forming the far side of the square, the Königsplatz has all the coldness and barrenness which Weinbrenner happily avoided in his Marktplatz; by the time of its completion this must have seemed very out of date, not least to Klenze himself. But as the Propylaeon indicates, Klenze never eschewed trabeated Classicism, however much his best later work belongs to – indeed to a considerable extent actually initiates – the Renaissance Revival.

His Walhalla[5] near Regensburg, built in 1831-42 but based on designs prepared a decade or more earlier, is the most grandly sited of all the copies of Greek and Roman temples which succeeded in the first half of the nineteenth century Jefferson's initial large-scale example at Richmond, Virginia. Like the finest ancient Greek temples, it is raised high on a hill – that is actually what is most truly

Classical about it, as it is also, paradoxically, what may today seem most specifically Romantic [22]. But the tremendous substructure of staircases and terraces, derived from Friedrich Gilly's project for the monument to Frederick the Great [15], could belong to no other period than this.

In the thirties Klenze, who had already visited Greece in 1823-4 before the establishment of a Wittelsbach monarchy gave employment to Bavarian architects there, was called to Petersburg. There, in 1839-49, rose his Hermitage Museum. The elaborate detailing of this, however Grecian it may be in intention, reflects the growing taste for elaboration in the second quarter of the century as his other Classical works do not. Still later, though not as late as the Propylaeon, is the Munich Ruhmeshalle of 1843-53, a U-shaped Doric stoa which provides in the Hellenistic way a setting for a giant statue of Bavaria by Schwan-

22. Leo von Klenze:
Regensburg (nr), Walhalla, 1831-42

taler. This is dull, and still in the old-established Grecian mode of the earlier years of the century. More characteristically, however, Klenze left all that behind him even before 1825, when Maximilian I was succeeded by Ludwig I. Museums are the most typical monuments of Romantic Classicism, as a whole range of them[6] from the Museo Pio-Clementino by Michelangelo Simonetti (1724-81) at the Vatican in Rome of 1769-74[6a] down at least to the Neuere Pinakothek in Munich of 1846-53 by August von Voit (1801-71) sufficiently illustrate. The two most purely Grecian examples, Smirke's British Museum in London [61] and Schinkel's Neues (later Altes) Museum in Berlin [29], were not yet designed when Klenze first turned his attention in the years 1822-5 to planning a gallery for paintings at Munich. Begun in 1826 and completed in 1833, the Pinakothek (Ältere or Alte Pinakothek) might be considered the earliest monumental example of revived High Renaissance design. Yet there is little about it that cannot be matched in published French Grand Prix projects or in the plates of Durand; Bonnard's ministry on the Quai d'Orsay in Paris, moreover, must have been rather similar. The Pinakothek was badly damaged in the Second World War, but has been well restored according to Klenze's original design, except for the ceiling decorations. Voit's gallery is completely gone.

Another building by Klenze, the Königsbau section of the Royal Residenz in Munich, fronting on the Max-Josephplatz at right angles to Fischer's theatre, is a more attractive early example of the Renaissance Revival. Begun in the same year 1826 as the Ältere Pinakothek, it was completed in 1833. The façade follows closely that of the Pitti Palace as extended in the seventeenth century, but carries the applied pilasters of the Rucellai Palace, and in designing it Klenze must have drawn heavily on the *Architecture toscane* of Grandjean de Montigny.[7] The planning inside is curiously free and

asymmetrical as Sigfried Giedion long ago noted, but then the original Pitti plan was hardly relevant for a nineteenth-century monarch's palace.

In 1836 Klenze completed this square, so characteristic a product of two generations of Romantic Classicism, by facing the eighteenth-century Palais Törring on the other side from the Königsbau with a *quattrocento* arcade in order to provide a monumental and harmonious Central Post Office. Another earlier square, the Odeonsplatz, with Klenze's Leuchtenberg Palais of 1819, his matching Odeon completed in 1828, and a range of shops of 1822, also by him, on the other side of the Ludwigstrasse, has almost as much Italian Renaissance feeling but is less derivatively Tuscan. It follows rather the work of his master Percier in Paris under the Empire.

The increasing eclecticism of Romantic Classical architects is well illustrated by the fact that the Court Church,[8] attached to the Residenz at the rear, built by Klenze in the same years as the Königsbau, 1826-37, was covered with a series of domes on pendentives, derived presumably from the Madeleine in Paris but detailed to suggest, as Vignon's do not, the ultimately Byzantine origin of the structural form. The immediate prototype, however, was probably one of Schinkel's projects for the Werder Church in Berlin (see below).

In the creation of the principal street of Ludwigian Munich, the Ludwigstrasse, a rival of Klenze, Friedrich von Gärtner (1792-1847), like Klenze ennobled by his sovereign, played a more important role. Born in Coblenz, Gärtner studied first at the Munich Academy, where he was later to be professor of architecture and, from 1841, director. After his studies in Munich, he travelled in France, Italy, Holland, and England, although he had no formal foreign training such as Klenze's. Gärtner's first major work, destined by its tall twin towers to dominate the long and rather

23. Friedrich von Gärtner: Munich, Ludwigskirche
and Staatsbibliothek, 1829-40 and 1831-40

monotonous perspective of the Ludwigstrasse, was the Ludwigskirche built in 1829-40 [23]. If Klenze's Court Church was Byzantinesque, Gärtner's church was Romanesquoid, though still in a rather Durandesque way. Even more Durandesque, and very much finer, is the long façade of Gärtner's State Library next door, which was built in 1831-40 [23]. Here the tawny tones of the brick and terracotta, as much as the slightly medievalizing detail of the arcuated front, give evidence of the Romantic rejection of the monochromy typical of the Greek Revival. But if this façade is warm in colour it could hardly be colder in design, throwing into happy relief the richer *ordonnance* of Klenze's nearby War Office (1824-6) with its rusticated arches and lower wings [24].

Rounding out the Ludwigstrasse are many other consonant structures. By Klenze is the Herzog Max Palais of 1826-30 on the right; by Gärtner the Blindeninstitut of 1834-8, farther down opposite the Ludwigskirche, and the University of 1834-40 together with the Max Joseph Stift that complete the terminal square. There stands also the inharmoniously Roman Siegestor of 1843-50 which is, rather surprisingly, also by Gärtner. Far more appropriate, if equally unoriginal, is his Feldherrnhalle of 1841-4 at the other end of the street above the Odeonsplatz, a close copy of the fourteenth-century Loggia dei Lanzi in Florence. The whole area constitutes what is perhaps the finest, or at least the most coherent, range of streets and squares of the later and more eclectic phase of Romantic Classicism. This exceeds in extent, though not in quality, Weinbrenner's Marktplatz in Karlsruhe of the preceding quarter century. This brilliant Munich period came to an end on Ludwig I's abdication in 1848; his successor Maximilian II's attempt to find a 'new style' for his Maximilianstrasse in the next decade was a dismal fiasco, for this 'new style' as applied by Friedrich Bürklein (1813–73), a pupil of Gärtner, in building up the new street in 1852–9 proved to be merely a fussy and muddled approach to the English Perpendicular, already employed with more success by Bürklein's master.

Before his death, the year before Maximilian II's accession, Gärtner had all but completed

Classicism deteriorated after the mid century, was Bürklein's railway station built in 1857–60. The whole station was largely but not entirely destroyed by bombing; originally it had a handsome shed with very heavy arched principals of timber.

Although the mode may be readily paralleled in other North European countries, the *Rundbogenstil* is peculiarly German. It was, indeed, the favourite mode of the thirties and forties in most German states;[9a] certainly it is comparable in local importance to the mature

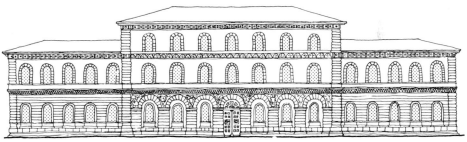

24. Leo von Klenze: Munich, War Office, 1824–6

the Wittelsbach Palace. This he had begun in 1843 using a very Durandesque version of English Tudor executed in red brick. Red brick also characterizes another example of contemporary eclecticism, the Bonifazius Basilika of 1835–40 by Ziebland. This was designed, as its name implies, in a Romantic Classical version of the Early Christian; but it is much less Roman in detail than the great French and Italian churches of the period of this generic basilican order (see Chapter 3).

Most of these variant aspects of later Romantic Classicism in Munich, whether Early Christian, Byzantine, Romanesque, Italian Gothic, or *quattrocento* in inspiration, are also examples of what was called at the time in Germany the *Rundbogenstil*.[9] A large and prominent example in Munich, late enough to illustrate how this special mode of Romantic

Gothic Revival of these decades in England as the German Neo-Gothic is not (see Chapter 6). Deriving from the more utilitarian arcuated models provided by Durand (and ultimately from the projects of his master Boullée and other French architects of the 1780s), the *Rundbogenstil* is still a phase of Romantic Classicism even if in it the Romantic element has risen close to dominance. But in its rigidity of composition, repetition of identical elements, and emphasis on direct structural expression it is wholly in the line of the earlier and more Classical rationalism.

The changing taste of these decades usually demanded ever more and busier detail. Rivalry with the archaeological pretensions of the Greek Revival, moreover, called for a certain parade of stylistic erudition. But the archaeological sources drawn upon were very various and to varying degrees effectively documented. From the Early Christian to the *quattrocento*, most of them were more or less Italianate. However, there were some architects who succeeded – like Gärtner at the Wittelsbach Palace – in using pointed-arched precedent in a characteristically *Rundbogenstil* way; others elaborated their detail with real originality rather than adhering closely to any precedent at all as architects elsewhere would do only later in the century.

On its *quattrocento* side the *Rundbogenstil* was perhaps most notably represented in Germany by the Johanneum in Hamburg of 1836-9 (completely destroyed in the Second World War), a large building surrounding three sides of a court and incorporating two schools and a library [25]. This was by C. L. Wimmel (1786-1845), like Hübsch a pupil of Weinbrenner, and F. G. J. Forsmann (1795-1878). This particular *Rundbogenstil* work might also be classified as belonging, like Klenze's Königsbau, to the international Renaissance Revival of which Hamburg was rather a centre. Moreover the extant Exchange there of 1836-41 by these same architects is of

richer and more High Renaissance character and no longer at all *Rundbogenstil*.

Many houses in Hamburg built by Gottfried Semper (1803-79), Alexis De Chateauneuf (1799-1853), who had studied in Paris, and others in the forties were of elegant Early Renaissance design – one by the former even having *sgraffiti* on the walls – more like Klenze's row of shops in the Odeonsplatz. The Rücker-Jenisch house of 1845 by the Swiss-born Auguste de Meuron (1813-98), a pupil of the same French architect A.-F.-R. Leclerc as De Chateauneuf, was certainly not *Rundbogenstil* but rather a version of the Travellers' Club in London. Thus it followed, in this anglicizing city, an epoch-making model by Charles Barry that dates from fifteen years earlier (see Chapter 4). However, De Chateauneuf's Alster Arcade beside the waters of the Kleine Alster and his red brick Alte Post (now the Weltwirtschafts-archiv) of 1845-7 in the Poststrasse are both prominent and excellent examples of the *Rund-bogenstil* of this period in Hamburg, the latter being slightly Gothic in its detailing.

The work of Hübsch, Weinbrenner's successor as State architect in Baden, despite his

25. Wimmel & Forsmann: Hamburg, Johanneum, 1836-9

very serious archaeological study of Early Christian and Romanesque architecture,[10] falls somewhere between Gärtner's Ludwigskirche and Ziebland's Bonifazius Basilika without achieving either the crisply Durandesque quality of the one or the relative archaeological plausibility of the other. In his civil buildings, such as the very simple Ministry of Finance designed in 1827 and built in 1829-33, the more ornate Technische Hochschule of 1832-6, the Art Gallery of 1840-9, and the Theatre of 1851-3, all in Karlsruhe, very considerable originality of composition was more and more confused as he grew older by the fussy elaboration of the terracotta ornamentation.

In his later work Hübsch frequently used not the round but the segmental arch – a highly rational form with brick masonry – and was usually somewhat happier than the Bavarians in handling the tawny tonalities of brick and terracotta which so generally replaced the pale monochromy of the Greek Revival in the thirties and forties. A minor but especially fine example of his most personal manner is the Trinkhalle of 1840 at Baden Baden [26], which is far better suited in its festive spirit to a

26. Heinrich Hübsch: Baden-Baden, Trinkhalle, 1840

watering-place than the Classical severity of Weinbrenner's Kurhaus there of 1821-3. Hübsch's churches are naturally more archaeological in character and definitely Romanesquoid rather than *Rundbogenstil*. Those at Freiburg (1829-38), Bulach (1834-7), and Rottenburg (1834) are typical. The *Rundbogenstil* railway stations of another Baden architect, Friedrich Eisenlohr (1804-55), at Karlsruhe (1842) and Freiburg preceded Bürklein's in Munich in date and were rather superior to it.

The *Rundbogenstil* was particularly dominant in the southern German states, overflowing also into Switzerland, where the Federal Palace in Berne, built in 1851-7 by Friedrich Studer (1817-70), is a particularly extensive and nobly sited example. It was, however, in Prussia in north Germany that the greatest architect who worked in this mode was active, and he owes his reputation largely to his Grecian work.

Karl Friedrich von Schinkel, the only architect of the first half of the nineteenth century who can be compared in stature with the English Soane, was the great international master of two successive phases of Romantic Classicism, first the programmatic Greek Revival, with which the post-Napoleonic period began almost everywhere in the second decade of the century, and then the more eclectic phase that followed. Born in 1781, a generation later than Soane, Schinkel's serious architectural production began only in 1816. His relatively early death in 1841 truncated his career; but his pupils and his spirit dominated Prussian and indeed a great deal of other German architecture for another score of years and more.

Somewhat as the long-lived Titian stands to the short-lived Giorgione stood Schinkel in relation to his near-contemporary and associate Friedrich Gilly, whose projects have already been mentioned [15]. Indeed, Schinkel showed almost as great a capacity to absorb and continue the revolutionary architectural ideals of the 1780s in France as Gilly – more, certainly, than most of the foreigners who visited Paris during the unproductive years following the Revolution, or even those who stayed on to study there.

Schinkel, however, soon to be one of the most architectonic of architects, made his earliest mark not with architectural projects but, like Inigo Jones in England before him, as a designer of theatre sets. Down to 1815 he executed no buildings of any consequence; but in his paintings of these years, even more perhaps than in his stage sets, he established himself as a High Romantic artist of real distinction. At their best these follow in quality very closely after the master works of German Romantic landscape by Caspar David Friedrich. Characteristically, buildings play an important part in Schinkel's pictures, and vast Gothic constructions in the 'Sublime' spirit of Wyatt's Fonthill Abbey are actually more prominent than Grecian or Italianate fabricks.

But if Gothic projects form a more important part of his production on canvas, and also on paper, in the first decades of the century than is the case with any other architect of the period, even in England, Schinkel made his formal architectural debut as a Grecian and a rationalist. Named by Frederick William III State Architect in 1815, his project of the next year for the Neue Wache [27], Unter den Linden, facing Frederick the Great's opera house, is especially notable in the use of square piers – a Ledolcian extreme of rationalist simplification – beneath the Grecian pediment. His intense Romanticism also reveals itself in the heads of Pergamenian extravagance that writhe forth from the frieze above. In the building as executed and still extant, Greek Doric columns replace the piers and winged victories the writhing heads. But the broad members that frame the cubic mass behind and, above all, the superb proportions of the whole reveal a surer hand than any other architect of the day in

27 *(above)*. K. F. von Schinkel: project for Neue Wache, Berlin, 1816

28 *(right)*. K. F. von Schinkel: Berlin, Schauspielhaus, 1819-21

Germany possessed. The urbanistic effect among existing buildings is equally notable and still very evident.

Schinkel's Berlin Cathedral, as rebuilt in 1817-22 beside the Baroque Schloss of Andreas Schlüter, was a modest work and much less successful; its replacement in 1894-1905 by the enormous Neo-Baroque structure of Julius Raschdorf was no tragedy.

There followed after the Cathedral a work of much greater scale, the Berlin Schauspielhaus, designed in 1818 and built in 1819-21 [28]. Here the complexity of the mass diminishes somewhat the clarity of the geometrical order in the separate parts; but Schinkel's rational-istic handling of Grecian elements is nowhere better seen than in the articulation of the attic by means of a 'pilastrade' of small antae or the reticulated organization of the walls of the side wings. The interior of the auditorium boldly combines very simple and heavily scaled wall elements with very delicately designed iron supports for the ranges of boxes and galleries. It is now being restored.

Characteristic of the many-sidedness of Schinkel's talent, if very much smaller and in-trinsically less happy, is the War Memorial, also of 1819-21, on the Kreuzberg in Berlin. This is a Gothic shrine of the most lacy and linear design, 111 feet high and entirely executed in cast iron.

The Singakademie in Berlin of 1822 and a large house in Charlottenburg for the banker Behrend, on the other hand, are very accom-plished exercises in a rigidly Classical mode such as his French contemporaries were current-ly essaying with markedly less elegance of pro-portion. The Zivilcasino in Potsdam, begun the next year, where an awkward site forced - or perhaps merely justified - an asymmetrical juxtaposition of the parts, illustrated an aspect of Schinkel's talent that has been particularly significant to twentieth-century admirers: the imposition of coherent geometrical order upon

an edifice markedly irregular in its massing. This was something the English were only playing at in these years when they erected Picturesque Italian Villas such as Nash's Cronkhill or loosely composed Castellated Mansions such as Gwrych [89].

It is characteristic of Romantic Classicism that Schinkel's masterpiece – and, with Soane's later Bank interiors, the masterpiece of the period – should be a museum.[10a] The Altes Museum, designed in 1823 and built in 1824-8, faced the Schloss across the Lustgarten, to which Schinkel's just completed Schlossbrücke gave a dignified new approach. The Museum quite outranked his rather undistinguished cathedral; yet at first glance it may seem one of the least original and most tamely archaeological of Romantic Classical buildings [29].

bored, and even shocked, by such stylophily because of the extraordinary logic and elegance of its total organization.

The frontal plane of superbly detailed Ionic columns is not weak at the corners, as colonnades seen against the light generally are, for here spur walls ending in antae firmly enframe the long, unbroken range. And if this frontal columnar plane is unbroken – and also seems to deny by its giant scale the fact that this is a two-storey structure – within the dark of the portico, originally made much darker and more Romantic by a mural designed by Schinkel and executed under the direction of Peter Cornelius, one soon becomes aware of a recessed oblong where a double flight of stairs leads to the upper storey. Moreover, lest this façade be read, like a stoa, as no more than a portico, there rises

29 and 30. K. F. von Schinkel: Berlin, Altes Museum, 1824-8

Substituting for the paradigm of the pedimented peripteral temple that of the stoa, Schinkel evidently counted on the prestige of a giant Grecian order to impress his contemporaries, quite as Brongniart had done at the Paris Bourse [11]. But the Museum retained the admiration of twentieth-century critics

over the centre, still farther to the rear, a rectangular attic.

It is characteristic of the purism of Schinkel's approach, a purism not archaeological but visual, that this attic masks externally a Durandesque central domed space [30]. Such circular central spaces, so recurrent in Romantic Classical planning, had been a favourite setting for classical sculpture, the principal treasure of most art collections of this period, ever since Simonetti's Rotunda was erected at the Vatican. None is finer than this in the proportional relationship of interior colonnade, plain wall above, and coffered dome with oculus. Most, indeed, are but feeble copies of the Roman Pantheon; this almost equals in distinction, if not in scale, its ancient original.

But the Museum, unlike the Munich Glyptothek, had to have picture galleries as well as sculpture halls; and Schinkel's organization of these, so much less palatial than Klenze's in his Pinakothek, was a technical triumph of the rationalistic side of Romantic Classicism. Screens at right angles to the windows, and thus free from glare, provided the greater part of the

also hardly equalled before the mid twentieth century. Tall windows in two even ranges express clearly the two storeys of galleries behind; the stuccoed walls between delicately suggest by their flat rustication – so like that Soane used on the Bank of England – the scale of fine ashlar masonry. But the giant order of the front is also crisply echoed in the flat corner antae just short of which the string-course between the storeys and the rustication of the walls are stopped. A prototype of such detailing can be seen in the Athenian Propylaea, no doubt familiar to Schinkel through publications; a derivation – or at least a superb twentieth-century parallel – is the way Mies van der Rohe handled the juxtaposition of steel stanchions and brick infilling in the buildings he erected for the Illinois Institute of

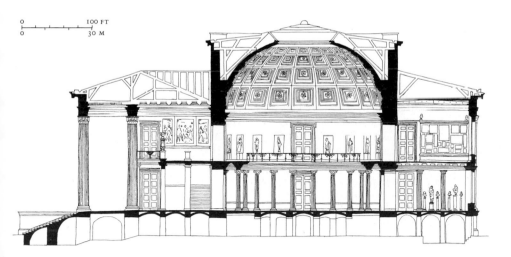

0 ⌐————————⌐ 100 FT
0 ⌐—'——'——'—⌐ 30 M

hanging space, a premonition almost of the movable screens of mid-twentieth-century art galleries [30].

The external treatment of the rear walls of the Museum, moreover, achieves a clarity of mathematical organization and a subtlety of structural expression in the detailing which was

Technology in Chicago in the 1940s and 50s (see Chapter 20).

The rapid deterioration of rationalist Grecian standards, which followed within a few decades even in the hands of Schinkel's ablest pupils, is to be noted in the Neues Museum, built in 1843–55 by F. A. Stüler (1800–65) behind the

Altes Museum. It is even more evident in the contiguous Nationalgalerie, also by Stüler but based on a sketch by Frederick William IV. This temple stands on a very high substructure in an awkward perversion of the theme of Gilly's monument to Frederick the Great and Klenze's Walhalla. It was finished only in 1876 by which time, even in Germany, Romantic Classicism was completely dead (see Chapter 9).

Behind his museum Schinkel himself had built in 1828-32, along the banks of the Kupfergraben, the Packhofgebäude. This range of utilitarian structures was definitely consonant, towards the Museum, with the Grecian rationalism of its rear façade. But for the warehouses at the remote end of the group Schinkel used a rather direct transcription of Durand's paradigm for an arcuated market.[11] Here, at almost precisely the same time as at Gärtner's State Library in Munich and Hübsch's Ministry of Finance in Karlsruhe, the *Rundbogenstil* makes an early appearance as an alternative to the trabeated Grecian. In comparably utilitarian works of a few years earlier, the Military Prison in Berlin begun in 1825 and the lighthouse at Arkona of the same date, Schinkel had already used dark brickwork unstuccoed, but with square rather than arched openings; while on his long-demolished Hamburg Opera House, begun also in 1825 and completed in 1827, there were arched openings throughout of a somewhat High Renaissance order, but far more severely treated than by Klenze on his Munich Pinakothek.

To the year 1825 belongs, too, the beginning of the Werder Church in Berlin, Gothic in its vaults, as also in its detail, and executed in brick and terracotta. Less just in its scaling than his earlier Gothic monument of cast iron, this church as executed makes one regret that the alternative domed project of 1822, derived either from Vignon's interior of the Madeleine in Paris or from one of Durand's paradigms, was not executed.

In 1826 began Schinkel's extensive and varied work for the Royal family at Potsdam,[12] the town destined to be the richest centre of later Prussian Romantic Classicism. Here he worked in close association with the heir to the throne who was later, after 1840, king as Frederick William IV. This romantic and talented prince – who actually wished he were an architect rather than a ruler – frequently provided Schinkel and, after his death, Schinkel's pupils with sketches from which (as we have seen in the case of the Nationalgalerie) various executed buildings were elaborated with more or less success. One of the great amateurs, his was a very late example of direct Royal intervention in architecture. Some of the modulation of Schinkel's style towards the Picturesque – still more evident in the work at Potsdam of his ablest pupil Ludwig Persius (1803-45) – may be credited to this princely patron.[12a]

In Berlin, in the later twenties, Schinkel was also remodelling and redecorating palaces for Frederick William's brothers, major works in scale but rather limited in architectural interest.[13] More characteristic of Schinkel's best Grecian manner is the somewhat later palace for Prince William built in 1834-5 by the younger Langhans (K. F., 1781-1869). This architect's still later theatre at Wrocłav (Breslau), begun in 1843, is worth mention at this point and also the old Russian Embassy of 1840-1 in Berlin by Eduard Knoblauch (1801-65), but Schinkel's comparable work is fifteen years earlier.

At Potsdam, even though much of what he did there also consisted of enlarging earlier buildings, Schinkel was freer than in Berlin. Collaboration with the gardener P. J. Lenné (1789-1866), who provided superb naturalistic settings in the tradition of the English garden, may have encouraged a looser and less Classical sort of composition. In many views, Charlottenhof with its dominating Greek Doric portico, remodelled from 1826 on as the residence of the

Crown Prince, may appear a sufficiently conventional Greek Revival country house. But if one considers the planning of the house and its close relation to the raised terrace, and also the relation to the solid block of the open pergola – 'an object of nature' in Durand's special sense – one sees that here, as earlier at the Zivilcasino, but from no necessity enforced by the site, Schinkel sought to apply the most stringent sort of geometrical order to an asymmetrical composition. For this, of course, the Erechtheum and to some extent the Propylaea on the Akropolis, those two fifth-century Greek examples of Romantic Classicism, provided precedents. At Schloss Glienecke[13a] near by, also begun in 1826 for another Prussian prince, Karl, whose palace in Berlin he was then remodelling, the Athenian derivation is very patent in the later belvedere of 1837 based on the Choragic Monument of Lysicrates. But it is the asymmetrical grouping of carefully organized elements here that reveals the extent to which Schinkel was able to absorb and actually to synthesize with the discipline of Romantic Classicism one of the major formal innovations of the Picturesque. The bold off-centre location

of the tower actually makes of this a sort of Italian Villa in the Cronkhill sense.

In the enlargement of the medieval Kolberg Town Hall in Pomerania, begun in 1829, Schinkel employed secular Late Gothic in a version as stiff and mechanical as that of Gärtner's Wittelsbach Palace of a decade later. A remarkable centrally-planned Hunting Lodge, built for Prince Radziwill at Ostrowo in 1827, on the other hand, illustrated a bold attempt to apply the principles of Durandesque structural rationalism to building in timber; the result is very different indeed from the contemporary American, Russian, and Swedish houses of wood designed as copies of marble temples.

In 1828 a series of designs for churches in the new suburbs of Berlin, several of them executed in reduced form in the early thirties, showed a drastic shift away from Classical models – still sometimes offered as alternatives and actually executed in two cases – towards the creation of a very personal sort of *Rundbogenstil*. All intended to be of brick with terracotta trim, these were less successful than the house he built of the same materials for the brick and terracotta

31. K. F. von Schinkel: Berlin, Feilner house, 1829

manufacturer Feilner in Berlin in 1829. In its perfect regularity and rigid trabeation this recalled the rear of the Museum [31]. But the employment of delicate arabesque reliefs in the jambs of the openings, quite in the *quattrocento* way, illustrated rather more attractively than the church projects the characteristic modulation in these years away from Grecian and towards Italianate models.

The happiest and most informal example of this modulation is to be seen in the Court Gardener's House of 1829-31 on the Charlottenhof estate [32]. The closely associated Tea House and Roman Bath of 1833-4 loosely enclose the square rear garden at the junction of two canals. As the plan of the house itself clearly

reveals, this was not a new construction but a remodelling, or encasing, of an earlier gardener's house; but more important to the total effect than the original solid block is the skilful disposition of the clearly defined voids in the three-dimensional composition, voids which include pergolas of varying height, loggias, and even an open attic below the main roof.

On the one hand, the inspiration for this must have come from Durand's illustrations of the 'employment of the objects of nature' or perhaps from other French works[14] more specifically dealing with Italian buildings in the countryside. On the other hand, rather more than most English Italian Villas in the line of Nash's Cronkhill, this seems to be based on

32. K. F. von Schinkel:
Potsdam, Court Gardener's House, 1829-31

some real knowledge of Italian rural, not to say rustic, building. But visually, as at Cronkhill and at Glienecke, the pivot of the whole composition is the tower around which the various elements, solid and hollow, are as carefully organized as in a piece of twentieth-century Neo-plasticist sculpture. This Gardener's House is as much the international masterwork of the asymmetrically-towered Italian Villa mode, one of the more modest yet extremely significant innovations of the first half of the nineteenth century, as is the Altes Museum of formal Grecian Classicism.

At Potsdam and near by Schinkel's pupil Persius, before his untimely death only four years after Schinkel's, produced many other compositions of this order, often by remodelling eighteenth-century buildings.[15] Two of the finest are the Pheasantry, which is specifically a towered Italian Villa, and the group that includes the Friedenskirche, carried out by others from Persius's designs in 1845–8 [33]. In this latter group the principal feature is a close copy of an Early Christian basilica, even to the inclusion of a real medieval apse mosaic brought from Murano; yet compositionally the group is a masterpiece of the classically ordered Picturesque, rivalling Schinkel's Gardener's House in subtlety and elegance. Even more personal to Persius is the delicacy of detailing and the unusual external arcade of his earlier Heilandskirche of 1841–3, with its graceful detached campanile, by the lakeside at neighbouring Sakrow.

Also notable are his steam-engine houses, particularly that for Schloss Babelsberg. The inclusion of medieval and even Islamic detail indicates the increasing eclecticism of taste around 1840; yet the disparate elements are so scaled and ordered as to compose into an asymmetrical pattern of Italian Villa character in which the minaret-like chimney provides the dominant vertical accent. Less Picturesque is the Orangerieschloss, based on a sketch by

Frederick William IV and executed after Persius's death by A. Hesse.

Schinkel's big Potsdam church, the Nikolaikirche, designed in 1829 and built up to the base of the dome in the years 1830–7, stands right in the town, not in the park like his work for the prince, and is a wholly formal monument. It was planned as a hemisphere above a cube in the most geometrical mode of Romantic Classicism. As in the case of Soufflot's dome of the Panthéon, this was undoubtedly influenced by Wren's St Paul's in London which Schinkel had seen on an English voyage in 1826. Unfortunately Persius had later to add corner towers, almost like the minaret chimney of his Babelsberg engine house, in order to load the

33. Ludwig Persius:
Potsdam, Friedenskirche, 1845–8

pendentives when he completed the church in 1842–50. These irrelevant features quite denature Schinkel's formal intention. The interior, however, was superior to those in most of the other churches of this period in various countries that were based more closely on the Roman Pantheon. It has not been restored.

Schinkel did not have such opportunities of building whole squares and streets as did his Baden and his Bavarian contemporaries.[15a] For all his efforts, the Berlin Lustgarten was probably never very satisfactory urbanistically because of the inadequate focus that was provided by his modest cathedral beside the massive Baroque Schloss and the awkward shift in the axis where the Schlossbrücke enters from Unter den Linden. At the other end of Unter den Linden the Pariser Platz inside K. G. Langhans's Brandenburg Gate shows little evidence of Schinkel's intended regularization of the surrounding buildings. All that he was actually able to carry out there was a remodelling of the Palais Redern in 1832–3, and this was demolished in 1906 to make way for the Adlon Hotel.

The façades of the Palais Redern gave a *quattrocento* Florentine impression because of their relatively bold over-all rustication; only the large openings were arcuated, however, the ordinary windows being lintel-topped. Significant of Schinkel's new interest in asymmetrical order was the disposition of the four arched openings; these were balanced in relation to the corner of Unter den Linden but unbalanced in relation to either façade alone; the other windows were quite regularly spaced.

If Schinkel seems to have adopted here a version of the Renaissance Revival – as, for that matter, he had already done much earlier in his somewhat similar remodelling of the Berlin City Hall in 1817 – at the Neues Tor, also of 1832, he provided two gatehouses which were in a sort of *Rundbogenstil* Tudor comparable to Gärtner's Wittelsbach Palace of fifteen years later. His trip to England[16] had fascinated him

with English architecture, old and new; there he had noted everything with intelligent interest – from medieval castles to the towering new cotton mills near Manchester with their internal skeletons of iron. He had no occasion, however, to make large-scale use of iron construction, though there is little doubt that had he lived on through the forties he would have done so with technical and aesthetic mastery.

At Schloss Babelsberg,[17] built for the rather tasteless brother of his own particular patron, later the Emperor William I, he essayed an English sort of castle, admittedly more in the contemporary Picturesque mode of the new Castellated Mansions of Nash and Wyatt than like any real medieval one. This was designed in 1834 and begun in 1835. Persius took it over on Schinkel's death, redesigning one of the principal towers, and it was finally finished after Persius's death by Heinrich Strack (1805–80) in 1849. Though certainly not inferior to Smirke's Eastnor or Cundy's Hawarden, if without the lovely site and the richly organic composition of Busby's Gwrych, Babelsberg is better appreciated in Schinkel's or Persius's drawings than in actuality. Schloss Kamenz, a rather Tudoresque remodelling of an earlier structure which Schinkel undertook in 1838, is more typical but no more successful.

Although playing but a very minor part in Schinkel's own production, his exercises in the Chalet mode should at least be mentioned. Not only do these illustrate the very wide range of his own eclectic inspiration, considerably wider than that of Durand and the French of the previous generation, they also represent one of the peripheral aspects of his achievement which his pupils, and German architects of the mid century generally, delighted to exploit. The happiest work of his followers, however, continued rather the Italian Villa line of Glienecke and the Court Gardener's House, a line in which Persius at least all but equalled his master.

The Grecian work of Schinkel's imitators and emulators tends to be overdecorated and lacking in geometrical order while their *Rundbogenstil* is in general awkwardly proportioned and incoherently ornamented (see Chapter 9). Outside Prussia, such Hamburg architects as Wimmel & Forsmann and de Chateauneuf illustrate better than other North Germans the real possibilities of the *Rundbogenstil*. De Chateauneuf had something of an international reputation, moreover, after winning the second prize in the competition held in 1839–40 for the Royal Exchange in London. His design for that was based on the Loggia dei Lanzi, and may well have provided the suggestion for Gärtner's Feldherrenhalle in Munich begun in 1841. He also worked in Oslo.

It is impossible and unnecessary to follow Romantic Classicism to all the other German centres. At Darmstadt the Classical Ludwigskirche of 1822–7 by Georg Moller (1784–1852),[17a] a pupil of Weinbrenner, is a handsome circular edifice with an internal colonnade below the dome. Thus it is rather like the 'central space' in Schinkel's Museum, but more broadly proportioned. A boldly arched entrance of almost Ledolcian character is set against the external circumference of blank wall rather than the more usual temple portico. The Artillery Barracks at Darmstadt of 1825–7 by Moller's pupil Franz Heger (1792–1836) provided a notably early example of the *Rundbogenstil*. Comparable was August Busse's Castellated Zellengefängnis in Berlin of 1842–9, the first German example of a penitentiary radially planned and with individual cells (see Chapter 5). Stüler's Schinkelesque Trinitatiskirche in Cologne, planned like an Early Christian basilica and built in 1857–61, was much finer than his Berlin churches (see Chapter 9).

Also *Rundbogenstil,* but of a more medievalizing order, was Semper's Synagogue of 1838–41 in Dresden. Its centralized massing is uncharacteristically plastic. His Palais Oppenheim there of 1845–8 at 9–11 An der Burgerweise, based on Raphael's Pandolfini Palace, was a handsome and very 'correct' example of the international Renaissance Revival to be compared, like de Meuron's house in Hamburg, with Barry's London club-houses. The Cholera Fountain of 1843 in Dresden was Gothic, however, providing further evidence of Semper's rather directionless eclecticism at this time.

His principal works of this period were the first Opera House[18] in Dresden of 1837–41, where Wagner's early triumphs took place, burnt and rebuilt by Semper later, and the nearby Art Gallery of 1847–54 which completes so unhappily the circuit of the eighteenth-century Zwinger by Daniel Pöppelmann. The one was a rather festive, the other a rather solemn example of the Renaissance Revival; both are more notable for their planning and their general organization than for any visual distinction [34]. The Opera House in Hanover, built by G. L. F. Laves (1789–1864) in 1845–52, is less original in plan but more sober, even a

34. Gottfried Semper:
Dresden, Opera House (first), 1837–41

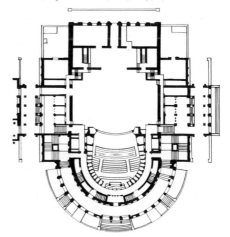

35. G. L. F. Laves: Hanover, Opera House, 1845–52

bit Schinkelesque, in design [35]. Its interior has been completely done over since it was bombed in the Second World War.

The historian tends always to press forward, forcing rather than retarding the pace of development in his written account. Klenze's Propylaeon, however, has already provided evidence of the late continuance of Grecian ideals in the German States; in Stuttgart the Königsbau of 1857–60 by C. F. Leins (1814–92), a pupil in Paris of Henri Labrouste, provides a worthier example, although this was actually begun twenty years earlier by J. M. Knapp (1793–1861). In Vienna, as late as 1873, the Parliament House of Theophil von Hansen (1813–91) provides a gargantuan example of what the French had first aspired to build almost a century earlier. Ambiguous in its massing, if still very elegant in its Grecian detail, this contrasts markedly with Hansen's other Viennese work of the third quarter of the century which is generally of High Renaissance design (see Chapter 8).

This Copenhagen-born and trained architect knew Greece at first hand, for he and his brother

H. C. Hansen (1803–83) worked in Athens for some years for the Wittelsbachs and the Danish dynasty that succeeded them. Along University Street in Athens a conspicuous range of porticoed structures is theirs. The University, built in 1837–42, is by the elder brother; the Academy, erected in 1859–87, was designed by Theophil and executed by his pupil Ernst Ziller; the National Library was also designed by Theophil in 1860 and completed in 1892. Conventional essays in the international Greek Revival mode, here made somewhat ironical by their proximity to the great fifth-century ruins, these lack the elegance and refinement of Theophil's Palais Dimitriou of 1842–3 (lately destroyed by the enlargement of the Grande Bretagne Hotel towards Syndagma Square) as also the more than Schinkelesque restraint of the earliest Romantic Classical building in Greece. This is Gärtner's gaunt but distinguished Old Palace,[19] designed in 1835–6 for Otho of Wittelsbach immediately after his assumption of the Greek throne and built in 1837–41 [36].

The Old Palace and its neighbour the Grande Bretagne still dominate the centre of modern Athens. The palace, in its regularity, its austerity, and its geometrical clarity of design, is a finer archetype of the most rigid Romantic Classical ideals than anything Gärtner built in Munich; indeed, perhaps those ideals were nowhere else ever followed so completely at monumental scale except in Denmark. One may even wonder irreverently if the fifth century had many civil buildings that were so pure and so calm!

Gärtner and the Hansens set the pace for a local Greek Revival vernacular of a rather North European order. In its detail this vernacular sometimes exceeds in delicacy that of the later centuries of antiquity, as illustrated here in the Stoa of Attalos in the Agora – at least as that has lately been reconstructed – or the Arch of Hadrian. Not all of the new construction was Grecian, however: Klenze's Roman

36. Friedrich von Gärtner:
Athens, Old Palace, 1837-41

Catholic Cathedral (Aghios Dionysios) in University Street is a basilica with Renaissance detail, built in 1854-63; the modest English Church of 1840-3 is rather feebly Gothic and based rather curiously on a design by C. R. Cockerell much modified in execution.

Of the leading Greek architects of the period, Lyssander Kaftanzoglou (1812 85), Stamathios Kleanthis (1802-62), and Panajiotis Kalkos (1800?-1870?), only Kleanthis was German-trained. This talented pupil of Schinkel followed his master's Italianate rather than his Grecian line, and the house he built in 1840 for the Duchesse de Plaisance[19a] on Kiffisia Avenue (now the Byzantine Museum) is a distinguished example of a Durandesque Italian villa, with simple arcading front and rear and low corner towers. Kaftanzoglou, trained at the École de Beaux-Arts in Paris and in Milan, was somewhat less able; but the large quadrangular Grecian structure that he designed in the fifties and built in 1862-80 to house the Polytechneion in Patissia Street more than rivals the academic buildings by the Hansens in University Street in the careful ordering of its parts and the

correct elegance of its details. Of Kalkos's work little remains in good condition today.

The new capital of remote Greece possesses more, and on the whole more impressive, Romantic Classical buildings than do Vienna and Budapest, capitals of the Austro-Hungarian Empire. In them ambitious urbanistic projects were initiated only later after the accession of Francis Joseph in 1848. The Theseus Temple in the Volksgarten in Vienna of 1821-3 by Peter von Nobile (1774-1854),[20] a Swiss who had made his reputation in Trieste, is hardly more than a large Grecian garden ornament conscientiously copying the fifth-century Hephaisteion in Athens line for line. His nearby Burgtor, begun the following year, is much worthier in its heavy, almost Sanmichelian, way. More characteristic, however, is the work of Joseph Kornhäusel (1782-1860) and of Paul Sprenger (1798-1854).

Kornhäusel's Schottenhof, opening off the Schottengasse, is a housing development built in 1826-32 in collaboration with Joseph Adelpodinger (1778-1849). This is of extraordinary extent and arranged very regularly around several large internal courts. The smooth stucco walls, restricted ornamentation, and regular fenestration, brought out to the wall surface by double windows, can be matched in many streets of the city that were built up in these decades. Behind such a façade in the Seitenstettengasse lies Kornhäusel's handsome but rather modest Synagogue of 1825-6. This has an elliptical dome and an internal colonnade that carries a narrow gallery. Much richer is his rectangular main hall of 1823-4 in the Albertina; as has been noted, this palace had already been enlarged in 1801-4 in Romantic Classical style by Montoyer. Kornhäusel's hall is finished in mirror and in pale yellow and pale mauve scagliola with chalk-white Grecian details and sandstone statues of the Muses by J. Klieber.

With Kornhäusel all is classical; Sprenger, on the other hand, employed a rather tight version of the *Rundbogenstil*, more Renaissance than medievalizing, for his considerably later Mint of 1835-7 in the Heumarkt in Vienna. More original, and with charming arched window-frames of terracotta in delicate floral bands, is his Landeshauptmannschaft of 1846-8 at 11 Herrengasse. This contrasts happily with the Diet of Lower Austria, projected in 1832-3 and built in 1837-44 by Luigi Pichl (1782-1856), next door at No. 13, a rather heavy and conventional example of Romantic Classicism; so also does No. 17, a very simple block originally built by Moreau for the Austro-Hungarian Bank in 1821-3. The later bank building across the Herrengasse at No. 14, built by Heinrich von Ferstel (1828-83) in 1856-60, well illustrates the modulation of the *Rundbogenstil* here, as in Germany, towards richer and more Gothicizing forms after the mid century. The glass-roofed passage extending through this to the Freyung is still very attractive, despite its shabby condition, and worthy of comparison with other extant examples of passages elsewhere in the Old and New Worlds (see Chapters 3, 5, and 8).[20a]

The great nineteenth-century Viennese building campaign of Francis Joseph began in 1849 with the initiation of the Arsenal. There the outer ranges (now mostly destroyed by bombing) were completed in 1855 from designs by Eduard Van der Nüll (1812-65), a pupil of Nobile and Sprenger, and his partner August Siccard von Siccardsburg (1813-68). The Army Museum of 1850-6 is by Ludwig Förster (1797-1863) and Theophil von Hansen (who had married Förster's daughter after moving from Athens to Vienna), and the chapel of 1853-5 is by Karl Rösner (1804-59). These are all in slightly varying *Rundbogenstil* modes, and they show, like Ferstel's bank, the changed taste of the mid century, most notably in their rather violent brick polychromy (see Chapter 8).

In Budapest the National Museum of 1837-44 by Michael Pollák (1773-1855) is a vast rectangle fronted in the conventional way by an octostyle Corinthian portico and with a somewhat Schinkel-like severity of treatment on the side wings. This is another major example of the museums which were such characteristic monuments of Romantic Classicism everywhere. Among many other large typical public monuments designed by Pollák, the Kommitat Building may be mentioned as of comparable size and dignity to his museum.

If first Greece and then Austria employed Danish Hansens in the forties and fifties, the earlier Romantic Classical tradition of C. F. Hansen, who in any case lived on until 1845, was still better maintained at home by his pupil M. G. B. Bindesbøll (1800-56). Where C. F. Hansen's inspiration was Roman and Parisian, Bindesbøll's seems rather to have been German, as was common in his generation. Certainly his masterpiece, again a museum and indeed a museum of sculpture, out-Schinkels Schinkel. The Thorwaldsens Museum[21] in Copenhagen was built in 1839-48 to house the sculpture and the collections of the thoroughly Romanized Bertil Thorwaldsen, which he had determined

37. M. G. B. Bindesbøll:
Copenhagen, Thorwaldsens Museum, Court, 1839-48

in 1837 to present to his native country. The mode, of course, is Greek but completely astylar like the rear of Schinkel's Berlin Museum; the general impression, particularly of the court with Thorwaldsen's tomb in its centre, is surprisingly Egyptian [37]. The mathematical severity of the architectural design is warmed by the murals on the walls, once largely washed away but now all renewed; they romanticize thoroughly its rigid geometrical forms. Even the purely architectural elements, moreover, were once polychromed, if the present restoration of the colour is correct.

The murals on the exterior of the museum were designed in 1847-8 and executed in 1850 by Jørgen Sonne in a sort of coloured plaster intarsia with heavy black outlines. Developing a happy idea of Bindesbøll's, these tell rather realistically the story of the transport of the sculpture from Rome to Copenhagen. The foliate work on the court walls was carried out by H. C. From in 1844 – laurel-trees, oaks, and palms. In the interiors, where Thorwaldsen disposed his own sculptures somewhat less formally than he had the Aegina sculptures in the Munich Glyptothek, the intricate and brightly coloured decoration of the barrel vaults is in that Pompeian mode which had been a part of the Romantic Classical tradition ever since the time of Clérisseau and Adam. This provides a happy contrast to so much Neo-Classic white marble statuary set against plain walls painted in strong flat colours. The finest of these ceilings have no modern rivals, even in Adam's eighteenth-century work, for the precise geometrical organization of the panels and the delicate refinement of the very low plaster reliefs. Bolder and wholly abstract are the floors of tile mosaic arranged in a bewildering variety of patterns, some imitated from Roman models but more of them so original in design that they suggest Op Art of the 1960s.

In his few other executed works and projects Bindesbøll showed himself considerably less Classical and Schinkelesque than in this museum; perhaps the museum reflects Thorwaldsen's taste as much or more than his own. Tending, like other Danes of his generation, towards the *Rundbogenstil* in his urban buildings, for his country houses he arrived at a very direct and logical rural mode in which rustic materials and asymmetrical compositions were controlled by a Romantic Classical sense of order and decorum. If, on the one hand, his interest in bold structural polychromy in the fifties parallels that of the English Butterfield, his domestic mode forecasts that of the English Webb (see Chapters 10 and 12). Bindesbøll's production was small, but the very simple *Rundbogenstil* Agricultural School of 1856-8 at 13 Bülowsvej in Copenhagen deserves mention, as also the striped brick church of 1850-2 at Hobro, which is Gothic.

J. D. Herholdt (1818-1902), living almost half a century longer than Bindesbøll, was naturally more productive. He was also a master of the *Rundbogenstil* hardly rivalled in his generation even by the ablest Germans. Late as is his National Bank at 17 Holmens Kanal in Copenhagen – 1866-70 – this is one of the finest examples anywhere of the more Tuscan sort of *Rundbogenstil*. His University Library of 1857-61 in the Frue Plads is less suave in design but much more original in its brick detailing. As late as the eighties he maintained the Romantic Classical discipline in his Italian Gothic Raadhus at Odense of 1880-3 as well as carrying out many tactful restorations

of Romanesque churches. Of his fine Copenhagen Station of 1863-4 the wooden shed now serves on another site as a sports hall.

G. F. Hetsch (1830-1903) also continued the Romantic Classical line, most happily perhaps in his Sankt Ansgarskirke of 1841-2, the Roman Catholic church in the Bredgade in Copenhagen. Ferdinand Meldahl (1827-1908), although capable of very disciplined Early Renaissance design in his office building at 23 Havnegade in Copenhagen of 1864, led Danish architecture away from Romantic Classicism and the *Rundbogenstil* towards a rather Second Empire sort of eclecticism after he became professor at the Copenhagen Academy in 1864 and its director in 1873 (see Chapter 8).

With its great individual monuments by C. F. Hansen and Bindesbøll and its streets of fine houses in the Romantic Classical vernacular, Copenhagen provides today a more attractive picture of the production of this period than almost any other city. Norway, at this time less prosperous than Denmark, has work by Schinkel himself. At least the designs for the buildings of the University at Christiania, erected in 1841-51 by C. H. Grosch (1801-65), a pupil of C. F. Hansen in Copenhagen, were revised by Schinkel just before his death, and the handling of the walls is quite characteristic of his work in the clarity and logic of the articulation. There are also De Chateauneuf's churches.

In Sweden, where the dominant influences in the early nineteenth century were first French and then German as in Denmark, there was no comparably brilliant development of Romantic Classicism. Rosendal, a country house built in 1823-5 by Fredrik Blom (1781-1851), is a pleasant and very discreet edifice that might well be by almost any French architect of Blom's generation. His Skeppsholm Church in Stockholm of 1824-42, circular within and octagonal without, is a typical but not especially distinguished work of its period. More characteristic are the modest wooden houses with

Grecian detail. These are similar to, but in their naive 'correctness' less extreme than, the temple houses of Russia and the United States. Their board-and-batten walls might, paradoxically, have inspired one aspect of Downing's anti-Grecian campaign in America in the forties (see Chapter 15).

In 1850 Stüler was called to Stockholm from Berlin to design the National Museum. Eventually completed in 1865, this is in a richer Venetian Renaissance mode than he usually employed at home. Such more definitely Romantic modes were generally exploited by native architects only much later. For example, the Sodra Theatre of 1858-9 in Stockholm by J. F. Åbom (1817-1900) is still quite a restrained example of the revived High Renaissance; while so excellent a specimen of the more Tuscan sort of *Rundbogenstil* as the Skandias Building in Stockholm by P. M. R. Isaeus (1841-90) and C. Sandahl dates from 1886-9, but must be compared with German work of at least a generation earlier.

Holland has even less of distinction to offer in this period than Sweden.[22] Yet the Lutheran Round Church on the Singel in Amsterdam, as it was rebuilt after a fire in 1826 by Jan de Greef (1784-1834) and T. F. Suys (1783-1861), a pupil of Percier, lends a distinctly Venetian air to the local scene with its great dome, despite the admirably Dutch quality of its fine brickwork. The original church was built in 1668-77 by Adriaen Dortsmann, and doubtless the odd plan, with main entrance under the pulpit and double galleries at the rear outside the main rotunda, derives from the older building.

The monumentally Classical Haarlemer Poort of 1840 in Amsterdam by J. D. Zocher (1790-1870) may also be mentioned, as it is nearly unique in Holland. This has the stuccoed walls that, in Holland as elsewhere, generally replaced exposed brickwork under the influence of international Romantic Classicism. The Academy of Fine Arts in The Hague, built by Z. Reijers in 1839 and demolished in 1933, dominated by an Ionic portico of stone, might well have risen in any French provincial city of the day. Very similar, except that the portico is Corinthian, is the Palace of Justice in Leeuwarden built in 1846-52 by T. A. Romein (1811-81). Handsome also, but like the Hague Academy less autochthonous in character than the Round Church, is the long stone façade beside the Rokin of the Nederlandsche Bank in the Turfmarkt (1860) by Willem Anthony Froger. On the whole, Holland is the exception that proves the rule. Almost alone in Northern Europe Dutch architects failed, in general, to accept Romantic Classicism as it was adumbrated most notably in the treatise of Durand; while local conditions, in any case, reduced monumental architectural production to a minimum in the decades between Waterloo and the mid century.

CHAPTER 3

FRANCE AND THE REST OF THE CONTINENT

Before considering English architecture in the years between Waterloo and the Great Exhibition of 1851, it will be well to turn to France. The drama of the supersession of a supposedly purely Classical school in painting by a purely Romantic one, the contrast between such giants as Ingres on the one hand and Delacroix on the other, cannot be matched in the tame course of French architecture in this period; only very rarely was the accomplishment of these great painters or of half a dozen others, ranging from Géricault and Bonington to Corot and Daumier, equalled in quality by a Henri Labrouste or a Duban. Although the art of Ingres is in many ways parallel to Romantic Classicism in architecture, no French architect of this generation really approaches him at all closely in stature, although he numbered several among his close friends. Nor are there among architects many Romantics of the boldness of Delacroix or 'independents' to compare with Corot.

The Empire left a vast heritage of unfinished monuments. It is properly to the credit of the July Monarchy of Louis Philippe that these were brought to completion a generation after their initiation; but all the credit for them has in fact generally accrued to Napoleon himself. The intervening Restoration of the returned Bourbons, tired, reactionary and bigoted, gave its support largely to the construction of religious buildings. Appropriately, the first important new commission under Louis XVIII was for the Chapelle Expiatoire in memory of his brother Louis XVI and Marie Antoinette. This chapel with its raised tomb-flanked forecourt, lying between the Rue Pasquier and the Rue d'Anjou off the Boulevard Haussmann, was begun in 1816 and completed in 1824 [38].

Somewhat less appropriately, it was Napoleon's favourite architect Fontaine – his partner Percier had by this time retired – who received the commission. But the character of the project and of the regime led him to modulate his earlier imperial style from the festive and the triumphal towards the solemn and the funereal. Not an unworthy example of Romantic Classicism, this nevertheless lacks the crispness and clarity of the best contemporary German work. Nor does it much recall – as it well might have done – either the delicacy of the *style Louis XVI* or the 'Sublime' grandeur of the many projects for

38. P.-F.-L. Fontaine:
Paris, Chapelle Expiatoire, 1816–24

monumental cenotaphs designed by the previous generation of architects and by those of Fontaine's own generation in their youth.

To restore the strength of the church, as the piety of the later Bourbons demanded, priests had to be trained in quantity. The next significant work undertaken in Paris after the Chapelle Expiatoire was the Séminaire Saint-Sulpice in the Place St Sulpice by É.-H. Godde (1781–1869); this was begun in 1820 and completed in 1838. So flat and cold are its façades that the observer may readily fail to note that the design somewhat approaches, perhaps unconsciously, the *quattrocento* Florentine. However, it quite lacks the archaeological character of Klenze's Königsbau in Munich, designed only a few years later, or the vigour and assurance of Wimmel & Forsmann's Johanneum in Hamburg. In fact, of course, it derives almost directly from Durand and not from any careful study of Grandjean de Montigny's *Architecture toscane*. Somewhat more definitely Early Renaissance in detail are the Baths at Mont d'Or, built by L.-C.-F. Ledru (1771–1861), a pupil of Durand, in 1822 and the Barracks in the Rue Mouffetard in Paris as extended in 1827 by Charles Rohault de Fleury (1801–75). Both exploit a rusticated Tuscan mode somewhat as Klenze was doing in Munich but much less conscientiously.

Shortly after the Séminaire, Godde undertook several Paris churches. Saint-Pierre-du-Gros-Caillou in the Rue St Dominique of 1822–3 replaced a church destroyed in the Revolution. Finer and considerably larger is Saint-Denis-du-Saint-Sacrament in the Rue de Turenne, built in 1823–35. Both are barrel-vaulted basilicas in the tradition of Chalgrin's Saint-Philippe-du-Roule; the latter is rather elegant in its dry severity, the former confused by various later additions behind the altar. Notre-Dame-de-Bonne-Nouvelle of 1823–30 is smaller and more modest, as are also two nearly contemporary Paris churches by A.-I. Molinos

(1795–1850), Saint-Jean-Baptiste in Neuilly of 1827–31 and Sainte-Marie-des-Batignolles in the Place du Dr Félix Lobligeois in Paris of 1828–9. All these churches lack externally the Grecian grandeur of scale of the London churches of the period built by the Inwoods and others (see Chapter 4), but the basilican plan provides interiors that are considerably more interesting than the galleried halls with which most English architects were satisfied at this time. Of course, such a highly original interior as that of Soane's St Peter's, Walworth, of 1822 is in a different class altogether.

A much larger and more prominent church than any of Godde's or Molinos's is Notre-Dame-de-Lorette in the Rue de Chateaudun, one of the few really distinguished products of this dull period. It was the result of a competition held in 1822 which was won by Lebas, Brongniart's collaborator on the Bourse [39]. This five-aisled edifice was built at very great expense in 1823–36 and sumptuously decorated with murals that added as much as a sixth to the total cost. The basic model is again the Early Christian basilica but here interpreted in thoroughly Classical terms, with a tall temple portico rivalling those of London at the front and no vaults or arches except at the east end. Evidence of a certain eclecticism is the rich coffering of the ceiling in panels alternately square and cruciform; so also is the introduction of a domed chancel before the apse. Both features are certainly of *cinquecento* inspiration.

To modern eyes, attuned to the late fifth- and sixth-century basilicas of Ravenna, Notre-Dame-de-Lorette certainly has a far less Early Christian air than Ziebland's Bonifazius Basilika in Munich of the next decade; but doubtless the great Imperial basilicas of Rome of the fourth and early fifth centuries, notably Santa Maria Maggiore with its trabeated nave colonnade, were originally something like it. In any case, Lebas's church is a highly typical monument of Romantic Classicism and a major one.

39. L.-H. Lebas:
Paris, Notre-Dame-de-Lorette, 1823-36

In France, as elsewhere, the accepted range of precedent now extended well beyond Greek and Roman antiquity to include Italian models of fifth- and of sixteenth-century date, if very little from the centuries between. Even before the construction of Notre-Dame-de-Lorette, the Belgian-born P.-J. Sandrié and Jacob Silveyra (1785-?) in building a big Parisian synagogue in the Rue Notre-Dame-de-Naza-reth in 1819-20 had also followed rather closely the basilican formula.

The most important Parisian church of the second quarter of the century, Saint-Vincent-de-Paul off the Rue Lafayette, is also a five-

40. J.-B. Lepère and J.-I. Hittorff:
Paris, Saint-Vincent-de-Paul, 1824-44

aisled classical basilica [40]. This was begun in
1824 by Lepère, but work was soon suspended.
When it was carried to completion in 1831-44
Lepère's son-in-law J.-I. Hittorff (1792-1867)
took over, and he has generally received credit
for the whole. In utilizing a rising site here,
which required terraces and flights of steps in
front, and in providing two towers, Lepère and
Hittorff gave their church more prominence and
a richer, if rather clumsily organized, three-
dimensional interest.[1] Hittorff's archaeological
studies in Sicily had made him an enthusiast for
architectural polychromy, and to contemporaries the great novelty about Saint-Vincent-
de-Paul was the proposal to use enamelled lava
plaques on the exterior.[2]

The French did not, like the Germans, turn
to the use of tawny brick and terracotta in the
second quarter of the century; but the interest

of Hittorff and his generation in applied polychromy relates their work a little to that of the
Romantic colourists in painting.[3] Unfortunately
almost none of this polychromy remains visible
now; and so the shift away from the monochromy that is characteristic everywhere of
Romantic Classicism before this period is less
evident in France than in other countries.

Especially fine is the open timber roof of
Saint-Vincent-de-Paul, although only a part
of the construction actually is exposed; while
the fact that the colonnaded apse is wide enough
to include the inner aisles as well as the nave
gives a quite unprecedented spatial interest to
the east end. Moreover, in this interior Hittorff
achieved a rich warmth of tone quite different
from the coldness of Godde's and Molinos's
churches of the twenties. His Cirque des
Champs Élysées of 1839-41 and Cirque d'Hiver
of 1852 were even more brilliantly polychromatic both inside and out. But the most conspicuous extant works of Hittorff, the Gare du
Nord of 1861-5, the Second Empire façades
surrounding the Place de l'Étoile, and the
decoration of the Place de la Concorde and the
Champs Élysées with fountains and other
features under the July Monarchy, provide
today little evidence[4] of this aspect of his talent
once so notable to contemporaries at home and
abroad.

Especially happy is the siting of Saint-
Vincent-de-Paul on the upper side of the new
polygonal Place Charles X (now Place Lafayette), of which the other sides were filled in
the twenties with consonant houses by A.-F.-R.
Leclerc (1785-1853),[5] a pupil of both Durand
and Percier, and A.-J. Pellechet (1798-1871).
Less characteristic of Romantic Classical
urbanism than the squares and streets of
Karlsruhe and Munich, this nevertheless well
illustrates the dignity and the regularity of the
houses then rising in the new quarters of Paris.
The very considerable new quarter in Mulhouse,
which was laid out and built up in 1826-8 by

J.-G. Stotz (1799-?), a pupil of Leclerc, and A.-J.-F. Fries (1800-59), a pupil of Huyot, is more comparable to Karlsruhe.

Most of the new churches in the suburbs of Paris and the French provinces followed basilican models. The parish church of Saint-Germain-en-Laye, which was brought at last to completion in 1823-7 by A.-J. Malpièce (1789-1864) and his partner A.-J. Moutier (1791-1874), a pupil of Percier, following the original designs of M.-M. Potain (1713-96) of the 1760s, is much more modest and somewhat less Roman. In Marseilles the younger M.-R. Penchaud (1772-1832), who designed in 1812 and built in 1827-32 the Palais de Justice at Aix on Ledoux's earlier foundations, erected in 1824 a large Roman basilica for the local Protestants, doubtless with some conscious reference to Salomon de Brosse's seventeenth-century Protestant Temple at Charenton of two hundred years earlier. By exception, however, the Protestant Temple at Orléans by F.-N. Pagot (1780-1844), a pupil of Labarre, which was built in 1836, is a plain cylinder in plan. Saint-Lazare in Marseilles, built by P.-X. Coste (1787-1879) and Vincent Barral (1800-54) in 1833-7, followed Notre-Dame-de-Lorette even more closely than does Penchaud's Protestant church.

In the quite modest parish church of Vincennes outside Paris, which rose in 1826-30, the very last years of the Restoration, J.-B.-C. Lesueur (1794-1883) was already using a rather Brunelleschian sort of detail that is not without a certain cool elegance. More definitely of the Renaissance Revival is Saint-Jacques-Saint-Christophe, the parish church of La Villette in the Rue de Crimée in Paris built by P.-E. Lequeux (1806-73) much later in 1841-4. It is one of half a dozen that Lequeux began in the forties, in addition to designing the town halls of this and several other quarters of Paris. Lequeux employed definitely *quattrocento* detail somewhat more lavishly than Lesueur had done

at Vincennes, and produced at La Villette one of the most satisfactory French churches of the Louis Philippe epoch. In building a small village church at Pollet near Dieppe in 1844-9, Louis Lenormand (1801-62), a pupil of his uncle Huvé, used Early Renaissance detail of a more French sort that may not improperly be called *François I*. Such detail was highly exceptional in ecclesiastical architecture even as late as the forties.

The housing of public services, initiated so actively by Napoleon, continued at a much reduced pace under Louis XVIII and Charles X. The Paris Custom House of 1827 by L.-A. Lusson (1790-1864), a pupil of Percier, with its great arched entrance rising from the ground and its similar transverse arches inside, was later transformed – three bays of it, at least – into a Protestant church by one of Lebas's pupils, the German-born F.-C. Gau (1790-1853), for Louis Philippe's German relatives in 1843. A similar reflection of Durand's utilitarian models may be seen in the vast Government Warehouse at Lyons, begun in 1828 by L.-P. Baltard (1764-1846), Lequeux's master, who had worked when very young with Ledoux on the Paris *barrières*. This contrasts notably in its consistent arcuation with the giant Corinthian colonnade that still fronts Baltard's Palace of Justice[5a] there, built in 1836-42, and parallels fairly closely the contemporary warehouses Schinkel was building in Berlin. More characteristic of the rather mixed official mode of the period is the Custom House of 1835-42 at Rouen by C.-E. Isabelle (1800-80), a pupil of Leclerc. This is of interest chiefly for the tremendous rusticated arch of the entrance which quite overpowers the rest of the *palazzo*-like façade.

For educational institutions most new construction was subsidiary to existing buildings. At the École Polytechnique, A.-M. Renié (c. 1790-1855), a pupil of Percier and Vaudoyer, provided in 1828 a new arcuated and rusticated entrance hardly worthy of the school where

Durand was now teaching a second generation of architects. P.-M. Letarouilly (1795-1855) made in 1831-42 additions that are less unworthy, but hardly more interesting, to Chalgrin's Collège de France, built originally in the 1770s. But his great contribution, of course, was the *Édifices de Rome moderne* – the first volume of which appeared in 1840. Finally completed with the publication of the third volume in 1857, this was the bible of the later Renaissance Revival in France as of several generations of academic architects throughout the rest of the world. The École Normale Supérieure by the youngest Gisors (H.-A.-G. de, 1796-1866), a pupil of Percier, is a large, wholly new building of 1841-7; this looks forward to the Second Empire a little in its high mansard roof and seventeenth-century detailing, extremely dry and sparse though that is (see Chapter 8).

Private construction was for the most part very dull, whether in city, suburb, or country. As an example of the country houses that were built in some quantity, a typical project of 1830 for one by Hittorff may be illustrated [41]. With its careful if rather uninteresting proportions, its rigid rectangularity, and the stiff chains of rustication that provide its sole embellishment, however, this rises somewhat above the general level of achievement of the period.

The *François I* character of the detailing of Lenormand's Pollet church has been mentioned. In domestic architecture such national Renaissance precedent had rather greater success even if nothing very novel or original developed from it. In 1825 L.-M.-D. Biet (1785-1856), a pupil of Percier, brought to Paris the court façade of an early sixteenth-century house from Moret and applied it to a *hôtel particulier* – always called with no justification the 'Maison de François I' – in a new residential area of Paris. This house shortly gave the name 'François I' to the entire quarter between the Champs Élysées and the Seine. The barrenness and brittleness of Biet's own elevations were more of a tribute to his respect for the old work than to his creative ability.

Within the next few years houses built by such architects as L.-T.-J. Visconti (1791-1853), another pupil of Percier, and Famin tended to grow ever richer. In 1835 P.-C. Dusillon (1804-60), an architect otherwise more active abroad than at home, used *François I* detail with the lushest profusion on a house at 14 Rue Vaneau. The façade rather resembles an interior of the so-called *style troubadour* turned inside out. Much the same may be said for the block of flats built by Édouard Renaud (1808-86), a pupil of Leroy, at 5 Place St Georges in

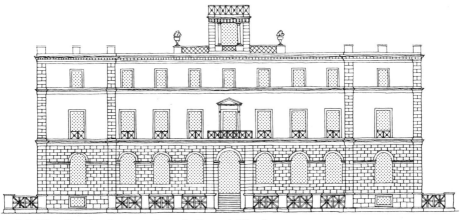

41. J.-I. Hittorff: project for country house for Comte de W., 1830

1841. But that was in distinct contrast to the severity of the earlier Parisian street architecture under the Restoration. That restraint was generally maintained under the July Monarchy for blocks of flats, even by men like Visconti and Lesueur whose private houses were often very rich indeed.

even the vitality – at that relatively low – of the revived 'Jacobethan' in contemporary England.

Even where a major sixteenth-century monument had to be restored and enlarged, as was the case with the Hôtel de Ville of Paris,[5b] the architects Godde and Lesueur were at some pains to regularize and chasten the unclassical

42. É.-H. Godde and J.-B. Lesueur:
Paris, extension of Hôtel de Ville, 1837–49

Two country houses of 1840 make a more extensive and plausible use of *François I* features. One is the Château de St Martin, near St Paulzo in the Nièvre, built by Édouard Lussy (1788–1868), a pupil of Percier; this is elaborately picturesque in silhouette but still rigidly symmetrical. Another by J.-B.-P. Canissié (1799–1877), a pupil of Hittorff, at Draveil, S.-et-O., is somewhat irregular both in plan and in composition. But the *style François I* in the France of the second quarter of the nineteenth century had neither the general acceptance nor

vagaries of Boccador's original design [42]. Most of the work by Lesueur was done after 1837; from 1853 Victor Baltard (1805–74), son of L.-P. Baltard, carried on; then the whole had to be rebuilt after it was burned under the Commune. The present rather similar edifice by Théodore Ballu (1817–74), a pupil of Lebas, was begun only in 1874, the year of his death, and eventually completed by his partner P.-J.-E. Deperthes (1833–98). Except for the high French roofs, looking forward like those by Gisors on the École Normale to the next period, the general effect of Lesueur's work here was very Italianate.

A somewhat similar character can be seen in a few wholly new structures of more or less *François I* inspiration, for example the Museum and Library at Le Havre built by C.-L.-F. Brunet-Debaines (1801-62), a pupil of Vaudoyer and Lebas, in 1845. In such a major commercial work of this period as the Galeries du Commerce et de l'Industrie in the Boulevard Bonne-Nouvelle, built by J.-L.-V. Grisart (1797-1877), a pupil of Huyot, and C.-M.-A. Froehlicher in 1838, it is hard to say whether the continuous arcading derived from French or from Italian sixteenth-century precedent. The iron-and-glass interiors were of more interest (see Chapter 7).

There has seemed no need to emphasize thus far, as regards its effect on architecture, the change of regime that took place in 1830, even though that date in the other arts of France has been thought by some to mark the triumph of a *romantisme de la lettre* over earlier Neo-Classicism.[5c] No comparable triumph succeeded in architecture, although it is evident that sources of inspiration other than the codified Antique were more frequently utilized after 1830 than before, if not with the same eclectic effect as in Germany. Yet, thanks to Victor Hugo and Guizot, Gothicism at least had acquired a less reactionary connotation than under the last Bourbons and was receiving the support, up to a point, of the July Monarchy (see Chapter 6).

For political reasons Louis Philippe desired especially to emphasize the continuity of his liberal monarchy with the more liberal aspects of the Empire and to reclaim for France the Napoleonic glories that the Restoration had denigrated. So Napoleon's ashes were brought back to the Invalides, where Visconti, hitherto chiefly active in the domestic field, prepared in 1842 a setting for them as funereal as the Chapelle Expiatoire but more sumptuous in its use of coloured marbles. Napoleon's Temple de

la Gloire (the Madeleine) and his Arc de Triomphe de l'Étoile were finally brought to completion, the one by Huvé in 1845, the other by Blouet in 1837, as has already been noted. Several new monuments, very much of the Empire type, were also erected in Paris.

Where Napoleon's Elephant Monument was to have marked the site of the Bastille, J.-A. Alavoine (1778-1834) and after his death L.-J. Duc (1802-79), a pupil of Percier, erected in 1831-40 the gigantic Colonne de Juillet, rather less imperial Roman and more French Empire than Napoleon's Colonne Vendôme, but like that all of metal. In the centre of the Place de la Concorde there rose, with echoes of Napoleon's Egyptian campaign (and less relevantly of Sixtine Rome), a real obelisk presented to Louis Philippe by the Khedive in 1833; thereafter, Hittorff ornamented in 1836-40 the square, the Champs Élysées, the Place de l'Étoile, and the Avenue de la Grande Armée with big fountains, lamp standards, and other pieces of elaborate urbanistic furniture.

While the Empire embellishment of Paris was thus finished up or complemented, the July Monarchy also developed a fantastically extensive activity in the construction of hospitals, prisons, and other such utilitarian structures. Vast and plain, these could hardly be duller in the eyes of posterity. Yet they derive quite directly from Durand's admirable paradigms for such structures and more remotely from the social, if not the aesthetic, aspirations of such men of high talent as Ledoux and Boullée, who initiated Romantic Classicism before the Revolution. If a funerary edifice – the Chapelle Expiatoire – best epitomizes the architecture of the Restoration, some enormous public institution is the contemporary, if inappropriate, architectural equivalent of the Romantic arts of Delacroix and Berlioz in the thirties and forties! Very conspicuous, and quite characteristic of these as a class, is the Hôtel Dieu, beside Notre-Dame in Paris, although this was actually built[6] very much later, in 1864–78, by A.-N. Diet (1827–90). It is the only one that can be readily seen without being jailed or certified; but most of them were amply presented in contemporary publications.

Penchaud, whose Marseilles Protestant church has already been mentioned, was one of the ablest and most productive provincial architects of the Restoration and Louis Philippe periods. His lazaret at Marseilles, built in 1822–6, is more Ledoux-like than the Aix Palace of Justice that he erected on Ledoux's foundations and considerably more original than his triumphal arch of 1823–32 at Marseilles, called the Porte d'Aix. On this arch, however, the liveliness of the relief sculpture provides something of the same Romantic *élan* as that of Rude on the Arc de l'Étoile – Rude's work dates, of course, from the Louis Philippe period. The Marseilles arch continues the Roman ideals of the Empire; the more significant lazaret revives the social and utilitarian ideals of the preceding Revolutionary period.

In Paris Lebas's Petite Roquette Prison for young criminals, in the Rue de la Roquette, designed in 1825 and executed with some modification of the original project in 1831–6, hardly rivals his great church in interest; but the polygonal plan with machicolated round towers at the corners recalls both the Roman-castellated mode of Boullée and the Millbank Penitentiary[7] in London of 1812–21 which Lebas had actually visited. Of more historical significance was the no longer extant Prison de la Nouvelle Force (or Mazas) commissioned in 1836 and built in 1843–50 by E.-J. Gilbert (1793–1874), a pupil first of Durand at the École Polytechnique and then of Vignon, the recognized leader in this field under Louis Philippe. Its radial cellular planning showed, like Barry's Pentonville Prison of 1841–2 in London, the significant influence abroad of the Eastern Penitentiary in Philadelphia built by John Haviland (1792–1852) in 1823–35. This plan was made known to Europeans by two reports on American prisons, one by William

43. Douillard Frères:
Nantes, Hospice Général, 1832–6

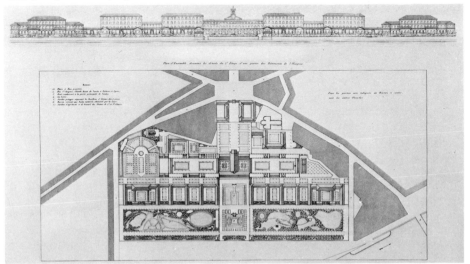

Crawford, published in London in 1834, and another by F.-A. Demetz and Blouet, published in Paris in 1837. On this prison J.-F.-J. Lecointe (1783–1858) was associated with Gilbert.

Much larger is Gilbert's Charenton Lunatic Asylum of 1838–45 at St Maurice outside Paris, which he designed and built alone. The vast and orderly grid of this institution provides a community that is almost of the order of a complete town. The innumerable bare and regular ranges of wards are dominated by the temple portico of the centrally placed chapel, an ecclesiastical monument of some distinction that is unfortunately inaccessible to visitors. Such work, often as extensive in the provinces as near the capital, was much admired and studied by foreigners even quite late in the century. To the French, moreover, it carried a special prestige: the line of descent was direct from Boullée to Durand and from Durand to Gilbert and his

provincial rivals, such as the brothers Douillard (L.-P., 1790–1869; L.-C., 1795–1878, a pupil of Crucy), who were responsible for the Hospice Général (Saint-Jacques) at Nantes built in 1832–6 [43]. In the estimation of contemporaries, this was one of the two main lines of development in this period, balancing socially the more aesthetic programme of polychromatic romanticization pursued by Hittorff, Henri Labrouste, and Duban.

Representational public buildings, although usually much less plain in design, are likely to be even more heavy-handed than the prisons and lunatic asylums. Their architects' strictly functional approach was capable of achieving a rather bleak sort of distinction which should not be unsympathetic in the twentieth century if only they were better known. The Palace of Justice at Tours of 1840–50 by Charles Jacquemin-Belisle (1815–69), with its unpedi-

44. F.-A. Duquesney:
Paris, Gare de l'Est, 1847–52

mented Roman Doric portico, is typical enough of a very considerable number of large and prominent civic structures. Lequeux's Paris town halls in the outlying *arrondissements* are just as dry but less monumentally Classical.

Happily there are some finer public buildings, mostly in Paris, structures not least interesting for their bold use of metal and glass. Among early railway stations only the Gare Montparnasse of 1848–52 by V.-B. Lenoir (1805–63) and the engineer Eugène Flachat (1802–73) and the Gare de Strasbourg (Gare de l'Est) of 1847–52 by F.-A. Duquesney (1790–1849), a pupil of Percier, long survived in Paris.[7a] The Gare de l'Est, its vast central lunette expressing clearly the original iron-and-glass train-shed, is a most notable early station. The detailing, of a somewhat High Renaissance – at least not Greek or Roman – order, is pleasant but undistinguished [44]. This detailing has been

effectively maintained in the modern doubling of the front of the station. The arched shed by the engineer Sérinet was long ago replaced.

The other great Parisian structure of the forties in whose construction the visible use of iron played a prominent part, the Bibliothèque Sainte-Geneviève in the Place du Panthéon, is especially distinguished for the originality and elegance of its detailing, even more as regards that of the masonry of the exterior than of the ironwork within [45]. Henri-P.-F. Labrouste (1801–75), a pupil of Lebas and A.-L.-T. Vaudoyer, who designed this library in 1839 and built it in 1843–50, is the one French architect of the age whose name is often mentioned, and no longer diffidently, with those of the great architects of the earlier decades of the century outside France, Soane and Schinkel, even if his contemporaries gave precedence it would seem to Gilbert and to Hittorff. Labrouste ranks for

45. H.-P.-F. Labrouste:
Paris, Bibliothèque Sainte-Geneviève, 1843–50

quality with a Dane of his own generation such as Bindesbøll and indeed his library is much more advanced both stylistically and technically than the contemporary Thorwaldsen Museum in Copenhagen.

Everywhere except in England this was a period, like the first quarter of the century, in which official architecture exceeded private in interest. Moreover, the priority that the erection of monuments of public utility, from markets and prisons to art galleries and libraries, received over the building of churches and palaces gave significant evidence of the rise of a new pattern of bourgeois culture. It is therefore quite appropriate that this library of Henri Labrouste's should be the finest structure of the forties in France. The Bibliothèque Sainte-Geneviève is also one of the few works of the second quarter of the century anywhere in the world that has been almost universally admired ever since its completion, if successively for a variety of reasons. The façade of the library, often ignored by those praising the visible iron structure of the interior [112], outranks in distinction almost all other contemporary examples of the Renaissance Revival anywhere in Europe; but it is worth noting that the flanking administrative block and the Collège Sainte-Barbe also offer a premonition of the next period in their prominent mansard roofs. (Henri's brother F.-M.-T. Labrouste (1799–1855) supervised the construction of the college.) The façade of Henri's administrative block is a composition of real originality and exquisite co-ordination of parts to which the term Renaissance Revival need hardly be applied; this is what *style Louis Philippe* really means, or ought at least to mean.

By Charles X's time the Salle des Cinq Cents at the Palais Bourbon, erected by the two older Gisors and Leconte in the 1790s, was in such a bad state that it was necessary to rebuild it, adding at the same time a library. J.-J.-B. de Joly (1788–1865) in 1828–33 followed closely

the original design; but behind the scenes, as it were, he used a great deal of iron to ensure a fire-proof structure. He also embellished the walls with a richly coloured sheathing of French marbles and, in the library, with murals by Delacroix. With less originality, but with respect for a major monument of the seventeenth century, H.-A.-G. de Gisors much enlarged the Luxembourg for Louis Philippe in 1834–41, repeating Salomon de Brosse's original garden façade, in order to accommodate a new chamber for the House of Peers. His chamber followed closely the earlier one there of 1798 by Chalgrin; the new chapel which he also provided at the Luxembourg has even more of the colouristic richness demanded by advanced taste in this period. The Luxembourg Orangery, later the Luxembourg Museum, which was built by Gisors in 1840 in an early seventeenth-century mode, used brick for the walls with only the dressings of stone, a rare instance of such external bichromy in the Paris of its day despite the lively interest in the employment of colour in architecture.

The present Foreign Ministry on the Quai d'Orsay was built in 1846–56 by Jacques Lacornée (1779–1856) who had completed in 1821–35 his master Bonnard's earlier Ministry near by that was begun for Napoleon in 1814. Superimposed arch orders produce a rich and rather Venetian version of the Renaissance Revival not unrelated to the treatment of the somewhat exceptional Empire building on which he had worked. Duc began to plan the restoration and enlargement of the Palace of Justice in Paris as early as 1840, but the handsomest and most conspicuous portions of this elaborate complex date from the Second Empire. J.-F. Duban (1797–1870) started in 1848 the restoration of the old Louvre, over which a hot controversy soon ensued; the New Louvre, begun by Visconti in 1852 and carried forward after his death in 1853 by Lefuel, would be the prime monument of the succeeding period (see Chapter 8). Duban's capacities in this period – he did his best work rather later [126] – are better appreciated in the building for the École des Beaux Arts he completed in 1838 and in the elegant Early Italian Renaissance design of the Hôtel de Pourtalès of 1836 in the Rue Tronchet, perhaps the finest Paris mansion of its day.

However, it was not with such *hôtels particuliers* but with *maisons de rapport*, that is, blocks of flats, that the streets of Paris, like those of other big cities, were mostly built up in these decades. The earlier ones, such as those in the Place de la Bourse, are carefully composed yet almost devoid of prominent architectural features [46]. In the later thirties and above all the forties, however, the detail grew richer and more eclectic, while the façades were in general

46. A.-J. Pellechet:
Paris, block of flats, 10 Place de la Bourse, 1834

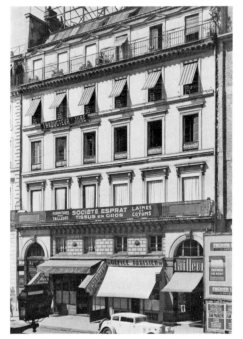

much less neatly organized. Not only were rich Italian or French Renaissance features popular but exotic oriental ornament was more than occasionally used. The planning became more complex and elastic also; but both in exterior design and in interior arrangement the type remained firmly rooted in late-eighteenth-century tradition. The Paris streets of the first half of the nineteenth century have a notable consistency of scale and character since the cornice lines, and even the shapes of the high roofs, were controlled by a well-enforced building code and their superficial eclecticism is little more than a matter of detail.

More than in other countries in this period, the major virtues of French architecture lay in the placid continuance of well-established lines. Traditions were being slowly eroded, but there was very little of that urgent desire to overturn the immediate past which coloured so significantly much English production of the thirties and forties. Nor was there the German capacity in this period for carrying over into medievalizing modes the basic disciplines of established Romantic Classicism. Not surprisingly, French leadership in architecture, established under Louis XIV and renewed under Napoleon, was largely lost; it came back, however, with the Second Empire (see Chapters 8 and 9). All the same, architectural controversy flourished at home in these decades.

Quite naturally, French influence still remained largely dominant in contiguous Belgium and parts of Switzerland. If Studer's work in Berne falls under the German rubric of *Rundbogenstil*, in French-speaking Lausanne and Neuchâtel important commissions went to Frenchmen. An Asylum for the former city was projected by Henri Labrouste in 1837–8; another for the latter town, several years later in date, is by P.-F.-N. Philippon (1784–1866), a pupil of J.-J. Ramée who had also worked with Brongniart. Both are characteristically respectable examples of *Louis Philippe* design.

Labrouste also provided a project for a prison at Alessandria in Italy in 1840.

In Belgium, under Dutch rule from the fall of Napoleon down to 1830, the Théâtre de la Monnaie in Brussels, begun in 1819 by the French architect L.-E.-A. Damesme (1757–1822), who had once worked on the Paris *barrières* with Ledoux, and completed by E.-J. Bonnevie (1783–1835), is a big but still typical example of the theatres built in the French provinces by architects of the previous generation. It was not improved by an enlargement and remodelling of 1856, but the original temple portico is noble in scale and handsomely detailed. Characteristically, Damesme also built the Brussels prison. When a new generation of Belgian architects appeared led by Joseph Poelaert (1817–79), who had studied with Huyot, more international influences were evident. For example, Poelaert's fine early school of 1852 in the Rue de Schaerbeek in Brussels shows little of Huyot but a good deal of Schinkel in its rationalistic handling of Grecian forms. Poelaert's boldness here, which even suggests that of Alexander Thomson in his Glasgow work of this decade and the next, prepares one a little for his later Palace of Justice designed in the sixties (see Chapter 8).

The long pre-eminence of Italy in the arts came to an end even before the end of the old regime. Architects still flocked there, finding in each generation new sources of inspiration as first Renaissance palaces and then medieval churches succeeded Roman ruins as the preferred quarry of travellers of taste. But not after Piranesi was there an Italian architect with real international influence. At the opening of the new century doctrine flowed from Paris, not from Rome; increasingly, moreover, architects turned to England and Germany for still fresher ideas and ideals.

Only a few Italian cities were notably ornamented in this period; on the other hand, none were blighted, and much ordinary building hardly even bears clear indications of its date. The characteristic and prominent productions of the period are, however, quite up to the highest international standards. They have thus far been underestimated, not least by the Italians themselves, partly because they are so much overshadowed in interest by earlier work, partly because they carry in Italy for the first time since the Gothic the onus – not entirely justified – of following a foreign lead.

The Pope, like other legitimate sovereigns who returned to power after Napoleon's fall, carried out existing projects, notably those for the Piazza del Popolo as planned by Valadier. He also initiated in 1817 the building of a new wing for the sculpture museum at the Vatican, the Braccio Nuovo by Raffaelle Stern (1774–1820). Completed in 1822 by Pasquale Belli (1752–1833), this is one of the finest galleries in the line of descent from Simonetti's Museo Pio-Clementino of which the first half of the nineteenth century saw so many [47]. Taller and less ornately embellished than Klenze's galleries in the Munich Glyptothek, and with rather stronger spatial articulation, this is none the less well within the Romantic Classical tradition as it had been established by the previous generation of French architects.

The principal architectural activity of the post-Napoleonic years in Rome and, indeed, of the whole later period of papal rule was the reconstruction after a fire of the great fifth-century basilica of San Paolo fuori-le-mura. Begun apparently by Belli in 1825, with whom were associated the younger Pietro Camporese (1792–1873) and F. J. Bosio (1768–1845), the supervision was taken over after Belli's death in 1833 by Luigi Poletti (1792–1869),[7b] who completed the job in 1856. Following closely the august original in its dimensions and proportions, San Paolo has a truly Roman Imperial scale; but the hardness of the materials, the polish of their surfaces, and the cold precision of their handling recalls rather the contemporary

47. Raffaelle Stern:
Rome, Vatican Museum, Braccio Nuovo, 1817-22

Paris churches of Lebas and Hittorff without matching their relatively rich colour. A more modest Roman monument of this period in a conspicuous location is the Teatro Argentina by Camporese.

The Teatro Carlo Felice in the Piazza de Ferrari in Genoa, built by C. F. Barabino (1768-1835) in 1826-7, is a more advanced and distinguished Romantic Classical structure of considerable originality, set in a very prominent location. Barabino was also responsible in 1835 for designing the Camposanto di Staglieno at Genoa with its Pantheon-like chapel and its endless colonnades. This project was carried out by his former assistant G. B. Rezasco (1799-1872) in 1844-61.

Naples[7c] has more interesting monuments of this period to offer than Rome or Genoa. Yet San Francesco di Paola, which was built from designs by Pietro Bianchi (1787-1849) in 1816-24 in resolution of a vow of Ferdinand I, can hardly be considered much more original than San Paolo [48]. The interior is another of the innumerable copies of the Pantheon that were erected all over Europe and America in this period; but the Berninian quadrant colonnades[7d] in front are better handled than at Voronikhin's Kazan Cathedral at Petersburg. The great saucer dome, moreover, is rather happily echoed in the two smaller domes on either side; they serve also to tie together the side colonnades and the pedimented portico. Above all, this church is most effective urbanistically. The colonnades enclose the square north of the Royal Palace in a quite Baroque way; while the church as a whole, because of the giant scale of its parts and its cleanly sculptural composition, stands as a discrete object in the best Romantic Classical way against the higher portion of the city that

earlier, very rich indeed in its gold-and-white decoration, but superbly ordered. Genovese also carried out an extensive and tactful remodelling and enlargement of the Royal Palace in Naples[7e] in 1837-44, notably the regularization of the long façade above the quay.

No other Italian city provides quite such prominent examples of individual Romantic

48. Pietro Bianchi:
Naples, San Francesco di Paola, 1816-24

rises behind. Less happy in the city picture is the front of the San Carlo opera house, carried out a little earlier in 1810-12 by Antonio Niccolini, who also rebuilt and redecorated the interior in 1816-17 and again in 1841-4. This has adequate open space only at the sides; and the curiously high-waisted façade, in any case rather underscaled in its parts, must be seen in a perspective sharper than is becoming to most post-Baroque monuments [49].

The throne room in the palace at nearby Caserta, decorated for Ferdinand II by Gaetano Genovese (1795-1860) in 1839-45, is a surprisingly worthy late pendant to de Simone's contiguous interiors of more than a generation

Classical monuments as do Rome and Naples. The setting of San Carlo in Milan, built by Carlo Amati (1776-1852) in 1844-7, a rectangular recession from the line of the present-day Corso Matteotti, provides no such approach to its dome as the Piazza Plebiscito does to San Francesco in Naples. The tall granite colonnades at the base of the contiguous blocks do, however, continue effectively the pedimented portico on either side of the little *piazza*. Only in Turin[7f] [50], almost more French than Italian always, were great squares and wide, arcaded streets carried out in this period, but without focal monuments of any particular distinction. These squares and streets vie with Percier and Fontaine's in Paris, yet

49. Antonio Niccolini:
Naples, San Carlo Opera House, 1810-12

50. Giuseppe Frizzi and others:
Turin, Piazza Vittorio Veneto, laid out in 1818; with
Gran Madre di Dio by Ferdinando Bonsignore, 1818-31

they also continue a local seventeenth-century tradition that was to remain alive down into the Fascist period.

The expiatory church in Turin, which paralleled in motivation Ferdinand I's in Naples, the Gran Madre di Dio, was proposed in 1814 and built on the farther bank of the Po by Ferdinando Bonsignore (1767–1843) in 1818–31 to celebrate the departure of the French and the return of the House of Savoy to its capital [50]. This is a far duller and less original example of a modern structure based directly on the Pantheon than is the Tempio Canoviano of 1819–20 at Possagno.[8] For this Thorwaldsen's rival, Antonio Canova, was the client and apparently also the designer.

It is not Bonsignore's church that is notable in the Turin scene but the vast Piazza Vittorio Veneto opposite, laid out by Giuseppe Frizzi (1797–1831) in 1818 and later surrounded by fine ranges of arcaded buildings mostly carried out between 1825 and 1830 [50]. At the upper end of this tremendous square two seventeenth-century arcaded quadrants connect with the Via Po. In Frizzi's Piazza the compound piers supporting the long arcades, though similar to those in the quadrants, are simplified and sharpened to conform to Romantic Classical taste. A typical Turin feature, new in this period, is the syncopation of the iron balconies of the upper storeys. The theme reappears on most of the houses in the contiguous district that was developed over the next generation with a consistency rivalling Paris and Vienna in the middle decades of the century. Such nineteenth-century Italian urbanism is rarely recognized to be of its own period, so successfully does it continue a tradition here two hundred years old.

The other principal square of this period, on the farther side of the new quarter and at the outer end of the present-day Via Roma, is the Piazza Carlo Felice. This was laid out by the engineer Lombardi and by Frizzi in 1823, and

has façades by Carlo Promis (1808–73) that also extend on both sides of the square along the broad Corso Vittorio Emmanuele II. Continuous arcades cross the street ends, as in the Piazza Vittorio Veneto, and the balconies are syncopated. The fine big trees in the square and along the Corso are a happy addition to the urban scene quite uncharacteristic of the rest of Italy.

The inner end of the Piazza Carlo Felice is not curved but semi-octagonal. Originally the outer end was open and defined only by rows of trees; later, in 1866–8, the handsome Porta Nuova Railway Station was built there by the engineer Alessandro Mazzuchetti (1824–94) and the architect Carlo Ceppi (1829–1921). Now this terminates the long central axis of the city which extends from the Royal Palace through the Piazza Castello, the Piazza San Carlo, and down the Via Roma to the Piazza Carlo Felice.

Turin has other monumental edifices of this period besides the Gran Madre di Dio. There are, for example, two later churches in the new quarter, San Massimo and the Sacramentine; the latter, by Alfonso Dupuy, was built in 1846–50 from a design of 1843, with portico of 1870 by Ceppi; the former in 1845–53 by Carlo Sada (1809–73). Both are domed, but less Pantheon-like than the Gran Madre. They lack, unfortunately, the elegance and delicacy of scale of the houses of the period in the streets that surround them.

Milan owes less than Turin to the architectural activity of this period. The present decoration of the interior of the opera-house, La Scala,[8a] which was built by Giuseppe Piermarini (1734–1808) in 1776–8, dates from 1830 and is by Alessandro Sanquirico (1774–1849). This is quite similar in the sumptuousness of its white-and-gold ornamentation to Genovese's later throne room at Caserta. The square gatehouses at the Porta Venezia, built in 1826 by Rodolfo Vantini (1791–1856), are boldly scaled and effectively paired. The Palazzo Rocca-Saporiti of 1812 by Giovanni Perego (1776–1817)[8b] in the Corso Venezia with its raised colonnade rivals in interest Cantoni's better-known Palazzo Serbelloni of the 1780s near by. The much smaller and considerably later Palazzo Lucini of 1831 in the Via Monte di Pietà by Ferdinando Crivelli (1810–55) is so expert an example of High Renaissance design that it can readily be taken for real *cinquecento* work. Paradoxically, such an extremely literate specimen of the Renaissance Revival is far less characteristic of Italy in the second quarter of the nineteenth century than of England or Germany. More typical of Italian taste in the thirties and forties are the buildings facing the flank of La Scala across the Via Verdi with their complex rhythm of fenestration and their very rich but still vaguely Grecian ornamentation. Eventually the Italians did, however, take up occasionally the Renaissance version of the

international *Rundbogenstil*, and none too happily. For example, the Casa di Risparmio (known vulgarly as the Ca' de Sass), built by Giuseppe Balzaretti (1801–74) in 1872 across the street from the refined and discreet Palazzo Lucini, is a stonier example of Tuscan rustication – as its nickname suggests – than was ever produced by the Northern Europeans who first revived the mode half a century earlier.

A charming ornament to a smaller city is the Caffè Pedrocchi[9] in Padua of 1816–31 by Giuseppe Jappelli (1783–1852), a pupil of Selva, and Antonio Gradenigo (1806–84). Delicate in scale, interestingly varied in the handling of solids and voids, and most urbane in the discretion of its carefully placed ornamentation, this is certainly the handsomest nineteenth-century café in the world and about the finest Romantic Classical edifice in Italy [51]. Exceptional in this period in the Latin world is the Neo-Gothic wing known as Il

51. Giuseppe Jappelli and Antonio Gradenigo: Padua, Caffè Pedrocchi, 1816–31

Pedrocchino attached to the café, designed by Jappelli and for the same client; this was added in 1837.

Trieste in this period, like the cities of Lombardy and the Veneto, is more Italian than Austrian architecturally. As a result it outshines Vienna in the extent and the quality of its early nineteenth-century construction. The new buildings were largely concentrated around the Canal Grande, a rectangular lagoon extending inland from the Riva Tre Novembre. At the head of this rises Sant' Antonio di Padova, built by Nobile in 1826-49, long after this former Trieste City Architect had been called to Vienna as head of the architecture section of the Akademie there. Occupying a position somewhat similar to that of the Gran Madre di Dio in Turin, Nobile's church is considerably more interesting, particularly as regards the generous spatial organization of the interior. The Canal Grande is flanked by contemporary palaces that are harmonious with one another in scale but quite varied in detail. The largest and finest, facing the sea on the left, is the Palazzo Carciotti. This was completed in 1806 by Matthäus Pertsch, a Milan-trained architect who had provided in 1798 the façade of the Teatro Verdi here in Trieste. With its raised portico and small dome, the Palazzo Carciotti is one of the most prominent and successful Italian buildings of the opening years of the century.

At the other side of the Latin world, the Iberian peninsula participated rather less than the Italian in the advanced architectural movements of the first half of the century. In Madrid the Obelisk of the 2nd of May, built by Isidro Gonzalez Velasquez (1764/5-?) in 1822-40, and the Obelisk of La Castellana (1883), by Francisco Javier de Mariateguí, are rather modest specimens of a widely popular sort of erection compared to Smirke's gigantic Wellington Testimonial in Dublin or Mills's Washington Monument. The Palace of the Congress of 1843-50 by Narciso Pascual y Coloner (1808-70) is a dull example of that nineteenth-century Classicism that hardly deserves the qualification 'Romantic'.

Italians, little employed elsewhere out of their own country in this period, provided the principal new public edifices of Lisbon. F. X. Fabri (?-1807) built the Palace of Arzuda, begun in 1802, and Fortunato Lodi (1806-?) from Bologna the Garret Theatre a generation later in 1842-6; both are as uninspired as the contemporary monuments of Madrid. As late as 1867-75 the Municipal Chamber of Lisbon by the local architect Domingos Ponente da Silva (1836-1901) maintained the Classical mode at its most conventional. Already, with the establishment of the Braganza headquarters in Rio de Janeiro early in the century, Portuguese vitality was passing to the New World (see Chapter 5). Yet if Lisbon has no individual Romantic Classical monuments of much interest, the lower city, extending from the Praça do Commercio to O Rocio, is a splendid example of late-eighteenth-century urbanism, initiated after the earthquake of 1755 by Eugenio dos Santos de Carvalho (1711-60).

In the eighteenth century Petersburg owed its grandeur as a Baroque city largely to the work of imported Italian architects; but with the rise of French and English influence in the later decades of the old century and the first of the new the day of the Italians was over, there as elsewhere (see Chapter 1). Alexander I's aspirations, after as well as before Waterloo, were wholly French, not Italian. The Committee for Construction and Hydraulic Works, indeed, which Alexander set up in 1816 to pass on the designs of all public and private buildings in his capital, had a French military engineer, General Béthencourt, as its chairman. Yet the principal architect of the post-Napoleonic decades, Karl Ivanovich Rossi (1775-1849), although he had an Italian family name and was of Italian origin, was Russian-born and

52. A. A. Monferran: Petersburg,
Alexander Column, 1829;
and K. I. Rossi: General Staff Arches, 1819–29

Russian-trained. Rossi's General Staff Arches of 1819–29 and the vast hemicycle of which they are the centre continue happily the urbanistic tradition of the older generation; but the detail is Roman not Greek, and the taste altogether coarser and more provincial than that of Thomon and Zakharov [52]. This is even more true of his Alexandra Theatre of 1827–32 and his Senate and Synod of 1829–34.

August Augustovich Monferran (1786–1858), to whom was assigned the building of St Isaac's Cathedral[10] in 1817, a vast pile that he completed only in 1857 [53], was French, despite the Russian form in which his name is here given, and actually a pupil of Percier. In his youth he had worked under Vignon on the Madeleine, moreover. Monferran lacked, like most of his own generation who remained in France, both the originality and the finesse of the earlier generation, just as Nicholas I lacked the taste of his brother Alexander I. A wealth of sumptuous materials, granites and marbles,

marks this church, however, and the dome is of some importance in technical history because it is entirely framed in iron (see Chapter 7).

Another typical monument in the Napoleonic tradition rose also from Monferran's designs, the Alexander Column of 1829 in the Winter Palace Square [52]. This may well be the largest granite monolith in the world – a typically Russian claim – but it quite lacks the elegance of Alavoine's still later Colonne de Juillet in Paris or the scale of Mills's Washington Monument. The Triumphal Gate of 1833 by Vasili Petrovich Stasov (1769–1848) is a trabeated Greek Doric propylaeon, somewhat comparable to Nobile's Burgtor in Vienna; more significant is the fact that, like the July Column in Paris and Monferran's great dome, not to speak of a curious Egyptian suspension bridge of this period in Petersburg, this structure is all of metal.

In 1840 the authority of the Committee of 1816 was terminated and in Petersburg, as so

53. A. A. Monferran:
Petersburg, St Isaac's Cathedral, 1817-57

generally elsewhere in Europe, coherent urban-istic control came to an end. The great archi-tectural period there was over as Moscow, with its nationalistic traditions, came more to the fore. Characteristically, the most important new church of the second quarter of the century, the Cathedral of the Redeemer of 1839-83, was built in the older capital and is the first major Russian example of Neo-Byzantine. One is not surprised to find that Konstantin Andreevich Ton (1794-1881), its architect, was German not French; for in a sense this represents a rather clumsy local variant of the German *Rundbogenstil*, continuing the particular eclectic line initiated by Klenze in his Munich Court Church more than a decade earlier.

CHAPTER 4

GREAT BRITAIN

In English terminology, the most productive period of Nash and Soane, the two greatest Romantic Classical architects of England, extending from 1810 down to the thirties, is loosely referred to as 'Regency', and the rest of the first half of the century as 'Early Victorian'. Neither term has much more specific meaning in an international frame of reference than does 'Restoration' or 'Louis Philippe' in France, not to speak of 'Biedermeyer', which is sometimes used for this period in Germany and Austria. 'Regency' production included the characteristic monuments of mature Romantic Classicism in England and also much work that makes manifest the Picturesque point of view. Early Victorian production illustrates the modulation of Romantic Classicism into the Renaissance Revival, and includes as well the most doctrinaire phase of the Gothic Revival (see Chapter 6).

Although current researches are somewhat amending the picture, it is accepted that private architecture has generally been more significant in England than public architecture. This was least true in the first three decades of the nineteenth century. Soane had been Architect to the Bank of England, in effect if not in fact an important branch of the State, from 1788. Nash succeeded Wyatt in the office of Surveyor-General – although he was only given the title of Deputy – in 1813. And in 1815 Soane, Nash, and Smirke, undoubtedly the three leading architects of their day if one excepts Wilkins, became the members of a new board set up by the national Office of Works, which was at a peak of its authority and activity immediately after Napoleon's downfall. Soane and Smirke, though not personal favourites of George IV,

were knighted like several of their German contemporaries. The principal building project of the day, the laying out and the construction of Regent Street and Regent's Park, the latter on Crown land, had the fullest personal support of George IV, as Regent and after 1820 as King.

Yet Soane's most important work between 1810 and 1818 was private, except for what he built as Architect to the Chelsea Hospital, and, in the case of his house and his family tomb, wholly personal. All that remains of consequence of his work at the Chelsea Hospital, the stables of 1814-17, might as well be private, for this is no great monument with columned portico and Pantheon-dome such as preoccupied most architects of Soane's generation and status abroad [54]. Rigidly astylar, boldly arcuated, and executed in common yellowish London stock bricks, with no more deference to the purplish walling bricks and bright orange-red rubbed dressings of Wren's earlier buildings at the Hospital than to his English Baroque style, this is as utilitarian as any project of Durand's. Moreover, in its very simple detailing this reflects, and quite consciously, something of that primitivistic aspect of international Romantic Classical theory deriving from the writings of Soane's favourite critical author, Laugier. Above all, in the proportioning and in the organization of the arcuated elements, the design of the stables is personal almost to the point of perversity. It was also far more acceptable to the abstract tastes of the mid twentieth century than in accordance with the ideals most widely respected in the England of Soane's own day.

Soane's Dulwich Gallery of 1811-14, outside London, is likewise built of common brick and has similarly primitivistic detailing. This structure is most characteristic of its period in being an art museum, indeed the earliest nineteenth-century example; but it could hardly be more different from the line of sculpture galleries that runs from Klenze's Glyptothek in Munich through Bindesbøll's Thorwaldsen Museum in Copenhagen. Nor does it much resemble the picture galleries of the period running from those in Schinkel's Altes Museum in Berlin through Klenze's Ältere Pinakothek in Munich to Voit's Neuere Pinakothek, also in Munich. It is least unlike the last of these, although that was designed forty years later; this similarity may help to suggest how confusingly advanced in style Soane, who was the eldest of the leading architects working in the post-Napoleonic decades, remained even in middle and old age.

But Soane's *Rundbogenstil* at Dulwich – to use the term out of its German context, as one might do even more aptly for the Chelsea Hospital stables – is a round-arched style with a difference. There are neither medieval nor *quattrocento* Italian overtones here. While Soane's approach was creatively personal in the detailing as well as in the over-all organization, that approach seems most closely parallel to Durand's rationalism, particularly in the technical skill with which the monitor-lighting was handled. The centrepiece of the Gallery is a mausoleum in which Soane's virtuosity in three-dimensional composition – an interest that sets him well apart from most of his generation on the Continent – and also at abstract linear ornamentation, produced here by plain incisions in the stone slabs of the lantern, reaches something of a climax.

54. Sir John Soane:
London, Royal Hospital, Chelsea, Stables, 1814–17

Even more of such ornamentation is to be seen on the family tomb in St Pancras churchyard of 1816 as also, though much more chastely handled, on the façade of his own house[1] of 1812-13 at 13 Lincoln's Inn Fields. The interiors of this house are full of spatial exercises, many of them minuscule in scale, which Soane developed later in various public structures. It may suffice here to mention the small breakfast-room with its very shallow dome, its varied and ingenious effects of indirect lighting, and its characteristic decoration by means of incised linear patterns and small convex mirrors.

In 1818 there began for Soane a new spate of public activity that continued down to 1823. A series of offices at the Bank of England[2] now carried further the spatial and decorative innovations of the interiors of the 1790s. Whether or not these were finer is a matter of

55. Sir John Soane:
London, Bank of England, Colonial Office, 1818-23

taste; but the continuous arched forms without imposts, the smoother surfaces, and the very abstract linear decoration certainly represent a more advanced stage of Soane's personal style [55]. Under the Act for Building New Churches of 1818,[2a] which generated great activity in the ecclesiastical field, Soane was one of the guiding architects; he built, however, only three churches for the Commission that was set up by the Act. St Peter's, Walworth, in south London, of 1823-5 is both elegant and ingenious in the way the galleries are incorporated into the internal architectural organization rather than treated as mere afterthoughts. The other two are less successful.

Almost all the other churches built under the Act, or by other means, in these years were rather conventionally Grecian, that is if sufficient funds were available; otherwise they were what is called 'Commissioners' Gothic' (see Chapter 6). The contrast that the former provide with the Walworth church helps to emphasize the highly personal character of Soane's achievement even in his least esteemed work. St Peter's was evidently designed from the inside out, and owes almost nothing to the architecture of any period of the past. The type-church of the age in England, however, comparable in historical significance to Lebas's slightly later Notre-Dame-de-Lorette in Paris, is St Pancras of 1818-22 in the Euston Road in London built by William Inwood (c.1771-1843) and his son (H. W., 1794-1843). Very evidently this was designed from the outside in, for its features are derived from the Erechtheum, a monument which the younger Inwood actually went to Athens to measure after the church had been begun.[3]

English tradition required a lantern above the temple portico at the front, and so the Inwoods devised a sort of Gibbsian tower for St Pancras out of elements borrowed from the Athenian Tower of the Winds. Urbane yet rather barren, the interior lacks even the tepid religious feeling of the French basilicas of the day. The architects, and contemporaries generally, were more interested in the caryatid porches – for there are not one but two – that flank the rear.

Other Inwood churches in London, such as All Saints in Camden Street of 1822-4 and St Peter's in Regent Square of 1824-6, are equally Greek in detail but less directly related to particular ancient monuments. They are also much less impressive. No more interesting are most of the Grecian churches built by other architects. St Mary's, Wyndham Place of 1823-4 by Smirke, however, is set apart by the circular tower placed on the south, a feature which he had already used on St Philip's, Salford, in 1822-5. His church at Markham Clinton in Nottinghamshire of 1833, cruciform in plan and with a fine octagonal lantern, is considerably more original, but it was rather a family mausoleum than an ordinary parish church.[3a]

A revolution was getting under way in Great Britain in the realm of church architecture at this very time, and the heyday of the temple church was destined to be brief. After the early thirties only Nonconformists continued to build them. But such a Congregational chapel as that built by F. H. Lockwood (1811-78) and Thomas Allom (1804-72) in Great Thornton Street, Hull, in 1841-3, its broad temple front flanked by lower side wings, still had real distinction. Such distinction was rarely achieved after this date, although rather similar structures continued to be erected for several more decades both in London and in the provinces.

In Scotland, where Greek sanctions lasted longer than in England, Alexander Thomson (1817-75) built in the fifties and sixties three of the finest Romantic Classical churches in the world. His Caledonia Road Free Church in Glasgow of 1856-7 was designed for those Presbyterians who had left the established Scottish church in 1843 [56]. This owes a great deal to Schinkel's suburban Berlin churches, which Thomson must have known through the *Sammlung architektonischer Entwürfe*. The composition is more Picturesque, in being markedly asymmetrical, and the superb tower at the corner reduces the temple front to a subordinate element in a sort of Italian Villa composition. Yet the idea for this sort of composition may well have come from Schinkel also, a derivation which the rather *Rundbogenstil* character and asymmetrical organization of certain of Thomson's earlier suburban villas seems to make still more probable. The interior of the church is very different from that of Soane's in Walworth, but it is equally architectonic in the Schinkelesque way the galleries are incorporated in the general scheme. This is real interior architecture, not just a gallery-surrounded hall like the Grecian churches in England built back in the twenties.

Thomson's more prominently located St Vincent Street Church of 1859, also in Glasgow, is not finer. But it utilizes a difficult site with striking success, and the exotic eclecticism of the spire is peculiarly personal to Thomson. His Queen's Park Church of 1867, in a southern suburb of Glasgow, was as perversely original as anything by Soane and perhaps Thomson's final masterpiece. Inside, he handled the light iron supports with clear logic and elegantly appropriate painted decoration. Both the heavy masonry tower – which was, of course, invisible from the interior – and the heavy clerestory were carried on these delicately proportioned metal columns with a frankness and boldness hardly equalled before the twentieth century. Externally Thomson detailed the trabeated masonry with the purity of a Schinkel and the originality of a Soane, yet he composed the façade in three dimensions in a fashion that was almost Baroque beneath his strange near-Hindu 'spire'.

Thomson's churches, late though they are, can be better understood as examples of

56. Alexander Thomson: Glasgow, Caledonia Road Free Church, 1856–7

Romantic Classicism, sharing important qualities with the boldest French projects of the
1780s, than in relation to any other stage of
nineteenth-century architectural development.
Yet it will be evident later that they also have a
good deal in common with the architectural
aspirations of their own quarter of the century
(see Chapter 9).

Soane in his latest work seems at times to have
produced what were almost parodies of his
characteristic Bank interiors, approaching in
their strangeness and their oriental allusions
the exotic spires of Thomson. As these things
do not survive, it is hard to know whether the
Court of Chancery at Westminster of 1824-5,
with its pendentives cut back so that they are no
more than a sort of plaster awning, or the
Council Chamber in Freemasons' Hall, with
its strange canopy-like covering, were effective
or not. But these interiors do help to explain
why the idiosyncratic, not to say cranky, Soane
left on his death in 1837 no such living tradition
behind him as did Karl Friedrich von Schinkel
in Germany.

Nash, Soane's rival as England's leading
architect in the second and third decades of the
nineteenth century, was a very different sort
of man. Until his marriage he was of no great
prominence; it was the Regent's favour which
then brought him to the fore. As an urbanist,
if not as a designer of individual buildings, he
was worthy of his opportunities – and no
architect of his generation had greater. His
distinction at what is today called 'planning'
resides not alone in the amplitude, the elasticity,
and the resultant variety of his schemes, but as
much perhaps in his ability as an entrepreneur
in carrying amazingly extensive operations to
completion. Few, moreover, succeeded better
than Nash in modulating Romantic Classicism
towards the Picturesque; and this was over and
above his important direct contribution to
Picturesque practice in the building of castles,
villas, and cottages.

At the beginning of the second decade of the
century the lease of the Crown's Marylebone
Estate fell in. Nash's scheme for its development, by far the most comprehensive, won the
day, evidently because he had the personal
backing of the Regent. Nash's scheme of 1812,

57. John Nash:
London, Regent Street and Regent's Park, 1812-27

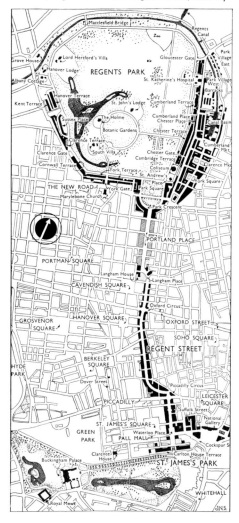

somewhat modified in ultimate execution, provided for a park – Regent's Park – surrounded by terraces of varying extent organized into a series of palatial compositions [57]. The traditions of homogeneous terrace design go back to the early eighteenth century, and terrace to face not a square or a street but open park-like country. This work around the park alone should have been enough to make Nash's reputation.

But in these unquiet years, when the world was briefly trying to live at peace with Napo-

58. John Nash:
London, Piccadilly Circus and Lower Regent Street, 1817-19

terraces facing out towards open scenery appeared soon after the middle of the century. But what Nash planned for Regent's Park, and in the main executed, vastly exceeded not only in its extent but also in its originality the early eighteenth-century terrace in Grosvenor Square, where the idea of over-all composition was probably first tried out, or the mid-eighteenth-century Royal Crescent at Bath by John Wood II (1728-81), which was the first leon, Nash sensed the Regent's ambition to embellish London in a way to rival the Emperor's plans for Paris. He therefore projected a street which should proceed, much as had been proposed even before this, along the line where the residential West End began, northward from the Regent's residence at Carlton House to the southern entrance of the new park. An early scheme for such a street, entirely lined with colonnades and interrupted by squares in which public structures would stand in splendid isolation, suggests his original aim of emulating the Rue de Rivoli and Parisian monuments like the Madeleine and the Bourse. As the project was gradually adjusted to the realities of the situation, most of its geometric regularity and practically all of its Parisian character disappeared. The colonnades survived only along the Quadrant leading out of Piccadilly Circus; the Duke of York's Column in Waterloo Place, rising between the two blocks of Carlton House Terrace, which eventually replaced Carlton House, is the one feature of Napoleonic scale and character. It is not by Nash but by the Duke of York's favourite architect, Benjamin Dean Wyatt (1775-?1850), and was built only in 1831-4.

Instead of an imitation of Paris, something vastly more original was created, an example of civic design whose full implications are perhaps not wholly digested even yet. Nash, the former partner of the landscape gardener Humphry Repton (1752-1818), in his new Regent Street as well as in his Regent's Park and its surrounding terraces, sought to carry out, not with natural scenery but with urban scenery, the principles of Picturesque landscaping. Yet his architectural vocabulary remained well within the accepted range of Romantic Classicism.

Waterloo Place is wholly formal, serving as a sort of forecourt to Carlton House when it was laid out in 1815. But going up Lower Regent Street the various buildings erected in 1817-19 were separately designed, to a harmonious scale but with no over-all regularity of shape and size. At Piccadilly, first the Circus, also of 1817-19, a circular *place*, and then the Quadrant of 1819-20 took care most ingeniously of a drastic leftward shift in axis. A relatively monumental façade, that of the County Fire Office, faced the head of Lower Regent Street; the other façades of the Circus were regular and plain in an almost Soanic way [58]. The

Quadrant gained great distinction from its projecting colonnades of Doric columns (made of cast iron) and from the skilful placing of a domed pavilion opposite its western end.

From there on the street, as carried forward in 1820-4, proceeded more directly, but with great variety in the individual façades - one terrace of houses over shops (1820-1) was by Soane. There were also special pavilioned structures to phrase several slight changes in direction and to mark the openings of intersecting streets. At Regent (now Oxford) Circus a second circle, similar to that at Piccadilly but elaborated by Nash with a Corinthian order, marks a major cross artery. Above this the street continues quite straight for a little way; then comes another sharp leftward shift in the axis. There Nash placed his All Souls' Church, which was built in 1822-4. Its curious fluted steeple still rises through the colonnade that crowns the tower to provide a pivot by which the eye is carried around the sharp corner. Almost at once another right-angled turn leads into the broad pre-existing esplanade of Adam's Portland Place. From here on all is formal again as at Waterloo Place.

At the upper end, between the top of Portland Place and the Park, was to be a large residential circus. Of this only the two southern quadrants were built - one of them the earliest portion of the whole scheme, initiated at the very start in 1812. As executed, there are above this - for this part of the scheme is all extant or accurately rebuilt - two regular terraces facing each other across Park Square.

In 1813, as has been said, Nash succeeded Wyatt in the Surveyor-General's office; but it was in the role of private entrepreneur rather than as an official that he executed the Regent Street scheme, hazarding his own rising fortune and using every device of subleasing to carry the project through. This he accomplished in the relatively short period of fifteen years, even though the renewal of the

59. John Nash and James Thomson: London, Regent's Park, Cumberland Terrace, 1826-7

war held up execution for several years immediately after the start. Of all this nothing remains below Portland Place but the planning and All Souls'. However, in the district east of Lower Regent Street, the Royal Opera Arcade still exists behind New Zealand House and, much larger and more conspicuous, the conventional temple portico of the Haymarket Theatre of 1821 stands at the end of what is now Charles II Street.

At the base of Waterloo Place, facing the Green Park, the two ranges of Carlton House Terrace, built in 1827, still rise above their cast-iron Doric basement colonnades. In the lower half of this square, south of Pall Mall, with the two clubs on either side - one by Nash, the other by Burton - and the Duke of York's Column silhouetted against the distant scenery of park and Government buildings between the two wings of Carlton House Terrace, Nash's urbanism can still be fully appreciated. The full grandeur of Napoleon's Paris or Alexander I's Petersburg is lacking, but so also is their archaeology. This obviously belongs to the nineteenth century. It establishes, for modern eyes, Nash's capacity as 'planner' quite as much as do his terraces around Regent's Park as these were carried out in 1820-7 by himself and by various younger architects working under his general supervision.

Curiously enough, the first Regent's Park terrace, built in 1821 while construction was still proceeding in Park Square, was at least nominally by young Decimus Burton (1800-81), the talented son of the builder James Burton, who was as active here in these years as in Bloomsbury. Dignified and severe, although not Grecian in detail like the handsomer Ionic York Terrace and its flanking Doric villa completed the next year, Cornwall Terrace certainly lacks the specifically Nashian qualities. Happily typical of Nash's response to urbanistic opportunities is the way he opened York Gate in the middle of York Terrace through to the Marylebone Road in order to incorporate visually the new façade provided by Thomas Hardwick (1752-1829) in 1818-19 for the Marylebone Parish Church.

Sussex Place of 1822, with its curved plan and its ten domes, is much more notably Picturesque; but the most spectacular composition of all is Cumberland Terrace, Nash's in general conception, but executed by James Thomson (1800-83) in 1826-7 [59]. This is far more palatial, at least superficially, than the rather humdrum Buckingham Palace that Nash was gradually erecting for the King from 1821 on.[4] When seen through the trees of the park or in sharp perspective from the ring road, this range of houses provides a Picturesque three-dimensional composition of a dream-like order - what matter if the conventional Classical elements are organized and executed in a very slapdash way?

The total scope of the Regent's Park development provided a 'New Town' in a rather complete sense inspired possibly by Ledoux's 'Ville idéale'. There were detached villas in the park, mews behind the terraces, a market-place to the east, modest two-storey houses near by in Munster Square and, finally, the two Park Villages, carried out by his protégé Sir James Pennethorne (1801-71) after Nash's ideas from 1827 on. These last are extensions of the Picturesque hamlet, consisting of groups of semi-detached villas, some of Italianate, some of Tudoresque character, loosely strung along curving roads, which provide the very prototype of the later-nineteenth-century suburb.

To most of his professional contemporaries, and not least to his associates on the Board of the Office of Works, Soane and Smirke, Nash seemed an opportunist and almost a charlatan. He differed as markedly from the archaeologically-minded Smirke as from Soane, even if he was as ready to borrow Greek orders from the one as incised detail from the other. Despite the independent position of Soane and of Nash, however, Britain could hardly have produced a line of archaeologist-architects from James Stuart to C. R. Cockerell – a line at least as distinguished as the French line from Leroy to Hittorff – without developing by this time Greek Revival doctrines quite as rigid and as self-assured as those of France and Germany. From the end of the second decade of the century the Grecian mode was, indeed, rather more firmly entrenched in Great Britain than anywhere on the Continent.

The historical importance of Wilkins's Downing College at Cambridge has already been noted. If Wilkins was never able to complete this, so that it remained but a fragment of an ideal Grecian college, he had greater opportunities later in London, opportunities which on the whole he muffed. His University College of 1827–8 in Gower Street impressed contemporaries because its central temple portico ran to *ten* columns in width. It is not otherwise distinguished, and the advancing wings of the quadrangle are not by him. His St George's Hospital at Hyde Park Corner, of the same date, is a much more modest building [60]. Yet it already shows some of the restlessness, if little of the elaboration, of later Grecian work on the Continent, such as Klenze's Hermitage Museum in Petersburg. The hospital, although the theme of the Choragic Monument of Thrasyllus is ingeniously exploited, lacks the delicacy and elegance of Decimus Burton's Ionic screen of 1825 across the way [60].

The hospital is, however, rather more original than Burton's nearby Constitution Hill Arch, also of 1827–8, now moved back towards the

60. London, Hyde Park Corner: Decimus Burton, Screen, 1825, Arch, 1825; William Wilkins, St George's Hospital, 1827–8; Benjamin Dean Wyatt, Apsley House, 1828

Green Park. This is one of the two erected in connexion with the new Buckingham Palace and in conscious rivalry of those Napoleon had set up in Paris and other Continental cities. The other one, originally forming the entrance to the court of the palace, is Nash's Marble Arch of 1828; that was moved to the corner of Hyde Park where Park Lane meets Oxford Street in 1851 after the palace was refronted by Blore in the late forties. Neither arch has the urbanistic value of Benjamin Dean Wyatt's Duke of York's Column or of the Nelson Column, erected in 1839 in Trafalgar Square by William Railton (1803-77), because of their very casual siting. Apsley House, as remodelled by B. D. Wyatt for the Duke of Wellington in 1828, rising too high beside the Burton screen, is not altogether an addition to the group at Hyde Park Corner.

Wilkins's largest and most conspicuous work, and the one which ruined his reputation, is the National Gallery of 1832-8. The long façade of this, extending across the top of Trafalgar Square, is excessively episodic and best seen in sharp perspective looking along Pall Mall East or from the south side of St Martin's-in-the-Fields. The order is not Greek, since the columns of the portico Henry Holland (1745-1806) erected in front of Carlton House in the early 1790s were re-used, and the little dome behind the central pediment is almost Byzantine in character. Comparison of this Picturesque-Classical composition with Cumberland Terrace is inevitable; the honours are all Nash's.

If Wilkins made the first Grecian spurt, it was Soane's pupil Smirke who held the course. In Trafalgar Square the unified range of buildings built in 1824-7 on the west side that once housed the Union Club and later the College of Physicians contrasts most strikingly with Wilkins's National Gallery. Heavy, dignified, and immaculately 'correct' in its Greek detailing, this block also shows considerable variety in the handling of standard Romantic Classical

elements without any such striving for Picturesque effect as the National Gallery. Later additions on the west have not seriously damaged Smirke's work.

It is highly typical that the most considerable Grecian edifice of London should be a museum and library. The British Museum, begun by Smirke in 1824, was not completed until 1847.[5] Its principal internal feature, moreover, the domed Reading Room built of cast iron in the central court (see Chapter 7), was designed and carried out in the mid fifties by Smirke's younger brother Sydney (1798-1877). Only the King's Library was finished rapidly within the twenties to house the library of George III. This is dignified and crisp, if somewhat less immaculately correct than Smirke's façade in Trafalgar Square.

The characteristic south front of the Museum, one of the most overwhelming examples of Romantic Classical stylophily, or love of columns – there are forty-eight of them – was one of the last portions of the whole to be completed [61]. The great temple portico and the colonnade that is carried round the inner sides and the ends of the flanking wings was probably not decided on until the thirties; such a redundancy of columns seems to belong well into the second quarter of the century – compare Elmes's St George's Hall in Liverpool [62] or Basevi's Fitzwilliam Museum in Cambridge. The façade of Smirke's General Post Office of 1824-9, with columns used only at the centre and the ends, and two ranges of good-sized windows between, was more characteristic of the usual Romantic Classical balance between columnar display and rationalistic provision for internal function.

Wilkins and Smirke were not alone in providing Grecian public buildings for the London of George IV. The London Corn Exchange of 1827-8 by George Smith (1783-1869) was an excellent example, less heavy than most of Smirke's work, less inconsequent than Wil-

61. Sir Robert Smirke: London,
British Museum, south front, completed 1847

kins's. Decimus Burton, who provided various
gatehouses at Hyde Park as well as the screen
at Hyde Park Corner in 1825 – the modest ones
at Prince's Gate are almost identical with
Schinkel's tiny Doric temples at the Potsdamer
Tor in Berlin – also provided the finest façade
in Waterloo Place when he built the Athenaeum there in 1829–30. This clubhouse is
severe and astylar externally but grand and
sumptuous within to a degree hitherto unknown. Henry Roberts (1803–76), a Smirke
assistant, followed his former master closely
in the design of the Fishmongers' Hall built in
1831–3. His great Ionic portico rises as splendidly above the solid substructure that flanks
the Thames as Klenze's Walhalla does above
its stepped terraces.

Corporate clients that came to the fore in the
thirties saw in the solemn Grecian mode the
best means of achieving representational monumentality in their buildings; moreover, they
were increasingly ready to employ leading
architects in order to obtain it. C. R. Cockerell
(1788–1863), the son of S. P. Cockerell, soon to
be Soane's successor as Architect of the Bank of
England, began his distinguished career as a
favourite servant of the financial world by providing the Westminster Insurance Office in the
Strand in 1831 with a range of Doric half-
columns. Six years later, in the London and
Westminster Bank in Lothbury, he attained a
greater effect of dignified restraint, with no loss
of plastic interest, in an astylar façade of great
originality.

The new railways, whose earliest stations had
been very modest indeed, were as interested as
insurance companies and banks in the representational dignity of Classical frontispieces.[5a]

At Euston Grove in London, before what was intended to be a double station planned by the engineer Robert Stephenson (1803-59) in 1835 to serve the London & Birmingham and the Great Western Railways, there rose from the designs of Philip Hardwick (1792-1870) the Euston 'Arch', a giant Greek Doric propylaeon;[5b] for the Birmingham terminal of the railway at Curzon Street Hardwick provided a second gateway that is more in the form of a Roman triumphal arch. This theme John Foster (1786-1846) expanded into a continuous Roman screen in front of Lime Street Station at Liverpool in 1836. At Huddersfield James P. Pritchett (1789-1868) and his son Charles fronted the main station block in 1845-9 with a Roman temple portico and flanked it with minor colonnaded features. The Monkwearmouth station by John Dobson (1787-1865) of 1848 is similar, but Grecian in its detailing.

More appropriate to modern eyes was the endless red-brick façade designed by Francis Thompson for Robert Stephenson's Trijunct Station in Derby in 1839-41. This was astylar but had various subtle projections and recessions of the wall plane and a comparable variety of levels in the very long skyline. Thompson also, in the stone towers he designed for Stephenson's Britannia Bridge of 1845-50, handled his material with a superbly rational directness [110]. The technical significance of such structures as examples of the new uses of iron which the railways encouraged must be considered later (see Chapter 7). Of comparable quality to Thompson's work is the enormous Royal Navy Victualling Yard at Stonehouse of 1826-35 by the engineer Sir John Rennie (1794-1874) - able son, like Robert Stephenson, of a more famous engineer father and also a brother-in-law of C. R. Cockerell. Despite the severity characteristic of the period, this has an almost Baroque plasticity and vigour of silhouette rarely achieved by contemporary architects before the mid-century.

Except for certain large provincial and suburban Nonconformist churches, the heyday of the temple portico came to an end about 1840. The last prominent example in London is the Royal Exchange, built by Sir William Tite (1798-1873) in 1841-4, but there is nothing Classical about other aspects of this prominent structure. The side, rear, and court façades are in a sort of Neo-Baroque that prefigures the bombast of the third quarter of the century (see Chapter 9).

Grecian public monuments were as characteristic of provincial cities in the twenties and thirties as of London, perhaps more so. Francis Goodwin (1784-1835)[5c] provided Manchester with a handsome town hall in 1822-4, now long since superseded. In the latter year he lost the competition for the new Royal Institution there to the young Charles Barry (1795-1860), hitherto most unsympathetically employed in building cheap Gothic churches for the Commissioners.[6] This edifice Barry erected over the years 1827-35. Happily it still stands, serving as the Manchester Art Gallery, an excellent example of Barry's command of that Grecian idiom which his more personal Italianate mode forced into obsolescence even before this building was finished (see below).

In 1828 Foster began the fine Grecian Custom House in Liverpool, completely destroyed, alas, in the blitz; while in 1831 Joseph A. Hansom (1803-82) won the competition for the Birmingham Town Hall with the most striking British example of the temple paradigm. This characteristic Romantic Classical edifice, raised on a high rusticated podium, was slowly executed by Hansom and his partner Edward Welch (1806-68) over the next fifteen odd years.

The more widespread the use of Greek forms became, the less vitality and character they seemed to retain. It is not the columnar detail, so much more correct than that at Regent's Park, which gives interest to the terraces - built from the twenties on - that George Basevi

(1794–1845) designed for Belgrave Square in London or to those of slightly later date designed by Lewis Cubitt (1799–1883) and by John Young in Eaton Square; it is the remarkable scale and extent of this newest urban development, rivalling that at Regent's Park, which was undertaken by the builder Thomas Cubitt (1788–1855), Lewis's brother, for the Grosvenor Estate behind Buckingham Palace gardens.

So also at Newcastle, where Thomas Grainger (1798–1861), with the presumptive assistance of Dobson[6a] as designer, laid out and built up a series of streets from 1834 on, it is not the more correctly Greek orders that make Grey Street a finer piece of urbanism than Nash's Regent Street; it is the light, creamy freestone that replaces London's stucco and the skilful organization of the ranges of buildings, all so much more carefully grouped and related to one another than in Regent Street, along the curving and rising slope.[6b] The Grey Column, built by John Green (?–1852) in 1837–8, is superbly placed in the best manner of the period as a focal accent at the top of the development just like the Duke of York's Column at the bottom of Lower

Regent Street. The cleaning of many buildings has of late much enhanced the attractiveness of central Newcastle.

It was not until the early forties that Greek Revival buildings began to be characterized by contemporaries as 'insipid'. But Basevi's façade of the Fitzwilliam Museum in Cambridge, begun in 1837 and largely completed with some emendations by C. R. Cockerell in 1847 after Basevi's death, well illustrates some of the changes that were already coming over Romantic Classical design. As at Wilkins's National Gallery, the silhouette is elaborately varied – here much more skilfully than in Trafalgar Square. As with Tite's Royal Exchange, there is also a most un-Grecian sort of plastic bombast. The orders are not Grecian but Roman, moreover, and the spirit is more Roman still, but Roman of the later Empire in the East, as at Baalbek or Palmyra.

St George's Hall in Liverpool [62], the latest of the major Romantic Classical monuments of England, was finished like the Fitzwilliam by C. R. Cockerell long after its original designer's death. It displays much less bombast and much

62. H. L. Elmes:
Liverpool, St George's Hall, 1841–54

truer grandeur in its scale. The young Harvey Lonsdale Elmes (1814-47) won two successive competitions, for a Hall and for Law Courts, in 1839 and 1840 respectively. Then, when it was decided to combine the two in one structure, he paid a visit to Berlin to study the work of Schinkel. Schinkelesque, indeed, is the long colonnade facing Lime Street Station, and even more so the curious square piers, free-standing in their upper half, that Elmes used elsewhere on the building.

The temple portico at the south end is conventional enough, but with its steps boldly raised above a massively plain foundation wall; the rounded end to the north is much more original and also rather French in feeling. French surely, but of the Empire rather than the contemporary July Monarchy, is the tremendous scale of the whole and the stately axial planning of the sort to be seen in many Prix de Rome projects of the preceding fifty years. The great hall is slightly larger than its prototype in the Baths of Caracalla.[7] As completed by Cockerell in the early fifties, the interior lost all the Grecian severity of the exterior. Together with the elegant elliptical concert hall, planned by Elmes but entirely executed by Cockerell, the great hall belongs to the next period of architectural development as much by its rich decoration as by its date.

It was in Scotland, not in England, that the Greek Revival had its greatest success and lasted longest. There seems to have been some special congruity of sentiment between Northern Europe in the first half of the nineteenth century and the ancient world. Edinburgh, which considered itself for intellectual reasons the 'Athens of the North', set out after 1810 to continue in a more Athenian mode the extension and embellishment of her New Town begun in the 1760s. The result rivals Petersburg as well as Copenhagen, Berlin, and Munich. Indeed, in Edinburgh, what was built between 1760 and 1860 provides still the most extensive

example of a Romantic Classical city in the world.[7a]

If the architecture of Edinburgh is largely Classical - the most conspicuous exceptions are the inherited medieval Castle on its rock at the head of the Old Town and the Walter Scott Monument in Prince's Street Gardens - the setting is extremely Picturesque. The fullest scenic advantage was taken of the castle-crowned hill, above the filled-in and landscaped North Loch, and of the two heights to the east and the south-east, Calton Hill and Arthur's Seat. The latter was kept quite clear of buildings, the former gradually turned into a sort of Scottish Akropolis. Perhaps fortunately, the largest structure there, the National Monument, a copy of the Parthenon by C. R. Cockerell and the local architect W. H. Playfair (1789-1857), was never finished; thus it appears to be a ruin and adds to the Picturesque effect of this terminus to the eastward view along Prince's Street. It was begun in 1822.

Calton Hill is approached, and the view of it framed, by Waterloo Place, the buildings of which were erected by Archibald Elliott (1763-1823) in 1815-19. This is no unworthy rival of the homonymous square in London, despite the lack of a central column. The view remains open to the high hill beyond, where Playfair's Observatory was rising in 1814-18 and later, in 1830, the Choragic Monument by Thomas Hamilton (1785-1858) dedicated to that very un-Grecian poet Robert Burns, as well as various other objects of visual interest. In St Andrew's Square in the New Town, however, is the Melville Column. This was built by William Burn (1789-1870) in 1821-2 and based, like the Colonne Vendôme in Paris, on that of Trajan.

These Scottish architects were perhaps more fortunate than Dobson in the material available to them; Edinburgh's Craigleith stone becomes with time a rather deep grey, but not so black as that in Newcastle when left uncleaned. Seen in Playfair's terraces, executed gradually from

63. W. H. Playfair: Edinburgh, Royal Scottish Institution, 1822–36,
National Gallery of Scotland, 1850–4, and Free Church College, 1846–50

1820 to 1860, which run around the base of Calton Hill on the south, east, and north, the effect may be rather dour; but the dignity and solidity of these Grecian ranges, rivalled in the contemporary circuses on the slopes to the north of the eighteenth-century New Town, are undeniably impressive.

From the completion of his Observatory in 1814 to the completion of the Scottish National Gallery forty years later Playfair continued to ornament Edinburgh with Classical (and on occasion with non-Classical) structures. Looking south along the cross-axis of the New Town, one sees just beyond Prince's Street his Royal Scottish Institution begun in 1822 [63], its rather massive Doric bulk happily crowned just after its completion in 1836 by the seated figure of the young Queen Victoria. Behind this lies his Ionic National Gallery of 1850–4, which is not unworthy of comparison with Smirke's British Museum begun more than a quarter of a century earlier. High to the rear, on the slopes

of the Old Town, rise the two towers of the Free Church College, also by Playfair and begun in 1846, framing with their crisp Tudorish forms the richer and more graceful spire (sometimes attributed to Pugin) of Tolbooth St John's, which was built by James Gillespie Graham in 1843.

Finer than any individual work of Playfair's, and splendidly sited on the south side of Calton Hill, is the High School by Thomas Hamilton (1784–1858). Begun in 1825, this complex Grecian composition shows how well the lessons of the Athenian Propylaea were learned by Scottish architects. More original, but still essentially Grecian, is Hamilton's Hall of Physicians in Queen Street of 1844–5.

Banking was not far behind State and Church as a patron of monumental architecture in Scotland. Before the astylar *palazzo* mode took over the financial scene, two banks grander than any in London had been erected in the Edinburgh New Town. The Commercial Bank of Scotland of 1846 in George Street by David Rhind (1808-83), despite its pedimented portico, is no longer Greek in detail; the British Linen Bank of 1852 in St Andrew's Square by David Bryce (1803-76), more plastically Roman still, has giant detached columns upholding bold entablature blocks, an idea deriving from C. R. Cockerell's rejected competition design for the Royal Exchange in London of 1839.

As the earlier mention of Thomson's churches in Glasgow will have indicated, the Greek Revival lasted even longer there than in Edinburgh. But such edifices as the Royal Exchange of 1829-30 by David Hamilton (1768-1843) or Clarke & Bell's Municipal and County Buildings of 1844 do not rival the work of Playfair and of the other Hamilton in the capital; there is, all the same, much good urbanism of this period. In his domestic work Thomson remained closer to the conventional norms of the Greek Revival than in his churches. However, in Moray Place, Strathbungo, of 1859, where he lived himself, he produced the finest of all Grecian terraces [64] and, still later, in Great Western Terrace an ampler if less original composition, as well as several others.

In England the Greek Revival was barely established as the dominant mode in the twenties before it was challenged. Barry, as has been noted earlier, began his career with the building of cheap Commissioners' Gothic churches, but his favourite mode was the Renaissance Revival. We have seen that in Germany the Renaissance Revival may be considered to begin with Klenze's Munich work of the mid twenties. Now, in 1827-8,

64. Alexander Thomson:
Glasgow, Moray Place, Strathbungo, 1859

Barry built the Brunswick Chapel, later St Andrew's, at Hove in the *quattrocento* mode – the exterior, that is, for the modest interior can hardly be thus characterized, and in its present form includes various changes since Barry's time. The façade looks rather nineteenth-century French to modern eyes; yet comparable French churches, such as Lequeux's Saint-Jacques-Saint-Christophe in Paris, are mostly from five to fifteen years later (see Chapter 3). Barry doubtless turned to some of the available French publications on the Italian Renaissance for his detail, most probably to the *Architecture toscane* of Grandjean de Montigny and Famin, but he certainly did not derive the design of his church from current Continental practice.

Following immediately upon the Brunswick Chapel, Barry built for Thomas Attree of

Brighton a symmetrical Italian Villa, later the Xavierian College, with an architectural garden setting. This was part of a scheme, otherwise unexecuted, for surrounding Queen's Park, east of the town, with a range of detached houses, some Italianate, some Tudoresque, in an extensive suburban development of the order of Nash's only slightly earlier Park Villages. The intended effect can best be seen in Decimus Burton's Calverley Estate at Tunbridge Wells carried out over the years 1828 to 1852.

Far more important, however, was the fact that Barry in 1829 won with a *palazzo* composition the competition for the new Travellers' Club. This was built in Pall Mall in the next two years beside the prominent corner site where Burton's astylar but still Grecian Athenaeum was rising. Raphaelesque on the front –

65. Sir Charles Barry: London, Travellers' Club and Reform Club, 1830-2 and 1838-40

although not as derivative from Raphael's Pan-dolfini Palace in Florence as was claimed at the time – but rather Venetian on the rear, this clubhouse notably eschews the flat barrenness and the giant orders of the Grecian mode to throw emphasis on the elegant aedicular treatment of the windows and the bold *cornicione* which crowns the top [65].

Very soon Charles Fowler (1791–1867),[7b] who owned the copy of Durand's treatise now in the Library of the Royal Institute of British Architects, was introducing a more utilitarian sort of Italianism in the Hungerford Market in London of 1831–3, now long gone, and in the Lower Market at Exeter of 1835–6. There the Durand-esque and almost basilican interiors, destroyed in 1942, contrasted markedly with the Greek Doric detailing of the façade of his Upper Market of 1837–8.

In 1836 Barry designed a larger edifice of the *palazzo* type, the Manchester Athenaeum built

in 1837–9. But this was overshadowed in size, in prominence, and in quality by the new Reform Club next door to the Travellers' in Pall Mall; for this he won the competition in 1837, and it was built in 1838–40 [65]. Here his model was obviously San Gallo's Farnese Palace in Rome. But there are many differences such as the unaccented entrance, the balustrade which sets the façades back from the pavement, the simpler and more San Gallesque top storey, the corner emphasis provided by prominent chimneys, not to speak of the metal-and-glass roofing of the central court.

Barry's two Pall Mall clubs provided architectural paradigms much followed through the forties and well into the third quarter of the century. Moreover, W. H. Leeds (1786–1866), in the text of a monograph on the *Travellers' Club-House* published in 1839, developed at some length the arguments for a Renaissance Revival. A little less evidently than the Con-

66. Sir Charles Barry: original design for Highclere Castle, Hampshire, *c.* 1840

tinental work of these years in Renaissance modes, but none the less truly, Barry's *palazzi* represent a continuation of Romantic Classicism. In the block-like unity of the external masses, the regularity of the fenestration, and the extreme orderliness of the planning his *palazzo* mode is at least as characteristic an aspect of later Romantic Classicism in Great Britain as is the *Rundbogenstil* on the Continent.

This is considerably less true of two other directions in which Barry first turned in the thirties. It would be premature, however, to discuss here the design with which Barry won the competition for the new Houses of Parliament in 1836 [92]. As the first major public monument to be designed anywhere in Gothic this constituted above all an epoch-making step in the English revolt *against* Romantic Classicism (see Chapter 6).

This is not so much the case with Barry's first and only important essay in the 'Jacobethan' mode – or the Anglo-Italian as he preferred to call it – the remodelling of Highclere Castle in Hampshire, proposed as early as 1837 and carried out over the next two decades [66]. Despite the Picturesque effect of its towered and bristling silhouette, this great country house rigidly maintains the quadrangular plan of the Reform Club and is almost as regular as that in composition, and even more coldly crisp in its detailing. Much the same can be said of Mentmore House in Buckinghamshire, built by Sir Joseph Paxton (1803-65) in 1852-4 in a very similar vein but more directly derived from Smithson's Elizabethan Wollaton Hall near Nottingham. In general, however, the extremely popular Jacobethan Revival of these years, even more than the contemporary revival of the *style François I* in France, represents a reaction not merely against the Greek Revival, as does the *palazzo* mode, but against the basic disciplines of Romantic Classicism since it was one of the major stylistic vehicles of the later Picturesque.

On the other hand, the utilization of pre-Gothic medieval forms in England in this period, so closely similar in its result to the Romanesquoid aspect of the *Rundbogenstil*, seems to have been only partly Picturesque in intention. From the twenties on a very considerable number of churches, mostly small, had Norman Romanesque detail, though there was rarely any attempt to break away from the hall-like tradition of the Late Georgian church in their plans. However, three rather large churches that are early medieval in inspiration but not Norman in detail deserve particular mention, for they are among the finest, though not the most historically significant, built in Britain in the early forties.

St Mary and St Nicholas's, Wilton, built by T. H. Wyatt (1807-80) and David Brandon (1813-97) in 1840-6 for Sydney Herbert and his Russian mother, might almost have risen in the Prussia or the Baden of this period. How-

67. J. W. Wild:
London, Christ Church, Streatham, 1840 2

ever, this Italian Romanesque basilica, with tall, detached campanile and rich internal polychromy of Cosmati-work brought from Italy, is rather more archaeological than Persius's or Hübsch's churches in Germany. On the other hand, the so much more original Christ Church of 1840-2 in Streatham, south London, by J. W. Wild (1814-92) is so similar to Prussian work that some knowledge on Wild's part of Schinkel's suburban-church projects of a decade earlier might almost be assumed [67]. Although the exposed yellow brickwork and the touches of external brick polychromy are notably premonitory of the next period, the splendid obelisk-like campanile and the crisp ranges of clerestory windows, for all their pointed tops, are quite as much within the range of Romantic Classicism as the German churches that this recalls. The handling of the galleries of the interior had local precedent in Soane's churches of the twenties as well as in Schinkel's of the thirties. Although the barrel vaults are presumably only of plaster, St Jude's, Bethnal Green, in London, built by Henry Clutton (1819-93) in 1844-6, has an impressive cruciform interior. The exterior here is notably Germanic with two thin towers flanking the great polygonal apse.

But these three churches, for all their individual excellence, are exceptional in England. They are related to the broad contemporary current of the Renaissance Revival that Barry had set under way only in rejecting Grecian sanctions even more completely than he. Barry was himself too versatile ever quite to repeat the strict *palazzo* formula of the Reform Club, although he almost came to that in the British Embassy in Istanbul of 1845-7. For this he provided sketches as early as 1842 and later emended the plans of the local executant architect, W. J. Smith. This structure, carrying the Renaissance Revival to, or even beyond, one edge of the western world as Grandjean de Montigny did to Rio de Janeiro at the other

edge, is considerably larger than the Reform Club and rather bleak, though splendidly sited and very dignified indeed. At Bridgewater House in London of 1847-57, however, Barry enriched the *palazzo* paradigm quite considerably, not only by the introduction of a good deal of carved work but also by breaking the continuity of the garden front towards the Park in order to emphasize the end bays. This personal compositional device is even more conspicuous on the river front of his Gothic Houses of Parliament (for which see below, pp. 150-1 and illustration 92).

It was for clubhouses and business buildings that Renaissance models were most generally used in England after 1840. For the remodelling of the Carlton Club in 1847 Sydney Smirke, who had provided the winning design in a select competition, looked not to San Gallo's Farnese Palace in sixteenth-century Rome as Barry had done at the Reform Club next door, but to Sansovino's Library in sixteenth-century Venice. Before this was finished in the mid fifties, C. Octavius Parnell (?-1865) and his partner Alfred Smith had erected across Pall Mall in 1848-51 the Army and Navy Club based on Sansovino's Palazzo Corner della Cà Grande. Both are now gone.

But if these architects in London were moving in the late forties towards an altogether richer and more plastic sort of High Renaissance design, from which almost all traces of the cold asceticism of Romantic Classicism had departed, most provincial architects were content to stick fairly close to the Farnese Palace model of the Reform Club well down into the sixties. This was most notably true in the design of edifices for financial institutions. In 1840 George Alexander (?-1884), who had made his own study of the *cinquecento* in Italy, designed the Savings Bank in Bath as a little Reform Club; the next year in the Brunswick Buildings in Liverpool A. & G. Williams applied the formula to a much larger block of general offices. Henceforth the mode was solidly established for almost a generation.

Barry usually gave a characteristically Italian Villa bent to the many country houses that he remodelled by introducing a tall loggia-topped tower (used to store water for the more elaborate sanitation now demanded) placed asymmetrically at one side of the main block. The first of these was at Trentham Park, near Stoke-on-Trent, where a second later rose in the stable court; the finest are those at Walton House near London of 1837 and at Shrubland in Suffolk of 1848–50. In these the inherited Georgian blocks became subordinate parts of rich three-dimensional compositions almost like the villas that Schinkel and Persius built at Potsdam. The rebuilding of Osborne House as a country retreat for Queen Victoria on the Isle of Wight gave Royal sanction to the Italian Villa mode. Unfortunately she did not employ Barry; the work was done in 1845–6 and 1847–9 by the builder Thomas Cubitt and the design was dictated, if not actually prepared, by Prince Albert.

Despite the continued use of Greek forms for certain purposes and in some areas, the controls of Romantic Classicism were loosening rapidly in Great Britain in the forties. A real change of style was at hand; but since certain stylisms, such as the conventional use of Renaissance forms, tended to continue indefinitely, it is hard to know just where to draw the line chronologically.

The Geological Museum in Piccadilly in London, built in the late forties by Pennethorne, Nash's protégé and his successor at the Office

68. Cuthbert Brodrick:
Leeds, Corn Exchange, 1860–3

of Works, was far more successful than the ball-room wing he added in the early fifties to Buckingham Palace. Even that, however, was a considerable improvement on the curious façade – more Neo-Baroque than Neo-Renaissance – with which Edward Blore (1787-1879) masked the front of Nash's edifice in 1847. The Museum was more successful precisely because its exteriors retained the regularity and severity characteristic of Romantic Classicism. Still later, the Free Trade Hall built by Edward Walters (1808-72) in Manchester in 1853-6 followed the lusher Sansovinesque Italianism of Smirke's Carlton Club, while his many hand-some warehouses there moved ever farther away from the severity of Barry's Athenaeum despite their generic *palazzo* character. Yet the Corn Exchange in Leeds, erected as late as 1860 by Cuthbert Brodrick (1825-1905), is still Romantic Classical in the cool regularity of its diamond-rusticated walls broken only by ranges of plain arches [68].

There can be little question, however, that his Town Hall in Leeds of 1855-9, despite the reiterative grandeur of its giant colonnades and the evident derivation of its principal interior from St George's Hall in Liverpool, is in English terms definitely 'High Victorian' [138]. If the Corn Exchange can hardly be considered typically Early Victorian in character, and in any case is some ten years too late in date, it might almost be called *Louis Philippe,* so close is it to some French work of the 40s.

Run-of-the-mill English railway stations of the forties, mostly designed by engineers and minor architects, clearly rank in their dullness with the most utilitarian French work of that decade. They indicate to what depths of con-ventionality late Romantic Classicism in Eng-land had sunk by this time. Yet Lewis Cubitt's long-demolished Bricklayers' Arms Station in London of 1842-4, with its entrance screen compounded of rustic Italian elements derived from the books of Charles Parker,[8] seems to have had considerable plastic interest. More-over, the great plain arches at the front of his King's Cross Station of 1850-2 [116] remain to signalize to every traveller a masterpiece of the period more than worthy of comparison with Duquesney's somewhat earlier Gare de l'Est in Paris [44].

On the whole, however, for all that King's Cross is one of the major late monuments of the rationalistic side of Romantic Classicism, it is better to consider railway stations in relation to their sheds of iron and glass, technically, that is, rather than stylistically (see Chapter 7). They illustrate especially well something which the stylistic preoccupations of the first half of the nineteenth century tended to mask from most contemporaries, the success with which new functional needs were satisfied in this period by the bold use of new materials and new types of construction.

Yet the most characteristic monuments of Romantic Classicism in Europe after those prime urbanistic symbols of Napoleonic or counter-Napoleonic triumph, the arches, the columns, and the obelisks that rose in all the great cities from Petersburg to Madrid, are the museums and libraries, starting with Soane's Dulwich Gallery, begun in 1811, and ending with Labrouste's Bibliothèque Sainte-Gene-viève, opened in 1850. These are useful, yes; moreover, they serve what were effectively new purposes, purposes closely related to the rising ideal of providing cultural opportunities for the general public. On the whole, however, they could be carried out – and so they usually were down to Labrouste's library – with established methods of construction; while their cultural significance – and in the case of the sculpture galleries from Klenze's Glyptothek in Munich, begun in 1816, to Bindesbøll's Thorwaldsens Museum in Copenhagen, opened in 1848, their very contents – seemed to justify, if not indeed to demand, the use of Greek or Roman forms.

CHAPTER 5

THE NEW WORLD

In varying degree Romantic Classicism left its mark on all the major cities of Europe. Paris without the Napoleonic monuments that Louis Philippe brought to completion is inconceivable, while Karlsruhe, Munich, Petersburg, and Edinburgh, not to speak of Helsinki, owe most of their architectural interest to this period.

In the New World, where the independence of the principal colonies of the European nations, British, Spanish, and Portuguese, was generally established in this period or just before it, one might expect that Romantic Classicism would have made a still more conspicuous contribution to the architectural scene. Yet the very youth of most of the countries of the New World, settled though many of them had been in the sixteenth and seventeenth centuries, and also the strong cultural links that they still maintained with the ancient traditions of their several homelands, tended to hold them back from entering fully into the new international movement of the day in architecture. What national libraries, moreover, were yet needed in Venezuela or Colombia, what sculpture galleries in the American Middle West? Columns and obelisks, if not triumphal arches, rose – frequently very belatedly – to celebrate national heroes of the various wars of independence; but outside the eastern United States the still very simple organization of society and the primitive means of transport required neither the institutional edifices of France – markets, hospitals, and prisons – nor the new railway stations of England.[1]

Yet in the United States, and not only along the eastern seaboard, the period of Romantic Classicism left a very rich architectural deposit.

The monuments of real distinction range all the way from such a church as Latrobe's Catholic Cathedral in Baltimore [8], one of the very finest ecclesiastical edifices of the first half of the century to be seen anywhere, to Haviland's Eastern State Penitentiary in Philadelphia of 1823-35, the first to be planned on the radial cellular system [69]. Studied and published by the English penologist William Crawford as well as by Demetz and Blouet,[2] this provided a new functional concept for penal architecture influential abroad from the time that Gilbert projected his Nouvelle Force Prison in the late thirties. Haviland's prison was Castellated like Lebas's Petite Roquette, not Grecian in detail; his New York prison of 1836-8, however, was Egyptian in detail, to which it owed its curious nickname, 'The Tombs'. That both Latrobe and Haviland were English-born and English-trained is certainly significant; the latter, who was a cousin of the painter Haydon and a pupil of H. L. Elmes's father James (1782-1862), had first tried his luck in Petersburg.

The characteristic and almost universal use of Grecian forms in domestic building, however, continuing in many parts of the country down to the Civil War of 1861-5, was the result of no foreign influence. Moreover, the Grecian details were not drawn by most architects and builders from the basic treatise of Stuart and Revett, available in America only to a very few, but at second hand from the local Builders' Guides[3] prepared by Haviland in Philadelphia, Asher Benjamin (1773-1845) in Boston, Minard Lafever (1798-1854) in New York, and various others. Such authors consciously Americanized what they borrowed from European sources in

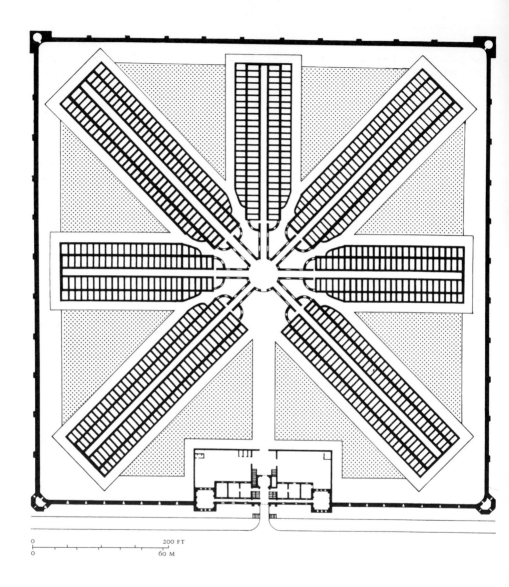

69. John Haviland: Philadelphia, Eastern Penitentiary, 1823–35

order to adapt Classical masonry forms to the ubiquitous wooden construction of the American countryside.

There are two levels of Romantic Classicism in America. Work at the upper professional level is found chiefly in the big eastern cities where architects operated who were either themselves foreign-born and foreign-trained or else pupils and emulators of such. The lower vernacular level is more conspicuous in America than in Europe because it includes a much greater proportion of building production than in older countries where so many structures of earlier periods remain extant. 'Carpenter's Grecian', so to call it, represents the perhaps naïve, but culturally significant, determination of all who built to employ, in some degree at least, the modern style of their day.

The frontiersman in the Oregon of 1850 when raising a tavern in the Willamette Valley thus shared with the new and old royalties of Europe the satisfaction of architectural patronage. Moreover, like so many English gentlemen of the eighteenth century or such a nineteenth-century prince as Frederick William IV, he often took a hand at design himself. In this he was assisted by memories of the relatively settled towns he had left behind in the Middle West, themselves largely products of this period architecturally, and also by the Builders' Guides issuing from the east in recurrent editions.

It was not alone the transient patronage of a Corsican soldier, for a few brief years heir to Louis XIV and overlord of Europe, nor the Building Committee of an autocrat on the banks of the Neva, controlling all public and private architecture in an Imperial capital for a quarter of a century, that really established Romantic Classicism as the last universal style before that of the mid twentieth century. It is the fact that Boston architects and builders, when Quincy granite (that most perfect of Romantic Classical building materials) became readily available in the mid twenties, arrived at a rational sort of trabeated design as distinguished as Schinkel's; while three thousand miles to the west, and a quarter of a century later, amateur builders working in wood produced almost the same sort of 'pilastrades', simplified well beyond the Americanized models of Greek antae they found in the plates of Asher Benjamin's books, as Schinkel had in Berlin.

The Grecian writ ran far south to Buenos Aires in Latin America, where the broad portico of the cathedral, designed by the French engineer Prosper Catelin and built in 1822, follows closely Grand Prix designs of the 1790s; and deep into the Antipodes as well, where Australia moved like the United States into nationhood and into the Greek Revival at much the same time, but at a slower pace and with less sophistication.

Washington, as the greatest fiat city of the period, might well have been, rather than Edinburgh, the Romantic Classical city *par excellence*. Even so, as it was laid out by a French engineer in the 1790s, the prototype of its plan was not the Baroque city but the French hunting park. And L'Enfant envisaged for it no walled-in streets and squares but rather the isolated block-like structures that once stood around his 'circles' as some still stand around Fischer's Karolinenplatz in Munich. In Washington, moreover, from 1803 when Jefferson made him Surveyor of Public Buildings until 1817, Latrobe generally had his headquarters; there his pupil Mills became Government Architect and Engineer in 1836, retaining the post until 1851.

The great monuments of the thirties still stand in Washington, mostly designed by Mills himself at the peak of his career. But at the Capitol [147], rising at the head of the main axis of the city, original elements of the edifice that was completed in 1827 by Bulfinch are now all but invisible between and below the wings and the dome added after 1851 by Thomas U. Walter (1804-87).[3a] Hoban's White

House, moreover, on the cross axis, remains, despite its restoration by Latrobe after the War of 1812 and two twentieth-century campaigns of enlargement and reconstruction, a quite Anglo-Palladian – indeed, almost Gibbsian – work. These focal edifices rather belie the Romantic Classical ideals eventually epitomized in the tallest of all nineteenth-century obelisks, Mills's Washington Monument. This was designed in 1833, begun in 1848, and not completed until 1884, when T. L. Casey, an Army engineer, sharpened the pitch of the pyramidon and crowned it with solid aluminium.

Immediately beside the White House, however, the Grecian granite of Mills's Treasury [70], worthy of Playfair if not of Schinkel, is overshadowed by the former State, War and Navy Department Building with its tremendous Second Empire plasticity [148]. Begun in 1836,

when Mills received his official appointment, the Treasury was largely completed by 1842; the west wing was added by Isaiah Rogers (1800–69) in 1862–5 after the original design.

Mills's career got under way decades before he was called to Washington (see Chapter 1). Churches in Philadelphia, Richmond, and Baltimore occupied him first, of which the most notable is the octagonal Monumental Church in Richmond begun in 1812. This is an austere structure with a strongly geometrical organization of the elements, but much less suave and refined than Latrobe's Baltimore Cathedral. Polygonal planning also gives original character to his Insane Asylum of 1821–5 in Columbia, S.C.; but this has, at the front, a giant Greek Doric portico such as was just becoming even more conventional in America than in Europe at this time.

70. Robert Mills:
Washington, Treasury Department, 1836–42

In an age so monumentally-minded it was a much earlier work, for which Mills won the competition in 1814, the monument erected in honour of Washington at Baltimore in 1815-29, that first made his national reputation. This was the first giant column to be erected in the New World. Superbly placed on a square podium of almost Egyptian severity at the centre of cruciform Mt Vernon Place, this Doric shaft is one of the most effective of the many that this period produced, even if it lacks the megalomaniac scale of his later obelisk in Washington. Mills claimed credit also for proposing the obelisk form for the Bunker Hill Monument[4] which Solomon Willard (1783-1861) erected in Charlestown, Mass., in 1825-43.

In Washington Mills's Government buildings include, besides the Treasury and the Monument, the Patent Office and the old Post Office Department, both begun in 1839. These are sober masonry edifices of wholly fireproof construction incorporating much vaulting. They are dominated by Grecian porticoes, like the Treasury, but without that more conspicuously sited structure's peristyles along the sides. Mills's smaller custom houses in various seaboard towns are simple and massive blocks of granite ashlar, the best preserved today being that in New London, Conn. These provided worthy symbols of Federal authority among the slighter edifices of wood and brick that filled the seaports of this period. Like Latrobe, Mills was as much engineer as architect, which helps to explain his preoccupation with fireproof construction; moreover, lighthouses and waterworks figured prominently in his total production.[5]

Mills, more than anyone else, set the high standard of design and construction for Federal buildings that was fortunately maintained by his successors until after the Civil War.[5a] These were Ammi B. Young (1800-74), who took over the Government post[6] in 1852, and Rogers, who followed him ten years later in 1862. In remote San Francisco the Grecian rule in Federal architecture continued very late, as the U.S. Mint there of 1869-74 rather surprisingly indicates. This was designed by Rogers's former assistant A. B. Mullet, who had succeeded him in office in 1865.

Related to the Romantic Classicism of Washington is certain Virginia work. Arlington House, as remodelled by the English-born and English-trained Hadfield, rises just across the Potomac River on a high hill-crest; by its tremendously overscaled Paestum-like temple portico, added in 1826 to give grandeur to a modest earlier mansion, this provides a more monumental note in the Washington scene than anything of this period inside the city except Mills's obelisk and his Treasury.

Just outside Charlottesville, Jefferson, after his retirement from the Presidency, devoted himself architecturally as well as educationally from 1817 until his death to the organization of the University of Virginia and the construction of its buildings. The layout, with pavilions for the various professors' use linked by porticoed galleries behind which the students' rooms are placed, culminated at the upper end in the Library and was originally open[7] to the view at the bottom [71]. Although most of the pavilions reflect earlier stages of Romantic Classicism – if not usually the Anglo-Palladian with which Jefferson's architectural career had begun half a century earlier – this is a more remarkable entity than his Virginia Capitol. Perhaps it has a lesser general historical importance, yet it is certainly not without special significance for America. This is most notably true of one of the pavilions whose design was suggested to Jefferson by Latrobe in 1819. Here for the first time a modern American dwelling, and one of quite modest size – for these pavilions were used as houses for the professors as well as providing classrooms on the ground storey – was encased within the shell of a prostyle Greek temple. Moreover, Jefferson accomplished this rather

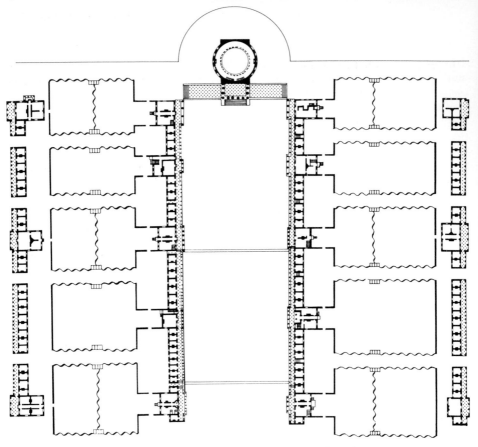

71 and 72. Thomas Jefferson: Charlottesville, Va, University of Virginia, 1817-26

more successfully than Beaumont in France in the late eighteenth century at the Temple de Silence, or Wilkins in England at Grange Park in 1809.

Not the least successful among the innumerable imitations of the Roman Pantheon, the building which originally served as the Library of the University, built in 1822-6, dominated the two ranges of colonnade-linked pavilions [72]. Here more drastically than by Wilkins at Downing College or Ramée at Union, the earlier Anglo-Saxon patterns of educational architecture were reconstituted in Romantic Classical guise, yet the University of Virginia did not have a very considerable influence, then or later. The central group at Amherst College in Massachusetts – two dormitories of 1821 and 1822 and a chapel between of 1827 – offers a modest group of quite different but equally notable quality on a splendid hill-crest site [73]. At other colleges, except Dartmouth, only individual structures usually survive from this period.

The temple house, initiated by Jefferson and Latrobe, had a tremendous success with builders

in the thirties and forties, particularly in the new territories west of the Alleghenies. But the finest and most exemplary came rather earlier and were architect-designed. Ithiel Town (1784–1844), for example, built the Bowers House in Northampton, Mass., in 1825-6 with an Ionic portico on the main block and fronted the lower side wings with antae. The big Corinthian Russell house, a pure temple with no side wings – the present wing was added later – rose in Middletown, Conn., to the design of his partner, A. J. Davis (1803-92), in 1828.

From such a 'Parthenon' as Berry Hill in Virginia, built by its owner James Coles Bruce in 1835-40, which is flanked by two lodges also of temple form, to innumerable more modest houses in the older towns of Ohio and Michigan, the roster of such edifices is infinitely extensive. It is also surprisingly varied in scale and in the materials used – most, but not all, are of white-painted wood – as also in the handling of the dominating columnar porticoes. In the South, for example, the characteristic plantation houses of Alabama, Georgia, Louisiana, and Mississippi are peripteral but unpedimented, with external

73. Amherst, Mass.,
Amherst College, Dormitories, 1821-2, Chapel, 1827

galleries splitting the height of the giant columns. Natchez in Mississippi has several fine examples; in Louisiana, Greenwood near St Francisville of about 1830 may be specifically mentioned, and also Oak Alley of 1836 at Vacherie near New Orleans.

The most ambitious Grecian houses of the Deep South are often very late in date, and architects were rarely employed to design them. Moreover, Greek detail was adopted in the South only very slowly and rarely used with the correctness of the Northern builders, who leaned so heavily on the plates of the orders in the books of Benjamin and others. Belle Meade, near Nashville, of 1853, being by the distinguished Philadelphia architect Strickland, is something of an exception in several ways; it had, for example, a fine portico of square antae executed in white marble that was almost Schinkelesque. Vast Belle Grove at White Castle, Louisiana, built by Henry Howard in 1857, was probably more effective in the romantically ruinous state in which it existed for many years before its final destruction than in its pristine condition so confusedly eclectic was the general composition, with Italianate as well as Classical elements quite casually mixed.

Unpedimented porticoes are not unknown in the North, both east and west of the Alleghenies, as in the Levi Lincoln house of 1836 (once in Worcester, Mass., now moved to nearby Sturbridge) by Elias Carter (1781-1864) with its convex-fluted Doric order. Such original touches, which many carpenters introduced out of plain ignorance and more sophisticated architects developed out of a conscious desire to nationalize and personalize even such absolute paradigms as those of the Greek orders, often lend variety and piquancy to the mode. The finest Grecian houses, such as Elmhyrst at One Mile Corner, Newport, R.I., built probably by Russell Warren (1783-1860) about 1833, certainly owed their originality to the studied intentions of architects. This house, in parti-

74. Russell Warren: Newport, R.I., Elmhyrst, c. 1833

cular, had a façade composed in overlapping planes that was not unworthy of Cockerell [74]. On the other hand, the Hermitage near Savannah, Georgia, designed by Charles B. Cluskey c. 1830, could almost be by Schinkel, so simple and pure is its design.

Trained architects, on the whole, were too rationalistic or too adventurous to follow closely the plain temple model in domestic or institutional work. Walter presumably surrounded Andalusia, the home of the philhellene banker Nicholas Biddle outside Philadelphia, with a Doric temple-shell in 1833 only against his own better judgement. In 1833-47 he also built for Girard College in Philadelphia, of which Biddle was the trustee who called the tune, an enormous Corinthian temple. Inside this he incorporated a variety of educational functions only with considerable difficulty, but he vaulted all the interiors in the manner of Latrobe and Mills in order to provide a completely fireproof structure.[8] Curiously enough, this was one of the first American buildings to be published abroad,[9] thus rivalling Haviland's prison, but it attracted no emulators in Europe. By the thirties, of course, these buildings by Walter were no novelties in Philadelphia.

Philadelphia, the former colonial metropolis and briefly the national capital, was much more than Washington the cultural centre of the country in the early decades of the century. Here Latrobe had had his start, significantly with a bank in the form of an Ionic temple. Now in 1818 Strickland,[10] a native-born American and quite untravelled, won in competition the commission for building the Branch Bank of the United States with a much more archaeologically correct temple. Like various European and British public monuments of the period, but unlike any bank abroad, this is a marble Parthenon. But the various needs of the banking business were skilfully provided for inside, and the principal barrel-vaulted interior is very fine indeed. Built in 1819-24, this bank (later a Custom House) rivals the Bavarian Walhalla and the Scottish National Monument, though lacking their splendid hill-top sites. It was just the thing to establish Strickland's national reputation. But his Merchants' Exchange in

75. William Strickland:
Philadelphia, Merchants' Exchange, 1832-4

Philadelphia of 1832-4, with a rounded end and a trabeated ground storey, provides more interesting and impressive evidence of his talent, perhaps the greatest in the generation following Latrobe in America [75].

Strickland's latest major work, the State Capitol in Nashville, Tennessee, of 1845-59, still a temple but with various accretions, has the high site his bank lacked, but it suffers otherwise from the general deterioration of the sense of Grecian style after the mid thirties, a deterioration quite as evident in American architecture as in European. This Tennessee temple was the last but one of a series of state capitols that followed the model of Jefferson's at Richmond, Virginia, rather than Bulfinch's dome-crowned Boston State House or the national Capitol in Washington. One of the finest examples that was correctly Greek in detail was that for Connecticut in New Haven; it was built by Town and his later partner Davis in 1827-31, and has long since been demolished. The one designed by Gideon Shryock (1802-80) in Frankfort, Kentucky, which survives was going up at about the same time.[10a]

In 1831-5 Davis built a larger and grander Greek Doric temple (no longer extant) as a Capitol for Indiana at Indianapolis, but provided it with a small central dome. The latest of all the temples built to serve as state capitols was a very modest one of 1849 at Benicia, California, where the columnar portico was reduced to two Doric columns *in antis* – it is worth noting that this was erected in the very year that Sutter's gold strike first put California on the map of the world.

Other state capitols of this period are Grecian but not of temple form; a good example is that Town & Davis built at Raleigh, North Carolina, which was begun in 1833. The finest of all is that for Ohio at Columbus,[11] begun in 1839-40 and carried to completion over the years 1848-61. Here the giant 'pilastrade', for which columns are substituted in the central third of the front, has a Schinkel-like directness and severity [76]. Not so happy is the flat-topped central lantern,

76. Thomas Cole and others:
Columbus, Ohio, State Capitol, 1839-61

which is also surrounded by a pilastrade. In conscientious pursuit of trabeated consistency the architects thus sought to mask the rounded shape of the dome within, as had been tried in various French projects of the late eighteenth century and by Schinkel in the Altes Museum already.

After Philadelphia, Boston was the architectural metropolis of this period; and from Boston, beginning in 1827, issued the later treatises of Benjamin purveying the Grecian orders to carpenters and builders all over the North and the Middle West. Here Bulfinch, however, established as the leading architect in the 1790s, long remained faithful to the ideals of Chambers and Adam (see Chapter 1).

At University Hall, built for Harvard College in Cambridge, Mass., in 1813–15, Bulfinch used granite for the ashlar of the walls as he had done for his Boston City Hall of 1810, but the white-painted wooden trim is not yet Grecian. The Massachusetts General Hospital in Boston, also of granite, was designed by him in 1816–17, just before he left for Washington to take over from Latrobe supervision of the construction of the Capitol. The hospital building (now known as the Bulfinch Pavilion) as executed by Alexander Parris (1780–1852) in 1818–20 is certainly a mature Romantic Classical edifice if not a typically Grecian one. Above the plain pediment of the central portico a square attic with corner chimneys supports the saucer dome, and the long side wings with three ranges of unframed windows display the fine granite ashlar of Boston in all its cold pride. Compared to Latrobe, however, Bulfinch remained a provincial if not a colonial designer, high as is the intrinsic quality of his best work.

A younger generation, hitherto much influenced by Bulfinch's established manner, took over leadership in Boston on his departure for Washington. Parris soon provided the first Greek temple in conservative New England when he built St Paul's Church (now the Epi-scopal Cathedral) in Tremont Street in 1819–21. Where Strickland's contemporary Philadelphia bank was Doric and of marble, this is Ionic with the portico executed in the Acquia Creek sandstone from Virginia which was then being much used in Washington. Solomon Willard carved the capitals. Parris's Stone Temple of 1828, the Unitarian 'Church of the Presidents' – the two Adams presidents – in Quincy, Mass., is not at all a temple in form but more comparable to the Grecian churches built in England in this decade. The Stone Temple outranks most of them in dignity, however, because of the superbly appropriate local material of which it is built. It was from this town that the Quincy granite came that was employed for the best Boston buildings of the next thirty years and more, and this church was a relatively early instance of its monumental use. Quincy granite had become more readily available after the first American railway was built from the quarries to the sea-shore by Willard solely to facilitate bringing it out by water.[12]

The first notable use of this granite away from Quincy had been for the Bunker Hill Monument in Charlestown, Mass., built by Willard in 1825–43. Not only Mills, as has been mentioned, but the sculptor Horatio Greenough[13] and also Parris claimed, and perhaps deserve, some credit for the particular form of this simple but grandiose obelisk, which rivalled those of the Old World a decade before Mills's in Washington was designed. On its completion, a steam-operated lift or elevator was provided in 1844 capable of carrying six people; this was one of the earliest examples of an important technical device that would later influence architecture profoundly (see Chapter 14).

Granite imposed rigid restrictions on detailing. But the new generation knew how to make of those restrictions an opportunity for developing a highly original sort of basic classicism such as even the most determined European

77. Alexander Parris:
Boston, David Sears house, 1816

rationalists rarely approached. The houses at 39-40 Beacon Street in Boston, later occupied by the Women's City Club, and the David Sears house at No. 42, the Somerset Club [77] – the latter by Parris and of 1816, the former probably by him and of 1818 – as also the granite terrace at Nos 70-75, possibly by Benjamin, are good examples of domestic work of this period. More important is Parris's Quincy (properly Faneuil Hall) Market in Boston, designed in 1823 for Mayor Josiah Quincy as the central feature of a considerable urbanistic development on the site of earlier docks. This domed and porticoed structure lacks the geometrical severity of the Sears house with its great bow on the front and its superbly placed scroll panel; but in the Market House Parris not only used cast iron for the internal supports but also experimented on the exterior with a trabeated framework of monolithic granite piers and lintels. The same sort of 'granite skeleton' construction (so to call it) was also used but with

78. James C. Bucklin: Providence, R.I., Washington Buildings, 1843

greater delicacy of proportion and elegance of finish – note the Soanic incised detail of the wooden window-frames – for the commercial buildings[14] which Parris designed and that various lessees shortly built along the streets that flank the Market House to the north and the south [197]. This was one of the major structural innovations of the period (see Chapter 14). The whole is now being restored.

Within a few years other Boston architects and builders were currently using this sort of construction, and it soon spread to several New England cities. However, more typical of the urban ambition of the twenties and thirties than the destroyed block of 1824 in Providence by J. H. Green (1777–1850), which followed line for line Parris's commercial work, are two other buildings there. The Providence Arcade of 1828 by Warren has not one, but two terminal porticoes of Ionic columns executed in granite and also a fine interior consisting of raised side galleries under an iron-and-glass roof. Few

extant galleries of this decade in Europe are as notable in scale and in finish. The Washington Buildings of 1843 by James C. Bucklin (1801–90), who was the contractor for the Arcade, had a plain range of three storeys of window-pierced red-brick wall above a trabeated granite ground storey, the whole dominated by a central pedimented feature [78]. This was a commercial project as grand as any in contemporary Europe in scale, in materials, and in finish, although without the originality of the trabeated all-granite bow-front of Rogers's contemporary Brazier's Buildings on State Street in Boston. Yet Bucklin's Westminster Presbyterian Church in Providence of 1846 is a straight Greek Ionic temple like so many other non-Anglican edifices of this period in England and America.

Where Romantic Classicism, and more specifically the Greek Revival, found its noblest opportunities in Europe in public monuments, in America after the days of Latrobe it was rather commercial, institutional, and even

79. William Clarke: Utica, N.Y., Insane Asylum, 1837–43

industrial[15] commissions that stimulated architects and builders to original achievement, while
public work grew more and more conventional.
For instance, the Lippitt Woollen Mill of 1836
in Woonsocket, R.I., and the Governor Harris
Manufactory at Harris, R.I., dating from as late
as 1851 can both be properly described as 'in the
Grecian vernacular'. They are most admirably
proportioned and very soundly built, with walls
of random ashlar masonry and boldly scaled
wooden trim, very plain, yet of generically
Greek character. The discipline of Romantic
Classicism accorded well with the requirements
of industrial building[15a] – not till the present
century would factories of comparable architectural quality be built – and they were often complemented by good low-cost housing, as in the
extant mill village at White Rock, R. I., of 1849.

No European public edifice has a grander
Greek Doric portico than that which dominates
the tremendous four-storey front block of the
Lunatic Asylum in Utica, N.Y., of 1837-43,
designed by no architect, according to the
records, but by the Chairman of the Board of
Trustees, William Clarke [79]. Still later, in
1850, after the Grecian mode was *passé* with
most architects if not with the general public,
Davis built in the Renaissance Revival mode
that he called 'Tuscan' the Insane Asylum at
Raleigh, North Carolina; this is distinguished
by his characteristic arrangement of the windows
in tall vertical bands. Such American institutions are not at all unworthy of comparison with
the best French productions of the period by
Gilbert and others, although generally of rather
smaller size [43].

Hotels in Europe had not as yet received
much architectural elaboration, nor did they in
general before the mid century. Such English
hotels of Grecian pretension as the Queen's by
W. C. and R. Jearrad at Cheltenham, which
opened in 1837, or the Great Western in Bristol
by R. S. Pope (1781-?), opened two years later,
are rather exceptional, being located at spas, and

in any case a decade later in date than the first
notable American example. It was in Boston, at
the Tremont House built in 1828-9, a Grecian
granite structure of dignified grandeur externally [80] and of considerable functional
elaboration internally [81], that Rogers and his
clients consciously initiated a new standard of
hotel design. For thirty years Rogers himself, in
various hotels from New Orleans – the St
Charles – to Cincinnati – the Burnet House – all
long ago demolished, personally maintained
and, at least in terms of functional organization,
continued to raise that standard. Not for nothing
did the big new London hotels of a generation
later label their bars and their barber-shops
'American'.

In 1832 Rogers began the Astor House in
New York; when completed in 1836 this
already outranked the Tremont House in every
way. Not least extraordinary must have been
the elaborately fan-vaulted hall. This reflected
that eclectic interest in Gothic of which Rogers's
wooden Unitarian Church of 1833 in Cambridge, Mass., provides extant evidence. The
last hotel that he built was the Maxwell House
in Nashville, Tennessee, of 1854-60.

Rogers's pre-eminence at hotel design was
signalized from the first by the publication in
1830 of a monograph on the Tremont House;[16]
thus the hotel joined the prison as a type of
building in which American influence became
important internationally. But Rogers's practice
was by no means confined to hotels; among other
things he gave both Boston and New York their
Merchants Exchanges long before he became
Supervising Architect in Washington. The
colonnade of the latter, a little like that of
Schinkel's Altes Museum, still survives at the
base of McKim, Mead & White's First
National City Bank in Wall Street to illustrate
Rogers's high competence at handling a standard Romantic Classical theme.

Resort hotels repeated the same Grecian
themes in wood, their columns being often

80 and 81. Isaiah Rogers: Boston, Tremont House, 1828–9

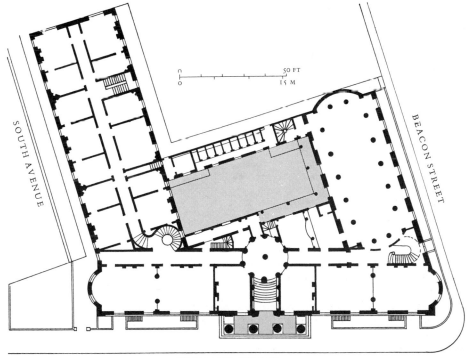

SOUTH AVENUE

BEACON STREET

50 FT

0   15 M

TREMONT STREET

82. A. J. Davis: New York, Colonnade Row, 1836

much attenuated in order to rise three and four storeys above the circumambient verandas. However, an early example, the first Ocean House of 1841 at Newport, R.I., had a colonnade only two storeys tall set against the main four-storey block. On the Atlantic House there of 1844 the fourth storey occupied the broad Greek entablature surrounding the entire main block, but the front portico of elongated Ionic columns was only hexastyle. Both of these hotels were burnt down many years ago, but quite a number of later examples of inferior quality remain in several forgotten spas and mountain resorts of the period, particularly in New York State.

New York City was drawing architectural talent in these years from other cities. Before Rogers moved there from Boston in 1834, mid way in the Astor House campaign, Town & Davis had arrived from Connecticut. Davis's Sub-Treasury in Wall Street begun in 1834,[17] however, is rather less successful than the earlier New England houses of similar temple form that he and Town had designed. Davis was himself more notably a protagonist of the Picturesque, despite all the very large and prominent Grecian buildings for which he was responsible (see Chapter 6). Yet his Colonnade Row in Lafayette Street of 1836, a terrace all of freestone with a free-standing giant Corinthian colonnade, equals in grandeur anything of the period that London or Edinburgh have to offer [82]. More typical of New York in this period than Colonnade Row, and of uncertain authorship, is the terrace of red-brick Grecian houses built on the north side of Washington Square in the thirties, of which a few happily survive and serve various aspects of New York University.

Some of the finest Greek houses are by provincial architects. One such is stone-built Hyde Hall in Cooperstown, N.Y., very crisp and severe as it was remodelled in 1833 by Philip Hooker (1766-1836) of Albany, who had built it originally in 1811. Still others are of uncertain authorship, notably the Alsop house of 1838 in Middletown, Conn. This is a symmetrical Grecian villa almost worthy of Schinkel's Potsdam, with very fine murals on the exterior as well as inside. The Alsop house (now the Davison Art Centre of Wesleyan University) was probably designed by a relative of the family who had access to the resources of the Town & Davis office; however, the painters employed were Italian or German. The Wooster-Boalt house of 1848 in Norwalk, Ohio, indicates the late continuance of real restraint and sophistica-

tion of design in the Middle West, something already lost in the sumptuous mansions of New Orleans and the Deep South. But many Middle Western houses illustrate rather the surprising elasticity of Carpenters' Grecian.

A mode that approaches the German *Rundbogenstil* – indeed, in the work of such foreign-trained architects as the Prague-born Leopold Eidlitz (1823-1908) relatively authentic examples of that mode – was not uncommon in the America of the mid century.[18] The Astor Library in Lafayette Street opposite Colonnade Row, built by A. Saelzer in 1849, is a good example. Less successful was Appleton Chapel at Harvard College in Cambridge, Mass., by Paul Schulze (1827-97), one of several young architects from Germany who had settled in America. Begun in 1856, this was a very reduced version of Gärtner's Ludwigskirche in Munich with only one tower. However, the largest and finest example was by a precocious student at Brown University, Thomas A. Tefft (1826-59).[19] This was the Union Station in Providence, begun in 1848 and gradually carried out by Bucklin and his partner Talman [83]. This station rivalled in extent and in the distinction and ingenuity of its rather Lombardic Romanesque detailing,

83. Thomas A. Tefft: Providence, R.I., Union Station, begun 1848

simply executed with ordinary red brick, the German ones by Eisenlohr and Bürklein in Baden and Bavaria; without much question it was the finest early station in the New World. Tefft also designed various New England churches of somewhat similar character, all dominated by very tall and simple spires. However, his churches in the East are outrivalled by such a Middle Western example as the Union Methodist in St Louis, built by George I. Barnett (1815-98) in 1852-4. Tefft's best works, other than the station, are not *Rundbogenstil* but Barryesque; such is the brownstone Tully-Bowen house on Benefit Street in Providence of 1852-3, for example. Others were building as fine ones there, however. The consistent use of brownstone and red brick well illustrates the sharp reaction that had set in by this time against the pale tones and untextured surfaces of the Greek Revival.

The towered Italian Villa[20] was introduced by John Notman (1810-65) in Bishop George

84. John Notman:
Philadephia, Atheneum, 1845-7

W. Doane's house at Burlington, N.J., in 1837 and soon actively propagandized by A. J. Downing (1815-52) in his influential books (see Chapters 6 and 15). Indeed, the Barryesque Renaissance mode was also probably first introduced by the Scottish-born Notman at the Philadelphia Atheneum[21] built in 1845-7 [84]. These non-Grecian, yet still basically Romantic Classical, modes were in relatively common use by 1850, though not very much earlier. Young, for example, who had made his reputation with the saucer-domed but otherwise Greek Custom House[22] that he built in Boston in 1837-47, substituted a somewhat Barryesque manner for Mills's Grecian as the current mode for Federal buildings[23] when he became Supervising Architect in 1853. But neither Notman nor Young was a Barry - nor even as competent at such design as the youthful Tefft - and the most notable result of the waning of the Greek Revival in the forties, in the East at any rate - it waned much more slowly in the South and West - was the rise of a rather considerable variety of Picturesque modes of suburban-house design, of which the Italianate was only one (see Chapters 6 and 15). In cities, the shift from the characteristic granite or, more usually, hard red brick with white trim to the chocolate tones of brownstone, used alone or with brick, is much more indicative of a general change of taste than any widespread exploitation of Renaissance forms.

A fine relatively early Italian Villa such as the Stebbins house of 1849 on Crescent Street, off Maple Street, in Springfield, Mass., by Henry A. Sykes belongs to the realm of Romantic Classicism like Schinkel's or Barry's country houses in this mode [85]. But on the whole the Italian Villa in America is rather one of the many vehicles of the Picturesque reaction against a doctrinaire Greek Revival. This fact was well illustrated in one by Eidlitz, also in Springfield, on Maple Street, that was built of brick with much wooden 'gingerbread' of a vaguely Tyrolean order and latterly, at least,

85. Henry A. Sykes:
Springfield, Mass., Stebbins house, 1849

painted a warm pink where Sykes's villa is painted white with brown trim. Sykes's originality within the Italian Villa mode is most happily illustrated by the former observatory at Amherst College, now known as the Octagon, whose stuccoed polygonal elements stand in such interesting contrast to the severe row of red-brick dormitories and chapel behind. Not often did the 1840s add so effectively to groups of buildings produced in earlier decades, and even Sykes's stone-built library at Amherst is less original.

Just as the Iberian peninsula was in general devoid of significant architectural activity in the first half of the nineteenth century, so in the Spanish and Portuguese lands beyond the seas there came no early wave of autochthonous Romantic Classicism to submerge and succeed the Baroque that had flourished there to the end

of the colonial period and beyond. In Brazil Dom Pedro, later the first Brazilian Emperor, under whose rule the centre of gravity of Portuguese civilization moved from Lisbon to Rio de Janeiro, imported in 1816 a group of French artists. They were expected to found a new post-Baroque Brazilian culture much as Alexander I's architects had done a little earlier in Russia. One was the French architect Grandjean de Montigny, author with Famin of that most influential work *L'Architecture toscane* to which all Europe turned for *quattrocento* models, who had been employed by Jerome Bonaparte in Westphalia as long as Napoleon's Empire lasted. He erected in Rio in 1826 the first home for the new Imperial Academy of Fine Arts, founded of course on the model of the Parisian École des Beaux-Arts, the Market, and the extant Custom House. He also trained a group of Brazilians who gave local architectural production an Empire flavour that lasted until it was superseded well after the mid century by a wave of Second Empire influence.

In vernacular building traditional treatments were often maintained in Brazil, notably the use of *azulejos* (glazed tiles) for wall surfaces and of rich painted colour for the ubiquitous stucco. But more sophisticated work can be very French indeed. For example, the Itamaratí Palace in

86. J. M. J. Rebelo:
Rio de Janeiro, Palacio Itamaratí, 1851–4

Rio of 1851–4 by J. M. J. Rebelo, a pupil of Grandjean de Montigny, might well be taken for a *hôtel particulier* erected in the new quarters of Paris in the earlier decades of the century [86]. Beautifully restored, this now houses the Brazilian Foreign Office – one says 'Itamaratí' as one says 'Quai d'Orsay'. Rebelo also built the Summer Palace at Petrópolis. The Santa Isabel Theatre at Recife, Pernambuco, built about 1845, which is so like a French provincial theatre of this period, is by another French architect who had settled in Brazil in 1840, L.-L. Vauthier.

In Chile, on the other side of the South American continent, C.-F. Brunet-Debaines (1799–1855), a brother of the architect who built the Museum and Library at Le Havre, was employed on government work in Santiago. But the schools that such French architects assisted in founding had more significance than the few buildings they were able to erect. Henceforth, Latin America would be less dependent in architecture on the Spanish and Portuguese homelands than on Paris. The character of the larger cities outside their colonial cores – if, indeed, more than a few early monuments remain extant – was henceforth determined by this fact. However, it is the Second Empire and not the First which left the more visible mark; for the various capitals, some like Montevideo in Uruguay almost without earlier architectural history, saw their greatest expansion in the later decades of the nineteenth century and the first of the twentieth.

The establishment of a Latin American architecture of really autochthonous character, as distinguished from the continuance of various local vernacular building traditions, had to await the mid twentieth century (see Chapters 22 and 25). Again French influence had a significant role to play. But between the arrival of Grandjean de Montigny in 1816 and Le Corbusier's first visit to South America in 1929 that continent took little part in the major architectural developments of the nineteenth and twentieth centuries. On the other hand, the United States, building on the professional foundations laid by Latrobe and exploiting to the full new structural materials and methods, rose before the nineteenth century was over to a position of world leadership (see Chapters 13, 14, and 15).

What is true of Latin America is not altogether untrue of the British Dominions in the New World and at the Antipodes, as also of various British Colonies throughout the rest of the world. No French architects were imported, of course, and the links with England remained very close and strong. As in all colonial situations, however, the transfer of new ideas from the homeland was slow and inefficient and the capacity of *émigré* architects usually rather low. No Latrobes or Havilands seem to have gone to the Dominions; and the Greek Revival was hardly accepted before the forties, when it was already passing out of favour in the States.

The first professional to work in Australia, Francis Greenway (1777–1837), who arrived in Sydney in 1814 as a convict and almost at once became Governor Macquarie's architect, remained faithful in most of his public work to the modes of his eighteenth-century youth in Bristol. But his house of 1822 for Robert Campbell, Jr, in Bligh Street in Sydney showed that he had real skill as a designer of up-to-date Regency villas. Canada had no early architect of comparable ability to serve the British community.

As the western world expanded in the nineteenth century, significant architectural achievement tended to move outwards from the old centres on the Tiber, the Seine, and the Thames; but that movement was always very uneven, and still remains so today. Russia was building more and finer structures of Western European character than Spain and Portugal; while the United States, not yet fantastically disparate in size and population, produced many more productive Romantic Classical architects than either Holland or Sweden. All the same, the architectural leadership of the western world remained for at least a generation longer in the old centres of Europe; our story must return to where it started in order to proceed beyond the mid century or even to complete the account of the period 1810–50.

Romantic Classicism came to no sudden end. If in Vienna a monumental Grecian Parliament house could rise as late as the seventies, so in the desert of Arizona the Crystal Palace Saloon of 1878 at Tombstone is still in the Greek Revival

vernacular. From the very first, on the other hand, there was some admixture of the Picturesque in Romantic Classicism. Almost all the architects that have been mentioned, both of the earlier and of the later generation, were more eclectic in their practice and even in their theories than this account of their major works has made altogether evident. But in the main, down into the forties, Romantic Classicism, while increasingly eclectic, remained a coherent style whose canons controlled most of the accepted variants to the Grecian.

The dissolution of the dominant stylistic discipline, hardly completed even in the fifties, had nevertheless begun very early indeed. In terms of historical significance, if not of absolute achievement, the Picturesque rises rapidly in comparative importance from the time of Wyatt's Fonthill Abbey in the 1790s. Beside Soane's crisp Bank interiors it is necessary to carry in the mind's eye the prophetic image which his renderer J. M. Gandy (1771–1843) provided of them as a Romantic ruin; nor should the vast dream-like Gothic cathedrals that Schinkel made the centre of one of his finest paintings be forgotten in the cool presence of his Grecian Schauspielhaus and Museum. Fortunately no one is likely in looking at Barry's *palazzi* to forget that they are contemporary with his Gothic Houses of Parliament; one does, however, tend to forget that the career of his associate Pugin as protagonist of the mature Gothic Revival ended well before Barry's did as the chief English protagonist of the Renaissance Revival. Earlier the Gothic Revival was hardly more than a special aspect of the Picturesque; with Pugin, however, it became a major movement in its own right and actually anti-Picturesque in theory, if rarely so in practice. To a considerable extent, moreover, the Gothic Revival usurped during the forties the centre of the stage in England, if hardly to the same degree in other countries even in the following decades.[23a]

CHAPTER 6

THE PICTURESQUE AND THE GOTHIC REVIVAL

The principal modern treatise on the Picturesque with a capital P, Christopher Hussey's of 1927, is subtitled 'Studies in a Point of View'. By the opening years of the nineteenth century the term had come to have a far more precise, if also a more complex, meaning than the adjective 'picturesque' as it is generally used today. But Hussey is perfectly correct: The Picturesque is no more a style than is the Sublime, it *is* a point of view. That point of view nevertheless influenced architecture[1] increasingly as the first half of the nineteenth century wore on. It had a solvent, and eventually a destructive, effect on the dominant Romantic Classical style as has already been suggested in discussing the later work of various leading architects in several countries.

The Picturesque had its early eighteenth-century origins[2] in England, and its most notable theorists were English. In the first quarter of the century, moreover, there was no British architect so resolutely Grecian that he did not, either on his own initiative or in deference to his clients' wishes, experiment with alternative modes in conscious pursuit of the Picturesque. Despite the stringencies of the Greek Revival as represented, early, in Wilkins's Downing College or, later, in Smirke's British Museum, Smirke had built several Castellated mansions in the years before Waterloo and Wilkins the Gothic screen and the hall range at King's College, Cambridge, in the twenties; while at the National Gallery in the thirties he handled standard Classical elements in a markedly Picturesque way. Nash was the initiator of one characteristically Picturesque mode, the asymmetrically towered Italian Villa, at Cronkhill in 1802; he also exploited in

87. John Nash: Blaise Hamlet, near Bristol, 1811

an exemplary way another longer-established one, the Rustic Cottage, in Blaise Hamlet in 1811 [87]. The score or more of Castellated mansions that Nash built were always Picturesque and irregular whether their detailing was Norman[3] or some sort of Gothic. Above all, he handled the urbanistic development which was his greatest achievement in a thoroughly Picturesque way. Soane's Picturesque was of a less usual order and his personal tendency was as much or more towards the Sublime, otherwise a largely forgotten category after 1810.

But from 1810 on new buildings in which the basic principles of Romantic Classicism were ignored and exotic stylistic alternatives to the Grecian exploited were generally larger, more prominent, and also more creatively original than they had ever been before. C. A. Busby (1788–1838) was responsible as late as 1827 for one of the finest, most formal, and most extensive examples of Romantic Classical urbanism, Kemp Town at Brighton. Yet in 1814 he exhibited at the Royal Academy his design for Gwrych Castle, completed in 1815, which he was building in North Wales near Abergele, presumably in collaboration with his client, Lloyd Bamford Hesketh, a notable amateur [89].

The next year Nash began for the Regent the transformation of his favourite residence, the Royal Pavilion[4] at Brighton. This was at that time an elegant early example of a Romantic Classical house as first remodelled and enlarged by Henry Holland[5] (1745–1806) just before the Napoleonic Wars began. Nash now made of it an extraordinary oriental confection (as had already been proposed by Repton[6] in 1806). Part Chinese, part Saracenic, and part

Indian, this is quite in the spirit of Porden's earlier Dome near by [88]. Festive and frivolous, the Pavilion resembles an oversized garden fabrick or sumptuously ornamented marquee; but the scale is fully architectural, even monumental, both externally and in the principal apartments. Not least interesting is Nash's frank use of visible iron elements. These are not masonry-scaled like the columns he employed later in the Regent Street Quadrant and on Carlton House Terrace, but delicate and playfully decorative. The pierced 'Chinese' staircases of 1815–18 have naturalistically coloured bamboo detailing and the tops of the four columns that carry the monitor over

88. John Nash:
Brighton, Royal Pavilion, as remodelled 1815–23

the kitchen of 1818–21 are embellished with copper palm-leaves [103].

The Pavilion had no real sequel; even the Regent, King as George IV from 1820, tired of it almost as soon as it was finished. Indeed, he forsook Brighton for good in 1823 just as the general building activity there,[7] commonly but incorrectly called 'Regency', was getting under way. Turning his attention to Windsor Castle, the King employed Sir Jeffrey Wyatville (1776–1840) to remodel the accumulated mass of heterogeneous construction there into a Picturesque mansion of the Castellated sort in which the real medieval elements were quite submerged. But Windsor, being much more obviously a remodelling than was the Pavilion when Nash completed it, is not a very exemplary specimen of a fake castle. Busby's Gwrych, set against a hanging wood, its round and square towers simply detailed and tightly though asymmetrically composed, is a better instance of that abstract sculptural massing which critics of the mid century would sometimes define as 'architecturesque' [89]. For this sort of three-dimensional composition the Italian Villa mode provided on the whole a better vehicle. Wyatville, for example, did his best to turn the vast regular mass of late seventeenth-century Chatsworth[8] into a more Picturesque adjunct to its landscape setting by Capability

89. C. A. Busby:
Gwrych Castle, near Abergele, completed 1815

Brown (1715-83), by adding a long service wing on the north side and terminating that with a very large and tall loggia-topped tower.

Well before George IV undertook the remodelling of Windsor, a relatively modest mansion linked the Castellated mode more closely to the rising enthusiasm for the Middle Ages. The author of the immensely popular Waverley novels, Sir Walter Scott, employed Blore in 1816 to build Abbotsford near Melrose in Roxburghshire in this vein – it was much extended along the same lines by William Atkinson (c. 1773-1839) in 1822-3. With its definitely Scottish features Abbotsford initiated a special mode, the Scottish Baronial, that eventually received Royal sanction when Queen Victoria acquired Balmoral Castle near Ballater in 1848, a modest residence built in the late thirties by John Smith of Aberdeen. At the time she and Prince Albert first occupied this Scottish retreat Balmoral was quite small, but it was reconstructed in 1853-5 on a vastly larger scale in the same Scottish Baronial mode by William Smith, son of the original architect, working in close collaboration with Prince Albert. Thus the Queen's two private residences, Osborne and Balmoral, both in part at least designed by the Consort, illustrated – in neither case very happily – the two major types of determinedly Picturesque design for edifices of some consequence, the Italian Villa and the Castellated; the viability of the Rustic Cottage mode was necessarily rather limited and hardly suitable for Royal use.

Castellated design was not restricted to the field of country-house building. At Conway, in Wales, the engineer Thomas Telford (1757-1834) in his suspension bridge of 1819-24 and, after him, Robert Stephenson and his associated architect Francis Thompson in the tubular bridge[9] there of 1845-9 castellated the piers out of deference to the nearby thirteenth-century Castle. Another example of Engineers' Castellated is the first Temple Meads Railway Station at Bristol, built in 1839-40 by I. K. Brunel (1806-59). Brunel, however, had preferred Egyptian forms for the piers of the Clifton Suspension Bridge[10] near Bristol that he designed in 1829 [105A].

Somewhat more appropriately, prisons were likely to be Castellated in the forties and fifties, thus echoing the design as well as the planning of Haviland's Eastern Penitentiary in Philadelphia. The Reading Gaol of 1842-4 by Sir George Gilbert Scott (1811-78) and his partner W. B. Moffatt (1812-87) and the Holloway Gaol in London of 1851-2 by J. B. Bunning (1802-63) are the most striking examples. Both are essentially Picturesque essays; but by the time the latter was built the accepted standards of fake-castle building had entirely changed. The reconstruction of Alton Castle in Cheshire about 1840, by A. W. N. Pugin (1812-52) was archaeological in intention; even more archaeological is Peckforton Castle in Shropshire, newly erected by Anthony Salvin (1799-1881) in 1846-50, and his extensive 'restoration' of Alnwick Castle in Northumberland carried out in the next decade. Thanks to its magnificent hill-top site and its present state of disrepair, Peckforton is in fact notably Picturesque; but the fine, hard, structurally expressive detailing of the beautiful pink sandstone may almost be considered anti-Picturesque – contemporaries praised it for its 'realism'.

The welter of alternative Picturesque modes is most entertainingly epitomized in the model village of Edensor,[11] built by Joseph Paxton in 1839-42 at Chatsworth. He was probably assisted by John Robertson, a draughtsman for that encyclopaedist of the Picturesque, J. C. Loudon.[12] One particular mode, however, had begun to take the lead before this 'point of view' came closest to dominance in the early decades of the new century. The use of Gothic[13] for new churches was common enough from the mid eighteenth century. Down to about 1820, however, this was usually without any real archaeological pretension. The mood of the protagonists of what was then called 'Gothick', whether architects or clients, was not very serious. Architects lacked accurate illustrations of old work such as the volumes of Stuart and Revett and other similar treatises were providing for the Grecian. In the first two decades of the new century the more thorough and general study of ancient Gothic monuments in England and the handsome publications of John Britton (1771–1857)[14] and of Nash's Gothic specialist, the elder Pugin,[15] were gradually changing the situation. Thomas Rickman (1776–1841), a pharmacist turned medievalist, began to put his knowledge[16] of old churches to practical use; his St George's, Birmingham, built 1819–21, is a not unsuccessful essay in revived Perpendicular. Several others had built or were building by this time churches whose relationship to monuments of the medieval past was about as close as that of most of the contemporary Grecian work to its ancient models. St Mary's, Bathwick, in Bath of 1814–20 is at once very early and exceptionally well-scaled. The local architect John Pinch (1770–1827) even vaulted it throughout in Bath stone.

The ultimate purging away of the frivolity of Georgian Gothick detail and the effective substitution of archaeological for Picturesque ideals in over-all composition was by no means always a gain. In two later Birmingham churches, St Peter's, Dale End, of 1825–7, and Bishop Ryder's of 1837–8, Rickman did not improve on St George's; while St Luke's, Chelsea, built in London by James Savage (1779–1852) in 1819–25, despite its great size and its stone vaulting, is as cold and dry as the Grecian churches of the day and quite inferior to Pinch's.

Edward Garbett's Holy Trinity, Theale, of 1820–5 – with tower added after the architect's death by John Buckler (1770–1851) in 1827–8 – is rather more interesting and also pre-

monitory of what was coming. Here the detail, imitated from Salisbury Cathedral, is thirteenth-century in character, not fifteenth-sixteenth-century, as in the churches of Pinch, Rickman, and Savage. Moreover, Theale is more boldly scaled and more plastically handled altogether than are theirs. The placing of the tower, far to the rear on the south side, while more Picturesque in its asymmetry than the standard position at the centre of the west front, is also an archaeological echo of the free-standing tower which still existed then beside Salisbury Cathedral.

Most Gothic churches built in the twenties and thirties under the Act of 1818 – Commissioners' Churches as they are called – were neither very satisfyingly Picturesque nor at all archaeological. The usual reason for preferring Gothic to Grecian, indeed, was to save money by avoiding the need for expensive stone porticoes! Barry's Commissioners' Churches around Manchester and in north-eastern London are among the better examples; but only his St Peter's, Brighton, of 1824–6 (not financed by the parsimonious Commissioners) is at all elaborate. Among the most successful contemporary examples are several by one of Soane's pupils, R. D. Chantrell, at Leeds. His Christ Church there of 1823–6 has considerable spatial grandeur in its tall nave and aisles, while the Perpendicular detailing is rich and even fairly plausible.

Generally preferable to the ecclesiastical Gothic of this decade is the collegiate work; of this more exists both at Oxford and at Cambridge than is generally realized. At King's College, Cambridge, Wilkins's Gothic screen fronting the quadrangle and the hall range at right angles to it are not altogether unworthy of the magnificent Perpendicular chapel and Gibbs's Fellows Building that form the other two sides. Wilkins won the competition for this work in 1823, and it was all completed by 1827. Still more appealing, because an effectively

90. Thomas Rickman and Henry Hutchinson: Cambridge, St John's College, New Court, 1825–31

independent entity, is Rickman's New Court at St John's College, also at Cambridge,[17] built by him with the aid of his pupil Henry Hutchinson (1800–31) in 1825–31 [90]. This is not very plausibly Gothic perhaps, but the papery planes of the light-coloured ashlar walls of the U-shaped quadrangle, now richly hung with creeper, form despite their total symmetry an eligibly Picturesque composition above and behind the open gallery across the south side.

By the thirties standards of Gothic design were generally rising, both in the greater degree of plausibility attained by the leading practitioners and in their more positive command of various borrowed idioms. Thus Barry's King Edward's Grammar School in Birmingham, designed in 1833 and built 1834–7, seems to have been a rather satisfactory Neo-Tudor design, notably Barryesque in the breadth of the composition and in the use of strong terminal features. This building was unusually literate in detail owing to the assistance of the younger Pugin, who was just about to make a tremendous personal reputation as a Gothic expert thanks to his books.[18]

Pugin's *Contrasts*, published in 1836, marks a turning point even more than does the acceptance in that year of Barry's Gothic design for the Houses of Parliament. Newly converted to Catholicism, Pugin believed the building of Gothic churches to be a religious necessity. His programme of Gothic Revival was far more stringent than any existing programme of Greek Revival or, *a fortiori*, of Renaissance Revival. If the Gothic were really to be revived, Pugin saw that its basic principles must be understood and accepted. Merely to copy Gothic forms was as futile, and to him as immoral, as merely to copy Grecian or *cinquecento* ones. The methods of building of the Middle Ages must be revived; architecture must again derive its character, in what he considered to have been the true medieval way, from the direct expression of structure; and at the same time it must serve the complicated ritual-functional needs of revived medieval church practices.

Some of Pugin's ideas are parallel to those of the most rationalistic eighteenth-century theorists on the Continent; they can perhaps be traced back, through his father, to French or even Italian sources (see Introduction).[18a] But Pugin's primary motivation was devotional and sacramental. Approaching all matters of building with passion, he could not but reject the frivolous emphasis on visual qualities that had always been characteristic of the Picturesque point of view.

The mature Gothic Revival that began with Pugin, essentially an English manifestation despite its presumptive French background and carried eventually wherever English culture extended – as far as the West Coast of the United States and to the remotest Antipodes – grew out of the Picturesque yet is itself basically anti-Picturesque. One must build in a certain way because it is right to do so, not because the results are agreeable to the eye. The Gothic Revival thus came to be, for about a decade, as absolute as the most doctrinaire sort of Grecian Classicism. When the Anglicans of the Established Church just after 1840 took over and began to apply rigidly the principles of the Catholic Pugin, a new church-architecture came into being. This is quite as characteristic of the nineteenth century as is Romantic Classicism, even though the mode was – nominally at least – entirely dependent on English medieval Gothic of the fourteenth century. Within a decade, however, Puginian Gothic, after being accepted and codified by the Cambridge Camden Society,[19] developed into a much more original mode, the High Victorian Gothic, very remote indeed from the models which Pugin had recommended as providing the only proper precedents for the Revival (see Chapter 10).

Here it will be well to consider two exceptional Gothic monuments, designed in the late thirties and built in the forties, one of them very large, the other rather small, which did *not* follow the new Puginian standards, even though in the case of one of them Pugin collaborated on the design from the first. The most Picturesque addition to the Romantic Classical scene in Edinburgh, curiously effective for its contrast to the heavy and severe Grecian structures near by, is the Sir Walter Scott Monument in Prince's Street Gardens [91]. This was designed in 1836 and executed in 1840-6 by G. Meikle Kemp[20] (1795-1844). His project had originally been placed below both Fowler's and Rickman's in a competition; as the local contender, however, he had eventually obtained the commission in 1838. The lacy elaboration of this florid shrine, if less appropriate to Sir Walter's own brand of medievalism than Abbotsford, is certainly in the richest Late Georgian tradition of the Picturesque.

91. G. M. Kemp:
Edinburgh, Sir Walter Scott Monument, 1840-6

Picturesque also are certain aspects of the Houses of Parliament, notably the contrast in shape and placing of the two towers at the ends and, above all, the silhouette of the Clock Tower, almost certainly one of Pugin's personal contributions to the design [92]. But essen-

functions as a pupil[21] of Durand might have developed. Equally regular are the façades and, in the case of the principal front towards the river, elaborately symmetrical as well.

The rich Late Gothic detail was provided in incredible profusion by Pugin, who designed

92. Sir Charles Barry:
London, Houses of Parliament, 1840–65

tially the Houses of Parliament, as might be expected of Barry, their architect, are one of the grandest academic productions of the nineteenth century. Summerson has suggested a relationship to Fonthill Abbey in the way the plan is organized round a central octagon; there may also be an echo of Wyatville's east front of Windsor in the composition of the river front. But except for the incorporation of the medieval Westminster Hall, the Crypt Chapel and the Cloister Court, which necessitated irregularity along the landward side, the plan is almost as regular and as rationally logical in its balanced provision for multiple

here under Barry against his developing taste for earlier and less lacy Gothic forms. Doubtless, like the towers, this detailing reflects the Picturesque, but the extreme regularity of the façades provides also the characteristic reiterations of Romantic Classicism. Pugin is supposed to have said that the river front was 'all Greek', a considerable exaggeration. But just as Highclere shows what Barry's basic principles of design could produce when expressed in the revived Jacobethan mode, so without too great a strain one can imagine this front executed with some sort of Renaissance detailing, if hardly in columnar Grecian guise.

Commissioned in 1836, the Houses of Parliament rose slowly. The House of Lords was opened in 1847; the House of Commons only in 1852, the year of Pugin's early death. Even at the time of Barry's death in 1860 the whole group was still not finished, although his eldest son (Edward Middleton, 1830–80) made but few personal contributions when he took over control and finally completed the job later in the decade. During this extended period of about thirty years the Puginian phase of the Gothic Revival had been initiated and run its entire course; even the succeeding High Victorian Gothic was more than half-way over by the mid sixties. Like the Napoleonic monuments of Paris, which were also a generation a-building, the Houses of Parliament belong historically to the period of their beginning. They are not quite pre-Victorian, since construction above ground began only in 1840 after considerable revision of the competition design, but they are definitely *Early* Victorian.

Not all of Pugin's own work is as remote in character from the Houses of Parliament as his mature principles would lead one to expect. His first church of any consequence, St Marie's, Derby, of 1838–9, is Perpendicular in style and very neat and flat in treatment. Nevertheless, both in its detailed 'correctness' and in Pugin's real command of the national Late Gothic idiom, this church marks a great advance over the work of Rickman and the other Gothic architects of the older generation who were still in practice. Scarisbrick Hall in Lancashire, a remodelling, is confused by the retention of earlier elements and also by a considerable addition made by Pugin's son (Edward Welby, 1834–75) in the sixties. But the portions carried out in 1837–52 are quite consonant with Pugin's work done in association with Barry. The great hall is a definitely archaeological feature of the plan yet also a feature that would be of great significance in the later development

of the nineteenth-century house (see Chapter 15).

If Scarisbrick is not exactly *anti*-Picturesque, comparison with such a great house as Harlaxton near Grantham, first designed by Salvin in the Jacobethan mode in 1831 and rising under Burn's supervision from 1838 on, reveals how little the Picturesque really influenced Pugin even at the beginning of his career. However, Neo-Tudor Lonsdale Square in London, begun by R. C. Carpenter (1812–55) in 1838, is still less Picturesque than Scarisbrick because of its extreme regularity. This example makes evident how far other young architects – and Carpenter was precisely Pugin's contemporary – were behind him in understanding and exploiting even Late Gothic forms; yet within a very few years Carpenter became the most 'correct' of Anglican church architects by following Pugin's lead.

In 1839 and 1840 Pugin designed two modest churches that provided favourite models for Anglo-American church-building for a generation and more. St Oswald's, Old Swan, Liverpool, built in 1840–2, adopts the fourteenth-century English parish-church plan with central western tower broach-spired, aisles, deep chancel, and south porch, each element being quite clearly expressed in the external composition. Internally the effect is low and dark, since Pugin provided no clerestory, roofed the nave with much exposed timber, and filled the traceried windows with stained glass. More original is St Wilfred's, Hulme, Manchester, built in 1839–42, because the tower – never completed, alas – was set at the north-west corner. The detail of St Oswald's is fairly elaborate, including a rather rich east window. St Wilfred's is simpler, with lancet windows to avoid the expense of fourteenth-century tracery.

A larger, more complete, and more expensively decorated example of the Old Swan model was St Giles's, Cheadle, of 1841–6 [93].

This has a quite magnificent, if hardly very original, spired tower and interior walls all patterned in colour. Here Lord Shrewsbury, Pugin's most important patron, eventually provided funds to furnish the church as the architect intended. Pugin's largest churches, unfortunately, never received the carved work, stained glass, and painted decoration that he planned for them. At St Barnabas's, Nottingham, of 1842–4, now the Catholic Cathedral

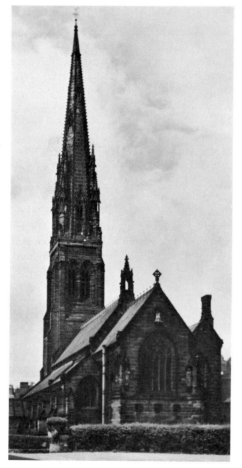

93. A. W. N. Pugin:
Cheadle, Staffordshire, St Giles's, 1841–6

there, he achieved externally a rather fine piling up of related masses at the rear, the whole crowned by a central tower. For lack of any decoration, however, this is grim without and barren within, despite all the spatial interest of the very complex east end.

Pugin, always his own severest critic, was most nearly satisfied with the church that he built for himself next door to his own house, the Grange, at Ramsgate.[22] The house dates from 1841–3, the church from 1846–51. Externally of Kentish knapped flint and internally of Caen stone with a very heavy roof of dark oak, this edifice is worthy of his highest standards of revived medieval construction. But it is rather less original and interesting in external massing and internal spatial development than such a big bare church as St Barnabas's. To the house we will be returning later (see Chapter 15).

Pugin's production is largely concentrated in the years 1837–44, between the two periods of his employment by Barry on the Houses of Parliament. By 1844 other architects, Anglican not Roman Catholic, were accepting his principles and soon rivalling his success. G. G. Scott, for example, never a really great architect but a notable self-publicist, after modest beginnings designed the Martyrs' Memorial at Oxford in 1841 in the form of a fourteenth-century Eleanor Cross and followed up that prominent commission by building the large suburban London church of St Giles's, Camberwell, in 1842–4. At that time he was still in partnership with Moffatt. Then, in 1844, he signalized the international standing of the English Gothic Revival by obtaining alone the commission for the Nikolaikirche in Hamburg, which he carried to completion over the years 1845–63.

Although the body of this church was all but completely destroyed by bombs, his tower and its spire still accent the Hamburg skyline [94]. It is interesting to compare this grand

94. Sir G. G. Scott:
Hamburg, Nikolaikirche, 1845–63

scenic object with the tower and spire of the Petrikirche, almost equally prominent, built in 1843–9 by de Chateauneuf and Fersenfeld [101]. Although built, with a curious echo of London's characteristic stock brick, of an unpleasantly yellowish brick, while the Petrikirche was of a handsome deep-red brick like de Chateauneuf's Alte Post, the silhouette is so enriched with elaborate fourteenth-century stonework – part English, part German in derivation – that it almost rivals in richness of effect Kemp's Walter Scott Monument in Edinburgh. Yet the scale is grand, the parts well related, and in every way it represents a more advanced, almost mid-century taste, in contrast to the simplicity and the geometrical clarity of de Chateauneuf's square brick tower with its plain triangular gables and its very tall and svelte metal-clad spire.

From 1845 down to 1855, when Henry Clutton (1819–93) and William Burges (1827–81) won the competition for Lille Cathedral in France and G. E. Street (1824–81) received the second prize, the pre-eminence of the English as designers of plausible Gothic churches was generally recognized abroad. Though few of the innumerable examples built by Scott and his rivals at home in the forties are in any way really memorable, by the middle of that decade all the characteristics of the English church had been drastically revised, largely thanks to the propaganda of the Cambridge Camden Society. There is no more typical nineteenth-century product than a Victorian Gothic church of this period built to the Camdenian canon; yet the real achievement of the most original architect who designed such churches, Butterfield, belongs to the next, or High Victorian, phase (see Chapter 10). The more Puginian Carpenter, the other favourite architect of the Society, who died in 1855, is hardly as interesting a designer – however 'correct' he may be – in such prominent works as St Paul's in West Street, Brighton, of 1846–8 and St

Mary Magdalen's, Munster Square, in London of 1849-51, as in what he built for Lancing College in 1851-3. There the plain high-roofed ranges with their fine smooth walls of knapped flint and very flat and simple cut-stone dressings have a quality of precision quite lacking in most contemporary churches. Almost finer is St John's College, Hurstpierpoint, although largely posthumous in execution.

Scott, Carpenter, and Butterfield all supplied designs for churches in various parts of the British Empire; other English architects emigrated to the Dominions and to the United States, carrying with them the doctrine of the Gothic Revival, just as French architects half a century earlier had carried a quite different sort of doctrine all over the western world. As a symbol of Britain's major world position, moreover, English churches now rose in many Continental cities, from German watering-places and French Riviera towns to remote capitals such as Athens and Istanbul. Remarkably alien in their foreign contexts, these express the vigour and the assurance, if rarely the real creative possibilities, of the Victorian Gothic.

The Established Church in England was the great patron of the revived Gothic although other denominations were not far behind. But the use of Gothic was by no means confined to churches, nor indeed to country houses as it had largely been in the late eighteenth century. No other Gothic public buildings rivalled the Houses of Parliament; but in 1843-5 Philip Hardwick, designer of the most Grecian of railway stations, with his son (P. C., 1822-92) built the Hall and Library of Lincoln's Inn in London of Tudor red brick with black brick diaperings and cream stone trim. This offered a foretaste of the external polychromy which would be the sign-manual of the next period of revived Gothic in England. An earlier, more severe, sort of Tudor, carried out in stone, served Moffatt, Scott's former partner, for a

mansion at No. 19 Park Lane. But this house was most exceptional; in the forties London architects and builders generally eschewed Gothic of any sort except for churches. Generically medieval, if not specifically Gothic, inspiration would eventually play a major part in forming the advanced commercial mode of the late fifties and sixties however (Chapter 15).

The success that Victorian Gothic, initiated by a Romanist and supported by the Catholicizing wing of the Church of England, had with non-Anglicans in England and throughout the English-speaking world is surprising. Ritualistic planning, almost the essence of the Revival to Pugin and Camdenian contemporaries, was naturally avoided; but the Gothic work of the best Nonconformist architects, such as the Independent Church of 1852 in Glasgow by J. T. Emmett, is by no means unworthy of comparison with Scott's, if not the more puristic Carpenter's. Samuel Hemming of Bristol even employed a few touches of Gothic detail on the prefabricated cast-iron churches that he exported all over the world in the early fifties.

The mature Gothic Revival, as has been said, is more anti-Picturesque than Picturesque, at least in the realm of theory; as a writer in *The Ecclesiologist* expressed the matter succinctly, 'The true picturesque derives from the sternest utility.' Yet the revived Gothic could only be expected to appeal widely to architects and to a public who had long fully accepted the Picturesque point of view. All its irregularity and variety of silhouette, its plastically complex organization and its colouristic decoration, its textural exploitation of various traditional and even near-rustic materials is profoundly opposed to the clear and cool ideals of Romantic Classicism, but fully consonant with the Picturesque.

The significance of the English Gothic Revival of the thirties and forties is manifold, and no two critics will agree how to assess it.

Certainly the functional doctrines of the Revival and its renewed devotion to honest expression of real construction remain of great importance, even though much of this runs parallel to – if, indeed, it does not follow from – the more rationalistic aspects of Romantic Classical theory. In this way the Revival made a positive historical contribution, if not perhaps as new and original a one as has sometimes been maintained.

Negatively, the English Gothic Revival was clearly of very great effectiveness as a solvent, not only of the rigidities and conventionalities of Romantic Classicism, but also of the older and deeper Classical traditions that had been revived by the Renaissance and maintained for several centuries. The lack of an equally effective solvent on the Continent helps to explain why the revolutionary developments of the next period, particularly in the domestic and in the commercial fields, were so largely Anglo-American.

Even in the twentieth century it may be said that part of the profound difference between a Wright and a Perret lay in the fact that one had the tradition of the English Gothic Revival in his blood – largely through reading Ruskin – while the other had not (see Chapters 18 and 19). Still later, the California 'Bay Region School' of the 1930s and 1940s implied a Gothic Revival background, however little its leaders may have been aware of it; the coeval 'Carioca School' of Brazil manifestly had no such background (see Chapter 25). It is therefore of more consequence to see how the ideals of the Picturesque, and concurrently the anti-Picturesque doctrines of the Gothic Revival, were accepted in the United States, than to give comparable attention to Europe, where neither the Picturesque nor the Gothic Revival were very productive of buildings of distinction. For that matter, most of the American buildings that fall under these rubrics are but feeble parodies of English originals. The Greek

Revival architects of America were no unworthy rivals of the Europeans of their day; the exponents of the Picturesque and the followers of Pugin – sometimes the same men – produced little of lasting value. But when seen in relation to the later development of the American house, the contribution of the Picturesque period, lasting in America down to the Civil War and even beyond, is of real significance (see Chapter 15).

There was not much eighteenth- or very early nineteenth-century Gothick of consequence in America. Latrobe's Sedgeley of 1798, Strickland's Masonic Hall in Philadelphia of 1809-11, and Bulfinch's contemporary Federal Street Church in Boston were none of them of much intrinsic interest, and all are now destroyed. Other early manifestations of the Picturesque were even rarer, and it was not until the thirties that a concerted Gothic movement

95. Salem, Mass.,
First Unitarian (North) Church, 1836-7

got under way. Haviland's Eastern Penitentiary of 1821-9 was very modestly Castellated; Strickland's St Stephen's in Philadelphia, a rather gaunt two-towered red-brick structure of 1822-3, more or less Perpendicular, represents but a slight advance in plausibility over his Masonic Hall.

The finest works of the next decade are a group of churches in and around Boston, all built of granite. Willard's Bowdoin Street Church of 1830 in Boston, and St Peter's of 1833 and the First Unitarian or North Church of 1836-7, both in Salem, Mass., are the best extant examples [95]. The material discouraged detail, but provided, when used rock-faced, an almost antediluvian ruggedness. Tracery is generally of wood and much simplified; the most characteristic decorative features are very plain crenellations and occasional quatrefoil openings. Thus, on the whole, these monuments are closer to Romantic Classicism than to the Picturesque and have little in common with English work of their own day or even of the preceding period. However, the wooden Gothic of this period is in general of a rather lacy Late Georgian order.[23]

The mid thirties saw some quite elaborate Gothic houses of stone, such as A. J. Davis's Blythewood of 1834 at Annandale, N.Y., and Oaklands, built by Richard Upjohn (1802-78) the next year at Gardiner, Maine. Both architects were capable of designing at the very same time Greek edifices of considerably higher quality – Davis's Indiana State Capitol of 1831-5 at Indianapolis and Upjohn's Samuel Farrer house of 1836 at Bangor, Maine, for example – but both were already leaders in the rising revolt against the Grecian.

Upjohn's Trinity Church in New York completed in 1846 is the American analogue of Pugin's St Marie's, Derby, and by no means inferior despite its plaster vaults [96]. With Trinity to his credit Upjohn, English-born but not English-trained, became the ac-

96. Richard Upjohn:
New York, Trinity Church, c. 1844-6

knowledged leader of the American Gothicists. At Kingscote, Newport, R.I., which he built in 1841, Upjohn easily rivalled Davis as a designer of Picturesque Gothic houses. But he was almost equally addicted to Italianate forms, even in the church-building field, for there his rigid denominational principles made him unwilling to use Gothic except for Episcopalians. His non-Gothic work ranges from a vague sort of *Rundbogenstil*, as illustrated in his Congregational Church of the Pilgrims in Brooklyn of 1844–6, once provided with a highly original spire of scalloped outline, and the more Germanic Bowdoin College Chapel in Brunswick, Maine, of 1844–55, to Italian Villas, such as that built in Newport, R.I., for

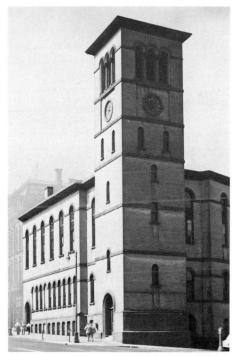

97. Richard Upjohn:
Utica, N.Y., City Hall, 1852–3

Edward King in 1845–7 (later Free Library), and even to public buildings in the Italian Villa mode, such as his City Hall in Utica, N.Y., of 1852–3 [97]. His basilican St Paul's in Baltimore,

Maryland, of 1852–6 – its style is rather surprising, since the parish was Episcopalian – is more successful than most of his later Gothic churches. His Corn Exchange Bank of 1854 in New York, round-arched if not exactly *Rundbogenstil*, was one of the most distinguished early approaches to the use of an arcaded mode for commercial building (see Chapter 14). Of very similar character and comparable quality was the H. E. Pierrepont house in Brooklyn completed in 1857.

But Upjohn's reputation, rightly or wrongly, is based on his Gothic churches. Externally these are usually quite close to contemporary Camdenian models; internally they are often distinguished by very original – and also very awkward – wooden arcades rising up to the wooden roofs above. St Mary's, Burlington, N.J., of 1846–54 is perhaps the most attractive and English-looking of his village churches, the modest cruciform plan culminating in a very simple but delicate spire over the crossing. Not least significant, moreover, are Upjohn's still more modest wooden churches[24] of vertical board-and-batten construction, such as St Paul's in Brunswick, Maine, of 1845. They illustrate, like his openwork wooden arcades, a real interest in expressing the stick character of American carpentry. This interest is intellectually similar to, but visually very different from, Pugin's devotion to the direct expression of masonry construction. At building churches in stone British immigrants like Notman and Frank Wills (1827–?)[25] were not surprisingly Upjohn's rivals in the quality of their craftsmanship.

Running parallel with Upjohn's career is that of Davis, but with the difference that he built few churches and, as Ithiel Town's former partner, continued on occasion, even after the latter's retirement in 1835, to provide Grecian as well as Gothic designs. He was perhaps most successful, however, with Italian Villas such as the Munn house in Utica, N.Y., or the E. C.

Litchfield house in Prospect Park, Brooklyn, N.Y., both of 1854. At Belmead, in Powhatan County, Virginia, built in 1845, he introduced Manorial Gothic to the southern plantation, but this mode never rivalled the Grecian peripteral temple in popularity in the South. Walnut Wood, the Harral house in Bridgeport, Conn., of 1846, was more typical and long retained all its original furnishings. With the building of Ericstan, the John J. Herrick house in Tarrytown, N.Y., in 1855 Davis brought the fake castle to the Hudson River valley – so frequently compared to that of the Rhine and favourite subject in these years of a new American school of landscape painters of the most Picturesque order. As a scenic embellishment Ericstan was not unlike the ruins that Thomas Cole introduced in his most Romantic and imaginary landscapes.

Despite Davis's ranging activity, extending westward into Kentucky and Michigan, elaborate Gothic houses, whether Castellated or manorially Tudor, were relatively rare in the America of the forties and fifties. But a type of gabled cottage with a front veranda and elaborate traceried barge-boards was rather popular. This is well represented by the extant Henry Delamater house in Rhinebeck, N.Y., and also by that of William J. Rotch of 1845 in New Bedford, Mass., both by Davis himself. The mode was energetically supported by Davis's great friend, the landscape gardener and architectural critic A. J. Downing (1815–52).

Downing was a characteristic proponent of the Picturesque point of view, leaning heavily on earlier English writers. The designs for Picturesque houses, some by Davis, some by Notman, one at least – the King Villa – by Upjohn, and others presumably by himself, illustrated in Downing's two house-pattern books[26] were quite as likely to be towered Italian Villas as Tudor Cottages or more pretentiously Gothic designs. Most significant of all are those called Bracketted Cottages by Downing for which he recommended the board-and-batten[27] external finish that Upjohn later took up for modest wooden churches. But these, which are neither very Picturesque – at least with the capital P – nor yet at all Gothic, are better considered in relation to the general development of Anglo-American house-design in the nineteenth century (see Chapter 15).

Rare in execution, as are indeed all the more exotic Picturesque modes, but also significant for its later influence, was the Swiss Chalet. Although chalets were illustrated in the English Villa books of P. F. Robinson (1776–1858)[28] and others from the twenties, the finest extant American example is fairly late, the Willoughby house in Newport, R.I., of 1854. Though this is by Hunt, it may be presumed to derive from Swiss[29] or German sources rather than from Robinson's or other English designs.

Thus at Newport, already rising towards its later position as the premier American summer resort, there were by the time the Civil War broke out in the early sixties examples of the Tudor Cottage (Upjohn's Kingscote), the towered Italian Villa (his Edward King House) – as for that matter also the more Barryesque symmetrical villa without tower, the Parish House of 1851–2 by the English-trained Calvert Vaux (1824–95)[30] – and the Swiss Chalet, not to speak of other quite formal houses which here in Newport began to show very early the influence of the French Second Empire. There were also several big hotels of this period, now all destroyed. Two Grecian examples have been mentioned earlier; but the second Ocean House, built by Warren in 1845, was Gothic, a gargantuan version of a Davis–Downing Tudor Cottage. On this the Tudoresque veranda piers were carried to a fantastic height in naïve competition with the columned porticoes of the previous Ocean House and the Atlantic House.

If there were in America no castles of the scale and plausibility of Salvin's Peckforton, no pavilions of the pseudo-oriental magnificence of Nash's at Brighton, the will to build them was none the less present. Ericstan has already been mentioned; while at Bridgeport, Conn., P. T. Barnum erected Iranistan in 1847-8 in conscious emulation of the Regent's pleasure dome at Brighton from designs he had obtained in England. This was carried out by Eidlitz. Longwood, near Natchez, Mississippi, by Samuel Sloan (1815-84), begun in 1860, is even more ambitiously oriental, but was left unfinished when the Civil War broke out the next year.[31] Rather curiously the Smithsonian Institution in Washington, set down like an enormous garden fabrick in L'Enfant's Mall near the Mills obelisk, was at the insistence of its director, Robert Dale Owen,[32] designed as a Norman castle by James Renwick (1818-95). Built in 1848-9 of brownstone, this is a very monumental manifestation of the Picturesque and one of the more surprising features of a capital otherwise mostly Classical in its architecture. On the whole the happiest American achievements in the Picturesque vein were the towered Italian Villas, from Notman's Doane house of the mid thirties down through Upjohn's City Hall in Utica of the early fifties and Davis's still later houses in the East and the Middle West (see Chapter 5).

The Gothic Revival in America, deriving after 1840 from Pugin and the Camdenians, was a much more alien movement than the Greek Revival. In the British Dominions and Colonies, even though the characteristic production of this period is in many ways more similar to that of the United States than to that of the homeland, the Neo-Gothic achievement appears somewhat less exotic. However, St John's in Hobart, Tasmania,[32a] by John Lee Archer, which was completed in 1835 in the most rudimentary sort of Commissioners' Gothic, is far inferior to the granite churches of its period in the Boston area. From that to Holy Trinity in Hobart, completed by James

Blackburn in 1847, the advance in mere competence is very evident, Yet, as in the case of Upjohn in America, the Norman church that Blackburn built for the Presbyterians of Glenorchy and even more his Congregational Church at Newtown, an asymmetrically towered Italian Villa edifice, may well be preferred to his Gothic work.

Greenway's Government House Stables of 1817-19 in Sydney, Australia, were already Castellated, but in a modest eighteenth-century way. M. W. Lewis's Camden church of 1840-9 was based on plans sent out by Blore and simply executed in red brick. In W. W. Wardell (1823-99), who emigrated as late as 1858, Australia finally obtained an experienced Neo-Gothic architect of real ability. He had already made his mark in England a decade before his departure with Our Lady of Victories, Clapham, in London; but even that very decent early church of his required no specific mention in the English section of this chapter. His Australian work is too late to be considered here (see Chapter 11).

Across the Atlantic, communications were doubtless quicker than with the Antipodes, and the cultural climate of Canada was undoubtedly more similar to that of the homeland. The first important Neo-Gothic work in Canada, however, was built for the French and not the British community. Notre Dame, the Catholic Cathedral of Montreal,[32b] was originally designed and erected by an Irish architect, James O'Donnell (1774-1830), in 1824-9 somewhat to the disgust of most French Canadians who considered O'Donnell's Gothic to be Anglican when in fact it was merely Georgian. Equipped later with western towers and redecorated internally with operatic sumptuousness in the seventies, it is not easy to realize just what Notre Dame was like when O'Donnell completed it. It was bigger, certainly, but not more advanced than the New England churches of a few years later.

In 1845 Wills arrived in Canada from England and began the Anglican Cathedral at Fredericton, New Brunswick, as a moderate-sized cruciform parish-church with central tower, the whole of rather run-of-the-mill Camdenian character despite its pretensions. Very similar, but considerably larger and richer, is the Montreal cathedral which he began a decade later in 1856. His American churches, though smaller and less elaborate, have somewhat more character. Canadians must have sensed Wills's inadequacy almost at once, for both Butterfield and G. G. Scott were asked to send out church designs in the forties. The former provided in 1848 a scheme for a more elaborate east end for Wills's Fredericton Cathedral, which had been started only three years before. Scott's Cathedral in St John's, Newfoundland, initiated in 1846, deserves a relatively important place in the roster of his churches as Butterfield's New Brunswick work does not. But this large edifice was completed only some forty years later by his son (G. G. II, 1839–97). Even the stone used here was imported from Scotland.

As in the United States, there is plenty of more-or-less Gothic domestic work in Canada, most of it relatively late. An early and rather pretentious secular edifice was the so-called Old Building of Trinity College, Toronto, erected in 1851 by Kivas Tully (1820–1905). This was a by no means incompetent example of Collegiate Gothic, but more like Wilkins's or Rickman's work of the twenties at Cambridge than the advanced Camdenian edifices of its own period. Canadian Neo-Gothic rose to a certain autochthonous distinction only in the next period (see Chapter 10).

If early illustrations of the Picturesque point of view and of the mature Gothic Revival are on the whole of minor interest in the English-speaking world outside Great Britain, that whole world from California to Tasmania was absorbing the propaganda of the English exponents of the Picturesque and the Gothic Revival. This had its effect in the succeeding period when the High Victorian Gothic of England was exploited to more considerable purpose than the Neo-Gothic of the Early Victorian period. By the time a great English critic came to the support of the Gothic Revival, John Ruskin (1819–1900), he had almost from the original publication of his *Seven Lamps of Architecture* in 1849 more readers beyond the seas than at home.[33]

Neither the Picturesque nor the Gothic Revival has the same importance on the Continent of Europe as in English-speaking countries. The Picturesque point of view was carried abroad[33a] by the great British artistic invention of the eighteenth century, the English garden – *jardin anglais, englischer Garten, giardino inglese, jardin inglès*, etc., to muster the various well-established and revelatory foreign terms for the more or less naturalistic mode that succeeded the architecturally ordered French gardens of the Le Nôtre type. By 1800 the Picturesque was as familiar in theory as were the international tenets of Romantic Classicism. But for all the garden fabrics that were built in Europe in the English taste, the point of view tended to remain alien. Moreover, from the continuance of Orléans Cathedral[34] in Gothic, ordered as early as 1707 by Louis XIV though not finally finished until 1829, to Schinkel's painted Gothic visions of the opening of the nineteenth century, there is no lack of evidence of Continental interest in Gothic forms. In France there was also a very considerable theoretical interest in Gothic methods of construction that can hardly be matched in eighteenth-century England (see Introduction). But there followed in the early decades of the nineteenth century no such effective crystallization of an earlier dilettante interest in the Gothic as in England, no popular fad for building fake castles, no flood of cheap Commissioners' Churches.

Yet, in France as in England, a new and more serious phase of the Gothic Revival did open in the late thirties, stimulated by the ideals of Catholic Revival of a series of writers from Chateaubriand to Montalembert. No great Gothic public monument like the Houses of Parliament in London was initiated in these years in Paris – nor for that matter at any later date – but several churches designed around 1840 were at least intended to be as exemplary as Pugin's; they were also considerably more ambitious in their size and their elaboration than most of those his Catholic clients and the Camdenians' Anglican ones were sponsoring in England at this point.

A curious example of the change in taste is the Chapelle-Saint-Louis at Dreux.[35] The original chapel was built in 1816–22 by an architect named Cramail (or Cramailler) as a Classical rotunda to serve as the mausoleum of the Orléans family. In 1839 Louis Philippe ordered its remodelling and enlargement in Gothic style by P.-B. Lefranc (1795–1856), desiring thus to associate the Orleanist dynasty with the medieval glories of French royalty in a manner already fashionable[36] with intellectuals to the left and to the right, if not with many architects. The new exterior, completed in 1848 just as the Orléans rule came to an end, is in a very lacy and unplausible sort of Gothick, not without a certain still rather eighteenth-century Rococo charm but quite inharmonious with the Classical interior. Like another Royal mausoleum of these years, the Chapelle-Saint-Ferdinand in the Avenue Pershing in Neuilly, built in 1843 in memory of an Orléans prince who had been killed in an accident near its site, the Chapelle-Saint-Louis has stained glass windows designed in 1844 by no less an artist than Ingres. These are even less appropriate in association with Lefranc's Gothic than with the Romanesquoid mode that the elderly Fontaine –who knew, like Talleyrand, how to maintain his position under several successive regimes –

used for the Neuilly chapel. They are hardly superior in quality, moreover, to the glass, whether imported from Germany or produced locally, that was being used in the early forties in England for Neo-Gothic churches.

A more important Gothic project of this date than the Chapelle-Saint-Louis was that for the large new Paris church of Sainte-Clotilde prepared in 1840 by F.-C. Gau (1790–1853), German-born but a pupil of Lebas. Doubts as to the extensive use of iron proposed by Gau held up the initiation of the construction of Sainte-Clotilde until 1846, so that several provincial Neo-Gothic edifices of some consequence were executed first. These may be compared, but only to their disadvantage, with Pugin's churches of around 1840 as regards their plausibility, their intrinsic architectonic qualities, and the elegance of their detail. However, several of them are larger and more ambitious – being Catholic churches in a Catholic country – than are even his various cathedrals.

In any case the character of real Gothic architecture in France, as in most other European countries, made unlikely a programme of revival based chiefly on parish churches in the way of Pugin's. The Continental Middle Ages had most notably produced cathedrals, and it was for new churches of near-cathedral scale that the re-use of Gothic was likely to be proposed. Notre-Dame-de-Bon-Secours, built by J.-E. Barthélemy (1799–1868) in 1840-7 on the heights of Ste Cathérine above Rouen, opens the serious phase of the Revival in France. It has a superb site and is best appreciated from a considerable distance, but the silhouette is not happy and the execution is rather hard and cold. Saint-Nicholas at Nantes was begun in 1839 just before the Rouen church by L.-A. Piel (1808-41), a confused Romantic character who died a monk, and taken over in 1843 by J.-B.-A. Lassus (1807-57), a pupil of Lebas and Henri Labrouste. It is very hard to accept this church as even in part the production of Lassus, the erudite archaeologist who brought out in 1842 the first volume of a major monograph on Chartres Cathedral and who undertook in 1845, together with the better-known E.-E. Viollet-le-Duc (1814-79), the restoration of Notre-Dame[36a] in Paris after sharing with Duban the responsibility for restoring the Sainte-Chapelle. Rather more plausible – at least in the sense that it merges fairly successfully with the original fourteenth-century nave to which it is attached – is the façade of Saint-Ouen at Rouen built in 1845-51 by H.-C.-M. Grégoire (1791-1854), a pupil of Percier.

Sainte-Clotilde was finally begun in 1846, as has been noted, and completed after Gau's

98. F.-C. Gau and Théodore Ballu: Paris, Sainte-Clotilde, 1846-57

death by Ballu in 1857 [98]. This ambitious urban church of cathedral scale lacks almost as completely as those just mentioned the personal qualities of design and the integrity of revived medieval craftsmanship that give character, if

not always distinction, to the churches of Pugin, Carpenter, and other leading English Gothic Revivalists of the forties. Nor does it have the grandeur of proportion of Scott's Nikolaikirche in Hamburg, to which it is more comparable in size and pretension [94]. The style is Rayonnant, or French fourteenth-century, and the material good freestone, but deadly mechanical and quite characterless in the detailing. The parts seem somehow too large for the whole. Ballu's west towers, for example, are excessively tall for so stubby a plan, and the chapel-surrounded chevet is too elaborate for even an urban parish church.

Two later churches by Lassus, Saint-Nicholas at Moulins, built in collaboration with L.-D.-G. Esmonnot (1807-80) in 1849, and Saint-Pierre at Dijon of 1853 hardly rival Sainte-Clotilde in size, elaboration, or even plausibility. Viollet-le-Duc was rather more of an executant architect than Lassus, even though in this decade and the next most of his vast energy and very considerable archaeological knowledge went into the restoration of medieval monuments. At Notre-Dame in Paris the Chapter House that he designed is a wholly new construction of 1847 not unworthy of comparison with the best work of Scott in these same years. The house [99] he built at 28 Rue de Berlin (now de Liège) in Paris in 1846-8 – his first executed building – may better be compared with the most advanced English secular Gothic of its date, Salvin's Peckforton, say, or Butterfield's St Augustine's College, Canterbury. The front is so simple and straightforward in composition that it fits between more conventional façades with no awkwardness, and the rather plain detailing has the 'realism' that was coming to be admired by this date in the most advanced English circles.

The Romanesquoid design of Fontaine's Chapelle-Saint-Ferdinand of 1843 has been mentioned. The use of such forms was in the forties even more exceptional in France than in England. In 1852 Didron estimated – probably with some exaggeration – that over two hundred Neo-Gothic churches had been built or were building in France, a record which compares statistically, if in no other way, with English church production in this period. None of them, however, is as impressive to later eyes as Saint-Paul at Nîmes, which follows with notable success the alternative Romanesquoid mode of Fontaine's chapel. C.-A. Questel (1807–88), a pupil of Blouet and Duban, the architect of this church, had evidently studied the Romanesque with the care and enthusiasm usually lavished on the Gothic by his generation, and the result is so great an advance over

99. E.-E. Viollet-le-Duc:
Paris, house in the Rue de Liège, 1846–8

Fontaine's work that the resemblance is merely nominal. Thus might the Camdenians have hoped to build had they considered the twelfth-century Romanesque of France as worthy of conscientious emulation as the fourteenth-century Gothic of England. Saint-Paul is a large cruciform edifice, rib-vaulted throughout in a proto-Gothic way, and crowned with a great central lantern. The detail is plausible in its design, neither too skimpy nor too elaborate, although the execution lacks any real feeling for medieval craftsmanship in stone. Questel's church, however, is as much of an exception as Fontaine's chapel. A Romanesque Revival did not get under way in the forties in France in the way it did to a certain extent then in Germany; other Romanesquoid churches of high quality all belong to the next period (see Chapter 8).

Minor evidence of French interest – and rising interest – in the Picturesque is not hard to find in these decades, but that is all there is. No Picturesque modes comparable to those of the Anglo-Saxon world became widely popular. In the first decade of the century the brothers Caccault built at Clisson[37] in the Vendée a whole village based on their memories of the Roman Campagna, a more considerable essay in the Italian Villa vein than anything carried out in England. But the asymmetrically towered Italian Villa[38] did not mature in France in the way that it did in England, Germany, and the United States. Séheult's *Recueil* of 1821, of which a second edition appeared in 1847, is one of the earliest and richest repositories of inspiration drawn from rustic Italian building; but the edifices Séheult illustrated, however Picturesque in other ways, are all symmetrical and quite in the Durand tradition. J.-J. Lequeu (1758–*c*.1824)[39] had produced bolder projects a generation earlier. These are often asymmetrical, generally quite wildly eclectic, and very vigorously plastic; but such things were rarely executed in France except as garden fabrics. Lequeu had no success at all in his later years.

Moreover, the Rustic Cottage mode seems to have struck no real roots in France, even though the painter Hubert Robert and the architect Richard Mique (1728-94), in designing the fabricks of Marie Antoinette's Hameau at the Petit Trianon in 1783-6, had followed native rather than English rural models. Under the Restoration and the July Monarchy inspiration came generally from English Cottage books. Visconti's Château de Lussy, S.-et-M., of 1844, though a fairly large structure, is really in the English Cottage mode with an asymmetrically organized plan and an irregularly composed exterior. This is almost unique and, in any case, quite undistinguished. A more vigorous flow of rustic influence entered France via Alsace and directly from Switzerland. The Chalet aux Loges of 1837 by Bonneau near Versailles was, as its name implies, a Swiss Chalet, but it quite lacked the integrity of structural expression and the originality of plastic organization of Eidlitz's Willoughby house in Newport, R.I., which is, of course, considerably later in date. Occasional imitations of the *style François I*, such as the already mentioned country house by Canissié at Draveil, S.-et-O., have some irregularity both of outline and of plan; but in general the *François I* of the July Monarchy, like so much of the Jacobethan of Early Victorian England, is Picturesque only in detail, not in general conception.

In 1840 the elder Bridant, who also built Chalets in the succeeding years around the lake at Enghien, a watering-place on the outskirts of Paris, built a Gothic 'Castel' on the plain of Passy, then a fairly open suburb. This was markedly asymmetrical and consistently medieval in detail. The contemporary fame of this enlarged garden fabrick – for such it really was – indicates its unique position in contemporary production, as unique as Moffatt's Gothic house in Park Lane in London. L.-M. Boltz, an architect of Alsatian if not German origin but a pupil of Henri Labrouste, had some success with a less feudal mode, half-timbered and asymmetrical, in the forties – a house of 1842 at Champeaux, S.-et-M., was typical.

This modest influx into France of Picturesque models from contemporary Germany as well as from contemporary England might lead one to assume that the Picturesque, if not the Gothic Revival, was more significant in Central Europe. In Germany and Austria, however, as also in Scandinavia, Picturesque and medievalizing tendencies mostly merged with Romantic Classicism in the *Rundbogenstil* rather than standing apart, constituting neither an opposition eventually rising to triumph in the English way, nor a mere gesture of aberrant protest as in France.

Schinkel's interest in Gothic has already been touched on, but none of his more ambitious Gothic projects ever got beyond the drawing-board (see Chapter 2). There are fewer such, in any case, belonging to his later than to his earlier years. Moreover, the Gothic of the early projects naturally belongs to the contemporary High Romantic world of Wyatt's Fonthill Abbey and Latrobe's alternative design for the Baltimore Cathedral, not to the ethical and archaeological milieu of Pugin and the Camdenians. Most of the virtues – by no means negligible – of his Berlin Werder Church of the twenties are not Gothic virtues – not at any rate as Englishmen of the succeeding decades understood them – they are rather Romantic Classical virtues. The principal interest of his earlier Kreuzberg Memorial lies in its cast-iron material, a material anathema to Pugin as a 'modernistic' innovation. The Babelsberg Schloss, based principally on the modern castles that he saw on his visit to England in 1826, makes no pretensions to archaeological correctness in the way of Pugin's Alton Castle of about 1840 or Salvin's still later Peckforton.

A few Castellated mansions of more local inspiration, such as Hohenschwangau in Upper

Bavaria, as reconstructed by J. D. Ohlmüller (1791–1839) in 1832–7, are closer in spirit to Pugin's and Salvin's ideals. Hohenschwangau, like certain castles built in this period on the Rhine, exploits the Picturesque possibilities of a fine site and the nostalgic overtones of a district with a romantic medieval past. Schloss Berg in Bavaria, which owes its present very domesticated Gothic character to the work done there by Eduard Riedel (1813–85) in 1849–51, hardly deserves mention in this connexion any more than do Schinkel's more or less medievalizing country houses, so crisp and regular is their design. Curiously enough, the old Schloss at Schwerin, as enlarged by G. A. Demmler (1804–86) from 1844, became a more elaborate and extensive example of *François I*[39a] than anything this period produced in France [100]. It is also notably Picturesque, with innumerable towers and gables disposed around

the sides of an irregularly polygonal court. Stüler carried this extraordinary pile to completion after Demmler left Schwerin in 1851. Not very Picturesque, but representing another sort of medievalism, were two Venetian Gothic houses Am Elbberg in Dresden, built with considerable archaeological plausibility by an architect named Ehrhardt in the mid forties. They provide a curious premonition of Ruskin and the High Victorian Gothic of England (see Chapter 10). Semper's Gothic Cholera Fountain of 1843 in Dresden has already been mentioned.

As in France, much energy went at this time into the restoration and completion of major medieval churches in Germany. Most notable in this connexion was the work on Cologne Cathedral begun in 1824 by F. A. Ahlert (1788–1833), continued by E. F. Zwirner (1802–61), and finally completed by Richard Voigtel

100. G. A. Demmler and F. A. Stüler: Schwerin, Schloss, 1844–57

(1829–1902) in 1880. Assisting Zwirner, who had worked earlier under Schinkel on the Kolberg Town Hall, was (among others) Friedrich von Schmidt (1825–91), after 1859 the most important Gothic Revivalist in Austria (see Chapters 8 and 11). No more than in France did this activity in 'productive archaeology' in Germany lead to new building of much interest, not at least until Schmidt reached Vienna after having taught in Milan.

Ohlmüller's Mariahilfkirche outside Munich, begun in 1831 and completed after his death by Ziebland, the next considerable essay in ecclesiastical Gothic in Germany after Schinkel's Berlin church, is certainly much less appealing than is his mountain castle. The hall-church form, authentically German though it was, produced a clumsily proportioned mass, at the front of which a stubby tower ending in an open-work spire seems to be 'riding the roof'. This church is as 'advanced', in the sense of being fairly plausible archaeologically, as Barthélèmy's Notre-Dame-de-Bon-Secours built a decade later, but that is about all one can say for it. It certainly does not stand up to comparison with Rickman's or Savage's English churches of the twenties.

De Chateauneuf's Petrikirche in Hamburg begun in 1843, or at least its tower, has already been mentioned [101]. This is superior in design, and in some ways also better built, to most of Pugin's churches of this date. It is, for example, rib-vaulted throughout in a quite plain but very competent way. The interior lacks, however, the strikingly simple proportions and the warm colour of the red brick exterior; above all, the complex spatial development of the transeptal members lacks clarity, although the plan was probably taken over from the medieval Petrikirche that had been burned. The Gothic churches of K. A. von Heideloff (1788–1865), beginning with his Catholic church in Leipzig built in the Weststrasse there in 1845–7, are hardly above the level of Ohlmüller's and certainly much less successful than the Petrikirche, though Heideloff had a much higher reputation than de Chateauneuf with contemporaries as a specialist at Gothic on account of his published studies of medieval architecture.[40]

In Berlin most of the new churches of this period by Stüler, Strack, and others were in a

101. Alexis de Chateauneuf and Fersenfeld: Hamburg, Petrikirche, 1843–9

Romanesquoid version of the *Rundbogenstil*. Of these elaborated and coarsened versions of Schinkel's suburban-church projects of a decade earlier, Stüler's Jacobikirche of 1844-5 was basilican in plan; his Markuskirche, begun in 1848, was of the central type but with a tall campanile rising at one side. The Berlin Petrikirche, built by Strack in 1846-50, was Gothic, however, and even clumsier than Ohlmüller's much earlier Mariahilfkirche, which it very closely resembles. Nor was Stüler's one important essay in Gothic, the Bartholomäuskirche, begun in 1854 and completed by Friedrich Adler (1827-?) in 1858, much better. In general, the first half of the century was well over before Gothic churches of any great size and pretension were built either in Germany or Austria. The largest and most prominent, the Votivkirche in Vienna [131], for the designing of which Heinrich von Ferstel (1828-83) won the competition in 1853 when he was only twenty-five, was not begun until 1856 nor completed until 1879 (see Chapter 8).

In England the Picturesque and the Gothic Revival were effective solvents of Romantic Classicism, because both, and particularly the latter, were consciously nationalistic, emphasizing in an increasingly nationalistic period the recovery of local rather than of universal building traditions. For a good part of their local acceptability they were dependent, moreover, on certain warm connotations which their visual forms had for English patrons. The Rustic Cottage, the Tudor Parsonage, the Castellated Mansion had all, supposedly, been autochthonous products of the insular past. On the other hand, even though the English of the eighteenth century had adopted as their own such foreign painters as Claude and Poussin, from whose canvases the Italian Villa mode principally derived both its forms and its prestige, that mode was certainly not English in its ultimate prototypes. It is readily understandable, therefore, that it was the Italian

Villa, of all the established vehicles of the Picturesque, which had the greatest success in a Germany romantically mad about Italy. But such superb compositions as the Court Gardener's House by Schinkel [32] or Persius's Friedenskirche at Potsdam [33], perhaps the highest international achievements in the Picturesque genre, owed only their basic concept, if even that, to England. Their elements were for the most part borrowed directly from Italian sources, and they were carefully composed according to a formal discipline consonant with the standards of Romantic Classicism.

The Swiss Chalet, an even more alien mode in England than the Italian Villa, was a native one in Central Europe. Hence one finds Schinkel first, and then his pupils, exploiting it with considerable virtuosity as the *Tirolerhäuschen*. Indeed, the particular form of wooden fretwork which came to be called 'gingerbread' in English, one of the favourite forms of later Picturesque detail everywhere in the western world from Russia to America, is more likely to be derived from Alpine chalets via nineteenth-century German than via nineteenth-century English intermediaries.

Romantic Classicism, being founded on the basic Western European heritage of Greece and Rome, could readily broaden its sources to include the Early Christian and the Italian Renaissance. But to men of the early nineteenth century the Gothic was not a universal European style as we are likely to consider it today; it was 'Early English' or 'altteutsch' or (with far more justification) 'l'architecture française'. The bigotry of the English Gothic Revival was so intense in the forties that Scott was denounced in *The Ecclesiologist* for even entering a competition for a church in Germany since, if successful, his clients would be Lutherans not Anglicans. Such insular narrowness made the Catholic Pugin's Gothic paradoxically intransmissible to Catholic countries abroad, quite as intransmissible in effect as the Jacobethan. Scott got his Hamburg commission by modulating, to the horror of puristic compatriots, his usual fourteenth-century English Decorated towards its German equivalent, on the whole a grander style at least as he exploited it there.

Continental nationalism, like Continental Neo-Catholicism outside France,[41] favoured earlier – or later – modes than the Gothic, down at least to the mid century. The *Rundbogenstil*, moreover, despite the fact that the precedent for its detail was quite as often Italian as local, received warm support from nationalists in Germany; when exported, moreover, as to the Scandinavian countries and the United States, it was properly recognized as a German product (see Chapters 2 and 5). In Latin countries, and particularly in Italy,[41a] Gothic continued to seem alien; hence there are few examples of revived medieval design of any sort there or in Spain and Portugal before 1850. Jappelli's highly exceptional work at Padua, mentioned earlier, is rich and delicate but not in the least plausible to Northern eyes in the way of Ehrhardt's somewhat similar Italian Gothic houses in Dresden.

A European consensus of taste had been achieved by the late seventeenth century, despite the division of Europe into Catholic and Protestant countries, and this consensus was maintained, and even grew in strength, for another hundred years and more. When it finally broke down in the second quarter of the nineteenth century, it necessarily broke down in different ways and to a different degree in each country. No new cultural synthesis was achieved, at least as regards architecture, before the mid twentieth century. The stylistic patchwork that the second half of the nineteenth century inherited was largely the product of the increasing nationalism of the two decades that preceded the mid century. This particularistic nationalism, rather than the concurrent increase in mere eclecticism of taste – for such

eclecticism had existed to a greater or lesser degree since the mid eighteenth century – explains the major difference in the architectural climate around 1850 from that around 1800; at least it is some part of the explanation. To be Roman in architecture, to be Greek, even to be Italian, one need not cease to be English or French or German. But to be Tudor one must be English, as to be *François I* one must be French, or so it seemed to most architects and their clients in the forties.

From this pattern of growing nationalistic divergence, this Late Romantic disintegration of the cultural unity that had remained strong and vital through the first few decades of the century, it is important now to turn to an aspect of architecture that derived from a different international absolute, that of science and technology. The English led in most technological developments affecting building methods from the mid eighteenth century on, both in the introduction of new materials and in the exploitation of new types of construction to serve new needs. But they led only because the Industrial Revolution, the result of certain technological as well as social changes and the cause of innumerable others, had its origins and its early flowering in England. Before the first half of the nineteenth century was over, other countries to which the Industrial Revolution came relatively late were rapidly catching up. After the fifties technological leadership in building passed from Britain to the United States and to the Continent. Some consideration of the increased use of iron and glass between 1790 and 1855 may well conclude the first part of this book.

CHAPTER 7

BUILDING WITH IRON AND GLASS: 1790–1855

Architectural history has many aspects. Ideas and theories, points of view and programmes can have real importance even when, as with the Picturesque and the earlier stages of the Gothic Revival, most of the buildings which derive from them or follow their prescriptions are lacking in individual distinction. Volume of production is also significant; the disproportion between the previous chapter and the four that precede it expresses fairly accurately the difference in the amount of building in the first half of the century belonging, at least by a broad definition, to the rubric of Romantic Classicism and the very much smaller amount up to 1840 at least and outside England – that can be considered essentially Picturesque or programmatically Neo-Gothic. But the history of architecture must include the history of building as a craft or technic; sometimes the story of technical development is – or has appeared to posterity to be – more important than any other aspect of a particular historical development. Such has recurrently been the case concerning the rise of the Gothic in the twelfth century in France; it has also seemed true in varying degree for the nineteenth century to many historians and critics.

The Industrial Revolution induced a parallel but gradual revolution in building methods; even today, after two hundred years, the potentialities of that revolution have not been fully actualized. The technical story, particularly as it concerns the structural use of ferrous metals, first cast iron,[1] next wrought iron, and then steel, begins well before 1800. There has already been occasion to mention, in passing, technical innovations in various edifices where those innovations had a determinant effect on

the total architectural result. But it is worth while, partly for the intrinsic interest of the subject, partly as preparation for subsequent structural developments of great importance later in the nineteenth and in the twentieth century, to go back to the beginning and to recount sequentially the episodes in the rise of iron as a prime building material, as also to touch at least on the concurrent use of other 'fireproof' materials and the vastly increased exploitation of glass. This sequence of episodes reaches a real culmination in the fifties with the construction of a considerable number of 'Crystal Palaces', first in London and then all over the western world, edifices that were almost entirely of iron and glass.

A marked change in the situation came about 1855. For one thing, it was in that year that Sir Henry Bessemer invented a new method of making steel in quantity so that it could be profitably used for large building components. However, the full architectural possibilities of the use of structural steel were hardly grasped before the nineties. There was also in the fifties an increasingly general realization that unprotected iron was not as fire-resistant[2] as had hitherto been fondly supposed. Then, too, and perhaps as significantly, a sharp shift in taste at this time, leading to a predominant preference for the massively plastic in architecture, made unfashionable both the delicate membering suitable to iron and the smooth transparent surfaces provided by large areas of glass quite as has happened again in the years since this book first appeared (see Chapters 8–11 and Epilogue).

The technical development of the use of ferrous metals in building continued unbroken beyond the fifties; indeed, most of the quantitative records of the first half of the century, in the way of distances spanned and volumes enclosed, were progressively exceeded in the sixties, seventies, and eighties (see Chapter 16). From the point of view of architecture, however, the story passes more or less out of sight for a generation. To a certain extent metal literally 'went underground' as new types of foundations were evolved for taller and heavier buildings; but more generally metal structure was masked with stone or brick, as was first proposed in the forties in England, to provide protection against the adverse effects of extreme heat in urban fires (see Chapter 14). When the use of exposed metal and glass became significant again in the nineties that use was to be a

major constituent of general architectural development as it indeed remained for two generations (see Chapters 16, 22, 23, and 25). But down to the 1850s the rise of iron and glass is best considered as a separate story.

This story is not confined to the most advanced countries. The tall, slim columns used by Wren in 1706 to support the galleries in the old House of Commons *seem* to have been of iron[2a]; but short ones, introduced in 1752, can still be seen in the kitchen of the Monastery of Alcobaça in Portugal, and a very early use of iron beams was in the Marble Palace at Petersburg built by Antonio Rinaldi (1709-94) in 1768-72. The main line of development, however, was undoubtedly English, French, and American. Definitely dated 1770-2 were the

101A. Thomas Farnolls Pritchard:
Coalbrookdale Bridge, 1777-9

iron members supporting the galleries in St Anne's, Liverpool.

A much more notable and better publicized use of iron followed shortly after this when metal replaced masonry for the entire central structure of the Coalbrookdale Bridge in Shropshire [101A]. This was begun in 1777 by Thomas Farnolls Pritchard (?-1777) with the active cooperation of Abraham Darby III, an important local ironmaster.[2b] Darby's Coalbrookdale Foundry cast the iron elements that were needed and the bridge was completed in 1779. Pritchard was an architect, and architects played a more important part in the story of the early development of iron construction than is generally realized. Soon, however, the importance of special problems of statics to which such construction gave rise and, above all, the need to measure accurately the strength of various components required the expert assistance of civil engineers, and often the engineers came to build on their own without the collaboration of architects.

At this point the story crosses the channel to France.[3] There Soufflot, the very technically minded architect of the Paris Panthéon - one of the edifices with an account of which this book began - assisted by his pupil Brébion, provided in 1779-81 an iron roof over the stair-hall[4] that he built to lead up to the Grande Galerie of the Louvre. In the next few years two rather obscure French architects, Ango and Eustache Saint-Fart (1746-1822), were occupied, respectively, with the introduction of iron framing and of 'flower-pot' (i.e. hollow-tile) elements supported on timber framework to produce more or less fireproof types of floors. Over the years 1786-90 the great French theatre architect J.-V. Louis (1731-1800), horrified by the recurrent fires at the Palais Royal, combined these two ideas when he designed the roof of the new Théâtre Français in Paris.

Now the main line of advance returns to England. In 1792-4 Soane avoided timber altogether in the fireproof vaults of his Consols Office at the Bank of England, using nothing but specially made earthenware pots;[4a] he also covered the twenty-foot oculus in the central vault with a lantern of iron and glass [6]. The architectonic qualities of this interior have already been stressed. Even more important for later architecture, however, although effectively invisible, had been the adoption just before this of French principles in a calico mill at Derby and the West Mill at Belper, both begun in 1792. These were planned and carried out by the millowner-engineer William Strutt (1756-1830) who used specially designed iron stanchions throughout carrying timber beams and, in the top storey only, 'flower-pot' vaults between the beams such as Saint-Fart had first introduced but flat brick vaults or 'jack-arches' elsewhere.

Other mills soon followed.[4b] The first to have iron beams as well as stanchions seems to be the Benyons, Marshall & Bage flax spinning mill in St Michael's Street, Shrewsbury. This was built in 1796-7 from the designs of Charles Bage (1752-1822), a friend and correspondent of Strutt. The much-publicized Salford Twist Company's cotton mill at Salford of 1799-1801, designed and built by Boulton & Watt of steam-engine fame - they knew Bage's mill since they had installed his steam-engine - was according to present evidence the second[5] to be erected with a complete internal skeleton of iron. By 1800, then, a system of fire-resistant construction using cast-iron stanchions and cast-iron beams, carrying what are sometimes called 'jack-arches' of brick, had been established in the world of English mill-building. By 1850 such construction was in use in Britain for almost all high-grade building. The system was significantly modified, however, after about 1845 by the substitution of rolled - that is wrought - iron beams, as proposed by Sir William Fairbairn (1789-1874),[6] since cast-iron ones had proved dangerously brittle.

102. Thomas Hopper:
London, Carlton House, Conservatory, 1811-12

103. John Nash:
Brighton, Royal Pavilion, Kitchen, 1818-21

Isolated columns of iron appeared in many edifices from the 1790s on. The most notable extant examples, perhaps, are those in the kitchen and in several of the rooms that were added by Nash to the Royal Pavilion at Brighton in 1818-21 [103]. His 'Chinese' staircases of 1815-18 there are entirely of decorative pierced ironwork and the framing of his big onion dome is also of metal, although of course in-

It is not necessary here to do more than sketch out the steps by which the new iron skeleton structure became generally accepted. In 1802-11 James Wyatt introduced it in the Castellated New Palace that he built at Kew for George III, an edifice of which little is otherwise known since it was demolished in 1827-8. In line with this curious conjunction of technical and stylistic innovation, already noted in Schinkel's somewhat later cast-iron Gothic monument of 1819-20 in Berlin, is Porden's profuse use of iron for the Gothic traceries and balustrades at Eaton Hall[7] in Cheshire in 1804-12, as also by Hopper in the even more ornate Gothic Conservatory at Carlton House in London in 1811-12 [102].

visible. From the early use of iron columns for gallery supports in churches, increasingly general by the early 1800s, there shortly developed the aspiration to exploit iron still more extensively in such edifices. In three churches that Rickman and the ironmaster John Cragg built in Liverpool, St George's, Everton, and St Michael's, Toxteth Road, both begun in 1813, and St Philip's, Hardman Street, completed in 1816, the entire internal structure is of iron.[7a] At St Michael's the new material is not restricted to the interior but appears on the outside as well. Rickman's increasing archaeological erudition and that of his contemporaries soon limited the use of iron in Gothic churches, however; by Pugin and the Camdenians it was rigidly proscribed. Structural elements of iron in churches of any architectural pretension became acceptable again only in the fifties (see Chapter 10).

Turning to what long remained the most notable field of metal construction, bridge building,[8] one finds a rapid increase in the numbers and the spans of English metal bridges from the mid 1790s on. In Shropshire, where the first iron bridge and the first all-iron-framed factory had been built, one of the greatest English engineers, Thomas Telford (1757–1834),[9] built the Buildwas Bridge with a span of 130 feet in 1795–6. At the same time the much longer and handsomer metal arch of the Sunderland Bridge in County Durham was rising to the designs of Rowland Burdon. He was assisted, it appears, by certain ideas supplied by Thomas Paine (1737–1809), better known for his political writings than as a technician, who had had some association with bridge-building in America. Burdon was a Member of Parliament and neither an architect nor an engineer. Telford, however, though not professionally trained as an architect, had worked for Sir William Chambers as a journeyman-mason on Somerset House in his youth; throughout his career he built masonry tollhouses and even, on occasion, modest churches in a competent if rudimentary Romantic Classical vein.

In connexion with his work on the Bridgewater Canal and on the road system of the Scottish Highlands, Telford designed and built innumerable bridges, the majority of them of stone. But some of his later iron bridges, more skilfully devised technically and more graceful visually than the Buildwas Bridge, deserve mention here. On the Waterloo Bridge of 1815 at Bettws-y-Coed in Wales he used an openwork inscriptional band and floral badges rather than architectural detail to give elegance and even richness to a modest cast-iron arch. A longer and simpler bridge of similar design but

unknown authorship built in 1816 still spans the Liffey in Dublin.

The same year as the Waterloo Bridge, at Craigellachie amid austere Scottish mountains, Telford bridged the Spey with a plain latticed iron arch. However one should mention that he elaborated the masonry abutments as battlemented towers in a wholly Picturesque way [104]. For the Menai Bridge, built in 1819–24

104. Thomas Telford:
Craigellachie Bridge, 1815

between North Wales and Anglesey, Telford used a new principle in metal construction, suspending his road-bed from metal chains [105]. This was a principle of great antiquity already exploited with success in America.[10] Telford's masonry towers at the Menai Bridge are of extremely elegant Romantic Classical design, tapered like Egyptian pylons and pierced with delicate arches. In the twin bridge to this at Conway, also in North Wales, the close proximity of the Edwardian castle led him to provide Castellated towers. In a yet later bridge at Tewkesbury of 1826 the latticed metalwork itself has the cuspings of Gothic tracery.

The Menai Bridge long remained the longest of its type in Britain. I. K. Brunel's Clifton

105. Thomas Telford:
Menai Strait, Menai Bridge, 1819-24

Suspension Bridge near Bristol [105A], for which he won the competition in 1829, but which was begun only in 1837, has already been mentioned because of the Egyptian detailing proposed for the piers. This bridge was finally completed only in 1864 by W. H. Barlow (1812-92) using the materials of Brunel's earlier Hungerford Suspension Bridge in London. Of early arched metal bridges there are very many and by all the leading English engineers of the first half of the century: John Rennie (1761-1821), I. K. Brunel (1806-59), George Stephenson (1781-1848) and his son Robert (1803-59), as well as Telford.[10a] The new railways required even more bridges than the canals constructed by the previous generation.

In France Napoleon's engineers built two arched iron bridges across the Seine. L.-A. de Cessart (1719-1806) designed before 1800 and Delon in 1801-3 executed the Pont des Arts, the first French bridge of iron, and Lamandé completed the Pont du Jardin du Roi in 1806.[11] Neither is comparable in span or in logic of design to the earlier English examples, thus reversing the pre-eminence which the French

had held as bridge-builders so long as masonry was used. The much later Pont du Carrousel in Paris, built by A.-R. Polonceau (1788-1847) in 1834-6, was considerably superior to these Napoleonic examples, though hardly epoch-making. But already in 1824, just as Telford's Menai Bridge was completed, Marc Séguin (1786-1875) was spanning the Rhône near Tournon with a suspension bridge hung on wire ropes[12] instead of chains.

From the early forties Séguin's cable principle was developed much further in America in bridges at Wheeling, W. Va., Pittsburgh, Penna., and Cincinnati, Ohio, by the German immigrant John A. Roebling (1806-69). Those at Wheeling[13] and Cincinnati are still in use. The more dramatically sited Niagara Falls Bridge of 1852, which attracted world-wide attention when it was new, is no longer extant [106]; its success, however, led to Roebling's being commissioned to build the famous Brooklyn Bridge[14] in New York. Begun by him in 1869 and completed by his son Washington A. Roebling (1837-1926) in 1883, this is still one of the principal sights of New York. It is sad to

105A. I. K. Brunel:
Clifton Suspension Bridge, 1837–64

record that work in the caissons sunk for the foundations of the piers killed the designer.

Bridges are at the edge of the realm of architecture. Fairly early, moreover, they came almost entirely under the control of men

106. John A. Roebling:
Niagara Falls, Suspension Bridge, 1852

without architectural training or standards – Roebling, for example, was such a one. Ordinary buildings, all of iron or with much use of iron, are more significant as the century proceeds, both in France and in England. Hopper's Carlton House Conservatory [102] has been mentioned. In 1809 the architect F.-J. Belanger (1744–1818), a pupil of Brongniart, replaced the domed wooden roof of the Halle au Blé in Paris, added in 1782 by J.-G. Legrand (1743–1807) and J. Molinos (1743–1831), with one of metal. The Marché de la Madeleine, designed by M.-G. Veugny (1785–1850) possibly as early as 1824 but not built until 1835–8, was apparently all of metal internally; its masonry exterior, however, was quite conventional. Already in 1835, in the fish pavilion which formed part of his rather Durandesque Hungerford Market in London, Charles Fowler had outstripped this in the direct and elegant use of light metal components, here with no surrounding shell of masonry at all.

Some further Continental examples of the use of iron in the late twenties and thirties deserve mention at this point. Alavoine – at whose suggestion Duc's Bastille Column, begun in 1831, was made of metal, though the metal is bronze not iron – designed in 1823 a flèche 432 feet tall to rise over the crossing of Rouen Cathedral in the form of an openwork cage of iron. Begun in 1827 and interrupted in 1848, this was finally completed by the younger Barthélèmy (Eugène, 1841-98) and L.-F. Desmarest (1814-?) in 1877. In 1829-31 Fontaine roofed the Galerie d'Orléans, which he built across the garden of the Palais Royal, with iron and glass. This structure, now destroyed, was more prominent and also much wider than most of the many *passages* and *galeries*[15] with glass roofs that had been built in Paris and elsewhere in France from the 1770s on. The most impressive extant French example is the Passage Pommeraye in Nantes, built by Durand-Gasselin and J.-B. Buron (?-1881) in 1843; in this the circulation moves upwards from one end to the other through three storey-levels. A modest Milanese example of 1831, the Galleria de Cristoforis by Andrea Pizzala (?-1862), might be mentioned here also, as it was the local prototype for the greatest of all these characteristic nineteenth-century urban features, Mengoni's Galleria Vittorio Emanuele begun in the sixties [129]. Of the many early nineteenth-

century ones that remain in other European cities, the Galerie Saint-Hubert in Brussels, built by J.-P. Cluysenaer (1811-80), a pupil of Suys, in 1847, is one of the largest and best maintained. Warren's Providence Arcade in Providence, R.I., has been mentioned earlier.

Related to the *galeries*, and sometimes also so-called, were the large Parisian enterprises of this period that were really early department stores. The Bazar de l'Industrie, built by Paul Lelong (1799-1846) in 1830, had a large glass-roofed and iron-galleried court of the sort that was to be continued in Parisian department stores down into the present century (see Chapter 16). Even larger and bolder were the similar courts in the department store known as the Galeries du Commerce et de l'Industrie, built by Grisart and Froehlicher in the Boulevard Bonne-Nouvelle in 1838, which has already been mentioned for its richly arcaded Renaissance façades [107]. Shop-fronts of iron were also frequent in Paris[16] by this time. Thus in France, as in England and America, the use of iron was closely associated with structures for business use, but more usually with sales emporia than with office buildings (see Chapter 14). Such, however, were not unknown in England and America, though they were

107. Grisart & Froehlicher:
Paris, Galeries du Commerce et de l'Industrie, 1838

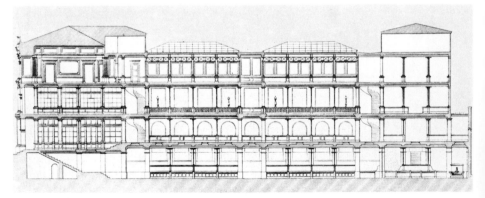

generally less extensive and made less use of glass-roofed courts.

Glass held in wooden frames had for some time been extensively employed for greenhouses. How early iron began to be substituted for wood is not clear, and not perhaps of much consequence.[17] Hopper's ornately Gothic Conservatory of iron and glass at Carlton House in London, demolished in the twenties, has been mentioned several times already [102]. In 1833, at the Jardin des Plantes in Paris, Charles Rohault de Fleury (1801-75) built a very large and handsome iron greenhouse without any stylistic decoration. The structure of the square pavilions was as transparent and rectilinear as the interior framework of Veugny's slightly later market seems to have been, and the ranges between were covered, just as so many wooden greenhouses had been, with transparent roofs rising in two quadrants. At Chatsworth in Derbyshire the Great Conservatory was built in 1836-40 by the 6th Duke of Devonshire's gardener, Sir Joseph Paxton (1803-65), with minor assistance from the architect Decimus Burton. This quite outclassed the largest earlier greenhouse, the Anthaeum at Brighton, designed in 1825 and built in 1832-3 for the horticulturist Henry Phillips, with a dome of

iron and glass 160 feet in diameter that collapsed before it was entirely completed. The Chatsworth conservatory was a still larger rectangle, 227 feet by 123 feet, with the exterior rising in a double cusp like the side ranges of Rohault's Paris greenhouse – or, for that matter, like the section of the Anthaeum. The columns and beams here were of iron, but the great arched principals of the 'nave' and the 'aisles' were of laminated wood and four-foot long panes of glass were held in wooden sashes arranged in a ridge-and-furrow pattern. A particular invention of Paxton's, whose name was given to such roofs, was the hollowing out of the wooden members at the base of the furrows to serve as gutters.

Decimus Burton's still extant Palm Stove at Kew, carried out by the contracting engineer Richard Turner of Dublin in 1845-7, with rounded ends and a higher central area, is more bubble-like than Paxton's because of the absence of ridges and furrows on its continuously glazed surface [108]. But both these great greenhouses were among the most striking monuments of their Early Victorian day and were never exceeded later in elegance though often in size. French rivals, long since destroyed, were the Jardins d'Hiver in Lyons and Paris of

108. Decimus Burton and Richard Turner:
Kew, Palm Stove, 1845-7

1841 and 1847 by Hector Horeau (1801-72), the latter a rectangle measuring 300 by 180 feet and 60 feet tall.

With the thirties begins the story of a new building type, the railway station,[18] in whose sheds the mid century was to realize some of the largest and finest examples ever of 'ferro-vitreous', or iron-and-glass, construction. The structures utilizing iron thus far mentioned have been of two sorts, some, such as bridges, markets, greenhouses, etc., with only subsidiary masonry elements, if any at all; others, examples of mixed construction with metal providing only the internal skeleton or the roof. Railway stations were generally – and before the fifties always – examples of mixed construction, but of a rather special sort. The iron and glass portions, that is the sheds, and the masonry portions are likely to be merely juxtaposed, not truly integrated. Such a masonry frontispiece as Hardwick's Euston Arch in London of 1835-7 had no connexion at all with the functional elements of the station behind – here by Robert Stephenson – although Euston was an extreme case. But a happy co-ordination of the masonry

and the iron-and-glass portions of stations was rarely achieved anywhere.

Of the earliest railway station, that at Crown Street in Liverpool of 1830, nothing remains; it was in any case a very modest structure.[18a] Of its successors at Lime Street the present station is the fourth on the site. Even the 'Arch' at Euston, the next major station to be built, is now gone, despite the strenuous efforts of the Victorian Society and others in Britain and overseas to save this symbolic portal to the Victorian Age. However, the first station at Temple Meads in Bristol, which was built by Brunel in 1839-40, is physically intact, though supplanted in present-day use by a larger and later one. Castellated as regards the masonry block in front, the shed here is equally medieval-izing; for its roof is of timber, not of iron, and based on the fourteenth-century hammerbeam roof of Westminster Hall in London, whose width it exceeds by a few feet only.

Of the once far finer Trijunct station at Derby [109], built in 1839-41, the last portions of Francis Thompson's brick screen have finally been destroyed; the three original sheds pro-

109. Robert Stephenson and Francis Thompson: Derby, Trijunct Railway Station, 1839-41

vided by Robert Stephenson, with Thompson's collaboration on the detailing, were each 56 feet wide in comparison to the 40-foot width of Stephenson's earlier ones at Euston. The tie-beam roof had much of the graceful directness and linear elegance of Rohault's greenhouse or Veugny's market.

More and more, the use of iron was being generally accepted as a technical necessity in the forties. At Buckingham Palace Blore, in adapting one of Nash's side pavilions as a chapel for Queen Victoria in 1842–3, used visible iron supports just as Nash had done so long before in the interiors of the Brighton Pavilion for her uncle. Yet generally the use of iron in important masonry structures in the thirties and the early forties was quite invisible, being confined to the floors and the substructure of the roofs. In 1837–9 C.-J. Baron (1783–1855) and Nicolas Martin (1809–?), for example, provided a complete iron roof above the vaults of Chartres Cathedral, a work of very considerable scale and technical elaboration that provided the immediate prototype for the iron roof of Gau's Sainte-Clotilde in Paris, designed in 1840 and begun in 1846. At the Houses of Parliament, the actual construction of which started only in 1840, Barry capped the whole with iron roofs – the external iron plates are actually visible, of course, but the fact of their being of iron is rarely recognized. Fireproof floors built according to various French and English patent systems were increasingly thought necessary in all high-grade construction. Queen Victoria's Osborne House on the Isle of Wight, constructed without the aid of an architect by the builder Thomas Cubitt, had them throughout, as did many other well-built country houses of the forties, at least in the passages and stair-halls.

Here and there in the commercial buildings of this decade the iron skeleton used inside came through to the exterior, as it had on one of Rickman's Liverpool churches a generation earlier. A small office building at No. 50 Watling Street in London, with visible iron supports and lintels in the upper storeys but with brick corner piers and brick spandrels, was a case in point, probably dating from early in the decade. By 1844 Fairbairn was recommending in a report that fireproof construction should be used in all warehouses. Increasingly this was done in Lancashire and, before long, elsewhere; Fairbairn himself had introduced it ten years earlier in the Jevons Warehouse on the New Quay in Manchester.

Closely associated with the development of iron construction is the development of prefabrication; indeed, the parts of an elaborate iron edifice, such as a bridge or a greenhouse, are necessarily prefabricated[18b] and merely assembled at the site. From the early forties, and perhaps even before that, lighthouses were frequently erected in ironmasters' yards in Britain, disassembled, shipped to Bermuda or Barbados, and then reassembled. In 1843 John Walker of London provided a prefabricated palace for an African king and, by the end of the decade, prefabricated warehouses and dwellings of iron were being supplied to gold-diggers in California and emigrants to Australia in very considerable quantity. A look at post-war prefabricated houses today perhaps helps to explain why almost none of these ancestors of a century earlier seems to have survived, at least in recognizable form. None the less, the advance of prefabrication remains a notable technical – though hardly architectural – achievement of the 1840s and 1850s.

To the mid and late forties belong several splendid examples of mixed construction in various countries that not only represent technical feats of a high order but are also fully architectural in character. Some are by architects, others by teams of architects and engineers working in close collaboration. In building the Britannia Bridge,[19] which crosses the Menai Strait near Telford's Menai Bridge, the Derby Trijunct team of Stephenson and Thompson in

1845-50 utilized with great success the rectangular tubes built up of wrought-iron plates that Fairbairn, the consulting engineer, recommended [110]. The Britannia Bridge was much damaged by fire in May 1970. The masonry entrances and the tall towers, taller than they need have been because of Stephenson's original intention to use suspensory members for additional support to his rigid tubes, were superbly detailed by Thompson. Contemporaries called them Egyptian, but the design has already been noted as fully consonant with Romantic Classicism though quite devoid of Grecian elements. At least the sculptor John Thomas's pairs of gigantic lions at the entrances are Nubian!

At the London Coal Exchange[20] built in 1846-9 in Lower Thames Street, the City Corporation's architect Bunning arrived at no such complete co-ordination of masonry and metallic design as did Stephenson and Thompson on the Britannia Bridge. The masonry exterior consisted of two *palazzo* blocks at a fairly sharp angle to one another and loosely linked by a very Picturesque round tower, freestanding in its upper stages. Behind this dome of the interior court could barely be glimpsed. Inside this court, however, no masonry at all was visible; one saw only an elegant cage of iron elements rising to the glazed hemisphere above [111]. The metal members were richly but appropriately detailed, and there was even more appropriate decorative painting by Sang in such panels as were not glazed.

In France two monuments of comparable distinction have already been mentioned, Henri Labrouste's Bibliothèque Sainte-Geneviève of 1843-50 and Duquesney's Gare de l'Est of 1847-52 [44]. Unfortunately the original shed of the latter, with arched principals of 100-foot span, was taken down when the station was doubled in size in the present century. Inside the library a central row of iron columns of somewhat Pompeian design – that is, resembling the slender, metallically scaled members seen in

110. Robert Stephenson and Francis Thompson:
Menai Strait, Britannia Bridge, 1845-50

111. J. B. Bunning: London, Coal Exchange, 1846–9

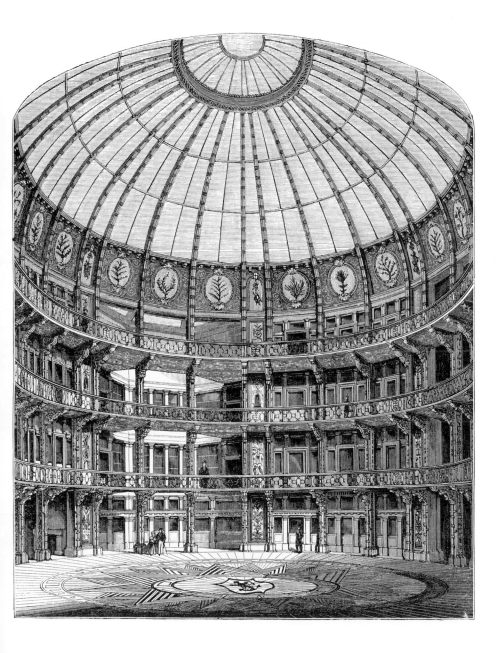

Pompeian wall paintings – still carries the two half-round roofs on delicately scrolled arches of open-work iron [112]. Since the masonry walls with their ranges of window arches are visible below, the effect is less novel here than it used to be in the iron-and-glass court of the Coal Exchange; but Labrouste achieved much greater integration between interior and exterior [45]. The Dianabad in Vienna, built by Karl Etzel in 1841–3, had a fine iron roof; the circular bracing of the iron principals, a frequent motif in large openwork members of cast iron at this time, was most appropriate to the *Rundbogenstil* detailing of the masonry walls [113].

Monferran's cast-iron dome on St Isaac's in Petersburg, completed about 1842, has already been mentioned [53]. This was rivalled before very long by several American examples,[21] most notably Walter's enormous dome, built in

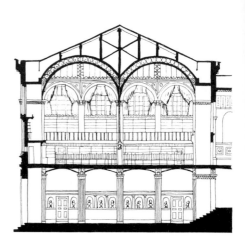

112. H.-P.-F. Labrouste: Paris, Bibliothèque Sainte-Geneviève, (1839), 1843–50

113. Karl Etzel: Vienna, Dianabad, 1841–3

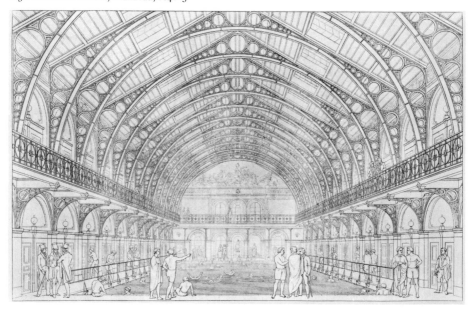

1855–65, above the Capitol in Washington [147]. Baroque in silhouette and rather Baroque in detail also, this may have encouraged – along with the rising taste for elaborately plastic effects of which it was itself a notable expression – the increasingly common practice of casting the exposed iron elements of American commercial façades in the form of rich Corinthian columns and heavily moulded arches.[21a]

Around 1850 cast-iron architecture was coming to its climax everywhere. James Bogardus (1800–74), a manufacturer of iron grinding machinery, not an architect or engineer, began to erect in Center Street in New York in 1848 a four-storeyed urban structure for his own use as a factory with an exterior consisting only of cast-iron piers and lintels. This was one of the earliest[22] and most highly publicized of the cast-iron fronts which Bogardus and various other ironmasters in New York and elsewhere made ubiquitous in the principal American cities before and after the Civil War. But his earliest completed iron front was that of the five-storey chemist shop of John Milhau at 183 Broadway erected within the year 1848. Another work by Bogardus, the range of four-storey stores built for Edward H. Laing at the north-west corner of Washington and Murray Streets in New York, was begun in 1849 and finished within two months, well before his own building was completed. These early cast-iron fronts were very logical and expressive in the way the attenuated Grecian Doric columns and plain architraves were used to form an external frame; but the Laing stores later lost most of the applied ornament that appealed so much to mid-century taste [114]. Later façades are richer and heavier, generally with Renaissance

114. James Bogardus: New York, Laing Stores, 1849

or Baroque arcading, as has just been noted. For the Harper's Building in New York, built in 1854, which incorporated the first American rolled-iron beams the architect John B. Corlies provided a design of ornate Late Renaissance character. Curiously enough, in executing this building Bogardus used for the upper four storeys the same castings as in the Sun Building that he had erected in 1850-1 in Baltimore to the designs of R. G. Hatfield (1815-79). To the typical cast-iron fronts of New York,[23] of which the most extensive and one of the simplest was that of the old Stewart Department Store on Broadway begun in 1859 by John W. Kellum (1807-71), that was later occupied by Wanamakers and burned during demolition in 1956, one may well prefer the delicacy of a Glasgow example, the Jamaica Street Warehouse[24] of 1855-6, or a remote Far Western department store like the Z.C.M.I. of 1868 in Salt Lake City, rivalling beyond the Rocky Mountains those of Paris. The cast-iron front is being preserved.

Great Britain and Europe saw few all-iron façades. This was in large part because the danger of their collapse when exposed to the extreme heat of urban conflagrations, a danger made real to Americans only by the fires of the seventies in Boston and Chicago, was appreciated very early. Yet it was not in America but in Britain that the greatest masterpieces of iron construction of the fifties were built. The succeeding turn of the tide against the visible use of iron also had its origins in Britain not in America, though the material early became ubiquitous there.

In 1850 Paxton was completing at Chatsworth a relatively small new greenhouse to protect the *Victoria regia*, a giant water-lily imported from Africa by the Duke of Devonshire. With its arcaded walls of iron and glass and its flat ridge-and-furrow roof, this seemed to Paxton to provide a suitable paradigm for the vast structure[25] needed by May 1851 to house the Great

Exhibition, the first international exposition, which was scheduled to open at that time. The Commissioners of the Exhibition had held an international competition that produced several extremely interesting ferrovitreous projects, notably an Irish one by Turner, Burton's collaborator at Kew, and a French one by Hector Horeau. Rightly or wrongly, all of them were rejected, and the Commissioners' own Building Committee, including the chief architectural and engineering talents of the age, then produced a project of their own. Reputedly in large part the work of the engineer Brunel and the architect T. L. Donaldson (1795-1885), this manifestly impractical scheme, a sort of *Rundbogenstil* super-railway-station intended to be built of brick – the project actually provided the inspiration for Herholdt's Central Station in Copenhagen of 1863-4, or so it would appear – was already out for bids when Paxton presented in July 1850 his own scheme based on the Chatsworth Lily House. Published in the *Illustrated London News* and offered with a low alternative bid by the contractors Fox & Henderson, this was accepted and – with much significant modification – erected in the incredibly short space of nine months.

Inside this vast structure, with its tall central nave, galleried aisles, and arched transept, Paxton and his engineer associates, Sir Charles Fox (1810-74) and his partner Henderson (to the two of whom a considerable part of the credit must go), created unwittingly a new sort of architectural space. So large as in effect to be boundless, this space was defined only by the three-dimensional grid of co-ordinates which the regularly spaced iron stanchions and girders provided [115]. These elements, designed for mass-production, and also in such a way that they could be disassembled as readily as they were assembled, had a new sort of mechanical elegance towards which the design of metal components had hitherto been moving only very gradually. The character of the casting process

115 Sir Joseph Paxton and Fox & Henderson:
London, Crystal Palace, 1850–1

made it only too easy to impose on cast-iron elements all sorts of more or less inappropriate decorative treatments from Gothic to Baroque; only rarely had stylistic detail been successfully reinterpreted, as by Bunning in the Coal Exchange, in terms of the fat arrises and broad radii that are suitable to the material and to the particular method of its production. Even at the Crystal Palace a few touches of ornament provided by Owen Jones (1806–89), who was also responsible for the highly original and rather Turneresque colour treatment, suggest the gap – and, alas, it was in the 1850s a widening gap – between the technicians' and the architects' ambitions for iron.

Contemporaries had no words for what the Crystal Palace offered. Even today, when the aesthetic possibilities of the new sort of space it contained as well as the technical advantages of its method of assembly from mass-produced elements have been more generally explored, it is not easy to describe Paxton's and Fox & Henderson's achievement despite the remarkably complete documentation that exists. The space inside the tall transept (an afterthought designed to allow the saving of a great elm), arched on laminated wooden principals, was more readily appreciated in its day than that in the long nave, because it was more familiar. It is not surprising, therefore, that when the Crystal Palace was disassembled and rebuilt in 1852-4 at Sydenham, where it lasted down to its destruction – ironically by fire – in 1936, the entire nave was arched although with principals of openwork metal rather than of laminated wood.

The Crystal Palace's structural vocabulary – though not, alas, the quality of its space – can be appreciated in the Midland Station at Oxford, built by Fox & Henderson with identical elements in 1852. There one can still see how the new methods enforced a modular regularity more rigid than that of Romantic Classicism and also encouraged a tenuity of material quite unknown to the Neo-Gothic as executed in masonry. Thus the visual result ran doubly counter to the rising fashions in architecture in the fifties (see Chapters 9 and 10). Within five years of the moment when the Crystal Palace was greeted with such general – though never universal – acclaim the climactic moment of the

early Iron Age was already over. In those few years, however, Crystal Palaces rose in many other major cities. The finest was perhaps that built in Dublin in 1852-4 by Sir John Benson (1812-74) with its bubble-like rounded ends; the least successful that in New York[26] of 1853 by G. J. B. Carstensen (1812-57), the founder of the Tivoli in Copenhagen, and Charles Gilde-meister (1820-69). The prompt destruction of this last by fire was a fearful early warning of the limitations of iron construction unsheathed by masonry. The burning of Voit's Glaspalast of 1854 in Munich,[26a] like that of the Sydenham Palace, occurred in our own day, as also the similar end of the Paleis voor Volksvlijt in Amsterdam, which was built by Cornelis Outshoorn (1810-75) in 1856.

The prestige of iron construction was never higher than in the early fifties. For Balmoral Castle, not yet rebuilt in its final form, the Prince Consort ordered in 1851 a prefabricated

116. Lewis Cubitt:
London, King's Cross Station, 1851-2

iron ballroom by E. T. Bellhouse of Manchester modelled on the houses for emigrants to Australia by Bellhouse that the Prince had seen at the Great Exhibition. In the Record Office in London, begun by Pennethorne in this same year, even more iron was used for the internal grid of separate storerooms and for the window-sash than in the great mill that Lockwood & Mawson built for Sir Titus Salt at Saltaire in Yorkshire in 1854. The internal structure of this last represented another major contribution by Fairbairn. Characteristically, however, the de-tailing of the external masonry of the Record Office is more or less Tudor, if rather crude and over-scaled, while that of the Saltaire mill is picturesquely Italianate.

In two new London railway stations, both happily extant, these years produced the chief rivals to the Crystal Palace. At King's Cross, planned by the architect Lewis Cubitt in 1850 and built in 1851-2, the two great arched sheds

somewhat resembled technically the transept of the original Crystal Palace, their principals having been of laminated wood. These had eventually to be replaced in 1869-70 with the present steel principals which are, however, still held by Cubitt's original cast-iron shoes. The masonry block of the station on the left, or departure, side is undistinguished but fairly inconspicuous. The great glory of the station is the front, with its two enormous stock-brick arches that close the ends of the sheds towards the Euston Road [116]. The idea had been Duquesney's at the Gare de l'Est, but here there is no irrelevant Renaissance detail, only grand scale and clear expression of the arched spaces behind.

Paddington Station, built in 1852-4, has no such grand exterior, being masked at the southern end by the Hardwicks' Great Western Hotel. The engineer Brunel here called in the architect M. D. Wyatt (1820-77) as collaborator,

117. I. K. Brunel and Sir M. D. Wyatt: London, Paddington Station, 1852-4

and for the metal members of the shed Wyatt devised ornamentation which – as Brunel specifically requested – is both novel and suited to the materials [117]. There is a slightly Saracenic flavour both to the stalagmitic modelling of the great stanchions and to the wrought elements of tracery that fill the lunettes at the ends and even run along the sides of the great elliptically-arched principals. But the detailing of these, if unnecessarily elaborate, is certainly quite original and not inappropriate to the materials or to the complex spatial effects of the three great parallel sheds crossed by two equally tall transepts. The cool spirit of Cubitt's station recalls that of earlier Romantic Classicism; the richer forms of Paddington are related to the rising 'High' styles of the third quarter of the century, of whose initiation the Great Western Hotel was one of the earliest indications (see Chapter 8).

By 1853 the craze for iron construction was so great that the Ecclesiological Society, forgetting their Puginian principles – Pugin had died the previous year, but not before issuing a severe critique of the metal-and-glass construction of the Crystal Palace – commissioned their favourite and most 'correct' architect, Carpenter, to design for them an iron church. It was not Carpenter's death two years later but the refusal of the English bishops to consecrate prefabricated structures for permanent use that brought to nothing this interesting project along the lines of Rickman's and Cragg's Liverpool churches of forty years earlier. The general flood of prefabrication, now producing all sorts of structures for the Antipodes and other remote areas that still lacked their own building industries, slowed down in 1854 when the demands of the War Office for barracks (on account of the Crimean War) deflected prefabricators from civil production.

In that year, however, Sydney Smirke began one of the last major monuments of cast iron in England, the domed Reading Room in the court

of his brother's British Museum. Awkward in proportion and encased in stacks, this is not to be compared in distinction of design with the Reading Room that Henri Labrouste added to the Bibliothèque Nationale in Paris in 1862–8[27] [118]. That superb interior, with its many light domes of terracotta carried on the slenderest of metal columns and arches, is a great advance over his earlier Bibliothèque Sainte-Geneviève [112]. The Reading Room in Paris has no proper exterior, however, any more than does that in London, for it is incorporated in a group of seventeenth- and eighteenth-century structures that Labrouste adapted and enlarged (see Chapter 8). Even more striking are Labrouste's stacks, visible from the Reading Room through a great glass wall, for in them the entire spatial volume is articulated by vertical and horizontal metal elements in a fashion somewhat like the interior of the Crystal Palace. But in the sixties such things were exceptional.

In 1853–8 L.-P. Baltard's son Victor (1805–74) built the Central Markets[28] of Paris with the assistance of F.-E. Callet (1791–1854) in a mode much less elegant but still franker, exposing his metal structure outside as well as in, at Napoleon III's personal insistence. Saint-Eugène, an almost completely iron-built church of Gothic design, was erected in Paris in 1854–5 by L.-A. Boileau (1812–96).[29] Boileau's Saint-Paul at Montluçon, Allier, completed in 1863, is a second French example of a cast-iron church, and he made designs for several others. His Notre-Dame-de-France off Leicester Square in London, a modest church of 1868, has been completely rebuilt since the last war.

However, to house the first Paris international exhibition, that of 1855, F.-A. Cendrier (1803–92) and J.-M.-V. Viel (1796–1863), both pupils of Vaudoyer and Lebas, provided in 1853–4 not another Crystal Palace, such as Dublin, New York, Copenhagen, Munich, Amsterdam, and Breslau, among other cities, had built or were building, but an example of

118. H.-P.-F. Labrouste: Paris,
Bibliothèque Nationale, Reading Room, 1862-8

mixed construction. The great iron-and-glass arched interiors were all but completely masked externally by a very conventional masonry shell. It was not until the Paris Exposition of 1878 that iron and glass were frankly exposed and decoratively treated on the exterior of such a structure in France (see Chapter 16). The curve of enthusiasm for iron was evidently taking a downward dip; in Britain the Age of Cast Iron came to an end even more suddenly and much more dramatically than in France.

In 1855 Sir Henry Cole, the prime mover of the Great Exhibition of 1851, had to provide on the estate at Brompton, in the part of London now called South Kensington that the Commissioners had just acquired from the proceeds

of the Exhibition, temporary housing for the collections that were being formed by the Government's Department of Practical Art. Having to build in great haste and in war-time, it is perhaps not surprising that Cole employed, properly speaking, neither an architect nor an engineer, but allowed the Edinburgh contracting firm of C. D. Young & Son to design as well as erect the structure subject to some nominal control from the engineer Sir William Cubitt (1785-1861). It was certainly a surprising product of a Government agency devoted to raising the standard of 'art-manufactures'! Although we can today appreciate some of the practical virtues of this edifice as a Museum of Science and Art, it must be admitted that it was inferior even to the general contemporary run of prefabricated structures to which it belongs technically. Christened the 'Brompton Boilers' by George Godwin (1815–88), editor of the *Builder*, it roused a chorus of disapproval as loud if not as wide-spread as the Crystal Palace had done of approval five years before.

After this time British and Continental interest in iron construction waned rapidly; for fifteen years or so exposed iron was chiefly exploited in the commercial façades of the United States, themselves now more and more masonry-like in scale and in detailing, as has been noted. Structural steel began to be used here and there from the early sixties, but the serious beginnings of the Age of Steel lay a quarter of a century ahead (see Chapter 14).

At least in England, its principal home, the Age of Cast Iron, so paradoxically interrelated with the Gothic Revival in its very early stages, came to an end in considerable part because of the triumph of the Gothic Revival around 1850 (see Chapter 10). For several decades the characteristic new architectural developments were stylistic rather than technical. Yet it was the later theories – not the practice – of a French medievalist, Viollet-le-Duc, which played a great part in the renewed interest in the frank use of metal on the Continent in the eighties and nineties (see Chapter 16).

PART TWO

1850-1900

CHAPTER 8

SECOND EMPIRE PARIS, UNITED ITALY,

AND IMPERIAL-AND-ROYAL VIENNA

Many historians, in despair, have merely labelled the period after 1850 'Eclectic' as if earlier periods of architecture – and notably all the preceding hundred years since 1750 – had not also been eclectic, although admittedly to a lesser degree. Within the eclecticism of the late eighteenth and early nineteenth centuries there can readily be distinguished the two major stylistic divisions with which Part One has dealt separately (in Chapters 1-5 and in Chapter 6, respectively). So also in the fifties, sixties, and seventies two principal camps are discernible among the architects. Their programmes were less clear than in the previous half century, and in one case much less widely accepted internationally. Yet the High Victorian Gothic of England, taken together with the later Neo-Gothic elsewhere, on the one hand, and what may be loosely called the international Second Empire mode on the other, subsume between them a fair part of the more conspicuous architectural production of the third quarter of the century.

Both the Victorian Gothic of this period and the Second Empire mode were 'high' phases of style. Perhaps for that reason neither of them controlled, in the way that Romantic Classicism had done in the earlier decades of the century, all or even any very extensive segments of

building activity; yet between them they gave colour to a very considerable proportion of it. The obvious stigmata of one or of the other, or even of both – external polychromy and high mansard roofs, respectively – are to be found on such modest things as mills and working-class housing blocks as well as on major public monuments. The High Victorian Gothic first developed in Anglican ecclesiastical architecture and always carried with it a rather churchy flavour – sometimes quite ludicrously, as in the case of Gothic distilleries, Gothic public-houses, and Gothic sewage plants. Continental Neo-Gothic was more largely confined to churches, especially in France. The international Second Empire mode found its inspiration in the grandiose extension of a palace in Paris; something of the Parisian and even the palatial clung to it when it was used – as often in the non-French world – for such things as factories and modest suburban villas.

Both the Victorian Gothic and the Second Empire had definite national homes, yet both were also full of elements of Italian origin. In that respect the High Victorian phase of the fifties and sixties was somewhat analogous to the Germanic *Rundbogenstil*, as well as being the direct heir of the earlier and more puristic Gothic Revival of the forties in England. Often the

Second Empire mode was even more Italianate, since it was in the main but a pompous modulation of the earlier Renaissance Revival. The one had its roots in the Picturesque, but it differed from earlier Picturesque manifestations in being a 'style' – or very nearly such – not merely the reflection of a point of view. The other had roots not only in Romantic Classicism but also farther back in the High Renaissance and the Baroque; some qualities of those earlier styles were both continued and revived. But neither High Victorian Gothic nor Second Empire were 'revivals' in the sense of those of the first half of the century; they lived with a vigorous nineteenth-century life of their own, not one borrowed from the past. In both cases one may more properly say that they *had* revived.

The Second Empire mode was the heir, or at least the successor, of the last universal style of the western world, the Romantic Classical. Moreover its wide international sway was hardly terminated by the end of Napoleon III's reign in France any more than its beginning had waited for his enthronement. Concerning that sway it should be noted, however, that considered as a definite 'style' the Second Empire mode is very far from characterizing as much of French production in this age as of that in several other countries. Indeed, somewhat paradoxically, its actual initiation may almost be said to have occurred outside France and before the political Second Empire actually began in 1852. In this chapter and the next, certain alternative developments in succession to the earlier Renaissance Revival have been associated with the Second Empire mode, sometimes a bit arbitrarily perhaps, for lack of a more appropriate place to deal with them.

Although France was less affected by the Picturesque in the first half of the nineteenth century than England, the Renaissance Revival had permitted some straying from the more rigid paths of Romantic Classicism in the thirties and forties (see Chapters 3 and 6).

The earliest French work of the twenties that may seem of Italian Renaissance inspiration is very severe and flat, approximating occasionally the effects of the German *Rundbogenstil* yet consistently disdaining that mode's tendencies towards either medievalism or originality in detail. Gradually, under Louis Philippe, there were changes: on the one hand, there arose an interest in later periods of the Italian Renaissance; on the other, there came an increasing and less peripheral use of sixteenth-century and even later native models. Common to both these developments was an evident desire for richer and more plastic effects.[1] What above all distinguishes the mature Second Empire mode, even more in other countries than in France, is the elaboration of three-dimensional composition by the employment of visible mansard roofs and of pavilions at the ends and centres of buildings, these last capped either with especially tall straight-sided mansards or, even more characteristically, with convex or concave ones. Such features are rare before 1850 in France and almost unknown elsewhere.[2]

The return of the mansard in France is harder to document than its appearance as a new element of architectural composition in other countries, for in France it had never passed out of use as a practical device for providing usable attics. With the increasing emulation of sixteenth-century French models in the second quarter of the century tall roofs of a more medieval sort began to be used with some frequency. Biet's 'Maison de François I' of 1825 did not have them; but ten years later they are very prominent on the *François I* house Dusillion built in the Rue Vaneau. Moreover, Lesueur in the late thirties could hardly avoid their use when extending the sixteenth-century Hôtel de Ville [42]. As noted earlier, it seems to have been H.-A.-G. de Gisors, at the École Normale Supérieure built in 1841-7, who first re-introduced on a prominent building mansards of seventeenth- or early eighteenth-century character, and in association with detailing that suggests, vaguely at least, the *style Louis XIV*. By the late forties the use of such mansards was fairly common in France, although they rarely received much emphasis. As early as 1848 they were introduced in America.

Had Dusillion in 1849–51 built the mansarded mansion for T. H. Hope[3] in Paris rather than in London therefore, or the Danish-born but Paris-schooled Detlef Lienau (1818–87)[4] his mansarded Hart M. Shiff house of the same date in France rather than in New York, neither would be considered especially notable today, as is equally true of the slightly earlier mansarded houses in Boston by Lemoulnier and in Philadelphia by Notman. But these novel features, moderate enough by French standards, suggested to the English and the Americans a way by which edifices of Renaissance character could be given something of the bold silhouette that high pointed roofs provide for Victorian Gothic structures. Like Barry's loggia-topped towers and his corner chimneys, mansards appealed directly to the mid century's characteristic desire to break sharply away from the flat-surfaced, and nearly flat-topped, cubic blocks of Romantic Classicism. Pavilion composition offered a similar resource for the plastic modelling of façades.

In 1851, following immediately after the Hope house, came the designing of the Great Western Hotel at Paddington in London by the Hardwicks. This was still, one should note, before the Second Empire actually began in France. Gawky though this hotel is, and very uncertain in its use of French precedent, contemporaries generally recognized its inspiration as derived from the period of Louis XIV. The complex massing and the broken skyline, with roofs of different heights and pavilion-like towers at the ends, are much more obviously a premonition of the Second Empire mode in the form the world outside France would shortly adopt it than were the English and American houses of a few years earlier. Unlike Dusillion, Lemoulnier, and Lienau, the architects of the Great Western Hotel, recognized masters of the dying Greek Revival as well as of the rising Gothic and Renaissance Revivals, were not French-trained.

If the international Second Empire mode had thus, in a sense, beginnings outside France, it is nevertheless true that its spiritual headquarters was in Paris. The prestige of the new Emperor's capital, a prestige rapidly regained after more than a generation of desuetude, quite as much as the visual appeal of multiple mansards and pavilioned façades, explains the world-wide success of the mode during, and even well after, the eighteen years that the Second Empire lasted.

It was in 1852 that Napoleon, then Prince-President, made himself Emperor. He had already signalized, a few months earlier, his ambition to revive the splendours not alone of his uncle's rule but those of earlier French monarchs by his decision to complete the Louvre[5] – or more accurately to connect the Louvre with the Tuileries. This was a project over which generations of architects had struggled on paper and at which several abortive starts had already been made. Visconti received the commission, not Duban, who had been engaged since 1848 on what was proving a highly controversial restoration of the old Louvre. Visconti was chosen not for his reputation as a private architect but largely because a succession of public projects for new library buildings in Paris that he had been asked to prepare under Louis Philippe and even under the Second Republic had all fallen through, and it was felt he deserved an important commission from the State. Perhaps also his Tomb of Napoleon I at the Invalides made him especially sympathetic to the emperor Napoleon III.

A viable scheme for the New Louvre was produced by the sixty-year-old Visconti with very great rapidity. Counting on the great size of the Cour du Carrousel to obscure the awkward lack of parallelism between the Louvre and the Tuileries, he planned two hollow blocks extending westward at either end of the existing western front of the old Louvre. Beyond these blocks narrower wings, in part built already, would connect with the two ends of the Tuileries Palace in which French rulers usually lived. In the middle of the court fronts of the side blocks there were to be large pavilions, echoing Le Mercier's in the centre of the west wing of the old Louvre, and other smaller pavilions to mark the salient corners towards the Place du Carrousel. Although the new constructions were intended to house various things – two ministries, a library, stables for the Tuileries, etc. – they were designed comprehensively with no specific indication of what would go on behind the long walls and inside the various pavilions. The New Louvre was not a palace or Royal residence; but like the old Louvre, which by this time housed several disparate activities – most notably the chief art gallery of France – it was meant to be representationally palatial.

In 1853 Visconti died and H.-M. Lefuel (1810-80), a pupil of Huyot, took over. Lefuel very much enriched the design and thereby provided the prime Parisian exemplar of the Second Empire mode, at least as the world outside France came to adopt it in the late fifties and sixties. Heavily though Lefuel leaned on the precedents provided by the various sections of the old Louvre, it is important to stress that his design did not represent, in the way of the first half of the century, a specific 'revival'. For one thing, the old Louvre, begun by Pierre Lescot in François I's reign and carried forward by a succession of architects in the next four hundred years, offered a wide range of suggestions but no one consistent model. The most characteristic and striking features of the New Louvre, the corner pavilions, were those that were most eclectic in inspiration and in their total effect most nearly original [119]. No part of the old Louvre is as boldly plastic as these pavilions with their rich applied orders set far forward of the wall-plane; only Le Mercier's Pavillon de l'Horloge on the old Louvre offered precedent for the great height of all the new pavilion roofs and in particular for the convex mansards, like square domes, over the central pavilions flanking the Cour du Carrousel.

Sumptuous as was Goujon's sculptural investiture of the earliest work in the court of the old Louvre, it was also delicate in scale and very flat; much of the sculptural decoration of the new pavilions follows Goujon fairly closely, but even more – some indeed nearly in the round – is so bombastically plastic as almost to justify the term 'Neo-Baroque'. Although there is actual early-seventeenth-century precedent for most of their individual details, the very bold stone dormers set against the high straight mansards of the corner pavilions are particularly novel in effect. For the next thirty years, and even longer, such features of the New Louvre would be imitated all over the western world yet, paradoxically, they had much less influence in France and almost none in Paris.

As far as the outside world – particularly perhaps England and the United States, but hardly less Latin America – was concerned the New Louvre was the prime architectural glory of Second Empire Paris and the symbol, *par excellence,* of cosmopolitan modernity. Burghers in Amsterdam and Montreal, vacationers in Yorkshire and silver-miners in the Rocky Mountains all expected to find echoes of it in the luxurious new hotels they frequented; Latin Americans continued to emulate it even into the twentieth century. Yet in the real Paris of the Second Empire, the Paris which is

119. L.-T.-J. Visconti and H.-M. Lefuel:
Paris, New Louvre, 1852-7

largely still extant today, the New Louvre is but one prominent structure among many and, as has been said, not even a very typical one.

The first Napoleon had had no time to carry out any considerable urbanistic reorganization of his French capital. But for the goodwill of his successors, notably Louis Philippe, the architectural projects that he was able to initiate would never have been brought to completion. His nephew, however, vowed to peace and not to war, had nearly two decades in which to build. Well before his reign began, moreover, he had definitely made up his mind to replan Paris more drastically than any great city had ever been replanned before.[6] Only a few fine squares, the Champs Élysées, and the Rue de Rivoli remain in Paris from earlier campaigns of urban extension and replanning; but the Paris of the Second Empire, the Paris of the boulevards and the great avenues, is the urbanistic masterwork of the third quarter of the nineteenth century, a period notably deficient in comparable achievement almost everywhere else except in Vienna.

For all the elaboration of the individual monuments with which the focal points of Napoleon III's Paris were ornamented, their settings are generally more distinguished than the 'jewels' mounted in them; an exception, of course, is the Place de l'Étoile where, however, the jewel was inherited from an earlier period [10]. This is because of the high standard of design that was maintained in the general run of new blocks of flats[6a] that lined the *places*, the boulevards, and the avenues [120]. Since in Second Empire Paris the urban totality is more significant than the individual buildings, and since over the years of the Empire – or for that matter down even to the eighties – there was very little stylistic development, the Parisian production of this period may well be presented more topographically than chronologically, as if one were outlining a tour[7] of its splendours.

There is one extant railway station of some distinction belonging to the period at which to arrive. Yet this station, Hittorff's Gare du Nord designed in 1861 and built in 1826-5, is perhaps less advanced than Duquesney's Gare de l'Est, which was just being completed as the Second Empire opened [44]. The flat Ionic pilasters of the façade and the great archivolt-surrounded openings between them are evidence of the firm resistance that Hittorff's generation put up against the lusher tastes of the mid century as expressed in Lefuel's work on the New Louvre. Even more characteristically Romantic Classical, and probably finer though less famous than the Gare du Nord, was Cendrier's Gare de Lyon, since demolished, which had been built almost a decade earlier at the same time as his Palais de l'Industrie in the early fifties.

Proceeding from Hittorff's station one strikes immediately the characteristic broad straight streets, often lined with trees, that were the new Second Empire arteries of Paris. The continuous ranges of grey[7a] stone buildings, their even skyline crowned with inconspicuous mansards, generally include shops below and always contain flats above. They are so designed as to attract very little attention to the individual structures,[8] almost as little as do the separate houses in London terraces. There is much less irregularity of outline than along Nash's Regent Street, for example, and a general consistency in the size and spacing of the windows. There is also very little noticeable variety in the handling of the conventional apparatus of academic detail so crisply carved in fine limestone. Even where, by great exception, some bolder architect such as Viollet-le-Duc used more original detail, the unity of character is

120. A.-F. Mortier: Paris, block of flats, 11 Rue de Milan, c. 1860

barely disturbed, so consistent are the basic patterns of the façades [170].

Since the plan of Paris has remained basically radial, the visitor has the choice of proceeding circumferentially along one of the lines of outer or inner boulevards or of turning inwards to the centre. It is more profitable, on the whole, to advance centripetally, for the outer boulevards are generally very monotonous. The Île de la Cité was the original core of Paris; the east-and-west axis of the Louvre, extended westward along the Champs Élysées all the way to the Étoile, already provided a central tract parallel to the Seine; the new cross axis was to be a north and south artery running from the Gare de l'Est to the Observatoire. On the Île the vast complex of the Palais de Justice, whose restoration and extension had been undertaken by Duc as early as 1840, received a notable Second Empire ornament in its western block, facing the Place d'Harcourt, which was built by Duc assisted by E.-T. Dommey (1801–72) in 1857–68. Rationalistic in its structural expression and Classical in most of its detailing, this façade and the hall behind it reflect the tastes of the period in the heavy scale of the parts and the rather cranky – and certainly studied – awkwardness of the modelling of the various conventional elements of the orders and minor features of detail. Duc's earlier work at the Palais de Justice, on the other hand, was detailed with very great grace and elegance, it may be noted.

The principal Second Empire construction on the east-and-west axis of Paris, the New Louvre, has been described already. Along the north side of the Louvre the Rue de Rivoli was extended eastward in 1851–5 the entire length of the palace with no change in the original Percier and Fontaine design except for the addition of high quadrantal mansards throughout the entire length of the street and its subsidiaries. Even a large new hotel⁹ was forced into this framework. Yet because of its island site, the high rounded roofs give this block as it is usually seen from the Place du Théâtre Français to the north something of the new plasticity; it thus provided eventually an appropriate terminus to the Avenue de l'Opéra, after that was finally completed under the Third Republic.

Facing the east side of the Louvre, Hittorff balanced the restored Gothic front of Saint-Germain-l'Auxerrois with the new front of the Mairie du Louvre built in 1857–61. Characteristic of this period in France is the avoidance of Gothic detail on this secular façade in favour of something vaguely *François I*; yet the pattern of the front of the church is carefully repeated, even to the rose-window in the high-pitched gable, and the new tower by Ballu, on axis between the Church and the Mairie, is Gothic.

Up to the Rond Point the Champs Élysées is flanked by open areas on the sides and decorated by fountains and other features designed by Hittorff (see Chapter 3). At the Rond Point there are a few very pretentious *hôtels particuliers*, but beyond that the avenue was built up – or more accurately, for the most part, would eventually be built up – like a very broad boulevard flanked by large blocks of flats with shops and cafés below. In the wooded area on the left between the main axis, the river, and the new quarter which had taken its name 'François I' from Biet's house, lay the Jardin d'Hiver of 1847 and the Palais de l'Industrie of 1853–4. Here also is the Rotonde des Panoramas of 1857 by G.-J.-A. Davioud (1823–81). Around the Arc de l'Étoile, at the far end of the Champs Élysées, are ranged pairs of dignified houses; these were designed by Hittorff with the collaboration of Rohault de Fleury in 1855 and executed in 1857–8 in a mode so academic as to be almost a revival of the *style Louis XVI* [10]. The general layout of the *place* was determined by Haussmann, expanding a much earlier scheme of Hittorff's.

What is most notable in all this mid-nineteenth-century construction along the main axis of the city is the continuity of taste between the Second Empire period and the period that preceded it. The only real echo of the New Louvre was in the big private houses round the Rond Point.

The Avenue de l'Opéra, extending northwestward from the Place du Théâtre Français, has become, since its completion in 1878, the major cross axis, rather than the earlier Boulevard Sébastopol to the east. The Place de l'Opéra, with a short spur of the avenue at its south end, was laid out in 1858 [121]; and the façades of the buildings around it began

to go up in 1860 from the designs of Rohault de Fleury[10] and Henri Blondel (1832-97). The Opéra[11] (more properly Académie Nationale de Musique) - after the New Louvre the most conspicuous product of the Second Empire - was begun in 1861 from the design with which J.-L.-C. Garnier (1825-98), a pupil of Lebas who also worked briefly for Viollet-le-Duc, won the second competition held in that year. Although the Garnier design is often thought to be particularly characteristic of the taste of the Imperial couple, it was actually very unpopular with the Empress Eugénie; she had expected the project of her friend Viollet-le-Duc to be accepted and was furious when it failed to win. Substantially completed externally by 1870, the Opéra was not finally finished and opened until January 1875, so that neither Napoleon III nor Eugénie ever entered it.

Here, at its heart, the contrast between setting and monument in Second Empire Paris is at its most extreme, even though this setting is far richer and more plastic than that provided by the severely flat houses that surround the Arc de l'Étoile. Just as there, however, the use of a giant order on all the big blocks that form the *place* reveals the distinctly academic taste of the leading French architects in this period; but Blondel's rounded pavilions, where two major streets come in on either side at an angle, provide an almost Baroque elaboration in the grouping of the various masses by which the complex space is defined [121]. Certainly the result is very different from the large open areas surrounded by discrete blocks of plain geometrical shape favoured by Romantic Classicism.

The Opéra is sumptuous in a rather different way from the New Louvre [122]. Yet in Garnier's work, as in Lefuel's, a generically Neo-Baroque effect is achieved with elements mostly High Renaissance in origin, but here Italian rather than French. The richly coloured marbles, the admirably placed sculpture by

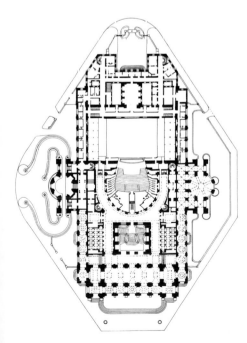

121 *(opposite)*. Charles Rohault de Fleury
and Henri Blondel: Paris, Place de l'Opéra, 1858-64
(before completion of the Avenue de l'Opéra)

122 and 123. J.-L.-C. Garnier: Paris, Opéra, 1861-74

Carpeaux, and above all the fashion in which the
masses pile up – from the ornate colonnade
crowning the main façade, through the half-
dome which expresses the auditorium externally, to the tall stage-house at the rear – is
much richer plastically than the somewhat
repetitive scheme of the New Louvre. The
whole, moreover, is made fully three-dimensional by the comparable organization of the
major elements at the sides and on the rear.
Thus Garnier provided a visual equivalent to
the complex ordering of his extremely elaborate
plan, a plan the undoubted virtues of which
can be fully appreciated only on paper [123].
Inside the Opéra the great staircase, the foyer,

and the actual auditorium drip with somewhat brassy gold and the profusion of detail has a curiously un-Renaissance spikiness and lumpiness [124]. This quality underlines how un-archaeological was Garnier's approach, how responsive he was (perhaps unconsciously) to the new tastes of the mid century that had produced the High Victorian[12] Gothic in England in the previous decade and fostered generally the international success of the Second Empire mode. When Eugénie asked him what the 'style' of the Opéra was - *Louis XIV, Louis XV, Louis XVI* - he replied with both tact and accuracy: 'C'est du Napoléon III'.

Like the lushness of the New Louvre, Garnier's lushness has an undeniably parvenu quality characteristic of the time and place; but the pace he set, however much emulated all over the world in later opera houses,[12a] and the peculiar capacity he showed for satisfying the taste for bombastic luxury of the third quarter of the century were never equalled by other architects, least of all by French ones. In the twin theatres flanking the Place du Châtelet,[13] which were built in 1860-2, Davioud, the architect of the Rotonde des Panoramas, made little attempt to vie with Garnier's Opéra; but they are considerably more successful in their own right than is the Vaudeville in the Boulevard des Capucines of 1872 by A.-J. Magne (1816-85), which does. Garnier's own Panorama Français of 1882 at 251 Rue Saint-Honoré had only a modest façade to the street.

Only one other work of Garnier himself rivals the Opéra, his Casino at Monte Carlo of 1878. The fine site that this occupies somewhat makes up for its tawdry finish in painted stucco, and the two-towered façade towards the bay has a properly festive air. The Casino and Baths he built at Vittel in 1882, his Observatory at Nice, and the Cercle de la Librairie of 1880 in the Boulevard Saint-Germain in Paris are considerably quieter in design. The Palais

124. J.-L.-C. Garnier: Paris, Opéra, foyer, 1861-74

125. H.-J. Espérandieu:
Marseilles, Palais Longchamps, 1862–9

Longchamps[14] of 1862–9 in Marseilles by
H.-J. Espérandieu (1829–74), who had worked
for Questel and for Léon Vaudoyer, two palatial
museum blocks joined by a curved colonnade
above an elaborate cascade, is more Neo-
Baroque than most work of the period [125];
but much of the credit should go to the sculptor
Bartholdi whose earlier fountain project
Espérandieu took over.

Despite what has been said of the houses at
the Rond Point, most Second Empire mansions
in Paris, at least those built by leading architects,
tend to be rather restrained in their general
design and often quite archaeologically correct
in their detailing. They are likely, moreover, to
follow French seventeenth- or eighteenth-
century models rather than those of sixteenth-
or seventeenth-century Italy. Already, in the
Hôtel de Pontalba, Visconti had copied Versailles closely in the interiors, while his exterior
followed the line of the early eighteenth-century
hôtels particuliers. (This was drastically remodelled in the eighties.) Labrouste, in the
Hôtel Fould, 29–31 Rue de Berri, which was

built in 1856–8, was rather plausibly Louis XIII;
while Alfred Armand (1805–88), a pupil of
Leclerc and a frequent collaborator with
Pellechet, in designing the Hôtel Pereire and
its twin in the Place Pereire about 1855
approached the *style Louis XVI* as closely as
Hittorff did round the Étoile. Nevertheless,
study of Parisian exemplars inspired many
foreign architects to design houses that could
hardly be anything else but Second Empire.

This is largely explained by the special
character of the publications[15] of C.-D. Daly
(1811–93), a pupil of Duban, and of P.-V.
Calliat (1801–81), a pupil of A.-L.-T. Vaudoyer,
by which current French work of this period
chiefly became known to the outside world.
Almost as was the case at the opening of the
century, when the volumes illustrating Prix de
Rome projects made the higher aspirations of
French architects better known to students
abroad than their ordinary practice, the publications of this later day seem to have focused
attention on certain aspects only of the French
architectural scene, aspects prominent enough,

but not altogether characteristic as regards public monuments and dominant official taste. Without knowledge of the French architectural past, without the inhibitions instilled early in French architects by their training at the École des Beaux-Arts, foreign architects readily derived from published sources a Second Empire mode considerably bolder than was generally approved for public use in French academic circles and made it very much their own. Even in public architecture foreigners evidently saw current work with different eyes from the French.

For example, the Tribunal de Commerce on the Île de la Cité, an agency provided in 1858–64 with a building of its own instead of mere quarters in the Bourse, was supposed by French contemporaries to express in its detailing the Emperor's personal enthusiasm for the *quattrocento* buildings that he had lately seen in Brescia. But posterity, like foreigners when the Tribunal was new, notes in this work of A.-N. Bailly (1810–92) the conspicuous Second Empire mansards and the almost Neo-Baroque dome – which at Haussmann's insistence was added to close the vista down the new north-south artery – not the uncharacteristically flat and delicately detailed façades. Far finer is the front of that section of the École des Beaux-Arts facing the Seine which was built by Bailly's master Duban in 1860–2, finer and doubtless also truer to the most exigent taste of the day. Rather directly expressive of its interior uses – it houses exhibition galleries, etc. – the detailing of this façade is quite original without being at all cranky like Duc's on the Palais de Justice, and the whole very subtle in composition [126]. Much of the cold severity characteristic of the previous half-century remains; but Duban was clearly trying to be creative, not archaeological, so that one cannot properly apply stylistic names from the past, not even to the extent that it is possible to do so in the case of the New Louvre

126. J.-F. Duban:
Paris, École des Beaux-Arts, 1860–2

and the Opéra. However, such high distinction of design as Duban achieved here was rather rare in Second Empire Paris; it parallels in this period the equally exceptional distinction of Henri Labrouste's Bibliothèque Sainte-Geneviève of the forties.[15a]

The accepted range of stylistic inspiration was so wide that it is often only a certain syncretism that gives buildings of this period, nominally in any one of half a dozen 'styles', a recognizably contemporary flavour. So also new methods of construction, rather than superseding masonry in toto and thereby demanding original expression as in Victor Baltard's Central Markets, were more characteristically fused with it, as in the reading-rooms of Labrouste's libraries. Of these only the later, that in the Bibliothèque Nationale, was built under the Second Empire [118]. Except for the Salle de Travail of 1861–9 and the Magasin or stacks, both so exciting to posterity, most of Labrouste's other work at this institution, begun in 1855, is as derivative as his private houses; for the most part it is actually hard to say where the old seventeenth- and eighteenth-century buildings stop and his nineteenth-century additions and those of his successor J.-L. Pascal (1837-1920) begin.

Despite the increasing use of metal in all sorts of buildings, there was undoubtedly less sympathy for it than earlier, and hence less success in finding appropriate expressions for its qualities (see Chapter 7). By exception, however, the Central Markets in Lyons of 1858 by Antoine Desjardins (1814-82), a pupil of Duban, have a somewhat Labrouste-like elegance in the arched and pierced metal principals spanning the three naves not equalled in Baltard's so much larger Central Markets in Paris that were lately demolished.

In church architecture something like full eclecticism reigned in Paris under Napoleon III, although Gothic was most popular in the provinces. The new Parisian churches generally occupy focal points where major avenues join or boulevards change direction; but, like the Opéra, they have little visual relation to the sober settings provided by the blocks of flats among which they are placed. Instead, each one seems intended to illustrate an alternative mode quite different from the standard urban vernacular of the day.

Saint-François-Xavier in the Boulevard Montparnasse was begun by the elderly Lusson in 1861 and finished by T.-F.-J. Uchard (1809-91) in 1875. With its basilican plan and cold Early Renaissance detail, this might well have been built under Louis Philippe. Saint-Jean-de-Belleville by Lassus, on the other hand, begun in 1854 and completed in 1859 after his death, while larger and rather better built than his churches of the forties, hardly represents any advance over Gau's Sainte-Clotilde, completed by Ballu only two years earlier. Neo-Gothic could hardly be duller. However, Saint-Denys-de-l'Estrée [169], the parish church of the suburb of St-Denis, designed by Lassus's associate and successor Viollet-le-Duc[16] in

1860 and built in 1864-7, is more comparable in quality to the contemporary High Victorian Gothic churches of England (see Chapter 11).

Victor Baltard's church of Saint-Augustin, also of 1860-7, is not located, like the Gothic edifices by Lassus and Viollet-le-Duc, in a working-class district or suburb, but occupies a very prominent if awkwardly narrow triangular site in the Boulevard Malesherbes near its intersection with the Boulevard Haussman. Considering the success of his Central Markets, it is not surprising that Baltard used iron here; but he did so with much less consistency and thoroughness than Boileau had done at Saint-Eugène (see Chapter 7). The arched iron principals of the roof accord very ill with the Romanesquoid-Renaissance design of the masonry structure below. The front, with its great rose window, is somewhat more effective. At least it provides a strong urbanistic focus among the standardized ranges of blocks of flats that line the boulevards in this quarter. Two other big Parisian churches are similar in quality although quite different in appearance. Ballu, in addition to finishing Sainte-Clotilde, built both Saint-Ambroise in the Boulevard Voltaire, which is certainly more acceptably Romanesque than Saint-Augustin, and also La Trinité in the Rue de la Chaussée d'Antin, which is much less plausibly *François I* than his later work at the Hôtel de Ville. La Trinité was built in 1861-7, Saint-Ambroise in 1863-9. Both are vast and pretentious, but neither has much positive character. Like so many comparable examples of the eclecticism of this period in other countries, it is by their faults and not by any characteristic virtues that they are recognizable as products of the 1850s and 60s.

Two Romanesquoid churches less prominently located, and hence less well known, are considerably more interesting. One is the parish church of Charenton, Seine, built by Claude Naissant (1801-79) in 1857-9; this is clearly composed and detailed with a somewhat eclectic elegance not unworthy of Labrouste or Duban. Much larger is Notre-Dame-de-la-Croix in the Rue Julien-Lacroix in the Menilmontant quarter of Paris. Built by L.-J.-A. Héret (1821–99), a pupil of Lebas, in 1862–80, this is a cruciform edifice with the vaulting ribs all of openwork iron like those of Saint-Augustin. For archaeological accuracy it compares not unfavourably with Questel's church at Nimes, begun some twenty years earlier, in the detailing of the masonry.

The only big Paris church of the sixties of much real distinction – the only French church, for that matter – is Saint-Pierre-de-Montrouge at the intersection of the Avenue du Maine and the Avenue d'Orléans. This was built by J.-A.-E. Vaudremer (1829–1914), a pupil of Blouet and Gilbert, in 1864–70. Romanesque and Early Christian – perhaps more specifically Syrian – in inspiration,[17] this basilica is notably direct in its structural expression, nobly scaled, expressively composed, and simplified almost to the point of crudity in its detailing [127]. Vaudremer's Santé Prison off the Boulevard Arago in Paris, which was commissioned in 1862 and built in 1865–85, is also Romanesquoid or at least in a sort of very simple *Rundbogenstil*. The still quite Durandesque character of this prison illustrates Vaudremer's close linkage, through the work of his two masters, who had both specialized in

127. J.-A.-E. Vaudremer:
Paris, Saint-Pierre-de-Montrouge, 1864–70

designing prisons and asylums under Louis Philippe, with the classicizing rationalism of 1800. His much later Lycées of the eighties, Buffon and Molière in Paris and those at Grenoble and Montauban, on the other hand, reflect the medievalizing rationalism of Viollet-le-Duc (see Chapter 11).

Vaudremer's work may have had some influence, around 1870, on the American Richardson, who was still a student in Paris when Saint-Pierre-de-Montrouge was begun (see Chapter 13). However, no significant line of development led forward in France from his sort of church design. In a smaller and later Parisian church, Notre-Dame in the Rue d'Auteuil of 1876-83, Vaudremer himself showed no further development of his personal style, though the interior here is not unimpressive in scale and proportions.

The vast and prominent church of the Sacré-Cœur on Montmartre in Paris was begun by Paul Abadie[18] (1812-84), a pupil of Leclerc, in 1874, well after the Second Empire was over, and largely finished before the end of the century by the younger Magne (Lucien, 1849-1916). This is Romanesque in inspiration, too, but painfully archaeological – 'painfully', because its architect, in carrying out the restoration of his principal medieval exemplar, Saint-Front at Périgueux, seems to have sought to provide 'precedent' for several of the features that he introduced here! Yet the bold exploitation of the remarkable site of this church, dominating Paris from the heights of Montmartre, and the bubble-like silhouette of its cluster of domes when seen from a distance give the Sacré-Cœur positive qualities lacking in most other French ecclesiastical work of the later nineteenth century except Saint-Pierre-de-Montrouge.

Architecture in France had been a highly centralized profession ever since the late seventeenth century. Under Louis XV a few provincial cities showed some capacity for independent activity, but this subsided during the unproductive years that followed the Revolution. Except to a certain extent in Lyons and Marseilles, local activity did not revive very notably in the first half of the nineteenth century. Under the Second Empire most French cities still remained content to follow the lead of Paris. There is hardly a large provincial town which did not – to stress first the positive side of the picture – lay out broad boulevards or straight avenues and line them with more or less successful versions of the *maisons de rapport* of Paris; on the negative side, the public buildings and churches were usually derived from, and too often very inferior to, obvious Parisian models.

In the centres of the biggest cities one can well believe that one has not left Paris. Occasionally, however, there are urbanistic entities which have more vitality than the rigidly controlled and tastefully restrained new squares and streets of the capital. The fairly modest square in front of the cathedral at Nantes, with its ranges of high-mansarded blocks, is a case in point. Better known is the rising slope of the Cannebière, continued in the Rue de Noailles and the Allées de Meilhan at Marseilles, with the columnar dignity of the Chamber of Commerce on the left near the Vieux Port at the bottom and the paired Gothic towers of Saint-Vincent-de-Paul closing the vista at the top. Public buildings in smaller cities sometimes have a rather illiterate sort of gusto in their boldly plastic massing and exuberantly coarse detailing closer to Second Empire work abroad than to that of Paris; these can have a theatrical charm not unlike the period flavour of Offenbach's operas, but they often date from well after 1870.

Espérandieu's Neo-Baroque Palais Longchamps at Marseilles has been mentioned [125]. Also at Marseilles is the enormous Romanesco-Byzantine cathedral of 1856-93, which was designed by the younger Vaudoyer (Léon,

1803–72), a pupil of his father and also of Lebas. Espérandieu became *inspecteur* on the job in 1858 and carried on the work after Vaudoyer's death. This is rather superior to Ballu's Paris churches, if not to Vaudremer's or so much Abadie's, but it is more striking plastically in its rather redundant combination of domed west towers, crossing dome, and transeptal domes; it is also exceptionally polychromatic for France. There is an almost High Victorian Gothic brashness in the treatment of the exterior walls with bands of alternately white and green stone. Here the aggressive assurance of the period speaks with an even louder voice than at the New Louvre and the Paris Opéra; this assurance is rivalled, moreover, by Espérandieu's own high-placed church of Notre-Dame-de-la-Garde, a major scenic accent of a boldness almost brazen.

The Marseilles Exchange, however, dominating its own tree-lined square, is rather similar to the Chamber of Commerce in the Cannebière as it rises among ranges of houses that are more Provençal than Parisian in the modesty of their painted stucco fronts. Originally begun in 1842 by Penchaud, the Exchange was largely built in 1852–60 by his pupil Coste, but its style remains *Louis Philippe* rather than Second Empire.

The great elaboration and consequent expensiveness of Second Empire modes of design, as generally executed in France in fine freestone, restricted their full exploitation to the capital and the largest provincial cities. There is a sort of economic striation, from the immense sums the Emperor and, after him, the authorities of the Third Republic – even though relatively impoverished – were willing to put into representational public construction at the top, through the level represented by what Parisian investors spent on blocks of flats or rich provincial cities on their principal monuments, down finally to the niggardly building budgets of small towns and villages. This striation provides a sort of analogue to the breakdown of that earlier unity which had been so marked and happy a characteristic of French architecture for at least a century and a half. That this breakdown was still relative in France is apparent when one turns to other countries where eclectic taste in this period was bolder and where the variation in expenditure on different sorts of buildings was at least as great.

French architectural prestige revived internationally in the fifties to remain surprisingly high for another two generations.[18a] However, the Second Empire mode was gradually succeeded internationally by another Parisian mode to which it is convenient to apply the name 'Beaux-Arts', from the École des Beaux-Arts out of whose instruction it stemmed. More and more foreigners went to Paris to study as the second half of the century wore on, until Paris became almost what Rome had been in the eighteenth century. In architectural education the influence of the École was especially strong in the New World; the training of English and most Continental architects was much less affected. The first two architectural schools to be founded in the United States, both by William Robert Ware (1832–1915) – himself, curiously enough, a practitioner of a fairly aggressive sort of Victorian Gothic (see Chapter 11) – that at the Massachusetts Institute of Technology in Boston opened in 1865 and the somewhat later school at Columbia University in New York, were both based on the methods of the École.[19] French winners of the Prix de Rome were increasingly imported to serve as teachers, and it was three generations later when the last of them left the United States. The influence of the École in Latin America was even more powerful, and the influence of its doctrines lasted in some countries well into the mid twentieth century.[20]

Both in the New World and the Old most cities grew like weeds in the third quarter of the century; the analogy is, indeed, a rather accurate one, for the growth was characteristically rank, uncontrolled, and destructive of earlier architectural amenities. Various European capitals, however, imitating Napoleon III's re-organization of Paris, took advantage of the clearing away of their fortifications to lay out something equivalent to the *grands boulevards*. Florence during the late sixties, for example, when it was for five years the capital of Italy, saw the laying out, following the basic plan of Giuseppe Poggi (1811-1901), of a range of avenues and squares that extend around the city to the east, north, and west on the site of the old walls. These districts, built up over the years 1865-77, display little or none of the new Second Empire afflatus. For the most part everywhere in Italy in this period the architecture is of generically Renaissance revival character. Only in the much later Piazza della Repubblica, carved out of the slummy heart of the old city in 1893-5, is there a heavy pomposity of scale that is curiously un-Florentine[20a] – the centre of nineteenth-century Athens might be Neo-Greek, but it was Munich, not Florence, that became characteristically Neo-Tuscan!

In the old Savoy capital of Turin, where the first half of the century had seen such notable urbanistic projects, a vigorous local tradition continued to control most of the new work.[21] However, at the farther side of the Piazza Carlo Felice the Porta Nuova Railway Station was built in 1866-8, as was mentioned in Chapter 3, by the engineer Mazzuchetti and the architect Ceppi in a rather original sort of *Rundbogenstil*. The vast iron and glass lunette at the front still provides a handsome termination to the long axis of the Via Roma, although the rear of the station has been rebuilt since the War. Along the Corso Vittorio Emmanuele II the earlier arcades of Promis were continued almost indefinitely; but the detailing of the façades grew continually richer in evident emulation of Second Empire Paris. This influence also affected the building up of the contiguous

quarter of the city. In the fine new square at the end of the Via Garibaldi, however, balancing the earlier Piazza Vittorio Veneto at the end of the Via Po, the Piazza dello Statuto opened in 1864, the façades by Giuseppe Bollati (1819-69) are not at all Parisian, but recall in a rather academic way the local Late Baroque of Juvarra. Especially effective, and rare in Turin, are the warm and tawny colours of the painted stucco walls here.

With the uniting of Italy and the eventual taking over of Rome as the capital of the kingdom of Italy on the downfall of Napoleon III in 1870, a tremendous expansion[22] of the old Papal city began. The two principal new streets extending eastward, the Via Venti Settembre and the Via Nazionale, were laid out in 1871 and built up over the next fifteen years. Vast and tawny-coloured like the Piazza dello Statuto in Turin, but much more varied in organization, is the Finance Ministry in the former street built by Raffaele Canevari (1825-1900) in 1870-7. Equally grand in scale and much more dignified are the quadrantal façades of the Esedra begun by Gaetano Koch (1849-1910) in 1880 at the head of the Via Nazionale facing Michelangelo's Santa Maria degli Angeli [128]. With the fountain by Alessandro Guerrieri and Mario Rubelli in the centre this provides a most impressive piece of late-nineteenth-century academic urbanism. It still offers a not altogether unworthy preface to the Baths of Diocletian – of which it actually occupies the site of the largest exedra – and to the new railway station [351], both so near, which epitomize between them the ancient and the modern worlds in the architecture of Rome.

Koch's Palazzo Boncampagni in the Via Vittorio Veneto, now the American Embassy, built in 1886-90, is also very dignified. It represents very well the occasional tendency in that decade towards restraint and sobriety in Renaissance design, a tendency that balances the contemporary stylistic development to-

128. Gaetano Koch: Rome, Esedra, begun 1880

wards the Neo-Baroque. In the Via Nazionale the two most prominent edifices[23] by Italian architects, the Palazzo delle Belle Arti of Pio Piacentini (1846–1928) built in 1878–82 and Koch's Banca d'Italia of 1889–92, are both quite academic in a respectable Renaissance way, and in the latter case impressively monumental as well. The same applies *a fortiori* to the two principal public edifices begun in Rome in the eighties – not the respectability, goodness knows, but the monumentality. The enormous Palazzo di Giustizia, in a new quarter across the Tiber, is an incredibly brash example of Neo-Baroque loaded down with heavy rustication, doubtless of Piranesian inspiration. This was designed by Giuseppe Calderini (1837–1916) in 1887 and built in 1888–1910 without the intended high mansards.

But the most overpowering new structure in Rome, dominating the whole city and blocking the view of both the ancient Forum and the Renaissance Campidoglio, is the Monument to Victor Emmanuel II, rising above the much enlarged Piazza Venezia at the head of the Corso. Largely the work of Count Giuseppe Sacconi (1854–1905),[24] who in 1884 won the third competition held for its design, this was begun in 1885 and continued after his death by Koch, Piacentini, and Manfredo Manfredi (1859–1927), being finally completed only in 1922 by Manfredi and others. Hardly Second Empire nor yet quite 'Beaux-Arts', this most pretentious of all nineteenth-century monuments well illustrates the final breakdown of the old standards of Romantic Classicism in Europe towards the end of the century. It can be compared only with Poelaert's Palace of Justice in Brussels, begun twenty years earlier, and entirely to the latter's advantage even as regards gargantuan assurance. But it was never really a typical work.

In general, Italian production of the second half of the century is of relatively slight interest; moreover, it often seriously upsets the balance of earlier urban entities by its heavy scale. The great exception, the one high-ranking Italian

129. Giuseppe Mengoni:
Milan, Galleria Vittorio Emmanuele, 1865-77

work of the period, is generally recognized to be the Galleria Vittorio Emmanuele II in Milan. In Genoa, behind the theatre, the Galleria Mazzini of 1871 also exceeds in length, in height, and in elaboration all the galleries and passages built in various European cities in the first half of the nineteenth century, yet it is not essentially very different from them in its scale or its detailing. The vast cruciform Galleria in Milan, however, extending from the Piazza del Duomo to the Piazza della Scala, with a great octagonal space at the crossing, is in concept and in its actual dimensions more a work of urbanism than of architecture [129]. Built with English capital by an English firm, the City of Milan Improvement Company Ltd, and even, presumably, with some English professional advice – M. D. Wyatt was a member of the English board – this tremendous project more than rivals the greatest Victorian railway stations of London in the height, if not the span, of its metal-and-glass roof. But the actual designing architect was Italian, Giuseppe Mengoni (1829-77), and the Galleria de Cristoforis provided him with at least a modest local prototype. Erected in 1865-77 and now completely restored to its pristine richness and elegance, the Galleria scheme involved the enlargement of the Piazza del Duomo and the lining of two

of its sides with related façades – executed only partly from Mengoni's designs – as also the regularization of the Piazza della Scala. Alessi's sixteenth-century Palazzo Marino, itself of almost Second Empire lushness, was enlarged to serve as the offices of the municipality and provided with a new façade in Alessi's extreme Mannerist style across one side of the square facing La Scala. This was carried out in 1888-90 by Luca Beltrami (1854-1933), who had studied in Paris at the École des Beaux-Arts, to serve as municipal offices.

Like all the other most prominent buildings of this period, Mengoni's Galleria makes its impression by its size, its elaboration of detail, and above all its unqualified assurance. From the triumphal-arch portal, rising as high as the nave of the medieval Duomo, to the gilded arabesques of the pilasters, all is obvious, expensive, and rather parvenu; yet the setting – at once so comfortable and so magnificent – that it provides for urban life, centre as it has always remained of so much Milanese activity, has not been equalled since.[25] The Galleria Umberto I in Naples is a late and rather inferior imitation whose ornate entrance most ungenerously overpowers the San Carlo Theatre across the street. This was built by Emmanuele Rocco (1825-?) in 1887-90.

After Paris the most extensive and sumptuous example of the re-organization of a great city carried out in this period is not in Italy but in Austria. Vienna had been relatively inactive architecturally in the first half of the nineteenth century under Francis I (see Chapter 2). His successor Francis Joseph, however, who came to the throne in 1848, set out in the following decades as *Kaiser und König* to see that his Imperial and Royal capitals should rival Napoleon III's Paris. In 1857 the fortifications surrounding the old city of Vienna were removed, and the following year Ludwig Förster (1797–1863) won the competition for the layout of the Ringstrasse that was to take their place.[25a] The execution of this project, with many modifications, took some thirty years [130]. Outside the actual walls there had been a wide glacis, and therefore the Ring could be developed not merely as a series of wide tree-lined boulevards like those of Paris but with large open spaces in which major public buildings were grouped. These edifices are even more various in style than the comparable ones in Paris, despite the fact that they were the work of a very closely knit group of architects. None of them is of

specifically Second Empire character, though the high mansards and the pavilion composition of the New Louvre were used fairly frequently on private buildings in Vienna and throughout the Austro-Hungarian Empire.

The earliest major project of Francis Joseph was the construction of the Arsenal, begun in 1849, where most of the leading architects of the period worked (see Chapter 2). All in various versions of the *Rundbogenstil*, this group of buildings culminates in the centrally placed Army Museum of 1856–77 by Förster and his Danish son-in-law Theophil von Hansen (1813–91). On this the very ornate detail is Byzantinesque and Saracenic in inspiration, yet it is not without a distinctive flavour that is unmistakably of this particular period. The brilliant polychromy of the red and yellow brick walls almost seems to echo, like Vaudoyer's Marseilles cathedral, the bolder effects of the contemporary High Victorian Gothic architects of England.

Ferstel's bank in the Herrengasse of 1856–60, also *Rundbogenstil*, has been mentioned earlier. The North Railway Station of 1858–65 by Theodor Hoffmann was *Rundbogenstil* of an

130. Vienna, Ringstrasse, begun 1858

even more ornate sort, with only a rather modest iron-and-glass-roofed shed set between its two massive masonry blocks. This was badly damaged by bombing in the last war but not totally destroyed. On the other hand, the South Station, built in 1869-73 by Wilhelm Flattich (1826-1900), a pupil of Leins in Stuttgart, was of rather conventional High Renaissance character.

The typical and, one may suppose, the preferred stylistic vehicle of most Viennese architects in these decades was, indeed, a rather rich High Renaissance mode. This, for example, Hansen used very effectively for the Palace of Archduke Eugene of 1865-7 and for the Palais Epstein at 1 Parlamentsring of 1870-3. He and Förster, and after Förster's death Hansen alone, as well as many other architects, employed this mode ubiquitously for various big blocks of flats along the Ring and elsewhere [130]. Good examples are such new hotels of the period as the former Britannia, still standing in the Schillerplatz, and the Donau, which once rose opposite the North Station. Both are by Heinrich Claus (1835-?) and Josef Grosz (1828-?) and were built in the early seventies. Their rather Barryesque raised end-pavilions, without mansards, and the heavily sumptuous detailing of the façades are most characteristic. The better known Sachers Hotel behind the Opera House, built by W. Fraenkel in 1876, is somewhat smaller and less lush, at least externally. The block at 8 Operngasse, built by Ehrmann in the early sixties, was topped with Parisian mansards, as are also the long blocks in the Reichsstrasse behind the Parlament and the University on either side of the Rathaus; these also have open arcades at their base somewhat like those in Turin.

As along the boulevards of Paris, there is a considerable homogeneity in the private architecture that lines the Ring and the many squares and streets that were built up at the same time. Only in the design of public monu-

131. Heinrich von Ferstel:
Vienna, Votivkirche, 1856-79

ments – often by much the same architects, it is worth noting – did a pompous and somewhat retardataire eclecticism rule. Consider the major works of Ferstel: his bank is *Rundbogenstil*; his Votivkirche [131] of 1856-79 is Gothic; his University something else again.

Ferstel's Gothic must be compared, not with the distinctly original High Victorian churches of its period in England (see Chapter 10), but with Gau's earlier Sainte-Clotilde in Paris (see Chapter 6). It is certainly a considerable improvement over that in the general justness of the scale and the plausible laciness of the fourteenth-century detail. But in English terms the Votivkirche is still Early rather than High Victorian. The painted decoration by J. Führich and others, somewhat more discreet than that in the chief *Rundbogenstil* churches of Vienna, relieves effectively the coldness usual in these big Continental examples of Neo-Gothic.

Ferstel's much later University of 1873-4, which stands next door to his church and balances Hansen's precisely contemporaneous Grecian Parlament (see Chapter 2), is a richly plastic pavilioned composition of generically Renaissance character. It also has a high convex mansard over the central block like those on the New Louvre, a feature echoed on the Justizpalast in the Schmerlingplatz, built by Alexander Wielemans (1843-1911) after the University in 1874-81. So much for the main works of one leading architect of the period. Not all Ferstel's contemporaries had quite so varied a stylistic repertory, however.

In Vienna, as in Paris, one of the most conspicuous and also one of the most successful and original of the new public buildings was the Opera House. This was built in 1861-9 by Van der Nüll & Siccardsburg in a mode quite unrelated to their earlier work at the Arsenal but one not easy to define. The Vienna Opera House is a somewhat simpler and less boldly plastic structure than Garnier's, both in its generally right-angled massing, with pairs of rectangular wings projecting on each side towards the rear, and in the rather flat, somewhat *François I* detail. Yet the vast curved roof, actually rather like that over the buildings along the Rue de Rivoli, does give it a distinctly Second Empire air [130]. Less grandly sited than the Paris Opéra, it was none the less balanced across the Opernring by one of the largest and handsomest of Hansen's private works, the Heinrichshof of 1861-3 [132]. This had a fine glass-roofed passage through its centre and ranges of flats behind the elaborate

132. Theophil von Hansen:
Vienna, Heinrichshof, 1861-3

Late Renaissance façades. It has unfortunately been demolished since the War to make way for a very poor modern block of offices.

Here by the Opera House, as at the Place de l'Opéra in Paris, the Viennese urban achievement of the age was concentrated. The Heinrichshof, with its accented centre balancing the high roof of the Opera House opposite and its corner towers corresponding to the mansarded pavilions of more definitely French-styled blocks of flats, offered a handsomer Austrian equivalent of the Second Empire mode than does the Opera House itself; for the Opera House lacks externally the richness and the bombast characteristic of the period at its most assured, while the auditorium within, re-opened in 1955, is today a much simplified reconstruction by Erich Boltenstern (b. 1896). Yet the masonry exterior of the Opera House is clean and fresh today thanks to Boltenstern's restoration and, with the great staircase and foyer regilded and refurbished generally, it offers a lighter and more festive vision of the period than do the vast majority of Viennese buildings whose stucco so often badly needs a coat of paint.

Hansen's Musikvereinsgebäude of 1867-9 in the Dumbagasse is academic in an almost eighteenth-century way, both as regards the general organization of the exterior and the restraint of the detailing. In his still later Parlament of 1873-83, as has been noted earlier, he produced the last grandiose monument of the Greek Revival. More characteristic, however, is his contemporaneous Academy of Fine Arts of 1872-6 in the Schillerplatz. This is externally in the Renaissance mode that he presumably preferred after he left Athens, but it has Grecian detailing inside of a delicacy and elegance that recall the thirties. Especially handsome is the colonnaded Aula in the centre, even though its rich painted ceiling of 1875-80 by Anselm Feuerbach is inappropriately Baroque in a rather Rubens-like way.

Another Austrian architect besides Ferstel was using Gothic for prominent Viennese edifices in this period (see also Chapter 11). After Ferstel's Votivkirche the next Neo-Gothic structure was the Academische Gymnasium in the Beethovenplatz; this was built in 1863-6 by Friedrich von Schmidt (1825-91), who had worked earlier under Zwirner on the restoration and completion of Cologne Cathedral. But the school was soon outshone in size and in elaboration by Schmidt's Rathaus of 1872-83. This stands between Hansen's Parlament and Ferstel's University but in a line with the Reichstrasse at their rear. The Vienna Rathaus is certainly not unrelated to G. G. Scott's Victorian Gothic and that of Waterhouse in England, particularly in the side wings that end, eclectically enough, in high-mansarded pavilions. But the general fussiness of the turreted front recalls rather pre-Puginian Gothic, say Porden's Eaton Hall of seventy years earlier (see Chapters 6 and 10).

Despite the total visual unlikeness of the Rathaus to its Grecian neighbour, the Parlament, both have a similarly obsolete air. It is as if Francis Joseph's presumptive intention in the fifties of outbuilding Napoleon III had been succeeded by a belated and rather provincial desire to outrival the larger structures in other countries in the two leading modes of the previous period, the Greek Revival and the Gothic Revival, neither well represented hitherto in Vienna.

Yet an equally prominent public monument of the seventies and eighties, the Burgtheater, which stands just opposite the Rathaus, is of a Late Renaissance, almost Neo-Baroque order, with a distinctly Second Empire flavour to its bowed front and generally very plastic composition [133]. This, the most distinguished of all the public monuments along the Ringstrasse, was built in 1874-88 by Semper, whose international career in Germany, England, and Switzerland wound up in Vienna after he was

133. Gottfried Semper and Karl von Hasenauer: Vienna, Burgtheater, 1874-88

called there in 1871 by Francis Joseph to advise on the extension of the Hofburg Palace. Except perhaps in its bowed front, this Viennese theatre does not much resemble the rebuilt Dresden Opera House of 1871-8 which Semper had just designed (see Chapter 9). Perhaps Semper and his Viennese partner Karl von Hasenauer (1833-94), a pupil of Van der Nüll and of Siccardsburg, were somewhat influenced by the plans on which they were working together for the extension of the nearby palace; these were, not inappropriately, in the Austrian Baroque of Fischer von Erlach's unfinished Michaelertrakt of the Hofburg dating from the first quarter of the eighteenth century. However that may be, the theatre, boldly scaled and tightly composed, is a far more successful building than the very derivative Neue Hofburg projecting out towards the Ring as that was executed in 1881-94 by Hasenauer after Semper's death. The post-War restoration of the theatre and the rebuilding of its auditorium are by Michel Engelhart (b. 1897).

Semper and Hasenauer's two vast Museums of Art History and Natural History face each other on a large square across the Burgring from the Neue Hofburg. Of identical design,

they were both largely built in 1872-81. In the treatment of the exteriors – they were finished internally only very much later – as also in some of Hansen's very latest work in Vienna, one senses a conscious rejection of the bold plasticity and the compositional elaboration characteristic of the preceding decades, and most notably of the Burgtheater. The Renaissance detail is by no means sparse, but there is an academic sort of primness and orderliness belonging to the last quarter of the century such as was noted in Koch's buildings in Rome, best represented in Vienna by the early work of Otto Wagner.

The Bodenkreditanstalt built by Emil von Förster (1838-1909), Ludwig's son, in 1884-7 is still more severe in its Florentine *quattrocento* way, recalling the more Tuscan aspects of the *Rundbogenstil*. With this may be contrasted the expansive Neo-Baroque of Karl König's Philipphof of 1883, introducing another mode very characteristic of the end of the century in both Austria and Germany.

Budapest, the second capital of the Austro-Hungarian Empire, was also much embellished with public buildings by Francis Joseph. Stüler from Berlin worked here, using a quiet version of the *Rundbogenstil* for the Academy of

Sciences in 1862-4. But the later and more ornate *Rundbogenstil* of Berlin and Vienna had already been echoed in Budapest by Frigyes Feszl (1821-84) in the Vigado Concert Hall of 1859-65. This could easily be by Ferstel, so similar is it to his bank in Vienna. The leading Hungarian architect of the period, Miklós Ybl (1814-91), who was trained in Vienna, also used the *Rundbogenstil,* but of a rather more Romanesquoid sort, for the Ferenczváros Parish Church which he built in 1867-78. However, his Renaissance Revival Custom House of 1870-4 is more nearly up to the Vienna standards of the day as then maintained by Hansen. The Opera House that Ybl built in 1879-84, with its boldly convex mansards, vies in its rich plasticity with Garnier's, but none too successfully. The Szent Lukásh Hotel by R. L. Ray (1845-99), a Swiss-born pupil of Garnier, is one of the largest mansarded Second Empire hotels anywhere in the western world.[25b] On the whole, the dominant influences in Hungary, as also in Bohemia, were Austrian and German, however, not Parisian, as is hardly surprising. No autochthonous note was struck; as is true of all Eastern Europe, the architecture of this age is as essentially colonial in character as in the outlying British Dominions or in Latin America, although the models emulated were rather different.

CHAPTER 9

SECOND EMPIRE AND COGNATE MODES ELSEWHERE

In the cities of Germany and of Northern Europe generally there were in this period no such comprehensive urbanistic developments as in Paris and Vienna. Some individual public monuments are, perhaps, not inferior to those that Napoleon III and Francis Joseph obtained from their architects; but these are rarely grouped into such coherent entities as the Marktplatz in Karlsruhe of the first quarter of the century or the Ludwigstrasse in Munich of the second quarter. The domestic building of the period is also considerably less consistent in character than in Paris and Vienna.

The architectural scene in Germany was overshadowed by the distinguished achievements of the previous period. The Schinkel tradition, although increasingly corrupted, lasted on almost indefinitely not merely in Prussia but in most German states. Stüler, Schinkel's ablest disciple in Berlin after the death of the short-lived Persius, remained an internationally respected practitioner. He was employed in Stockholm and in Budapest, as has been noted, not to speak of German cities, down to his death in 1865. By him and by many others the *Rundbogenstil* was employed quite as late as in Austria-Hungary both in the various German states and also in the Scandinavian countries. Such a very large and prominent public building as the Berlin Rathaus of 1859-70 by H. F. Waesemann (1813-79) well indicates the long-continued hold of this mode on German officialdom. Nor was this particularly inferior in quality to much similar work produced in the earlier heyday of the *Rundbogenstil* before 1850. As in Austria, however, alternative modes were growing increasingly popular, even though none rose to a local dominance comparable to that of revived Renaissance in Vienna. The taste of the period for elaboration, both in general composition and in detail, is everywhere evident regardless of the mode employed.

French influence was not absent; indeed specifically Second Empire features were perhaps more common than in Austria. G. H. Friedrich Hitzig (1811-81), a former assistant of Schinkel's, had actually studied in Paris. After Stüler, he was the most prominent and successful architect of the period in Berlin, and in the fifties he built a few mansarded houses there. Along the new Viktoriastrasse in the Tiergarten quarter, where he did a great deal of work in 1855-60, one house among the eight that he built was mansarded; the others and most of those he was erecting near by in the Bellevuestrasse, the Stülerstrasse, and other streets at the same time, were, however, in a much elaborated Schinkelesque vein. Suburban houses of the sixties occasionally followed Parisian modes also; but far more were clumsy variants of Schinkel's and Persius's Italian Villas, or else in some sort of equally clumsy Gothic.

Public buildings in Germany were only occasionally designed in the mansarded mode and, in general, only after the mid sixties. The Baugewerkschule in Stuttgart, built in 1866-70 by Josef von Egle (1818-99) its director, had projecting centre and end pavilions with crudely Parisian detailing. It is curious to realize that it was contemporary with Leins's belated but rather distinguished Grecian Königsbau there. In Cologne the High School of 1860-2, and the Stadttheater of 1870-2 by Julius Raschdorf (1823-1914), both destroyed in the last war,

134. Julius Raschdorf: Cologne, Opera House, 1870–2

were heavily mansarded and very plastically modelled; the latter, at least, on which H. Deutz collaborated with Raschdorf, had some real compositional interest in the tight interlocking of the masses [134]. Despite their very evidently French character, both were considered by contemporaries to be 'German Renaissance' – as, for that matter, was Wieleman's Justizpalast in Vienna – because of the specific precedent of much of the detail. German Renaissance was by this time the newest fashion, but to later eyes these buildings in Cologne were no more characteristic examples of it than the one in Vienna. Raschdorf is better known in any case for his much later Neo-Baroque work, notably the Berlin Cathedral, for which he prepared the design in 1888, although it was not built until 1894–1905.

The Military Hospital by F. Heise in Dresden of 1869 was considerably more French in the strong articulation of the mansarded centre and end pavilions and also in its quite Parisian detailing than Raschdorf's contemporary buildings in Cologne. More prominent in Dresden by far, however, is the Hoftheater, which is not at all French in character. This was designed in 1871 by Semper after his earlier theatre there had been destroyed by fire; its construction was supervised by Semper's son Manfred after he settled in Vienna, and completed in 1878. Gone was most of the festive grace and delicacy of his Hamburg and Dresden work of the forties, even though the auditorium was not dissimilar to the one that had been destroyed. Yet in the arrangement of the interior and the disposition of the masses this rivals in clarity of organization the opera-houses of Garnier in Paris and of Van der Nüll & Siccardsburg in Vienna. The plans undoubtedly owed a great deal to the elaborate studies Semper had made for Ludwig II in 1865-7 for an opera-house to be built in Munich especially for the production of Wagner's operas.

general stylistic stasis of this period in Germany. His Museum of Decorative Art in Berlin, begun in 1877 and completed in 1881 by Heinrich Schmieden (1835-1913), resembled Hitzig's houses of the fifties in its Grecian elaboration; it also recalled Klenze's Hermitage Museum, built more than a generation earlier

135. Friedrich Hitzig: Berlin, Exchange, 1859 63

The relative importance of Berlin was, of course, rising well before its establishment as the imperial capital in 1871. Friedrich Hitzig's most considerable public building in Berlin, the Exchange, built in 1859-63 at the same time that the Rathaus was in construction, was neither Schinkelesque nor *Rundbogenstil* but in a rather academic sort of Late Baroque [135]. Hitzig seems to have been consciously recalling what Knobelsdorf built for Frederick the Great and thus presaging the more overt Neo-Baroque of the last decades of the century. His later Reichsbank of 1871-6, on the other hand, was in general considerably more Classical despite its banded and diapered walls in two colours of brick.

The public buildings of Martin K. P. Gropius (1824-80) are also indicative of the

in Petersburg. Gropius & Schmieden's still later Gewandhaus in Leipzig of 1880-4, however, was less reminiscent of Schinkel or Klenze and more conventionally academic. This concert hall was renowned for its superb acoustics.

It is easy to forget how much the architects of these decades, apparently obsessed with stylistic elaboration, were also concerned to incorporate in their buildings all sorts of technical advances. Iron may show less than in the previous period, but it was quite consistently used behind the scenes. Central heating, extensive sanitary equipment, vertical transportation, and various other things that are taken for granted today first became accepted necessities in these decades. But it was only in the commercial field – and in England and the United States above all – that

such technical innovations influenced architecture very positively or visibly (see Chapter
14), however much they must actually have
preoccupied architects who now seem so
imitative and retardataire. The Anhalter Bahnhof in Berlin by Franz Schwechten (1841–
1924), however, built in 1872-80, did represent
a real advance over the principal English railway station of this period, St Pancras in London
of 1863-76, in the clarity and coherence of its
organization. One can hardly say that the shed
roof of the Anhalter Bahnhof was in the *Rundbogenstil*; yet it was much more happily related
in scale and shape to the masonry elements of
the station than are the two parts of that in
London, world-famous nonetheless until the
nineties for the unrivalled span of its shed.

Architectural activity in Bavaria was of a
very different order. The Ludwigsschlösser,[1]
the country palaces that Ludwig II of Bavaria
erected for his private delectation after he
succeeded Maximilian II in 1864, were the
retreats of a monarch mad about Louis XIV.
Linderhof, built in 1870-86, emulated the local
Bavarian Late Baroque, and was thus even
more premonitory of a favourite German mode
of the eighties and nineties than Hitzig's Berlin
Exchange [136]. Herrenchiemsee, projected in
1868 but begun only in 1878, is a direct imitation of Versailles. Neuschwanstein, on the other
hand, is a wild Wagnerian fantasy of a medieval
castle occupying a superb mountain site.

It must be assumed that the architect of the
first two, Georg von Dollmann (1830-95), was
little more than the draughting agent of his
master's dreams of grandeur. More interesting
than the exteriors are the incredibly rich interiors of Linderhof, operatic recreations of the
Bavarian Rococo. Appropriately enough these
were designed by Franz von Seitz (1817-83),
then director of the Munich State Theatre,
who was famous for his stage-sets. At Herrenchiemsee, however, several of the interiors
were exact copies of the main apartments of

Louis XIV at Versailles. These were executed
by Julius Hoffmann (1840-96), who began to
work under Dollmann in 1880 and succeeded
him in 1884. More original were certain other
rooms at Herrenchiemsee designed by F. P.
Stulberger after 1883 in an even more elaborate
and fantastic Neo-Rococo than those by Seitz
at Linderhof.

Ludwig II had another obsession besides the
majesty of Louis XIV and that was the genius
of Richard Wagner. This cult is almost
nauseatingly reflected at Neuschwanstein for
which Riedel, who had built Schloss Berg in
1849-51, prepared the original design in 1867.
Construction there began in 1869, was taken
over by Dollmann in 1874, and only completed
as regards the exterior in 1881; much of the
decoration is still later. Despite Ludwig's
romantic love of the real Romanesque of the
Wartburg, Neuschwanstein really differs very
little from the fake castles of the first half of the
century, except in its very ingenious adaptation
to a most precarious site. It is the later interiors,
designed by Hoffmann in the early eighties,
that attempt to realize the Wagnerian legends
both in the architectural detailing and in endless murals. The whole culminates in the
Byzantinesque throne room of 1885-6 intended
by Ludwig to be a sort of 'Grail Hall' from
Parsifal. The results of his other obsession are
more gratifying to the eye.

Never again would any ruler, however - at
least not in Europe - be so spendthrift a patron
of architecture. Considering the deterioration
in quality evident in these palaces and castles of
the seventies and eighties from the work done
for Ludwig's grandfather Ludwig I or for
Frederick William IV of Prussia in the thirties
and forties, this was just as well. Fortunately
the activities of William II were less related to
the building arts; and Hitler, a thwarted architect, had too little time.

Far more typical of the turn German architecture in general was taking in the seventies

than the Ludwigsschlösser were such things as the von Tiele house in Berlin by Gustav Ebe (1834–1916) and Julius Benda (1838–97). In its crawlingly rich German Renaissance detail and its irregularly gabled silhouette this prepared the way far more definitely than Rasch-dorf's contemporary Cologne buildings for a veritable flood of such coarse work all over Germany in the next decade. This characteristic German mode has analogies with the English style-phase of the seventies and eighties somewhat perversely known as 'Queen Anne'; more

136. Georg von Dollmann: Schloss Linderhof, near Oberammergau, 1870–86

specifically it often resembles very closely what is called 'Pont Street Dutch' in England. But leadership comparable to that provided in England by Webb and Shaw was entirely lacking, and even lesser talent of the order of George's or Collcutt's (see Chapter 12).

Usually executed in dark-coloured brick with stone trim, this prime manifestation of the bourgeois ambitions of the Bismarckian Empire produced a spate of buildings of all sorts that have come to look very grim indeed with the accumulated smoke of years. Old photographs indicate that many of them once had a certain lightness and even a quite festive air, Wagnerian in the *Meistersinger* vein rather than in that of the *Ring* as at Neuschwanstein. But the materials used were always hard and mechanically handled and the execution of the detail at once fussy and metallic. No positive originality in general composition or in planning made up, as with much comparable work in England, for the anti-architectonic character of the basic approach.

A prominent late example is the Rathaus[2] in Hamburg built in 1886–97. This vast and turgid edifice contrasts most unhappily with the suave High Renaissance design of Wimmel & Forsmann's contiguous Exchange built in the thirties. Its tall tower, moreover, has neither the richness of outline of Scott's on the Nikolaikirche nor the simple directness of de Chateau-

neuf's on the Petrikirche, with both of which it still disputes a central position on the Hamburg skyline.

The nationalistic 'Meistersinger mode', so to call it, had only too long a life, lasting well into the twentieth century. But it was early challenged by a new modulation of German taste in the eighties, parallel to that which the English also experienced, towards an eighteenth-century revival – here in Germany definitely Neo-Baroque – of which Linderhof was probably the first really sumptuous and striking example. Ebe & Benda early deserted the German Renaissance for a German Baroque at least as chastened as that of Hitzig's much earlier Exchange when they built their Palais Mosse in Berlin of 1882–4. In 1882 Paul Wallot (1841–1912), who had also worked earlier in the Meistersinger mode, won the competition for the Reichstag Building with an overpoweringly monumental Neo-Baroque project recalling Vanbrugh more than Bernini or Schlüter. Erected by him in 1884–94, this was soon matched at the other end of Unter den Linden by Raschdorf's cathedral.

Unlike Napoleon III and Francis Joseph, the German emperors William I, Frederick I, and William II did not succeed in making their capital an important exemplar of nineteenth-century urbanism. Moreover, the influential position that Germany had occupied in the

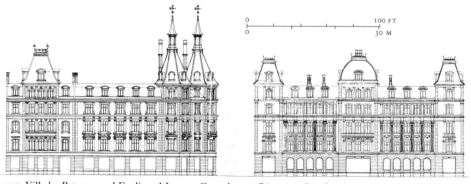

137. Vilhelm Petersen and Ferdinand Jensen: Copenhagen, Søtorvet, 1873–6

international world of architecture in the first half of the century was less and less maintained after the death of Stüler. Not until the twentieth century did Germans again make a significant contribution to European architectural history (see Chapter 20).

With the deterioration of German leadership in the seventies and eighties went also a general decline in the architectural standards of the Scandinavian countries that had so successfully based their later Romantic Classicism and their *Rundbogenstil* on German models of the thirties, forties, and fifties. In Denmark the work of Meldahl was increasingly inferior to that of Herholdt. Although he was only nine years younger than Herholdt, his direction of the Copenhagen Academy, beginning in 1873, coincided with the feeblest and most eclectic period in Danish architecture, from which recovery started only in the nineties with the early work of Martin Nyrop (1849-1925) in Copenhagen and of Hack Kampmann (1856-1920) in Aarhus (see Chapter 24).

A characteristic urbanistic development of the seventies in Copenhagen, the Søtorvet built in 1873-6 by Vilhelm Petersen (1830-1913) and Ferdinand Vilhelm Jensen (1837-90), is French not German in its ultimate inspiration. This grandiose pavilioned and mansarded range of four tall blocks forms a shallow U-shaped square along a canal [137].

Its definitely Second Empire character may not, all the same, have derived directly from Paris but via German or English intermediaries, so much more typical is this of the international than of the truly Parisian mode of the third quarter of the century.

As late as 1893-4 the much more conspicuous Magasin du Nord department store, built by A. C. Jensen (1847-1913) and his partner H. Glaesel in the Kongens Nytorv in Copenhagen, also carried the high mansarded roofs of the new Louvre, both flat-sided and convex-curved, above its end and centre pavilions. The detailing was chastened, however, by memories of local palaces and mansions in the nearby Amalie quarter of the city, where Jensen had worked on the completion of the eighteenth-century Marble Church. The Magasin du Nord thus combines two characteristic aspects of the architecture of the period, evident in most countries but rarely thus joined: a reflection of Napoleon III's Paris, elsewhere reaching its peak around 1870, and a revival of the style of the seventeenth and eighteenth centuries, generally beginning about a decade later.

In Sweden also there was some Second Empire influence, although nothing very notable resulted from it. The Jernkontovets Building in Stockholm erected by the brothers Kumlien (A.F., 1833-?; K.H., 1837-97) in 1873-5 has a high mansard and pavilions combined with a

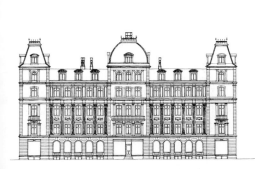

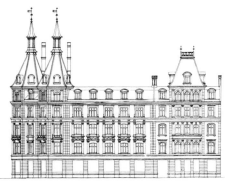

respectably academic treatment of the façades that is quite different from the bombast of the Søtorvet. Bern's Restaurant in Stockholm of 1886 by Åbom, whose more conservative Renaissance Revival theatre of thirty years earlier has been mentioned, is similarly Parisian, particularly in the decorations that were provided by Isaeus.

With I. G. Clason (1856–1930) the tide of eclecticism in Sweden turned more nationalistic. The Northern Renaissance of his Northern Museum, built in 1889–1907, parallels somewhat belatedly the Meistersinger mode in Germany; but it also shows a more refined and delicate touch, somewhat like that of George and of Collcutt in England. As in most other countries, the revival of the native sixteenth-century style was soon succeeded by a revival of the Baroque, here rather academically restrained. This phase is most conspicuously represented in Stockholm by the grouped Parliament House and National Bank of 1897–1905 by Aron Johansson (1860–1936). In the nineties Ferdinand Boberg (1860–1946) was also initiating a new movement somewhat comparable to that led by Nyrop in Denmark (see Chapter 24).

The modes of Second Empire Paris left rather more mark on Holland than did those of the First Empire, particularly in the work of Cornelis Outshoorn (1810–75), whose iron-and-glass Paleis voor Volksvlijt in Amsterdam of the late fifties has been mentioned earlier. That is long gone, but the related Gallerij, a U-shaped range of mansarded blocks linked by a sort of veranda of cast iron, till lately bounded the south of the Frederiksplein. His enormous Amstel Hotel, near by on the farther side of the Amstel, was built in 1863–7. At Scheveningen the Oranje Hotel (1872–3), also by him, was one of several typical resort establishments there of an international Second Empire order, as was also his hotel at Berg-en-Dal near Nijmegen (1867–9). Fairly generally, high

mansards rose in the sixties and seventies over the narrow house-fronts in the new quarters of Dutch cities. However, the opposing Neo-Gothic is more significant historically in Holland, and the secular work of Cuijpers, although rather like Clason's, as well as his churches, is better considered in that connexion (see Chapter 11). As in the Scandinavian countries, the nineties saw new beginnings in Holland, in this case with the appearance of Berlage and Kromhout (see Chapter 20).

The principal Anglo-American developments in the second half of the century were in the specialized fields of domestic and commercial building (see Chapters 14 and 15). England, moreover, had from 1850 to the early seventies a lively stylistic development of her own, the High Victorian Gothic, rather different from the later Neo-Gothic of the Continent. This was also very influential in the Dominions and in the United States (see Chapters 10 and 11). Nevertheless, the international Second Empire mode flourished on both sides of the Atlantic among Anglo-Saxons to a greater extent, perhaps, than anywhere in Europe. It is not, of course, possible to subsume all non-Gothic work of these decades in England under the Second Empire rubric any more than on the Continent. Yet, with certain notable exceptions, the most vigorous and conspicuous buildings of a generically Renaissance character were clearly inspired by Paris, and often specifically by the New Louvre, as Prosper Mérimée noted and wrote to Viollet-le-Duc while on a visit to London in the mid sixties.

The most considerable English public monument built just after the mid century, the Leeds Town Hall of 1855–9, is by Cuthbert Brodrick [138]. That Brodrick was an architect markedly French in his leanings has already been noted in describing his Leeds Corn Exchange, which is later in date but earlier in style than his Town Hall (see Chapter 4). But this major early work, for which Brodrick won the commission in a

138. Cuthbert Brodrick: Leeds, Town Hall, 1855–9

competition in 1853, is not easily pigeon-holed stylistically. The great hall inside derives quite directly from Elmes's in Liverpool, designed almost a quarter of a century earlier, though not opened until 1856. The exterior recalls in its grandiose scale the English Baroque of Vanbrugh more than it does anything that had even been proposed since the megalomaniac French projects of the 1790s. The Leeds Town Hall is certainly no longer Romantic Classical, no longer Early Victorian; yet except for the rather clumsy originality of some of the detail and the varied outline of the tower – a late emendation of the original project of 1853 – it is hard to say how or why it is so definitely High Victorian, and rather a masterpiece of the High Victorian at that. Wallot in Berlin in the eighties approached Brodrick's mode of design in the Reichstag but had little of his command of scale or his almost Romantic Classical control of mass.

When Brodrick designed his town hall very little was known in England of Visconti's project of 1852 for the New Louvre, and Lefuel had not yet begun to elaborate the design. So vigorously individual an architect as Brodrick was hardly likely, moreover, to find inspiration in the Hope house of Dusillion or the Hardwicks' Great Western Hotel. But the wave of Second Empire influence arrived in England well before the Leeds Town Hall was finished. When the English swarmed to Paris to visit the International Exhibition of 1855 the character of the New Louvre became generally known to architects and to the interested public. The Crimean War in the mid fifties served, moreover, to bring English and French officialdom into close contact. To English ministers and civil servants, even more than to architects and ordinary citizens, the existing governmental accommodations in Whitehall contrasted most unfavourably with those Napoleon III was providing in the New Louvre. When a competition was held in 1856–7 for a new Foreign Office and a new War Office to be built in

Whitehall, it is not surprising that most of those entrants who were not convinced Gothicists should have modelled their projects more or less on the work of Visconti and Lefuel.

Barry, the head of the profession, did not enter the competition; but unofficially – for he was still an employee of the Government at the Houses of Parliament – he prepared at this time a comprehensive scheme for the development of the whole length of Whitehall from Parliament Square to Trafalgar Square. In this project he crowned all his façades – including the already once-remodelled Treasury – with mansards, introduced stepped-back courts like that of the New Louvre, and marked the corners and the centres of the court façades in the most Louvre-like way with pavilions crowned by still taller mansards. Had this project of Barry's been followed, London would rival Paris and Vienna in the extent, the consistency, and the boldness of her public buildings of this period. In fact, practically nothing ever came of it nor, indeed, of the official competition; for by this period earlier traditions of urbanism had all but completely died out and architectural initiative was largely in private hands.

When the competition was judged in 1857, the designs that received the top prizes both for the War Office and for the Foreign Office were in the pavilioned and mansarded manner; they derived, however, at least as much from the Tuileries as from the New Louvre. It was the rising prestige of Napoleon III, of course, that called public attention at this time to the Tuileries which was his residence – as it had been, for that matter, the residence of most French monarchs for several centuries. Otherwise no one in England would probably have thought of reviving any of the various periods represented in its conglomerate mass or of emulating its pavilioned and mansarded composition.

Since neither of these projects for ministries was ever executed, and their respective architects – Henry B. Garling (1821–1909), on the one hand, and H. E. Coe (1826–85) and his partner Hofland, on the other – never built much else of consequence, it is not necessary to linger over them. However, their designs and other Second Empire ones that received minor premiums were extensively illustrated in professional and general periodicals, and they provided favourite models in the sixties both in England and in the United States. The Paris originals, on which graphic data was not only scarcer but also less readily accessible, were not on the whole so influential. This helps to explain why French influence *appears* to have been stronger in the Anglo-Saxon world than on the Continent, even though there was surely no greater amount of contact with Paris.

There was also in England at this time a general tendency, even more evident than in Austria or Germany, to enrich and elaborate plastically the long-established Renaissance Revival mode. This is less specifically inspired by Paris. An excellent example was provided by the extensive range of terraces, designed by Sancton Wood (1814–86) in 1857, that flanked Lancaster Gate in the Bayswater Road in London with their boldly projecting bay windows linked by tiers of colonnades. In other examples, such as the National Discount Company's offices at 65 Cornhill built by the Francis Brothers in 1857, the capping of the whole block with a boldly dormered mansard[3] was more obviously of Second Empire inspiration, though the façades below are merely of a much enriched *palazzo* order.

When the Moseley Brothers designed in 1858 the vast Westminster Palace Hotel near Westminster Abbey at the foot of Victoria Street, a caravanserai intended to exceed the Hardwicks' Great Western Hotel of 1850–2 in international luxury, they took over its pavilioned and mansarded design. To judge from the relative dignity and sobriety of their detailing, they would seem to have studied contemporary

139. Sir Charles Barry: Halifax, Town Hall, 1860–2

Parisian work – not the New Louvre but the quieter *maisons de rapport* along the boulevards rather than merely basing themselves on the prize-winning Government Offices projects as so many others were content to do at this time. This hotel, which proved a failure, now serves as a block of offices, and has been remodelled almost beyond recognition.

The next year Barry designed the Halifax Town Hall, his last work. He did not himself propose to cap this, like the Government Offices in his Whitehall scheme, with French mansards; those that were executed are an emendation by his son, E. M. Barry, who carried the building to completion in 1862 after his father's death in 1860. But the richly arcaded articulation of the walls and the emphatic forward breaks of the great tower and of the more modest pavilion at the other end clearly emulate, without directly imitating, the ornate plasticity of Lefuel's New Louvre. Nevertheless, the boldly asymmetrical composition, dominated by a single corner tower, is more in the Italian Villa tradition [139].

This tower – but not the site – was lined up with the axis of Prince's Street, which enters Crossley Street at this point. The assured quality of its design and above all that of its tremendous spire, more than worthy of Wren in the ingenuity with which the silhouette of a Gothic steeple was built up out of Renaissance elements, makes the Halifax Town Hall thoroughly English and one of the masterpieces of the High Victorian period. Totally devoid of Gothic elements, it has more Gothic vitality than Barry's Houses of Parliament, at this time just approaching completion nearly thirty years after they were first designed.

E. M. Barry went on to crown two London station hotels, that at Charing Cross in 1863-4 and that at Cannon Street in 1865-6, with mansards; but these were far from being masterpieces, and Charing Cross which survives has been much modified. The Grosvenor Hotel, built beside the new Victoria Station in 1859-60

by Sir James T. Knowles (1831-1908), is far more original. He covered the whole enormous mass with a very tall convex mansard, giving further emphasis to the broad pavilions at the ends by carrying their roofs still higher and capping them with lanterns. Beyond this nothing was French. The detail indeed, defined by its architect as 'Tuscan', i.e. *Rundbogenstil,* is highly individual, partaking of the coarse gusto and even somewhat of the naturalism of the most advanced Victorian Gothic foliage carving of the period (see Chapter 10).

Similar mansards, but flat-sided not bulbous, and similar detail characterize a pair of tall terraces that Knowles built in 1860 on the north side of Clapham Common, south London. These constituted a subtle suburban attack on Early Victorian traditions of terrace-design that soon had metropolitan repercussions. His Thatched House Club in St James's Street in London of 1865 has a great deal of very rich carving by J. Daymond in the naturalistic vein, but is less interesting in general composition.

Knowles's Grosvenor was still new when John Giles outbid it with the Langham Hotel, begun in 1864. Given a rather finer site than Knowles's at the base of the broad avenue of Portland Place across from Nash's All Souls', Langham Place, Giles rose boldly – many critics have thought too boldly – to the occasion [140]. Certainly he overwhelmed Nash's delicate and ingenious steeple by the angled projection and the tall square corner tower – since bombed away at the top – with which he faced it. Equally certainly his massive north façade, with its boldly modelled flanking pavilions and its profusion of lively animal carvings, would overwhelm the urbane refinement of the nearby Adam terraces flanking Portland Place had many of these not been replaced by far bigger buildings. For all its gargantuan scale and the somewhat elephantine playfulness of the detail (not to speak of the dinginess to which the 'Suffolk-white' brickwork and the stone trim

140. John Giles: London, Langham Hotel, 1864-6

have now been reduced), the Langham is a rich and powerfully plastic composition, most skilfully adapted to a special site, and more original than most of what was produced in the sixties in Paris. The carved animals at the window heads, so varied and so humorous, deserve an attention they rarely receive; these scurrying creatures almost seem to come out of Tenniel's illustrations, but may actually derive from Viollet-le-Duc.

That this degree of architectural originality, presented with such bold assurance and even bombast, should within a decade or two have come to seem tasteless and actually ugly – as,

indeed, it has seemed to many ever since – is not of major historical consequence. The age that achieved it rejected as tasteless and insipid the architectural production of the previous hundred years, and most notably Late Georgian work of the sort to which the Langham stood in close proximity. What *is* of consequence is that such High Victorian buildings, even when not Gothic, possessed a vitality and a contemporaneity within their period that was very largely lacking in parallel work on the Continent, most of which in any case is a decade or more later in date. In their parvenu brashness, the Grosvenor and Langham balance the contemporary achievement of the Gothic church architects – an achievement generally more acceptable even today as it was already to high-brows and aesthetes in the sixties – without necessarily equalling it (see Chapter 10).

In the English hotel boom of the early and mid sixties which these big London hotels set off, some variant of the anglicized Second Empire became the accepted type of design; indeed, a mansarded French mode continued to be used as late as the nineties[4] for such a big London hotel as the Carlton built by H. L. Florence (1843-1916) in 1897. Many of these Frenchified London hotels of the seventies and eighties are now gone or have been turned, like the earlier Westminster Palace and the Langham, to other uses – among these the former Grand Hotel in Trafalgar Square of 1878-80 by

H. Francis and the front block of the former Cecil Hotel in the Strand built by Perry & Reed should at least be noted here, since they remain conspicuous and may not be replaced for some years still.

It is a resort hotel, however, the Cliff (now the Grand) at Scarborough in Yorkshire, built by Brodrick at the height of the boom in 1863-7, just before he retired to live in France, that remains internationally the most notable example of the type [141]. And the type could be found in such remote spots as the famous 'ghost town' of the Comstock Lode, Virginia City, Nevada, where the large and elaborate hotel is no more, or Leadville, Colorado, where the more modest and much later Vendome Hotel, built by Senator Taber for his 'Baby Doe', is still in use, as well as in big European

141. Cuthbert Brodrick: Scarborough, Grand Hotel, 1863-7

cities such as Amsterdam, Frankfurt, Brussels, and Budapest.

The site of Brodrick's Grand Hotel is a superb one on the edge of the Scarborough cliffs above the North Sea, as different as possible from the setting of the New Louvre. Its corner pavilions are capped, not with ordinary high mansards, but with curious roofs like pointed domes, richly crowned with elaborate cornices. In the intricacy of their silhouette these are not unworthy rivals of Barry's Halifax tower. The massive walls are not of freestone in the manner of Paris nor yet of pallid Suffolk brick with light coloured stone or cement trim as in London. Instead, they are of warm red brick with incredibly lush decorative trim of tawny terracotta – a combination that M. D. Wyatt also used on the most elegant

143. J.-A.-F.-A. Pellechet: Barnard Castle, Co. Durham, Bowes Museum, 1869-75 (photograph copyright *Country Life*)

142. Sir M. D. Wyatt: London, Alford House, 1872

Second Empire mansion in London, Alford House, which stood from 1872 until 1955 in Prince's Gate at the corner of Ennismore Gardens [142].

Public and private architecture could hardly hope to rival the pretentiousness of the new hotels, and in Britain rarely attempted to do so.

At Liverpool T. H. Wyatt in 1864-9 carried a U-shaped range of comparable pavilioned and mansarded blocks that housed the Exchange around the open space at the rear of the Town Hall, somewhat as Outshoorn carried his Gallerij around the Paleis voor Volksvlijt in Amsterdam; but that is now all gone.

In the English countryside, the Bowes Museum at Barnard Castle in County Durham, built in 1869-75 by J.-A.-F.-A. Pellechet (1829-1903), and Waddesdon Manor in Buckinghamshire by another French architect, G.-H. Destailleur (1822-93), largely of 1880-3, are unique examples of extensive mansions completely in the Second Empire mode [143]. In London Montagu House, designed in 1866 by the elderly Burn for the Duke of Buccleuch, once raised in Whitehall the mansarded pavilions that Barry and the winners of the Government Offices competition had proposed in 1857, but this is demolished. Fortunately the other two, being museums, should survive.

Of the most notable Second Empire ensemble in London nothing is now extant [144]. Facing the gardens of Buckingham Palace and extending southward from the group of Late Georgian monuments around Hyde Park Corner, were the terraces of Grosvenor Place. These were designed[5] in 1867 and built in the following hand. English were the porches, however, which made plain that these pretentious ranges were rows of dwellings like those in nearby Belgrave Square. English, also, were the red stone bands, novel touches echoing the fashion-

144. London, 1-5 Grosvenor Place, begun 1867

years. They provided one of the more striking features of the London skyline inherited from the Victorian period. Rivalling the high roofs and, almost, the tall steeples of the Victorian Gothic, the mansards over the end houses were carried to fantastic heights and capped with pointed upper roofs, providing several storeys of attics; while the centre houses had convex mansards like square domes taken straight from the New Louvre.

Below these Alpine crests, elaborated at the base with rich stone dormers, the enormous houses were all of fine Portland stone – hardly to be found in any earlier nineteenth-century London terraces except those of Ennismore Gardens – and detailed with a plausibly Parisian flair – it is even said that draughtsmen were sent to Paris to study Second Empire work at first

able 'structural polychrome' of the contemporary Victorian Gothic, just as the tall mansards echoed its pointed roofs (see Chapter 10).

Beyond the first two blocks of Grosvenor Place the new construction of the sixties stopped; but it started again at the far end and still surrounds the two triangles of Grosvenor Gardens, of which Knowles's hotel occupies part of the southern side. It is characteristic of the Parisian inspiration of the whole that on the east side of the Gardens great blocks of flats – 'mansions' in a Victorian euphemism – replaced the usual London terraces of individual tall houses, but these now serve as offices as did at the last the houses in Grosvenor Place. For one of these blocks red brick was used, but set like a mere panel-filling within stone frames according to a French rather than an English tradition.

145 Francis Fowke: London, Victoria and Albert Museum, Court, begun 1866

There are no other comparably pretentious examples of Second Empire terraces in London except Cambridge Gate (1875) by Thomas Archer and A. Green (?-1904), an unhappy intrusion among Nash's stuccoed Regent's Park ranges despite its handsome execution in fine ashlar of Bath stone. Characteristically, London domestic architecture of the late fifties and sixties merely elaborated the Renaissance Revival formulas of the previous decade. Not only were the chosen models generally later and richer as in Vienna; wherever possible bolder plastic effects were achieved by a more extensive use of ground-storey colonnades, first-storey porches, and projecting bay windows, as on Wood's magniloquent terraces at Lancaster Gate or those of 1858 by C. J. Richardson (1800–72) that followed them in Queen's Gate.

The high standards of the earlier period were maintained only in business *palazzi*, not those of London's City, but the ones in Northern cities like Bradford and in Scotland. There good freestone was readily available and a certain cultural lag, as well as a regional sobriety of temperament, led to the maintenance of a more Barry-like tradition. Notable everywhere for their academic virtues are the various National Provincial Bank buildings by Barry's pupil John Gibson (1819–92). The earliest, but not the most typical, is the head office in Bishopsgate, which was begun in 1863.

A special school of Renaissance design is associated with Sir Henry Cole's Department of Practical Art, and this produced the various buildings that he sponsored in the new London cultural centre in Brompton (now usually called

South Kensington).[5a] The Exhibition of 1862, on the southern edge of the estate belonging to the Commissioners of the Great Exhibition, was housed in a structure designed by Francis Fowke (1823–65), an army engineer. As at the Paris Exhibition of 1855, the metal and glass construction of this was masked externally with masonry walls but, unlike Cendrier's and Viel's Palais de l'Industrie, the whole was pavilioned and mansarded in the Second Empire mode. A still more elaborate Second Empire project was prepared by Fowke for the Museum of Science and Art (later Victoria and Albert), Cole having evidently accepted all too abjectly the criticism of his earlier temporary structure, the notorious 'Brompton Boilers' (see Chapter 7). As Fowke died at this point the Museum [145], begun in 1866, as also the associated Royal College of Science (Huxley Building), built in 1868–71, were carried out in a much less French vein under another army engineer, H. G. D. Scott (1822–83). The walling material is a fine smooth red brick, very rare in nineteenth-century London, beautifully laid up with thin joints. With this is combined an enormous quantity of elaborate pale cream terracotta, as on some Central European buildings deriving from Schinkel's Bauakademie in Berlin of 1831–6.

In these South Kensington structures, planned by an engineer, the emphasis is on the sculptural embellishment designed and executed by Godfrey Sykes and other artists associated with the Department. This team-work, by-passing as it did over-all control by an architect, was not very successful in achieving the coherence of Knowles's and Giles's hotels, although those were built for much less sophisticated clients. Much the same team, but with still more sculptors collaborating, was responsible for the Albert Hall, the vast circular auditorium built in 1867–71 on the northern edge of the Commissioners' Estate facing the most characteristic monument of the age, G. G. Scott's Victorian Gothic Albert Memorial.

The engineer Scott's really notable achievement here in the metal construction of the vast dome is unfortunately swamped by the profuse investiture of sculptural detail in terracotta, intrinsically elegant though much of that is.

In the sixties there was some coherence in the planning of the Commissioners' Estate as a whole, with a garden court surrounded by a great hemicycle of terracotta arcading by M. D. Wyatt lying behind the 1862 Exhibition Building and below the Albert Hall. In Vienna the cultural edifices were admirably grouped along the Ringstrasse with plenty of open space between them, however much they may have lacked intrinsic architectural quality. In sad contrast is the way the following decades allowed this considerable tract to become clogged up until almost no urbanistic organization at all remains. Extensive rebuilding has not improved the situation.

Other European countries tended in this period, like Denmark, Sweden, and Holland, to follow Paris and Vienna rather than London. Only a few works of the sixties and seventies need be singled out from the welter of pretentious public and private construction that turned Brussels, for example, into a 'Little Paris'.[5b] The Boulevard Anspach as a whole suggests the Cannebière in Marseilles, although the mansards on the buildings that line it are more plastically handled; the Exchange, in its own square half-way down the boulevard, was built by L.-P. Suys (1823–87) in 1868–73, and this provides the focus of the mid-nineteenth-century city, as does Garnier's Opéra in Paris. A provincial variant of the Opéra in many ways, despite its quite different function, this is somewhat more academic in composition yet also rather coarser in its profuse ornamentation. Brussels as a whole is dominated, however, by one of the grandest and most original monuments erected anywhere in this period.

The Palace of Justice,[6] built by Joseph Poelaert (1817–79) in 1866–83, occupies so high

146. Joseph Poelaert: Brussels, Palace of Justice, 1866–83

a site and is mounted on so mountainous a sub-structure that almost the whole of its gargantuan mass is visible from all over the city. Although generically Classical, a good deal of the external treatment has an indefinable flavour of the monuments of the ancient civilizations of the East, somewhat like that of the exotic Glasgow churches Alexander Thomson built in the late fifties [146]. Even more than Thomson's relatively small and delicately scaled work, the Palace of Justice also suggests the megalo-maniac architectural dreams of such a Romantic English painter as John Martin. Heavy and almost literally cruel, it has a Piranesian spatial elaboration and a plastic vitality of the most exaggeratedly architectonic order. Thus it puts to shame the urbane Renaissance costuming of most Continental public architecture of this period and the usual Neo-Baroque of the next.

The existence of this extraordinary edifice in a minor European capital prepares one a little for the important part that Brussels was to play in the nineties, even though there could hardly be two architects further apart in spirit than Poelaert and Victor Horta, who initiated there the Art Nouveau (see Chapter 16). So also in Glasgow, the originality of Thomson's Queen's Park Church of the sixties at least opened the way for the notable international contribution to be made by the Glaswegian C. R. Mackintosh in the nineties. But it was Alphonse Balat (1818-95), not Poelaert, who was Horta's master and also in these decades professor of architecture at the local Academy. Balat's Musée Royale des Beaux Arts of 1875-81 already represents a reversion to a more restrained and academic classicism with none of Poelaert's force and vitality. Yet this building is not without a certain correct elegance of detail and conven-tional skill in composition for which his houses of the sixties, with their Barry-like handling of the High Renaissance *palazzo* theme, prepared the way. The real eclecticism of this period lies less significantly in the variety of nominal styles

employed than in the variety of ways of employ-ing them. It is this, rather than the concurrent multiplication of fashionable modes, that makes it so difficult to characterize broadly the produc-tion of the period between the mid century and the nineties.

In several other European countries the situation was made even more complicated than in Belgium by a very considerable cultural lag such as has already been noted in Scandinavia. While the Rütschi-Bleuler House in Zürich of 1869-70 by Theodor Geiger (1832-82) had the fashionable Second Empire mansard, here high and concave, at nearby Winterthur Semper's Town Hall of precisely the same date, with its dominating temple portico, might at first sight be taken for a provincial French public edifice of the second quarter of the century. At the Zürich Polytechnic School, where Semper became a professor in 1855,[7] the large building begun in 1859 that he erected with the local architect Wolff is equally retardataire in style. His Observatory there of 1861-4 is a delicate, picturesquely composed exercise in the *quattro-cento* version of the *Rundbogenstil*, rather like his Hamburg houses of twenty years earlier.

If a German architect of established interna-tional reputation could be thus affected by the conservative tastes of his Swiss clients, it is not surprising that in the Iberian peninsula almost nothing of interest was built in this period. It may, however, be mentioned that the building for the National Library and Museums in Madrid, designed in 1866 by Francisco Jareño y Alarcón (1818-92) and almost thirty years in construction, while still of the most conventional Classical character as regards its façades, has convex mansards over the end pavilions of quite definitely Second Empire character. Charac-teristically, the Chamber of Commerce in Madrid, completed in 1893 by E. M. Repulles y Vargas (1845-1922), illustrates the general return of official architecture to still more con-ventional academic standards towards the end of the century. But in the seventies there began in Barcelona the career of a Spanish – or more accurately Catalan – architect, Antoni Gaudí, who was destined to produce around 1900 some of the boldest and most original early works of modern architecture. Gaudí's real links in the seventies and eighties, spiritually if not so much actually, are with the High Victorian Gothic not the Second Empire, although the earliest project on which he worked reflected the Palais Longchamps at Marseilles (see Chapter 11).

The situation in the United States was naturally most like that in England. As has already been noted, a French-trained Danish architect, Lienau, prefigured the Second Empire mode in the Shiff house in New York as early as 1849–50. By the mid fifties mansards of rather modest height, often with shallow concave slopes, had appeared in Eastern cities on many houses not otherwise particularly Frenchified. Richard M. Hunt (1827–95), the first American to study at the École des Beaux-Arts and actually an assistant as well as a pupil of Lefuel, returned from Paris to America in 1855. But he brought to New York[8] not the nouveau riche Second Empire mode but rather the basic academic tradition of the French official world, despite the fact that he had himself worked in 1854 on the New Louvre. Although some of the earliest work of H. H. Richardson, who returned from Paris a decade later after working for several years for Labrouste's brother Théodore, was of Second Empire character, he showed himself from the first more responsive to influences from contemporary England (see Chapters 11 and 13). On the whole, the Second Empire mode, as it was practised in America through the third quarter of the century, derived almost as completely as the local Victorian Gothic from England. Most American architects were kept informed of what was going on abroad through the English professional Press, and so they naturally followed the models that were offered in the *Builder* and the *Building News* rather than those in the publications of César Daly.[9]

The Civil War of 1861–5 did not bring architectural production to a stop; indeed, it

147. Thomas U. Walter:
Washington, Capitol, wings and dome, 1851–65; central block by William Thornton and others, 1792–1827

seems to have had a less inhibiting effect than the aftermath of the financial crash of 1857 in the immediately preceding years. In Washington the building of Walter's new wings of the Capitol, initiated in 1851,[10] and of his cast-iron dome, designed in 1855, continued until its completion in 1865, right through the war years at President Lincoln's express order [147]. There is nothing specifically French about this new work at the Capitol, even though Walter had the assistance from 1855 of the Paris-trained Hunt. On the other hand, the original more-or-less Romantic Classical edifice that had finally been brought to completion in 1827 by Bulfinch after so many changes of architect was largely submerged. The new wings echo in their academic porticoes the broader portico of the original late eighteenth-century design; but the cast-iron dome (see Chapter 7), rivalling in size the largest Baroque domes of Europe, has a high drum and a Michelangelesque silhouette of the greatest boldness in contrast to the Roman saucer shape of that designed by Latrobe and not much raised in execution by Bulfinch.

It was not in Washington that the Second Empire mode was first introduced for public buildings; Washington, indeed, would never again be the centre of architectural influence that it was in the Romantic Classical period, although the new state capitols begun in the sixties and seventies were mostly capped with imitations of Walter's dome. A 'female seminary' on the Hudson River, endowed by a brewer, and the new City Hall in Boston, Mass., both dating from the opening of the sixties, are the first monumental instances of the new mode that dominated the field of secular public building until the financial Panic of 1873 brought the post-war boom to a close. James Renwick,[11] who designed the very extensive Main Hall for Matthew Vassar's new college at Arlington near Poughkeepsie, N.Y., in 1860, was specifically instructed by his client to imitate the Tuileries – not the New Louvre – and so he did in an

elaborately pavilioned composition of U-shaped plan crowned by various sorts of high mansards. This overshadows in significance his earlier Charity Hospital of 1858 on Roosevelt Island in New York, already mansarded but very plain, and his Corcoran Gallery of 1859 in Washington, with a rich but muddled façade still rather flatly conceived. That is now restored for use as a museum and called the Renwick Gallery.

Renwick was at least as eclectic as such Europeans as Ballu and Ferstel. Having made his first reputation with the building of the Episcopal Grace Church in New York in 1843-6 – if not very Camdenian, this is at least a fair specimen of revived fourteenth-century English Gothic – he continued in the Gothic line with the Catholic St Patrick's Cathedral in New York, begun in 1859 and completed (except for the spires) in 1879. That vast two-towered pile, however, is Gothic in a very Continental way, resembling Gau's and Ballu's Sainte-Clotilde in Paris and Ferstel's Votivkirche in Vienna more than anything English of the period. In the late forties Renwick had also been the agent of Robert Dale Owen's 'Romanesque Revival' aspirations in designing the Smithsonian Institution in Washington (see Chapter 6).

For such things as the Smithsonian and his churches Renwick had plenty of visual documents on which to lean, either archaeological treatises on the buildings of the medieval past or illustrations of contemporary foreign work. But for Vassar College, very evidently, he was dependent for his inspiration on rather generalized lithographic or engraved views of the Tuileries. Nor could he, at this relatively early date, borrow much from published illustrations of contemporary English work in the new international Second Empire mode. The particular plastic vitality of the Americanized Second Empire is already notable in this early example, however, even though the rather crude articulation of the red brick walls is remote from anything French of any period from the sixteenth century to the nineteenth. Later buildings by Renwick in the same mode are more ornate and also closer to Parisian standards, but their architectonic vitality is considerably less.

The Boston City Hall,[12] built by G. J. F. Bryant (1816–99) and Arthur D. Gilman (1821–82) in 1862–5, is a smaller but suaver edifice. Although it is a compactly planned block, the articulation of the walls by successive Roman-arched orders, coldly but competently executed in stone, is boldly plastic below the crowning mansards. However, just before this, for the Arlington Street Church of 1859–61, the first edifice erected in the Back Bay district that Gilman was just laying out,[13] he had turned not to France but to eighteenth-century England for inspiration, basing himself chiefly on those churches by Gibbs that had been the most popular American models in later Colonial times.

A leading opponent of the Greek Revival, Gilman, like most Continental architects of the day, evidently knew better what he meant to leave behind than whither he wished to proceed. His Boston church initiated no national wave of Gibbsian church architecture; indeed, the sixties were the heyday of Victorian Gothic design for churches in the United States. His City Hall, on the other hand, set off a nation-wide programme of public building in the Second Empire mode; for Boston was now for a score of years the artistic as well as the intellectual headquarters of the country in succession to Philadelphia. In this programme municipalities, state authorities, and the Federal Government all participated actively during the decade following the Civil War. The buildings erected for the Federal Government in Washington and elsewhere were the work of Alfred B. Mullet (1834–90) who had succeeded Rogers as Supervising Architect in 1865. He had been trained in Rogers's office and worked first on the west wing of the Treasury.

These vast monuments were mostly constructed during General Grant's presidency. Parisian in intention, yet American in their materials, they are withal rather similar to Second Empire work in England. Few were completed before the mode went out of favour as changes in architectural control sometimes make evident. In the case of the New York State Capitol in Albany, for example, begun in 1868 by Thomas Fuller (1822–98) and his partner Augustus Laver (1834–98), who had both come from England via Canada, Eidlitz and Richardson took over jointly in 1875, modifying the design of the building very notably above the lower storeys away from the Second Empire mode. It was brought to completion by them and Isaac G. Perry by the century's end. The very tall tower on the Philadelphia City Hall, begun in 1874, was finished over a decade later. This tower, whose crowning statue of William Penn still tops the local skyline, has hardly anything in common with the Louvre-like pavilions below. Yet the whole is nominally the work of one architect, John McArthur, Jr (1823–90). The sculptor was Sandy Calder's grandfather, it might be mentioned.

Undoubtedly the association of these prominent buildings with the unsavoury Grant administration and the fact that there were – at least in the two cases mentioned above – major financial scandals involved in their slow and incredibly costly construction played an important part in the early rejection of a mode so associated with the public vices of the decade after the Civil War. Not many of them are extant today other than the Boston, Albany, and Philadelphia structures just mentioned and the State Department Building in Washington [148], now the Executive Office Building.

In New York, Boston, and other large cities the vast granite piles in this mode that served as post offices are almost all gone. In Chicago the Cook County Buildings built by J. J. Egan in 1872–5 have also long since been replaced. In San Francisco Fuller & Laver's extensive group of Municipal Buildings was destroyed in the fire that followed the earthquake of 1906. This must have been the largest, the richest, and plastically the most complex production of the whole lot, with its triangular site, boldly articulated massing, and central dome.

Though threatened by every intervening generation, the State, War and Navy Department Building built by Mullet in 1871-5 has now at last been sympathetically restored. It is perhaps the best extant example in America of the Second Empire - or as it is sometimes called locally, the 'General Grant' - mode [148]. The

tiers of Roman-arched orders in fine grey granite tower up storey above storey to carry mansards of various different heights above the complex pavilioned plan. Cold and grand, almost without sculptural decoration, this could hardly be less like the New Louvre or the old Tuileries in general texture; nor is there any of the playful semi-Gothic detail of Knowles's and Giles's London hotels or the festive colouring and lush ornament of Brodrick's at Scarborough. But the complex massing of the mansards, especially over the centre, and the dignified restraint of the detailing are unequalled.

148. Alfred B. Mullet:
Washington,
State, War and Navy Department Building, 1871-5

The contrast of the Executive Office Building with its *pendant* on the other side of Lafayette Square, Mills's Grecian Treasury, finally completed by Rogers a decade earlier, is still shocking to many. Yet it is most revealing to read here the representational aspirations of an age that found its most significant expression, not in its public buildings, but in the new sky-scrapers which first rose in New York at just this time, Hunt's Tribune Building and the Western Union Building by his pupil George B. Post. Both, incidentally, were heavily man-sarded, and the one by the American-trained Post was much more typically Second Empire than the French-trained Hunt's (see Chapter 14).

In urban domestic architecture, both on large mansions and on the more usual terrace houses, mansards became characteristic but not ubiquitous in the late fifties and remained so down to the mid seventies and even later in the West. Boston's Back Bay district, laid out by Gilman in 1859, has a few mansions along Commonwealth Avenue that resemble some-what the *hôtels particuliers* of Paris, and also several mansarded terraces by Bryant & Gilman and other architects in that avenue and in Marlborough and Beacon Streets. The materials used are un-Parisian – brownstone like Gilman's nearby church or dark-red brick with brown-stone trim – and the detail is rarely very plausibly French. In general, inspiration still came from London, even if nothing so extensive and spectacularly monumental as Grosvenor Place and Grosvenor Gardens was ever pro-duced. In New York Lienau's finest terrace, that built in Fifth Avenue between 55th and 56th Streets in 1869, was considerably hand-somer than are the Boston examples, being of white marble with very literate ranges of superposed orders. Hunt's New York work was often so authentically Parisian as quite to lack the bombast of the international Second Empire mode. Especially interesting were his Stuyvesant Flats in 18th Street, New York, of 1869-70. This block was a very early example of an apartment house of the Parisian sort in America, where they did not generally flourish before the eighties, later even than in London.

For the more characteristic free-standing houses that were built outside cities, in suburbs,

in towns, and even in the country, the Second Empire mode was also very popular. Interpreted in wood, painted brown or grey stone colours, these have a distinctly autochthonous character. Generally symmetrical and tightly planned, they did not advance the development of the American house in the way of the rival 'Stick Style'; but in their emphasis on complicated three-dimensional modelling, especially the modelling of the roofs, they prepared the way for one important aspect of the later and more original 'Shingle Style' (see Chapter 15).

The Second Empire episode in the United States is a curious one. On the one hand, it was a consciously 'modern' movement, deriving its prestige from contemporary Paris, not from any period of the past like the Greek, the Gothic, or even the Renaissance Revivals – of which last, of course, it was in some limited sense an heir. On the other hand, the considerable originality of the mode as it was actually employed was largely unconscious and due to the lack of accurate visual documents, or even a codified body of precedent, to be followed. At this time contemporary conditions demanded, as in Europe, the construction of many public edifices, Federal, state, and municipal, to house a complexity of functions. It would have been almost impossible to compress these within the rigid rectangles of the Greek Revival even had the Greek Revival not already been rejected by most critics twenty years or more earlier.

Yet the Second Empire episode was neces-sarily brief, lasting little more than a decade. The crass assurance it reflected, particularly the special arrogance of the post-war politicians in Washington, the state capitals, and in the bigger cities, was much shaken by the Panic of 1873. The mode did not therefore, as in much of Europe, continue in America into the eighties and nineties.

The episode has a longer-term significance, nevertheless. Slight as was the actual relation-ship to the Second Empire mode of the first two

Americans to be trained at the École des Beaux Arts, Hunt and Richardson, their personal influence and their prestige encouraged a growing trek of architectural students to Paris; their recommendations alone would hardly have had much effect had not fashion already established Paris rather than London in general esteem as the centre for modern architectural achievement and inspiration. From the mid eighties on, the long-maintained dependence on England in architectural matters began to be notably weakened; for a generation and more very many American architects would seek their roots abroad, but henceforth in France, or even Italy, not England.

It is not surprising that in the British Dominions there was no such direct French influence in this period as in Latin America. Urban entities like the Colmena and its terminal square in Lima, Peru, pavilioned and mansarded throughout, rival European examples like the Søtorvet in Copenhagen or the Galerij in Amsterdam. Before they gave way to skyscrapers, the *hôtels particuliers* along the Paseo de la Reforma in Mexico City were more numerous and more plausibly Parisian than along Commonwealth Avenue in Boston or Bellevue Avenue at Newport. But both in Canada and in Australia the Second Empire mode arrived from England late and in a more corrupted form than in America. The mansarded Windsor Hotel of 1878 in Montreal hardly rivalled the Palmer House of 1872 in Chicago by J. M. Van Osdel (1811-91), to which the rich merchant Potter Palmer was as proud to give his name as to the incredible fake castle that he built for his own occupancy a decade later. The Princess Theatre in Melbourne, Australia, built by William Pitt in 1877, with its three square-domed mansards, has an appealing nonchalance, like that of the contemporary edifices of the mining towns high in the American Rocky Mountains – the hotel in Virginia City, Nevada, that has been mentioned

earlier, or the much more modest Opera House in Central City, Colorado, for example. But the public architecture of the third quarter of the century in Australia was more restrained in design just because it was generally so very retardataire.

The Parliament House in Melbourne, begun in 1856 by John G. Knight (1824-92) and completed in 1880 by Peter Kerr (1820-1912), has academic virtues not unworthy of Kerr's master Barry, though its giant colonnades recall rather those of Brodrick's contemporary Town Hall in Leeds. The Treasury Buildings in Melbourne, by John James Clark (1838-1915) of 1857-8, are not unworthy of comparison with High Renaissance work of the period on the Continent. Other public buildings of the sixties and seventies are of more definitely Victorian character, but Early Victorian rather than High. For example, Clark's Government House of 1872-6 in South Melbourne is a towered Italian Villa consciously modelled on Queen Victoria's Osborne House of a generation earlier. Both in Australia and in Canada the Victorian Gothic had more vitality in this period (see Chapter 11).

There is little profit in pursuing farther in the outlying areas of the western world evidence of direct influence from Paris (of which there is, for example, some in Russia) or autochthonous variants of the Second Empire mode. In this generally rather unrewarding period the best work mostly falls under the High Victorian Gothic rubric, or else it illustrates specifically the development of commercial and domestic architecture in the Anglo-American world (see Chapters 10 and 11; 14 and 15). In an attempt to give an over-all picture too many buildings of low intrinsic quality and little present-day interest have already been cited.

What makes especially difficult the proper historical assessment of the widespread influence of Paris in the decades following 1850 is that this influence, whether direct or indirect, rarely produced buildings on the Continent of real distinction or even of much vitality. Only in England and the United States, where the mode was quite reshaped by a different cultural situation and the bold use of local materials, is it of much independent interest. The more plausibly Parisian the work outside France, the less vigour it usually possesses. Some of it can be very plausible indeed, as for example the street architecture of Mexico City and Buenos Aires, even if what appears to be carved French limestone in the Argentine capital is usually but a triumph of imitative craftsmanship on the part of stucco-workers imported from Italy. In general, Mexican and Argentine Second Empire is very dull, as dull as in Belgium, say, with no Poelaerts to redress the balance. Yet along the Malecón in Havana, Cuba, where the traditional galleried house-fronts were re-interpreted in a generically Second Empire way with Andalusian lushness, the results are much more notable, not least because the soft local stone has been very richly weathered by the strong sea breeze. As was mentioned earlier, the use of *azulejos* in extraordinary tones of brilliant green and purple gives autochthonous character to similar work in Brazil.

The international Second Empire mode has so far found no historian or even a sympathetic critic. Perhaps no other mode so widespread in its acceptance and so prolific in its production has ever received so little attention from posterity. Yet beside it the contemporary stream of the Victorian Gothic mode, which has been recurrently studied, must seem more than a little parochial and also excessively dependent on the individual capacities – not to say the caprices – of its leading practitioners. Within the areas in which the Victorian Gothic was employed, however, an area effectively confined to the Anglo-Saxon world geographically and to certain kinds of buildings typologically, it was capable of major architectural achievement. Moreover, thanks to the line of spiritual descent from the leaders of the generation of architects active in the third quarter of the century to those of the next, the more creative aspects of the architecture of the turn of the century derive in not inconsiderable part from the later Victorian Gothic.

The Lefuels and Hansens, or such men as Brodrick, Poclaert, and Gilman, trained no worthy pupils.[13a] But the disciples of the Victorian Gothic leaders not only include such very able young men who actually worked in their offices as Webb and Shaw and Voysey but also, in some sense at least, so great an American architect as Richardson, whose formal training had been wholly Parisian (see Chapters 11, 12, and 13). The advance of domestic architecture in the second half of the nineteenth century and, to a somewhat lesser extent, also that of commercial architecture therefore owed a great deal to the Victorian Gothic, at least in England and the United States of America (see Chapters 14 and 15).

CHAPTER 10

HIGH VICTORIAN GOTHIC IN ENGLAND

By 1850 Neo-Gothic was accepted as a proper mode for churches throughout the western world. Only in England, however, had it become dominant for such use. Moreover, Gothic was a more than acceptable alternative there to Greek or Renaissance or Jacobethan design for many other sorts of buildings also. Only in the urban fields of commercial construction and of terrace-housing was its employment still very rare. On the Continent the nearest equivalent in popularity and ubiquity to the Victorian Gothic was the German *Rundbogenstil*. Neo-Gothic, although used more and more everywhere after 1850 for churches, attracted few architectural talents of a high order (see Chapter 11).

There are several reasons why the Gothic Revival was able in England, and almost only in England, to pass into a new and creative phase around 1850. One was certainly the ethical emphasis of its doctrines, an emphasis more sympathetic to Victorians than to most Europeans of this period, but not without its appeal on the Continent towards the end of the century. Another reason was the informality, not to say the amateurishness, of architectural education in Britain, encouraging personal discipleship and the cultivation of individual expression rather than providing for the continuance of an academic discipline.

Related to this is the private character of architectural practice in England as compared to its more public responsibilities and controls on the Continent. The desirable professional positions in France, and to almost the same degree in many other European countries, were those offered by the sovereign or the State. But after the time of Soane and Nash official employment usually carried neither prestige nor opportunity in England, the Houses of Parliament notwithstanding – it was not Barry's work there but his clubs and mansions that established his high professional reputation. As in the eighteenth century, a social and aesthetic *élite* still provided both critical esteem and the most desirable commissions for Victorian architects; by 1850 a large part of that *élite* was very church-minded and thoroughly Gothicized. Not until the mid sixties was there any significant change; even then those responsible for this change, both the architects and their patrons, had mostly been brought up in the churchly Gothic Revival tradition.

The High Victorian Gothic opened with the building of a London church. All Saints', Margaret Street, designed in 1850,[1] largely completed externally by 1853, and consecrated in 1859, was the result of no imperial fiat, like the Votivkirche in Vienna or the big churches of the sixties in Paris, nor did it occupy like them an isolated site approached by wide new boulevards. Intended as a 'model' church by its sponsors, the Ecclesiological Society, and financed by private individuals, All Saints' is set in a minor West End street at the rear of a restricted court flanked by a clergy house and a school [149]. But for its tower, the tallest feature of the mid-century London skyline, it would have been hard to find; but once found, it could never be ignored.

The architect of All Saints', Butterfield, had been for some years, together with Carpenter, the favourite of the ecclesiologists because of the Pugin-like 'correctness' of his revived fourteenth-century English Gothic. Now, un-doubtedly encouraged by his sponsors he embarked on new paths. As soon as the walls began to rise, their startling character became apparent; for the church is of red brick, a material long out of use in London, and that red

149 and 150 *(opposite)*. William Butterfield: London, All Saints', Margaret Street, Schools and Clergy House and interior, 1850-9

brick is banded and patterned with black brick, a theme varied on the tower by the insertion of broad bands of stone. 'Permanent polychrome', achieved with a variety of materials, thus made its London debut. In the interior, moreover, the polychromatic effect was even richer and more strident, with marquetry of marble and tile in the spandrels of the nave arcade and over

the chancel arch, not to speak of onyx and gilding in the chancel itself [150]. The very exiguity of the site forced expansion upwards; the nave is tall, the vaulted chancel taller, and the subsidiary structures flanking the court are even higher and narrower in their proportions.

Preceding the designing and building of All Saints' there was significant complementary activity in the English architectural world. In 1849 a young critic, John Ruskin (1819-1900), brought out an important book, *The Seven Lamps of Architecture*, in which many of the recommendations ran parallel to, if indeed they did not influence, the innovations so soon introduced at All Saints'. Notably, Ruskin urged the study of Italian Gothic: If All Saints' is, in fact, not specifically Italian in the character of its polychromy, it was accepted as such by most contemporaries. The real foreign in-fluences here, as in the profile of the fine plain steeple, are German if anything; but Butter-field's moulded detail continued to follow quite closely English fourteenth-century models.[1a]

In that same year 1849 Wild[2] was building on an even more obscure London site in Soho his St Martin's Northern Schools with pointed arcades of brick definitely derived from Italian models. Furthermore, he was being acclaimed for doing this by the very ecclesiological leaders who had condemned his Christ Church, Streatham [67], as 'Saracenic' ten years before. With the publication of the first volume of Ruskin's next book, *The Stones of Venice*, in 1851 (the two less effective later volumes came out in 1853) and the appearance of *Brick and Marble Architecture of the Middle Ages in Italy* by G. E. Street (1824-81) in 1855, Italian influence rapidly increased. Street's name, moreover, introduces the third of the three men most responsible for the sharp turn that English architecture was taking in the fifties.

Without exploiting polychromy, Butterfield also designed in 1850 and built in 1851-2 St Matthias's off Howard Road in Stoke

Newington, a London suburb, another church of novel character. Unconfined by a closed-in urban site, this also showed in its great scale and the bold silhouette of the gable-roofed tower – long left standing above the bombed ruin of the church – how the timid Early Victorian Gothic of the forties could be invigorated. Moreover, at St Bartholomew's at Yealmpton in Devonshire, built in 1850, Butterfield introduced in a country church striped piers of two different tones of marble and considerable coloured marquetry work. A former fellow assistant of Street in G. G. Scott's office, William H. White (1826–90), at All Saints' in Talbot Road, Kensington, in London, begun in 1850, also used the new polychromy that soon became the principal, though by no means the only, hallmark of High Victorian Gothic.

A large country house of stone by S. S. Teulon (1812–73), Tortworth Court in Gloucestershire, built in 1849–53, has no polychromy, although its architect was soon to be the most unrestrained of all in its employment. His patrons, moreover, would be notably 'lower' in their churchmanship than the members of the Ecclesiological Society who commissioned Butterfield. But in the boldly plastic massing of Tortworth, leading up to a tall central tower of the most complex silhouette, Teulon exemplified the new architectural ambitions, ambitions that would soon be finding as striking expression in secular work as in ecclesiastical building whether 'high' or 'low'.

Street had been a favourite of the High Church party since he first began building small country churches and schools of a most 'correct' sort on leaving Scott's office. He was also the author of several critical articles, notable for their cogency, published in *The Ecclesiologist*. In these he commented, for example, on the applicability of the arcades of Wild's school to commercial building; he also attacked the curious habit of the forties, most prevalent with the ecclesiologists, of designing urban churches on confined sites as if they were to sprawl over ample village greens. Street began his first important church, with associated school buildings, All Saints', Boyn Hill, at Maidenhead, in 1853. Here he made use of red brick and almost as much permanent polychrome as Butterfield at All Saints', Margaret Street. He also handled the detail, particularly on the schools, with something of the sort of brutal 'realism' (to employ a catchword of the period) Butterfield used on his subsidiary buildings.

In the same year in London, Street's former employer Scott, long established as the most successful, if hardly the most 'correct', of Early Victorian Gothic practitioners, and since 1849 Architect to Westminster Abbey, built in Broad Sanctuary contiguous to the façade of the Abbey a Gothic terrace. That the use of Gothic should have been encouraged here by the Abbey authorities is not surprising. But they themselves may well have been surprised at what their architect produced; for this is no flat range of Neo-Tudor fronts in stock brick, but a plastic mass of stonework bristling with oriels and turrets and capped with a broken skyline of stepped gables. Nothing here recalls the rather French thirteenth-century Gothic of the Abbey itself; instead the effect is Germanic, recalling the medieval houses of the Hansa cities. The work was executed with a boldness of detail less personal in character than Butterfield's or Street's, but quite as striking to the casual observer.

Scott's houses had little influence, however. Gothic terraces were no more popular in the fifties and sixties in England than in the preceding decades. In residential districts the flood of more-or-less Renaissance stucco continued to spread, little affected by the High Victorian Gothic. As we have seen, the Second Empire mode also had only a very limited success in this field of construction, a field dominated not by architects but by builders.[2a]

In 1853 also Scott provided for the Camden Church in the Peckham Road in South London – Ruskin's own family church – a new east end in a round-arched and banded medievalizing mode; Ruskin himself collaborated on the window design, or so it is said. There is sufficient Gothic 'realism' in the detail here to justify considering this a round-arched variant of the High Victorian Gothic, but it is definitely of Italian inspiration. It seems also to be related to the later *Rundbogenstil* of this decade in Germany and Austria; nor is it altogether without resemblance to such a contemporary French church as Vaudoyer's Byzantinesque cathedral of Marseilles as begun a few years later.

Several far more important and better publicized interventions in architecture on the part of Ruskin followed immediately. In considerable part because of his personal influence with an Oxford friend, the Gothic design of the Irish architects Sir Thomas Deane[3] (1792–1871) and Benjamin Woodward (1815–61) was accepted for the University Museum at Oxford in 1855. Woodward had already proved himself a would-be Ruskinian in detailing their design of 1853 for the Museum of Trinity College, Dublin, in a Venetian (though largely *quattrocento*) way. As the Oxford Museum rose to completion in the next four years, Ruskin was in continuous contact with Woodward, providing himself the design for at least one window as well as encouraging the delegation to the Irish O'Sheas of much of the responsibility for the ornamental decoration – of which only a small part was, in fact, ever executed. The work of the O'Sheas is better appreciated in Dublin, where the decoration both of the Trinity College building and of the Kildare Street Club of 1861 was carved by them in a very free and yet boldly naturalistic vein.

The most interesting feature of the University Museum – and one that it is surprising to find Ruskin, who hated iron and all it stood for in the nineteenth-century world, involved with – is

151. Deane & Woodward: Oxford, University Museum, 1855–9

the court with its roof of iron and glass [151]. How different this is, however, from what ironfounders without architectural control were providing at the same time in the Brompton Boilers! Yet it is even more different from Hopper's or Rickman's iron Gothic of fifty years earlier [102]. For all the elaboration of the ornament, which is very metallic in character but also very close to Early Gothic precedent, what is most notable is the highly articulated character of the structure, as if the architects had asked themselves: 'How would medieval builders have used structural iron had it been readily available to them?' Is this, perhaps, the first echo in England of the theories of Viollet-le-Duc, the French architect who was to exercise an international influence equal to Ruskin's over the next generation? Probably not, as his own enthusiasm for iron was only publicized later (see Chapter 16). Whether or not there is specific influence from Viollet-le-Duc here, his great archaeological publication, the *Dictionnaire raisonné*,[4] had begun to appear the year before. Very soon the structural expressiveness of 'Early French' detailing, studied by English architects at first hand as well as in the woodcuts of the *Dictionnaire*, began to supplant Italian polychromy as the hallmark of advanced fashion in the higher aesthetic circles.

A more modest Oxford building by Deane & Woodward, the Union Debating Hall of 1856-7, has more vigour on the whole than does the Museum, particularly in its characteristically

notched brick detailing. It also had the advantage of murals by the young Pre-Raphaelites. One of these, who had just left Street's architectural office to turn briefly to painting, was William Morris (1834-96).[5] His ceiling here initiated the most distinguished career of architectural decoration of the second half of the century. Morris as a critical writer was destined, moreover, to be at least as influential on later architects as Ruskin or Viollet-le-Duc.

Of the same date, 1856, is perhaps the most successful of Butterfield's extant churches, that at Baldersby St James, near Beverley in Yorkshire, with its contiguous group of vicarage, schools, and cottages. All of stone externally, the polychromy here is rather a sort of 'poly-

152. William Butterfield:
Baldersby St James, Yorkshire, St James's, 1856

texture' most effectively handled in the banding of the tall pyramidal spire above the plain square tower [152]. Internally a delicate harmony of pink and grey-blue bricks, with accents of creamy stone, replaces the acid chords of All Saints' in London, a harmony rivalled in the Welsh church of St Augustine's at Penarth near Cardiff built a decade later in 1866. At the same time, Teulon at St Andrew's in Coin Street off Stamford Street south of the Thames in London was using the boldest of brick-and-stone banding externally and, inside, elaborate patterns of light-coloured brickwork. Moreover, the rather Germanic planning of this church, demolished since the Second World War, was highly unorthodox by ecclesiological standards. Already it was evident that within the High Victorian Gothic there were to be two streams, one High Church in its patronage and led by architects of considerable learning and sophistication like Butterfield and Street, another more characteristically Low Church and often quite secular; this was generally coarser and more philistine, not to say outright illiterate.

Yet not all the best work of the High Church architects was ecclesiastical. By 1857 J. L. Pearson (1817-97) had already built some respectable if not very interesting churches distinguished chiefly by their very fine spires; but his first work of positive High Victorian character was Quar Wood, a country house he built in Gloucestershire in that year. The skilful asymmetrical massing around the stair tower here, the plastic variety provided by several different types of steep roofs, the crisp precision of the detailing, all combine to produce a modest mansion that is as different in effect from Teulon's mountainous Tortworth as both are characteristic of the beginnings of the High Victorian Gothic.

Two more houses begun after Quar Wood, both within the broad frame of reference of the maturing High Victorian Gothic, could hardly differ more from one another. In remodelling Eatington Park in Warwickshire in 1858 John Prichard (1818-86) attempted to mask an underlying Georgian mansion with a profusion of bold innovations in the detailing. Stone polychromy, applied sculpture, bold plastic membering of wall, roof, and chimneys, all are used here more abundantly than ever before. The Red House at Bexley Heath in Kent, on the other hand, which Philip Webb (1831-1915), who had been a fellow pupil with Morris in Street's office, built for Morris in 1859-60, is notable for its extreme simplicity. So also is the house now known as Benfleet Hall that he built in 1861 at Cobham in Surrey for Spencer Stanhope, another of the young artists who had collaborated on the murals of the Oxford Union. This has a more advanced plan than the Red House.

These houses have no external polychromy, only plain red brick beautifully laid; there is no sculptured detail at all; and the few breaks in the loose massing of the walls and roof are closely related to the informal ease of the rather novel plans. Only the high roofs of red tile are similar to those of Pearson's Quar Wood. But in the plain, very 'real', detailing and the segmental-headed white-painted window-sash of an early eighteenth-century sort, set under pointed relieving arches, the relationship is close to the secular work of somewhat older men – to Butterfield's vicarages of the forties [213] and more notably to his clergy house and school at All Saints', Margaret Street [149]. Webb had himself worked on some of the latest of the rather similar vicarages and schools that Street had been building for a decade. His first big country house, Arisaig, built of local stone in the remote Scottish Highlands forty miles beyond Fort William in Inverness-shire beginning in 1863, may properly be considered High Victorian Gothic also [215]. It is especially interesting, like Benfleet Hall, for its plan (see Chapter 15).

Down to about 1860 the development of the High Victorian Gothic was on the whole convergent. Henceforth, ambitious young architects tried harder to have personal modes of their own like Butterfield; yet, conversely, many formed loose stylistic alliances in which individual expression became merged in some sort of group expression. The boldest and the most unruly were no longer likely to be of the High Church party, but rather of the Low. St Simon Zelotes of 1859 in Moore Street in London by Joseph Peacock (1821-93) hardly compares with the work of Butterfield and Street in distinction; but its internal polychromy of white and black brick outbids that of their best London churches, also built at the end of this decade.

Butterfield's St Alban's in Baldwin's Gardens off Holborn in London, erected 1858-61, is all rebuilt now. But something of its splendidly tall proportions, if not the rich brick and tile marquetry of the wall over the chancel arch, can still be apprehended. The contrast in quality with Peacock's work was once amazing. Street's St James the Less in Thorndike Street off the Vauxhall Bridge Road in London, also of 1858-61, is less fine but still much superior to Peacock's work [153]. The tall square tower, set apart like a campanile, has a curiously gawky roof based on a Genoa model and the interior is somewhat cavernous. But in the richness of its red and black brick patterns, used both inside and out, and in the naturalistic carving of the nave capitals this church of Street's rivals Butterfield's All Saints' and St Alban's and is, unlike the latter, still completely intact.

Various younger men of Webb's generation were beginning to make important contributions in church design also. G. F. Bodley (1827-1907), trained in his kinsman Scott's office rather than in Street's, built St Michael's, Brighton, in 1859-62. This must have been very striking for the boldness of its scale and for the vigour of its structural expression before it was

153. G. E. Street:
London, St James the Less, Thorndike Street, 1858-61

overshadowed by the tall later nave beside it added by William Burges (1827-81).[6] But it is not the parody of 'Early French' detailing in the square archivolts and spreading capitals of the nave arcade, so soon to be abjured by Bodley, that is significant here but the fact that this was the first church to receive an over-all decorative treatment, including stained glass, at the hands of Morris and his associates, who included the painters Ford Madox Brown and Edward Burne-Jones.

There is still finer glass of this period designed by Burne-Jones in the east window of Waltham Abbey in Essex, where the rear wall was rebuilt in the heaviest 'Early French' taste by Burges in 1860-1. As a painter Burne-Jones is hardly to be compared with Ingres; yet as a designer of stained glass the superiority of such early windows of his as these at Waltham Abbey to the ones by Ingres at Dreux and at Neuilly is amazing. It is not the least claim to distinction of the High Victorian Gothic that it nurtured this brilliant revival of decorative art led by Morris. Many churches of the sixties and seventies are worth visiting solely for their windows by Morris, Brown, and Burne-Jones to which there are apparently no worthy Continental parallels.

A quite different sort of contemporary church is White's Holy Saviour, Aberdeen Park, in London, of 1859. Externally this is quiet and rather shapeless; but inside the red brick of the exterior gives way to a subtle harmony of patterned brickwork in beiges, browns, and mauves – assisted in the chancel by some additional decorative painting – that is unequalled in High Victorian polychromy. Also rather different from standard High Church Anglican work of the day is the Catholic church of St Peter in Leamington of 1861-5 [154] by Henry Clutton (1819-93). He had won the competition for Lille Cathedral in France in 1855 with a design prepared in collaboration with Burges, but was not allowed to supervise the construction because he was a Protestant; English Roman Catholics were not so bigoted. Internally the characteristic articulation of Puginian planning was given up; nave and apse form one continuous vessel, almost basilican in effect, under a barrel roof that ends in a half dome. Unfortunately, the painted decoration of the walls and the ceiling here has all been destroyed; the effect must once have been much less barren than it is today. Externally, plain red brick is most happily combined with stone trim treated with great simplicity and yet with extreme subtlety. The inspiration is Early French, perhaps influenced by Viollet-le-Duc,[7] although Clutton knew old French work at first hand; but the smooth concavities and the

delicately varied chamfers are handled with the greatest originality and justness of scaling. The fine tower, at once sturdy in its detailing and svelte in its shape, has lost the original pyramidal roof.

154. Henry Clutton:
Leamington, Warwickshire, St Peter's, 1861-5

Not unworthy of the church, and vastly superior to Clutton's rather dull country houses, is the contiguous rectory here, a rectangle in plan with the long gable broken only by elegantly chamfered pairs of brick chimneys [154]. The expanses of plain brick wall are regularly but not symmetrically pierced by coupled windows divided by colonnette mullions of stone. In simplicity of massing this rectory surpassed the Red House and Webb's other – and in some ways better – early house for Spencer Stanhope, Benfleet Hall. In their simple dignity such things contrast sharply with the more ambitious secular work of the day, by this time reaching peaks of elaboration almost exceeding Prichard's Eatington Park.

Teulon's Elvetham Park in Hampshire of 1861, for example, is perhaps the wildest of all High Victorian Gothic houses;[7a] this mansion is so complex in composition and so varied in its detailing that it quite defies description. Polychromy runs riot, forms of the most various but indefinable Gothic provenience merge into one another, and the result seems almost to illustrate that original mode of design which Thomas Harris (1830–1900)[8] had just christened 'Victorian' in describing a project he published in 1860 for a terrace of houses at Harrow.

However, several churches of the mid sixties rivalled Elvetham Hall, if not Harris's 'Victorian Terrace'. There was, for example, Teulon's own St Thomas's, Wrotham Road, of 1864, piling up to its heavy central tower among the railway yards of Camden Town in London; and there was also his much more peculiar St Paul's, Avenue Road, also of 1864, in the approaches to Hampstead. This was purged early of its original internal decoration but it long remained externally an almost unrecognizable variant of the standard Victorian Gothic church. Both have been demolished since the war. At St Mary's in the London suburb of Ealing, built in 1866–73, Teulon used iron columns for the nave arcade; a still wilder Low Church architect, Bassett Keeling (1836–86), did the same in two London churches, St Mark's in St Mark's Road, Notting Dale, and St George's on Campden Hill (where they have since been replaced), both begun in 1864. Nor were Teulon and Keeling by any means the only architects to revive the use of iron columns in the sixties; even Burges introduced them once in a church, St Faith's at Stoke Newington, now demolished, and also in his less attractive but extant Speech Room at Harrow School of 1872.

Of a quite different order is another London church, St Martin's in Vicars Road, Gospel Oak, also begun in 1864. This is by E. B. Lamb (1805–69), an architect who had already begun to show rather High Victorian tendencies in the thirties. There is no polychromy here, and the inspiration from the past is neither Italian nor French but the still heterodox English Perpendicular. The massive plasticity of Lamb's personal mode, with much large-scale chamfering and a consistent use of segmental-pointed arches in several orders, is happier where it was exploited more simply on the nearby rectory. The interior of his church, which has a sort of central plan with wide transepts and only a slightly prolonged nave, is a forest of timberwork ingeniously bracketed and intersected in a fashion peculiar to Lamb. Only perhaps in an international context, in relation to the contemporary American 'Stick Style', is this sort of structural articulation intelligible (see Chapter 15). But the solid, compactly planned, and simply detailed rectory has virtues not unworthy of comparison with Clutton's at Leamington, if not perhaps with Webb's more delicately scaled and functionally articulated early houses.

Two churches by Street, St John's at Torquay of 1861–71[9] and St Philip and St James's at Oxford, which was completed in 1862, are more standard products of the early sixties. The former is notable for the very rich marble polychromy in the chancel and the full complement of windows by Morris and Burne-Jones; the latter is more 'Early French' with a tall tower rising in front of the polygonal apse and a curiously unorthodox but effectively 'real' way of running the nave arches into the east wall with no imposts at all. The device was repeated at All Saints', Clifton, now destroyed, where the variety of colours of the fine local stones – orange and blue Pennant and cream Bath – permitted a more truly structural polychromy than usual and one of remarkable tonal harmony. All Saints' was begun in 1863.

Both Burges and Pearson erected distinguished churches at this time, Burges in Ireland, Pearson in London. St Finbar's Church of Ireland Cathedral in Cork, designed in 1863 for a competition and built in 1865–76, is of unusual size for a British church of this period and, what is more unusual for a nineteenth-century cathedral, it was completed without serious modification of the original project. Provided with a fine open site and a full complement of towers, two flanking the west front and a taller one over the crossing, this rivals in elaboration the big Continental Gothic churches of the period (see Chapter 11). Moreover, the detailing is of a distinctly French twelfth-century order with very few eclectic or Italianate touches, thus recalling the winning design for Lille Cathedral that he had prepared with Clutton in 1855. Yet the contrast with contemporary Continental Gothic – especially with Lille Cathedral as finally executed by others – is almost as great as in the case of the rather more original English churches of this period by Butterfield or Street.

In the interior of St Finbar's Burges developed the theme of articulation, a theme more characteristically Early English than 'Early French', with remarkable plastic vigour; while the handsome wooden roof, so rare a feature in medieval France, lends to the whole an unmistakably Victorian air. Less subtle, less aesthetic, than other churches of the sixties by younger men, St Finbar's has the sort of athletic strength that is characteristic of much High Victorian Gothic expressed here in unusually literate, not to say archaeological, terms.

Burges's church opened the road again towards a more 'correct' imitation of the medieval High Gothic, a road along which Pearson soon proceeded more rapidly and more doggedly than he. Yet Pearson's own South London church of 1863–5, St Peter's in Kennington Lane, Vauxhall, is more typically High Victorian than St Finbar's. The carved capitals and the heavy scale of the stone detail are rather 'Early French'. But walls and vaults are of London stock brick and there is some polychromy of the quieter, less Butterfieldian, sort resembling a little White's at St Saviour's.

The continuity of the chancel and rounded apse with the nave echoes the 'unified space' of Clutton's Leamington interior. Puginian articulation of plan and mass was henceforth somewhat out of date.

The Albert Memorial[10] in Hyde Park in London is a monument generally – and not unjustly – considered the perfect symbol of this High Victorian period, more perfect than the Houses of Parliament (in the early sixties at last approaching completion) were of the previous Early Victorian period. In 1861 Queen Victoria's beloved husband, the Prince Consort, died. In the competition for a national memorial to rise in Hyde Park near the site of the Crystal Palace, held the next year, G. G. Scott almost inevitably won first place. Construction of the Albert Memorial began in 1863 and took nearly ten years. By the time it was completed in 1872 critics of advanced taste were already condemning it, yet it represents precisely what Scott most liked to do and what he undoubtedly did best – in his own words, this his 'most prominent work' represented his 'highest and most enthusiastic efforts'. It is, moreover, an epitome of the aspirations[11] most widely held when it was designed [155].

The contrast between this elaborate shrine and Scott's modest and essentially archaeological Martyrs' Memorial of 1841 at Oxford is very great – what a long distance the English Gothic Revival had travelled in a score of years! Among Early Victorian memorials the Prince Consort's cenotaph is rather more like Kemp's Scott Monument in Edinburgh [91] than like the Oxford one. But where Kemp's is soft and monochrome, this is hard and almost kaleidoscopically polychromatic. Scott's theme is still that of the fourteenth-century English Eleanor Crosses, as is certainly appropriate for a monument to a Royal spouse; but the inspiration came in the main from relatively small reliquaries and other medieval works in metal embellished with enamels and semi-precious stones.

155. Sir G. G. Scott: London, Albert Memorial, 1863–72

The Martyrs' Memorial was purely English, the specific precedents for the Albert Memorial mostly Continental: Italian, French, German, and Flemish. The materials are cold and shining, polished granites, marbles, and serpentines of various colours; and much of the detail is executed in gun-metal left plain or gilded. A profusion of white marble sculpture at various scales leads up to the seated bronze figure of the Prince by J. H. Foley, finally installed in 1876, over which is a vaulted canopy of brilliantly coloured glass mosaic. Enamels, cabochons of marble or serpentine, and intricately crisp detail of the most metallic character carry out Scott's basic idea of a ciborium enlarged, like Bernini's in St Peter's, to fully architectural scale.

Beside the Albert Memorial most of Scott's other work of this period lacks interest. His churches, particularly, are likely to be dull and respectable, reflecting the new eclectic tastes of the day only in a rather inconspicuous way. His Exeter College Chapel at Oxford of 1856-8 is a sort of Sainte-Chapelle; St John's College Chapel at Cambridge of 1863-9 is equally monumental but somewhat less French in character and also more original in its proportions. His secular work at Oxford and Cambridge is also dull, lacking the Ruskinian touches that give a certain vitality to the Meadow Buildings built for Christ Church in 1863 by Sir Thomas Deane and his son Thomas Newenham Deane (1828-99).

Far finer, however, is their Kildare Street Club in Dublin, facing the Trinity College Museum across an expanse of lawn; for this continues the best Ruskinian tradition of the work that they did earlier with Woodward, as has been noted already.[12]

A very striking example of the Gothic of the early sixties in England, superior to anything at Oxford or Cambridge, is the Merchant Seamen's Orphan Asylum of 1861 by G. Somers Clark (1825-82), now the Wanstead Hospital, in a suburb north-east of London. This is

actually more what is supposed to be 'Ruskinian', because of its Venetian detailing, than the very original Dublin clubhouse with its consistent theme of segmental arches and its bold naturalistic carving; but, like that, the Wanstead building is generically High Victorian in the asymmetrical massing, the strong colours of the black-banded red brickwork, and the surprising richness of the decoration Clark lavished on a utilitarian structure.

In the early sixties several younger men, most of them trained in Street's office, were already turning away from the stridency of the work of the High Victorian leaders towards a simpler and suaver mode. Webb's houses of this period have been mentioned, and will be again (see Chapter 15). Here the plain row of small London shops that he built at 91-101 Worship Street, Finsbury, in 1861 might be described. In them the material is not even red brick, but London stocks excellently laid. Almost nothing is overtly Gothic, yet a sense of medieval craftsmanship controls the handling of both the wide shop-windows below and the sash-windows in the upper storeys. Above all, the general composition is quiet and regular, more like Clutton's Leamington rectory than the asymmetrical articulation that is characteristic of Webb's own houses of these years.

A similar quietness controls the design of the wing that W. Eden Nesfield (1835-88), son of Barry's collaborator on Italian gardens, William A. Nesfield (1793-1881), and a pupil not of Street but of Burn and Salvin, was adding to the Earl of Craven's seat, Combe Abbey in Warwickshire, beginning in 1863. This was Nesfield's first major work. Despite his studies of French Gothic,[13] which he had published the previous year with a dedication to Lord Craven, and the tracings he is supposed to have made from the illustrations of Gothic detail in Viollet-le-Duc's *Dictionnaire*, the arches at Combe Abbey were round, not pointed, and the major architectural theme was the English late medieval 'window-wall' of many lights divided by stone mullions and transoms.

In a completely new house, Cloverley Hall, that Nesfield began in 1865 together with his partner Richard Norman Shaw (1831–1912), the great window-bays and the other ranges of stone-mullioned windows in the beautifully laid salmon-pink brick walls were even more the principal theme of the design. But in the decorations, delicate in scale and elegant in craftsmanship, a new sort of eclecticism made its appearance. Basically the house derives from those manor houses of the sixteenth century that were uninfluenced by Renaissance ideas; but in the detailing of Cloverley there were Japanese motifs, notably the sunflower disks that Nesfield called his 'pies', reflecting the new interest in oriental art that such painters as Whistler and Rossetti were taking. Except for its relatively early date, Cloverley Hall has no place in a discussion of High Victorian Gothic, for it is characteristically Late Victorian (see Chapter 15).

Nesfield's partner Shaw, however, built in the sixties two churches that were still High Victorian in style, one in Yorkshire, the other at Lyons in France. Holy Trinity at Bingley of 1866–7 was one of the finest examples of the 'Early French' phase of the Victorian Gothic [156]. Externally it built up to a very tall central tower, superbly proportioned and simply detailed, that more than rivalled in quality Street's at Oxford. Internally the fine random-ashlar stonework – there was no polychromy – the very bold and structural detailing of the square archivolts and the simply carved capitals illustrated even better than does Webb's domestic work in brick the new and more sophisticated attitude towards the building crafts. The principles involved go back to Pugin; but now for the first time in Webb's and Nesfield's and Shaw's work of the sixties one senses a real respect, at once intelligent and intuitive, for the differing nature of different materials. Such a

156. R. Norman Shaw:
Bingley, Yorkshire, Holy Trinity, 1866–7

respect would continue to give special virtue to the work of the most distinguished English and American architects of the late nineteenth and early twentieth centuries (see Chapters 12, 13, 15, and 19).

The Lyons church, which Shaw began in 1868, is perhaps the finest of the many Victorian churches built on the Continent for local English colonies, but very different indeed from that at Bingley. A city church set between tall blocks of flats, this is also very tall in its proportions and has a more urban character than that of the Yorkshire church. French freestone does not lend itself to the particular type of semi-rustic craftsmanship that was now rising to favour with the younger English architects; hence the Lyons church is less significant than the Bingley one in that respect. But Shaw was not primarily a church architect, nor did he long remain a High Victorian (see Chapter 12).

More characteristic of the various new directions that the Victorian Gothic was taking in the mid sixties, directions that soon also led quite away from the High Victorian, are two new churches both designed well before Shaw's at Bingley and Lyons were begun. At All Saints' in Jesus Lane, Cambridge, begun in 1863, the spikiness of the Italianizing Victorian Gothic and the rugged structuralism of the 'Early French' – rarely carried farther than in Bodley's own early work – gave way to something much more English in inspiration. There is, for example, a very deep chancel and only one aisle, not to speak of a battlemented tower at one side, out of which rises a small stone spire. In fact, Bodley returned here to the fourteenth-century Decorated models preferred by Pugin, some so 'late' as to suggest the still forbidden Perpendicular.

Bodley now made even more use of the decorative talents of Morris and his associates than at St Michael's, Brighton. His St Martin's-on-the-Cliff, Scarborough, completed in 1863, is a finer church than either St Michael's or All Saints'. Falling between them in style as well as in date, this has less historical importance, but it also was richly decorated by the Morris firm. At All Saints' painted polychromy, but of a rather subtle order much superior to most of that of the forties, entirely replaced permanent polychrome. The brocade patterns stencilled on the walls seem almost to be designs of Pugin strengthened in their outlines and their colours by Morris. Although Bodley's mature career as one of the two principal Late Victorian church architects did not really get under way until

1870, Victorian Gothic was evidently coming full circle at All Saints', and the High Victorian phase was nearly over.

The other important new church of this period, St Saviour's, Penn Street, in the Hoxton district of the East End of London, was begun in 1865 by James Brooks (1825–1901). Unfortunately this was very badly damaged by bombing, and has since been demolished. St Saviour's was of brick and included some polychromy like Brooks's slightly earlier East End church, St Michael's in Mark Street, Shoreditch, of 1863–5. But what was really significant

157. James Brooks:
London, St Saviour's, Hoxton, 1865–7

at St Saviour's was the unified interior space, ending like Clutton's Leamington church and Pearson's Vauxhall church in London in a rounded apse [157]. Notable also were the Webb-like quietness of the general composition and the straightforward handling of the main structural elements. In another, happily unbombed, church by Brooks in the East End of London, St Chad's, Nichols Square, in Haggerston, which was begun in 1867, the same qualities can be seen in a more mature state. Moreover, the rather plain windows and the simple moulded brick trim are echoed at domestic scale on the nearby rectory.

The fine vessel of the interior of St Chad's, with its simple nave arcade of stone, clean red-brick walls, quietly structural wooden roof over the nave, and brick-vaulted chancel, contrasts strikingly with the hectic elaboration and dramatically vertical proportions of Butterfield's last London church of any great interest, St Augustine's, Queen's Gate, of 1865-71. Two churches of the late sixties outside London, All Saints' at Babbacombe near Torquay, which was built in 1868-74, and the earlier mentioned St Augustine's at Penarth, begun in 1866, are much more satisfactory examples of Butterfield's middle period.

Brooks continued through the seventies to develop the implications of his East End churches with great success. The largest and most notable is that of the Ascension, Lavender Hill, in Battersea, which was begun in 1873 and completed by J. T. Micklethwaite[14] (1843–1906), a former assistant of G. G. Scott, in 1883. The vast lancet-pierced red-brick hull of this church is one of the landmarks of the South London skyline; the interior, which is perhaps a little bare, has nevertheless a monumentality of scale rare in English churches of any period. However, this monumentality is rivalled both inside and out in St Bartholomew's, Brighton[14a] [158], completed in 1875 by Edmund E. Scott (?-1895), and considerably later in Brooks's own London church of All Hallows, Shirlock Street, begun in 1889 and never provided with its intended vaults.

Victorian Gothic, whether Early or High, is primarily an ecclesiastical mode. The leading Neo-Gothic architects were happiest when building churches; their few secular works – if parsonages, colleges, and schools can really in this period be called secular – generally have a churchy tone. But it is characteristic of the High Victorian Gothic as opposed to the Early Victorian Gothic, and a *fortiori* to Neo-Gothic

158 *(below)*. Edmund E. Scott: Brighton, St Bartholomew's, completed 1875

159 *(right)*. E. W. Godwin: Congleton, Cheshire, Town Hall, 1864-7

on the Continent, that it became for some twenty years, from the early fifties to the early seventies, a nearly universal mode.[15] A good many houses have already been cited; and certainly no churches of this period provide finer specimens of High Victorian Gothic than the warehouse at 104 Stokes Croft in Bristol, which was built by E. W. Godwin (1833-86), a friend of Burges, in the early sixties [200], or the office building of 1864-5 at 60 Mark Lane in London by George Aitchison (1825-1910). The one is an especially subtle attempt to follow Ruskin's polychromed Italianism, the other more 'Early French' in its detail, but both use

round-arched arcading throughout their several storeys (see Chapter 14).

Godwin in two rather modest town halls, one at Northampton of 1861-4, which is very rich in sculptural detail, the other at Congleton, Cheshire, of 1864-7, which is more severe and 'Early French' in character, produced two further High Victorian Gothic[16] works of the highest quality [159]. Unfortunately by the time the taste of the authorities in the larger English cities caught up in the late sixties with the advanced position of the High Church architectural leaders, those leaders had left that position far behind. As a result, many of the

biggest and most conspicuous public edifices are very retardataire. Gothic designs won only low premiums in the Government Offices competition in 1857, although both Street's and Deane & Woodward's, on which Ruskin may have advised, were of considerable distinction. When Alfred Waterhouse (1830-1905) two years later won the competition for the Manchester Assize Courts he elaborated the design of this large public structure, based on Deane & Woodward's Oxford Museum, with some features borrowed from their project of 1857.

At best Waterhouse had a rather heavy hand and an uncertain sort of eclectic taste somewhat like G. G. Scott's. He lacked the cranky boldness of a Butterfield, the sophistication of a Street, and the sense of craftsmanship of such men as Webb and Godwin who were his own contemporaries. But he did have real capacity as a planner of large and complex buildings, something at which most of the leading church architects had little or no experience. Thus his Manchester Town Hall, begun ten years later than the Assize Courts in 1869, while lacking all the refinement of Godwin's smaller and earlier ones, is a large-scale exercise in High Victorian Gothic of some interest. But inevitably Victorian Gothic was a mode less well suited to this kind of monumental exploitation than the contemporary Second Empire mode as naturalized in England and America. For all the skill of Waterhouse in the organization of plan and general composition and in the bold detailing of materials inside and out, the Manchester Town Hall is a late and inferior work – late, that is, in the phase of style which it represents, though not so late in the highly successful career of its architect. It may properly be compared, and to its own manifest advantage moreover, with Schmidt's Rathaus in Vienna.

The other most conspicuous High Victorian Gothic public monument, the Law Courts in London, is the work of Street, an older and a more distinguished architect; but it came very late indeed in Street's career, so late that he died before it was finished in 1882. Designed originally for a competition held in 1866, many years dragged by during which the site was twice changed – once southward to the river's edge and then back to the north of the Strand – before it was even begun in 1874. Other work of the late sixties and early seventies by Street indicates how completely his own taste had turned away from this sort of French thirteenth-century Gothic even before the Law Courts were started.

At St Margaret's in Liverpool, for example, which he designed in 1867, Street reverted to English fourteenth-century models; thus, like Bodley at All Saints', Cambridge, he seemed to be returning to the particular stylistic ideal with which the ecclesiologists had started out twenty-five years before. In the Guards' Chapel at the Wellington Barracks in London, however, now entirely rebuilt except for Street's apse, he remodelled in 1877 the interior of an engineer-built Grecian edifice with incredible sumptuousness in a sort of Byzantinoid Italian Romanesque, using a stone-and-brick banded barrel vault and a glittering investiture of gold mosaic to the east that still outshines the comparable work of Continental architects in the *Rundbogenstil*. Then, in remodelling the interior of St Luke's, West Norwood, near London, built by Francis Bedford (1784–1858) in 1823–5 and equally Grecian, he used in 1878–9 even more Italianate detail. Despite the bold banding in brick and stone, this is certainly not Gothic or Byzantine, but rather recalls the Tuscan Proto-Renaissance or even the *quattrocento*.

Certain buildings by Deane & Woodward and by Scott at Oxford and Cambridge have already been mentioned; much more exists by Scott, Waterhouse, and various others, very little of it of any distinction, yet sometimes fitting not too uncomfortably into the general scene. The most striking example of Victorian Gothic architecture at Oxford, fortunately on

an isolated site opposite the Parks, where it had no neighbours earlier than the Museum, is Butterfield's Keble College, a complete entity in itself, largely built in 1868–70. With its walls so violently striated with bricks of various colours, Keble would have been a most disturbing increment to any existing college; on the other hand, Butterfield's quieter stone-banded chapel at Balliol of 1857 is that college's happiest Victorian feature, the rest being largely the work of Waterhouse.

Since Keble was founded by Butterfield's pious High Church friends for clerical students, the chapel, which was added to the group in 1873–6, understandably dominates the whole. Tall and richly decorated, this has many of Butterfield's virtues, but it quite lacks the directness and the poignance of his best work of the fifties and early sixties. The hall and library are less monumental than the chapel, fitting more easily into the ranges of sets that surround the two quadrangles. The over-all composition is fairly regular, and there is less coarse or fussy detailing than Scott and Waterhouse used in their 'Collegiate Gothic'. Moreover, the scale of Keble is modestly domestic and, despite its considerable size, the features are simple and crisp; but in the relatively clean air of Oxford Butterfield's polychromy has received less of the desirable mellowing than it gets in London. The banded walls certainly lack the harmony that the softer colours of the materials used in his country church interiors generally produced.

By the time Keble was completed – indeed in advanced circles well before it was begun – such polychromatic brashness was out of date. Yet at Rugby School, where Butterfield's buildings of 1868–72 awkwardly adjoin various earlier nineteenth-century Gothic structures, the polychromy is even louder; moreover, it is still less mellowed by time. Although Butterfield lived on through the rest of the century and continued to build many churches and some schools, this first and boldest of High Victorian Gothic architects was more and more left behind after the mid sixties by the evolving taste of his own High Church milieu.

There are other High Victorian Gothic collegiate groups which are, or would have been if carried to completion, far finer than Keble. Being at less renowned institutions than Oxford, they are less well known. University College on the sea-front at Aberystwyth in Wales is by J. P. Seddon (1827–1906), from 1852 to 1862 a partner of John Prichard. This, structure was begun in 1864 to serve as a hotel, incorporating as its most inappropriate nucleus a small Castellated villa built by Nash for Uvedale Price

in the 1780s. The failure of the hotel project, the slow and faltering start of the college, and the necessary repair and rebuilding after two fires have left a complex pile of most disparate character, even though it is almost all by Seddon. But certain aspects of the building, the bowed section on the sea-front – originally the hotel bar, later the college chapel! – and the entrance and stair tower on the rear are among the grandest and most boldly plastic fragments produced in this period [160]. Neither Oxford nor Cambridge has anything of comparable quality.

For Trinity College in Hartford, Conn., Burges prepared in 1873 a splendid plan

160. J. P. Seddon:
Aberystwyth, University College, begun 1864

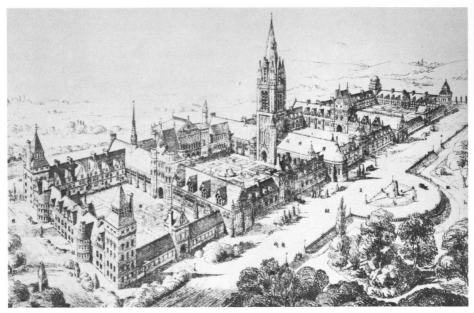

161. William Burges:
Hartford, Conn., project for Trinity College, 1873

worthy of its fine new site on a high ridge south of the city [161]. Unfortunately only one side of one quadrangle was finished according to his designs; but that is perhaps the most satisfactory of all his works, and the best example anywhere of Victorian Gothic collegiate architecture. The brownstone from nearby Portland, Conn., favourite material all over the eastern states during what Lewis Mumford has called the 'Brown Decades', is especially well suited to Burges's heavy and well-articulated detail. The rough quarry-facing of the random ashlar contrasts tonally with the more smoothly cut trim in a fashion that is polytonal if not polychromatic. The roughness of the stone walls also enhances the massive proportions of the long north-south range and the paired towers with their boldly pyramidal roofs. Yet for the classrooms this masonry is articulated into banks of large mullioned windows. There is

plenty of functionally logical variety in the handling of the different sections as executed under the supervision of the local architect F. H. Kimball. Burges also had in Hartford a Scottish-born admirer of his work, G. W. Keller (1842-1935). Keller rather successfully emulated Burges in the construction of a Memorial Arch in the park in Hartford, one of the very few examples of such a Classical monument completely translated into Gothic terms, and in other local buildings.

Burges undoubtedly enjoyed more what he did for the Marquess of Bute, beginning in 1865, in restoring Cardiff Castle and Castell Coch in Wales. 'Restoring' should be put in quotation marks, for by the time Burges got through with them both were almost as much fake castles as any built in the first half of the century. They lie somewhere between Fonthill Abbey and Peckforton in intention and are considerably more sumptuous internally than either. Though Cardiff Castle, which had been drastically remodelled by Holland, was gradually re-castellated with considerable success, the work there never reached completion. It is chiefly the incredibly rich interiors that are of interest today, however, even if the interest is of a rather theatrical order.

Castell Coch near Llandaff, restored in 1875, has interiors of equal fantasy, almost comparable to those of Neuschwanstein; that is, they are more like settings for Wagnerian opera than anything the Middle Ages actually created. But the quality of the imagination and of the execution is of a very much higher order than Ludwig II commanded. Externally Castell Coch is a sober and plausible restoration-reconstruction of a smallish castle, chiefly of archaeological interest but most romantically sited and solidly built. Beside its integrity the more famous restorations by Viollet-le-Duc at Pierrefonds, if not at Carcassonne, appear rather harsh and obviously modern.

The McConochie house, built in Cardiff for Lord Bute's estate agent, is one of the best medium-sized stone dwellings of the High Victorian Gothic, superior in almost every way to Burges's own house at 9 Melbury Road in London. That was built later, in 1875-80, by which time the operatic medievalism of the interiors was quite out of date (see Chapter 12). Here in the Cardiff house the tight asymmetrical composition, the excellent detailing of the handsome stonework, and a generally domestic rather than Castellated air prepared the way for Burges's fine collegiate work in the United States. It dates from the sixties.

English architects in the sixties were capable of exploiting a wide range of different aspects of the High Victorian Gothic in almost precisely the same years. Only the size and departmentalized organization of G. G. Scott's office, the largest of the period and more like the 'plan-factories' of the twentieth century (see Chapter

24), can explain how he could be nominally responsible for such a quiet, well-scaled, and advanced church as St Andrew's, Derby, designed in 1866 – some say by Micklethwaite, who was working for him at the time – and also for such a strident, complex, and over-elaborated edifice as the Midland Hotel fronting St Pancras Station. The design for this was prepared in 1865 for a competition held, curiously enough, two years after the shed had been begun by the engineers W. H. Barlow (1812-1902) and R. M. Ordish (1824-86). Such a drastic divorce of engineering and architecture could hardly be expected to produce a co-ordinated edifice, yet both aspects of St Pancras have considerable independent interest. The shed, ingeniously tied below the level of the tracks and rising, for purely coincidental technical reasons, to a flattened point of slightly 'Gothic' outline, has the widest span of any in the British Isles and, until the nineties, in the world. It is, therefore, a nineteenth-century spatial achievement of quantitative, if not so much of qualitative, significance. The masonry block at the front is one of the largest High Victorian Gothic structures in the world It long had ardent admirers, and it has come to have them again, for it epitomizes almost as notably as the Albert Memorial the aspirations of Scott and his generation. The contrast to its neighbour, Lewis Cubitt's Kings Cross Station, begun some fifteen years earlier, or even to Paddington, where the engineer Brunel and the architect Wyatt collaborated so happily, is striking. The taste of English railway authorities, as of most patrons of architecture, had been revolutionized by the general triumph of the High Victorian Gothic in the late fifties and early sixties. Yet on its completion in the mid seventies St Pancras was even more out of fashion in advanced circles than were Street's Law Courts, the construction of which only began at that time, so rapidly did taste continue to change in the late sixties and early seventies.

By 1870 church architecture, for example, was in general much chastened. Externally Teulon's St Stephen's, The Green, on Rosslyn Hill in Hampstead of 1869-76 is not polychromatic but all of purple-brown brick with some creamy stone trim. It builds up, moreover, somewhat like Shaw's Bingley church begun a few years earlier, to a tall rectangular crossing tower with rather quiet, more or less 'Early French', membering. Inside Teulon achieved in the brickwork a kind of golden harmony of tone resembling that of White's interior in St Saviour's, Aberdeen Park, completely eschewing the bold and almost savage patterns of contrastingly coloured bricks he had favoured since the early fifties. In the tremendously tall interior of Edmund Scott's already mentioned St Bartholomew's, Brighton – aisleless, chancelless, and provided with broad, flat internal buttresses – the traces of brick polychromy are hardly noticeable on the walls of a space so grandly proportioned [158]. The later ciborium here is not by Scott.[16a]

Burges in the two Yorkshire churches which he began in 1871 at Skelton and at Studley Royal, both near Ripon, the latter with a very fine rectory near by, still aimed at a rather satiating luxury of both coloured and sculptural decoration in the interiors. But Pearson at St Augustine's, Kilburn Park Road, London, initiated at this time a new line of vast plain churches [162]. That line would culminate in the archaeological correctness of his Truro Cathedral in Cornwall, started in 1880 and finally completed by his son (F. L., 1864-1947) in the present century. His last work, the cathedral of Brisbane, Australia, designed shortly before his death in 1897, was only begun by his son in 1901.

As Pearson's Kilburn church was built in 1870-80, it should perhaps more properly be considered Late Victorian than High. But Pearson retained here and to the end of his life, particularly in his tall towers and spires, a truly High Victorian love of grand and bold effects.

However archaeological he became, and with his passion for rib-vaulting he could from this time on be rather more archaeological in a Franco-English way than Viollet-le-Duc in France or Cuijpers in Holland, his spaces are usually nobly proportioned and his masses crisply composed no matter how 'correctly' they are membered. At Truro, where the cathedral rises suddenly out of narrow streets, its granite still almost unweathered, Pearson's handling of the relationship of the three tall towers carries vigorous plastic conviction; Burges had attempted the same effect at Cork with rather less success when the High Victorian was still at its highest. Brisbane Cathedral is plainer and tougher than Truro despite its very late date.

It would be inappropriate in this chapter to carry the story of Victorian Gothic much further. Scott and Street died in 1878 and 1881 respectively, though Butterfield and Bodley

163. G. F. Bodley:
Pendlebury, Lancashire, St Augustine's, 1870-4

outlived Pearson. Butterfield seems to have frozen for life in the mode of his early maturity, and as a result produced ever feebler work after the mid sixties; Pearson was able to maintain a leading position with a younger generation grown chaster and more archaeological in its standards without forsaking his pursuit of those more abstractly architectonic values which gave distinction to his earlier work. It was above all Bodley, however, with his Late Decorated verging on Perpendicular, who set the pace in Anglican church-architecture from this time forward. His personal style, still tentative at All Saints, Cambridge, in the mid sixties, was mature by the time he built St Augustine's at Pendlebury in Lancashire in 1870-4. Crisp and almost mechanical in its detailing, this tall rectangular mass, buttressed by an internal arcade, is impressive both inside and out [163], yet it wholly abjures most of what had for two decades given vitality to English Neo-Gothic.

With various modulations what might, rather ambiguously, be called 'Bodleian Gothic' remained the favourite of Anglicans in and out of England well into the twentieth century. The continuing admiration for the work of Sir Ninian Comper (1864-1960) beyond his death suggests that it has only lately been finally superseded; but most of Comper's best work actually dated from before Bodley's death in 1907. For example, his principal London church, St Cyprian's in Glentworth Street, was built in 1903. This crisp and clean example of revived Late Gothic, with its elegant gilt font-cover and screen, may wind up this account more appropriately than the vast unfinished cathedral at Liverpool begun by Sir Giles Gilbert Scott (1880-1960), a grandson of the first G. G. Scott, in 1903 also. But neither is Victorian Gothic; both are rather manifestations of one aspect of twentieth-century 'traditionalism' (see Chapter 24).

CHAPTER 11

LATER NEO-GOTHIC OUTSIDE ENGLAND

The High Victorian Gothic produced in the United States no such roster of distinguished – or at least prominent and highly characteristic – monuments as in Britain. The period of its florescence was much briefer, and few assured and sophisticated talents came to the fore. If, in the case of Richardson, one such did appear, his maturity came only in the mid seventies, when the High Victorian Gothic was all but over. Why the period was so much shorter in the United States, in effect only the decade 1865–75, is not altogether clear. One reason, undoubtedly, is that the speed of transmission of new architectural ideas from England to America had increased so much by the seventies that the influence of the later English modes which succeeded the High Victorian Gothic around 1870 reached America very promptly indeed (see Chapters 13 and 15). Another quite different reason is that a wave of nationalism in America, parallel to those current in North European countries at the time, encouraged from the mid seventies developments that were more autochthonous. Leadership in commercial and in domestic architecture crossed the Atlantic almost precisely at the moment when, in 1876, the centenary[1] of American political independence was being celebrated.

The phenomenal success in the United States of Ruskin's treatises, *The Seven Lamps of Architecture* of 1849 and *The Stones of Venice*[2] of 1851–3, should be emphasized; from 1855 Street's *Brick and Marble Architecture* was also available. Yet, despite the warm reception of such relevant writings, few if any reflections of the High Victorian Gothic can be discerned in American production before 1860, for Ruskin's message at first appealed chiefly to those

interested in painting. The earliest use of 'permanent polychrome' on the so-called Church of the Holy Zebra (All Souls' Unitarian in New York), commissioned in 1853, was uninfluenced by Ruskin. Its architect, Jacob Wrey Mould (1825–84), who came to the United States to build this church, was a pupil of Owen Jones (1809–74), not in touch with either Camdenian or Pre-Raphaelite circles.[3]

The years immediately following the Panic of 1857 and, quite understandably, the Civil War years 1861–5 were relatively unproductive of new buildings, as has already been noted. The first that can really be considered overtly Ruskinian was the National Academy in New York, built by Peter B. Wight (1838–1925) in 1863–5, though he won the competition for it in 1861. Its Venetian Gothic mode, with pointed arches boldly banded and walls diapered in coloured stones, was still the subject of considerable contemporary controversy as it would hardly have been in England by this date.

Wight was still a very young man. Established Gothic Revivalists in America did not swing over as rapidly as in England from the Early Victorian to the High. Richard Upjohn was no Butterfield; James Renwick when designing St Patrick's Cathedral in New York in 1859 followed contemporary Continental rather than English models, as has been noted, presumably because his clients were Catholics.

At best the sort of High Church Anglican patronage which sponsored Butterfield's and Street's innovations in Victorian England was rather less important in the United States – or Canada and Australia, for that matter. Enthusiasm for the High Victorian Gothic, although widespread in the later sixties and early seventies, was rarely exclusive as is evidenced by the disparate interests and activities of the members of the prominent and successful firm of Ware & Van Brunt. It has already been noted that when William Robert Ware founded in 1865 the first American architectural school at the Massachusetts Institute of Technology in Boston, he based its instruction on that of the Paris École des Beaux-Arts.[4] His partner Henry Van Brunt (1832-1903) was one of the first to follow Richardson's lead away from the High Victorian Gothic in the seventies. So little were either of them dyed-in-the-wool Gothicists in these decades.[5]

However, Ware & Van Brunt designed and built in Cambridge, Mass., one of the largest and most conspicuous of mature High Victorian Gothic edifices in America, Memorial Hall[6] at Harvard College, first projected in the late sixties and erected in 1870-8. This somewhat cathedral-like edifice has walls of red brick liberally lashed with black and a massive central tower now denuded by fire of its high roof [164]. The manner is more than a little Butterfieldian, but the quality is not even up to G. G. Scott.

Before Memorial Hall was designed, a competition held in 1865 for the First Church (Unitarian) in Boston in the new Back Bay residential district had brought out a variety of rather feeble attempts by Boston architects to follow the High Victorian Gothic line. The winning design of Ware & Van Brunt, executed in 1865-7, while not of the wilder Low Church order of Teulon's or Keeling's London work of these years, is hardly comparable to Street's or Butterfield's, much less to the contemporary production of younger architects such as Brooks, Bodley, or Shaw. Its best feature was the material, the richly mottled and textured local Puddingstone from nearby Roxbury.

The High Victorian Gothic of the sixties and early seventies in the United States was no more restricted to the ecclesiastical field than in England. Despite its churchy look, Memorial

Hall served a variety of secular purposes from refectory to concert hall; only the wide transeptal lobby was strictly memorial in purpose. But there was rarely even such relative devotion to the Gothic in this period in the United States as the major works of Ware & Van Brunt display. For example, the untutored Elbridge Boyden (1810-98), best known for introducing the cast-iron commercial front into New England in 1854, could build two buildings for the Polytechnic Institute of Worcester, Mass., in the same year 1866 of which one, the Washburn Machine Shop, is mansarded with crude, vaguely Second Empire, detailing; while the other, Boynton Hall, is in a very provincial sort of High Victorian Gothic. Hunt, product of a Parisian education, designed the Yale Divinity School in New Haven in 1869 in a frenzied, rather Teulonian, Gothic; while in his precisely contemporary Lenox Library in New York, built in 1869-77, he followed closely the estab-

164 *(left)*. Ware & Van Brunt:
Cambridge, Mass., Memorial Hall, 1870–8

165. H. H. Richardson:
Medford, Mass., Grace Church, 1867–8

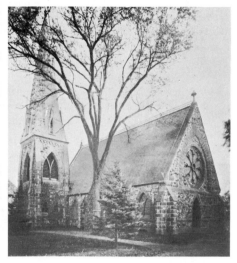

lished mode of the École where he had been trained.

It is not really surprising, therefore, that Richardson, returning from Paris and the École des Beaux-Arts at the end of the Civil War and entering a competition for a new Unitarian church to be built at Springfield, Mass., offered a High Victorian Gothic project that seems to derive rather directly from the work of Keeling and other Low Church English practitioners. What *is* surprising, however, considering the lack of special interest to later eyes in his Unity Church as executed in 1866–8, is the fact that he won the competition! The warm colour and texture of the rock-faced brownstone from nearby Longmeadow laid up in random ashlar, a certain masculine scale in the details, and an attempt at least at a boldly asymmetrical composition evidently struck his contemporaries as very promising, however. (The church was demolished in 1961.)

It was not in the Unity Church, but in Richardson's second church, Grace Episcopal in Medford, Mass., happily still extant, of 1867–8, that one recognizes strong personal expression. The more massively pyramidal character of the asymmetrical composition and, above all, the great boulders of which the walls are built, with heavy trim of rough quarry-faced granite, announce an original approach [165]. Yet this approach was evidently still nurtured on the English High Victorian Gothic models that Richardson knew through the wood engravings in imported periodicals. It is even specific enough here so that one can describe this Medford church as Burgessy rather than Butterfieldian or Street-like; it is certainly no longer Keelingesque like the church in Springfield. Incidentally, when Richardson visited England in 1882 it was the work of Burges, who had just died, that he went out of his way to see – by that time, however, he found it rather disappointing.

If Richardson's first churches were Gothic, his Western Railway Office at Springfield, built in 1867 for a client associated with the Unity Church commission, was generically Second Empire. Yet this was still more directly derived from current English work that was closely related to that mode, notably the Francis Brothers' National Discount Building of 1857 in the City of London, than from anything Parisian. His brick and stone Dorsheimer[7] house of 1868 in Delaware Avenue in Buffalo, N.Y., is also Second Empire rather than Victorian Gothic, but very restrainedly so, and hence rather more French in effect. Other work by Richardson dating from the late sixties, such as the B. H. Crowninshield house in Marlborough Street in Boston of 1869–70, was more experimental in design, often recalling wild English work of the early years of the decade. Although built of wood and of very modest size, Richardson's most interesting house of this period was the one that he built for himself in 1868 at Arrochar on Staten Island near New York.[8] This combined the use of a high mansarded pavilion with a sort of imitation half-timbering related to the contemporary American 'Stick Style' (see Chapter 14).

In Farnam Hall at Yale College in New Haven [166], begun in 1869, the German-trained Russell Sturgis (1836–1909),[9] who had been for a time Wight's partner, somehow arrived at an almost Webb-like – or at least Brooks-like – simplicity and sophistication of late High Victorian Gothic design, in marked contrast to the stridency of Hunt's precisely

contemporary Divinity School there. This, however, is almost unique. The most characteristic work of the day was produced by such home-trained architects as Ware & Van Brunt, Wight, Edward T. Potter (1831–1904), and his brother William A. Potter (1842–1909).[10] Wight's National Academy in New York has been mentioned. His Mercantile Library in Brooklyn, N.Y., completed in 1869, of red brick with ranges of pointed-arched windows regularly but asymmetrically disposed, is similar – and not inferior – to much of G. G. Scott's secular work. E. T. Potter's Union College

166. Russell Sturgis: New Haven, Conn., Yale College, Farnam Hall, 1869–70

Library in Schenectady should also be mentioned.[10a] His Harvard Church in Brookline, Mass., of 1873-5 is more conventional for its period. Largely renewed internally after being gutted by a fire in 1931, this shows how effectively such American materials as the popular brownstone from Portland, Conn., and the light-coloured Berea sandstone from Ohio, enlivened by accents of livid green serpentine from Pennsylvania, could produce a polychromy richer and more enduring than the endemic Butterfieldian or Teulonian red brick, with banding of bricks dipped in black tar, that had been in general use for a decade. Along this line Richardson himself followed for a while (see Chapter 13). At the same time William A. Potter, who became very briefly Supervising Architect in Washington in succession to Mullet in 1875, produced a few post offices, such as the one in Evansville, Ind., that are characteristic and rather distinguished examples of secular High Victorian Gothic executed in stone. (Both Potters, however, gave up the High Victorian Gothic to accept Richardson's leadership within the next few years.)

The Boston & Albany Railroad station in Worcester, built by Ware & Van Brunt in 1875-7, with its tall and striking tower and its vast segmental-pointed arches at the ends of the shed, provided one of the happiest illustrations of what the rather illiterate approach of even the most highly trained Eastern architects of this period could produce. By working in an almost primitive way, along lines suggested by the half-understood work of the bolder English innovators, something was often achieved of which few Continental architects were capable in this period. In less sophisticated hands, whether of provincial architects or of builders, the results were naturally still cruder, though sometimes equally vital and fresh. In church design,[11] where ecclesiological control of planning was not accepted outside the Episcopal denomination, galleried auditorium schemes with rows of exposed iron columns were often executed with a violence of polychromy and a gawkiness of notched detailing that exceeded Teulon or Keeling at their most extreme. One of the most prominent extant examples is the squarish New Old South Church at Copley Square in the Back Bay district of Boston, which was built in 1874-5 by Charles A. Cummings (1833-1905) and his partner Sears. Its impressive tower resembling an Italian campanile has now been much reduced in height and chastened in silhouette.

Even more extreme than most churches, but of the highest quality, is the intensely personal work of Frank Furness (1839-1912)[12] in Philadelphia. His building for the Pennsylvania Academy of Fine Arts in Broad Street was erected in 1872-6 in preparation for the Centennial Exhibition. The exterior has a largeness of scale and a vigour in the detailing that would be notable anywhere, and the galleries are top-lit with exceptional efficiency. Still more original and impressive were his banks, even though they lay quite off the main line of development of commercial architecture in this period (see Chapter 14). The most extraordinary of these, and Furness's masterpiece, was the Provident Institution in Walnut Street, built as late as 1879 [167]. This was most unfortunately demolished in the Philadelphia urban renewal campaign several years ago, but the gigantic and forceful scale of the granite membering alone should have justified its respectful preservation. The interior,[13] entirely lined with patterned tiles, was of rather later character than the façade and eventually much cluttered with various intrusions, but it was equally fine in its own way originally. Later work by Furness is of less interest, and his big Broad Street Station of 1892-4 has also been demolished. No small part of Furness's historical significance lies in the fact that the young Louis Sullivan picked this office - then known as Furness & Hewitt - to work in for a short period after he

167. Frank Furness: Philadelphia,
Provident Life and Trust Company, 1879

left Ware's school in Boston. As Sullivan's *Autobiography of an Idea* testifies, the vitality and originality of Furness meant more to him than what he was taught at the Massachusetts Institute of Technology, or later at the École des Beaux-Arts in Paris (see Chapter 14).

In the realm of house-design the more-or-less Gothic-based 'Stick Style' represented a largely autochthonous American development not without considerable significance and interest (see Chapter 15). In public architecture there was little serious achievement even at the hands of English-trained architects such as Calvert Vaux (1824–95) and his partner F. C. Withers (1828–1901)[14] or second-generation Gothicists like Upjohn's son (Richard M., 1828–1903). The younger Upjohn's Connecticut State Capitol[15] in Hartford begun in 1873, the only major American example of a High Victorian Gothic public monument of any great pretension or luxury of materials, is grandly bold but stylistically ambiguous, with its completely symmetrical massing and its tall central dome, compared to Burges's contemporary project for Trinity College there.[16] Doubtless G. G. Scott would not have disdained it, all the same.

Still more comparable to Scott's own thwarted ambitions for a High Victorian Gothic governmental architecture, which led him as late as the seventies to enter various Continental competitions, is an earlier group of buildings in the New World outside the United States, the Parliament House [168] and associated structures at Ottawa, Canada, designed by Fuller & Jones and Stent & Laver in 1859 and built in 1861–7. F. W. Stent had come out from England some considerable time before this, having last exhibited at the Royal Academy in London in 1846. Thomas Fuller (1822–98), also English, had settled in Toronto in 1856. Of their respective partners, Augustus Laver (1839–98) and Herbert Chilion Jones (1836–1923), less is known. In the course of the work

Fuller and Laver joined forces, moving on shortly to the United States, as has been noted.

The main block at Ottawa, which was by the first-named firm, has been rebuilt after a fire in the present century in a considerably chastened vein except for the big chapter-house-like library at the rear, which is original. But the variety of form, the gusto of the detail, and the urbanistic scale of this project made of the Dominion Capitol a major monumental group unrivalled for extent and complexity of organization in England.[17] The buildings flanking the vast lawn extending in front of the Parliament House are by Stent & Laver. These

168. Fuller & Jones:
Ottawa, Canada, Parliament House, 1859-67

are somewhat less exuberant in scale and more provincial in the character of their detailing than the Parliament House was originally.

Most of the Neo-Gothic in Canada up to this time is more properly to be considered Early rather than High Victorian (see Chapter 6). An exception to this, perhaps, is University College in Toronto, begun in 1856 by F. W. Cumberland (1821-81), who had come out from England in 1847. Yet its rich and rather bombastic Norman design is closer to English work of the earlier decades of the century than to the round-arched Ruskinian Gothic of the fifties.

Australia, the other major British Dominion, had nothing comparable to Canada to offer in this period. Wardell's English, Scottish, and Australian Bank in Melbourne is a passable example of secular High Victorian Gothic but no more than that. St John Evangelist's, which he built at Toorak south of Melbourne in 1860-73, is handsomer but very simple – still almost Puginian, indeed – and all of monochrome ashlar. The enormous Catholic cathedral of Melbourne, St Patrick's, which Wardell began in 1860, is more Continental in character, with two west towers like Renwick's St Patrick's in New York and also a tall crossing tower completed only in 1939. The Catholic cathedral of Adelaide, St Francis Xavier's, begun in 1870 and still without its intended western spires, reputedly goes back to a design prepared by Pugin before his death in 1852. But even the later design of his son E. W. Pugin, on which the executed work was actually based, must have been much modified over the years by W. H. Bagot (b. 1880), H. H. Jory (b. 1880), and Lewis Laybourne-Smith (b. 1888), who successively supervised the job. It is certainly no happier an example of High Victorian Gothic than is Wardell's Roman Catholic cathedral in Melbourne.

The Anglican cathedral in Melbourne, St Paul's, having been begun in 1850 from designs by Butterfield, ought to be finer. But Butterfield had made the drawings as early as 1847, before even he was a High Victorian, and the laggard execution of the church by Joseph Reed evidently entailed much modification of the original designs. Moreover, the spires by John Barr date only from 1934. For the very late Anglican cathedral at Brisbane, St John's, perhaps the finest of the lot, which was begun in 1901 by F. L. Pearson from earlier designs by his father J. L. Pearson as has already been mentioned, Butterfield had also prepared designs in 1884.

The architecture of the Dominions remained Colonial in spirit, as these notes on a few Australian churches indicate, well into the present century. First the able Frank Wills, moreover, the English-born architect of Montreal Cathedral, and then Fuller & Laver were drawn away from Canada to the United States, where opportunities were greater. Despite the great interest of the Government Buildings at Ottawa, it was in the United States rather than the British Dominions that the High Victorian Gothic proved a stimulus to such highly original achievement as Furness's in the seventies.

The High Victorian Gothic episode in American architecture balanced almost precisely the Second Empire episode. Both were disowned, even by many of their most successful protagonists, by the late seventies. It was the Gothic, however, that prepared the way for the more original developments of the last quarter of the century; as has already been stated, those who had practised chiefly in the Second Empire mode continued to take their lead from Paris. Yet there are paradoxes in the situation which must not be ignored. Richardson, the most creative new force in the seventies and eighties, continually urged young aspirants to an architectural career to study at the École des Beaux-Arts as he had done. Charles F. McKim (1847-1909), Richardson's first effective assistant, was Paris-trained; partly because of that training, it was he who became in the mid eighties the leader of the reaction against the Richardsonian. Sullivan, the first truly great modern architect not alone of America but of the whole western world, was also in part Paris-trained, even though he was always highly critical of the doctrine of the École and much stimulated by Furness. Finally, it was even more the later writings of the French Viollet-le-Duc than those of the English Ruskin that encouraged bold and imaginative thinking about architecture in America in the seventies and eighties when his *Entretiens* became available in translation and were first widely read.[18]

Were this a history of architectural thought rather than of architecture – that is of what was actually *built* in the nineteenth and twentieth centuries – Viollet-le-Duc would play a much larger part. But his production,[19] while not negligible, is curiously ambiguous. His many 'restorations' are no contribution to nineteenth-century architecture; rather they represent a serious diminution of authenticity in the great monuments of the past subjected to his ministrations. These include most notably Notre-Dame in Paris, the refurbishing of which he continued alone after the death of Lassus in 1857, and the Château de Pierrefonds, Oise, the rebuilding of which began the next year and continued down to his death in 1879; but the whole list is very long indeed, including Carcassonne, Vézelay, and Saint-Denis, to mention only some of the best known things.

Viollet-le-Duc's new parish church for the suburb of St-Denis, Saint-Denys-de-l'Estrée

169. E.-E. Viollet-le-Duc:
St-Denis, Seine, Saint-Denys-de-l'Estrée, 1864–7

in the Boulevard Jules Guesde, built in 1864-7, has considerable interest, however. Unlike most English High Victorian Gothic churches, it is vaulted throughout; but the vaulting does not have that look of a student exercise which characterizes Lassus's of the previous decade at Saint-Jean-de-Belleville in Paris. The broad square bays of the nave are well lighted by groups of lancets in the clerestory, and there is a sturdy sort of articulation of the elements not unlike that in the early work of Burges [169]. Externally the rather complex plan, with a large rectangular Lady Chapel projecting behind the altar, produces a gawky and confused composition; but the detailing is simple and virile as in the interior. A massive western tower rises over the entrance porch, culminating in a tall slated roof rather than a stone spire. But the plate tracery of the large west window over the porch and the lancets of the stage above are stony enough and have a quite Street-like scale and vigour of form. It is perhaps unfortunate that Viollet-le-Duc built so few new churches; certainly most other French Neo-Gothic work is very inferior to this, as such a large and prominent church as Saint-Epvre at Nancy, begun in 1863 by M.-P. Morey (1805-78), a pupil of Leclerc, well illustrates.[19a]

In secular work Viollet-le-Duc was too often content to parallel the current Second Empire mode with a good deal of the eclecticism, but little of the plastic boldness, of the English and the Americans. Such more or less Gothic blocks of flats as those that he built in the late fifties and sixties in the Rue de Condorcet and at 15 Rue de Douai in Paris are somewhat more comparable to the secular High Victorian Gothic in England [170]. These are certainly praiseworthy for the urbanistic politeness with which they fit between more conventional Second Empire neighbours despite their distinctly 'Victorian' detail,[20] but there is little originality of conception. On paper Viollet-le-Duc did show great boldness, however, in certain projects proposing the use of metal structural elements that he published as an adjunct to the text of the *Entretiens* (see Chapter 16).

In the late fifties and sixties the vigour of the 'Early French' detailing of certain English architects and the related logic of structural

170. E.-E. Viollet-le-Duc:
Paris, block of flats, 15 Rue de Douai, *c.* 1860

expression then called 'real' was often derived in part from a study of Viollet-le-Duc's *Dictionnaire*. But Shaw's book of *Continental Sketches* of 1858 and Nesfield's similar book of 1862 make evident how intense and how idiosyncratic was their own first-hand study of medieval work across the channel. Certainly the 'Early French' detail of the English leaders is generally of higher quality than even Viollet-le-Duc's best.

If there was very little Gothic work done in the third quarter of the century in France comparable in quality or in interest to that of the Anglo-Saxon countries, yet there was a general movement there away from the somewhat mincing attitudes of the forties and early fifties. Just as the Medieval Revival in America, considered in a broad sense, came to its climax in the mature work of Richardson (see Chapter 13) – which is much more Romanesque than Gothic in so far as it leans at all on the past – in France the Romanesqoid works of Vaudremer and Vaudoyer offer the highest achievement in non-Renaissance modes[20a] [127]. The same may even be said up to a point of most of the other countries of Europe. Yet the Germanic *Rundbogenstil* of the third quarter of the century was, for all the size, prominence, and elaboration of such public monuments as Waesemann's Berlin City Hall or Hansen's Vienna Waffenmuseum and the real excellence of Herholdt's Danish work, already a sinking rather than a rising mode.

In Germany and Austria more Neo-Gothic edifices, both secular and ecclesiastical, were built after 1850 than before; several of them have already been mentioned. These are, however, rather examples of contemporary eclecticism than of a concerted movement. In addition to his school and his Rathaus, however, Schmidt built in Vienna some eight Gothic churches ranging in date from the Lazaristenkirche of 1860-2 to the Severinkirche of 1877-8. Most of them are brick-vaulted hall-churches –

that is, of the characteristic medieval German plan and section, with aisles of the same height as the nave. However, the largest and most interesting, the Fünfhaus Parish Church of 1868-75, is centrally planned. This is an aisled octagon rising to a ribbed dome with hexagonal

171. Friedrich von Schmidt: Vienna, Fünfhaus Paris Church, 1868-75

chapels grouped around the irregularly polygonal apse [171]. The spatial complexity of the interior is of real interest, and the walls are painted to suggest polychromatic brickwork of almost English brashness. Two front towers flanking the gabled entrance bay are set close against the dome to provide a very Baroque sort of composition – this is really, therefore, a sort of Sant' Agnese in Agone or Karlskirche carried out with a G. G. Scott vocabulary of Neo-Gothic elements.

In Hungary the eighties saw a very belated manifestation of secular Neo-Gothic. The Parliament House, begun in 1883 by Imre Steindl (1839-1902) and completed in 1902, was surely inspired by Barry's in London begun nearly a half-century earlier, but in character it is (not surprisingly) more like Schmidt's Vienna Rathaus. Thus did outlying countries in the later decades of the century continue to take up modes long obsolescent in the major architectural centres.[21]

The Gothic of C. F. Arnold (1823-90) at Dresden, as seen in his secular Kreuzschule of 1864-5 or the two-towered Sophienkirche of the same years, is inferior to Schmidt's, both in command of the idiom and in architectonic organization, as indeed is most such German work of these decades. The Johanniskirche in Dresden of 1874-8 by G. L. Möckel (1838-1915), however, has a rather fine tower set in the transeptal position so much favoured in Victorian England. This is bold in scale and carefully detailed in a literate twelfth-century – not to say 'Early French' – way much as Burges or Pearson might have designed it in England. More characteristic of German work of these decades is the Munich Rathaus, built in 1867-74 by G. J. von Hauberrisser (1841-1922) and extended by him in 1899-1909. Excessively spiky, this seems almost to have borrowed back from G. G. Scott the more Germanic features of his Broad Sanctuary terrace in London of fifteen years earlier. But the Neo-Gothic of the seventies and eighties in Germany is in general no more aggressive and gawky than the popular Meistersinger mode that revived so turgidly the forms of the Northern Renaissance (see Chapter 10).

Holland, which made almost no significant architectural contribution in the first half of the nineteenth century, now produced in P. J. H.

Cuijpers (1827-1921) a sort of Dutch Viollet-le-Duc. In addition to undertaking important restorations, he built many vast new Gothic churches of brick which he exposed once more in reaction against the earlier nineteenth-century practice of stucco-coating. Cuijpers was learned and ambitious, and in such work he could be rather more original than Viollet-le-Duc in France, if less so perhaps than Schmidt in Austria. His Vondelkerk, a church of 1870 near the Vondel Park in Amsterdam, is not centrally planned like Schmidt's Fünfhaus church in Vienna, but he obtained a somewhat similar spatial effect by making the crossing octagonal. The brickwork of the piers and the vaults is very richly treated but in a fashion as much polytonal as polychromatic. The banding is in bricks of different sizes and textures rather than of different colours, and the result has something of the subtlety of the interior of White's Aberdeen Park Church in London.

A larger and later Amsterdam church by Cuijpers, the Maria Magdalenakerk in the Zaanstraat of 1887, was considerably more impressive, both inside and out. Occupying one of those narrow triangular sites so often assigned to important urban churches in this period, the exterior built up grandly to the rather severe crossing tower at the rear. Inside, Cuijpers made the most of the difficulties of the site also. The east end was conventionally Gothic in plan, and the choir was brick-vaulted, as is the Vondelkerk throughout. But the taller nave, covered with a wooden roof of ogival section, was much more effective spatially because of the way it was widened by triangular elements at the front where the aisles were cut off owing to the narrowing of the site [172]. The later painted decoration in this church was harmonious in tone with the brickwork, and the whole had a breadth of attack comparable to some of the best English churches of the seventies, such as Pearson's in Kilburn or Edmund Scott's in Brighton, without resembling any of them very much.

172. P. J. H. Cuijpers:
Amsterdam, Maria Magdalenakerk, 1887

Curiously enough for so dedicated a church-builder, Cuijpers's secular work is more conspicuous, and hence better known, than are his churches. The two largest and most prominent nineteenth-century buildings of Amsterdam are both by him. In these, the Rijksmuseum built in 1877-85 [173] and the Central Station of 1881-9, he moved away from the emulation of thirteenth- or fourteenth-century ecclesiastical Gothic towards a more elastic sixteenth-century sort of design, rather similar to the English mode of these decades known as 'Pont Street Dutch' (see Chapter 12).

The similarity to the Northern Renaissance mode of this period in Germany is nearly as great, as also to such somewhat later Scandinavian buildings as Clason's Northern Museum in Stockholm and Nyrop's Town Hall in Copenhagen [329]. But Cuijpers's touch is lighter than that of the Germans, and his precedent rather more Late Gothic than Mannerist, while his two chief works precede those that they most resemble in Sweden and Denmark by a decade or more. In both cases the

173. P. J. H. Cuijpers: Amsterdam, Rijksmuseum, 1877-85

frank incorporation of iron-and-glass elements is notable, a vast shed at the station and two almost equally vast covered courts in the museum. Above all, being the Gothic Revivalist he was, Cuijpers saw to it that the craftsmanship was excellent throughout; while his handling of scale, though ambiguous as in much work of these decades everywhere, is surprisingly successful. Both are very large buildings, placed in isolation where they can be seen from a distance and with carefully studied silhouettes varied by towers and other skyline features; yet the membering is delicate and almost domestic, quite as in the rather comparable English work of George [182] or Collcutt (see Chapter 12).

In Italy projects of restoration led, as elsewhere, to the designing of certain fairly ambitious new façades in Gothic to complete medieval churches. The most conspicuous is that of the cathedral of Florence. After various abortive earlier moves, this was finally begun by Emilio de Fabris (1808–83) in 1870 and completed after many vicissitudes by his chosen successor Luigi del Moro in 1887. The earlier and less successful façade of Santa Croce in Florence had been carried out in 1857–63 by Niccoló Matas (1798–1872). It is characteristic of the international architectural scene in these decades that neither of these carefully archaeological compositions in polychrome Italian Gothic comes alive in the way that Italianate High Victorian Gothic often did in the hands of English architects, or a few American ones, in the fifties and sixties.

Churches were built for Anglicans in most of the principal cities of Europe in the mid nineteenth century, usually by English architects and always in Victorian Gothic. Sometimes, as in the case of the Crimean Memorial Church by Street[22] at Istanbul and Shaw's English Church at Lyons, these were by the most distinguished English designers of the day, but more often they were by hacks who lived abroad and specialized in such work.

Among the 'English churches' of this period that provided good samples of the High Victorian Gothic for foreigners – many were still to all intents and purposes Early Victorian – are two by Street[23] in Rome, one for the English community, the other not 'English' at all in fact but built for American Episcopalians. The former, All Saints', in the Via del Babuino, with a tower built only in 1937(!), provides internally a moderately successful example of his later work, although it is unimpressive and largely invisible externally. It was begun in 1880, a year before Street's death, and opened in 1885.

Far finer is St Paul's, the American church, prominently located among the contemporary

174. G. E. Street:
Rome, St Paul's American Church, 1872–6

banks and blocks of flats of the Via Nazionale and built in 1872-6. Boldly banded in brick and stone and with a tall square campanile at the front corner, this is indeed a richer and more striking example of an Italian Gothic basilica than the Middle Ages ever produced in Rome [174]. The interior, with a rich apse mosaic by Burne-Jones on a glittering gold ground, has an originality and a coherence that is quite lacking in such Italian churches as were redecorated in the later nineteenth century. Late though this is in Street's *œuvre*, it remains one of his best works.

If the English High Victorian Gothic was to some extent an article of export – and, of course, this account has hardly touched on the vast outlying areas of the British Empire, notably including India, to which it was exported in the greatest quantity – it was nevertheless largely without real influence outside the United States and the British Dominions. In the world picture, it was the British architectural critics of this period, Ruskin and Morris, who would have a vital influence, but that influence came for the most part rather later, around 1890 (see Chapter 16). Cuijpers, however, was a reader of Ruskin from the fifties.

Still to be discussed is the early work of one great architect, also reputedly a reader of Ruskin, whose career began in the seventies with a sharp revulsion from the Second Empire mode towards the Neo-Gothic. The Spanish (or more precisely Catalan) architect Antoni Gaudí i Cornet (1852-1926) was one of the most intensely personal talents that either the nineteenth or the twentieth century has produced. His style hardly matured before the nineties, and what are generally considered his typical works must be discussed later in connexion with the Art Nouveau (see Chapter 16). But what he had accomplished already in the seventies and eighties can be better appreciated here in relation to the contemporary work of those decades in other countries.

Gaudí's earliest work was at the Parc de la Ciutadella in Barcelona, laid out in 1872, where he assisted the master of works Eduardo Fontseré, while still a student, in various projects for its embellishment. The elaborate Cascade there, incorporating an Aquarium, on which he worked in 1877-82 derives in the main from Espérandieu's at the Palais Longchamps in Marseilles [125]. But some details, both plastic and incised, have a flavour more comparable to those of the wildest and most eclectic English and American Second Empire work of the previous decade than to anything French.

The first commission for which Gaudí was wholly responsible is the house of Don Manuel Vicens at 24-26 Carrer de les Carolines in Barcelona. This was erected in 1878-80, immediately upon his graduation from the local Escuela Superior de Arquitectura, and in it no trace of Second Empire influence, French or international, remains. A large suburban villa built of rubble masonry liberally banded with polychrome tiles, the Casa Vicens passes beyond the extravagances of a Teulon or a Lamb in the sixties into a world of fantasy that only one or two High Victorian designers such as the Scottish Frederick T. Pilkington (1832-98) ever entered. Yet Gaudí's general inspiration came definitely from the medieval past. In Spain that past included the semi-Islamic Mudéjar, however, and much of the detailing which appears most original to non-Spanish eyes is, in fact, dependent on local precedents of one sort or another. For example, the floral tiles are merely what the Iberian world knows as *azulejos* and has continued to use down to the present time, especially in Portugal and Brazil (see Chapter 25).

In all the flamboyance of the decoration of the Casa Vicens, the most personal note is in the ironwork. This is naturalistic in theme and bold in scale; it also includes curious linear elements that wave and bend in a way which is more than a little premonitory of the Art Nouveau of the nineties (see Chapter 16). The rather later entrance grille is a masterpiece of decorative art of the period, rivalled only by Morris's wallpapers.

The very utilitarian warehouse Gaudí built for La Obrera Mataronense of 1878-82 at Mataró, with its great arched principals of laminated wood, should be mentioned to balance the Casa Vicens. Here his prowess as a truly imaginative constructor – almost a straight engineer – was very evident, as also the fact that the unfamiliar forms he repeatedly used – the curve of the arches here was parabolic not semi-circular or pointed – were not a matter of personal crankiness but selected for statical reasons: Gothic in theory, that is, like some of Soufflot's vaulting, though not very Gothic in appearance.

In 1884, however, Gaudí was made director of works for a large new Gothic church in Barcelona, and from this time forward a considerable part of his activity, extending down through his restoration of the cathedral of Palma on the island of Mallorca in 1900-14, was that of a Gothic Revivalist, if an increasingly unconventional one. Towards such a career his almost fanatical piety inclined him quite as much as was in the case with Pugin and later also with Cuijpers – Viollet-le-Duc, by exception, was strongly anti-clerical. Unlike Pugin's or Cuijpers's, however, Gaudí's career as an ecclesiastical architect was rather unproductive. Yet from the first he designed and executed church furnishings and, while still a student in 1875-7, he assisted the architect Francesc de Paula del Villar i Carmona (1845-1922) on a project for adding a porch to the monastery church of Montsarrat.

In 1881 Villar was made architect of the proposed Expiatory Temple of the Holy Family (Sagrada Familia),[24] for which a large square site had been obtained between the Carrers de Mallorca, de Marina, de Provença, and de Sardenya in an outlying part of Barcelona, and

the construction of the crypt of a great cruciform Gothic church was started in 1882. Two years later Gaudí took over charge of the work, as has been said, completing the crypt by 1891 almost entirely according to Villar's original and quite conventionally thirteenth-fourteenth-century Gothic design. There followed the construction of the outer walls only of the chevet; these were finished by 1893. The further history of the church will be considered later; for Gaudí's style underwent extraordinary changes in the nineties as he designed and built one transept façade of the church and its towers – which is all that exists of Gaudí's own work above ground even today (see Chapter 17).

Contemporaneously with Gaudí's construction of the crypt and the chevet walls of the Sagrada Familia came four secular works, two of them also quite Neo-Gothic in character and two others of very great originality. The Bishop's Palace at Astorga of 1887-93 and the Fernández-Arbós house, known as the Casa de los Botines, in the Plaza de San Marcelo at León of 1892-4 might well be mistaken for provincial High Victorian Gothic done in England or America twenty or thirty years earlier. But the city mansion of Don Eusebi Güell at 3-5 Carrer Nou de la Rambla (now Conde del Asalto) in Barcelona, built in 1885-9, is an edifice of very great distinction, rivalled for quality in this period only by the finest late work of Richardson in America (see Chapter 13). The Teresian College at 41 Carrer de Ganduxer in Barcelona is also quite remarkable in its simpler way.

Far suaver than his earlier Casa Vicens, the Palau Güell is quite strikingly novel all the same. At the base yawn a pair of parabolic arches, their tops filled above a plain reticulated grille with sinuous seaweed-like ornament of the most extravagant virtuosity [175]. The 'Dragon Gate' of the Finca Güell of 1887 in the Avenida Pedralbes is still stranger, with a nightmare quality which those of the house in town happily lack. On either side of the entrance arches and in the projecting first storey the façade of the Palau Güell is no more than a rather plain rectangular grid of stone mullions and transoms. In scale this grid is more like Parris's Boston granite fronts of the twenties than like English window-walls, but it is detailed in a cranky medievalizing way that is more comparable to Webb's handling of stonework [176]. The rear façade towards the court includes in the middle a broad bay-window with curved corners protected by sun-screens as original but less fantastic than the grilles at the entrance. The most extraordinary features of the exterior, however, are the chimney-pots rising in profusion above the flat roof like an exhibition of abstract sculpture and entirely covered with a mosaic of irregular fragments of glass, rubble, or coloured tiles. In them the wild originality of his earlier houses was continued, and such crowning features remained characteristic of his later secular work.

The interiors of the Palau Güell are extremely sumptuous. There is much use of marble arcades of parabolic arches carried on round columns, both arches and columns being detailed with the greatest mathematical elegance and simplicity, yet with considerable variety. Some of the ceilings are of marble slabs

175. Antoni Gaudí: Barcelona, Palau Güell, 1885-9

176. Antoni Gaudí: project for Palau Güell, Barcelona, 1885

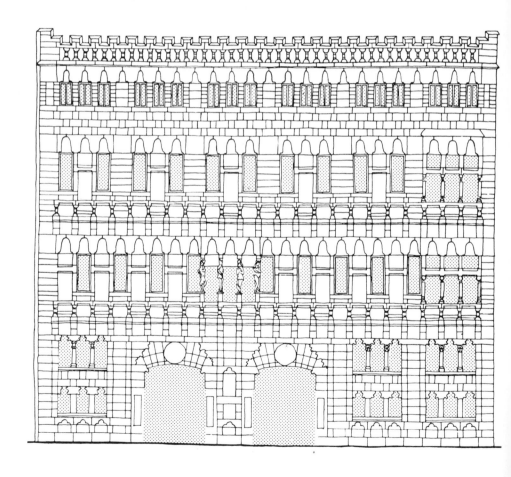

carried on visible iron beams, but in the principal apartments there are incredibly elaborate confections of woodwork in the Moorish tradition.

The College of Santa Teresa de Jesús, built in 1889-94 immediately after the Palau Güell, is naturally much more modest than that great merchant's palace which continues the line of those that late medieval and Renaissance magnates often erected. Rubble walls banded and stripped with brickwork are pierced alternately with ranges of narrow windows and with small square ventilators closed with quatrefoil grilles. The widely spaced windows are capped with steep parabolic 'arches' formed by cantilevering inward successive brick courses. The third storey is all of brickwork panelled with blind 'arches' between the windows and carried up into large, flat, triangular finials along the skyline. Less ingratiating than the Palau Güell with its luxurious use of fine materials inside and out, this college building is as regular in composition and no more medieval in appearance to a non-Spanish eye; in fact, however, it leans even more heavily on Mozarab and Mudéjar precedent than does the Casa Vicens. A certain amount of relatively plain wrought-iron grillework recalls that at the entrances of the earlier houses.

Only perhaps in England and America did the line of descent from the Gothic Revival lead so far away from the standard medievalism of the mid century in the seventies and eighties. But these early works of Gaudí represent only a part – to most critics the less important half – of his production. For strangeness they can be matched in work of equal consequence within this period only by Sullivan's earliest commercial façades in Chicago (see Chapter 14). Teulon and Harris had reformed by the seventies; Lamb and Pilkington were forgotten. In character Gaudí's work of the seventies and eighties could hardly be more different from the mature style of the English Shaw. Yet

Shaw, at his occasional best, could compete with Gaudí in the quality of his achievement; while his influence, both at home and in the United States, was of very considerable historical importance, as Gaudí's was not, even in Spain (see Chapters 12, 13, and 15).

For all that Gaudí was actually represented at the Paris Exhibition of 1878 – by a glovemaker's vitrine! – and later by pavilions designed for the Compañía Transatlántica in the Naval Exhibition of 1887 at Cadiz and in the Barcelona International Exhibition of the following year, his work was hardly known at all except to his compatriots before the nineties. In the mid twentieth century, however, his reputation began to rise again, as the flood of publications since 1950 makes evident. The reasons for this will be suggested later, since they apply chiefly to the work that he did after 1900 (see Chapters 16 and 20).

In the European picture as a whole a less notable shift of direction occurred around 1870 than in England and America. There was naturally continuity in the Vienna of Francis Joseph, since the Imperial government called the tune in Austrian architecture and the King-Emperor's reign went on without a break – indeed, it lasted for another generation and more. What is surprising is that the end of the Second Empire and the beginning of the Third Republic brought so little change in France. There was, of course, a short hiatus in production like that which followed the fall of the first Napoleon. As around 1820, however, so around 1875 the story picks up again almost as if there had been no break at all. Gradually interest in exposed metal construction, long in decline, began to revive; by the time of the Paris Exhibition of 1889 feats of metal construction in that, not so much the Galerie des Machines as the Eiffel Tower, became the talk of the world (see Chapter 16).

In the fugue-like composition of nineteenth-century architectural history different themes have differing durations. The English theme of High Victorian Gothic, picked up in any case only by the Anglo-Saxon sections of the orchestra, came effectively to an end with the early seventies; the Second Empire theme, whether it be considered in a specialized sense or in a broader one, was employed at least selectively by the whole western world and not least boldly by the Anglo-American section; moreover, it continued in most countries, with certain modulations, for at least a decade longer than the High Victorian Gothic. Yet both in England and America, the important new themes of the seventies and eighties were rooted not in the Second Empire but in the Victorian Gothic, even though they represent something much more original than mere variations on that earlier theme.

The third quarter of the nineteenth century is notable for the superficial diversity of its production. In principle there may, perhaps, be no more difference between Visconti's and Lefuel's New Louvre and a Butterfield church than between Nash's Blaise Hamlet and his terraces around Regent's Park, to cite merely work by one early nineteenth-century architect. Yet thanks to the fugal character of the general historical development, which meant that new modes were added to the architectural repertory – as they had been at least since the twenties – more rapidly than old modes were dropped, the over-all picture

became extremely complicated after 1850. It belies the most valid and idiosyncratic achievements of this period, however, to stress too much its apparently limitless eclecticism.[25] The account given in the last four chapters undoubtedly exaggerates the importance of certain modes, if that importance be measured statistically in terms of quantity of production. Qualitative considerations have led to a drastic selectivity, emphasizing relatively limited but vital aspects of architectural production at the expense of others that were far more ubiquitous but generally very dull. With different criteria of selection, using different standards of architectural quality – attainment of archaeological plausibility, say; or success or failure in the incorporation of new technical developments; or realization of programmatic aims – several very different pictures could be, and indeed frequently have been,[26] given of the architecture of the western world in these decades.

At the expense of emphasizing architectural developments peculiar to the Anglo-Saxon world in this same, possibly unbalanced, fashion the next chapter is organized around the career, after 1870, of Norman Shaw, whose early work in the High Victorian Gothic has already received some attention. The chapter following that centres on the achievement of the American architect Richardson, whose beginnings have also been described in this chapter.

CHAPTER 12

NORMAN SHAW AND HIS CONTEMPORARIES

In England and America there followed immediately upon the 'High Styles' of the fifties and sixties phases of stylistic development that cannot readily be matched in other countries of the western world. This is true both of the quality of the achievement and also of its significance for what came after. Beginning just before 1870 in England and but little later in the United States, these two phases developed in far from identical ways. In both cases their conventional names, 'Queen Anne' and 'Romanesque Revival', are misnomers. It was a long time before the Queen Anne of the seventies actually became a revival of early eighteenth-century architecture in the same sense as the Greek, Gothic, or Renaissance Revivals. The supposed Romanesque Revival in America of this period was not at all archaeological either. It is therefore less inaccurate to label these modes by the names of their principal protagonists: 'Shavian' for Richard Norman Shaw (even though that proper adjective refers more familiarly to George Bernard Shaw) and 'Richardsonian' for Henry Hobson Richardson. Shaw, however, shares responsibility for the effectiveness of the mutation away from the High Victorian with other men, notably his early partner Nesfield, Webb, Godwin, and J. J. Stevenson.[1] Of all this group, Shaw was unquestionably the most successful, the most typical, and the most influential, though not the most original.

Except for Pugin, no architect since Robert Adam had so much effect on English – and for that matter also on American – production. Moreover, his influence lasted for some thirty-five years, rather longer than did Adam's. Yet it is not possible to define the Shavian mode simply as it is the Adamesque or the Puginian. An architectural Picasso, Shaw had many divergent manners which he developed successively, but of which none – except the High Victorian Gothic – was ever entirely dropped. Each of these manners, down to the very end of his long practice, found in turn a following. His latest and most conspicuous work, the Piccadilly Hotel, built in London in 1905–8 between Piccadilly and the Regent Street Quadrant [188], is more characteristic of the Edwardian Age of the opening twentieth century than his early church at Bingley is of the High Victorian. Outside church architecture the intervening Late Victorian can hardly be defined better than in terms of his various manners, and even in church architecture he had a real contribution to make, if a lesser reputation than Pearson or Bodley.

Yet Shaw cannot be rated with Soane or Schinkel as a nineteenth-century architect of absolutely the first rank; nor yet with his American contemporary Richardson, even though Richardson's career came to an end a score of years before his. Shaw's work reflects all too clearly, despite his own vast and sanguine assurance, the general uncertainties of the years after 1870. Webb, though less successful and famous, eventually had more influence, not so much on English architecture in general as on the more creative and original men of the next generation. The later history of European architecture would be much the same – if not that of American architecture – had Shaw never existed; but the modern architecture that first came into being about 1900 in various countries of Europe owed something directly, and even more indirectly, to Webb. In this way

Richardson also has more significance than Shaw, despite the brevity of his influence abroad, for Sullivan and Wright in America both learned from him.

Norman Shaw was born in Edinburgh in 1831. Brought early to London, he was taken on in his early teens by Burn, the Edinburgh architect then settled in London who had so great a success designing Jacobethan and Scottish Baronial mansions for the high aristocracy in the forties and fifties. Shaw also studied at the Royal Academy, winning in 1853 their Silver Medal, and in the next year their Gold Medal with the award of a Travelling Studentship that took him to Germany, Italy, and France. The project which won him the first medal was a surprising production for its period, and quite without relation to his own High Victorian Gothic work of the next decade that has been described earlier (see Chapter 11). A vast design for a college with central domed block and side pavilions loaded with giant orders, this project is more Vanbrughlike than Second Empire. In some sense Shaw's career was to come full circle stylistically; but even in the Gaiety Theatre in the Strand in London of 1902-3 and the still later Piccadilly Hotel he would hardly be as whole-heartedly Neo-Baroque again.

In 1858 Shaw published, as has been mentioned before, what is perhaps the most attractive of High Victorian source-books, *Architectural Sketches from the Continent*, based on his European studies; doubtless on the strength of this book he became at this time, or shortly after, Street's principal assistant – chief draughtsman, one might call it – in succession to Webb.[2] There he remained for four years, leaving in 1862 to form a partnership with Nesfield, whom he had first known in the early fifties in Burn's office. As has already been noted, Nesfield was the son of Barry's collaborator in garden design for all his major country house commissions. Younger than Shaw, Nes-

field had gone to Burn's office in 1850 a year or two after leaving Eton, and in 1853 had moved to the office of his uncle Anthony Salvin, another successful builder of aristocratic country houses. Nesfield, in this year 1862, issued a book rather like Shaw's of four years earlier as has been noted in describing the work he did for Lord Craven at Combe Abbey. Other aristocrats with whom he had connexions through his father had already begun to employ him on more modest jobs.

Building lodges and other accessories to great country estates, and in 1864 one in Regent's Park where everyone might appreciate his highly personal touch, Nesfield revived in effect the Picturesque Cottage mode of half a century earlier. But the materials he used were more various,[3] including tile-hanging and pargetting, and his designs had a general finesse that was much more craftsmanlike than those of the slapdash Nash and his rivals in this genre [87]. In Nesfield's first major work, Cloverley Hall in Shropshire, begun in 1865, several characteristic features appear for which his lodges hardly prepared the way (see Chapter 15). There a tall great hall provided the principal interior, and the areas of mullioned windows in the Tudor tradition were so extensive as to constitute real 'window-walls' [216]. The significance of his refined ornamentation of Japanese inspiration at Cloverley was indicated in Chapter 10.

In 1862, moreover, when Japanese art was just beginning to be an inspiration to advanced painters in Paris and in London and the Japanese Government first sent examples of characteristic work to an international exhibition, Godwin, who was just then throwing off the influence of Ruskin, had already stripped bare the interiors of his own house in Bristol and decorated them only with a few Japanese prints asymmetrically hung. By 1866 Godwin was designing wallpapers of notably Japanese character for Jeffry & Co. and from 1868

'Anglo-Japanese' furniture for the manufacturer William Watt.[4] But *japonisme*, though a major contemporary theme in the arts,[4a] influenced Shaw and other architects very little. The return to eighteenth-century modes was more important.

Half a century earlier the prestige of a ranking novelist, Sir Walter Scott, had helped to launch one of the most popular Picturesque modes, the Scottish Baronial, when he asked Blore to imitate the old Border castles in designing his house at Abbotsford. Now in 1861 Thackeray, a novelist many of whose novels were set, not in the Middle Ages, but in early eighteenth-century England and Virginia, designed for himself a house in Palace Green in London opposite Kensington Palace, much of which is more or less of that particular period. This house echoes the modest red-brick manor houses of the time of Queen Anne on both sides of the Atlantic, but it could hardly be less plausible. At the same time Wellington College by John Shaw (1803–70), which was begun in 1856, was reaching completion in a much richer, almost Second Empire, version of the Wren style of 1700.

The serious adumbration of a Queen Anne mode really began a few years later with a small public commission of Nesfield's. His lodge at Kew Gardens, designed in 1866 and built in 1867, though simple, is already almost an archaeological exercise in early eighteenth-century[5] brickwork [177]. This Kew lodge he followed up a few years later with a big but remote country house, Kinmel Park near Abergele in Wales, built in 1871–4 though possibly designed rather earlier. To this we will be returning shortly. Shaw had nothing to do with Kinmel Park, since his partnership with Nesfield came to an end in 1868; that was just after the completion of Cloverley Hall on which he certainly collaborated even if his personal contribution there cannot now be readily distinguished.[5a] Already in 1866, before Shaw

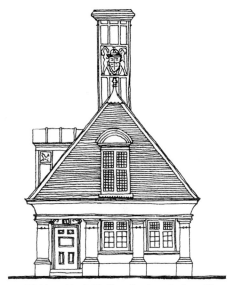

177. W. Eden Nesfield: Kew Gardens, Lodge, 1867

parted from Nesfield, however, his own career had opened with the designing of the Bingley church [156] and of Glen Andred, near Withyham in Sussex, a house of great originality of character [178].

Glen Andred is little more related to the new Queen Anne mode of the Kew lodge than it is to the Gothic of the Bingley church. It does, however, seem to derive somewhat from earlier Nesfield work, or possibly from Devey. Where the High Victorian Gothic had rejected English precedent in favour of Italian and French models, this first Sussex house of Shaw's is peculiarly regional in character. The tile-hung walls above a red-brick ground storey, the white-painted wooden casements, almost as extensive as the 'window-walls' of Cloverley, the loose asymmetrical organization of the massing are all related to a local Sussex and Surrey vernacular of no particular period [178]. The entrance front is more formal, carefully balanced if not precisely symmetrical, and here the pargetting in the central gable is of Jacobethan character.

178. R. Norman Shaw:
Withyham, Sussex, Glen Andred, 1866-7

But the great stair-window and the graceful massing of the tiled roofs, quite in the finest tradition of the Picturesque but handled with a new ease and casualness, are more important elements of Shaw's first manner, which can be called 'Shavian Manorial'. The hall across the front between the two projecting wings is modest in size, with the principal living rooms loosely grouped round it. Thus this may be considered an early example of what I have rather clumsily called the 'agglutinative plan', but as the plan has never been published the extent of its influence must remain uncertain.

There was little logic to Shaw's regionalism. Already in 1868 he was applying his Sussex vocabulary of materials and forms to the Cookridge Convalescent Hospital at Horsforth near Leeds in stony Yorkshire. In general, however, he kept this manner for work near London, using it even as late as 1894 for a house called The Hallams near Bramley in Surrey. He also introduced tile-hanging on some of his houses in London such as West House, at 118 Campden Hill Road, of 1877 and Walton House in Walton Street of 1885 as well as - rather more

appropriately - on the suburban Hampstead house that he built in the same year for Kate Greenaway at 39 Frognal.

Shaw's first client had been the artist J. C. Horsley, R.A., for whom he made some alterations in the early sixties and whose son later entered his office. Glen Andred was for another painter, E. W. Cooke, later R.A., and West House was for George Boughton, R.A. Kate Greenaway, better known today than these forgotten academicians, was an illustrator of children's books much patronized by Ruskin. F. W. Goodall, R.A. (1870), Marcus Stone, R.A. (1876), Luke Fildes, R.A. (1877), Edwin Long, R.A. (1878, and again in 1888), Frank Holl, R.A. (1881), are other successful painters and fellow academicians - Shaw became an A.R.A. himself in 1872 and an R.A. in 1877 - for whom he built houses (with the dates of the commissions). All but Goodall's house at Harrow Weald were either in Melbury Road in Kensington in London or else in Fitzjohn's Avenue near his own Hampstead house of 1875 at 6 Ellerdale Road. Where the prosperous artists - themselves presumably aping the aristocracy - led, magnates and City men were now quick to follow. The Newcastle steelmaster Sir William Armstrong had Shaw build Cragside near Rothbury in Northumberland for him as early as 1870.

Leyswood, near Withyham in Sussex,[5b] begun in 1868 at the same time as the Cookridge Hospital, was one of Shaw's most influential works [217]. More archaeologically manorial than Glen Andred, it provided a mass of suggestions that English and American architects borrowed again and again over the next twenty years and more. Because of Shaw's later leadership, it is natural for posterity to note what was new here; contemporaries, used to the wild vagaries of the High Victorian Gothic, saw Leyswood rather as a reaction against the 'modernism' of the fifties and earlier sixties. Tile-hung upper storeys and barge-boarded gables, richly half-timbered – the half-timbering a mere sham applied over solid brickwork! – long banks of casements that approach the twentieth-century 'ribbon-window' and great mullioned bays providing 'window-walls' as extensive as Nesfield's at Cloverley clothed an interior that was not at all medieval but a more developed example than Glen Andred of the 'agglutinative plan' [179]. The main reception rooms were grouped about a central hall, from one side of which rose elaborate stairs arranged in several flights about an open well. Webb had already essayed this sort of planning in a more orderly way at Arisaig, begun in 1863 [215]; but it was Shaw's version, not Webb's, that was generally imitated (see Chapter 15).

Shortly after Leyswood, and following fairly closely its manner although with fewer Late Gothic elements of detail, came the house later called Grim's Dyke built at Harrow Weald in 1870-2 for F. W. Goodall, afterwards the country house of the composer W. S. Gilbert, and Preen Manor in Shropshire also designed in 1870. Then followed Hopedene, near Holmbury in Surrey, and Boldre Grange, near Lymington in Hampshire, in 1873; Wispers, Midhurst, in Sussex, in 1875; Chigwell Hall in Essex, and Pierrepoint, near Farnham in Surrey, in 1876; Merrist Wood near Guildford in Surrey, and Denham at Totteridge in Hertfordshire, in 1877; and so on down into the nineties.

179. R. Norman Shaw:
Leyswood, Sussex, 1868

DINING ROOM

DRAWING ROOM

KITCHEN

LIBRARY

COURT

After their showing each year at the Royal Academy Exhibition Shaw's brilliant pen-and-ink perspectives of these houses were published photo-lithographically in the professional press; moreover, from 1874 the plans were usually given as well, the first published being that of Hopedene. Not surprisingly these were the most influential of Shaw's works abroad, providing in the late seventies and early eighties one of the most important sources of the American 'Shingle Style' (see Chapter 15). Beside them, moreover, Webb's more prominent London works of the late sixties, the house for George Howard, later Earl of Carlisle, built in 1868 near Thackeray's in Palace Green, Kensington, and the small office building at 19 Lincoln's Inn Fields, also of 1868, appear somewhat cranky and overstudied, still rather too Gothic in detail and lacking the comfortable air of his country-house work. However, the modest London studio-house at 14 Holland Park Road, Kensington, which was designed in 1864 and built in 1865 for Val Prinsep, like Morris and Spencer Stanhope one of the crew of artists who worked on the decoration of the Oxford Union, must have been more like the Red House and Benfleet Hall before it was recurrently enlarged by Webb in the following decades. Another London studio-house for the water-colour painter G. B. Boyce at 35 Glebe Place, Chelsea, which was begun in 1869, is in rather better condition today and quite exemplary in its quiet way despite some changes by Webb and others.

At this point came Nesfield's Kinmel Park. Shaw and other advanced architects must have been aware of the character of the designs for this house from 1870 or 71, even though it was neither shown at the Royal Academy nor published then and took some four years to complete. Kinmel is much more complicated stylistically than Nesfield's Kew lodge of 1866-7, but it offers the next step in the development of the new Queen Anne mode. At first

sight it might appear to be related rather to Second Empire work, for the main block on the entrance side is symmetrical, high-roofed, and dominated by a bold central pavilion. Moreover, the detailing of the red-brick façades with their profuse light-coloured stone trim is almost as French of Louis XIII's time as it is English of Queen Anne's day. The garden front, which is carefully ordered but not symmetrical, and the service wing to the south, much more loosely composed and with a profusion of small-paned double-hung sash-windows and dormers, are more definitely English and also more original.

Webb had been using such windows and even approaching the Late Stuart vernacular in his houses for a year or two before Kinmel was begun. This was most evident at Trevor Hall [218], built at Oakleigh Park near Barnet in Hertfordshire in 1868-70, for that modest country house was quite symmetrical in design although almost devoid of any sort of 'period' detail, whether Gothic or Late Stuart. To more acclaim, Webb had also been responsible for designing with William Morris a little earlier, in 1866 and in 1867, the Armoury in St James's Palace and the Refreshment Room in the Victoria and Albert Museum. The former, particularly, is a very original masterpiece of nineteenth-century decoration, hardly at all related to the contemporary High Victorian Gothic, yet reflecting the eighteenth century only as regards the treatment of the wainscoting and the door and window casings (which may be of eighteenth-century date). The Refreshment Room is also very fine and accessible to the public [180].

Just after 1870, while Kinmel was still in construction, the main line of development moved from the country into London. The Education Act of 1870 required the building of innumerable new schools, particularly by the London School Board. Among the architects successful in the first competitions that

180. William Morris and Philip Webb: London, Victoria and Albert Museum, Refreshment Room, 1867

were held for designs for these schools were E. R. Robson (1835–1917) and J. J. Stevenson (1831–1908); they used a non-Gothic vocabulary in London stock bricks trimmed with red bricks cut or moulded along seventeenth-century vernacular lines.[6] This mode was not unrelated to the more definitely Queen Anne models provided by the Kew lodge and by Kinmel, but the new London schools were more irregular in composition and naturally much more cheaply built. Robson, appointed architect to the London School Board in 1871, soon made this mode the official one for schools in London County and this, of course, before long influenced Board School design nationally.

In 1871 Stevenson, like Shaw a Scot out to make a London reputation, built a new house for himself in what is now Bayswater Road. This he named the Red House, like Morris's at Bexley Heath of a decade earlier, in order to call attention to the fact that its brickwork was not covered with stucco but exposed like that of the Thackeray and Howard houses in Palace Green. In fact, however, it was built like the Board Schools of brownish stock bricks with red-brick detail elaborately moulded, gauged, and cut in the Late Stuart way. Although Stevenson's house had little of the real elegance of Kinmel or the natural ease of Shaw's manors, its novelty and its fairly conspicuous location would have attracted attention in any case. But Stevenson, a very accomplished publicist, saw the advantage of proclaiming for this hybrid mode a name, 'Queen Anne', which was evidently no less applicable to Nesfield's Kew lodge and Kinmel or even to his friend Robson's schools. Thus was a revival formally launched.

Two new buildings in London by Shaw, begun in 1872 and in 1873, were definitely in the new mode. Only at this point, indeed, does the term Queen Anne begin to make any sense as applied to Shaw's work. Despite the valid claim to priority that Stevenson made for his Red House in a paper read in 1874 at the Architects' Conference 'On the recent reaction of taste in architecture' in which he claimed the Queen Anne mode was a 'Re-Renaissance' (sic) and his own relative success from this time on as a fashionable London house-architect, the Queen Anne became Shaw's from the moment that he first turned his hand to it in 1872. Whether the original idea came to him from Devey or from Nesfield – he had possibly worked on the designs for the lodges of 1866 at Kew and Kinmel – or was merely an attempt to outbid a rival Scotsman on the London scene makes no real difference.

New Zealand Chambers, the office building which Shaw erected in 1872-3 in Leadenhall Street in the City, was certainly totally unlike anything the Age of Anne ever saw except for the cut-brick detailing of the pedimented entrance. Boldly projecting red brick piers divided the tall façade into three bays, while between them rose oriel windows broken by ornately sculptured spandrels imitated from the mid-seventeenth-century ones on Sparrow's House at Ipswich. The small panes and thick white sash-bars of these windows made the scale surprisingly domestic in contrast to the usual boldness of High Victorian commercial work, and the whole composition was effectively tied together by an ornately pargeted cove cornice that ran straight across the top (see

Chapter 14). Above this the rather simple range of continuous dormers in the roof was very much in the spirit of the 'ribbon-window' bands on his country houses.

So dazzled were contemporaries by the lush exuberance of Shaw's ornament on the spandrels and the cove that they hardly noticed the way in which the bold articulation of this façade by the brick piers, with the areas between nearly all window, frankly reflecting the internal iron construction, provided most satisfactory lighting for the offices; nor that Shaw, while keeping his scale intimate in all the detailing, was not afraid to stress the verticality of his façade by avoiding emphasis on the storey lines. Only the weaker features of the design – the arbitrary asymmetry of the entrance, the profuse ornamentation, and the underscaling – were generally imitated.

Lowther Lodge, built in 1873-4, a large free-standing mansion in Kensington Gore, still survives – it is now the home of the Royal Geographical Society – as New Zealand Chambers does not. Here the vocabulary of cut and moulded brick is more consistently Late Stuart, although the general composition, with many gables, two tall polygonal bay-windows, quantities of dormers, and tall fluted chimney stacks, is as romantically complex as that of Shaw's manors in Sussex and Surrey. However, both the front and the rear façades, when studied, will be found to approximate symmetry in their principal portions as does the front of Glen Andred; and the main rooms inside, the hall at the front and the drawing-room behind, are quite symmetrical and have recognizably Early Georgian (rather than specifically Queen Anne) fireplaces and door and window casings although their grouping is still, so to say, agglutinative.

In a Surrey house of the same date, 1873, like Trevor Hall unhappily demolished, Webb moved rather farther in a similar direction. Joldwynds near Dorking was quite as symmetrical as Trevor Hall but even less Gothic. The vocabulary of tile-hanging on the upper storeys, with weather-boarding in the gables, was as authentically regional as that of Shaw's nearby houses, but the vaguely eighteenth-century vernacular of the detailing was much simpler than Shaw's repertory of moulded and cut brickwork at Lowther Lodge.

Nesfield, in designing what is now Barclays Bank in the Market Square of Saffron Walden in Essex, remained more eclectic, staying closer to the manorial mode of Cloverley Hall yet using again various Japanese motifs in the rich decoration. This was built in 1874. Godwin, who had just moved to London with the actress Ellen Terry and was now largely occupied with designing stage sets, developed further in the rooms of their rented house in Taviton Street in 1873-4 the Anglo-Japanese mode of his interiors of ten years earlier in Bristol. In 1874 he also arranged an exhibition of paintings in a similar spirit for his friend the painter Whistler at the new Grosvenor Galleries.[7]

In the mid seventies, however, it was Shaw, not Nesfield or Godwin, who occupied the centre of the architectural stage. In the Convent of the Sisters of Bethany of 1874 in St Clements Road at Boscombe near Bournemouth he disguised his use of concrete, then a relatively new building material, with his familiar Sussex vernacular. He did the same in a slightly later series of designs for cottages made of patented prefabricated concrete slabs.[8] It is worth noting, moreover, that the internal iron skeleton above the bold cantilever on the front of his Old Swan House [181] of 1876 at 17 Chelsea Embankment in London provides in effect an example of what would later be called 'skyscraper construction' since it carries completely the weight of the brickwork of the upper walls; this was a decade before the 'invention' of this sort of construction in Chicago (see Chapter 14). Shaw's interest in technical developments and

his enthusiasm for new materials and methods was evidently very great, always provided that he could bend them to his particular sort of retrospective pictorial vision. When he built the Jury House for the Paris Exhibition of 1878 of patent cement bricks, for example, he designed the façade very elegantly in his Late Stuart manner just as if it were of cut and moulded clay bricks. Godwin and Whistler, however, were showing at this same exhibition an Anglo-Japanese room of highly original character in association with Watt the furniture manufacturer.

Shaw's excellent church of this period at Bournemouth, St Michael's and All Angels, Poole Hill, begun in 1873, is Late Victorian in the crispness and clarity of its design but less archaeological than those of this date by Bodley. It seems to indicate that he could have made a great reputation as a church builder had he not been absorbed with secular work. But by the seventies secular work once again provided the field of major prestige in England, as it had hardly done since 1840, and so Shaw concentrated on it. Having revolutionized country-house design, he now turned, more definitely than at Lowther Lodge – by its size and open siting more a country house set in the city – to urban and suburban domestic work. In these his conquest was even more complete, at least in England and, as regards the suburbs, in America.

The Old Swan House and its neighbour Cheyne House at the outer end of the Chelsea Embankment, respectively of 1876 and 1875, are both mansions rather than ordinary terrace houses. They also represent a considerably further advance along the road towards a formal eighteenth-century revival than Lowther Lodge. Old Swan House is completely symmetrical, and the upper storeys are also quite regularly fenestrated in the early eighteenth-century way [181]. However, the total effect is still highly Picturesque because of the way

181. R. Norman Shaw:
London, Old Swan House, 1876

these upper storeys are cantilevered forward; from the cantilever depend, moreover, elaborate oriels of much earlier character very similar to those Shaw had introduced at New Zealand Chambers. Such oriels he long continued to employ; they are not only a principal feature of his own house in Hampstead, built in this same year, but also of the much later Holl and Long houses. Cheyne House occupies an irregular curving plot with the entrance in Royal Hospital Road; but Shaw used all his considerable ingenuity to give it symmetrical façades, even though the plan actually has little of the orderliness of that of Lowther Lodge.

If these two Chelsea houses seem to presage an early return to the serenity of Georgian street architecture, Shaw's J. P. Heseltine house of 1875 at 196 Queen's Gate in South Kensington unleashed a flood of the most individualistic house-design London had ever seen. Stucco-fronted houses of Builders' Renaissance design were still being erected on contiguous sites when this tall gabled façade rose, totally oblivious of old and new neighbours. Cut brick, moulded brick, terracotta, all of the brightest red, surround very large mullioned windows in a composition that is gratuitously asymmetrical at the base but symmetrical in the upper storeys below the crowning gable. For fifteen years such houses proliferated in the Chelsea, Kensington, and Earls Court districts of western London. The best are by Shaw himself, such as those at 68, 62, and 72 Cadogan Square – the first of 1879, the others of 1882 – and those at 8-11 and 15 Chelsea Embankment of 1878-9; but more are by other architects, and the vast majority by builders. In the Chelsea Embankment range River House at No. 3 is by Bodley; Nos 4-6 are by Godwin; and No. 7 is by R. Phéné Spiers (1838-1916), an architect whose Parisian training did not restrain him from following Shaw.

Collingham Gardens of 1881-7 by Sir Ernest George (1839-1922) and his then partner Harold A. Peto (?-1890), a sort of square with variously designed houses, all gabled, opening on to a lawn in the centre, provides a still more complete illustration of what may be called Neo-Picturesque urbanism. Not at all Shavian, the detailing of many of these houses is very similar to that of Cuijpers's Rijksmuseum and none of it Queen Anne. The contiguous mansions that George & Peto built in 1882 near by in Harrington Gardens, one for W. S. Gilbert at No. 19 [182], another for Sir Ernest Cassel, the banker, are the most elaborate single London examples of their domestic work. The house of the composer of the Savoy Operas approaches very closely the German Meister-singer mode of the period, but the touch is much lighter – intentionally whimsical perhaps? – and both the organization of the whole and the execution of the profuse detail is very superior to what one finds in most contemporary German work (see Chapter 9).

182. George & Peto:
London, Ernest Cassel and W. S. Gilbert houses, 1882

Stevenson's best and most Shavian houses in London are two that he built in 1878 in partnership with A. J. Adams in Lowther Gardens behind Lowther Lodge; however, those he built at 40-42 Pont Street have a certain interest because the mode that he exploited here is often called 'Pont Street Dutch', so ubiquitous is it in this part of Chelsea. This name also emphasizes the characteristic tendency of the late seventies and eighties towards varying the English late seventeenth-century vernacular mode by the introduction of Dutch and Flemish elements of detail, usually executed in terracotta, as George & Peto did in most of the Earls Court

houses mentioned above. Thus, by the late seventies, the long-established London tradition of coherent terrace design came to an end. That was, on the whole, a real urbanistic misfortune, however excellent some of the best individual houses by the above-mentioned architects may be.

Shaw's venture into the suburbs initiated a new domestic tradition of positive value and also a tradition of 'planning' that has continued with some modification down to the present, both in England and abroad. At Bedford Park, Turnham Green, then well beyond the western edges of built-up London, Shaw laid out in 1876 and largely designed an early 'Garden Suburb' (see Chapter 24), in fact, almost a 'new town', similar in some ways to the New Towns of the decades since the war, but without any industries of its own. Small houses, mostly semi-detached, i.e., in pairs, stand in their own gardens, simply and casually built of good red brick with a certain amount of modest Queen Anne detailing. The scheme is very complete, including a church by Shaw that is most ingeniously styled to harmonize with the domesticity of the houses, a club, a tavern, shops, and so forth.[9] Godwin's assistant Maurice B. Adams (1849-1933) and E. J. May (1853-1941) also worked here, as well as Godwin himself; indeed, some of the best houses are not by Shaw but by Godwin.

With characteristic versatility, while the construction of Bedford Park was proceeding in this simplified version of his middle manner, Picturesque but distinctly anti-Gothic, Shaw was also erecting at Adcote in Shropshire in 1877 a large Tudor manor house in reddish stone. This is notable for its restrained, almost 'abstract', detailing and for the tall mullioned window-wall of the hall bay, more than rivalling that of Cloverley Hall. Flete, a still larger house in Devon begun the year after Adcote, is also Tudor. Dawpool in Cheshire, demolished in 1926, was begun in 1882 in much the same mode but was even more extensive and elaborate than Flete. J. F. Doyle (1840-1913) of Liverpool collaborated on this.

The Bedford Park church of 1878, St Michael's, is more or less Queen Anne, at least not at all Gothic. But at Ilkley in Yorkshire Shaw's St Margaret's of the previous year is a remarkably personal essay in the Perpendicular, low and broad and elegantly detailed. In quality this is well above his earlier Bournemouth church and rather more original in its proportions than the standard work of Bodley and his imitators at this time. Somewhat similar, and still more original, is St Swithin's in Gervis Road in Bournemouth, also of 1877; while All Saints', Leek, of 1886 carries almost to the point of parody the Shavian stylization of English Late Gothic proportion towards the

broad and low – visually, that is; ritualistically they are quite as 'High' as Bodley's.

Next Shaw produced his finest and most creatively conceived church, Holy Trinity, Latimer Road, comparable in quality to his early church at Bingley but wholly different in character. This was built in 1887-9 for the Harrow Mission in a poor district of western London. The interior of Holy Trinity is a single vessel, very broad and moderately low, covered by a flat-pointed wooden ceiling which is tied by vigorous horizontal members of iron cased in wood and heavily buttressed externally [183]. Behind the chancel, which is no more than a square dais on which the altar is raised, rises an ecclesiastical version of the Shavian window-wall, broad and low like the space it terminates but arched and lightly traceried at

183. R. Norman Shaw:
London, Holy Trinity, Latimer Road, 1887-9

the top. The result could hardly be more different from Shaw's domestic Queen Anne of these years. It is on such things as this church, in which his basic architectural capacities are revealed unconfused by frivolous elaboration of detail, that his claim to high talent, occasionally to genius, must be based.

If Shaw did not cease to design churches while continually extending the range of his secular practice, it is a still more notable testimony to the breadth of his approach that he built in 1879, in Kensington Gore between the Albert Hall and Lowther Lodge – and with a characteristic disregard for both – the first really handsome block of flats erected in London; the first, that is, unless one prefers the Second Empire ones of the late sixties in Grosvenor Gardens. The tall and extensive

184. R. Norman Shaw:
London, Albert Hall Mansions, 1879

mass of this block, like that of most of his houses of the period, is extremely picturesque in silhouette because of the very tall scrolled gables that face the Park. But these are quite regularly spaced and the walls below them, with the multitudinous segment-arched, white-sashed windows all evenly phrased in threes, illustrate Shaw's Queen Anne of the seventies at its most disciplined [184].[10]

As has been noted, Shaw was by now the preferred architect of most of his fellow Royal Academicians. Webb had built houses for several of the Pre-Raphaelite painters who were his friends and associates. Less successful and more advanced painters employed Godwin. Small though it is and now much remodelled, the White House in Tite Street round the corner from the Chelsea Embankment, which Godwin built for his friend Whistler in 1878, had one of the most original façades of the decade. As its name implies, although all of brick, it was not 'red' like Morris's and Stevenson's famous houses, but 'white' because the walls were so painted,[11] recalling perhaps the white-painted Colonial farmhouses of Whistler's New England youth. The sparse detail was related in its vaguely eighteenth-century character to the Shavian Queen Anne but it was much more delicate and linear, indeed almost Late Georgian in inspiration. Most significantly, the composition of the façade as a whole, and even more evidently the asymmetrical placing of the door and windows, owed a great deal to those abstract principles of Japanese art which both Whistler and Godwin had been studying for almost twenty years.

Whistler had to sell his house almost as soon as it was finished in order to pay the costs of his unhappy libel suit against Ruskin, a legal battle in which the Late Victorian and the High Victorian came to violent grips. But Godwin went on to build several more studio houses in Tite Street at Nos 29, 33, and 44 in the next few years and also the Tower House in 1885.

Similar, but inferior, is No. 31 by R. W. Edis, which John Singer Sargent later occupied. Also in Tite Street is the commonplace terrace house at No. 16, of which the interiors were decorated by Godwin for Oscar Wilde,[12] the greatest aesthete of them all. Wilde's influential ideas in this field, carried to America on a lecture tour in 1881-2, were largely derived from Godwin, it may be noted.

When Shaw turned again to commercial work it was to design in 1881 the offices for the bankers Baring Brothers at 8 Bishopsgate in the City of London. This small building was as discreet, as orderly, and almost as domestic as Cheyne House. But the next year, so chameleon-like was his development, he gave the more conspicuous Alliance Assurance Building at the corner of St James's Street and Pall Mall opposite St James's Palace broad, low, banded arches of brick and stone below and elaborated the vertical articulation of the upper storeys with profuse sculptural ornament.[13] Very tall scalloped gables provide a Neo-Picturesque effect comparable to the ubiquitous 'Pont Street Dutch' houses of his London rivals and to much contemporary Northern Renaissance work in northern Europe. To emphasize his various-ness further, there is diagonally across the street a later edifice for the same clients, built in colla-boration with his pupil Ernest Newton (1856-1922) in 1903, so quietly academic in the Neo-Georgian taste of the early twentieth century that one can hardly believe it is also the work of Shaw.

His next important secular works after the first Alliance building, both begun in 1887 like the Latimer Road church, contrast with each other almost as markedly as they do with that. Characteristic of the essentially private pat-ronage – patronage from successful artists, patronage from business, patronage from the professional classes – responsible for the best English architecture of this period is the fact that Shaw's first public commission came at

this advanced stage of his career. London's old Metropolitan Police Offices in New Scotland Yard, of which the original block was built in 1887-8 and the second block to the south added in 1890, have a splendid site on the Thames Embankment. Remembering, it would seem almost for the first time, his own Scottish birth – or possibly in apposite reference to the familiar name of the London police head-quarters – Shaw designed Scotland Yard somewhat like a Scottish castle with corner tourelles and tall scrolled gables, but using throughout heavy and rather academic later seventeenth-century detailing of a much less regional sort [185]. Red brick and stone in combination make it also as colouristic as the Alliance building, the solidity of the propor-tions makes it weighty, and the high gables and turret roofs give it great variety of outline. As a result, the total effect is almost High Victorian in its vigour and its massiveness. Shaw is said to have regretted the need to build a second block; certainly it must have been more im-pressive when the original block stood alone like an isolated riverside fortress. The police have moved to Victoria Street but the building survives.

Scotland Yard seems to look backward some-what, at least in relation to that gradual de-velopment towards orderliness and restraint of an eighteenth-century sort which can be discerned in Shaw's work of the seventies despite all its variousness. On the other hand, the house he built also in 1887-8 for Fred White,[14] an American diplomat, at 170 Queen's Gate, so near to that strikingly aberrant terrace house of the previous decade at No. 196, seems to look forward into the early twentieth century, when the eighteenth-century Georgian would provide the basis for a quite archaeological revival. This plain rectangular block of red brick, orderly and symmetrical on the long façade rowards Imperial Institute Road and also on the end towards Queen's Gate, with

185. R. Norman Shaw: London, New Scotland Yard, 1887-8

186. R. Norman Shaw:
London, Fred White house, 1887-8

187. Philip Webb:
Smeaton Manor, Yorkshire, 1877-9

three ranges of large sash-windows below an academic cornice, is therefore as much a historical landmark, if not an original creation, as was Glen Andred twenty years before [186]. The suave and well-scaled ornamentation is concentrated at the doorway in the eighteenth-century manner, and the hip roof is unbroken except by regular spaced dormers. Yet, curiously enough, the plan is somewhat less completely regular and symmetrical than one might expect from the exterior; for example, the large drawing-room towards Queen's Gate is L-shaped.

Only the excellence of the craftsmanship here, based not on the Sussex vernacular but on the most sophisticated work of around 1720, the prominence of the tall chimneys, and the wide central dormer with its curved top reveal Shaw's hand and suggest, perhaps, an early date; otherwise such a house might well have been built forty years or so later by many other architects, English and American (see Chapter 24). However, Webb at Smeaton Manor[15] in Yorkshire, built in 1877-9, had already arrived at an almost identical regularity and formality

of design [187]. Characteristically, however, he did not elaborate the exterior with borrowed eighteenth-century detailing, and the house remains almost undatable on internal evidence, like much of his best work.

Scotland Yard is an all but unique example of an English public building of distinction erected in the eighties. Before continuing with the account of Shaw's work in the nineties, two prominent features of the London skyline, the most striking additions made since Butterfield's spire of All Saints' rose in Margaret Street in the fifties and the Victoria Tower of the Houses of Parliament was completed in the sixties, should be mentioned. Both the Imperial Institute, towering over Shaw's contiguous Fred White house in South Kensington, which was built in 1887-93 in honour of Queen Victoria's first jubilee, and the Catholic cathedral of Westminster, not begun until 1894, are especially notable for their very tall dome-topped towers. The cathedral, which was designed by J. F. Bentley (1839-1902), a pupil of Clutton, has also a magnificent domed interior. The Institute, built by T. E. Collcutt (1840-

1924), was perhaps of less over-all interest but extremely refined and elegant in its detailing compared to the contemporary work of George & Peto, which it most closely resembled. Curiously enough, the very underscaled membering and even so dainty a trick as the occasional single courses of red brick in the stonework do not make the extant 280-foot tower petty. It may be compared to its own very great advantage with Haller's contemporary tower, in a somewhat parallel Northern Renaissance vein, on the Hamburg Rathaus. Collcutt's own earlier tower on the Town Hall at Wakefield in Yorkshire of 1877-80 was less successful than this London landmark, which has happily survived the rest of the building.

Bentley's tower has a similar silhouette, but is more boldly striated by broad bands of brick and stone. The detail, partly Byzantine, partly Early Renaissance despite his distinguished early career as a Late Victorian Gothic church architect, is, like Collcutt's, rather underscaled. This goes still further to prove the extent to which this period in England saw all architecture, even that of cathedrals, in domestic terms. However, well before Bentley began his cathedral - it is not even yet completed as regards the internal decoration - Shaw had turned towards considerably more monumental forms at Scotland Yard, and even to quite academic design.

At Bryanston, a large country house in Dorset begun in 1889 for Lord Portman, Shaw modelled the main block on Sir Roger Pratt's Coleshill House of the mid seventeenth century; the side wings here are quite Gibbsian. This is the earliest example of what the English call 'Monumental Queen Anne' - to distinguish this sort of work henceforth from the freer and more vernacular Queen Anne of the seventies and eighties - and the Americans 'Georgian Revival'. Two years later Shaw built Chesters in Northumberland. This mansion is equally academic if less derivative from particular sources; but it is also highly original in plan and conception. The composition of the incurved façade planes, moreover, is as knowing and as ingenious in its formal way as anything he ever built in a more rambling vein.

Later in the nineties Shaw's stylistic uncertainty - or, if one wishes to call it so, his versatility - was notably illustrated in two large commercial buildings built in Liverpool. The façade of Parr's Bank in Castle Street, built in 1898 in collaboration with W. E. Willink (1856-1924) and P. C. Thicknesse (1860-1920), is of the suavest academic order. Its proportions are surer than in any of his other works except Chesters, and yet he striated its light-coloured stonework with bands of green marble in a way few later architects working in this vein would ever have thought of doing. Two years later, in the offices that he built in collaboration with Doyle for Ismay, Imrie & Co., later the White Star Line - for whom he also designed the interiors of the liner *Oceanic* - he provided what was externally almost a copy of Scotland Yard, and yet inside he exposed the riveted metal structural members in a fashion at once frank and highly decorative.

If Shaw had had the opportunity to rebuild Nash's Regent Street Quadrant completely according to the designs that he prepared in 1905 the loss of the original work might not be so serious. Approaching seventy-five, he turned here to a Piranesian Classicism. The colonnaded section finished in 1908, which forms the northern front of the Piccadilly Hotel, though flanked at both ends by an emasculated version of Shaw's design carried out in 1923 by his admiring biographer Sir Reginald Blomfield (1856-1942), rivals in boldness anything English architecture had produced since the days of Vanbrugh and Hawksmore. Even more spectacular, and also incomplete, since the gable at the east end was never built, is the Piccadilly façade of the hotel with its tremendous open colonnade raised high against the sky [188]. The Classical serenity of this feature is characteristically contrasted with the voluted silhouette of the tall gable over the projecting wing at the west end, and the exuberance of the whole puts most other Edwardian Neo-Baroque to shame.

To summarize Shaw's achievement or even to epitomize his personal style is almost impossible. He was, for example, in no ordinary sense of the word merely an eclectic; yet his modes were very various, more various than those of almost any other nineteenth-century architect of equal rank. After his borrowings in the mid sixties, however, they were all his own – his own, at least, until hordes of other architects in England and America took them up, one or two at a time, often vulgarizing them beyond recognition. He was probably not the most talented English architect of his generation and certainly not the most original. How much he owed to Nesfield at the start it is impossible to say, though at least two of the characteristic

Shavian modes seem to have been originally of his invention – if not, indeed, of Devey's!

Yet ironically Nesfield's own later work appeared to contemporaries almost like an echo of Shaw's if it was known at all. He never had any such success as did Shaw, and died relatively young in 1888. Godwin also was somehow never able, after 1870, to repeat the public triumphs that had been his in the competitions of the early sixties. In his later life he turned more and more to designing sets and costumes for the theatre and died in 1886, two years before Nesfield. Webb survived till 1915, although he retired from practice in 1900; his spirit, moreover, lived on in a quite different way from Shaw's. It was through emulation of the craftsman-like integrity of Webb's work that the attitudes, rather than the forms, of Pugin's earlier Gothic Revival were transmitted to the first modern architects quite as much as through study of the writings of his friend and close associate Morris.

188. R. Norman Shaw: London, Piccadilly Hotel, 1905-8

CHAPTER 13

H. H. RICHARDSON AND McKIM, MEAD & WHITE

The story of Shaw's career is a fascinating one, far more interesting in fact than the general history of English architecture in the last quarter of the nineteenth century. It was a success-drama in four or five acts, of which the last was by no means the least brilliant. Richardson's career was less eventful, even though, at its peak in the mid eighties, he was at least as successful as Shaw. It was also incomplete, since death brought his production to an end at that peak when he was only forty-eight. Yet Richardson's achievement must be considered greater than Shaw's, qualitatively if not quantitatively, because his work was better integrated and his development more intelligently directed. Moreover, his influence operated on two levels: on one it was as wide, if more evanescent, than Shaw's – say, what Shaw's might have been if *he* had died at the age of forty-eight, that is, in 1879 – on another level it was more like that of Webb, affecting deeply the most creative American architects of the next two generations.

Henry Hobson Richardson was born in 1838 in St James Parish in Louisiana. Upon graduation from Harvard in 1858 Richardson, bilingual on account of his Louisiana birth, not unnaturally proceeded to Paris to the École des Beaux-Arts, entering there the atelier of L.-J. André (1819-90), a pupil of Lebas who had become a professor at the École in 1855. But after two years the outbreak of the Civil War in the United States cut off his remittances from home and he had to find work in order to maintain himself. His experience in the office of Théodore Labrouste, notably in working on the designs for the Asile d'Ivry outside Paris, was perhaps of more ultimate value to him than

what he learned in André's atelier and at the École. Several of his earliest works in America, designed immediately after his return from Paris in 1865, have been discussed already (see Chapter 11). It was with the Brattle Square (now First Baptist) Church on Commonwealth Avenue at Clarendon Street in the new Back Bay residential district of Boston, the commission for which he won in a competition held in 1870, that his career seriously began. During the years that this was in construction, 1871-2, he had in his office a young assistant, Charles F. McKim (1847-1909), who had returned from Paris at the outbreak of the Franco-Prussian War in 1870. It may well be that the forceful McKim helped Richardson to crystallize the divergent elements evident in his earlier work into a coherent personal style. The Brattle Square Church somewhat resembles in its round-arched medievalism such a Paris church of the sixties as Vaudremer's Saint-Pierre-de-Montrouge, which Richardson himself may have seen and admired in the early stages of its construction. But the squarish T-shaped plan, without aisles but with transepts, would have been as unusual in France at this period as in England. The material is the richly textured Roxbury Puddingstone rising in broad plain surfaces to the medium-pitched gables. The detail strikes a sort of balance between the French Romanesquoid and the English High Victorian Gothic, the forms being more French, the execution more English. The varied polychromy of the deep voussoirs of the arches is possibly English, but with a personal note in the great variety of the coloured banding. The corner placing of the tall tower, with its fine frieze by the French sculptor Bartholdi, is

English in spirit, but its shape is rather more campanile-like than any English church tower had been since the forties.

A similar stylistic crystallization can be seen in the very extensive plant of the State Hospital at Buffalo, N.Y., a commission also won by Richardson in competition in 1870. This was largely re-designed before construction began in 1872 and was in building throughout the whole decade. It was, functionally, the sort of commission for which Richardson's French training best prepared him, and the planning is French. The other sources of the design seem to have been mostly English, particularly the projects of Burges.

Two buildings in Springfield, Mass., where Richardson had been working on and off since his return from Paris, are even more significant than the Buffalo asylum for the rather definite evidence they offer as to his chief contemporary sources of inspiration at this point. The spire of the North Congregational Church there – commissioned as early as 1868, but built in 1872-3, after being re-designed in 1871 or 72 – is a rather squat pyramid of quarry-faced brownstone with four corner spirelets rising from the same square base, apparently a version of the spire Burges designed for his Skelton church begun in 1871 or that of Street's St James the Less. The tower of the Hampden County Court-house of 1871-3 also comes from Burges, in this case from the project that he entered in the London Law Courts competition of 1866. The general composition owes more to the slightly earlier English town halls at Northampton and Congleton by Godwin, who was also Burges's collaborator on the Law Courts project. But the magnificent scale of the random ashlar walls of quarry-faced Monson granite, their coldness relieved by bright red pointing, is as personal to Richardson as the similar brownstone masonry of the North Congregational Church at Springfield and the Buffalo Hospital.

Richardson's American Express Building,[1] his first work in Chicago, which was begun in 1872, and his contemporary Andrews house in Newport, R.I., both showed comparable evidence of generic influence from contemporary England (see Chapters 14 and 15). In this same year, 1872, Richardson won the competition for Trinity Church[2] in Boston, which was to occupy a conspicuous site on the east side of what became Copley Square, the one open space in the Back Bay district. Preceding by a year the Panic of 1873, which slowed building almost to a standstill, this commission and that for the Buffalo Hospital kept him busy through five lean years. As Trinity rose to completion over the years 1874-7, this big Boston church established Richardson's reputation as the new leader among American architects [189]. Even before Trinity was finished others were producing crude imitations of it; and over the next twenty years many prominent American churches, particularly in the Middle West, followed in some degree the new model that it provided.

Trinity is in plan an enlarged and modified version of the Brattle Square Church. A deep semicircular chancel provides a fourth arm, and a great square lantern rises over the crossing. The elaborate porch, so archaeologically Provençal Romanesque, was added by Richardson's successors, Shepley, Rutan & Coolidge, in the nineties, as were also the tops of the western towers; the present decorations of the chancel are much later and by Charles D. Maginnis (1867-1955).

The materials of Trinity are pink Milford granite in quarry-faced random ashlar for the walling and the Longmeadow brownstone that he had first used on the Unity Church in Springfield for the profuse trim. The detail changed in character as the work proceeded; in the earliest portions executed it is heavy and crude, with the foliage carved in a naturalistic High Victorian Gothic vein. But the logic of

189. H. H. Richardson:
Boston, Trinity Church, 1873–7

of the round arches that Richardson had been consistently using since he designed the Brattle Square Church in 1870 led him towards Romanesque models. The pyramidal massing of Trinity from the east derived from Auvergnat churches, and there is even Auvergnat polychromy on the apse; the lower portion of the original west front was based on St-Gilles-de-Provence; and the executed lantern was an adaptation of that on the Old Cathedral of Salamanca in Spain.[3] Only the last influence seems to have been specifically recognized by contemporaries, yet most of them, supposing all worthy nineteenth-century architecture to be necessarily derivative from this or that style of the past, believed that Richardson had initiated a Romanesque Revival here. But Richardson remained really as responsive to contemporary English ideas as he had been earlier. For example, the curious double-curved wooden roof with kingpost trusses derives from published examples of similar roofs built or projected by Burges. Equally symptomatic of English influence is the use of stained glass by Morris and Burne-Jones in the north transept windows. That glass, however, is inferior in richness of tone to the small windows in the west front designed by the American artist John LaFarge.

LaFarge was also responsible for the painted decoration on the walls and the roofs.

To take over Fuller & Laver's New York State Capitol at Albany when already partly built in the way that Richardson and Eidlitz – a foreign-born exponent of Romanesque of the earlier *Rundbogenstil* sort, it will be recalled – were asked to do in 1875 was a thankless job; but this call for Richardson's aid illustrates the rapidity with which he achieved a national reputation. More important, both historically and intrinsically, than what he was able to carry out in Albany – chiefly the Senate Chamber – were a second house that he built in Newport, R.I., in Shepard Avenue in 1874-6 and a building in Main Street in Hartford, Conn., of 1875-6 (see Chapters 14 and 15). The Sherman house is the first example of a 'Shavian manor' successfully translated into American materials; the Cheney Block (later part of the J. Fox Store) is not Shavian at all, but very similar to the arcaded façades common in England since the late fifties [202].

To the late seventies belong two remarkably fine buildings, still obviously related to slightly earlier English work, but more personal than either the Newport house or the Hartford commercial building. With the Winn Memorial Library in Woburn, Mass., of 1877-8 Richardson initiated a line of small-town public libraries that reached its climax in the Crane Library in Quincy, Mass., of 1880-3 [190]. The high window-bands of the stack wings, a monumental stone version of Shaw's 'ribbon-windows', and the stone-mullioned 'window-wall' at the end are more significant than the round stair-turrets and the cavernous entrance arches – Early Christian from Syria[4] in origin,

190. H. H. Richardson:
Quincy, Mass., Crane Library, 1880-3

not Southern French Romanesque, it should be noted – that romanticize their generally compact massing. The highly functional planning is asymmetrical yet very carefully ordered, perhaps the one remaining trace of his Paris training.

In building Sever Hall, a classroom building for Harvard College in Cambridge, Mass., in 1878–80 Richardson abandoned rock-faced granite and brownstone, materials whose common use would, a little later, mark the extent of his influence on other architects, for the red brick of the nearby eighteenth-century buildings in the old Harvard Yard. He even imitated the plain oblong masses of these Georgian edifices under his great red-tiled hip-roof; but the front, with its deep Syrian arch and two tower-like rounded bays, and the rear, with a broader and shallower central bow, are wholly Richardsonian. There is a rather Shavian pediment over the centre of the front, however; while the moulded brick mullions of the banked windows and the very rich cut-brick panels of floral ornament seem to reflect current English work by Stevenson and by Godwin as well as by Shaw. Yet the whole has been amalgamated into a composition quite as orderly as anything English 'Annites' had yet produced. At the same time Sever Hall is almost as vigorous and masculine in scale as his contemporary libraries of granite and brownstone.

Two domestic buildings of 1880, one entirely shingled, the other of rough glacial boulders, are even more personal works; and both, particularly the former, represent the American domestic mode of this period that is called 'Shingle Style' (see Chapter 15). The John Bryant house in Cohasset, Mass., of 1880 first illustrated his emancipation from the direct Shavian imitation that had begun with the Sherman house and continued in several projects – probably mostly designed by Stanford White – that were prepared in the later seventies but never executed. Quite a series of later

shingled houses by Richardson followed the Bryant house between 1881 and 1886 [221].

The contemporary Ames Gate Lodge[5] in North Easton, Mass., has a sort of antediluvian power in the bold plasticity of its boulder-built walls – a theme exploited once before in Grace Church in Medford, Mass., of 1867 it will be recalled – as remote from the Romanesque as from the Queen Anne. A similarly absolute originality of a more gracious order can be seen in the Fenway Bridge of 1880–1 in Boston; its tawny seam-faced granite walls happily echo the easy naturalistic curves of the landscaping of the parkway by his friend F. L. Olmsted (1822–1903)[6] of which it is a prominent feature.

1881 saw the initiation of a more monumental building for Harvard, Austin Hall,[7] then the Law School, which was completed in 1883. Rich Auvergnat polychromy and a great deal of rather Byzantinesque carved ornament somewhat confuse the direct structural expressiveness of the thoroughly articulated masonry walls; as a result Austin Hall provided a variety of decorative clichés for imitators to abuse. Much more modest and also much more significant was the station at Auburndale, Mass., also of 1881, built for the Boston & Albany Railroad. This was the first and the finest of a series of small suburban stations notable for the simplicity of their design and for the compositional skill with which the open elements, carried on sturdy but gracefully shaped wooden supports, were related to the solid masonry blocks of granite and brownstone beneath sweeping roofs of tile or slate. If Shaw was called on in the nineties to design the interiors of an ocean liner for the White Star Line, Richardson was ready to provide the designs for a railway carriage for the Boston & Albany. This was neither Romanesque nor Queen Anne in inspiration, but had domestically scaled interiors lined with small square oaken panels and with no carved ornament of any description.

191 *(below)*. H. H. Richardson: Pittsburgh, Penna., Allegheny County Jail, 1884–8

192 *(right)*. H. H. Richardson: Chicago, Marshall Field Wholesale Store, 1885–7

Stations, libraries, and houses formed the bulk of Richardson's production from 1882 until his death. But two much larger buildings, which he himself judged to be his master works, were also fortunately initiated, one in 1884 and the other in 1885, well before his last illness began, though both had to be finished by his successors Shepley, Rutan & Coolidge after his death. The Allegheny County Buildings[8] in Pittsburgh, Penna., consist of a vast quadrangular courthouse dominated by a very tall tower that rises in the centre of the front and a gaol across the street to the rear. Except for the courtyard walls, interesting for the variety and the openness of their ranges of granite arcading, the courthouse offers on the whole only a sort

of summary of his talents; the detail, above all, is afflicted with an archaeological dryness that must be due to the increasing dependence of his assistants on published documents of medieval carving. The courthouse provided, however, the model for many large public buildings in the next few years. Among these, the City Hall in Minneapolis, Minn., begun by the local firm of Long & Kees in 1887, is not unworthy of comparison with the original, particularly as regards the tower. That of Toronto in Canada, built by E. J. Lennox in 1890–9, is less interesting but even more monumental; it also signalizes the supersession of English by American influence in Canadian architecture at this point, as does the almost

equally Richardsonian Windsor Station in Montreal begun by the American architect Bruce Price in 1888.

The Pittsburgh Jail is a masterpiece of the most personal order, Piranesian in scale, nobly expressive of its gloomy purpose, and as superb an example of granite masonry as exists in the world [191]. It epitomizes Richardson's genius where the courthouse merely summarizes his talents.

Richardson's highest achievement, however, was in the field of private building not in that of the public monument. By a happy coincidence his ultimate masterpiece rose in Chicago where, at this very moment, technical advances in construction were being made that would soon bring to a climax the whole story of nineteenth-century commercial architecture (see Chapter 14). Chicago retains Richardson's last great masonry house, that of 1885-7 for J. J. Glessner, almost as perfect a domestic paradigm of granite construction as the Pittsburgh Jail. To her shame, however, Richardson's Marshall Field Wholesale Store, built during the same years, was torn down half a century ago to provide a car park.

The Field Store occupied an entire block with a dignity and a grandeur no other commercial structure had ever attained before [192]. Internally it was of iron-skeleton construction; externally the arcaded masonry walls represented a development from those of the Cheney

Building of ten years earlier [202]. Segmental arches covered the broad low openings in the massive ground storey, all built of great ashlar blocks of rock-faced red Missouri granite. The next three storeys, built of brownstone, were combined under a single range of broad arches, yet also articulated within these arched openings by stone mullions and spandrels. Above this stage the rhythm doubled, with the windows of the next two storeys joined under narrower arches.[8a] The scale of the quarry-faced ashlar was graded down as the walls rose, quite as were the window sizes, and the non-supporting spandrels were filled with small square blocks. The full thickness of the bearing masonry walls was revealed at all the openings. Finally there came a trabeated attic of somewhat Schinkel-like character over which appeared almost the only carved detail on the building, a boldly crocketed cornice. That was 'Early French', i.e., of twelfth-century Gothic rather than Romanesque or Byzantine inspiration.

The result was a monument as bold and almost as Piranesian in its scale and its forcefulness as the Pittsburgh Jail; but the walls were also as open, as continuously fenestrated, as those of the Pittsburgh Courthouse. The logical and expressive design of commercial buildings with walls of bearing masonry could hardly be carried further. But in the very year that the Field Store was finished Holabird & Roche, in designing the Tacoma Building, also in Chicago, first showed how the exterior of such edifices might express instead a newly developed sort of construction that allowed the internal metal skeleton to carry the external cladding of masonry (see Chapter 14).

In one last commercial building, much more obscurely located and built of far less expensive materials, which was started just before Richardson's death – it was only commissioned after his last illness had begun – he carried the logic of the design of the Field Store one step farther. It was almost as if he had already sensed, like Holabird & Roche, the implications of the Home Insurance Building in Chicago of 1883-5 by their former employer William Le Baron Jenney, in which the new sort of construction was first used but not at all expressed. On Richardson's Ames Building in Harrison Avenue in Boston a tall arcade rose almost the full height of the wall beneath a machicolated attic; the depth of the reveals around the sash at the sides of the brick piers was minimized; and above the ground storey the spandrels were of metal panels set almost flush with both piers and sash.

When Richardson died in 1886 the evidence of his great late works indicates that his powers were at their highest. His office, moreover, had never been busier. How Richardson might have developed further it is impossible to say. In the hands of his imitators the Richardsonian mode did not grow in any very creative way during the decade or more that it continued a favourite for churches, public buildings, and even houses built of masonry. Those who had been closest to Richardson when his style was maturing, McKim and White, rarely imitated him; even before his death, in fact, they had already set under way a reaction against the Richardsonian. Their buildings and not his provide the real American analogue to the later work of Shaw in England. Moreover, their leadership superseded his for many younger architects from coast to coast almost before he was dead.

Leaving aside the modes inherited from the sixties, in any case transmuted almost beyond recognition by the early eighties if not yet entirely obsolete, there were at the time of Richardson's death three main currents in American architecture as against the four or five more or less Shavian modes then popular in England. One was the Richardsonian.[9] This was practised with some success by various Boston firms such as Peabody & Stearns and Van Brunt & Howe. It had been carried to Kansas City, Missouri, by Van Brunt, moreover, and it was being developed with some originality by other Middle Westerners such as George D. Mason (1856–1948) in Detroit, D. H. Burnham (1846–1912) and his partner J. W. Root (1850–91), H. I. Cobb (1859–1931) and his partner Frost, and several other firms in Chicago. The very able designer Harvey Ellis (1852–1904),[10] working for L. S. Buffington (1848?–1931)[10a] in Minneapolis, should also be mentioned. Another current was represented by the development leading towards the Chicago skyscrapers of the nineties, in Richardson's last years more in the hands of technicians than of architects (see Chapter 14).

The third, and for the next few years the most expansive, current was what can already be called the Academic Reaction. This was parallel to, yet already pushing well ahead of, Shaw's somewhat coy approach to a program-matic revival of eighteenth-century forms; and McKim, Mead & White were its acknowledged leaders.[11] During the years that White was working for Richardson he seems to have been devotedly Shavian. Certain unexecuted house projects from the Richardson office which White signed, done for the Cheney family of Manchester, Conn., the clients for Richardson's Cheney Block in Hartford, make this particu-larly evident. When White replaced Bigelow in the firm of McKim, Mead & Bigelow, on his return from the European trip that he took after leaving Richardson in 1878, he found McKim designing Shavian houses with a con-siderably less sure decorative touch than his own. The McKim, Mead & White country houses that followed, however, such as that for H. Victor Newcomb in Elberon, N.J., of 1880–1 [224], that for Isaac Bell, Jr, in New-

193. McKim, Mead & White:
New York, Villard houses, 1883–5

port, R.I., of 1881-2 [222], and that for Cyrus McCormick in Richfield Springs, N.Y., of the same years, represent in several ways a real advance over Richardson's Sherman house.[12] Such an advance is equally to be observed in various houses built around Boston in these years by W. R. Emerson (1833-1918) and by Arthur Little (1852-1925), the very earliest of which doubtless influenced Richardson when he designed the Bryant house (see Chapter 15).

For McKim, Mead & White's Tiffany house in New York of 1882-4, all of tawny 'Roman' brick with much moulded brick detail, the inspiration was largely Shavian[12a] also; only the rock-faced stone base and the broad low entrance arch were at all Richardsonian. In the New York house that they began the same year, however – really a group of houses arranged in a U around an open court across Madison Avenue from the rear of St Patrick's Cathedral – for the railway magnate Henry Villard an entirely different, even quite opposed, spirit appears [193]. The Villard houses, although on Villard's insistence still built of brownstone rather than of light-coloured limestone, are as much a High Renaissance Italian *palazzo* as anything Barry or his contemporaries on the Continent ever designed in the preceding sixty years. Reputedly Joseph M. Wells (1853-90), an assistant in the McKim, Mead & White office who later refused membership in the firm, was responsible for the decision to follow Roman models of around 1500, most notably the Cancelleria Palace. Though he had been abroad, this was best known to him through the plates of Letarouilly's *Édifices de Rome moderne*.

This type of design represented a conscious reaction against the Neo-Picturesque, whether Richardsonian, Shavian, or *François I*, a return to disciplined order of the most formal sort. It represented also a return to close archaeological imitation of a style from the past such as had ended in America, on the whole, with the decline of the Greek Revival a generation

earlier. Curiously enough this turn was also something of a declaration of independence from Europe, since the American Academic Reaction as initiated in the design of the Villard houses seems to have had no contemporary sources abroad. However much Shaw's Queen Anne had, for about a decade, been moving towards an equivalent formality – of a more eighteenth-century sort – Shaw had neither gone so far as yet in this direction nor did he ever turn to the Roman Renaissance for his models. Continental parallels in the eighties are not hard to find in the work of such men as Balat in Belgium, Koch in Italy, and Wagner in Austria; but their current production was probably not known in the United States, whose foreign relations in architecture had always been largely restricted to England, France, and Germany.

This American return to order was at first more significant for its absolute aspect than for its archaeological bent. Although McKim, Mead & White used a Renaissance arcade at the base of their Goelet Building erected in Broadway at 20th Street in New York in 1885-6, the upper storeys of this modest skyscraper offer a very free, and at the same time a highly regularized, expression of the hive of offices behind, and even of the metal grid of the internal skeleton. Certain houses by McKim, Mead & White in New York of these years were even freer from the imitation of specific Italian precedents; while their Wm. G. Low house of as late as 1886-7, on the seashore south of Bristol, R.I., was a masterpiece of the 'Shingle Style' despite the tightness and formality of its plan (see Chapter 15). Carefully ordered under its single broad gable, which even subsumed the veranda at the southern end, the Low house was yet quite without reminiscent detail or, indeed, much of any detail at all [225]. In a group of small houses at Tuxedo Park, not at all academic in their exterior treatment, Bruce Price (1845-1903) was re-organizing the open plan of the Americanized Queen Anne in a schematically symmetrical way at just this time also [226, 227].

The possibility of a revival of the American Colonial and Post-Colonial in all their successive phases from the medievalism of the seventeenth-century origins to what can be called the 'Carpenters' Adam' of 1800 had been in the air ever since the early seventies when McKim had added a Neo-Colonial room to a real Colonial house in Newport, R.I. In the local Colonial architecture Americans found obvious parallels to the seventeenth- and eighteenth-century precedents that Shaw was exploiting in England.[13] The 'Shingle Style' employed various features and treatments – such as the all-over covering of shingles itself – that recall American work of the periods before 1800. But because of the continued strength of inherited Picturesque ideals there was little programmatic imitation of formal eighteenth-century house design before the mid eighties. Even such a highly orderly example as Little's Shingleside House at Swampscott, Mass., of 1880-1 was still quite unarchaeological. Interestingly enough, this seems also to have been the first up-to-date American house to be published in a foreign magazine[14] since the *Allgemeine Bauzeitung* in 1846 presented examples of Greek Revival terrace-houses in New York.

Well before the completion of the Bramantesque Villard houses in New York in 1885, McKim, Mead & White were already building in Newport, R.I., the H. A. C. Taylor house, now destroyed, which was as Neo-Georgian, in its American Colonial way, as the Fred White house that Shaw began in London in 1887. For this the American architects adopted the symmetrical Anglo-Palladian plan of the mid eighteenth century and capped the resultant rectangular mass with the special gable-over-hip roof of Colonial Newport. Elaborately embellished with Palladian windows and with

much carved detail of a generically Georgian order, the Taylor house provided a new formula of design for domestic work that soon superseded almost completely the 'Shingle Style'. From the Taylor house stems that mature Colonial Revival which was to last longer in the end in America than had the Greek Revival.

Down to the early nineties, however, McKim, Mead & White were rarely so programmatic in their Neo-Colonial work, and their principal public building of the late eighties, the Boston Public Library, was entirely Italianate [194]. In 1887 they were commissioned to build this major monument on the west side of Copley Square. There it was to face the Trinity Church that had initiated the Richardsonian wave more than a decade earlier – a monument in whose designing, moreover, both McKim and White had actually participated. The Library as built in 1888-92 was a major challenge to the Richardsonian, at least as contemporaries then generally understood and employed what they thought was Richardson's mode. The contrast it offers to the church opposite is almost as great as to the prominent but low-grade High Victorian Gothic structures that flanked the new site to north and south, the New Old South Church by Cummings & Sears of the mid seventies, still standing across Boylston Street, and the contemporaneous Museum of Fine Arts by John H. Sturgis (?-1888) and Charles Brigham (?-1925) which long occupied the south side of the square.

Trinity is dark and rich in colour, a complex pile rising massively to its large central lantern. Moreover, it was flanked at the left on the Boylston Street side, where Richardson took Picturesque advantage of the corner cut off his site by Huntington Avenue, with an asymmetrical organized and domestically scaled parish house. The Library is light coloured and monochromatic, all of a smooth-cut Milford granite ashlar almost white in tone even before cleaning,[14a] lighter than the rock-faced

194. McKim, Mead & White:
Boston, Public Library, 1888-92

pink Milford granite of Trinity. It is, moreover, a simple quadrangular mass, capped by a pantiled[15] hip-roof of moderate height; the scale throughout is monumental and the detail sparse but eminently suave. Yet if the contrast with Richardson's Trinity of 1873-7 is so great – and even greater with the ponderous vernacular Richardsonian as that was long illustrated south of the Library in the all-brownstone S. S. Pierce Store just built by S. Edwin Tobey in 1887 – the continuity with the work that Richardson carried out in the mid eighties is equally notable.

For example, none of Richardson's own late work was polychromatic. Three of his more prominent edifices, the Allegheny County Buildings in Pittsburgh and the Glessner and MacVeagh houses in Chicago, were all of

light-coloured granite, while the Warder house in Washington was of smooth-cut limestone such as Wells had wished to use for the Villard houses. Above all, the quadrangular block of the Boston Library with its regular arcuated fenestration parallels rather closely the design of Richardson's just completed masterpiece, the Marshall Field Store. Thus, in fact, Richardson's former assistants, for all the Renaissance precedent of their detailing – and the courtyard of tawny Roman brick is almost more Bramantesque in treatment than the Villard houses – were only proceeding farther in a direction that he himself had already taken.

Since most contemporaries, in their innocence, thought the Richardsonian merely a Romanesque Revival, it is understandable that they saw in such things as the Villard houses and the Boston Public Library an alternative – and anti-Richardsonian – Renaissance Revival. Nor can it be denied that the handling of the exterior of the Library derives from the sides of Alberti's Tempio Malatestiano in Rimini almost as directly as the arcade in the court is copied from that of the Cancelleria Palace in Rome.[16]

The stair-hall, the reading-room, and even the minor corridors reveal clearly their Letarouillian origins when they are studied in the architects' drawings, drawings which imitate the very style of draughtsmanship of Letarouilly's plates. The stair-hall, executed in yellow Siena marble, has walls decorated allegorically by the French painter Puvis de Chavannes, now come to be esteemed again as a great muralist; the delivery room has an entirely different sort of illustrative Shakespearean frieze painted by Edwin A. Abbey; the hall in the top storey contains John Singer Sargent's most ambitious murals. The associated sculpture by Augustus St Gaudens and others is less interesting; but these notable decorative increments from the hands of painters and sculptors of considerable reputation help to explain why for a generation this building was thought to have set under way a real 'American Renaissance' in which all the arts participated. Of this 'Renaissance' an international exhibition represented the moment of early triumph.

When, in 1891, it was decided to hold in Chicago the first American international exhibition in recognition of the 400th anniversary of the discovery of America by Columbus, the initial architectural responsibility lay with the Chicago firm of Burnham & Root. They were then working on some of the most remarkable early Chicago skyscrapers. Their Monadnock Building, completed in 1891, was the last very tall building to have exterior walls of bearing masonry (see Chapter 14). The more typical Chicago skyscrapers of this period by Burnham

& Root, the Women's Temple and the Masonic Building, were of generically Richardsonian character; and Richardsonian influence was never greater in Chicago than in the five years following his death. Root, however, was too great an architect in his own right to be thus pigeonholed merely as a Richardsonian follower, nor was his work with Burnham confined to Chicago. The principal buildings of the World's Columbian Exposition,[17] moreover, as they rose in 1892-3, proved to be neither Richardsonian nor expressive of metal construction in the way of some of those at the Paris Exhibitions of 1878 and 1889 (see Chapter 16).

Burnham in 1891 called in various leading Eastern architects to assist him in designing the World's Fair, as the Chicago exhibition was usually called. Then in that same year John Root, who was the designer of the pair, died. So it came about that the Easterners, not so much the ageing Hunt, dean of the profession, as the energetic and executive McKim, called the tune; McKim even provided Burnham with a new designer in the person of Charles B. Atwood (1849-95) to replace Root. The Fair, with the landscape architect Olmsted to collaborate on the planning, came out a great 'White City', the most complete new urbanistic concept[18] to be realized since the replanning of Paris and of Vienna in the third quarter of the century [195].

The metal-and-glass construction[18a] of the regular ranges of vast exhibition buildings was almost entirely hidden by the elaborately columniated façades of white plaster that were reflected, dream-like, in Olmsted's formal lagoons. The architects' inspiration was generically academic, not specifically Italianate or Classical, and only one or two small State pavilions followed Colonial Revival models. The dominant scale was very large indeed, and the façades of the various buildings, although by many different architects both Eastern and

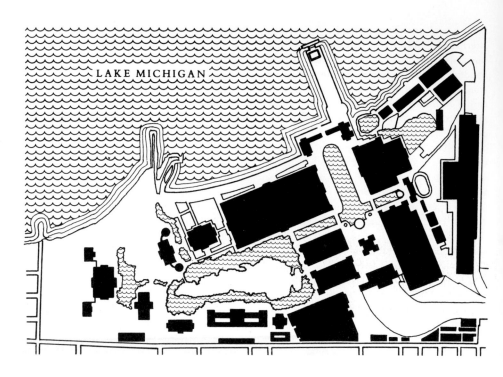

Western, were surprisingly harmonious. The young men back from the École in Paris must have worked overtime to bring up to McKim's increasingly academic standards the projects of various well-established architects who had been doing more or less Richardsonian work for the last decade.

Despite the major importance of the Shavian influence in America around 1880, after the designing of the Villard houses in 1882-3 American architects moved far more rapidly than Shaw himself along the path towards abstract order and stylistic dscipline. As noted, the Taylor house introduced, in an American version, the formal eighteenth-century revival – whether one calls it 'Monumental Queen Anne' or 'Neo-Georgian' – well before Shaw began his house for Fred White: it is even perhaps significant that this was done for an American client. The World's Fair of the

early nineties brought to the fore a more Classical and ordered sort of Neo-Academicism than Shaw ever reached. By the standards of the next generation, for example, Atwood's Fine Arts Building at Chicago [196], though based on a Prix de Rome project of 1857, was more advanced than Shaw's Piccadilly Hotel of 1905-8 [188]. The Paris Exhibition of 1889 was notable for its great feats of metal construction, Eiffel's Tower [238] and Contamin's Galerie des Machines (see Chapter 16). But the façades of the Grand Palais built for the Paris Exhibition of 1900, executed permanently in stone, seem merely a solider realization of the plaster 'dream-city' that Burnham and McKim had conjured up on the Chicago lake-front earlier in the decade (see Chapter 17).

Whether or not there was really influence from Chicago on Paris in the late nineties, there can be no question that the influence of the

195 *(left)*. D. H. Burnham and F. L. Olmsted: Chicago, World's Fair, 1893

196. Charles B. Atwood: Chicago, World's Fair, Fine Arts Building, 1892–3

Fair in America was very great indeed. While the buildings of the Fair were rising in 1892 the young Frank Lloyd Wright built his Blossom house in Chicago in rather obvious emulation of McKim, Mead & White's Taylor house (see Chapter 15). The following year he submitted in competition a completely academic project for a Museum and Library in Milwaukee. Moreover, this project, based on Perrault's east front of the Louvre, was more suave in its academicism than the buildings that Richardson's successors, Shepley, Rutan & Coolidge, who had already gone over like most of the Easterners to the McKim camp, were erecting that year for the Chicago Art Institute and for the Chicago Public Library on Michigan Avenue, the one begun in 1892, the other in 1893.

It is the great historical paradox of this period in Chicago that at the very time the academic triumph of the Fair was being prepared, nineteenth-century commercial architecture was also reaching its climax there. Even before Richardson died, his tradition had split in the mid eighties. One side of it, that related to his own French training and his dependence on various styles of the past, limited though that was, as also his growing concern with architectonic order, went forward under the leadership of McKim (see Chapter 24). The other side, derived from his sense of materials, at once intelligent and intuitive, and his interest in functional expression – the qualities that were most notable in his shingled houses and his commercial buildings – provided the platform from which first Sullivan and then Wright in the late eighties and the nineties advanced to the creation of the first modern architecture (see further Chapters 14 and 15, below).

If the importance of Richardson and, indeed, that of Shaw – as regards the development of domestic architecture – are to be fully appreciated the stories of the general development of the commercial building and of the dwelling-house in England and America down to 1900 must be known. Of the two, that of commercial architecture is the simpler and also the more dramatic. The culmination of this story in the American skyscrapers of the nineties has been recognized, from the time when so many foreign visitors came to Chicago in 1893 on account of the Fair, as one of the major and most characteristic of the architectural achievements of the whole period with which this volume deals.

CHAPTER 14

THE RISE OF COMMERCIAL ARCHITECTURE

IN ENGLAND· AND AMERICA

The line of technical development which runs from the cast-iron-framed textile mills of the 1790s in England to the steel-framed sky-scrapers of the 1890s in America seems to posterity a simple and obvious one. But, in fact, various lags and cul-de-sacs make the story long and complex. The most significant technical advances in iron construction of the first half of the century were not in the com-mercial field, and the account in this chapter is by no means merely a repetition and a con-tinuation of the story of iron construction down to 1855 that has been provided earlier (see Chapter 7).

The great difference between the English textile mills of the 1790s in which metal skeleton construction was first introduced and Sullivan's Guaranty Building in Buffalo, N.Y., of a century later is that the English work represented simply a technical advance in construction quite without architectural pre-tension. If not literally anonymous, the mills were definitely the work of millwrights rather than architects; the skyscraper, on the other hand, is a prime architectural monument of the nearly two centuries that this book attempts to cover, and the masterpiece of one of the greatest and most creatively original designers that the nineteenth and twentieth centuries have produced [208]. But the skyscrapers of the 1890s do represent also the culmination of developments in construction that began with the English innovations of the 1790s, even if those developments are far from being the whole story of nineteenth-century commercial architecture. How office buildings were gradu-ally received into the realm of architecture and, by the end of the nineteenth century, had risen so high in that realm that few productions of the 1890s in other fields of building can com-pare in quality of design with the great early skyscrapers is perhaps more significant for western culture in general than the purely technical aspect of the story. The weaving together of these two strands makes the full story one of the most interesting in the history of nineteenth-century architecture.

Nineteenth-century commercial building need not be very precisely defined. It includes several slightly different sorts of edifices suit-able for the needs of business, all consisting of a succession of identical upper storeys sub-divided into offices or store-rooms, with or without shops or representational premises below. Highly specialized and very lucrative concerns such as banks and insurance com-panies, to whom prestige of various sorts increasingly appeared a major desideratum, were the first to seek dignity and architectural display by employing architects of established reputation. Such agencies also desired buildings that were fire-resistant quite as much as did contemporary mill-owners. Already in Soane's earliest work at the Bank of England he adopted, as has been noted, certain French technical advances that had just been employed by Louis in the Théâtre Français in Paris before these advances were first utilized in an English textile mill (see Chapters 1 and 7). Along Regent Street, around 1820, Nash and others housed less pretentious types of business in structures of mixed character and of less completely fireproof construction. But the premises on the ground floor here generally required wide shop-windows of the sort that the new use of iron supports made possible, even though the upper storeys were still nearly identical with those of domestic terraces.

197. Alexander Parris:
Boston, North Market Street, designed 1823

In Boston in the mid twenties Parris was designing for the streets flanking his Market Hall commercial façades of a much more novel character, using not iron but granite in mono-lithic posts and lintels to provide a masonry skeleton filled with wide and close-set windows in all the storeys [197].[1] In later Boston work of the next two decades in this tradition architects such as Isaiah Rogers and various builders employed iron for internal supports and some-times also on the exterior at ground-floor level. But the granite 'skeleton' front preceded the skeletonized all cast-iron front in the United States of America by precisely a quarter of a century.

In England in the forties complete internal skeletons of iron carrying jack arches of brick or tile, hitherto used chiefly in textile mills, were increasingly adopted for superior com-mercial work, but the characteristic exteriors of commercial buildings[2] remained entirely of bearing masonry construction. However, in one case at least, a small block at 50 Watling Street in London which was probably built before 1844, the iron came through to the outer surface in the continuous window-bands of the upper storeys, even though the corner piers and the sections of wall between the storeys were of solid brickwork.

From C. R. Cockerell, titular Architect of the Bank of England after Soane's retirement in 1833, and other architects such as Hopper, banks and insurance companies in London and other large cities obtained in the thirties and forties distinguished buildings all of masonry. In one especially fine edifice, erected in 1849-50 purely for use as offices, Bank Chambers behind Cockerell's monumental Branch Bank of England of 1845-8, in Cook Street in Liverpool, he closely approached the directness of tra-beated masonry expression of the contemporary Boston architects and builders [198]. The fireproof construction was of vaulted masonry throughout, moreover, with iron used only for the skylights over the stair-wells.

For the general character of commercial architecture down to the late fifties, however, A. & G. Williams's Brunswick Buildings of 1841-2, also in Liverpool, were more significant. In this very large quadrangular block of general offices they followed the *palazzo* model pro-vided by Barry's newly completed Reform Club almost as closely as George Alexander had already done in his Bath Savings Bank the year before. The *palazzo* mode soon became the favourite one for imposing commercial architecture in Britain and, before long, in the United States as well.[3] With its regular rows of good-sized windows and its special prestige of having housed a commercial aris-tocracy in Renaissance times, this had certain aspects of suitability, both real and symbolical, to the needs of business-men. It also had

198. C. R. Cockerell:
Liverpool, Bank Chambers, 1849–50

serious disadvantages which soon led to a gradual modulation away from the earlier formulas of design.

The wide spacing of the windows demanded by correct *palazzo* precedent was awkward for offices requiring that maximum of natural light which was so readily provided by Parris and others in their granite buildings in Boston and by the unknown designer of 50 Watling Street in London. Therefore windows were soon much enlarged and also set closer together. Sometimes, moreover, as in a large cotton warehouse built in Parker Street in Manchester in 1850 by J. E. Gregan (1813–55), the increasingly heavy frames were applied only to every other opening. Properly, such 'palaces' ought not to be more than three storeys high, but the rapidly rising value of good sites in urban business districts made it ever more desirable to carry office buildings to four and five storeys like the terrace houses of the period.

Already in the Sun Assurance Offices in Threadneedle Street in the City of London, designed in 1839 and built in 1841–2, which do not in fact conform at all closely to the standard *palazzo* formula, Cockerell not only opened the ground floor with an arcade of haunched-segmental arches but also linked his two topmost floors behind an engaged colonnade in order to reduce the apparent height of the façade to three storeys. Across the street in the long range of Royal Exchange Buildings Edward I'Anson (1812–88) in 1844–5 lifted his whole palace front above a tall glazed arcade and tied the top-storey windows into a sort of frieze as Barry had already done in the second storey of the Reform Club [65]. In Manchester I'Anson's cousin Edward Walters (1808–72) in the Silas

Schwabe Building of 1845 at 41 Mosley Street linked the windows of the first and second storeys by an applied arcade.

The building with an exterior entirely of cast iron that James Bogardus (1800–74) designed and built for his own use in New York in 1848–50 was well publicized at the time,[4] and is still famous although long since demolished. On the corner of Washington and Murray Streets in New York another Bogardus building, the Laing stores erected in two months in 1849, long survived [114]. Although there was never any such general use of cast-iron fronts in Great Britain as in America in the fifties and sixties, it seems probable from contemporary evidence that some architect, probably Owen Jones, built one at 76 Oxford Street in London a year or so before 1851. However that may be, an ironfounder named R. McConnell provided the structural elements for an office building that still stands[5] at 36 Jamaica Street, Glasgow, in 1855–6 with an exterior all of cast iron. A curious feature of the architect John Baird's design is the delicate iron membering that forms a series of arcades between the structural piers. This decorative device, structurally meaningless in iron except for bracing although employed at the Crystal Palace, is probably an imitation of the masonry arcading that was, in the mid fifties, gradually modifying the *palazzo* paradigm beyond recognition.

In 1849 Wild used two ranges of Italian Gothic arcades on his St Martin's Northern Schools in London, and the perspicacious *Street* remarked in an article on the obvious suitability of the theme for commercial fronts, as has already been noted. In Manchester in 1851 Starkey & Cuffley in a pair of shops employed ranges of three arches on each of the two fronts in the four storeys, binding them in with coupled columns marking the ends of the party walls.

The lifting of the window tax in 1851 encouraged great increases in window area. In jubilant recognition of this H. R. Abraham the next year made all his windows triplets in the first and second storeys of the W. H. Smith Building at 188–192 Strand in London, but without using any arches at all. Two years later, however, in a building for Heal's furniture store in Tottenham Court Road in London, James M. Lockyer (1824–65) carried a *quattrocento* arcade all across the first storey.

By this time architects and public alike had become aware of a different High Renaissance formula from Barry's (see Chapter 4). Beside the Reform Club in Pall Mall Sydney Smirke's new front of the Carlton Club, designed in 1847, was coming to belated completion in the mid fifties. Moreover, its Sansovinesque arcades were already echoed in the first storey of Parnell & Smith's Army and Navy Club of 1848–51 across the way. These London models were closely followed by William B. Gingell, (1819–1900) in his West of England Bank in Corn Street, Bristol, of 1854 and quite outranked by the great Venetian *palazzo* that David Rhind (?–1883) erected in 1855 in Edinburgh for the Life Association of Scotland.

Possibly the fine warehouse at 12 Temple Street in Bristol with three groups of triplet arches in each of the upper storeys was by Gingell and of this date. There was none of the Sansovinesque lushness of his bank here, but the fine workmanship of the quarry-faced Pennant stone walls laid up in random ashlar, with smooth-cut Bath stone trim and coloured voussoirs banding the arches, bore some resemblance to the Bristol General Hospital he was building in 1853–7, notably in the very bold rustication of the ground-storey arches.

However that may be, two London buildings of 1855 advanced nearly as far towards the all-arcaded front. Hodgson's Building by Knowles in the Strand at the corner of Chancery Lane had the general character of a *palazzo*, but all the windows were arched, as in buildings of the *Rundbogenstil*; moreover their trim sank into the wall rather than projecting from it, so that the wall sections between were reduced visually to mere piers, even though they had no imposts. The Crown Life Office, in New Bridge Street, Blackfriars, was built in 1855-7 by Ruskin's friends Deane & Woodward, with whom he was most closely associated precisely in those years. The round-arched medieval arcading of this façade, with the piers hardly narrower than on Knowles's building yet articulated by bases and imposts, may surely claim Ruskinian sanction. Here, at any rate, was the first important contact between advanced High Victorian Gothic and the commercial world, a contact destined to be very fruitful over the next fifteen years or so. Henceforth even architects of no aesthetic pretension were ready to exploit arcading.

The English development of arcaded masonry façades can be closely matched in America, specifically in Philadelphia.[6] There S. D. Button (1803-97), Napoleon Le Brun (1821-1901), and others in buildings of 1852-3 in Chestnut Street - that at 239-241 by Button long survived - consistently used arched openings between slim piers; and Notman in 1855 provided for the Jackson Building at 418 Arch Street a façade even more completely articulated by iron arcading on all four floors than the Crown Life Office. By this time, moreover, the trabeated design of Bogardus's earlier iron fronts in New York had likewise given way to ornate arcading emulating masonry fronts.[7]

Iron remained behind the scenes in most of the English arcaded buildings. In Waterhouse's Fryer & Binyon Warehouse in Manchester of 1856, however, whose upper walls had the polychrome diapering of the Doge's Palace so much admired by Ruskin, the first storey was opened up by an arcade on coupled iron columns. In the Wellington Williams Warehouse of 1858 in Little Britain in London, the obscure City firm of J. Young & Son used arcades in all the five storeys with iron columns

to support the outer orders; thus the width of the piers could be considerably reduced, and the effect of over-all articulation was much enhanced as in the Philadelphia buildings.

Deane & Woodward's very Ruskinian project of 1857 for the new Government Offices, with its endless Italian Gothic arcading, and a small warehouse in Merchant Street in Bristol of 1858 by Godwin gave some impetus to the use of pointed instead of round arches. But on the whole the best designed among the innumerable arcaded façades in England retained the rounded form, however Gothic their other detailing may be. In one of the largest and finest examples of the early sixties, moreover, Kassapian's Warehouse in Leeds Road, Bradford, perhaps by Lockwood & Mawson, the detailing is academically Roman[7a] [199].

199. Lockwood & Mawson(?):
Bradford, Yorkshire, Kassapian's Warehouse, c. 1862

200. E. W. Godwin: Bristol, 104 Stokes Croft, c. 1862

Different as they are, this Bradford façade and that of Godwin's contemporary warehouse at 104 Stokes Croft in Bristol, so much more subtly Ruskinian than anything by Deane & Woodward, are the two masterpieces of the genre at its best moment [200]. Of very high quality also is 60 Mark Lane in the City of London built by George Aitchison in 1864-5. There the existence of a complete iron skeleton, presumably but not certainly present in most of the other examples, is fully documented. Moreover, on the rear the metal comes through to the outer face of the wall much as it did at 50 Watling Street, built some twenty years earlier.

In Philadelphia William Johnston had begun in 1849 the seven-storey Jayne Building in Chestnut Street,[8] introducing a new vertical formula of design for commercial façades. Above a conventional ground floor, narrow granite piers in the forms of clustered colonnettes rose the full height of the building, merging into Venetian Gothic tracery below a terminal parapet. Whether or not Samuel K. Hoxie, the contractor who provided the Quincy granite for this and other Philadelphia buildings, was familiar with the 'granite-skeleton' work of Parris, Rogers, and others in Boston is not clear. But in the next few years a good many façades with a similarly vertical and 'skeletonized' treatment were built in Philadelphia by J. C. Hoxie and his sometime partner Button. That across the street from the Jayne Building has already been mentioned, since the openings between the piers are covered with segmental arches throughout. Button's building at 723–727 Chestnut Street of 1853 and also his Leland Building at 37–39 South Third Street were even more 'proto-Sullivanian', so to put it. Louis Sullivan probably saw and admired such things as the Jayne Building and the Leland Building when he was working for Frank Furness in Philadelphia in the seventies; certainly they are very premonitory of his characteristic work of the eighties and even the nineties.

Various other ways of reducing the wall to little more than a masonry cladding of the iron structural members were also in use in England as well as in America by this time. A notable small edifice in the City of London, of uncertain date and authorship but probably by Thomas Hague and of 1855, is at 22 Finch Lane, with another front to the court at the

side. On both these façades the two lower storeys are joined together visually by setting back the horizontal spandrel between them, and the moulded stonework of the very narrow piers is of almost metallic scale and crispness.

Still more striking is Oriel Chambers[9] in Water Street in Liverpool, built in 1864–5 by Peter Ellis (fl. 1835–84), and another smaller building by him at 16 Cook Street of a year or two later. On the front façades of these the masonry is scaled down quite as much as at 22 Finch Lane but given a more decorative treatment, in both cases of distinctly metallic character. At Oriel Chambers, oriels of plate glass held in delicate metal frames are cantilevered out in every bay of all the upper storeys, producing a regular rhythm broken only by

201. Peter Ellis: Liverpool, Oriel Chambers, 1864–5

the stepped cresting on the top [201]. At 16 Cook Street all the stone spandrels are set back, thus emphasizing even more strongly than at Oriel Chambers the continuous vertical lines of the mullions. But the plain over-all pattern is again awkwardly elaborated across the top, this time by arches that link the mullions together. The rear walls of both of Ellis's buildings are even more open in design and directly expressive of the metal skeleton. Towards the narrow court at the side of Oriel Chambers only every third iron pier is clad with masonry; those between rise free behind the glass of the horizontally sashed windows whose upper planes are slanted inward. This is, in effect, an early example of the 'curtain-wall' (see Chapter 22).

If in some technical respects the Chicago skyscraper of the nineties seems almost to have come to premature birth in Liverpool in the sixties, as in some other respects it had done in the Philadelphia commercial buildings of the fifties, the immediate influence of these buildings by Ellis seems to have been almost nil. Eventually Owen Jones, in a façade at Derby of 1872, and Thomas Ambler, in a corner building at 46–47 Boar Lane in Leeds of 1873, did come to use only iron and glass, omitting all masonry; but more characteristic commercial work of these years is to be seen in such warehouses by unknown hands as the one at 1–2 York Place in Leeds, with an arcade crisply detailed in moulded brick rising through all the upper storeys, somewhat as on the Philadelphia buildings of the fifties, or a larger example in Strait Street in Bristol, with a much heavier arcade subsuming several upper storeys, handsomely executed in stones of different colours and textures and very boldly and simply detailed. Such things, however, very soon seemed to the English not advanced but retardataire as contemporary attention focused on the Queen Anne of Shaw's New Zealand Chambers of 1872–3.

Richardson's very un-Shavian American Express Building[10] in Chicago of 1872–3 first brings that Mid-Western metropolis into this story. That had no arcading, but the windows were very closely set, sometimes (it would appear) with only light metal colonnettes as mullions between them. There was also a directness and a 'realism' of treatment throughout comparable to that of Richardson's more monumental work of this date, notably the Hampden County Courthouse and the Buffalo State Hospital, both designed in the previous year and at this time in construction. But Richardson's dependence on English commercial work of the preceding fifteen years became closer still in his first really fine business building, the Cheney Block (now part of the

202. H. H. Richardson:
Hartford, Conn., J. Fox Department Store
(Cheney Block), 1875–6

J. Fox Department Store) built in Hartford, Conn., in 1875–6 [202]. Here the wide ground-storey arcade, including a mezzanine, and the narrower arcade above, subsuming several storeys – as on the very proto-Richardsonian warehouse in Strait Street in Bristol – are carried out with typically Richardsonian stoniness in quarry-faced brownstone. But the banded arches introduce a bold note of High

Victorian Gothic polychromy, and the carved detail is in the harsh but richly naturalistic vein – also High Victorian Gothic in spirit – of the ornament on the earliest executed portions of Trinity Church in Boston, which must be of the same date.

Already, in New York, the skyscraper[11] had been born in these years, and leadership in commercial architecture had crossed the Atlantic for good and all. None of the structures dealt with so far in this chapter except the Jayne Building were more than five or six storeys high, since it could not be expected that business clients would climb more than four or five flights of stairs. But the average height of buildings in the financial districts of cities had, even so, almost doubled since the eighteenth century, partly because of the general rise in the number of storeys, partly because of much increased storey heights. Vertical transportation of human beings, which would allow the erection of office buildings considerably more than five storeys high – industrial buildings were often much taller already – became increasingly feasible during the forties and fifties. Hoists for goods were a commonplace of English warehouse design after 1840, and in 1844 the Bunker Hill Monument had a passenger-hoist operated by a steam engine. In New York J. P. Gaynor in the Haughwout Store on Broadway provided in 1857 the first passenger lift or elevator in an ordinary urban structure. This was of the type developed by Elisha G. Otis. A lift of another sort was available in the Fifth Avenue Hotel in New York later that year. Those of 1860 in the Westminster Palace Hotel in London apparently did not function, at least for some years. The Equitable Building, for which Arthur Gilman and Edward Kimball, with George B. Post (1837–1913) as the associated engineer, won the competition in 1868, was the first office building in New York to have a lift from the time of its completion in 1871. Immediately after this lifts were

introduced in several other comparable structures, and one- or two-storey mansards were often added to the tops of existing buildings. A great change was thus at hand in New York in the early seventies.

Despite the Panic of 1873, the mid seventies saw the construction of what may properly be considered the first skyscrapers, the nine-storey (260-foot) Tribune Building and the ten-storey (230-foot) Western Union Building. Both were therefore about double the height even of the tallest office structures, such as the five-storey (130-foot) Equitable Building erected during the preceding boom period. These first skyscrapers rose to altitudes reached hitherto in America only by church spires, as general views of the New York skyline around 1875 make evident. Neither Hunt's New York Tribune Building, which was later carried many storeys higher, nor Post's Western Union Telegraph Building, both now demolished, incorporated any other technical innovations;[12] nor was their design at all closely related, like that of Richardson's Cheney Block in Hartford, to the advanced English commercial work of the previous decade. Paradoxically, the French-trained Hunt's building was somewhat the more English of the two in character; but, for all the direct expressiveness of the window grouping in triplets in each bay, the detail throughout was coarse and gawky, and the silhouette of the very tall mansard and the asymmetrically placed tower was from the first overbearing. The later addition of so many more storeys made the building even more top-heavy in appearance. The Tribune Building was of interest chiefly for its relatively great height, eventually unnoticeable among the taller skyscrapers built around it later. Its almost complete avoidance of any sort of archaeological styling, however, such as the Romanesquoid of Richardson's Cheney Block or the violently polychromatic and spiky Gothic of Hunt's own Divinity School at Yale, on which construction was still at this date proceeding, was worth remark also.

The Western Union Building of Post was nominally French, but its rather heavy-handed Second Empire treatment owed more to earlier English and American designs in this mode than to anything Parisian [203]. Yet the exterior was more orderly, if less expressive, than that of Hunt's skyscraper and the mansards on top piled up as grandly to the centrally placed tower as on the big contemporary Post Office

203. George B. Post:
New York, Western Union Building, 1873-5

near by. But stylistically both Post's and Hunt's buildings were out of date almost as soon as they were finished; and after the hiatus caused by the depression of the seventies the locus of the main line of the skyscraper story moved westward to Chicago.

Chicago, already the metropolis of the Middle West, had almost no architectural traditions at this time. First developed as a city in the thirties, the need for rapid building in timber had led to the invention or development of what is called 'balloon-frame' construction,[13] in which relatively light studs or scantlings, rising wall high, form a cage or crate whose members are fastened together by a liberal use of machine-made nails. Balloon-frame construction, thus, is a typical offshoot of the industrial revolution that became feasible only with the mechanization of the saw-mill and of the manufacture of nails. Theoretically, there might be thought to be some analogy between this New World method of carpentry, so different from the heavy framing of the Old World, hitherto always used in America as well, and metal construction. There is no evidence, however, that Chicago took to iron with any greater enthusiasm in the fifties and sixties than did New York or various other cities; indeed, St Louis seems to have had more and finer examples of cast-iron fronts, particularly in the early seventies. As late as that, moreover, the cities of the American Northwest were obtaining cast-iron fronts prefabricated from Britain, just as San Francisco had obtained many of her warehouses and immigrant dwellings in 1849-50.

At the opening of the seventies a terrific conflagration[14] all but wiped out Chicago. The need for rapid rebuilding drew thither ambitious architects and engineers from all over the East, but the immediate results of their activities were anything but edifying. Architectural leadership was still centred in Boston and New York; in any case, that leadership had rarely been more confused than in the early seventies when even Richardson was only just maturing his personal style. Richardson's own Chicago building for the American Express Company, modified in execution by Peter B. Wight, attracted no local following; nor did he build again in Chicago until the mid eighties, by which time various versions of the Richardsonian were already reaching Chicago at second or third hand.

If the Chicago architectural scene had any virtues around 1880 they were largely negative ones: no established traditions, no real professional leaders, and ignorance of all architectural styles past or present. Among the architects who had settled in Chicago in the seventies was a Dane, Dankmar Adler (1844–1900). Into his office in 1879, first as chief draughtsman but soon as partner, came the young Bostonian Louis Sullivan. As has been noted before, Sullivan had been trained first in Ware's school at the Massachusetts Institute of Technology and later, until he revolted against its rigid doctrines, at the École des Beaux-Arts in Paris. Having worked for Frank Furness, wildest of American High Victorians, Sullivan picked Chicago not alone for its evident professional opportunities but also because he liked the idea of working where there were no hampering traditions. (Moreover, his parents had moved there from Boston.)

The earliest building of much originality designed by Sullivan, the Rothschild Store in Chicago of 1880-1, seems at first sight a turgid compilation of barbarisms. Examined more closely, however, and compared with the Leiter Building on its right, which was built two years earlier by the engineer-architect William Le Baron Jenney (1832–1907), the two sorts of innovation that Sullivan essayed here can be readily recognized. On the one hand there is the ornament,[15] indefinable in historic terms yet with a certain similarity – almost certainly accidental – to the Anglo-Japanese detail of Nesfield and Godwin. At this stage in Sullivan's career the originality of his ornament must be remarked but can hardly be admired. Below his elaborate ornamental cresting, on the other hand, Sullivan handled the main architectonic elements of this façade with considerable novelty and most admirable logic. Although the building is not tall – no skyscraper, that is, even by the modest standards of 1880 – Sullivan did not hesitate to follow the lead of the Philadelphia commercial architects of the fifties in emphasizing the vertical. This he accomplished by carrying the slim mullions that subdivide his bays across the spandrels, somewhat as Ellis had done fifteen years before in his buildings in Liverpool, rather than by using a multiplicity of heavy masonry piers.

Sullivan's next Chicago building, the Revell Store erected for Martin Ryerson in 1881-3, continued the theme of the Rothschild Store, but extended it over a much larger corner block with considerable chastening of the ornamental treatment at the top. The Troescher Building of 1884, which came next in sequence, is very much finer. Widely-spaced piers of plain brickwork rise the full height of the façade above a slightly Richardsonian ground-storey arcade of rock-faced stone;[15a] between them there are no oriels, as on Ellis's Oriel Chambers or his Ryerson Building[16] of the previous year, but broad horizontal windows separated by recessed spandrels. These spandrels are rather like Ellis's on his other building at 16 Cook Street, but their actual prototypes are to be found, more probably, in Philadelphia buildings by Button such as the one at 723-727 Chestnut Street. The ornament here, now still further chastened, is largely confined to these spandrels. The curved cresting across the top, however, recalls a little the turgid crown of the Rothschild façade.

Sullivan's early buildings were not very tall, and they did not advance the technical development of the skyscraper. In these same years, however, other Chicago architects were doing so to notable effect. For the ten-storey Montauk Block of 1882-3, tall, but no taller than the first New York skyscrapers of ten years before, Burnham & Root introduced spread foundations to carry its great weight on the muddy Chicago soil, out of which earlier buildings had, literally, to be hoisted every few years. In design they were content, however, with a range of ten almost identical storeys of plain brick pierced by regularly spaced segmental-arched windows. Obvious as this treatment may seem, it took courage to use it at a time when most architects were still trying to disguise the embarrassing height of buildings only half as tall by grouping their storeys together in twos and threes.

The Home Life Insurance Building begun in 1883 was also only ten storeys tall.[17] But in erecting it Jenney invented, or at least introduced in Chicago, what is specifically called 'skyscraper construction', that is a method of carrying the external masonry cladding on metal shelves bolted to the internal skeleton. Jenney, however, probably thought he was merely tying together his metal skeleton and his brickwork, not carrying the latter entirely, though this was found to be the case when the structure of the building was carefully examined during its demolition. The Home Insurance Building, in any case, looked far more as if its external walls were bearing than do any of Sullivan's early works. Jenney, moreover, fought shy of the frankness of Burnham & Root's treatment of the Montauk Block; instead he phrased his storeys in groups, almost as if several buildings of normal three- or four-storey height had been casually piled one on top of the other.

Before the Home Insurance was finished in 1885 two more major commercial monuments were rising in Chicago, Richardson's Marshall Field Wholesale Store [192], one of the last few important buildings in Chicago with walls entirely of bearing masonry, and Burnham & Root's Rookery Building (see Chapter 13). Both were begun in 1885, Richardson's being finished in 1887 and Burnham & Root's a year later in 1888. The exterior of the eleven-storey Rookery Building is not an example of the stripped 'functionalism' that these architects had introduced in their Montauk Block but rather Root's personal parallel to the Richardsonian. In the court walls, however, the architects used – and with complete awareness of its implications – the new structural method of Jenney's Home Insurance Building, carrying the brickwork above the sides of the central glass-roofed lobby entirely on the internal metal[18] skeleton.

With the advent of Richardson in 1885, the two main lines of development in commercial architecture, as regards design and as regards construction, might seem to have been brought together in Chicago. It is well therefore to note again that McKim, Mead & White in their Goelet Building on Broadway in New York of 1885-6 provided almost as frank an expression of the skyscraper, or tall office building of many identical storeys, at least above their Renaissance ground-floor arcade, as did Burnham & Root in the Montauk Block. Their windows, however, were phrased in triplets like Hunt's on the Tribune Building and also grouped vertically within tall bay-width panels of moulded brick rising all the way up to the cornice. This was a logical solution of the design problem that cannot be castigated as 'traditional' or even as 'un-functional'. Moreover, another New York building, Babb, Cook & Willard's De Vinne Press of 1885 in Lafayette Street, is not altogether unworthy of comparison with the Field Store. It lacks the regularity and the grandeur of scale of Richardson's masterpiece, but George F. Babb used his fine red brick in a belated *Rundbogenstil* way, and not without some conscious reminiscence, one may presume, of Durand's exemplars of the beginning of the century.

Richardson's last commercial work, the Ames Building in Harrison Avenue in Boston of 1886-7, on which the arcade was carried the full height of the building and the reveals much reduced, had no immediate influence in Chicago (see Chapter 13). Sullivan's first really great work, the Auditorium Building (now Roosevelt College) in Chicago, derived largely from Richardson's published project for the Field Store, at least as regards the exterior.[18a] Designed

in 1886 and built in 1887-9, this is a vast and complex edifice, or group of edifices, with a hotel on the Michigan Avenue front, an opera-house entered in the middle of the Congress Street side, and offices along Wabash Avenue at the rear. The walls are all of bearing masonry still. In order to incorporate more storeys than Richardson had ever done, Sullivan carried up his heavy rock-faced granite base through two mezzanine levels and increased the number of floors subsumed by the main arcade which rises from the first storey [204]. He also used light

204. Adler & Sullivan:
Chicago, Auditorium Building, 1887-9

stone throughout, instead of the red granite and the brownstone of the Field Store, with its surfaces all smooth-cut above the mezzanines. This flattening of the wall-plane was carried even further on the tower which rises above the portal of the opera-house in Congress Street. On that wide arched panels of very slight projection are filled with articulated screens of stone in which the windows are arranged in a continuous grid with no evident storey lines. The eaves gallery at the top of the tower, a stubby colonnade set in a long horizontal panel with a continuous ribbon-window behind – the window in fact of the Adler & Sullivan office – is so like Thomson's on the front of his Queen's Park church of the sixties in Glasgow that it is hard to believe Sullivan did not know it. Yet other evidence indicates that he continued to abjure all contemporary European influence at this point in his career. But not all traditional influence: the small change of Classical beaded and dentilled mouldings, perhaps introduced by Wright, is often found in the work of these years.

In the interiors, particularly the bar and the banquet hall at the top of the hotel, Sullivan's ornament changed even more markedly than his exterior design. Actually, however, the change had begun several years earlier. The adumbration of Sullivan's personal style of ornament, to which he later attached so much importance, can be followed, almost month by month, in the dated sketches for the redecoration of McVickar's Theatre in 1884–5. Wright claimed in later life that he had first brought Owen Jones's *Grammar of Ornament*[19] to Sullivan's attention in 1888; but internal evidence suggests that he had known it much earlier, if it hardly supports the somewhat fanciful suggestion that Jones's page of Celtic ornament especially appealed to the Irish Sullivan.[20] However that may be, even the extant decorative work, some of it doubtless as late as 1888 and possibly detailed by Wright

under Sullivan's direction, makes certain that Sullivan's near-Art-Nouveau style of ornament had already fully matured at least four or five years before the Art Nouveau began in Europe.

Together with the Auditorium, though commissioned a year later, there was also rising in Chicago in 1887–9 the Tacoma Building of William Holabird (1854–1923) and Martin Roche (1855–1927), two young architects trained in Jenney's office. Here the exterior walls on the two fronts were entirely carried by the metal skeleton within, only the rear walls and some of the interior partitions being of bearing masonry like the walls of the Auditorium. Moreover, this fact was made evident in the frank if not particularly distinguished treatment of the two fronts. Vertical ranges of oriels were carried the full height of the building, and there was only a minimal brick and terra-cotta sheathing of the structural verticals and horizontals. A vaguely Richardsonian sort of cornice capped the whole, but the general effect was closer to Ellis's Oriel Chambers of the sixties in Liverpool or to some of Sullivan's earlier buildings than to the Field Store.

Despite the general swing of Eastern architects towards the Neo-Academic in these years, some who were doing commercial work were not out of step with what was happening in Chicago. For example, there are office buildings and warehouses in Boston and New York of relatively modest height built in the late eighties and early nineties that emulate in brick the arcading of the Field Store with almost as much success as Sullivan. Similar things exist in many Middle and Far Western cities, for example, a big bank building on the Public Square in Cleveland, Ohio, by Burnham & Root.

In the Middle West, moreover, McKim, Mead & White were building in 1888–90 two very large business buildings, still with bearing masonry walls, for the New York Life Insurance Company, one in Omaha, Nebraska, and one in Kansas City, Missouri, of effectively identical design. Unlike the already characteristic Chicago 'slabs' – the quadrangular plan of the Rookery Building is exceptional – these are U-shaped, and each has a tower rising above the main mass at the rear of the court. The treatment of the walls with tall arcading follows even more evidently from Post's Exchange than Sullivan's at the Auditorium; as on the contemporary Boston Public Library, moreover, the detailing is of High Renaissance character like Post's.

Before these towering blocks were finished in the West the new 'skyscraper construction' had been introduced in New York by Bradford Lee Gilbert (1853–1911). His Tower Building of 1888–9, as its name implies, was a tower, not a slab, with more or less Richardsonian detailing. It is worth noting that the Tower Building – ten storeys, 119 feet – was *not* as tall as the first New York skyscrapers built in the early seventies with bearing walls. Indeed, Post's World or Pulitzer Building of 1889–90 in New York with twenty-six storeys, the tallest built up to then – 309 feet – still had bearing walls. Of course, the Eiffel Tower, completed in 1889, exceeded in height by a great deal all the skyscrapers of its day whatever their construction; its 300 metres was not overtopped until the Empire State Building in New York rose from the designs of Shreve, Lamb & Harmon in the early 1930s at the end of the second wave of skyscraper building following the First World War.

Post's Western Union Building of the early seventies was in the Second Empire mode; his World Building was still French, but what can now be called 'Beaux-Arts'. It was designed like a series of three- or four-storey Renaissance palaces, one on top of the other, and crowned with a large and ornate dome. The next New York skyscrapers all followed the new structural method introduced by Gilbert in the Tower Building; but by the mid nineties the archi-

tects who designed them mostly used rather heavy Renaissance detail with little of the restraint characteristic of McKim, Mead & White even on their Mid-Western insurance buildings. Typical examples of the period were Bruce Price's American Surety Building at Broadway and Wall Street, begun in 1894, and his St James Building of 1897–8 at 1133 Broadway, both in New York, and Post's Park Building in Pittsburgh, completed in 1896. The Havemeyer Building in New York of 1891–2 among others by Post had still been somewhat Richardsonian.

The maturing of an original sort of skyscraper design around 1890 is a Mid-Western, and almost specifically a Chicago, story to which New Yorkers other than Post made little contribution. Boston's architectural leadership had ended with the death of Richardson; despite the prominence of McKim, Mead & White and their large Eastern following, leadership in this field passed almost at once to Chicago. It was most appropriate that Richardson's masterpiece, the Field Store, should have been built there; the inspiration his works provided, as is evident in the Auditorium Building, was playing a real part in the Mid-Western development.

In 1889–90 Jenney built for Levi Z. Leiter a large building on South Clark Street in Chicago later occupied by Sears, Roebuck & Company. In this he not only used the new 'skyscraper construction' for the exterior walls but also – with the presumptive aid of his assistant and later partner William Bryce Mundie (1863–1939) – arrived at an expression of its structural character almost as logical as that of the Tacoma Building yet much more monumental. Like most other Chicago designers in these years, Jenney and Mundie were influenced here by the Field Store. The uncompromisingly block-like shape of this tremendous building, with its heavy plain entablature and pilaster-like corner piers, is Richardsonian both in its scale and in its simplicity [205]. The various groupings of

205 *(below)*. William Le B. Jenney: Chicago,
Sears, Roebuck & Co. (Leiter) Building, 1889-90

206 *(right)*. D. H. Burnham & Co.:
Chicago, Reliance Building, 1894-5

207 *(opposite)*. Adler & Sullivan:
St Louis, Wainwright Building, 1890-1

stone mullions that clad the main piers and sub-divide the bays, lithe and light though they are, were clearly envisaged as Romanesque colon-nettes and even carry modest foliate capitals. Despite the dichotomy of the solidly Richard-sonian silhouette and the open screen-like treatment of the walls, the effect is coherent and dignified. In this respect the Sears, Roe-buck Building is superior to Sullivan's very Richardsonian[21] Opera House Building in Pueblo, Colorado, of 1890 which was burned

in the 1920s. The Walker Warehouse in Chicago of 1888-9 better displayed his great talent.

Three buildings of the early nineties, two in Chicago by Daniel H. Burnham's firm and one in St Louis by Sullivan, illustrate the wide range of creative possibilities in skyscraper design at this point. The most advanced is the Reliance Building, at least in terms of direct structural expression. Though two lower storeys had been built in 1890, this was even-tually carried to its present thirteen storeys by

D. H. Burnham & Company in 1894–5.[22] The Reliance is a refined and perfected version of Holabird & Roche's Tacoma Building [206]. The light-coloured terracotta cladding of the vertical members, particularly on the flat oriels, is reduced to a minimum; the terminal member is a thin slab, not a cornice or an entablature; and the only stylistic reminiscence is in the cusped panelling – neither Romanesque nor Renaissance, but slightly Late Gothic in character – of the spandrels. The designer, surprising as it may seem, was Charles B. Atwood.

Burnham & Root's other significant skyscraper of this particular moment, the sixteen-storey Monadnock Building, completed in 1891,[22a] the last tall Chicago slab with bearing walls of brick, was and still remains more famous than the Reliance; doubtless it is also finer, although some influential mid-twentieth-century critics favoured the Sears, Roebuck Building of Jenney & Mundie and the Reliance because they were more advanced technically. The smooth shank of the Monadnock, varied only by the slight projection of the recurrent oriels, has a most subtle and elegant taper or reverse entasis. The final bending outward of the brickwork to provide a cove cornice unifies the whole formal concept with extraordinary effectiveness. Few large buildings have achieved such monumental force with such simple means. There is no detail, whether derivative or original, other than the use of special brick-shapes at the corners and on the oriels.

Sullivan's Wainwright Building of 1890–1[22b] in St Louis, Mo., in which he and Adler used 'skyscraper construction' for the first time, no longer dominates two- and three-storey neighbours as it did when newly built; thus the prominence that the relatively great height gave it in the city picture of the nineties can hardly be realized today. But Sullivan undoubtedly sought to emphasize what seemed to contemporaries, as they do not to posterity, its very tall proportions [207]. Continuous pilaster-like

piers of brick, quite like those on his Troescher Building of 1884, clad the vertical elements of the steel skeleton, yet identical brick piers with no major structural members inside them also serve as intervening mullions. But at the base the wide windows of the ground storey and the mezzanine reveal the true width of the actual bays of the steel skeleton as the treatment of the shank of the building does not. The piers are considerably broader than most of those on the Sears, Roebuck Building; but they are also topped, like Mundie's, with ornament that forms a sort of capital. Moreover, the attic storey above is quite hidden by a deep band of the richest Sullivanian decoration elsewhere restricted, as on the Troescher Building, to the recessed spandrels. The 'cornice' above this frieze-like member is merely a slab, but a much thicker one than that which caps the Reliance Building. Nothing of Richardson's direct influence is left; but by now Sullivan had learned from the Field Store the basic lessons of scale and order, applying them here in a visually sure but not particularly frank way to the new type of metal-skeleton construction. The plan is U-shaped, like those of the McKim, Mead & White buildings in Kansas City and Omaha, but the court is at the rear so that the block appears unified from the surrounding streets.

In Sullivan's next important work, the Schiller Building in Chicago of 1891-2, he adopted - exceptionally for him - a truly tower-like shape. Here the masonry piers that cladded the structural steel stanchions were not doubled by identical mullions between; instead these piers are linked by arches below a sort of frieze. The 'frieze' was really a very ornately arcaded eaves-gallery, not a flat band as on the Wainwright Building, occupying the attic below the thick slab cornice. The building has been demolished since this book was written.

Interchange of ideas was continuous in these years between the various Chicago architects' offices, while the influence of the Academic Revival in the East, dominant in almost all the buildings at the World's Fair of 1893 save Sullivan's own Transportation Building, was still negligible in the commercial field. Thus Sullivan's Stock Exchange Building of 1893-4 in Chicago borrowed its rather clumsy ground storey and mezzanine, with a cavernously Richardsonian arched entrance, from Burnham's Ashland Block of 1892 and its oriels from Holabird & Roche's Tacoma Building of 1887-9. These oriels alternate with horizontal openings of the type known as 'Chicago windows' sharply cut through the smooth light-coloured terracotta of the wall plane. 'Chicago windows', with a wide fixed pane in the centre and narrower sashes that open on either side, were used by most Chicago architects in this decade and the next. A heavy moulded cornice, not just a thick slab, crowns the whole above a colonnaded eaves-gallery somewhat like the one at the top of the Auditorium tower.

What should probably be considered Sullivan's masterpiece, the Guaranty Building in Buffalo, N.Y., followed in 1894-5 [208]. One of the most significant new themes in the design of this skyscraper, whose premonitory character can only be fully appreciated in relation to the use of *pilotis* in later modern architecture (see Chapter 22), is already to be found in a project of Sullivan's of the previous year for the St Louis Trust & Savings Bank. This is the special treatment of the ground storey with the terracotta sheathed piers isolated from the wall plane by bending back the tops of the shop-windows. The piers are thus nearly free-standing and seem to lift the shaft of the building above them right off the ground allowing circumambient space to penetrate under and into the main volume of the building. Thus the fact that the edifice is a hollow cage is very strongly suggested, and the wide shop-windows do not appear to undermine the walls above them as in so much commercial work of the nineteenth century.

There are several reasons, not intrinsic to Sullivan's design, that explain why the Guaranty remains the most effective of the early skyscrapers. Since this area in Buffalo has not filled up with buildings of equal or greater height in the way of downtown St Louis and the Chicago Loop, the Guaranty still rises high above most of its modest neighbours, in effect a tower as well as a slab, although actually of U-shaped plan like the Wainwright. In this city, moreover, which has in the last eighty

208. Adler & Sullivan: Buffalo, N.Y., Guaranty Building, 1894-5

years remained considerably cleaner than Chicago, the colour of the tawny terracotta sheathing has not been so much obscured by grime as on the Stock Exchange Building. These were happy local conditions that Sullivan could not foresee.

The plastic treatment of the crown of the Guaranty was perhaps suggested to Sullivan by the effectiveness of the cove at the top of Burnham & Root's Monadnock Building. Here the crowns of the arched façade bays – two to each structural bay, as the wide spacing of the piers at ground-storey level so clearly reveals – are related to the outward curve of the top of the wall below the terminal slab. The profuse and melodious curvilinear ornament, subsuming the round attic windows, echoes and complements the plastic theme. This is an example, rare even in Sullivan's most mature work of the mid and late nineties, of the successful integration of architectonic and decorative elements. The character of the terracotta cladding of the piers and spandrels of the Guaranty, moreover, covered all over as they are with lacy geometrical ornament in low relief, seems to lighten the whole, for this cladding is read as a mere protective shell around the underlying steel structural members and not as solid self-supporting brickwork like the piers of the Wainwright Building.

Just as the Wainwright Building may be contrasted on the one hand with the still greater solidity of the Monadnock Building – in that case justified by the bearing-wall construction – and on the other with the openness of the Reliance, so it is of interest to compare the Guaranty with two other big business buildings of 1895 by other Chicago architects. In the Ellicott Square Building, also in Buffalo, Burnham was strongly influenced by his close association with McKim at the World's Fair. With the assistance of his designer Atwood, whose short life ended this same year, he adopted the elaborate Renaissance membering and the

heavy masonry vocabulary of the New York skyscraper architects, although he retained the quadrangular plan and the glass-roofed central court of the Rookery. On the other hand, in Chicago Solon S. Beman (1853-1914) in the Studebaker (now Brunswick) Building came very close to providing an all-glass front, despite the profusion of Late Gothic frippery with which he detailed his terracotta cladding of the metal structural members.

Adler had parted from Sullivan in 1895, but Sullivan's career as a skyscraper builder continued for a few more years at a very high level. In his next skyscraper, the Condict Building in New York of 1897-9, he reduced considerably the size of the mullions in the middle of the bays so that they became mere colonnettes, and even omitted them entirely in the first storey. But this logical differentiation between pier and mullion, related to the treatment of his Rothschild Store of 1880-1, still gets lost at the top in a flurry of ornamentation that is as turgid in its very different and almost *quattrocento*[23] way as the top of that very early façade. The ground storey was originally like that of the Guaranty, but has been replaced by new shop-fronts.

The next year Holabird & Roche built three contiguous buildings on Michigan Avenue in Chicago for Harold McCormick [209]. The two southerly ones are excellent examples of the work of the Chicago School; they are a little less extensively glazed than Beman's Studebaker Building or Holabird & Roche's own McClurg Building of 1899 but with crisp and simple, if quite conventional, moulded brick detail on the piers and rather plain cornices of wholly academic character. Standard Chicago windows are used throughout. The third façade on the north, that of the Gage Building at 18 South Michigan Avenue, while fronting a structure also by Holabird & Roche, is itself by Sullivan. A different arrangement of the windows, a bolder moulding of the terracotta cladding of the piers – there were no intervening

209. Holabird & Roche: Chicago, 19-20 South Michigan Avenue, 1898-9;
(right) Louis H. Sullivan: Gage Building (façade only), 1898-9

mullions now, any more than on his Troescher Building of 1884 - and a strategic spotting of the chicory-like ornament - as well as, originally, a rich picture-frame-like band around the ground-storey shop-window - produce an entirely different effect. This effect is no less expressive of the underlying structure, but it represents a fuller and subtler deployment of architectural resources than Holabird & Roche provided on the façades next door.

The Gage Building was Sullivan's penultimate major work. With the Carson, Pirie & Scott Department Store his career as an architect of big commercial buildings came to an end. Designed in 1899, the three-bay and nine-storey section facing Madison Street was built in 1899-1901 for Schlesinger & Mayer. The store was carried further in 1903-4 for the later owners with the erection of the twelve-storey section facing State Street.[24] This building, which was Sullivan's swan song, has also seemed to many critics his masterpiece [210]. It lacks, however, the unity of the earlier Guaranty Building, having been built in two - indeed actually in three - successive campaigns. Despite the prominence of its site in the Chicago Loop, the store is inevitably over-shadowed today by later and taller neighbours; nevertheless, it occupies a special place in the Sullivanian canon and among the works of the Chicago School.

There is no vertical emphasis except on the rounded pavilion at the corner where continuous colonnettes rise the full height between

210. Louis H. Sullivan: Chicago, Carson, Pirie & Scott Department Store, 1899–1901, 1903–4

the rather narrow bays; this feature was intended from the first but not built until 1903-4. The wide Chicago windows are crisply cut through the white terracotta sheathing just like the windows between the oriels on the Stock Exchange Building. The underlying grid of the structural steel frame – always more horizontal than vertical in effect, as the Reliance Building so clearly reveals – completely controls the surface pattern of the fenestration. On the Guaranty Building Sullivan emphasized the structural piers at their base by bending back the shop-windows of the ground storey; here it was the topmost storey that he set back, revealing the tops of the piers like little freestanding columns beneath the terminal slab in the spirit of his earlier eaves galleries. This treatment – most unfortunately replaced in 1948 by a flush parapet – increased very notably the effect of hollow volume in much the same way as at the base of the Guaranty.

At the base here, however, the shop-windows are carried up two storeys and given picture-frame-like surrounds, somewhat as on the Gage Building. In the cast-iron ornamentation of these frames, now much simplified, as also in that of the canopy on the north side and around the entrances in the rounded corner pavilion, Sullivan reached a peak of virtuosity in applied decoration that long seemed to most critics quite at odds with the severe rectangularity of the façades above. There can be no question, however, that Sullivan considered ornament of the greatest importance in architecture and gave to its invention and elaboration his best thought and energy. It is certainly an interesting coincidence, moreover, rather than a matter of influence either way, that in these very years in Europe the newest architectural mode, the Art Nouveau, also put heavy emphasis on a somewhat similar sort of curvilinear decoration, often in association with exposed metal construction, and most notably on department stores (see Chapters 16, 17).

Sullivan's ornament never had much influence either at home or abroad. Although Sullivanian skyscrapers of varying size and quality exist in many Middle Western and Far Western cities, most of them built in the first two decades of the new century, only the Rockefeller Building in Cleveland, built in 1903-6 by Knox & Elliot and extended laterally in 1910, really employs ornament, although of a drier and more geometrical order deriving from Owen Jones's *Grammar*, in anything like Sullivan's way. On Sullivan's own late buildings, mostly tiny banks in small Middle Western towns, and in comparable work by his former assistant George G. Elmslie (1871-1952)[24a] and William G. Purcell (b. 1880) the ornament tends to get more out of hand than on any of his skyscrapers of the nineties except perhaps the Condict Building. The best of Sullivan's is the National Farmers' Bank at Owatonna, Minn., built in 1908; Purcell & Elmslie's Merchants' National Bank in Winona, Minn., completed in 1911, might easily be mistaken for Sullivan's work, for it is of comparable quality.

In the skyscrapers of the late nineties and the first two decades of the twentieth century designed in other Chicago architectural offices, such as D. H. Burnham & Co., Jenney & Mundie, and Holabird & Roche, there was rarely any attempt to vie with Sullivan as an ornamentalist but rather a continuance of the straightforward sort of design of the last-named firm's Michigan Avenue buildings of 1898-9. A particularly fine and very large example is their Cable Building in Chicago of 1899. In the Fisher Building of 1897, also in Chicago, the Burnham firm more or less repeated the formula of the Reliance Building, but with a profusion of rather archaeological Late Gothic detail, eschewing the New York influence apparent in the Ellicott Square Building of 1895. Jenney & Mundie, rather more than the others, tended to follow the leadership of the New York architects of the day in using Renaissance detail.

On the whole, the Chicago School continued to be vigorous, if not especially creative, down to the First World War, all the way through a period during which New York skyscrapers, still usually conceived as shaped towers rather than as plain slabs, received a succession of different stylistic disguises as they rose higher and higher. The forty-seven-storey (612-foot) Singer Building[25] of 1907 by Ernest Flagg (1857-1947) with its curious bulbous mansard – 'Beaux-Arts' of a quite aberrant sort – was followed by the campanile-like 700-foot Metropolitan Tower in Madison Square of 1909 by Napoleon LeBrun & Sons;[26] and that in turn by the cathedral-like Late Gothic elaboration of the Woolworth Building[27] of 1913 by Cass Gilbert (1859-1934), fifty-two storeys and 792 feet tall, which is still one of the major landmarks of down-town New York [337]. A new flurry of skyscraper building followed in the twenties (see Chapter 24). The story with which this chapter is concerned, however, had reached its climax with the Chicago skyscrapers of the nineties, even though they were soon overshadowed in height and in contemporary esteem by the taller and more spectacular towers of Manhattan. Moreover, most of the big cities of the country, including Chicago, eventually sought to imitate the New York mode. But size is not, even in this period, a measure of quality, and the tallest skyscrapers are not the best, any more than the longest bridges are the most beautiful. So far the results of the revival of skyscraper building in the last twenty-five years have confirmed this judgement (see Chapter 25).

A difficult question remains to be asked, even if it cannot be very satisfactorily answered: Why was the nineteenth-century development of commercial architecture, from Nash's Regent Street to Sullivan's skyscrapers, so completely an Anglo-American achievement? A few reasons may at least be suggested. On the Continent business activity was less concentrated

in special urban districts in the nineteenth century, and was hence less likely to develop its own architectural programme. The big new nineteenth-century blocks in cities like Paris and Vienna and Rome generally serve a variety of purposes and almost always consist of residential flats in the upper storeys. In England and in America, on the other hand, most dwellings were still not flats but houses before 1900, and these fled farther and farther from the commercial areas as the nineteenth century progressed. The high property values in the central urban districts of the big Anglo-American cities, rising very rapidly in the second half of the century, encouraged the exploitation of their sites with taller and taller buildings. These values also helped to drive out the earlier inhabitants, leaving such areas as the City of London and the Wall Street district of New York all but deserted after office hours.

Neither the office blocks of London and the big provincial English cities of the fifties and sixties nor, a fortiori, the skyscrapers of New York of the seventies and those of Chicago of the nineties can readily be matched elsewhere – except, of course, to some extent in the British Dominions and Colonies. Yet European cities do offer certain nineteenth-century commercial structures that are of real interest. The covered passages and galeries, from the modest ones of the early decades of the century in Paris to Mengoni's great Galleria Vittorio Emanuele II in Milan [129] of the sixties, offered an urbanistic device of real significance. This is barely to be appreciated in the various extant English and American examples, such as the still flourishing Burlington Arcade in London or the Arcade in Providence, R.I., whose restoration some years ago led to a renewal of its commercial viability.

Related to these structures serving multiple business purposes was the gradual development of the department store, a grouping together of various separate shops under one management and one roof, of which the Galeries du Commerce et de l'Industrie in Paris of 1838 were a relatively early example [107]. Exploiting like the *galeries* the possibilities of iron-and-glass roofing, the early Continental examples of the department store had their more modest English and American counterparts such as Owen Jones's Crystal Palace Bazar of 1858 in London or the Z.C.M.I. in Salt Lake City, founded by the Mormon leader Brigham Young himself and housed in cast iron in 1868.

The most notable later nineteenth-century department stores were in Paris and Berlin. In Paris the still extant Bon Marché of 1876 in the Rue de Sèvres by L. C. Boileau (1837–?), son of the builder of several Second Empire churches of iron, and the engineer Eiffel and the Printemps at the corner of the Rue de Rome and the Boulevard Haussmann of 1881–9 by Paul Sédille (1836–1900) were remarkable in conception if without much distinction of design. However, the Bon Marché is now completely masked externally by a masonry façade of the 1920s, and little of interest remains visible inside the Printemps. Of the portion of the Wertheim Department Store in Berlin built by Alfred Messel (1853–1909) in 1896–9 nothing survives.

Just after 1900, when the metal-and-glass construction of the interiors of department stores came to be generally exposed externally, this line of development came to its climax [243, 247]. This climax is so closely associated with the decorative and architectural development called Art Nouveau that the later Continental department stores may better be discussed in connexion with that (see Chapters 16 and 17). Being of exposed metal, however, not of masonry-sheathed 'skyscraper construction' and relatively low, these stores are closer in character to the cast-iron commercial buildings of the third quarter of the century in America and Britain than to the tall Chicago structures of 1890–1910.

Steel construction of the American type, with the internal skeleton carrying a protective cladding of masonry, has gradually spread since the opening of the century to all parts of the world that produce or can afford to buy structural steel. It was, for example, used early in London by the Anglo-French architects Mewès & Davis in building the Ritz Hotel there in 1905. Yet it remains typically American. In most other countries reinforced concrete rivals or completely takes its place as the characteristic material for building large structures of all sorts. The story of reinforced concrete had its technical beginnings in the mid nineteenth century; but it was not before the nineties that it first began to be exploited on a large scale and for conscious architectural effect. The first important reinforced concrete buildings, French like the best department stores of around 1900 that survive, will be mentioned later (see Chapter 18).

The whole picture of architecture in the twentieth century, so different from the picture of architecture before 1850, was modified by the developments that culminated in the Chicago skyscrapers. However important this has been for all later architecture both technically and aesthetically, it is important to stress here, as with the mid-century monuments of iron and glass, that the successive stages in the development are not solely, or even primarily, of premonitory and historical interest. From Parris's granite buildings in Boston of the twenties, through the arcaded English commercial work of the fifties and sixties, to Richardson's Field Store and Sullivan's skyscrapers in Chicago, St Louis, Buffalo, and New York, enlightened commercial patrons demanded and often received the best architecture of their day. The functional and technical challenges of commercial building seem to have brought out the creative capacities of three generations of architects as no other commissions did so consistently. Compare Parris's

Grecian temple church, St Paul's in Boston, with his granite 'skeleton' fronts beside the Quincy Market [197]; set Godwin's Stokes Croft Warehouse beside his town halls [200, 159]; measure Richardson's Field Store even against his Pittsburgh Jail [192, 191]. Then the strictly *architectural*, as well as the technical and social, significance of the century's major commercial monuments will be evident.

This chapter has summarized what was probably the greatest single innovation in nineteenth-century architecture, the rise of a new type of building to a position of prestige and of achievement comparable to that of churches and palaces in earlier periods. The same cannot be said of domestic architecture. The house was hardly a nineteenth-century invention like the office building. It was, however, modified almost beyond recognition as the century progressed, at the hands of several generations of creative architects. Around 1900 there are few if any churches, for example, to rival Sullivan's skyscrapers in quality; but there are some houses, especially several by his disciple Wright and by his English contemporary Voysey.

CHAPTER 15

THE DEVELOPMENT OF THE DETACHED HOUSE

IN ENGLAND AND AMERICA FROM 1800 TO 1900

In the long story of man's dwellings from prehistory to the present, the Anglo-American development that took place in the hundred years between the 1790s and the 1890s is of considerable significance, particularly as it provides the immediate background of the twentieth-century house. Architectural history has generally been little concerned, in dealing with periods earlier than the eighteenth century at least, with the habitations of any but the upper classes. The study of rural cottages in various regions of the world has been more a matter for anthropological investigation; the housing of the urban poor, when that was other than the makeshift adaptation of grander structures fallen into decay, remains for most early periods a matter of mystery. We know that ancient Rome had its blocks of middle-class flats of many storeys; although the links are not easy to recover, there was certainly some continuity in Mediterranean lands between that form of urban housing in antiquity and what can be traced from the medieval period down to the nineteenth century. Northern Europe in the late Middle Ages saw rather the development of individual urban dwellings with party walls, ancestors of the terrace-houses that first appeared in England in the seventeenth century.

The detached house of moderate size, so familiar today, the principal type of dwelling to undergo notable development in the nineteenth century in Anglo-Saxon countries, has no such remote Classical origins as the Continental flat or apartment. It made its appearance as the dwelling of the yeoman when economic conditions in late medieval England encouraged the rise of a class between the feudal landowner and the peasant parallel to the skilled artisan class in the towns. The conditions of settlement of the British colonies in America, particularly in New England, encouraged the continuation through the seventeenth century of this type of dwelling almost to the exclusion of any other sort, since towns were then small and large estates rare. Around 1700 in America, though considerably earlier in England, relatively advanced contemporary modes began to have some influence on the design of such houses. With a lag of as much as a quarter of a century, the architectural developments of the home country were generally followed in the colonies; nor did political independence much affect the dependent cultural relationship in this field after the American Revolution.

The effects of the Picturesque point of view on the development of the house in England around 1800 were several (see Chapter 6). On the one hand, the newly fashionable attitude gave prestige to modest detached dwellings, raising the social status of the 'cottage' from an agricultural labourer's hovel to a middle-class habitation or even on occasion a holiday 'retreat' for the upper classes – at first by adding the French adjective *orné* [211]. At the same time the status of the 'villa' tended to be reduced from a large Italianate mansion in its own estate to a moderate-sized house at the edge of town. In much of the prolific architectural literature of the period, the hierarchy of residential building types was Rousseauistically inverted

211. J. B. Papworth: 'Cottage Orné', 1818

as rustic models, both native and Italian, were proposed for emulation in edifices of fairly considerable size. Thus several modes of informal design that had made their eighteenth-century debut in garden ornaments received more serious attention from architects as they came to be considered suitable for medium-sized dwellings and even sometimes for quite large mansions. As we have already seen, the towered Italian Villa was first introduced as a modest detached house by Nash at Cronkhill in 1802. It was similarly utilized by Schinkel [32] and Persius at Potsdam a generation later, although Royalty still preferred to dwell there in Grecian dignity or Castellated pomp (see Chapter 2). Somewhat later, however, the Italian Villa provided (none too happily) a Royal retreat when Prince Albert decided on this mode for Osborne House on the Isle of Wight in the mid forties.

Not all Picturesque modes were equally adaptable to middle-class dwellings. The Indian found its most notable realizations in a large country house, S. P. Cockerell's Sezincote, and a Royal folly, Nash's Brighton Pavilion [88]. There were, however, considerably later Ameri-

can examples[1] on a somewhat more modest scale, such as Iranistan at Bridgeport, Conn., built for Barnum in 1847–8, and Longwood, near Natchez in Mississippi, designed by Samuel Sloan in 1860 that have been mentioned earlier. But the Indian mode contributed the veranda, henceforth an integral feature of American domestic architecture, though rare after the Picturesque period in England. Verandas very early lost their Oriental detail, however. In front of Rustic Cottages they were often supported by bark-covered logs, but they could also acquire the formal character of Italian loggias, Tudor arcades, Swiss galleries or, most frequently, Classical porticoes and 'pilastrades' when adapted for use with other current modes.[1a] In some cases the veranda, carried on occasion to two storeys in height, became the main theme of the exterior, yet was detailed so simply that no stylistic name properly applies [211].

Even the Castellated mode, although used mostly for rather large houses [89], encouraged loose asymmetrical massing of the sort that is still more characteristic of the towered Italian Villa.

The Picturesque was thoroughly eclectic, in both possible senses of the word, as well as occasionally original. On the one hand, the point of view encouraged the parallel use of diverse modes. In theory, these were to be chosen according to their suitability to various sorts of natural settings, but in practice several were often employed side by side, as in Nash's Park Villages in London, begun in 1827, and in the contemporary and later development of comparable suburban areas both in England and in America. On the other hand, the combination in one design of features derived from several different modes was allowable, even praiseworthy – low-pitched roofs with very broad eaves borrowed from the Swiss Chalet, towers from both the Castellated Mansion and the Italian Villa, bay-windows from the Tudor

Parsonage, and verandas from the Indian were all part of a common repertory exploited rather indiscriminately. Basic to the Picturesque point of view and often determinant of choice of mode and even of individual features was the preoccupation with the natural setting; verandas, loggias, bay-windows and prospect towers were desirable, even necessary, features because they made possible the fuller enjoyment of the circumambient scene.

All these features affected house-plans in detail; but domestic planning in general was not as consistently re-organized as might have been expected, if only because the Picturesque point of view was so predominantly visual rather than practical in its usual concerns. Asymmetrical massing allowed, even forced, asymmetrical planning, however, thereby encouraging functional differentiation of the disposition and the sizes of various rooms [212].

212. T. F. Hunt: house-plan, 1827

Yet very often, behind irregular exteriors, the plans were only slightly dislocated from the formal patterns of the preceding Palladian period. Although the increased articulation of most house-plans allowed the introduction of windows on several sides of many rooms, more significant at this stage was the frequent use of irregular shapes for the larger rooms, their main rectangular spaces complicated by external oriels and by internal inglenooks. None of these individual changes can be very precisely dated, at least in the current state of knowledge of the development of the house-plan in this period. Almost all of them were generally familiar in England by 1810. Tudor Parsonages, whether or not occupied by members of the clergy, were likely to be most adeptly planned.[2] In them the well-defined needs of a family of relatively high social status but low income encouraged a more efficient grouping of the rooms and a clearer distinction of separate functions – entrance hall, drawing-room, dining room, study, kitchen, scullery – than had been common earlier in such medium-sized dwellings.

In the first third of the century the various Picturesque modes of house-design were very widely exploited in England for middle-class habitations in the new suburbs, having generally made their first appearance a decade or so earlier in lodges or other accessories to large private estates. They were also popular at the new seaside resorts, such as Sidmouth in Devon and Bournemouth in Hampshire, where they often housed more exalted clients. At Sidmouth, for example, what is now the Woodlands Hotel was remodelled from a barn into a bargeboarded Cottage Orné by Lord Gwydyr in 1815; the nucleus of the Knowles Hotel there was Lord Despencer's cottage of a few years earlier; and the Royal Glen Hotel, a modest Castellated house then known as Walbrook Cottage, was built early enough to house Queen Victoria as a baby. Although the prestige of the Picturesque declined rapidly in high aesthetic circles after 1840, the rigorous principles of Pugin and the ecclesiologists had little effect on the operations of suburban builders, who continued for decades to follow the various well-established modes of a generation earlier.

As Latrobe's 'Gothick' Sedgley, built outside Philadelphia in 1798, and various other Neo-Gothic structures in Philadelphia and Boston of the first decade of the new century make evident, the Picturesque came early to the United States. Yet it was hardly before the thirties that the various Cottage and Villa modes began to compete at all with the Greek temple and the formal post-Palladian house modernized by the use of Grecian detail; only with the appearance in 1842 of *Cottage Residences* by A. J. Downing (1815-52)[3] were they enthusiastically propagated.

Earlier, new developments in the planning of the ubiquitous moderate-sized free-standing houses were not very notable in America. In the 1790s the influence of Adam, and possibly of the French, encouraged some experimentation with variously shaped rooms; but this largely died out as the necessary rectangularity of the Greek temple house, only extended by one or more wings in the largest examples, reimposed the formal Anglo-Palladian plan with central stair-hall and four nearly equal-sized corner rooms. For smaller houses with pedimented fronts, however, a sort of terrace-house plan was increasingly popular, with stair-hall at one side, two principal living rooms one behind the other, and a narrower kitchen wing extending to the rear. A planning innovation that first appeared in America in the 1790s, by no means unknown earlier in England especially in urban terrace-houses, was the opening together of two rooms – front and back parlours – by means of broad sliding doors. This became increasingly common after 1800. Moreover, the temple portico provided the equivalent of a shallow veranda across the front of the house and was sometimes replaced or supplemented

by a deeper colonnaded porch at the sides or rear. The veranda, indeed, had reached the southern states fairly early in the eighteenth century, arriving from the East via the West Indies. In its usual two-storeyed form it was easily merged with the monumental colonnades demanded by the Grecian mode [72].

Thus, even before a rather belated wave of strong Picturesque influence began to drive out the temple house in the forties, early nineteenth-century American houses had certain definitely post-Colonial characteristics in their plans. Of later house-planning in the United States in the forties and fifties almost everything that has been said about English planning in the preceding decades applies [214]. By this time in England, however, newer planning ideas were being introduced by leading architects in relatively large houses. At Scarisbrick, for example, where the remodelling and extension of the existing Georgian house began in 1837, Pugin revived the medieval great hall (see Chapter 6). A few years later in his own house, The Grange of 1841-3 at Ramsgate,[4] by no means a mansion in size or scale, the more modest two-storey hall incorporates the staircase and also provides, with the galleries above, the central core of communication. Parallel with these examples, which were of Gothic inspiration, Barry at Highclere adapted the glass-roofed central *cortile* of the Reform Club to domestic use, associating with it the main staircase rising in a contiguous vertical space.

At the hands of High Church architects the parsonage, by definition no mansion but a modest free-standing gentleman's residence, was also undergoing a characteristic development. No longer Tudor, of course, it was still not forced to be archaeologically Decorated in its planning, since there were few if any relevant medieval models to imitate. The doctrine of 'realism' condemned the shabby construction and careless use of materials that had too often been characteristic of Picturesque house-building in the previous decades, while the need for economy discouraged the ornamentation usual on contemporary churches.

Such a vicarage as that which Butterfield built in 1844-5 to go with his 'first' church, St Saviour's at Coalpitheath, Gloucestershire, is a model of simple masonry construction. In the random ashlar walls are set wide banks of plain mullioned windows, Gothic only in the arching of their heads, where they can serve best to light the various rooms [213]. The massing also is

213. William Butterfield:
Coalpitheath, Gloucestershire,
St Saviour's Vicarage, 1844-5

irregular yet orderly with several high gables, a porch, many tall chimney stacks, and a broad bow-window elaborating the basically rectangular block. But, in the language of the ecclesiologists, 'the true Picturesque derives from the sternest utility', and so all these projecting features were such as could be readily justified functionally, like the ritualistic articulation of contemporary churches. The plan of Butterfield's vicarage has the virtues of those of the Picturesque Tudor Parsonages in the variety of room-sizes and shapes provided and also in the opportunities that the windows offer to enjoy surrounding nature. There is also at Coalpitheath a very modest version of

Pugin's stair-hall at The Grange, not a mere lobby but a central space designed for easy horizontal and vertical communication.

Any serious revival of medieval craftsmanship in masonry was all but impossible in America; in any case it was largely irrelevant in a land where most houses were built of wood. But in reaction to the white-painted clapboards and the smooth Grecian trim of the previous decades, echoing however humbly the marble of Greece, Downing in the early forties proposed and many at his behest adopted variant treatments for the exterior sheathing of Picturesque villas and cottages that were rather more expressive. The distinguished native craftsmanship evident in the more monumental edifices of the Greek Revival executed in fine ashlar of granite or other light-coloured stone, or else in smooth red brick, died out. Such materials had no more appeal than did crisp white-painted wood to a generation indoctrinated with the Picturesque point of view. Yet clapboards remained the usual surfacing material for wooden houses, even if they were now painted, not white, but in the stony hues – grey or beige – that Downing recommended in his books with actual coloured samples.

The treatment Downing preferred was board-and-batten.[5] This he made a constituent element of the very original Bracketted mode that he offered as an American alternative to the imported Italian Villa and Tudor Parsonage which he was energetically engaged in naturalizing. Board-and-batten provides a stronger pattern of light and shade, and also the verticalism that appealed increasingly to mid-century taste. This sheathing also offers a sort of symbolic expression of the light 'balloon-frame'[6] construction that was beginning to come into general use by the fifties, though this method of wooden framing was apparently never known to Downing, since he died in 1852 before it reached the eastern states where he lived and worked.

With their board-and-batten walls, their ample verandas, and their bay-windows, what are still usually called 'Downing houses' constitute a largely original American creation in

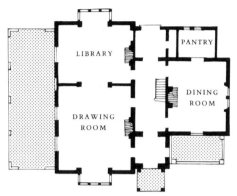

214. A. J. Downing: house-plan, 1842

spite of the frequent use of Tudoresque detail on barge-boards and veranda supports and even of elaborately moulded terracotta chimney pots. Yet in their planning the houses designed by Downing and his architect friends Davis and Notman do not advance much beyond the models published in the English books of the previous decades that were their immediate prototypes [214]. The verandas are usually wider and more prominent, however, and the front and rear parlours are likely to open into one another, as sometimes also into a modest central hall.

In America as in England, the Picturesque period came to no sudden end. The recurrent publication of Downing's books even after the Civil War[7] indicates how long his models remained favourites with American builders and their small-town and suburban clients. However, even before the Civil War a mansarded Second Empire mode was beginning to become popular (see Chapter 9). With the wide acceptance of this and of the High Victorian Gothic

there developed a rather sharp split between autochthonous and imported types of house-design, drastically though the imported types were usually Americanized outside the bigger eastern cities. To this situation we must return later.

Something has already been said of the major turn that took place in the development of the English house around 1860 (see Chapters 9 and 12). When seen in relation to the parsonages that his master Street and also Butterfield had been building in the previous fifteen years, Webb's Red House built in 1859-60 for William Morris is considerably less revolutionary than has sometimes been supposed. Had this been built in Gloucestershire rather than in Kent, it would certainly have been of stone like Butterfield's Coalpitheath Vicarage; as it is, the entrance porch is no simpler or less Gothic than Butterfield's. The particular window forms, moreover, can be matched in Butterfield's Clergy House and School at All Saints', Margaret Street, and the somewhat rustic ease of composition in his cottages at Baldersby St James. Yet the planning here is highly individual, suited to the special needs of a client who was an artist and a writer, not a parson.

The next house that Webb built, now known as Benfleet Hall, Cobham, begun in 1860 for the painter Spencer Stanhope, has been less publicized, and it never had the rich furnishings that Morris and his associates designed and executed for the Red House. Yet it is perhaps more significant in the general history of the Anglo-American house. There is here, for example, a small stair-hall of the order of Pugin's at the Grange or Butterfield's at Coalpitheath around which the other ground-storey rooms are loosely grouped. The particular character of the plan can, in fact, best be matched at Hinderton, a small country house in Cheshire that is hardly more of a mansion than Benfleet, which Waterhouse built in 1859. This house is in Waterhouse's gawkiest High Victorian Gothic,

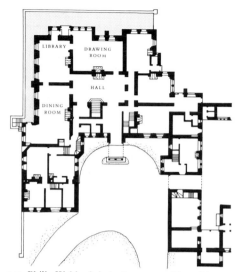

215. Philip Webb: Arisaig, Inverness-shire, 1863

with none of the simplicity and delicacy of Webb's early houses. It is rather unlikely that Webb was actually emulating it, but the plan was twice published[8] and hence soon known abroad.

Webb's Arisaig in Inverness-shire was begun in 1863 [215]. Built of local stone, it is somewhat more conventionally Gothic externally; moreover, it is of country-house size, a mansion rather than a modest artist's dwelling like the Red House or Benfleet Hall. The plan has two major aspects of interest: the two-storeyed hall, with gallery above, occupies a central position and the principal rooms on both storeys are very efficiently grouped about it within the bounding rectangle of the main block of the house. In other words, Arisaig's hall seems to derive as much from the Highclere sort of glazed central

216. Nesfield & Shaw:
Cloverley Hall, Shropshire, 1865–8

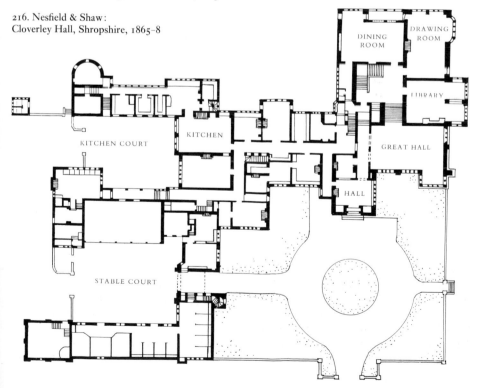

court as from Pugin's revival of the medieval great hall.

Cloverley Hall, which was built by Nesfield and Shaw in 1865-8, attracted much favourable contemporary attention largely because of the superb craftsmanship of the brickwork and the originality of the *japoniste* ornament (see Chapter 12). It is destroyed now except for the extensive service and stable wings and the gate lodge; but the amount and the character of the fenestration, providing in some areas what amounted to window-walls of stone-mullioned and transomed lights, and the character of the plan make it still memorable. It was also the first of the many notable Late Victorian manor houses which both Nesfield and Shaw would build when working alone.

Like Arisaig, Cloverley was a large country house. The medieval great hall, first rather modestly revived by Pugin at Scarisbrick, here returned at full scale; but it was placed in a corner of the main block – as was occasionally its position in the sixteenth century – so that it might receive light from one end as well as from the side [216]. From the entrance, however, one passed by this hall through the 'screens' under a gallery to arrive at a stair-hall, more in the manner of Waterhouse's and Webb's, around which the other principal rooms were compactly grouped. There was also here a very skilful play with levels, the hall being lower than the rest of the main floor, and therefore part-way down to the basement – containing a billiard room and so forth – which was entirely above ground at the rear of the house.

While Cloverley Hall was still in construction, Shaw had begun his own personal career as a house-builder at Glen Andred in 1866-7 [178], where he introduced a more vernacular manner (see Chapter 12). Following this came his Leyswood in 1868-9, a mansion as large as Cloverley Hall and in some of its decorative features more archaeologically Late Medieval. As at Cloverley Hall, the amplitude of the fenestration, however, arranged here in long mullioned bands as well as in tall window-walls, has seemed more significant to posterity than the stylistic detailing[9] [217]. Above all, Leyswood marked a further stage in the development of the 'agglutinative plan' [179], of which the first well-publicized example was Waterhouse's at Hinderton. Here the great hall and the stair-hall of Cloverley are combined to form a central spatial core of communication, somewhat as at Webb's Arisaig, but the shape of this is quite irregular and the reception rooms are grouped very loosely about it, more as at Benfleet Hall. Projecting well out of the main block, the dining-room and the drawing-room both receive light from three sides. Moreover, the space of these rooms is articulated, as in certain Picturesque houses of forty and fifty years earlier, by ingle-nooks, oriels, and various other irregularities. Perspectives of Leyswood – not the plan[10] – were published in the supplement to the *Building News* of 31 March 1871 and made at once a tremendous impression both in England and in America [217].

In a house by Webb of the same date as Leyswood, Trevor Hall at Oakleigh Park, Barnet, in Hertfordshire, the arrangement of the rooms about the central hall was much more compact [218]. The whole formed a square and allowed quite symmetrical treatments of the three principal fronts. This house is now destroyed except for the gate lodge. Less interesting in plan but significant for its very modest size is Webb's Upwood Gorse, Caterham, Surrey, built for Queen Victoria's dentist Sir John Tomes also in 1868. The consistency and the simplicity with which the local vernacular of brick below and tile-hanging above is handled in connexion with plenty of white-painted Queen Anne sash-windows regularly but not symmetrically spaced offers a curiously close prototype of the American 'Shingle Style', even though the initiators of that mode a decade later can hardly have known

217. R. Norman Shaw:
Leyswood, nr Withyham, Sussex, 1868

of this house since it was never published. It was rather Shaw's houses of the next decade, of which his drawings were exhibited each year at the Royal Academy and given great prominence in the professional Press, that provided the exemplars which architects generally imitated both at home and abroad; from 1874 on the plans were usually illustrated as well as Shaw's own very virtuoso pen-drawn[11] perspectives [217].

Webb's houses for the painters Val Prinsep and G. B. Boyce in Kensington and Chelsea, of 1865 and 1869 respectively, were the first English 'studio-houses' – houses, that is, in which the studios, naturally equipped with very large windows, were the principal rooms. These provided a more usable alternative to the great halls that Shaw generally provided in his country houses; but it was the larger artists' houses of the seventies and eighties which Shaw built for

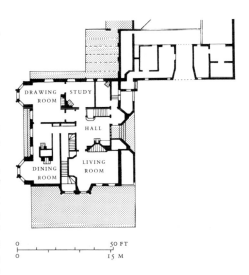

218. Philip Webb:
Barnet, Hertfordshire, Trevor Hall, 1868–70

his fellow academicians that received the most contemporary publicity.

By the mid seventies Shaw was moving in the formal and symmetrical direction initiated by Webb at Trevor Hall, and soon carried much further by Nesfield at Kinmel Park, as regards both the planning and the external organization of his larger London houses. Lowther Lodge in Kensington Gore of 1873-4 is the first of his domestic commissions that may properly be called Queen Anne rather than Manorial. The even more formally designed Cheyne House and Old Swan House, of 1875 and 1876 respectively, on the Chelsea Embankment followed shortly after [181]; but he long continued to build more loosely composed houses in the country, as has been noted earlier.

Before turning to the results of Shaw's very notable influence in the United States in the seventies, something should be said of the situation there in the preceding decade. The Second Empire mode had been increasingly popular for houses from the mid fifties and was especially fashionable during the boom period that followed the Civil War. It had no positive contribution to make to the general Anglo-American development in these decades, however. In the domestic field more or less Gothic modes were its significant rivals; first Downing's wide-verandaed version of the Tudor Cottage; then, after 1860, what Vincent Scully has christened the 'Stick Style'.[12]

On houses in this mode, which is really hardly Gothic at all, a sort of imitation half-timbering panels the exterior walls, suggesting, like Downing's board-and-batten sheathing, the underlying wooden stud-structure of balloon-frame construction. This construction came to be generally used in the East as well as in the Middle West, where it originated, after it had been explained by William E. Bell in his *Carpentry Made Easy* in 1858. More striking is the open stickwork of the ubiquitous verandas. This can be seen in an early form on the Olmsted house in East Hartford, Conn., of 1849 by the English architect Gervase Wheeler,[13] who obviously derived it from Picturesque models in England dating back at least to the thirties. In the J. N. H. Griswold house of 1862 in Bellevue Avenue in Newport, R.I.,[13a] by the French-trained Hunt, now the Newport Art Association, the 'sticks' of the wall surface are so sturdy that they may well be the actual framing members.

Very characteristic of the maturity of the mode is the Sturtevant house at nearby Middletown, R.I., built by Dudley Newton (1845? - 1907) a decade later in 1872. Here the gawky vigour of the Stick Style, its intense woodenness, and its descent from several different Picturesque modes – not least the Swiss Chalet – is very evident [219]. Extensive surrounding verandas are of the very essence of the mode; but the internal planning, while informal and often asymmetrical, is rarely very open. Several books by Eugene C. Gardner (1836-1905)[14] of Springfield, Mass., give a sophisticated architect's rationale of the mode. But the exemplars that G. E. Woodward[15] offered in the sixties are more typical, and were more widely imitated in actual production; for the Stick Style had almost run its course by the time Gardner began to present his excellent house designs. Woodward was no architect, and for the most part the Stick Style should not be considered an architect's mode. It represented rather a popular attempt, remarkably successful for a few years, to create an American domestic vernacular, suited to the materials in general use and to the current methods of building, comparable to Downing's earlier Bracketted mode. Like the Second Empire vogue the Stick Style died out, at least in the East, during the general hiatus in building production after the financial Panic of 1873.

By that time Shaw's influence had begun to reach America.[16] Moreover, the possibilities of agglutinative planning about a great hall had

219. Dudley Newton:
Middletown, R. I., Sturtevant house, 1872

been realized by Richardson well before a Shaw plan – that for Hopedene – was first made available in the *Building News* in 1874. It is, of course, possible that McKim, in passing through England on his way home from Paris in 1870, had seen (or merely heard of) the character of Webb's, Nesfield's, and Shaw's houses of the sixties and transmitted that information to Richardson, but that is two years too late.

An undated project, probably of *c.* 1868–9, by Richardson for a house to be built for Richard Codman includes his first 'great hall'[17] of the Shavian sort; but the Codman plan is already in advance of, or at least rather different from those of Shaw. This hall, out of which the stairs would rise in an L at the rear, was to be very large in relation to the other rooms, and thus

definitely a principal living area not a mere foyer or centre of circulation. The drawing room and dining room were to open out of the hall in such a way that some sort of spatial continuity would have extended through all the reception rooms of the ground storey. There was to be a large veranda at the rear in the well-established local tradition. The exterior as shown in the elevations is not at all Shavian but rather related to the Stick Style, like Richardson's own house at Arrochar on Staten Island of 1868.

Richardson's first executed country house, the F. W. Andrews house of 1872–3 at Newport, R.I., was much more Shavian in plan. Four or five rooms were grouped about a relatively smaller central stair-hall and most of these were articulated by bay-windows and ingle-nooks.

But the main block was also surrounded by verandas, features which are rare and always of modest extent on Shaw's houses. The Andrews house was burned a long time ago, but from the existing elevations it would appear that the external treatment represented a sort of transition between the Stick Style, then at its apogee, and Shaw's Surrey vernacular translated into American materials. The verandas were still detailed in a Stick Style way, and flat stickwork interrupted the continuity of the wall surfaces; but the clapboarding of the lower walls evidently took the place of the brickwork Shaw used – it was almost certainly painted red – and the wooden shingling of the upper walls was a happy substitute for English tile-hanging. Shingles were, of course, an old though largely forgotten American sheathing material long used especially for roofs.

By the time Richardson came to design his next large house, that for William Watts Sherman on Shepard Avenue in Newport in 1874, the perspectives of several of Shaw's manors had appeared in the *Building News* and the plans of two. As a result, probably, of his assistant Stanford White's Shaw-like skill with the pencil, the Sherman house was notably Shavian externally. Above the ground storey, which is of Richardsonian random-ashlar masonry in pink Milford granite with brownstone trim, the walls and the high roofs are covered with shingles cut in various decorative shapes suggested by those of Shaw's tile-hanging. Many of the casement windows are grouped to form window-walls in the ground storey and arranged in long horizontal bands above. The half-timbering of the front gable, with painted decoration on the intervening plaster, was taken straight from Shaw's Grim's Dyke; the carved ornament on the barge-boards is almost Nesfieldian in its suggestion of *japonisme*. Thus the whole is as perfect a specimen of Shaw's Manorial mode as anything any architect other than he or Nesfield ever

produced in England. The house has since been twice enlarged, by White in 1881, by Newton very much later, but always with due respect for the character of the original design.

The plan has more of the independent virtues of that of the Codman project. The hall provides a principal portion of the living area, and the other main rooms open into it through wide doors; thus there was from the first a flow of space throughout the whole ground storey. The library at the rear corner, later replaced by a ballroom, ended in a Shavian rounded bay with a continuous window band, a feature Wright would copy later. Yet otherwise the house was less articulated than Shaw's earlier ones, having rather the compactness, though none of the symmetry, of Webb's Trevor Hall.

The mid seventies saw many other American reflections of Shaw's Manorial mode and soon of his Queen Anne also, none of them so successful as the Sherman house. But the deep business recession that followed the Panic of 1873 led to a general mood of repentance after the extravagances, architectural and otherwise, of the post-war boom. From the resultant nostalgia for the simpler ways of the American past there began to develop at this time a great interest in the houses of the Colonial period, an interest that readily merged with the parallel interest in the modest English vernacular of the seventeenth and eighteenth centuries. To an extent difficult for posterity to appreciate, the nascent 'Shingle Style',[18] which crystallized towards the end of the decade with the renewal of building activity, was to its protagonists already a sort of Colonial Revival. Although its origins are partly Shavian, it represents above all a reaction, as did Shaw's Manorial mode in England, against the 'modernism' of the High Victorian Gothic and the Second Empire, now grown thoroughly unfashionable except in the West.

Boston was still the architectural metropolis of the United States, and it was around Boston, especially in the work of Emerson and Little, the latter a serious early student of old Colonial work, that this crystallization of the Shingle Style first took place (see Chapter 13). But it was at once taken over and given a somewhat more Shaw-like elaboration by the New York firm of McKim, Mead & White, formed in 1879. From the early eighties, and for over a decade, the Shingle Style was widely practised by architects from coast to coast, and not least happily in the Far West. The characteristic use of shingles as an all-over wall-covering emphasized the continuity of the exterior surface as a skin stretched over the underlying wooden skeleton of studs, in contrast to the way the preceding Stick Style had echoed that skeleton in the external treatment. The shingles properly provide the name for a most characteristically American domestic mode; but it was in planning that American architects made a really original contribution in what was the most significant development of the detached house since the Picturesque period.

One of the first mature examples of the Shingle Style, the Morrill house by Emerson on Mount Desert in Maine of 1879, illustrates the virtuosity of the new planning [220]. Rooms of varied shape and size are loosely grouped about the hall and open freely into one another. The variant levels of the different areas are related to the landing level of the elaborate staircase. Above all, it should be noted that the verandas are not mere adjuncts or afterthoughts, as they were even on Richardson's Andrews house, but major elements, both space-wise and visually, of the whole composition. Such houses parallel in their three-dimensional complexity the massing of the Italian Villas of the earlier nineteenth-century decades with their loggias, pergolas, and prospect towers, yet they bear little or no visual resemblance to them, since the later houses are always much more plastically modelled and less articulated in composition. The windows are generally of double-hung small-paned sashes of a type at once Queen Anne and Colonial, but they are frequently grouped in

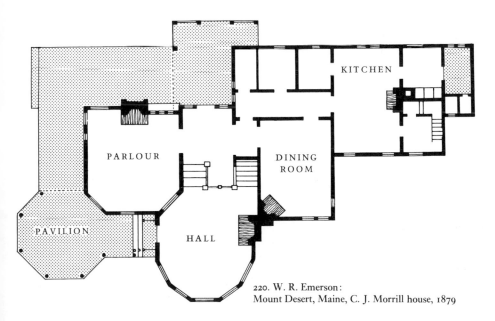

220. W. R. Emerson:
Mount Desert, Maine, C. J. Morrill house, 1879

the Shavian way, as well as being ingeniously placed in order to vary the internal lighting effects, so that the pattern of fenestration is not at all of an eighteenth-century orderliness.

Richardson certainly did not initiate the Shingle Style; but he took it over in 1880 and made it very much his own, using it for all his later country and suburban houses. Dropping all detail, whether Richardsonian Romanesque, Shavian Manorial, Queen Anne, or American Colonial, he retained much of the ease and casualness of Shaw's best early houses. But there is also a great deal of similarity to the simple massive look of the old Colonial houses also. Spiritually, so to say, if not so much visually, Richardson's shingled houses most resemble Webb's best work; of these Richardson

presumably had no knowledge, although it is just possible that he might have seen some when he was in England in 1882, well after the Shingle Style was fully established.

Richardson's Stoughton house in Brattle Street in Cambridge, Mass., of 1882–3 is perhaps his best shingled one, at least in the relatively untouched form in which it, almost alone, alas, has come down to us [221]. It certainly shows little evidence of the interest that he is known to have taken in Burges's and Shaw's work while he was abroad just before this. The entrance, originally, was through the loggia recessed into the main mass of the house (it is now from Ash Street on the left). The living-hall extends, as in the Sherman house, from front to back and the stairs sweep up in a quarter-circle over the entrance. The drawing room at the corner and the dining room behind the loggia both open into the hall through wide doors; the small library alone is isolated from the general flow of space. Externally, the shingled surfaces, broken only by banks of double-hung windows, model the complex

221 *(opposite)*. H. H. Richardson: Cambridge, Mass., Stoughton house, 1882–3

222 and 223. McKim, Mead & White: Newport, R.I., Isaac Bell, Jr, house, 1881–2

mass into a unified L, and the almost submerged stair-tower by its rounded form links together the two gabled wings at right angles to one another. There is no ornament of any sort, and the weathered grey of the shingles is unvaried but for the dark green paint of the window frames.

McKim, Mead & White's houses of the early eighties, several of them equally fine, are usually rather more elaborate in their massing and are likely to be enlivened with much imaginative detail.[19] Some of the detail recalls this or that style of the past, but all of it is thoroughly personalized by White's delicate hand. One of their best houses is the one for Isaac Bell, Jr, built in 1881–2 in Bellevue Avenue in Newport, R.I. [222]. This is less unified externally than

the Stoughton house but more open in plan [223]. A wide veranda, with very elegant bamboo-like supports, extends around two fronts, expanding into a two-storeyed open

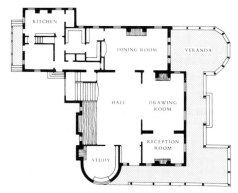

pavilion on the right. This pavilion provides a
semicircular void to balance the round tower
at the rear left corner. The patterns of the
original cut shingles on this house, although
obviously suggested by English tile-hanging,
were much softer and more graceful, almost
bringing to mind birds' plumage.

Inside, the hall is articulated by a wide inglenook, rather dark and low, in sharpest contrast
to the great flight of stairs beyond down which
floods light from the window-wall at the half
landing. Twenty-five-foot sliding doors, hung
from above, make it possible to open the
drawing room through almost its entire length
into the hall. The Bell dining room, connecting
at its end through French windows with the
curved portion of the veranda, has some of the

finest of White's orientalizing detail. This is
much more original than that in the new library
he decorated at this time in the Sherman house
or the dining room he added to Upjohn's
Kingscote, both also in Newport.

McKim, Mead & White's slightly earlier
H. Victor Newcomb house of 1880-1 in
Elberon, N.J., is at once clumsier and more
Shavian externally than the Bell house; but the
spatial treatment of the living-hall is most
original and very significant for later developments [224]. The main rectangular space, of
which the shape is emphasized by the ceiling
beams and by the abstract geometrical pattern
of the floor, seems to flow out in various directions into other rooms and into several bays and
nooks; but the actual room-space is sharply

224. McKim, Mead & White:
Elberon, N.J., H. Victor Newcomb house, 1880-1

defined by a continuous frieze-like member that becomes an open wooden grille above the various openings. There can be little question that the major influence here is from the Japanese[20] interior, but from the Japanese interior understood as architecture. This is not just a superficial matter of Nesfieldian *japonisme* such as White was employing so much in his ornament in these years. The Kingscote dining room has somewhat similar spatial qualities but more eclectic detailing and richer materials: marble, mahogany, Tiffany glass tiles, cork panels, stained glass.

In 1879 Cyrus McCormick had his Chicago mansion built by the German architect Adolph Cudell (1850–1910) and his partner Blumenthal in the form of a very corrupt Second Empire *hôtel particulier*. It is good evidence of the rapidity with which taste changed at this time that two years later he called on McKim, Mead & White to build for him in Richfield Springs, N.Y., one of the finest and most carefully composed of all their Shingle Style houses. This house was notable not only for the subtly Japanese character of the various sorts of veranda supports but even more for the way the composition was unified under the broad front gable by the long horizontal line of the veranda roof repeating that of the stylobate-like stone wall of the terrace below. It is most unfortunate that this house, long in a state of near-collapse, has been demolished.

Little's contemporary Shingleside House of 1881 in Swampscott, Mass., has been mentioned already. Soberer than the Bell or the McCormick houses in its rectangular shape and almost total lack of exterior detail, this had a galleried two-storey hall with a window-wall as the principal living area. In the combining of different levels this house recalled a little Cloverley Hall, but it was completely Americanized in scale and in detail without being archaeologically Neo-Colonial except for the interior wainscoting.

By the mid eighties J. Lyman Silsbee (1848–1913) had introduced the Shingle Style to Chicago, and other Eastern architects were building good houses of this order in such Western towns as Cheyenne, Wyoming; Colorado Springs, Colorado; and Pasadena, California. In Philadelphia Wilson Eyre (1858–1944) developed the mode with a very characteristic personal difference, often eschewing the use of shingles. If his exteriors are rather English in their frequent use of brick and real half-timbering, his plans are most original. The long rooms of varied and irregular shape are strung out on either side of halls from which rise stairs within grilled enclosures of a sort that appeared in England only in the houses of the nineties by Voysey and his contemporaries.

The heyday of the Shingle Style was brief, even though it continued in use well down into the nineties. The Colonial Revival implications, present from the first, soon encouraged more and more comprehensive use of eighteenth-century detail, and this supported the general tendency of the mid eighties in America away from the irregular and towards more formal order (see Chapter 13) Something of this change could be seen in Richardson's latest houses in masonry such as the Glessner house of 1885–7 at 18th Street and South Prairie Avenue in Chicago, which still stands, and the contemporary Mac Veagh house, long since destroyed, also in Chicago, both of which were almost symmetrical as regards their front façades. The most drastic examples, of course, of this Academic Reaction were such houses as McKim, Mead & White's Villard group in New York [193] and their H. A. C. Taylor house in Newport with its formal Anglo-Palladian plan of central hall and four corner rooms. Despite its even tighter plan, however, their W. G. Low house in Bristol, R.I., completed in 1887 – several years after the Neo-Colonial Taylor house – can properly be cited again as a masterpiece of the Shingle Style [225]. This illustrated

225. McKim, Mead & White: Bristol, R.I., W. G. Low house, completed 1887

very well how the loose massing of the houses of the early eighties could be organized into a carefully balanced composition without succumbing to any historical mode of design, whether Italian Renaissance or American Colonial.

Particularly interesting in this connexion are the small houses at Tuxedo Park, N.Y., which Price designed for Pierre Lorillard in 1885-6, some years before he began to build Renaissance skyscrapers (see Chapter 14). Lorillard's own house has a rather tight plan of the Neo-Colonial sort; but the exterior with its paired chimneys on the front, a Richardsonian entrance arch between them, and the verandas and terrace treated as voids carefully related to the

226. Bruce Price:
Tuxedo Park, N.Y., Pierre Lorillard house, 1885-6

227. Bruce Price:
Tuxedo Park, N.Y., William Kent house, 1885-6

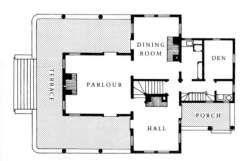

solid mass behind is still in the earlier tradition [226]. In such other houses by Price at Tuxedo as those for William Kent and Travis C. Van Buren, the loose open plans of the immediately preceding years were organized into T and X patterns, and the verandas and terraces were even more formally treated as important elements in compositions made up of well-defined voids and solids [227].

This brings us to the beginning of the career of Frank Lloyd Wright, already introduced as an important coadjutor of Sullivan from 1888 to 1893. Although Wright's mature career begins only about 1900 (see Chapter 19), his apprentice years as a builder of houses provide a very significant episode that is closely related to the earlier story of the nineteenth-century house in England and America. By the late eighties a full-dress Colonial Revival was under way in the East. But it was the particular combination of freedom and order that had been achieved by Richardson in his latest houses, by McKim, Mead & White in their Low house, and by Price in his Tuxedo houses which was the immediate tradition from which Wright's domestic architecture drew far more than from the work of Sullivan.

Born in 1867, Wright had had a little over a year in the Engineering School – there was no architectural school – at the University of Wisconsin when he came to Chicago at the age of twenty in 1887. He first found work in the office of Silsbee whom Wright's uncle Jenkin Lloyd Jones had brought to Chicago a year or two earlier to design All Souls' Unitarian Church, of which he was minister. The young architect's first work, nominally a Silsbee commission, was the Hillside Home School built in 1887 for his aunts near Spring Green, Wisconsin. This was a rather provincial specimen of a Shingle Style house and was later demolished by Wright himself.

Shifting over the following year to the Adler & Sullivan office, Wright by 1889 was married and ready to build a house for himself on the strength of a five-year contract with his new employers. This house, at 428 Forest Avenue in Oak Park, Ill., still extant[20a] but much pulled about, derives almost entirely from Price's cottages at Tuxedo except that the plan is much less formal. In the interior, the wide openings between the rooms are not framed by architraves but seem to have been produced by pulling back the walls beneath the continuous frieze. In this treatment, rather Japanese in concept, Wright would seem to have been influenced by White's handling of the hall of the Newcomb house, even though that is rather oriental also in some of the detailing and Wright's is not.

Wright's next important work is the James Charnley house at 1365 Astor Street in Chicago, built in 1891–2. This was actually a commission of the Adler & Sullivan firm, but one of which he had entire charge. A city house built of tawny Roman brick like that used for the court of the Boston Public Library, this is as formal[21] as anything McKim, Mead & White had yet designed. But there is no High Renaissance or Colonial reminiscence whatever in the external detailing. The Charnley house is rather a conscientious attempt to emulate in a modest three-storey residence the highly original design of Sullivan's newly completed Wainwright Building in St Louis.

Wright was also accepting various private commissions on the side, mostly very small ones, by this time. The George Blossom house of 1892 at 4858 Kenwood Avenue on the south side of Chicago, however, is of more consequence. Externally, this follows rather closely McKim, Mead & White's Taylor house in the curved Ionic entrance porch and the recurrent Palladian windows, not to speak of the use of yellow-painted clapboards and white-painted trim of simplified academic character. Even the plan is for the most part symmetrically ordered. But behind the formal range of entrance lobby and two small corner rooms at the front the

whole centre of the house opens up as a single great living-hall. In this living-hall a wide inglenook is lined up on axis with the entrance, the elaborate staircase rises in several flights across one end, and wide openings connect with the library and the dining room. The dining room, which ends in a curved bay with a continuous window-band, is almost a copy of the original library of Richardson's Sherman house. In another Wright house of 1892, that for A. W. Harlan, also on the south side of Chicago at 4414 Greenwood Avenue, which Sullivan happened to see, he recognized his assistant's hand and this brought about the break between the two before Wright's contract ran out.

When Wright set up for himself in 1893 there were two paths open to him. That he actually considered following the path of Academic Revival, so heavily publicized by the success of the World's Fair, is evident from his project of this year for a Library and Museum in Milwaukee (see Chapter 13). But when Burnham at this point offered to send Wright to Paris to study at the École des Beaux-Arts and then to the new American Academy which he and McKim were planning to start in Rome, in preparation for taking him on as designing partner, the young architect turned the opportunity down.

The W. H. Winslow house of 1893–4 in Auvergne Place in River Forest, Ill., always considered by Wright his 'first', shares many qualities with the Blossom and Harlan houses, but is altogether a much more mature and original work [228]. The front is completely symmetrical and as formal as that of the Charnley house of two years before.[21a] Broad and low, of fine Roman brickwork with a rich band of moulded terracotta the full depth of the upper-storey windows below the wide eaves, the general effect of this has usually been considered very Sullivanian. But as Wright himself was responsible for the Adler

228. Frank Lloyd Wright:
River Forest, Ill., W. H. Winslow house, 1893-4

& Sullivan work that this house most resembles – the Charnley house, certainly; and the Victoria Hotel of 1892 at Chicago Heights, probably – it is more accurate to consider that the Winslow house represents a continuation of his own manner of the previous year or two. The plan is more axial and less open than that of the Blossom house, the still rather Richardsonian dining room with its rounded bay being placed here at the centre of the rear. The stair-case, still so prominent in the Shingle Style way in the Blossom house, is here pushed out of sight between walls.

Wright's next important house, that of 1897 for Isidore Heller at 5132 Woodlawn Avenue on the south side of Chicago, perhaps shows some Japanese[22] influence in the succession of eaves-lines, one above the other. It is the development of the plan, however, that is more significant, as also the effect of the planning

229. Frank Lloyd Wright:
Chicago, Isidore Heller house, 1897

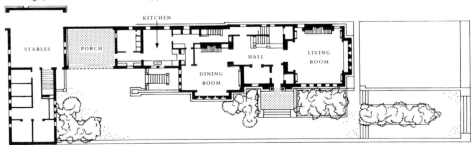

on the treatment of the exterior [229]. The two principal rooms are linked by a modest stair-hall into which they both open through wide apertures – no more mere doorways than in his own house of 1889 but tall breaks in the continuity of the walls. Although these rooms have inglenooks, they are not casual and cosy in the Shingle Style way but carefully ordered; both, indeed, are of regular cruciform shape. These shapes, moreover, are given external expression in the plastic articulation of the external massing, an articulation that the multiple eaves echo above.

Two years later, in the Joseph W. Husser house, now destroyed, in Buena Park on the north side of Chicago, Wright's personal development of domestic planning was carried much farther [230]. Here the main living rooms

the more Richardsonian bays of the Blossom and Winslow dining rooms.

Between the two houses just described, in which Wright's planning developed so rapidly and so boldly towards unified but articulated space, came the River Forest Golf Club in River Forest, Ill. The front wing of this, built in 1898,[23] showed a comparable maturing of his vocabulary of wooden construction. The two Chicago houses were both of brick with rather lush Sullivanian terracotta decoration below the eaves not unlike that on the Schiller Building. At the Golf Club the characteristic feeling of the Shingle Style for rough natural wood surfaces was renewed by Wright and made more architectonic in scale. Below continuous window bands protected by his characteristic hovering eaves, the lower walls and the terrace

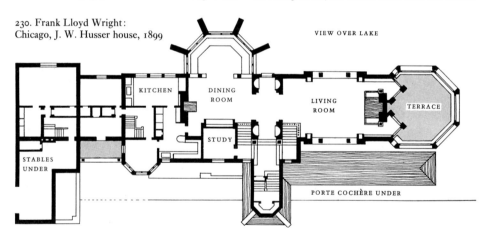

230. Frank Lloyd Wright:
Chicago, J. W. Husser house, 1899

VIEW OVER LAKE

KITCHEN

DINING ROOM

LIVING ROOM

TERRACE

STUDY

STABLES UNDER

PORTE COCHÈRE UNDER

were all raised to the first storey in order to have a good view of Lake Michigan, and the interior space was continued uninterrupted along the main axis of the house from the dining-room fireplace, across the landing, and through to the living-room fireplace. But the dining room was also articulated along a cross axis, extending outward into a large polygonal bay facing the lake, somewhat like

parapets were sheathed with boards and battens, not applied vertically as by Downing but horizontally. Uncovered terrace, covered veranda, glazed foyer, all were closely related spatial areas, the last two unified by the continuous roof. The only solid element was the broad stone chimney marking the point where the main axis and the subsidiary axis of the low side-wings crossed. In 1901 the building

231. Frank Lloyd Wright: River Forest, Ill.,
River Forest Golf Club, 1898, 1901

was much enlarged by Wright, but quite in the original spirit [231].

In 1900, the last year of the nineteenth century, with which this account of Wright's beginnings may properly close, he built two houses side by side in Kankakee, Ill. He also designed for the *Ladies' Home Journal* 'A Home in a Prairie Town' which was published in February, 1901. The larger of the two Kankakee houses, that for B. Harley Bradley at 701 South Harrison Avenue, is a large, loosely cruciform composition with low-pitched gables projecting in blunt points well beyond the ends of the wings. The smaller Hickox house, next door at 687 South Harrison Avenue, has a more advanced plan under similar roofs. Wood stripping suggests the stud structure underneath the stucco of the walls as do also, and rather more directly, the wooden window mullions [232]. The living room here, flanked by semi-octagonal music and dining rooms, extends across the 'garden front' and opens by french doors on to the uncovered terrace [233]. Here the articulated but unified space of the Husser house was reduced in scale and sim-plified until it provided a quite new concept of domestic planning, later to be widely influential internationally (see Chapter 22). Towards that new concept much of the development of the Anglo-American house since as far back as the 1790s may seem – not too exaggeratedly – to have been tending.

The *Ladies' Home Journal* project for a 'House in a Prairie Town', from which the term 'Prairie Houses' for Wright's characteristic production of the next decade derives, is larger than the Hickox house, but the living area was intended to be very similarly unified and articulated. In one version Wright even proposed carrying this space up two storeys in the centre, somewhat like one of Shaw's manorial halls. As on the River Forest Golf Club, the long lines of the low hip roofs shelter very long window-bands – out of Shaw, via Richardson, presumably. Although the *Ladies' Home Journal* house was intended to be stuccoed like the Kankakee houses, the window mullions echo the underlying wooden stud structure. As at the Golf Club, the chimneys would be the only really solid elements, passing up through the crossing

232 and 233. Frank Lloyd Wright:
Kankakee, Ill., Warren Hickox house, 1900

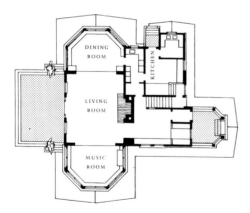

volumes defined by the two levels of roof. The
lower line of eaves extends, somewhat as on
McKim, Mead & White's McCormick house,
over the *porte-cochère* on one side and over the
veranda on the other, a treatment Wright tried
out somewhat clumsily on the Bradley house.

In considering the significance of these
Wright houses of 1900 it must be recognized
that even in America they were highly exceptional. Despite the fact that the 'Prairie house'
project was published in a general magazine of
national circulation, its immediate influence
was very slight indeed. For all the vigour of the
two great Chicago achievements of the nineties,
Sullivan's skyscrapers and Wright's earliest
houses, the main direction of American architecture in 1900 was quite different. So also in
England of these years, where Shaw's house
for Fred White and his Bryanston had introduced by the nineties almost the same sort of
Academic Revival as had McKim, Mead &
White's Villard and Taylor houses, the work
of Voysey, the English architect who was most
comparable to Wright, was also exceptional.

The line of architectural development had already split as sharply as in America, with the difference that the longer-lived Shaw himself had taken the lead in the academic direction that Richardson's pupils, McKim and White, took in America.

Although Charles Francis Annesley Voysey (1857–1941)[24] was ten years older than Wright, it is understandable with English conditions that his architectural career got under way little earlier. From 1874 to 1880 he worked as a pupil in the office of Seddon; from 1880 until he set up for himself in 1882 he was assistant to Devey.[25] In 1883 Voysey sold his first designs for wallpapers and printed fabrics, but for several more years he did little building. His first house, The Cottage at Bishop's Itchington in Warwickshire, was built only in 1888; in the next two years various projects of his, increasingly original in character, were published in the British Architect; of these the one for a house[26] at Doverscourt of 1890 was the most advanced.

By the late eighties Nesfield and Godwin were both dead and leadership in English architecture, particularly as regards the domestic field, rested more firmly than ever in Shaw's hands. The forces of innovation in English art were concentrated in the decorative field, thanks in part to Webb's continuing activities with the Morris firm. But there is some question how well younger men like Voysey really knew Webb's architectural work; almost none of it was published, and some of the best is hidden in remote parts of Scotland and the North of England. The work of A. H. Mackmurdo (1851–1942) was perhaps somewhat better known, but he was much more active with furniture, chintzes, and wallpapers than with building in the eighties. A project for a 'House for an Artist' that he published in his magazine The Hobby Horse in 1888 was of considerable promise, however. In any case Voysey soon rivalled Mackmurdo as a designer of furniture, wallpapers, and chintzes, and quite outclassed him as an architect. Mackmurdo's most significant influence was probably abroad (see Chapter 16).

The existence of an earlier project dated 1888 for Voysey's house for J. W. Forster at Bedford Park has led to some confusion. The executed house dates from 1891. Sometimes known as the Grey House, it is very different indeed from its neighbours, many by this time fifteen or more years old, by Godwin, Shaw, and their pupils. For one thing, its walls are covered with roughcast, already used by Voysey on The Cottage at Bishop's Itchington; for another, it is a three-storey rectangular box, severe and rather formal beneath its low hipped roof, not quaint and irregular like even the simplest of the earlier houses. The casement windows are arranged in bands between stone mullions, regularly but not symmetrically, and the eaves troughs are supported by delicately curved iron brackets. Otherwise there is no external detail.

The plan of the Forster house is also compact and regular, with entrance on the left side and living room across the front. In other words this house represents as much of a reaction against the picturesqueness of the earlier Queen Anne as does Shaw's Fred White house, yet is quite without eighteenth-century reminiscence.[27]

More interesting and more prominent than the contemporary storey-and-a-half house known as The Studio at 17 St Dunstan's Road in West Kensington are a pair of terrace-houses, also designed in 1891 but begun only the next year, at 14–16 Hans Road off the Brompton Road in London. Here Voysey dropped the roughcast he had originally proposed and used Webb-like red brickwork with the windows characteristically arranged in bands between plain stone mullions. The elegantly original detailing of the projecting stone porches and the curved line of the

parapets at the top are related to his contemporary decorative work and in notable contrast
to the almost 'Monumental Queen Anne'
treatment of Mackmurdo's slightly later house
next door at No. 12.

A moderate-sized country house, Perrycroft,
Colwall, near Malvern, begun in 1893, may be
considered Voysey's first mature production,
introducing in executed work the personal
mode of design for which the Ward project of
1890 had already shown the way, and from
which he never moved very far in later years.
This is comparable, not to Wright's 'first'
house in River Forest of the same date, but to
his more advanced work of the end of the
decade, the River Forest Golf Club and the
Hickox house. Roughcast walls, windows arranged in bands between plain mullions,[28] a
regular composition approaching but not quite
reaching symmetry, these all follow from the
Grey House and the Studio. But, being in the
country, the house could spread out more.
Moreover, the roofs were raised to a medieval
pitch – 45 degrees – so that their conspicuously
heavy slating is as much a part of Voysey's
simple craftsman-like mode as are the off-
white roughcast walls. The planning is closer
to Webb's than to Wright's, the rooms being
less symmetrically shaped and not opening at
all into one another as in the Ward project.

A rather larger house, begun in 1896 on the
Hog's Back near Guildford in Surrey for the
American Julian Sturgis, presumptive original
of Santayana's *Last Puritan*, has a somewhat
less balanced composition with a prominent
cross gable near one end [234]. The characteristic stone-mullioned lights of several of the
rooms are here so extensive in their grouping
as to constitute window-walls of the earlier
Shavian sort.

In what is doubtless Voysey's finest work,
Broadleys on Lake Windermere, designed in
1898, the roofs are lower once more, and the
window-walls are concentrated in three rounded bays along the lakeside terrace [235]. Here
the hall in the middle is carried up two storeys,
quite as Wright would propose in one version
of his first *Ladies Home Journal* house [236].
In its horizontality, its concentration of fenestration, and its avoidance of medieval feeling, this
house represents the extreme point of innovation
and originality in Voysey's work.

His own house, The Orchard at Chorley
Wood in Hertfordshire, was completed in
1900. Externally this resembles closely his
earlier houses, but The Orchard has two
cross gables and hence a stronger feeling of
symmetry. Towards this the more regular and
carefully balanced spacing of the window
bands further conduces. In studying the

234. C. F. A. Voysey:
Hog's Back, Surrey, Julian Sturgis house, 1896

vocabulary of this house, a vocabulary destined to be parodied *ad infinitum* by architects and then by builders in the next twenty-five years, one can understand his feeling that he was a reformer not an innovator – the last disciple of Pugin, so to say, to whose secular work a line can be traced back via Webb, Street, and Butterfield. In Voysey's special sense of continuity, which grew on him in later years, lies his great difference from Wright; for Wright was certainly determined, from the time he designed the Winslow house, to be as great an innovator – as much of an architectural creator – as was Sullivan in his skyscrapers. None the less, to look forward a little, such a house by Voysey as that now called Little Court at Pyrford Common in Surrey, built in 1902, is quite worthy of comparison with Wright's masterpieces of that year (see Chapter 19). It shows little further development beyond his houses of the late nineties, however, except for a certain increase in horizontal emphasis.

Just before and just after 1900, Voysey's work was very much better known and more influential in England, and increasingly in other countries,[29] than was Wright's either at home or abroad at that time. Moreover, many

235 and 236. C. F. A. Voysey: Lake Windemere, Broadleys, 1898-9

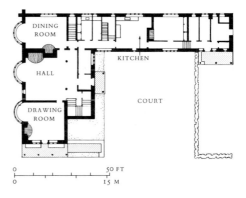

contemporaries in England were building rather similar houses. One of them, M. H. Baillie Scott (1865–1945), who also worked a good deal on the Continent, developed his planning much farther in the direction of Wright-like openness along the lines suggested by Voysey's project of 1890 for the Ward house. The many houses, both executed and projected, that Baillie Scott published in *Houses and Gardens* in 1906 made his planning known to the young architects of the Continent [237].

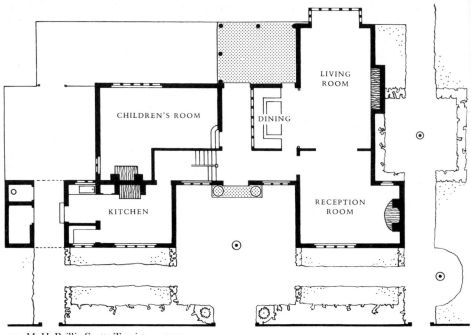

237. M. H. Baillie Scott: Trevista, c. 1905

Characteristic is his Blackwell house on Lake Windermere of about 1900 with an enormous two-storey living-hall elaborated spatially by various inglenooks and so forth. The plan was published by Muthesius in 1904, and may well have influenced Adolf Loos in Vienna and other Europeans even before his own book appeared (see Chapters 20 and 21). After 1906 Baillie Scott's work became quite Neo-Georgian, and it is hard to believe that the projects published in the later version of his *Houses and Gardens* in 1933 are by the same man.

The name of W. R. Lethaby (1857-1931), later the biographer of Webb and an influential writer on architecture, should also be at least mentioned here. When Lethaby left Shaw's office, where he had been chief assistant, he began his career by building Avon Tyrrell in Hampshire in 1891, a large brick country

house closer to Webb's than to Shaw's in character. But his main contribution was not in the field of domestic architecture.[29a]

Already by the mid nineties, the most successful English house-builder, more than rivalling Voysey in the quantity and occasionally even in the quality of his domestic work, was Sir Edwin L. Lutyens (1869-1944). Beginning like Voysey in the late eighties by building cottages, his first house of real distinction was the one he built for his cousin and frequent collaborator, the garden-designer Gertrude Jekyll, at Munstead Wood near Godalming in 1896. Several other good houses followed shortly, including notably The Orchards, Godalming, in 1898; but this early period of his work really culminates in Deanery Gardens at Sonning in Berkshire of 1901 [341]. In these houses are preserved all the best of the Shavian

Manorial – the great timber-framed bay-window of the two-storeyed hall at Deanery Gardens is exemplary – simplifying and regularizing that mode under the influence of Webb and even approaching Webb's standards of craftsmanship in the execution.

Like Webb in his later work, Lutyens used almost from the first a good deal of stylistic detail in interiors; he also turned towards the Neo-Georgian in his exteriors considerably earlier than Baillie Scott when designing such houses as Overstrand Hall in Norfolk and Tigbourne Court at Witley in Surrey, both built in 1899 two years before Deanery Gardens. Lutyens became from about 1906 the leading architect of his generation in England, and his later work will be treated elsewhere (see Chapter 24). His increasing material success after the opening years of the century, rivalling Shaw's in the previous generation, is to a certain extent the measure, though not the cause, of Voysey's decline in popularity.

C. R. Ashbee (1863–1942) and George Walton (1867–1933)[30] were other domestic architects active in the nineties and the early years of the new century. The latter belongs to the Glasgow School, of which Mackintosh was the principal figure, and like Mackintosh he was more decorator than architect (see Chapter 17). One house in England, The Leys at Elstree of 1901, may be mentioned here. The interiors are fine examples of the Arts and Crafts mode, as it is usually called, more stylized than Voysey's but less original than Mackintosh's. The plan is organized symmetrically around a large two-storey hall rivalling Baillie Scott's of the period in its complex spatial development.

Ashbee was one of the first Europeans to appreciate the significance of Wright, and was appropriately chosen by Wasmuth to write the introduction to his second publication of Wright's work in 1911 (see Chapter 19). Three houses by Ashbee side by side in Cheyne Walk in London, No. 37 of 1894 and Nos 38–39 of 1904, represented the chronological span of his significant architectural production and illustrated clearly his characteristic progress from the Shavian to an originality at least comparable to Voysey's.[30a] Closely associated with the Arts and Crafts Exhibition Society, Ashbee was like most of these men except Voysey[31] and Lutyens generally more active in the field of decorative art than in building. Right through this period English decorative art exercised a major influence on the Continent (see Chapters 16 and 17). So close is Mackintosh's tie with the Continent that his schools and even his houses are better discussed in relation to the Art Nouveau.

Of all these English architects who have just been mentioned, Voysey was the most creative in the field of domestic architecture and, except for Lutyens, the most productive down at least through the early years of the twentieth century; after 1910 he built almost nothing at all. Yet Voysey did not die until 1941, by which time a younger generation, to his confusion, had accepted him as one 'father' of a modern architecture that he disapproved as strongly as did Lutyens. In 1940 he returned almost from the grave to receive the Gold Medal of the Royal Institute of British Architects.

From the Picturesque cottages of the opening decades of the nineteenth century to the early masterpieces of Wright and Voysey around 1900 is a far cry, further perhaps in the drastic revision that it represented of so old-established a building type as the dwelling-house than from Parris's Market Street buildings in Boston of 1824 to Sullivan's Carson, Pirie & Scott Store in Chicago as completed eighty years later in 1904. Yet in Anglo-American domestic architecture, quite as was the case with commercial architecture, real achievement recurred all through the century.

PART THREE

1890-1955

CHAPTER 16

THE BEGINNINGS OF THE ART NOUVEAU: VICTOR HORTA

The two preceding chapters, in entering the nineties, crossed what is perhaps the major historical frontier within the two centuries covered by this book. The skyscrapers of Sullivan and the early houses of Wright and Voysey – despite Voysey's own disavowal of modernism – are among the first major manifestations of the period of architectural history that extends down towards our actual present.[1] The contemporaries of these men who were the new leaders on the Continent in the nineties had as sharp a sense of the novelty of the innovations they were making as did Sullivan or Wright, and the most characteristic stylistic formulation of this decade in Europe was appropriately known from an early date[1a] as 'Art Nouveau'. Before discussing the Art Nouveau itself, two related developments that precede it must be considered at least briefly. In France, various feats of metal construction of the sixties, seventies, and eighties had prepared the way for the Art Nouveau on the technical side, and these have, moreover, considerable intrinsic interest in their own right. English innovations in decorative art of the eighties and early nineties are accepted by most historians as perhaps the most important immediate sources of the Art Nouveau,[2] and English architecture and architectural theory of the later decades of the nineteenth century certainly offered a generic stimulus to Europeans between 1890

and 1910 that was of vital consequence to subsequent developments. The channels for this British influence can be documented.

By the early nineties advanced English work had begun to be well known on the Continent. From 1888 the German architect Alexander Koch (1848–1911) was publishing annually his *Academy Architecture* to bring current English production, and many significant projects also, to the attention of designers abroad. *L'Architecture moderne en Angleterre* by the French architect Paul Sédille (1836–1900) appeared in Paris in 1890. The architect Hermann Muthesius (1861–1927), who was stationed at the German Embassy in London from 1896 to 1903 primarily to study low-cost housing, issued two folio volumes devoted to *Die englische Baukunst der Gegenwart* in 1900–2, another on *Die neuere kirchliche Baukunst in England* in 1902 and, in 1904–5, three thick quarto volumes on *Das englische Haus*. These richly illustrated books made much of the story of the development of English architecture in the second half of the century available in German long before it was pieced together by the English (see Chapters 12 and 15).

Voysey never worked abroad; but his houses, known internationally from an early date thanks to their publication in the *Studio*, an English periodical founded in 1893, were soon much studied on the Continent, and to a lesser extent in America. Voysey's contemporaries Baillie Scott and Charles Rennie Mackintosh (1868-1928), however, received several foreign commissions from as early as 1898; Mackintosh and his highly original ideas – he was no Voyseyan 'reformer' but a very bold innovator – received more support abroad than at home and were more influential on the Continent than in Great Britain.

Historians of modern architecture have generally emphasized, and rightly, the special importance of the advances in metal construction[3] that were made in France in the later decades of the nineteenth century. The great name of the period is not that of an architect but of an engineer, Gustave Eiffel (1832-1923). At the International Exhibition of 1855 in Paris and again at the World's Fair of 1893 in Chicago the vast metal-and-glass structures were masked externally by real or imitated masonry façades. Between these dates, however, came a series of French exhibition buildings that were increasingly bold in scale and frank in design; with the construction of most of them Eiffel was directly concerned. Yet his bridge over the Douro at Oporto in Portugal of 1876-7 quite overshadowed the Galerie des Machines that he and Krantz built for the Paris Exhibition of 1867, as his later Pont de Garabit of 1880-4 outclassed the pavilions that he designed for the Exhibition of 1878 and that portion of the Bon Marché Department Store on which he collaborated in 1876 with the younger Boileau. In the exhibition buildings the metal-work was completely exposed and in that of 1878[4] a serious attempt was made to develop appropriate embellishments, quite as Wyatt had done for Brunel at Paddington Station in London twenty-five years earlier. The rather tawdry result helps to explain why innovations in architectural design had so little public support in France in this period – a period when the bold innovations of the Impressionists were revolutionizing another art in Paris.

Beside Eiffel's gallery, the 'Anglo-Japanese' room[5] which Whistler and Godwin showed at this same exhibition must have seemed infinitely sophisticated, and even the Late Stuart detailing of the cement-brick front of Shaw's Jury House most agreeably urbane. Such things might well have turned the attention of foreign architects towards England earlier than was generally the case. Sédille, one of the less tradition-bound French professionals of this period, did visit England in the eighties, publishing his book on current English architecture, which has just been mentioned, ten years before Muthesius's. His selections, however, were not very discriminating, nor is there evidence that he profited much from what he saw. The Printemps department store of 1881-9, which was designed well before his trip, certainly shows no English influence.

For the Paris Exhibition of 1889[6] Eiffel early proposed and, in 1887, was commissioned to build the tremendous all-metal tower[7] which still dominates Paris [238]. As has been noted, this 984-foot edifice was, down to the erection of the Empire State Building in New York by Shreve, Lamb & Harmon more than forty years later, the tallest structure in the world. The Eiffel Tower, which appropriately carries its designer's name, is no more a building in the ordinary sense than are his great bridges, however. Although scraping so much higher skies than did Holabird & Roche's Tacoma Building in Chicago, which was erected in precisely the same years, the Paris tower was far less significant either technically or functionally. Except the painter Seurat, most contemporaries disliked it, considering it a monstrous blemish on the Parisian skyline; today, of course, it is rightly deemed a nineteenth-century masterpiece, but a masterpiece of engineering rather than of architecture.

As with Eiffel's pavilion at the Exhibition of 1878, there is considerable ambiguity in the design of the Eiffel Tower. Seen from a distance

238. Gustave Eiffel: Paris, Eiffel Tower, 1887-9

however, the arbitrarily arched forms that link the legs are very conspicuous and also the coarse ornamentation of curvilinear strapwork – recalling a little Wyatt's at Paddington Station of nearly forty years before, but much less just in scale – with which the basic forms are bedecked. The close similarity of this mixture of frank construction and applied decoration to the Art Nouveau approach to the design of metal structures will shortly become evident. Over-impressed, perhaps, by the more functional engineering feat of construction at the 1889 Exhibition provided by the wide-spanned metal-and-glass Palais des Machines of the engineers Contamin (1840-93), Pierron, and Charton – in which the contribution of the associated architect C.-L.-F. Dutert (1845-1906) was relatively unimportant – certain later critics have preferred that structure to the Eiffel Tower. Yet it is the tower which clearly has more of the magnificence of Eiffel's bridges despite its irrelevant and (from a distance) almost invisible ornamentation. The tower, moreover, is premonitory of the Art Nouveau; the Galerie des Machines rather of later modern architecture (see Chapters 20 and 22).

One other line of innovation in France in these decades deserves mention. In 1871 Jules Saulnier built a factory for Chocolat Menier near Paris at Noisiel, S.-et-M., with an exposed metal skeleton. The iron frame consists of diagonally set members rather similar to the late medieval timber-framing of France, and the infilling of the panels is of varicoloured bricks and tiles. This structure attracted the attention of Viollet-le-Duc, who saw in it a realization of certain of his theoretical ambitions for nineteenth-century architecture. He not only mentioned it very favourably in the second volume of his *Entretiens*, which appeared in 1872, but had already suggested similar and variant combinations of iron and masonry. In a colour plate,[7b] for example, he showed a striking urban façade with its visible iron

its four legs have much of the vigorous spring of his bridges and the tapered shaft of crisscrossed metalwork seems – but in fact is not – an almost inevitable expression of large-scale construction in metal.[7a] Seen from nearer to,

framework filled with brilliantly coloured glazed tiles. By the nineties quite a few buildings in France had exploited very successfully this structural system;[8] it is perhaps more important, however, that Viollet-le-Duc's text and illustrations made the idea familiar internationally.

When one learns that Horta or Gaudí or various Americans 'read Viollet-le-Duc' in the seventies and eighties one must assume that the *Entretiens*, of which the first volume appeared in 1863, is meant – and perhaps even more specifically the accompanying plates mentioned in the previous paragraph. These last could be 'read' by architects to particularly good purpose. The *Entretiens* were available to most Europeans in the original language and to the English and the Americans in translation.[9]

The characteristic employment of metal by Art Nouveau architects in the nineties and the first decade of this century undoubtedly owed a great deal both to the inspiration of Eiffel's large engineering structures, culminating in his tower of 1887-9, and to the vigorous critical support of Saulnier's ideas which Viollet-le-Duc provided, not to speak of the related projects of his own that he published. The knot is tied tighter – although with a different sort of structural development – when one notes that de Baudot, of all French architects most particularly the disciple and heir of Viollet-le-Duc as well as a former pupil of Henri Labrouste, was the first to exploit ferro-concrete architecturally and not merely technically (see Chapter 18). Moreover, he employed as contractor to construct his epoch-making concrete church of Saint-Jean-de-Montmartre in Paris of the nineties (see Chapter 17), Contamin, one of the engineers responsible for the Galerie des Machines at the Exhibition of 1889. But the European Art Nouveau was even less a matter of structural innovation, pure and simple, than Sullivan's contemporary skyscrapers in America (see Chapter 14).

This brief and curious episode in the history of art,[10] starting in the early nineties and subsiding little more than a decade later, has always been called in English by a French name, perhaps because it never became acclimatized in England but was always considered a dubious import from Belgium and France. Despite the diffidence of the English – which the Americans also shared – the Art Nouveau was an international mode. It was most usually called in France by the English name 'Modern Style', while to the Germans it was 'Jugendstil' and to the Italians 'stile Liberty'. The German term comes from the magazine *Jugend*, whose illustrations and typography were fairly consistently in the new mode; the Italian from Liberty's, the shop in London whose orientalizing fabrics became widely popular at this time (but with overtones from the obvious pun involved). In Italian it is also, and much more descriptively, the 'stile floreale'.

The Art Nouveau is not primarily an architectural mode. Yet many of the finest and boldest large edifices built between 1890 and 1910, however, beginning with Sullivan's skyscrapers, are certainly related to its ethos; and the Art Nouveau leaders produced quite a few buildings of real distinction that can be defined by no other term. Like the Rococo of the early and mid eighteenth century – which the Art Nouveau sometimes closely resembled and to whose revived forms it was often vulgarly assimilated – it was most successful as a mode of interior decoration. Generally linear rather than plastic,[11] the Art Nouveau was also very closely associated with the graphic arts; indeed they provide many of the most characteristic examples, as well as the earliest items that can be considered possible prototypes.

How far back the ultimate sources of the Art Nouveau should be sought, and precisely where, has long been a subject of active research. In the graphic arts there are certainly significant similarities to be noted in William

Blake's[12] way of designing book pages. Through the Pre-Raphaelites, moreover, a line of descent from Blake can be traced down to the eighties and nineties when, indeed, his characteristic pages were sometimes reproduced in facsimile. But oriental,[13] specifically Japanese, influence certainly played some part also in the gestation of the mode. There is early evidence of that influence on western architecture in the decorative work of Godwin and Nesfield in England, beginning already in the sixties, as also in the painting of the Impressionists in France (see Chapters 10 and 12). But the earliest designs that can be readily mistaken for Continental work of 1900 are certainly by the English architect-decorator Mackmurdo and date from just after 1880. Many of the textile and wallpaper patterns that Mackmurdo, Heywood Sumner (1853-1940), and others created for the Century Guild, founded in 1882, already have the characteristic semi-naturalistic[14] forms, swaying lines, and asymmetrical organization of the mature decorative mode of the nineties. Even more striking is the design of Mackmurdo's title-page of 1883 for his book on the London churches of Sir Christopher Wren[15] a curious conjunction, this, of two opposed stylistic developments of the eighties, the one towards the Baroque and the 'Monumental Queen Anne', the other towards a wholly novel mode of ornamentation.

English products, such as were shown by the Arts and Crafts Exhibition Society from its foundation in 1888, soon reached the Continent. Moreover, even before the *Studio* began publication in 1893 Koch's *Academy Architecture* (from 1888), which has already been mentioned, and (from 1890) his review *Innendekoration*, as well as less specialized English magazines such as (from 1884) Mackmurdo's *Hobby Horse* and (from 1891) *The Yellow Book*, with its highly stylized and very curvilinear illustrations by Aubrey Beardsley, were eagerly studied all over western Europe. The younger men were reading William Morris, too, and responding enthusiastically to his ethical and social demands for a reform of the household arts. At the same time the novel styles of certain of the Post-Impressionist painters, especially Munch and Toorop, offered a stimulus to architects.

This matter of the relationship between advanced painting and advanced architecture in the nineteenth century, a relationship destined to be of rather greater importance in the early twentieth, deserves some broader comment and recapitulation here. A hundred and fifty years before, when Romantic Classicism was being born in Rome, painters, sculptors, and architects shared common ideals and worked with a full understanding of each other's problems (see Chapter 1). The backgrounds of David's bas-relief-like early paintings show architecture in the most advanced taste of the day, and no more beautiful Romantic Classical furniture was actually produced than that which he invented for his Classical scenes and occasionally introduced in his modern portraits. The Classical sculptor Thorwaldsen at the Glyptothek in Munich and later at the Thorwaldsen Museum in Copenhagen collaborated closely with the architects Klenze and Bindesbøll. Schinkel was himself a Romantic painter of some distinction before he matured as a Romantic Classical architect, and he collaborated later on the mural for the front of the Altes Museum with the painter Peter Cornelius, as did Klenze on the decorations of the Glyptothek in Munich.

With the gradual decline of Romantic Classicism architects and painters had more difficulty in developing parallel programmes; and the results of collaboration between them in the decoration of buildings were rarely as happy as the backgrounds the architects sometimes supplied to the painters. Ingres's stained-glass windows of the forties in the Chapelle d'Orléans at Dreux and the Chapelle Saint-Ferdinand at Neuilly have been mentioned. More successful are the murals by Delacroix in Joly's library at the Chambre des Deputés in Paris; but there is hardly that real visual harmony between picture and setting that the previous period had often achieved. However, the rising interest in architectural polychromy and the extension of the range of acceptable stylistic models to include the Early Renaissance and even the Middle Ages were both encouraged by the turn that the art of painting was beginning to take on the Continent around 1815. Hübsch, for example, was a sort of Nazarener among architects. Later Ingres was a close friend of Hittorff, even though he never collaborated with him to any good purpose (see Chapter 3), much less with Viollet-le-Duc, with whom he was also on good terms. The degree of stylization that Early Christian, Romanesque, or Gothic architectural modes properly demanded was not yet acceptable in figural art. Indeed, the rather *quattrocento* early pictures of Ingres were much too 'Gothic' for most of his comtemporaries and are generally less esteemed than his more Classical work even today.

Above all, the ever-rising importance of landscape in the painting of all countries was necessarily without real parallels in architecture, except in so far as the increasing desire to open up houses towards the circumambient view reflects a similar preoccupation with the natural scene. As to Realism, the principal artistic movement of the mid century in French art, that could only be echoed in architectural theory. Impressionism is even more difficult to relate to architecture.[16]

In England in the fifties, however, a loose alliance did exist between the new Pre-Raphaelite painters and some of the leading High Victorian Gothic architects, both supported for a time by the critic Ruskin. In the sixties and seventies Morris on the one hand, developing as a decorator out of the Pre-

Raphaelite *milieu* of Rossetti and Ford Madox Brown, and Whistler on the other hand, chiefly nurtured in the advanced artistic world of Paris but also influenced in England by Rossetti, collaborated closely with architects – Morris with Webb and with Bodley, Whistler with Godwin. As has been noted, the strikingly novel results of the latter collaboration were displayed in Paris in their 'Anglo-Japanese' room at the Exhibition of 1878. Europeans became generally aware of Morris's decorative work only somewhat later it would appear.

In France in these decades fewer painters than in England commissioned talented individualists of the order of Shaw or Webb or Godwin to build their houses.[17] If they were Realists or Impressionists they could not have afforded to do so; if they were prosperous Academicians they would not have wished to. Even in England, Millais, after he became really successful, preferred to build a dull house in South Kensington of quite conventional character rather than to employ Shaw or Webb or Godwin.

In the eighties the most advanced European painters, not merely those of France but more generally, turned away from Realism and even from Impressionism in order to concern themselves more with pattern or with expression. The two French leaders of this reaction whose art seems to posterity most architectonic, Cézanne and Seurat, did not affect architecture or design at this time at all. Even Van Gogh and Gauguin, whose styles have a more decorative inflection, were less influential than such almost forgotten painters as the Dutch Toorop and the Belgian Khnopff, the better-known Belgian Ensor, or the Swiss Hodler and the Norwegian Munch, not to speak of the English Beardsley.

The general admiration in *avant-garde* circles for the work of these artists – with which went paradoxically a continuing and even growing estimation of the anti-architectonic pictures of the Impressionists and Neo-Impressionists

both French and native – ran parallel everywhere with the rapid rise and spread of the Art Nouveau. In some sense, indeed, the Art Nouveau may be considered the equivalent as a mode of design of what is somewhat ambiguously called Impressionism in music – the work of Debussy, Delius, etc. Some of the chief critical supporters of the new painters in the nineties such as Julius Meier-Graefe were also active proponents of the Art Nouveau. Yet advanced painting, in fact, provided little more than a sympathetic atmosphere for the birth of the Art Nouveau, somewhat as the young painters and critics of the third quarter of the eighteenth century had done in Rome for the gestation of Romantic Classicism in architecture.

Why the Art Nouveau should have been initiated full-fledged by Victor Horta (1861–1947)[18] in Brussels in 1892 remains a mystery. The rather similar stylistic crystallization in Sullivan's architectural ornament, henceforth almost equally organic and sinuous in character, had begun several years earlier even before the interiors of the Auditorium were designed in 1887–8. These will hardly have been known in Belgium, for few foreigners were aware of Sullivan's work at all until they came to Chicago to visit the World's Fair in 1893. Illustrations of the remarkable ironwork on Gaudí's Palau Güell in Barcelona are not likely to have reached Brussels either, though several of its interiors were published in *The Decorator and Furnisher* in New York in 1892. In any case Gaudí's ultimate style was only beginning to take form in the early nineties. A certain amount of quite original decoration was being done in New York from the beginning of the eighties by Louis Comfort Tiffany (1848–1933),[19] but it is unlikely that it was known abroad. Tiffany's 'Favrile' glass came a good deal later and is precisely contemporaneous with the international Art Nouveau, of which it continued to be for a decade and more one of the most distinguished products.

It is generally assumed that Horta knew the rather similar glass designed earlier by Émile Gallé (1846–1904) in France and that he already had some familiarity with the work of such painters as Ensor, Khnopff, and Toorop, if not with that of Hodler, Munch, or Beardsley. Yet such familiarity would hardly by itself have counterbalanced the academic training he received from his master and later employer Balat (see Chapter 9). This explains, however, the still Classical character of his Temple des Passions Humaines, erected in 1884 in the Parc du Cinquantenaire in Brussels. Horta did no building on his own between 1885 and 1892. Presumably, however, it was knowledge of the theories and the projects of Viollet-le-Duc acquired in those years that encouraged him to make frank and expressive use of iron in association with masonry when he really began to practise. Yet the influence of Viollet-le-Duc hardly provides an explanation for the specific character of his innovations in ornament or the consistency of style that he achieved almost at once.

Against such rather negative assumptions, a more positive one may be set. In the Tassel house in Brussels, completed in 1893, Horta's first mature work, he introduced an English[20] wallpaper between the exposed metal structural elements of the dining-room walls. It is highly likely, therefore, that the new English decorative products were already known to him the previous year[21] when he designed and began this epoch-making house.

The Tassel house at 6 Rue Paul-Émile Janson, just off the Avenue Louise, initiated a new architectural mode as definitely as one modest terrace-house could possibly do. How long before 1892, when the Tassel house was begun, Horta may have been designing on paper in this way does not seem to be known. When one considers how important the innumerable projects of the mid and later eighteenth century are to our understanding of

the architectural revolution that established Romantic Classicism as the successor to the Baroque, the absence of such clues concerning the gestation of the Art Nouveau is most exasperating; but considerable research by students of the period has so far brought little that seems relevant to light.

In plan there are no very great novelties in the Tassel house, although the interior partitions of the principal floor are bent to give varying shapes and sizes to symmetrically disposed spaces that open rather freely into one another. The major innovation lay in the frank expression of metal structure and in the characteristic decoration, particularly that of the stair-hall [239]. There at the foot of the stair an iron column rises free and svelte out of which iron bands branch at the top, like vines from the trunk of a sapling, to form brackets under the curved openwork beams of iron above. Other lighter and less structural bands interlace to form the stair-rail. The organic, swaying, and interweaving lines of the metalwork, both structural and decorative, were originally rather boldly echoed in purely ornamental curvilinear decoration painted on the walls, and they are still so echoed in the patterns of the extant floor mosaic.

These patterns in the stair-hall are each unique, not repeated like those on the English chintzes and wallpapers they so much resemble. The lines, whether moving freely in space like those of the ironwork, painted on the curved wall, or inlaid in the flat floor plane, all form part of complex organic motifs. The result is therefore more comparable to Mackmurdo's title-page of 1883, or even to some of the repoussé brasswork on his furniture. (Like the very few buildings Mackmurdo designed, this furniture is quite rectilinear otherwise, it might

be noted.) During the brief life of the Art Nouveau hardly even Horta himself, much less those who followed in his footsteps, achieved an ensemble more exemplary than this stair-hall. It is truly a work of interior architecture, not merely a matter of applied decoration as is most of the ornament used in association with the English wallpaper in the dining-room.

The façade of the house is much less striking than the interiors. However, the linear curves of the internal structural elements are reflected plastically, so to say, in the bowing forward of the entire central window area. This is so extensive as to approach, but not to equal, English window-walls of the preceding decades. In the upper storeys the lights in this broad bay-window are subdivided only by iron colonnette-mullions and topped with exposed iron beams. There is no archaeological reminiscence of any past style here; yet it must have been from local stucco-work of the Rococo period that Horta drew the inspiration for his carved stone detail. It certainly does not derive either from England or from Viollet-le-Duc. Horta was, and continued to be, much less happy in devising such plastic ornament than in his metalwork; but he felt obliged to apply it here and there on capitals, cornices, brackets, and so forth, just as conventional architects of the time used the common coin of the Renaissance or Gothic vocabularies.

The Tassel façade may be almost unnoticeable today unless one looks carefully for its exposed metalwork and its rather original detailing, but it evidently had an almost instant appeal in the Brussels of the nineties. The somewhat similar Frison house at 37 Rue Lebeau was built in 1893-4, and in 1895 three more houses were begun, of which the finest is the much larger Hôtel Solvay at 224 Avenue Louise.[22] This house was built, together with a laboratory started a year later, over a period of several years for the famous chemist Ernest Solvay. It remains the most complete of Horta's

239. Baron Victor Horta:
Brussels, Tassel house, 1892-3

domestic commissions, since it retains all the original furniture designed by the architect, though long a *maison de couture*. The broad façade is much more plastic than that of the Tassel house with the walls curving forward in the first and second storeys to enframe two tall flanking bays subdivided by metal colonnettes and transoms [240]. The ironwork of the balconies is especially rich and characteristic. In the interiors the exposed metal structure and various elaborate incidental features, such as the lighting fixtures, participate fully in the

240. Baron Victor Horta:
Brussels, Solvay house, 1895–1900

general pattern of organic curvature. Although plant-like in feeling, Horta's metalwork is quite as abstract as Gaudí's grilles in the entrance arches of the Palau Güell [175] and often achieves a comparable distinction considered as craftsmanship.

The house of Baron Van Eetvelde of 1895 at 4 Avenue Palmerston – the extension to the left numbered 2 is considerably later – has a quite different exterior from the Solvay house. The front has an almost Sullivanian range of arched bays consisting entirely of exposed metalwork. Inside, the salon is even more of a masterpiece than the stair-hall of the Tassel house. A circle of iron columns, curving up into elliptical arches, supports a low dome of glass across which long leaf-like bands of transparent colour continue the sinuous structural curves below. In a happy floral metaphor the lighting fixtures bend and droop, each electric bulb shaded by a coloured glass bell of over-blown tulip shape. Not since Nicholas Pineau developed the *pittoresque* version of the Rococo in the second quarter of the eighteenth century had such elegant consistency and originality been seen in the decorative exploitation of plant-like elements.

Horta's other fine houses in Brussels range in date down to the Wiener house of 1919 in the Avenue de l'Astronomie. After the very elegant and restrained Hallet house of 1906 at 346 Avenue Louise they became so dry and so formal that the term Art Nouveau hardly applies to them, however. There are two much earlier examples at 23–25 Rue Américaine, begun in 1898, which are of special interest because Horta occupied them himself. The virtuoso elaboration of the interwoven structural and decorative ironwork of the oriel on the one to the left and the continuous ribbon-window set behind iron mullions in the top storey of the other are among the most striking and original external features he ever designed. These years around the end of the century un-

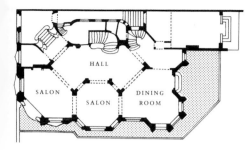

241. Baron Victor Horta:
Brussels, Aubecq house, 1900

242. Baron Victor Horta:
Brussels, Maison du Peuple, interior, 1896-9

There the flow of space between the several interlocking octagonal reception rooms of the ground storey comes very close to that found in certain early houses by Wright (see Chapters 15 and 19).

Certainly Horta's most important single work was the Maison du Peuple of 1896-9,[22a] built for the city authorities of Brussels on a curiously-shaped site of which Horta took the fullest advantage. Extending around a segment of a circular *place* and part way along two radial streets, the façade formed a continuous but

doubtedly represent the peak of his career. His most advanced domestic planning was to be seen in the Aubecq house of 1900 at 520 Avenue Louise, demolished in 1950 [241].

irregular series of curves, mostly concave, but with the main entrance placed in one of the shorter convex portions. The greater part of the exterior wall consisted of a visible skeleton of iron with solid masonry sections defining the ends and the entrance bay. The vertical stanchions were not curved, but many of the horizontal members were slightly arched. Decorative metal elements at some of the intersections attempted, not altogether successfully, to give to the structural grid the over-all organic quality so happily achieved in the Van Eetvelde entrance hall. As in his houses, Horta had difficulty in assimilating the carved detail of the stonework, here associated with wall panels of brick, to the metalwork; where the two came close together, as in the entrance arch of mixed materials, the result was rather awkward.

Comparison with Sullivan's work of these years is inevitable - there is really nothing else of the precise period with which the Maison du Peuple can properly be compared. With Sullivan the main structural members of metal are always covered with terracotta and the visible metalwork is almost entirely decorative. Yet there is considerable similarity in the way Sullivan handled the metal mullions at the entrances of the Carson, Pirie & Scott Store, mullions which rise into and interweave with the ornament above, to Horta's attempt to merge the structural and the decorative in his framework of visible metal elements here.

His greatest success at this was certainly in the auditorium at the top of the Maison du Peuple. In this the openwork iron beams that supported the roof, forming a sort of hammerbeam system with the side galleries, had graceful and expressive but essentially structural curves [242]. To these the decorative railings of the galleries provided a delicate and harmonious counterpoint in their intricately plantlike detailing. Around the structural frame the auditorium was enclosed only by glass or by very thin panels held in metal frames, rather like the 'curtain-walls' of the mid twentieth century; thus there was in this permanent edifice a good deal of the volumetric lightness previously associated with temporary exhibi-

tion buildings only. It was, most unfortunately, demolished in 1967.

Among Horta's commercial buildings in various Belgian cities the most conspicuous was the Innovation department store of 1901 in the Rue Neuve in Brussels [243]. The front, almost entirely of metal and glass though set in a granite frame, was a remarkable example of Art Nouveau decorative design at fully architectural scale. The Innovation completely overshadowed the equally bold but extremely coarse

243. Baron Victor Horta:
Brussels, A l'Innovation Department Store, 1901

and clumsy Old England Department Store just off the Place Royale in Brussels, also almost entirely of iron and glass, that was built by Paul Saintenoy (1832-92) considerably earlier. In the Gros Waucquez Building in the Rue de Sable of 1903-5 and the Wolfers Building of 1906 in the Rue d'Arenberg, as in his houses of those later years, Horta's treatment is much more restrained than in the department store. Stone piers subdivide their façades, curves are fewer and more structural, and there is much less ornament and almost no exposed iron.

It is a historical paradox that Horta's architectural career should have continued long after the Art Nouveau was forgotten, bringing him in the end such public esteem and material success as few other innovators of his generation ever knew. Yet his later work, beginning with his Palais des Beaux-Arts in Brussels, designed in 1914 just before the First World War but begun only in 1923, and continuing down to his Central Station there, begun in 1938 and only lately completed, is of purely local significance. What brought him a peerage and a street named after him – that at the side of his Palais des Beaux-Arts – was not his early work of the Art Nouveau years, standing with Sullivan's skyscrapers like a landmark at the beginning of modern architecture, but this later official work which is almost totally without intrinsic interest and, in the case of the station, actually rather monstrous. The contrast with Sullivan's barren later years after 1904 is very striking.

Despite the poetic justice that there might be in ignoring a Belgian who long falsely claimed the credit for the invention of the Art Nouveau, one cannot turn to other countries without mentioning the name of Henri Van de Velde (1863-1957).[23] In 1892, when Horta designed the Tassel house, Van de Velde had not even begun to practise architecture. His first work, which is his own house of 1895-6 at Uccle near Brussels, though still rather conventional externally in a simple, almost peasant way perhaps influenced by Voysey, included furniture more functional than Horta's, if much less elegant and imaginative. He also brought to Brussels – and later to Paris, Berlin, and Weimar – an interpretation of Ruskin's and Morris's sociological approach to the arts that had a wide and growing influence, for he pursued his mature career as decorator, architect, and educator largely outside Belgium[24] (see Chapters 17 and 20).

CHAPTER 17

THE SPREAD OF THE ART NOUVEAU:

THE WORK OF C. R. MACKINTOSH AND ANTONI GAUDÍ

The initiation of the Art Nouveau by Horta in 1892 was sudden and its spread extremely rapid. Almost concurrently forms very similar to those he had invented began to appear in other European countries. Rarely has a new idea in the visual arts been taken up internationally with so little lag. Advanced artistic circles at this time were evidently thoroughly prepared to accept major innovations and new periodicals, starting up almost one a year, provided vehicles for their transmission: *Pan* in 1895, for example, *Jugend* in 1896, *Dekorative Kunst* in 1897, and *Die Kunst* in 1899, to mention only German magazines. Had the Art Nouveau not already been invented by Horta the year before, three works of art dated 1893, Aubrey Beardsley's 'Cello Player', an illustration in black and white, Toorop's picture 'Three Brides', and Munch's 'The Cry', first a painting but widely available as a colour-lithograph the following year, might well have supplied the impetus for other designers to do so; doubtless such inspiration did encourage rivalry rather than direct imitation of Horta. In Germany a Munch exhibition in Berlin in 1892 and a Toorop exhibition in Munich in 1893 called attention to the long waving curves and the general linearity of style of these artists. In 1893, moreover, the *Studio* began to bring to designers and architects everywhere well-chosen illustrations of current English decorative work.

England itself was least responsive to the new Continental mode. It is, indeed, improper to call the Bishopsgate Institute in Bishopsgate in the City of London, built in 1893-4 by C.

Harrison Townsend (1850-1928), Art Nouveau. Yet, despite its evident dependence on Webb, the way in which Townsend took the characteristically stylized but basically naturalistic patterns of contemporary English wallpapers and chintzes and used them in relief at architectural scale is as drastic an innovation as are the bits and pieces of more abstract stone carving that Horta used on his Brussels houses

244. C. Harrison Townsend:
London, Whitechapel Art Gallery, 1898-9

of these years. Townsend remained a 'fellow-traveller' rather than a member of the international Art Nouveau group for a decade. For example, the façade of his Whitechapel Art Gallery in the Whitechapel Road in the East End of London, designed in 1897 and built in 1898-9, is an improved version of that of the Bishopsgate Institute [244]. The broad and almost Richardsonian arch is placed off centre, the ornament is freer and bolder, and the few windows are organized in a continuous band below the plain wall of the upper portion.

Less successful, though perhaps more advanced, is Townsend's Horniman Museum of 1900-1, a free-standing edifice in London Road, Forest Hill, South London. This has less external ornamentation, except for the façade mosaic by Anning Bell, but there is a very plastically conceived tower with rounded corners placed at one side of the front façade. His church of St Mary the Virgin, consecrated in 1904, at Great Warley in Essex, is very simple, indeed rather Voysey-like as regards the buttressed and rough-cast exterior. However, the elaborate decorations inside by Sir William Reynolds-Stephens (1862-1943) offer the most virtuoso example of Art Nouveau in England – at least they are about as close to the Continental mode as the English came.[1] No other English architect came nearer the Art Nouveau than Townsend; in quality, moreover, his work excels most of that done on the Continent by the various imitators and emulators of Horta, even if it lacks the humble integrity of Voysey's best houses of these years.

The earliest and, later, the most versatile Art Nouveau architect of France[1a] was Hector Guimard (1867-1942). But his first work of consequence, the complex block of flats in Paris called the Castel Béranger[2] at 16 Rue La Fontaine, which was completed after several years of construction in 1897, still represents a very ambiguous exploitation of the new ideas coming from Brussels. It must be remembered,

however, that even the elements of the decoration deriving most definitely from Horta antedate other Art Nouveau work outside Belgium. Also notable is the fact that the façade of the Castel Béranger was premiated by the City of Paris in 1898, for this indicates the rapidity with which the new mode won approval in France.

In 1896, while the Castel Béranger was building, Siegfried Bing, a Hamburg art-dealer whose wares included Japanese prints – now even more in demand than at any time since their introduction to Europe in the late fifties – and also the new English decorative products, decided to open a shop in Paris. Bing's Maison de l'Art Nouveau at 22 Rue de Provence was designed for him by L.-B. Bonnier (1856-1946) in the Belgian mode, which thereby acquired its familiar name. This shop was of no great architectural interest, however, except that it was the first of the multitude that were produced in the next ten or fifteen years. Not only in Paris but in most Continental cities large and small, and even in England and in America, where the Art Nouveau otherwise hardly penetrated, these shop-fronts can still be noted; one of the finest has even been transferred from Paris to the Philadelphia Museum of Art in America.

Bing also enlisted the services of Van de Velde, still quite immature as a designer compared to Horta, but very articulate as a critic. Influenced more intellectually than visually by the English, Van de Velde's personal development as a decorator now proceeded very rapidly. The lounge he designed for the Dresden Exhibition of 1897, for example, was an accomplished if somewhat heavily scaled example of an Art Nouveau interior and much more elaborate than those completed in his house at Uccle the year before.

By the time the Maison du Peuple in Brussels opened two years later in 1899 and Horta's early career reached its apex of achievement, the Art Nouveau was already a favourite mode with young French designers and generally in rising favour in *fin de siècle* Paris. As a result even established architects were not averse to introducing its curves in interior decoration and for the detailing of exposed metal structural elements, although most of them had little understanding of its real possibilities. The giant stone colonnades of the Grand Palais in Paris, designed in 1897 and built in 1898-9 for the Exhibition of 1900, were presumably intended to rival those of the plaster palaces of the Chicago World's Fair of 1893; but behind them the architectural team of H.-A.-A. Deglane (1855-1931), L.-A. Louvet (1860-1936), both pupils of Richardson's master, André, and A.-F.-T. Thomas (1847-1907) provided a vast iron-and-glass interior detailed in a coarse sort of Art Nouveau quite unrelated to the academic treatment of the colonnaded exterior.[3]

The entrance feature, designed by René Binet (1866-1911), and the Pavillon Bleu by E.-A.-R. Dulong (1860-?), the principal Exhibition restaurant in the Champ de Mars, were even more whole-heartedly *à la mode*. One can hardly regret, however, that these gaudy structures, unlike the Grand Palais, were only temporary.[3a] A much superior example of Art Nouveau decoration, Maxim's Restaurant in the Rue Royale, remains intact as it was decorated in 1899 by Louis Marney. This is full of period flavour and still splendidly maintained, but it has no real existence as interior architecture. Soon the Art Nouveau would be vulgarized in dozens of cafés, large and small, all over Europe. Of these the Brasserie Universelle in the Avenue de l'Opéra in Paris by Niermans, which was carried out some two or three years after Maxim's, was perhaps the most sumptuous; in this case, however, the new mode was eclectically combined with a lush Neo-Rococo.[3b] Maxim's has lately been copied in Chicago.

The architect Charles Plumet (1861-1925), working with the decorator Tony Selmersheim

(b. 1871), built in 1898 at 67 Avenue Malakoff the first of a series of houses in which Art Nouveau decoration was grafted on to a general scheme of design that was more or less Late Gothic. This has long been demolished. Such eclecticism, based more usually on eighteenth-century models, is characteristic of the rapid Parisian dilution of the Art Nouveau and doubtless played a great part in its early descent into the obsolescence of the *démodé*. Yet Auguste Perret (1874-1954), in a large block of flats built in 1902 at 119 Avenue de Wagram, exploited in masonry a heavier and richer sort of Art Nouveau than Plumet's with considerable success [245]. This edifice is in curious contrast to the flats of ferro-concrete at 25 bis Rue Franklin, designed by Perret in 1902 also, with

245. Auguste Perret:
Paris, block of flats, 119 Avenue Wagram, 1902

which his career is generally considered to begin. Even the latter, moreover, have considerably more Art Nouveau feeling in their panels of faience mosaic than is usually recognized (see Chapter 18). The block in the Avenue Wagram is quite typical of French production in these years but of much higher than average quality.

The most accomplished French Art Nouveau designer remained Guimard, the first to take up the mode. His most conspicuous works, however, the Paris Métro entrances of 1898-1901, lie outside the normal realm of architecture [246]. These are executed entirely in metal of the most sinuous and vegetable-like character, and their extreme virtuosity is the more surprising in that they consist of metal castings produced in series. His no longer extant Humbert de Romans Building of 1902 in the Rue Saint-Didier in Paris, on the other hand, illustrated the usual difficulties of Art Nouveau architects when working with masonry. The exterior was neither Neo-Rococo nor Neo-Flamboyant but curiously crude and gawky in

its originality, like his Castel Béranger, with none of the Art Nouveau grace that even Plumet sometimes evoked with success, or the rather lush ornamentation of Perret's block of flats in the Avenue Wagram. The auditorium inside, however, employed curved structural members even more boldly than Horta had done in that of the Maison du Peuple. Here Guimard succeeded in giving a masculine vigour to the rather feminine forms of a mode already passing its brief prime.

As late as 1911, however, Guimard remained faithful to the Art Nouveau in an extensive range of contiguous blocks of flats that he built at 17-21 Rue La Fontaine near the Castel Béranger. For his own flat there he designed ironwork as boldly abstract as advanced mid twentieth-century sculpture in metal, but also as suavely elegant as comparable Rococo detail of the eighteenth century. The exteriors, moreover, which are entirely of stone, have a great deal of the refinement and restraint of Horta's Hallet house of 1906 in Brussels. They are, however, more plastically treated with boldly

246. Hector Guimard:
Paris, Gare du Métropolitain, Place Bastille, 1900

247. Frantz Jourdain: Paris, Samaritaine Department Store, 1905

moulded bay windows and attic storeys. Except for Perret's, few Parisian blocks of flats of the period rival these in interest or in quality of design and execution.

Three Paris department stores of the early years of the century continued to use the metal-and-glass interior structure of Boileau and Eiffel's Bon Marché with notable success. In presumable emulation of Horta's Innovation in Brussels, moreover, the architects of two of these extended considerably the external use of exposed metal introduced by Sédille at the Printemps in the eighties. These two stores remain, with Guimard's Métro entrances, the most prominent Parisian examples of the Art Nouveau. The main branch of the Samaritaine[4] in the Rue de la Monnaie near the Pont Neuf was built in 1905 by C.-R.-F.-M. Jourdain (1847-1935). This has several fine galleried courts inside in the tradition of the Galeries du Commerce et de l'Industrie of the 1830s, but it is even more distinguished for the sturdy scale and the straightforward design of the external metal frame [247]. The actual structural members are hardly bent at all by the exigencies of the mode; but they were characteristically ornamented not only with decorative metalwork but also with inset panels of polychrome faience, now painted over. On the north front, however, other panels, here of faience mosaic, remain visible; these are of even greater delicacy and elegance than Perret's foliate panels in his block of flats of 1902-3 in the Rue Franklin.

The contemporary Grand Bazar de la Rue de Rennes, now the Magasins Réunis, at 134-136 Rue de Rennes by H.-B. Gutton (b. 1874) is generally fussier in design than the Samaritaine. Gutton achieved, however, a more completely volumetric expression, emphasizing the lightness and the thinness of metal-and-glass construction somewhat as the early monuments of the 1840s and 1850s in England had done. New shop-windows below and the removal of the open grillework that once rose against the sky have now much diminished its effectiveness. Binet's earlier galleried court of 1900 at the Printemps was burned out in 1923 unfortunately. With the lifts rising in the corners and the staircases swooping down in great splashing curves, this court was altogether superior to his Entrance to the Exhibition of 1900 and even to Frantz Jourdain's small later courts in the Samaritaine. It seemed somehow to epitomize what a great metropolitan department store *ought* to look like somewhat as Garnier's Opéra epitomizes what later generations came to expect of an opera-house. If Prince Danilo supped with the 'Damen' of Maxim's, we can be sure the 'Merry Widow' and the 'Pink Lady' did their shopping here.

It was the Art Nouveau structures at the Exhibition of 1900 which first focused public attention on the new mode, occasioning also that rapid Parisian vulgarization which brought its early end. At the exhibition, besides the crude but conspicuous things designed by Binet and Dulong that have been mentioned, there was the Pavillon Art Nouveau Bing by Georges de Feure (1868-1928), a designer rather than an architect, which had rooms by Edward Colonna, back from working for years in America, and others of the best artists and craftsmen employed by Bing; but their exhibits represented decoration, not interior architecture properly speaking. However, by 1900 the Art Nouveau was not at all the strictly Parisian manifestation that it must have seemed to most of those who visited the exhibition. The Germans, notably, had already taken it up with great enthusiasm, beginning shortly after 1896.

The Studio Elvira of 1897-8 in Munich by August Endell (1871-1925) had a plain stucco façade cut by a few strategically placed windows of varied shape; but this façade was splashed across the centre with a very large abstract relief of orientalizing character resembling something halfway between a dragon and a cloud. Endell's studio, if not the first manifestation of the Art

Nouveau in Germany, was certainly the most striking; moreover, it followed immediately upon the showing of Van de Velde's Lounge at the Dresden Exhibition of 1897. Already, however, in that portion of the Wertheim Department Store in Berlin in the Leipzigerstrasse which was begun in 1896, Alfred Messel (1853–1909) had used a great deal of exposed metal and glass and even perhaps modified the detail a bit towards the Art Nouveau. This was five years before Horta designed the Innovation Department Store in Brussels and ten years earlier than Jourdain's Samaritaine in Paris. Messel made the spacing of his heavily moulded masonry piers quite wide and opened up completely the bays between. The result was at least as close to Sullivan's Gage Building of 1898–9 as to the Paris department stores of a decade later. In those portions of this department store that Messel added in 1900–4, however, the façades, although highly stylized, were of rather Late Gothic character and certainly quite remote from the Art Nouveau.

In 1899 Van de Velde moved from Paris to Berlin. There he designed the Hohenzollern Kunstgewerbehaus, a shop parallel to Bing's Maison de l'Art Nouveau in Paris in its interests and its activities. In the next year he carried out the Haby Barber Shop and the Havana Cigar Store, two of the most extravagant of all Art Nouveau shop interiors. With the opening of the new century, however, in his full-scale architecture Van de Velde moved almost as rapidly away from the Art Nouveau as did Messel, although in a different direction (see Chapter 20). By this time strong counter-influences were reaching Germany from Glasgow and Vienna.

Although not disdaining the Art Nouveau as completely as did the English and the Americans, the Austrians showed little of the enthusiasm of the French and the Germans. There is in Vienna one block of flats[5] of about 1900 so completely Art Nouveau that it might well have been designed by Horta himself. But the leading Austrian architects, old and young, reflected the new Belgian mode only with considerable diffidence and restraint. Otto Wagner (1841–1918), long a well-established academic architect and indeed Professor of Architecture at the Akademie, introduced more and more Art Nouveau detail in the Stadtbahn stations that he built over the years 1894–1901, most notably in the one at the Karlsplatz with its curved metal frame and inset floral panels. However, even this seems tentative and hardly rivals in interest Guimard's contemporary Métro stations in Paris.

Wagner's so-called Majolika Haus, a block of flats at 40 Linke Wienzeile built in 1898–9, is much more distinguished and original [248]. Although the ironwork of the balconies is here and there curvilinear in detail and the faience plaques that completely cover the wall are decorated with great swooping patterns of highly colourful flowers, the architectonic elements of the façade are nevertheless very

248. Otto Wagner: Vienna, Majolika Haus, 1898-9

crisp, flat, and rectangular. That Vienna would very shortly become the focus of a reaction against the Art Nouveau does not seem surprising in the light of this façade. Moreover, on an office building erected in the Ungargasse for the firm of Portois & Fix in 1897 by Max Fabiani (1865-1962), who had been Wagner's assistant in 1894-6, the coloured faience slabs which sheathe its surface are arranged in a purely geometrical chequer-board pattern; only the ironwork has a slightly Art Nouveau flavour. In the late nineties it would be hard to say whether Art Nouveau influence was arriving or departing but for the projects other Viennese architects were publishing in the review *Ver Sacrum* started in 1898.

The design of the art gallery built in the Friedrichstrasse in Vienna in 1898-9 for the Sezession, a newly founded society of artists in revolt against the Academy, by J. M. Olbrich (1867-1908) seems more influenced, however, by English work. The pierced dome of floral metalwork alone vies in virtuosity with Horta and Guimard, and the pattern of this is actually quite English in character. The closest connexion is with the personal style of Wagner, whose assistant he was at the time. Curiously enough, there are later Wagner projects that seem to derive from this façade of Olbrich's. The original bronze doors[5a] were by Georg Klimt, a brother of the Austrian Post-Impressionist who can be grouped, up to a point, with the Dutch, Belgian, Norwegian, and Swiss Post-Impressionists mentioned earlier (see Chapter 16). Olbrich was called to Darmstadt in Germany to work at the artists' colony sponsored there by the Grand Duke Ernst Ludwig in 1899 and Darmstadt, like Vienna, soon became a centre of reaction against the Art Nouveau under his leadership (see Chapter 20).

Both in Vienna and in Darmstadt the influence of the Scottish designer Mackintosh helped most to crystallize an alternative mode. Mackintosh first exhibited a room on the Continent at Munich in 1898, the same year that Baillie Scott was called by the Grand Duke to decorate an interior in the palace at Darmstadt. In 1900 Mackintosh was invited to design a room in the Sezession Exhibition in Vienna. That exhibit undoubtedly encouraged Viennese architects, already diffident towards the Art Nouveau, to turn very sharply away from it. This Adolf Loos (1870-1933) had already done in designing a completely rectilinear shop interior in Vienna in 1898. Loos, Wagner after about 1901, and Wagner's pupil Josef Hoffmann (1870-1956) were all leaders in the international reaction against the Art Nouveau (see Chapter 20). The position of Mackintosh, however, is rather hard to state so categorically and must be considered here in more detail.

At home in Scotland Mackintosh's early decorative work of the mid nineties approached Continental Art Nouveau more closely than that of any other Briton, not excluding Townsend. Indeed, he was castigated by his compatriots and his English contemporaries for participating in so exotic a movement. But Mackintosh also came nearer to possessing genius than most of the men of his generation associated with the Art Nouveau, not even excluding Horta. That genius, all the same, was of so ambivalent a nature that he could seem for a few years to go along with the general stream of Continental fashion and yet, almost at the very same time, provide also a real protest against its excesses and its superficialities by the craftsmanlike integrity and the almost ascetic restraint of his best work. That protest the Austrians and the Germans were not slow to heed.

Mackintosh made his first mark in Glasgow, which had earlier been the home of the highly original 'Greek' Thomson (see Chapter 4). By the nineties, moreover, interest in contemporary French painting was probably livelier there than it was in London. But Glasgow was also as notorious as Chicago, that major focus of architectural achievement in the America of the nineties, for its presumed philistinism. Touches of Mackintosh's hand can be distinguished in work of the office of John Honeyman (1831–1914) and his partner Keppie, where the young architect was employed at the start of his career, notably in the Martyrs' Public School in Glasgow of 1895. But it was in the decoration of the first of a series of Miss Cranston's 'tearooms' (*scottice*, restaurants), the one in Buchanan Street remodelled by him in 1897-8, that Mackintosh's personal talents were first effectively exploited. His very earliest decorative compositions and the murals that he and his wife provided here, full of heavy and presumably Gaelic symbolism, are parallel to, rather than derivative from, the work of the Belgians. They are, in fact, much closer to the drawings of Beardsley and the paintings of Toorop[5b] and Munch than to the plant-like ironwork and almost Neo-Rococo carved stone ornament then characteristic of Horta. But the same long swinging curves are present, the same linearity, and the same avoidance of stylistic influence from the past.

In this same year 1897 Mackintosh's firm had the good fortune to win the limited competition for the Glasgow School of Art with a project that was entirely their young designer's [249]. Thus he very soon had an opportunity to prove himself architect as well as decorator in a way that only two or three of the Europeans associated with the Art Nouveau had been able to do up to this point. The school was built during the next two years, just as Horta was finishing his Maison du Peuple in Brussels. The only element in the design that relates to the contemporary Art Nouveau of the Continent is the ironwork. This is quite incidental to the major architectonic qualities of the building, moreover, since it is purely decorative, not structural. It is also extremely restrained in its abstract curves, like Fabiani's of this date in Vienna, and largely devoid of vegetable or floral reminiscence.

The entrance to the Glasgow Art School seems to derive from Webb, but, like that of Townsend's contemporary art gallery in London, it is rather less traditional in character than Webb's work of this period. The somewhat wilful asymmetry and the plastic elaboration of the central part of the façade contrast nevertheless with the straightforwardness of the general treatment. There are two ranges of very wide studio windows – reputedly derived from a Voysey project – like 'Chicago windows' but larger, with the reinforced-concrete lintels above them frankly exposed, and little else in the whole composition. To later eyes this façade, expressing so clearly the uncomplicated plan that it fronts, tends to appear deceptively simple and obvious. But Mackintosh's very sensitive proportions and the delicate touches of linear detail provided by the ironwork create a design at once very direct and very subtle.

The north end of the building is a tall plain wall of rather small-scaled random ashlar broken only by a few strategically spotted windows of various shapes. At once medievally dramatic and quite abstract, this façade makes one appreciate all the more the almost classical serenity and horizontality of the main front. The Art School is clearly the manifesto of an architectural talent of broad range and great assurance – very different from that of Voysey.

Mackintosh was not alone in Glasgow in these years. A real 'school' existed, chiefly in the field of decoration, of which George Walton was another notable exponent.[5c] Like Baillie Scott and Ashbee, Walton had some success as an architect in England (see Chapter 15) as Mackintosh did not, even though he executed a few interiors below the Border. But local support was not what it should have been for any of them in either Scotland or England. While the Art School was in construction, however, Mackintosh was asked in 1898 to

249. C. R. Mackintosh: Glasgow, School of Art, 1897-9

250. C. R. Mackintosh: Glasgow, School of Art, 1907-9

provide the already-mentioned room in Munich, first of many that he showed at various exhibitions in Germany and Austria. This interior was very different indeed, both in the basic rectangularity of the forms and in the delicacy of the membering, from Van de Velde's Art Nouveau Lounge at the Dresden Exhibition of the previous year. Thus, even before Van de Velde reached Berlin in 1899, a new line of influence from Glasgow into Germany – and soon into Austria also – was established whose general tendency was in opposition to the lusher currents flowing from Brussels and Paris.

When Olbrich settled in Darmstadt – just *before* Mackintosh's room was shown at the Sezession – he soon rejected almost completely in the work he carried out at the Grand Duke's Art Colony the still slightly Art Nouveau leanings – in any case already closer to the English designers than to Horta or Van de Velde – of his newly completed Sezession Building (see Chapter 20). Even though his Pavilion of the Plastic Arts of 1900–1 at Darmstadt retained curved elements, those were quasi-structural as well as decorative. The general rectangularity and the broad horizontal windows of the Ernst Ludwig Haus, a block of artists' studios also by Olbrich, designed in 1899, suggest comparison with Mackintosh's Glasgow School of Art. Whether or not, in fact, Olbrich knew Mackintosh's building – he might have seen drawings for it – his approach here was certainly very similar.

Mackintosh had a good many further opportunities as a decorator, both at home and abroad, but only too few commissions to design whole buildings. However, his two houses near Glasgow, Windy Hill at Kilmacolm of 1899–1901 and Hill House at Helensburgh of 1902–3, are both very notable. Externally they have a certain generic similarity to Voysey's, with their moderate pitched roofs of dark slate, rough-cast walls, and plain stone trim. His prototypes are not English but Scottish, however – the simple

seventeenth-century houses of the minor lairds. As one would expect from his interiors, moreover, the façades of Mackintosh's houses are much more carefully and abstractly composed than Voysey's; they even include some simple geometrical features that are not at all reminiscent of the past in their design. Like Voysey's houses, Mackintosh's show no real novelties in planning, although the disposition of the rooms is always straightforward and commodious. The interiors are very original and rather less forced than those he was producing for exhibitions on the Continent.

Mackintosh built very little after 1903 except the Scotland Street School of 1904 in Glasgow, the north wing of the Glasgow Art School in 1907–9, and the finest of the various tea-rooms that he remodelled for Miss Cranston. This was the Willow Tea Room in Sauchiehall Street of 1904, for which he remade the façade as well as reorganizing the interior. Internally this tea-room was arranged on several interrelated levels subdivided by ingenious screenwork; the exterior was a flat surface of white stucco cut by broad horizontal openings, one to a storey. The Scotland Street School is equally straightforward in design, the rather plain façade with its ranges of horizontal windows being flanked by rounded stair-towers articulated into continuous stone grids by mullions and transoms, like the bay windows of Voysey's Broadleys but much taller.

The south wing of the Glasgow Art School is more remarkable, quite worthy of the original front but much more stylized [250]. Where the front is strongly horizontal the new end façade, like that on the north, is markedly vertical, in part because of the way the ground falls off. But the tall oriels, glazed at the outer plane of the stonework, are striking features, and the whole composition is tense and dramatic. The library inside is a *tour de force* of spatial subdivision somewhat like the Willow Tea Room. Most notable is the way the rectangular stick-work makes manifest the complex articulation of the total volume. This sort of handling of interior space was unique up to this time as a product of conscious design, although already present inside Paxton's Crystal Palace in the mid nineteenth century. Certainly there is no evidence here of a decline in Mackintosh's creative powers; indeed, quite the contrary. Yet this library proved to be his swan song; for want of further commissions Mackintosh's career all but closed at much the same time that the Art Nouveau was coming to an end on the Continent. Not since Ledoux perhaps had so great a talent been thus thwarted by circumstances, although just what the thwarting circumstances were, other than Mackintosh's own temperament, is not so evident as in the case of the revolutionary French architect.

The Art Nouveau, so extensively propagated by exhibitions, is often thought to have terminated with an exhibition, that held at Turin in 1902. This is more than a slight exaggeration, as various already mentioned buildings executed as late as 1911 will have made evident. Yet after the early years of the century the decline of the Art Nouveau was almost universal except in provincial places and in outlying countries such as those of Latin America and eastern Europe. At Turin the Belgian section had characteristic Art Nouveau interiors by Horta. Mackintosh, wholly detached by now from the Art Nouveau, contributed a Rose Boudoir, typically light in colour and delicate in line with the predominant verticals and horizontals relieved by little abstract knots, so to say, of curvilinear decoration. Raimondo D'Aronco (1857–1932), the Italian architect responsible for the principal pavilions, wavered between a rather plastic, somewhat Neo-Baroque, version of the Art Nouveau, not unrelated to the seventeenth-century work of the great local architect Guarino Guarini, and a crisper mode much influenced by Mackintosh and the Viennese.

D'Aronco's finest building, however, was not at Turin but the Pavilion of Fine Arts that he designed for the Udine Exhibition the next year. Moving sharply away from the turgidity of much of his work at the earlier exhibition, he produced for Udine a façade that was unified in design, frankly impermanent in its materials, and at once festive in spirit and dignified in tone. This was a most distinguished piece of exhibition architecture in a period when leading designers gave a great part of their attention to such rather ephemeral things – largely, doubtless, because so few opportunities to build permanent structures came their way. In Istanbul, D'Aronco built a small mosque in 1903, prominently located by the Galata Bridge, and also several blocks of flats that signally fail to maintain the promise of his Italian exhibition buildings. The very awkwardly sited mosque, raised on top of an existing structure, is as Viennese in character as the Udine pavilion.

Other Italian architects,[5d] however, remained faithful for some years to the *stile floreale*, their version of the Art Nouveau. In Milan the Casa Castiglioni, a *palazzo* or mansion-like block of flats at 47 Corso Venezia built by Giuseppe Sommaruga (1867–1917) in 1903, is a very large and ponderous example. The detail is extremely bold, inside and out, the materials rich, and a very large part of the interior is given up to a monumental stair-hall of almost Piranesian spatial complexity. A Milanese hotel at 15 Corso Vittorio Emmanuele of 1904–5 by A. Cattaneo and G. Santamaria is of a comparable extravagance. Finer perhaps, certainly simpler, is the Casa Tosi of 1910 at 28 Via Senato in Milan by Alfredo Campanini (1873–1926).[5e]

To judge from the rather *stile floreale* character of some work of this period in Latin America, Italians as well as Iberians may well have carried the Art Nouveau there. In Cuba and Brazil, especially, memories of Colonial exuberance encouraged a profusion of carved or moulded ornament beyond even the excesses of the

French around 1900. The most prominent example, but not the most characteristic, is the Palacio de Bellas Artes in Mexico City begun for President Diaz by Adamo Boari after 1903 and completed in 1933 by Federico Mariscal; this is 'Beaux-Arts' – not inappropriately, perhaps! – in all except its detailing; in the latest portions this reflects the Paris of the Exposition des Arts Décoratifs of 1925 rather than the Art Nouveau Paris of 1900.

In Spain itself the international current of the Art Nouveau was not very influential outside Barcelona. Gaudí, whose earlier work of the seventies and eighties has already been described (see Chapter 11), continued to be as much apart from the contemporary Spanish architectural scene as he was from the international Art Nouveau. His finest late works, moreover, all but post-date the demise of the Art Nouveau in the major European capitals. Nor is there any such close, if ambiguous, linkage between Gaudí's career and the general rise and fall of the mode as in the case of Mackintosh. One can only say that his personal style is more closely related to the Art Nouveau than to the new stage of modern architecture that was already succeeding it by the time he produced his final masterpieces. The premonitory character of his early ironwork has been discussed and illustrated already [175].

Gaudí's work on the church of the Sagrada Familia[6] in Barcelona went on more or less continuously from 1884 to 1914 and began again in 1919 after the First World War. The most conspicuous portion that he was able to execute, one of the transept façades, was designed and largely built in the nineties. Dominating Barcelona with its four extraordinary towers – not finally completed until after Gaudí's death in 1926 – this façade, begun in 1891, breaks quite sharply with the Neo-Gothic of Villar's crypt and his own chevet. The portals with their steep gables have a generically Gothic *ordonnance*; but the extraordinary pro-

fusion of sculpture, mostly executed after 1903, gives a highly novel flavour. While conventional enough as regards the figures, this is otherwise either naturalistically floral or else meltingly abstract. It resembles the Art Nouveau in many minor details, but is generally bolder in scale, more fully three-dimensional and, in places, somewhat nightmarish.

Although only about two-thirds as tall as the cluster of towers intended by Gaudí to rise over the crossing, the four openwork spires above this façade – with the two in the centre taller than those on the sides – reach a wholly disproportionate height in relation to the roof that should ultimately cover the still unbuilt transept. At the top they break out into fantastically plastic finials whose multi-planar surfaces are covered with a mosaic of broken tiling in brilliant colours. The prototypes for these finials are the chimney-pots of the Palau Güell, but here their note of free fantasy is raised to monumental scale. The inspiration of the towers, so remote in character from anything that the Art Nouveau ever produced, came from certain native buildings which Gaudí had seen in Africa: these strange primitive[7] forms he first exploited in a project of 1892-3 for the Spanish Franciscan Mission in Tangier which was never executed.

In posse the Sagrada Familia is perhaps the greatest ecclesiastical monument of the last hundred years; beside it such a suave late example of monumental Neo-Gothic in England as Liverpool Cathedral,[7a] begun by Sir Giles Gilbert Scott in 1903, lacks both vitality and originality of expression, if not nobility of scale. However, Gaudí's church still remains a fragment, and a very incoherent one at that, even though he prepared in 1925, the year before his death, a brilliant new project for the nave. Gaudí really stands or falls by the few secular buildings that he was able to carry to completion, beginning with the Palau Güell of 1885-9 [175], and not, as many compatriots assume, by the unrealized – perhaps unrealizable – plans for the Sagrada Familia. (Construction has gone slowly forward, however, on the other transept for several decades now.)

Gaudí's next Barcelona mansion after the Palau Güell, that built at 48 Carrer de Casp for the heirs of Pedro Mártir Calvet in 1898-1904, is much less impressive. Baroque rather than medieval in its antecedents, this is interesting chiefly for the detailing of the ironwork; but even that is no more remarkable here than that at the Palau Güell of a decade earlier. It is of interest, however, as illustrating the support which Gaudí received all along from his fellow citizens, that the Casa Calvet was awarded a prize in 1901 as the best new façade in Barcelona, quite as Guimard's Castel Béranger was premiated three years earlier in Paris.

A wholly new spirit, quite comparable in its total originality to the Art Nouveau, first appears in the work that Gaudí did for Don Eusebio Güell at the Park Güell (now the Municipal Park of Barcelona), carried out over the years 1900-14, and in the walls and the gate he built in 1901-2 for the suburban estate of Don Hermenegildo Miralles in Las Corts de Sarriá. In the latter all the forms are curved and no stylistic reminiscence whatsoever remains, but it is a production of minor importance compared to the park. The park is mostly landscaping, but partly architecture in that it includes several small buildings and much subsidiary construction. A sort of Neo-Romantic naturalism, exceeding in fantasy that of the most exotic landscape gardening of the eighteenth century, controls the whole conception. Sinuous and megalomaniac near-Doric colonnades of concrete support a sort of flat vault that is of great interest technically;[8] yet these colonnades also suggest artificial ruins of the eighteenth-century sort raised to giant scale. The other porticoes and grottoes, however, recall no architecture of the past. Their rubble columns seem rather to emulate slanting tree-trunks, but in fact their profiles were worked out statically with the most careful study of the forces involved.

The ranges of curving benches surrounding the great open terrace over the Doric hypostyle, although covered with a mosaic of the most heterogeneous bits and pieces of broken faience, seem like congelations of the waves of the sea; the roofs of the lodges, also tile-covered, toss in the air like cockscombs. A strange biological plasticity, rather like that of the small-scale carved detail of Horta's or Guimard's buildings very much enlarged, turns whole structures into malleable masses as in some Gulliverian dream of vegetable or animal elements grown to monumental size. Everything but the ironwork is moulded in three dimensions, and even the ironwork tends towards a heavy scale more comparable to that of the structural members of metal used in Belgian or French work of the day than to the delicacy of Art Nouveau decorative detail.

Gaudí's major secular works belong to the same years as the execution of the park. It is hard to believe that the Casa Batlló at 43 Passeig de Gracia in Barcelona, a small block of flats, is not a completely new structure but a remodelling carried out in 1905-7. This fact perhaps explains the relative flatness of the façade. Yet Gaudí made the lower storeys extraordinarily plastic and open, using a bony articulation of curvilinear stone members, and the high roof in front that masks the roof terrace is of even more cockscomb-like character than those on his park lodges [251]. The upper storeys of the façade glitter with a fantastic plaquage of broken coloured glass considerably more subtle in tonality than his usual mosaic of faience fragments.[9] But architecturally the façade is handled more like Horta's, with most of the windows nearly rectangular even though bulging balconettes of metal project at their bases. The effect, as with Horta, is slightly Neo-Rococo. But the sort of Rococo which this façade recalls is not circumspect French eighteenth-century work but the lusher mode that was exploited in southern Germany – and still more appositely in Portugal and Spain. The entire wall surface seems to be in motion, and all its edges waver and wind in a way that even interior panelling did rarely in eighteenth-century France. This effect of total motion is even more notable in the interiors, which seem to have been hollowed out by the waves of the sea.

The rear façade of the Casa Batlló is remarkable for its openness. The wide window-walls in the paired flats open on to sinuous balconies extending all the way across. Above, there is a simpler plastic cresting than on the front; over this the curious forms of the chimney-pots provide a range of abstract sculptural features covered with polychrome tiling, always a favourite terminal theme of Gaudí's.

Much larger than the Casa Batlló is the edifice built for Roser Segimon de Milá in 1905-7 at 92 Passeig de Gracia, appropriately known in Barcelona as 'La Pedrera' (the quarry). Surrounding two more or less circular courts, this large block of flats occupies an obtuse corner site, and the entire plan is worked out in curves as well as all the elements of the exterior [252]. The façade of the Casa Milá is not a thin plane, curling like paper at the edges and pierced with squarish holes like that of the Casa Batlló; instead ranges of balconies heavier than those on the rear of the Casa Batlló sway in and out like the waves of the sea beneath the surf-like crest of the roof, making the whole edifice a very complex plastic entity [253]. From a distance La Pedrera looks as if it were all freely modelled in clay; in fact, it is executed in cut stone with boldly hammered surfaces that appear to result from natural erosion.

There is no external polychromy of glass or tile here, and the frescoed colour used on the court walls has suffered such serious deterioration that it is difficult to know what it was like originally. On the other hand, Gaudí's detail

251. Antoni Gaudí:
Barcelona, Casa Batlló, front, 1905-7

was never more carefully studied nor more consistent; there are no straight lines at all, and in the forms of the piers rising from the ground to support the balconies of the first storey he suggested natural formations with real success

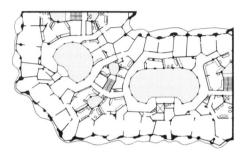

252-4. Antoni Gaudí:
Barcelona, Casa Milá, 1905-7, with plan of typical floor and detail of ground storey

[254]. These elements look as if they had been produced by the action of sea and weather rather than by the chisel, quite as does some of the mid-twentieth-century sculpture of Henry Moore.

The marine note is seen at its strongest and most naturalistic in the ironwork however. Strewn over the balcony parapets and across various openings, like seaweed over the rocks and sand of the seashore, the railings and grilles are full of intense organic vitality with none of the graceful droopiness of Guimard's Métro entrances. Gaudí's metalwork frequently suggests the work of various mid-twentieth-century sculptors in welded metal, quite as his handling of masonry does later sculpture in stone. Indeed, his iron grilles often exceed such sculptors' metalwork in richness and variety of form, as also in the fine handcraftsmanship of the execution.[9a]

The detailing on the Casa Milá, whether of the masonry or the ironwork, avoids the nightmarish overscaling of the somewhat similar elements at the Park Güell, and also the coarseness of the broken faience mosaic surfaces that he used so much there and elsewhere but here restricted to the roof-tops. As regards the masonry, moreover, it is really wrong to speak of detailing, for the very fabric of the structure, not just its edges and its trimmings as on the Casa Batlló, has been completely moulded to the architect's plastic will.[9b] Whether or not it be correct to consider the Casa Milá an example of the Art Nouveau – and technically it is not – La Pedrera remains one of the greatest masterpieces of the curvilinear mode of 1900, rivalled in quality only by the finest of Sullivan's skyscrapers [208] which it does not, of course, resemble visually at all.

Despite the esteem in which his work has always been held by his fellow-citizens of Barcelona, Gaudí had only a few local imitators of interest. However, such detailing on early twentieth-century buildings there as may appear at first to be conventionally Art Nouveau is often in fact a bit Gaudian. Only his assistants Francesc Berenguer (1866-1914) and J. M. Jujol Gibert (1879-1949) seem to have understood Gaudí's mature style. At least the house by Jujol at 335 Diagonal in Barcelona, though quite small and simple, and the Bodega Güell at Garraf of 1913 by Berenguer are of a quality worthy of comparison with Gaudí's own best work.[9c] The big Palau de la Musica Catalana, built by Luis Doménech i Montaner (1850-1923) in 1908, is a quite notable example of the architecture of the period, bold and coarse and rich. With a steel skeleton and walls in part continuously glazed, it is very advanced technically.

In Glasgow Mackintosh after 1908 was a prophet with far less honour than 'Greek' Thomson had received there in an earlier day. But the counter-current that he had helped to set going on the Continent was in full swing, particularly in Austria and in Germany (see Chapters 20 and 21). Even in Horta's own Brussels, Josef Hoffmann had been called from Vienna as early as 1905 to build the suburban Stoclet mansion [284] at 373 Avenue de Tervueren (see Chapter 21).

Despite the ephemeral nature of much of its production and the completeness with which it was ultimately rejected everywhere, the Art Nouveau has very great historical importance. The Art Nouveau offered the first international programme for a basic renewal of architecture that the nineteenth century actually set out to realize. Most earlier programmes, moreover, even if not primarily revivalistic, aimed chiefly at the reform of architecture; this was still true of Voysey and his English contemporaries in these very years, though not, of course, of Sullivan and Wright, working in isolation in the American Middle West. Thus the Art Nouveau was actually the first stage of modern architecture in Europe, if modern architecture be understood as implying primarily the total rejection of historicism.

The proto-modernity of earlier stages of nineteenth-century architectural development is almost always ambiguous, since the leaders of the various successive movements rarely intended to break with the past entirely. The characteristic ideal of nineteenth-century architects, as of their late eighteenth-century predecessors, had been to react against what they considered the decadence of the building arts current in their day by returning to the principles of some earlier and supposedly purer or more vital age. The very considerable amount of innovation that many European architects before Horta introduced in their work was not exactly unconscious; but it was more a matter of achieving personal expression by adapting old forms to new needs, new materials, and new methods of construction than of creating a wholly original modern style.

Well before the nineties a very few men had consciously sought absolute originality and total freedom from the disciplines of the past. But such architects found little or no public support for their programmes of architectural revolution nor even fellow-artists to share in their highly individualistic campaigns. After the relatively universal acceptance of the doctrines of Romantic Classicism there had followed chiefly a succession and a multiplication of divergencies; now, in the nineties, a real pattern of convergence appeared. But this convergence was premature. The renewal of ornament and of the accessories of architecture outran the renewal of the more basic elements of the art of building towards which the technical developments of the nineteenth century had been leading.

Thus the Art Nouveau stands apart from the architecture of the preceding hundred years and from the modern architecture of the following seventy which extend down towards the present. It did not bring the one to an end, as the profusion of so-called 'traditional' buildings of the early twentieth century makes very evident (see Chapter 24), nor did it provide much more than a preface to the major new developments that mark the early decades of the present century (see Chapters 18–21). That the Art Nouveau was completely rejected on

principle by 'traditionalists' is not surprising: It was the first serious attack on the position they continued to maintain.[9d] But the very rapidity with which the Art Nouveau rose to popularity and descended to vulgarity led to its denigration in the name of 'taste' by almost all architects and critics soon after it reached its climax around 1900. In recompense, interest in the Art Nouveau began to revive early, by the early thirties, after a much shorter period of neglect than that which other phases of nineteenth-century architectural development underwent.

The place of the Art Nouveau in the story of modern architecture, if only as an episode of youthful wild-oat-sowing, is now well established. Most of its exponents actually lived long enough to receive in their later years embarrassing praise for youthful work they had quite disowned if not forgotten. It is a curious paradox that although most of the leaders of the Art Nouveau survived for decades – and Van de Velde died only in 1957 – not one except Gaudí[10] maintained after 1910 the position of relative pre-eminence that had been his in 1900. A wholly new cast of characters, many of them no younger, came to the fore in the first decade of the twentieth century; they constitute the first generation of modern architects, properly speaking.

CHAPTER 18

MODERN ARCHITECTS OF THE FIRST GENERATION IN FRANCE:

AUGUSTE PERRET AND TONY GARNIER

No better name than 'modern' has yet been found for what has come to be the characteristic architecture of the twentieth century throughout the western world, well beyond its confines in Japan, India, and Africa, and by the 1960s also in the various Communist countries. Alternative adjectives such as 'rational', 'functional', 'international', or 'organic' all have the disadvantage of being either vaguer or more tendentious. Whether the Art Nouveau or such things as Sullivan's skyscrapers and Voysey's houses all truly belong, in their rather sharply differing ways, to a first stage of modern architecture or are transitional and prefatory may still be debated; but from the earliest years of this century several continuous lines of development can certainly be traced. These lines were in the main convergent through the twenties, if increasingly divergent in the middle decades of the century. By stressing generic changes rather than specific achievements the development can be presented almost anonymously, somewhat as the nineteenth-century development of commercial architecture was outlined earlier in this book (see Chapter 14). But it is more humanistic, and at least as true to the detailed facts, to consider modern architecture as deriving from the individual activities of a few leaders rather than from some Hegelian historic necessity. Of those leaders one group, born in the late 1860s, constituted the first generation; a group born some twenty years later formed a second generation; since the 1930s still another generation has come to maturity.

A somewhat similar succession of three generations could be distinguished in the case of Romantic Classicism, the last universal style in architecture. What sets the twentieth-century situation apart from that of the earlier period has been the marked prolongation of the activity of the first generation, two of whose leading members, Wright and Perret, lived on and remained active well beyond 1950. Wright continued in vigorous production down to his death in 1959. Of the leaders of the second generation, who first moved towards the centre of the stage in the early twenties, all were long-lived; two of them at least, Le Corbusier and Mies van der Rohe, were rather more productive after 1946 than earlier (see Chapter 21).

While some influence from their juniors can be noted in the latest works of the modern architects of the first generation, a real difference between their approach to architecture and that of the second generation continued. Those who then came forward after the mid thirties owed perhaps as much to the first generation as to the second, yet they also manifested some significant characteristics that are their own. The modern architecture of the last seventy years may well be presented historically in terms of the work of two generations of leaders (see Chapters 18-23), and after that of the production of the decades following the Second World War (see Chapter 25). But modern architecture, even very broadly interpreted, included only a small fraction of all building production down to the last war; the work of the supporters of 'tradition' in the twentieth century bulked much larger in quantity, even if it very rarely rivalled the modern work in interest or quality (see Chapter 24). An Epilogue touches on the scene in the sixties, but not the seventies.

The leaders of the first generation of modern architects remained great individualists to the last. It is therefore not easy to draw any general stylistic picture from their production, even for the years before the twenties when they were the only modern architects. The leaders of the second generation drew their inspiration, in most cases, not from one but from several of the older men; yet their work was so convergent that by the mid twenties a body of doctrine had come to exist deriving partly from their theories and partly from their few executed buildings and their many projects. With the increasing acceptance of this body of doctrine critics were by the thirties ready to recognize the existence of a new style as coherent, as consistent, and almost as universally emulated by younger architects everywhere as the Romantic Classical had been at the opening of the nineteenth century (see Chapter 22).

Towards the constitution of this new style each of the great architects of the first generation had made a notable contribution; yet their executed work, and even more their theories, remained independent of it. To appreciate that work only in the light of what they had in common with their juniors is to miss much of the richness and all of the idiosyncrasy of their achievement. In considering the work of these older architects for its own sake, what sets it apart from the Art Nouveau, whose protagonists were in many cases their exact contemporaries, must first be indicated and evaluated. For example, their rejection of ornament, at most but relative, provides only a minor and negative point of differentiation. In their positive preoccupation with structure and its direct architectonic expression, and

also their reform and revitalization of planning concepts, however, they went much further than most of the Art Nouveau designers of 1900. It is true that such architects as Horta and Jourdain, when working with metal and glass, were concerned with the expression of structure, but that expression was usually more decorative than architectonic [242, 247]. Traditional materials, such as stone and brick, in the hands of Art Nouveau architects and their spiritual brothers often lost all their natural character, being treated like so much clay. The sense of materials, both new and old, and the determination of their proper use preoccupied most of the leading architects of the first generation, something for which the English and the Americans more particularly prepared the way.

The new importance of structure and its expression, the preoccupation with a particular building material, is nowhere more evident than in the work of Auguste Perret (1874-1954), the only great French architect of this generation. Belonging as he did to the family contracting firm of A. & G. Perret, which specialized early in the use of reinforced concrete, he saw as his principal task the development of formulas of design for concrete as valid as those so long established in France for building with stone. The other architects of his generation came more gradually and less single-mindedly to the exploitation of new materials – it is paradoxical, for example, that the characteristic Art Nouveau interest in exposed metal construction came generally to an end about 1905 – and their work as a result is more various and less doctrinaire. Because of Perret's clear definition of his goal and his single-minded advance along a predetermined line, his somewhat limited architectural achievement may well be considered before the protean manysidedness of Wright's in America and the ambiguity of Peter Behrens's in Germany, not to speak of the important contributions of Wagner and Loos in Austria, and of Berlage and de Klerk in Holland (see Chapters 19, 20, and 21).

Auguste Perret came of Burgundian stock, but by the accident of his father's exile from France after the Commune he was born in Brussels. His education was entirely French. He left the École des Beaux-Arts to enter the family's building firm without waiting to receive the Government's diploma,[1] somewhat as Wright went out into the practical world after less than two years of engineering school. His career began almost at once, for he built his first house at Berneval in 1890. Several blocks of flats and an office building in Paris followed in the next eight years; the Municipal Casino at St-Malo, built in 1899, was the first work of any real consequence. There he and his brother Gustave (1876-?) used reinforced concrete for an unsupported slab floor of 54-foot span. Executed otherwise in local granite and wood, this building has a certain bold simplicity as remote from 'Beaux-Arts' as from Art Nouveau work of the period.

Reinforced concrete,[1a] that is concrete strengthened by internal reinforcing rods of metal, seems to have been invented by a French gardener named Joseph Monnier in 1849, but he used it only for flower pots and outdoor furniture. In 1847 François Coignet (1814-88) built some houses of poured concrete without reinforcement; in 1852 for a house at 72 Rue Charles Michel in St-Denis, Seine, Coignet first employed his own system of *béton armé*, to use his term. That term has since remained current in French – the German term is *Eisenbeton*, the Italian *cimento armato*. During the next four decades ferro-concrete, to give it its simplest English name, was developed very gradually by Coignet and by François Hennebique (1842-1921) with no very notable architectural results. Detailed research is still revealing many instances of its early use by various men in different countries; but neither in the scale of its employment nor in the achievement of new and characteristic modes of expression did its history in these decades rival that of iron in the first half of the nineteenth century (see Chapter 7).

In 1894, just as the Art Nouveau was reaching France, ferro-concrete was used for the first time in a structure of some modest architectural pretension by J.-E.-A. de Baudot[2] (1836-1915) for a school in the Rue de Sevigné in Paris. This is overshadowed in interest, however, by the church he began to build in 1897. Saint-Jean-de-Montmartre at 2 Place des Abbesses in Paris has very little connexion with the Art Nouveau except for its drastic novelty. On the contrary, de Baudot employed for his structural skeleton very much simplified Gothic forms. Actually, it is incorrect to call the material used here *béton armé*; it is more properly *ciment armé* since there is no coarse aggregate as in concrete. Like his master Viollet-le-Duc's projects, Saint-Jean is curious rather than impressive and not at all to be compared in intrinsic interest with Gaudí's Sagrada Familia. Worth noting, however, is the use of faience mosaic to decorate the concrete structural members, something de Baudot had already tried out on his earlier school. The authorities were dubious of the strength of de Baudot's structure, as well they might have been considering the iron-like delicacy of the membering, and a hiatus of several years held up the construction after 1899, the church being completed only in 1902-4. As has been mentioned already, the contractor was Contamin working with Soubaux, his partner of the period.

Before Saint-Jean-de-Montmartre was finally finished in 1904, Perret had already demonstrated the architectural possibilities of the new material rather more effectively in the block of flats that he built in 1902-3 at 25 bis Rue Franklin in Paris. Despite the echo of the Art Nouveau already noted in the foliage patterns of faience mosaic filling the wall-panels on the exterior, most of the interest of the building resides in its structure and its planning. Like that of Anatole de Baudot's church, the structure is visibly a discrete framework, but made up entirely of vertical and horizontal elements with no curved members of either Gothic or Art Nouveau inspiration. However, the concrete is nowhere exposed but always covered with glazed tile sheathing. Within the wall-panels the windows are crisply outlined by plain projecting bands of tile; this provides an early instance of that *encadrement*, or framing, on which Perret came to insist in all his work after the mid twenties.

The skeletal structure of 25 bis Rue Franklin allowed great freedom in planning [255]. Around a small court, sunk into the front of the building, the principal living areas of each flat all open into one another, somewhat as in Wright's Hickox house of 1900 but with less spatial unification [233]; the result is closer to Horta's treatment of the main floor of his Aubecq house of 1900 in Brussels [241].

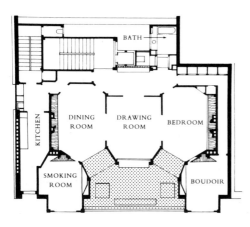

255. Auguste Perret:
Paris, block of flats, 25 bis Rue Franklin, 1902-3

The next year Perret built another block of flats at 83 Avenue Niel in Paris, with an internal skeleton not of concrete but of metal and façades of stone treated somewhat like those of his Art Nouveau flats of the previous year in the Avenue Wagram (see Chapter 17). He returned, however, at once to the use of ferro-concrete and rarely deserted it again.

The Garage Ponthieu, which was built in 1905-6 in the Rue de Ponthieu in Paris, is a much more striking example of the possibilities of the new material than the earlier block of flats; moreover, the concrete is here exposed [256]. Inside, galleries carried along both sides of the L-shaped space provide a second level for parking motor cars and the whole interior is almost as light and open as if it were built of metal, thus recalling a little de Baudot's church. The façade, likewise, is as skeletal as if executed with a metal frame. But Perret's determination, somewhat comparable to Sullivan's in the Wainwright Building in St Louis of fifteen years before, to organize the expression of a new type of construction along basically Classical lines is as evident as the maximal fenestration. The thin slab which projects at the top provides a sort of cornice and the range of small windows underneath it a sort of frieze, while the arrangement of the elements of the façade below is very formal indeed. The rose-window-like glazing of the big central panel is somewhat rudimentary and rather less Classical in feeling than the rest, but the essentials of Perret's concrete aesthetic are all adumbrated here as they were not in the more tentative block of flats in the Rue Franklin.

In the solid, marble-sheathed façade of the Théâtre des Champs Élysées in the Avenue Montaigne in Paris, Perret's largest and most conspicuous early work, his classicizing intentions are even more evident, but the expression of concrete-skeleton structure is much less complete; these intentions are underlined, moreover, by the large stylized reliefs by Antoine

256 Auguste Perret:
Paris, Garage Ponthieu, 1905–6

Bourdelle that provide the only external decoration. Originally, in late 1910, the commission for this theatre was given to Van de Velde. He at once proposed that it should be built of ferro-concrete with the Perret firm as contractors. During the course of the following year Perret suggested various changes in the plan to make more practical its construction with a concrete skeleton. When he later offered an alternative design for the façade this was preferred by Van de Velde because it seemed then so expressive of the underlying structure, as it hardly does to posterity. By September Van de Velde made a final report as consulting architect and withdrew completely. Needless to say, there has been controversy ever since as to the degree of Perret's res-

ponsibility for this major monument of twentieth-century Paris; as built, however, there can be little question that it is very largely of his design. How different a theatre by Van de Velde would have been is at least suggested by the one that he erected in 1914 for the Werkbund Exhibition in Cologne (see Chapter 20).

The foyer of the Théâtre des Champs Élysées expresses the possibilities of ferro-concrete in a more architectural way than do the interiors of the earlier block of flats and the garage. The actual structural members of the skeleton are visible in the free-standing columns, as are also the beams that they support; the walls are very evidently only thin panels between the piers. A few simple mouldings are used to assimilate the new expression to the conventions of academic design – too few to satisfy contemporaries, though too many for later taste.

There is less clarity of expression in the great auditorium because of the profusion of murals contributed by various Symbolists and Neo-Impressionists – Maurice Denis and K.-X. Roussel most notably – and by the over-all gilding[2a] of the principal structural members, which are also elaborated by semi-Classical detailing. Even so, the fact that the dome is carried on the four pairs of tall slender columns is very evident, and the swinging curves of the successive balconies gave early evidence of the ease with which ferro-concrete lends itself to bold cantilevering.

The presumed necessity of achieving monumentality undoubtedly compromised the purity of Perret's expression of structure throughout the Théâtre des Champs Élysées. During the War, which followed so soon after the inauguration of the theatre in 1913, an important industrial commission of Perret's produced what would be for the next generation of architects a more exemplary work. The warehouses built at Casablanca in North Africa in

1915-16 – there are also others there of 1919 – required no representational display; they are almost 'pure' engineering in concrete. But the lightness of their walls, pierced with abstract patterns formed by ventilating holes, and the elegance of their thin shell vaults of segmental section displayed the potentialities of a quite new structural aesthetic, at once delicate and precise, with no echoes at all of the massive masonry buildings of the past.

The interior of the Esders Clothing Factory at 78 Avenue Philippe-Auguste in Paris, erected just after the War in 1919, and several smaller industrial buildings for the metal-working firm of Wallut & Grange at Montataire, Oise, of 1919-21 were more readily studied by younger architects and, in the case of the Esders factory, much grander in scale than the North African warehouses. Even more elegant than the warehouses, and equally 'pure', was the atelier of the decorator Durand built in Paris in the Rue Olivier-Métra in 1922. This has a shell vault rising from the floor broken, along one side only, by a long skylight over widely spaced ribs that continue the half-round curve of the vault.

By this time, of course, ferro-concrete was in general use for industrial building throughout most of the western world. In France the vast parabolic-vaulted aircraft hangar at Orly, Seine, designed by the engineer Eugène Freyssinet (1879-1962) in 1916, overshadowed in size and boldness anything built by Perret. This very exceptional utilitarian construction, magnificent in form yet quite without architectural pretension, was destroyed during the Second World War. To Tony Garnier's work in Lyons we shall turn later.

In America Frank Lloyd Wright used ferro-concrete for his modest E.Z. Polish Factory in Chicago in 1905, just as Ernest L. Ransome was completing the first mature example of a large plant of ferro-concrete frame construction, the United Shoe Machinery Plant in Beverly, Mass., begun in 1903.[3] All over the Middle West, moreover, grain elevators[4] were rising in the form of gigantic linked cylinders.[4a] In Switzerland the great engineer Robert Maillart (1872-1940) in his factories and bridges was using concrete in several new ways as different from the elevators as from the usual timber-like frames of the French and the Americans or the shell vaults of Perret and Freyssinet. Everywhere the importance of ferro-concrete as the prime building material of the twentieth century was receiving increasing recognition; for it was a material more universally available than structural steel and also so elastic in its potentialities that these have hardly even yet been fully exploited.[5] In the early twenties, when a younger generation of architects all over Europe turned their major attention to ferro-concrete as the most modern of building materials, Perret was the architect who had the most to offer them – how limited had been Wright's exploitation of concrete up to this time we shall shortly see (see Chapter 19). When Perret erected the church of Notre-Dame at Le Raincy, a Paris suburb, in 1923-4[5a] concrete came of age as a building material in somewhat the same way that cast iron had done in a series of major English and French edifices of the 1840s (see Chapter 7).

The Le Raincy church is not revolutionary in plan, being a basilica with aisles and an apse; unlike de Baudot's church, however, it has no specific elements of Gothic reminiscence in the interior [257]. Instead it provides what the medieval builders of Saint-Urbain at Troyes or King's College Chapel in Cambridge had obviously sought to achieve, a complete cage of glass supported by a minimal skeleton of solid elements. The broad segmental shell vault of the nave, with smaller vaults running crosswise over the aisle bays in the Cistercian way, is carried on no walls at all but only on the slightest of free-standing columns reeded vertically by the forms in which they

257. Auguste Perret: Le Raincy, S.-et-O., Notre-Dame, 1923–4

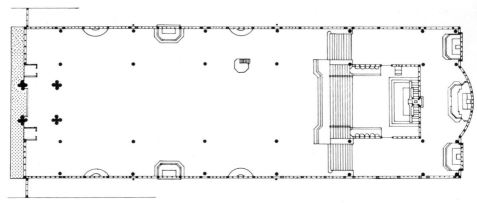

258. Auguste Perret:
Le Raincy, S.-et-O., Notre-Dame, 1923-4

were cast [258]. Quite separate from this supporting skeleton is the continuous enclosing screen of pre-cast concrete units, pierced and filled with coloured glass designed by Maurice Denis. This is carried round the entire rectangle of interior space and bowed out at the east end in a segmental curve to form a shallow apse behind the altar. Only at the front is the clarity of the conception compromised by the awkward impingement of the clusters of columns that shoot up to form the tower.

Deserting the dilute Classicism that was his natural bent, Perret allowed the clustered piers of his tower to rise into the sky, supporting nothing at the top, in order to approximate the outline of a Gothic spire. Even more than in the interior, where one is aware only of the lowest stage, the verticalism and the medieval suggestion of this feature, so over-ingeniously composed of standard ferro-concrete elements, seems quite at odds with the severe concrete-and-glass box that provides the body of the church. Few other ferro-concrete churches[6] of the twenties, least of all Perret's own Sainte-Thérèse at Montmagny, S.-et-O., of 1925-6 and other French ones by his imitators, rival Notre-Dame at Le Raincy. The largest and

boldest, Sankt Antonius at Basel in Switzerland, built by Karl Moser (1860-1936) in 1926-7, seems somewhat heavy and factory-like. Its plain rectangular tower, however, rising free at one corner of the church, is much simpler and more original than Perret's spire and has been frequently and successfully emulated by other architects. Of quite a different order are the Expressionist churches of the German Dominikus Böhm, which have, in the long run, survived aesthetically as well as Perret's (see Chapters 20 and 25).

Two remodelled Paris banks, one of 1922 for the Société Marseillaise de Crédit in the Rue Auber and another of 1925 for the Crédit National Hôtelier, gave evidence of Perret's capacity to extend the implications of ferro-concrete design to more conventional problems. These interiors are almost wholly devoid of ornament, and they largely depend for their effectiveness, like the foyer of the Théâtre des Champs Élysées, upon the careful proportioning of the exposed elements of the skeleton construction. In 1924 the Palais de Bois, a temporary exhibition building at the Porte Maillot in Paris, showed how this sense of direct structural expression could be exploited in a building all of timber. This was much more successful than the theatre that Perret built in 1924-5 for the Paris Exposition des Arts Décoratifs. Of a quite different order was the Tour d'Orientation at Grenoble, also of 1924-5. Here Perret was far happier in achieving something comparable to the richness of medieval spires with standard structural elements and pre-cast panels than in the tower of his church at Le Raincy, for this is much more structurally conceived and quite devoid of Gothic reminiscence in the outline.

The mid twenties also brought to Perret, by this time widely recognized in advanced circles as the leading French architect, several commissions for houses, chiefly for artists, in France and even as far afield as Egypt. Characteristically French in his preoccupation with large, not to say monumental, problems, house-design was not Perret's forte in the way it was that of his American and Austrian contemporaries Wright and Loos. Moreover by this date certain young architects, particularly Le Corbusier and two or three others in Paris, had set under way a revolution in domestic architecture as drastic as Wright's of twenty-five years earlier (see Chapter 22).

Perret's best houses, such as the Mouron house at Versailles of 1926 or the Nubar house in the Rue du 19 Janvier at Garches of 1930, have an almost eighteenth-century dignity and serenity. The 'stripped-Classical' apparatus of terminal cornices, *encadrements* around the openings, and occasional free-standing columns is doubtless logical as an expression of the construction, but it is also very conservative in effect. Yet the ferro-concrete construction encouraged Perret to introduce very wide openings leading out on to surrounding terraces and to open up the main living areas even more than he had done in the flats of 1902-3 in the Rue Franklin. Such treatments were still rather advanced for Europe, however common they may have been in America for a quarter of a

259. Auguste Perret: Paris,
block of flats, 9 Place de la Porte de Passy, 1930

century and more. The characteristic quality of Perret's domestic work is seen at its best in a small block of flats at 9 Place de la Porte de Passy in Paris facing the Bois de Boulogne that he built in 1930 [259]. This has a façade towards the park so superbly proportioned that it might almost be by Schinkel and a flow of space inside the individual flats that is worthy of Wright, although much more formal in organization.

Now Perret began to receive the official commissions that are generally given in France only to men well on in years. The building designed in 1929 that he erected for the technical services of the Ministry of Marine in the Boulevard Victor in Paris is one of the largest and most typical of his later works [260]. The complex rhythms and subtle three-dimensional play of this façade are entirely produced by the actual structural elements. The skeleton divides the long façades into a series of horizontal panels within which are set the vertical frames of the windows separated by pre-cast slabs; in one storey the windows even extend the full width of the bays.

To a considerable extent Perret had succeeded in achieving what he had long con-

260. Auguste Perret:
Paris, Ministry of Marine, Avenue Victor, 1929-30

sciously sought, that is, a vocabulary of design in concrete as direct, as expressive, and as ordered as the masonry vocabulary of the seventeenth and eighteenth centuries – a *style Louis XX*, so to say – still very French in a quite traditional way, yet unmistakably of this century. In the Garde Meuble or National Furniture Storehouse in the Rue Croulebarbe in Paris, begun the next year, the vocabulary is – from principle – all but identical; yet fewer windows and more solid panels were necessary here so that the general effect is flatter and blanker. The curved colonnade across the open side of the court is almost archaeologically reminiscent of the eighteenth century, despite the breadth of its spans and the ingenuity of its detailing. The small concert hall of 1929 in the Rue Cardinet for the École Normale de Musique is less pretentious but also less impressive.

Concrete to Perret, after all these years of employing it, was not a crude or a substitute material. By the use of coloured aggregates which he found various means of exposing

he was able to vary the texture of his poured and pre-cast elements with considerable subtlety and elegance. In the later buildings the workmanship is usually of the highest quality – it was by no means so in the early twenties – with arrises brought to a sharp edge in pure cement and such classicizing details as the flute-like facets on piers and the capital-like treatment of their tops carried to a finish comparable to that of chisel-cut freestone.

Thus Perret was eventually able to avoid the industrial brutality of much work in concrete where the material is left as it comes from rough timber forms with crumbling arrises and pock-marked surfaces. Such lack of finish is acceptable in large-scale engineering work but certainly awkward when seen close to as in Notre-Dame at Le Raincy. On the other hand, Perret kept well away from that slickness of surface – especially popular with younger architects in the twenties – that is produced when concrete is covered with a smooth stucco rendering and painted.[7] Such slickness was, of course, generally very soon lost as the original surface grew cracked and stained; only too rarely is it properly maintained by frequent patching and repainting. Concrete was to Perret a worthy material, like stone, and therefore deserved the effort and the cost required to give it an expressive finish requiring little or no maintenamce.

The reticulated wall system of the big government buildings was also used for a block of flats at 51-55 Rue Raynouard, built in 1932, where Perret himself lived and also maintained his atelier. The necessary adaptation of his formalized open planning to a trapezoidal site produced suites of interior space of considerable complexity yet perfect orderliness. Though Perret was still without a governmental diploma, the atelier[8] he ran here was associated with the École des Beaux-Arts. It almost seemed as if he wished thus to demonstrate how much trucr a representative he was of real French tradition than those who were its official, though unworthy, custodians. Thus the older he grcw the farther his work drew away from that of the more revolutionary modern architects of the second generation. By 1930 it had definitely begun to date; yet it was only in the last twenty-five years of his life that there came to him the greatest opportunities for realizing his ambitions.

In comparison with Perret's own pioneering of 1902 23 his late work seems to lack vitality. For all the thought that went into its finish, for all the virtuosity of certain features – such as the self-supporting curve of the broad stair that spirals down into his atelier in the Rue Raynouard – his very ambition to create a new French tradition gave his later buildings something of the banality of those designed by the more conventionally 'traditional' architects of his generation. This applies in particular to his principal work of the thirties in Paris, the never-finished Musée des Travaux-Publics in the Avenue du Président-Wilson which he began in 1937. Here the ingeniously pseudo-Classical – yet also truly structural – apparatus of external engaged columns and the intricate plan, spreading out from a circular auditorium at the apex of the site, are quite in the Beaux-Arts manner. But the grandeur of scale in the interiors and the exciting upward sweep of the boldly curving stairs lent interest, and even novelty, to a scheme that was in many ways extremely conservative.

After the Second World War Perret was asked to provide plans for the rebuilding of several bombed cities: Le Havre in 1945; Amiens in 1947; and the Vieux-Port district of Marseilles in 1951. For Amiens he designed a rather useless skyscraper, long unoccupied, that derived more indeed from his decorative Tour d'Orientation at Grenoble than from the skyscrapers of the New World. This was one of his few complete failures, if for no other reason than the competition its tall and awkward silhouette offers to the cathedral, whose towers had so long dominated the city's skyline. The executed Marseilles buildings are not of his own design any more than are most of those at Amiens.

At Le Havre, however, his control of the rebuilding was more complete. The Place de l'Hôtel de Ville, or at least the three sides completed between 1948 and 1950 by his associates, outweighed by a great deal the failure of the Amiens skyscraper [261]. Ranges of four-storey buildings, all carried out in the reticulated vocabulary of his Government buildings of the early thirties in Paris, surround a large sunken plaza; the Hôtel de Ville in the near Beaux-Arts manner of his Musée des Travaux-Publics occupies the fourth side. Shops open towards the square under a continuous colonnade. Behind, rising out of small courts, are taller towers occupied by flats; these lend great three-dimensional interest to the formal and absolutely symmetrical layout of this section of the rebuilt quarter. Since his death

261. Auguste Perret:
Le Havre, Place de l'Hôtel de Ville, 1948-54

similar ranges of buildings have been carried out along the quais to the south. On the whole the extensive work of the team[9] is superior to the public monuments by their captain, the Hôtel de Ville and the church of St Joseph, both designed in 1950 and completed before Perret's death in 1954.

Impressive as was Perret's Le Havre in the international roster of post-war urban rebuilding, it long seemed out of date, a mere realization in the 1940s and 1950s, one might almost say, of the aspirations of the early decades of the century. Since that period had few such opportunities as Perret's here to realize urbanism on this scale, however, what he accomplished was a welcome addition to the city-building achievements of this century.

Until the second generation appeared on the scene in the twenties France produced little modern architecture of much interest besides Perret's work. The department stores of the

early years of the century, still strongly under the influence of the Art Nouveau, have already been mentioned (see Chapter 17). After Perret the most important architect was Tony Garnier (1867-1948), and he is of more significance for a vast project that he prepared in his youth than for the executed work of his maturity. In the later decades of the eighteenth century, when the Romantic Classical revolution in architecture was getting under way, projects were often of more interest than executed buildings for their premonitions of what was to come, and this was particularly true in France. It was true there again in the early decades of the twentieth century, down at least to Le Corbusier's project for the Palace of the League of Nations of 1927-8.

Ledoux's 'Ville idéale' summarized his own aspirations and also provided a wealth of ideas from which later generations of Romantic Classical architects could draw inspiration. So, at the opening of the twentieth century, Garnier's very complete scheme for a 'Cité industrielle'[10] contained a wealth of ideas on which architects drew down to the 1920s. Like that of the 'Ville idéale', the interest of the 'Cité industrielle' is threefold: sociological, urbanistic, and architectural. Henceforth the industrial city would be more and more accepted as normal and not exceptional. Its needs both general and specific – so notably recognized by Garnier, all the way from the provision of adequate workers' housing to various sorts of industrial plants – would become more and more important preoccupations of most modern architects. In coping generally with the manifold needs of an industrial community Garnier also faced in detail many very different individual architectural problems with considerable ingenuity.

Garnier's solutions in the main were very simple and direct, but they often had a merely negative character, as of buildings of academic design scraped of all surface paraphernalia, rather than displaying any fresh and creative approach. But an important part of the main architectural development for some twenty years was to be such a purging of inherited excess. Garnier reduced architecture to basic, if not particularly unfamiliar, terms; on his foundations the next generation began, in the twenties, to build something much more positive; thus his influence was parallel to that of Loos (see Chapters 20 and 21). His contribution to the twentieth century's repertory of forms was less than Ledoux's had been to that of the nineteenth a hundred years earlier; notably inferior in quality to Ledoux's was his own actual production, moreover.

Garnier's appointment as Architect of the City of Lyons in 1905, a position which he retained until 1919, might seem to have provided the perfect opportunity to realize his dreams as, but for the Revolution, should Ledoux's appointment by Louis XV to build

the Royal Saltworks at Arc-Senans. But neither the Municipal Slaughterhouse of Lyons at La Mouche, executed in 1909-13, the Herriot Hospital at Grange-Blanche, designed in 1911 and begun in 1915, nor the Olympic Stadium of 1913-16 at Lyons realize much more than the obvious practical implications of the detailed projects for various buildings in his 'Cité industrielle'.[11] The slaughterhouse is bold structurally but clumsily industrial in its handling, with none of the refinement of Perret's factories; the more highly finished stadium has irrelevant Classical touches in the detailing, simple though it is, of the concrete elements.

Garnier's work after the First World War began with the hospital, which was completed only in 1930, and included a large low-cost housing project in the États-Unis quarter of Lyons designed as early as 1920 but executed only in 1928-30. Both are quite overshadowed by the comparable work of the next generation in these years – that in other countries at least, if not that in France. The Moncey Telephone Office at Lyons of 1927, the Textile School at La Croix-Rousse of 1930, and the Hôtel de Ville of the Paris suburb of Boulogne-Billancourt of 1931-4, on which another architect, J.-H.-E. Debat-Ponsan (b. 1882), a pupil of Victor Laloux, collaborated, differ very little from the scraped academicism of most French public architecture of this period. The houses Garnier built in 1909 at St-Rambert and in 1910 at St-Cyr (Mont d'Or) are among his best executed works; all the same, except for their early date, they are hardly very notable.

Two blocks of flats built by Henri Sauvage (1873-1932) in 1925 in the Rue des Amiraux and in the Rue Vavin in Paris, faced with glazed white brick and stepped back in sections to provide terraces for the upper floors, are well above the level of quality of Garnier's later work without approaching that of Perret's. That in the Rue des Amiraux, being for working-class occupancy, is more significant of the international aspirations of the period. Although less drastically novel than the low-cost housing of the twenties in Holland and Germany, this has survived very well because of its permanent grime-proof surfacing. It has been rather unjustly forgotten, largely because it lies off the main line of international development (see Chapter 21).

Most French production in the twenties remained completely subject to academic discipline although it was often tricked out with the sort of modish decoration that flourished particularly at the Paris Exposition des Arts Décoratifs of 1925. Yet at the same time Paris, as the world capital of modern art, was one of the three great foci of architectural advance. The linkage between advanced painting and the Art Nouveau in the nineties was discussed earlier (see Chapter 16). Perret employed Symbolist and Neo-Impressionist painters as collaborators, beginning with the Théâtre des Champs Élysées before the First World War. But there is no real parallel between his architecture and that of Garnier or Sauvage on the one hand and the art of the great twentieth-century masters of the École de Paris on the other. Picasso, Gris, Braque, Matisse, and Derain had no effective influence on architecture. Characteristically Perret employed Bourdelle, not Maillol, when he needed sculpture. With the next generation the situation entirely changed; but the new architects of the twenties, not only in France but everywhere, for all their greater sophistication and their close association with advanced painters and sculptors, still owed at least as much to Perret and to Garnier if not to Sauvage.

To the most creative new architects who appeared around 1920 Garnier's project for the 'Cité industrielle' offered both a challenge and an inspiration, but Perret was by far the more important influence. Somewhat later, towards 1930, that influence became almost ubiquitous in France, and its effect grew increasingly banal as the ferro-concrete Classicism of Perret's later work gradually replaced the official and inherited tradition of the École des Beaux-Arts, by that time nearly obsolete even in France.[12] As has so often happened in France before, a youthful rebel, after being accepted late in life by the academic authorities, was only too ready to supply a new discipline that had itself already become academic. Thus is cultural continuity maintained in France at the expense of variety and recurrent new growth. The situation was rather different in America, as we shall soon see.

CHAPTER 19

FRANK LLOYD WRIGHT

AND HIS CALIFORNIA CONTEMPORARIES

Wright in America found himself, in his seventies, as generally accepted a master as did Perret in France, but his influence never became at all academic in the way of Perret's after 1930. There could hardly be a greater contrast between the careers of two contemporaries in the same field. Both were very productive over a length of time that is more than a third of the whole period covered by this book, but this is about all that they did have in common. Perret's career progressed gradually over several decades to wide and even official acceptance. Wright's career, on the other hand, had very notable ups and downs, and he only once received a governmental commission.

After the years of preparation discussed earlier (see Chapter 15) there followed some ten years of great success. But this success was largely restricted to a particular region, the Middle West, and to a particular field, the building of good-sized suburban houses. Following that, in a decade interrupted by the First World War, Wright's influence rapidly increased, not at home but abroad, although he had considerably fewer, if much larger, commissions. Then, paradoxically, in the twenties, while the United States swung into the biggest building boom in history, there began a decade in which Wright's production all but ceased. Many assumed that his career had closed and that his work had passed into history as had Voysey's and Mackintosh's by that time. This, of course, was not at all true. In the mid thirties Wright's activity revived, and his production continued at a rising rate until his death. Moreover, there was little sign of any decline into personal academicism such as marked the late work of Perret in the same decades.

Where Perret had, in effect, only a double architectural career, being largely occupied on the one hand with industrial commissions close to the dividing line between architecture and engineering, and on the other hand with public buildings, Wright's career was increasingly multifarious. Beginning chiefly as a domestic architect, he never ceased to build houses; but by the 1950s there were few fields, including that of urbanism, which he had not entered, if only to present challenging projects and announce controversial theses. Disciple of a great skyscraper architect, author of a succession of skyscraper projects, Wright had to wait a full half century after Sullivan completed his last skyscraper in Chicago before he built his first, the Price Tower in Bartlesville, Oklahoma, in 1953-5. None of his planning projects came to posthumous execution, but that for Florida Southern College was at least of urbanistic scope.

Perret consciously summarized and continued earlier French tradition; but Wright wished to initiate a new tradition, one which he preferred to call 'Usonian' rather than American. Perret's disciples, emulators, and imitators in his later years were able to some extent and for a while to take control of French architecture. Wright's disciples, despite the fifty years during which he maintained offices that were also training ateliers in Oak Park, in Chicago, in Tokyo, in Wisconsin, and in Arizona, were rarely able to make any significant mark of their own; nor did his influence have much more specific effect on the character of modern architecture in America than it had generically on that of the world outside. Where Perret's influence, particularly outside France, was very largely restricted to architects working with ferro-concrete, the material that he had been the first to master architecturally – and even in concrete construction this influence inhibited quite as often as it liberated – Wright's influence was protean on the international scene. From the day when the German publisher Wasmuth first made Wright's work available to Europeans at the opening of the second decade of the century this was true, down to the time, twenty-five years ago, when the Italian architect, critic, and historian Bruno Zevi (b. 1918) tried to invert chronology so that Wright's 'architettura organica'[1] might seem to have succeeded rather than preceded the 'funzionalismo' or 'International Style' of the second generation of modern architects.

Before turning to a more detailed consideration of Wright's work after 1900 one further comparison with the *œuvre* of Perret may be made. Although Wright never confined himself to one material or to one method of construction – indeed, his versatility in this respect continued to increase right down to his death – he was from the first especially interested in the possibilities of concrete. He published in *The Brickbuilder* for August 1901 a project for a small village bank, still very Sullivanian in its rich detailing, that was intended to be executed entirely in concrete. This was only two years after Perret had first used the material with little or no attempt to develop its architectural possibilities and a year before his block of flats in the Rue Franklin was designed. His E.-Z. Polish Factory of 1905 at 3005-17 West Carroll Avenue in Chicago has already been mentioned. The Unity Church in Oak Park of 1906 [266], entirely of concrete surfaced with a special

pebble aggregate and decorated with integral ornament, precedes by many years Perret's church at Le Raincy [257]. Perret's ultimate development of various refined finishes for exposed concrete came still later. Admittedly, however, the Oak Park church is a much smaller and less striking edifice than Perret's; and the work of Kahn and other industrial architects soon overshadowed Wright's modest factory. Moreover, it was only with the twenties that Wright, like the Europeans, really gave major attention to building in concrete.

Wright's creative powers in the first decade of this century were largely concentrated on his 'Prairie Houses'. Their essentials were already present in the two Kankakee houses of 1900 [232] and the first house designed for the *Ladies' Home Journal* (see Chapter 15). But these essentials received more masterly – one might well say more classic – expression two years later. The large W. W. Willits house at 715 South Sheridan Road in Highland Park, Ill., of 1902 is of wooden-stud construction, but covered like the Kankakee houses with stucco [262]. The C. S. Ross house off the South Shore Road on Lake Delavan in Wisconsin, also of 1902, has the rough board-and-batten sheathing of the River Forest Golf Club [264, 231]. Both offer versions of the cruciform plan [263] with the interior space 'flowing' round a central chimney core and also extended outward on to covered verandas and open terraces quite as in Price's Tuxedo Park houses of fifteen years earlier [227].

Another major work of 1902 is the Arthur Heurtley house at 318 Forest Avenue in Oak Park, Ill. There the principal living areas, which are on the upper floor as in the Husser house of 1899, form an articulated L within the basic square that is defined by the overhanging roof. The brick walls of the lower storey have broad projecting horizontal bands and the wide, low entrance arch remains quite

262 and 263. Frank Lloyd Wright: Highland Park, Ill., W. W. Willits house, 1902

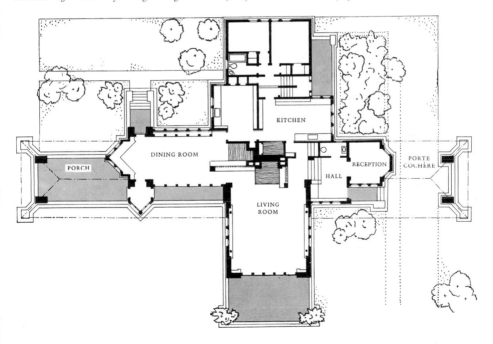

PORCH

DINING ROOM

KITCHEN

RECEPTION

PORTE COCHÈRE

HALL

LIVING ROOM

264. Frank Lloyd Wright:
Delavan Lake, Wis., C. S. Ross house, 1902

Richardsonian. The upper storey consists largely of continuous ranges of wooden-mullioned casement windows.

No continuous progression is observable in the series of suburban houses built in the remainder of this decade before Wright went to Europe in 1909; but he produced many other brilliant illustrations of both the cruciform and the square plan as well as a more elongated sort extending along a single axis. Of the many fine examples of the Willits or Ross type around Chicago, the small house for Isabel Roberts at 603 Edgewood Place in River Forest of 1908 is one of the best; there the living room in the front wing is carried up two storeys, as was proposed for one version of the *Ladies Home Journal* house. The larger F. J. Baker house at 507 Lake Avenue in Wilmette of 1909 also has a two-storeyed living room; but here the tall cross element of the plan which this feature provides was moved to one end of the house so that the plan is of a T or L shape rather than cruciform.

The E. H. Cheney house at 520 North East Avenue in Oak Park of 1904 is square like the Heurtley house near by. It is raised off the ground on a sort of extended square stylobate so that the living area, which runs all across the front as at the Hickox house, can open freely through french doors on to the walled terrace in front. In the T. P. Hardy house at 1319 South Main Street in Racine, Wis., of 1905 a declivitous lakeside site encouraged a vertical rather than a horizontal organization of the interior with a two-storey living room as the spatial core.

A very different feeling pervades the small, squarish house at 6 Elizabeth Court in Oak Park that Wright built for Mrs Thomas Gale in 1909. Here flat slabs - which had been proposed in a somewhat earlier project (perhaps for execution in concrete) for the Yahara Boat Club in Madison, Wis. - replace the low-pitched hip or gable roofs of the characteristic Prairie Houses. Moreover, parapeted balconies and other simple rectangular features elaborate

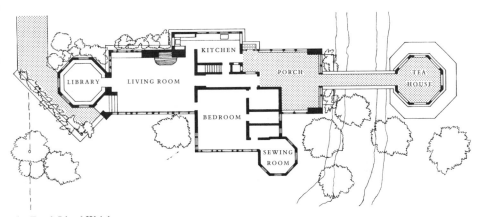

265. Frank Lloyd Wright:
Glencoe, Ill., W. A. Glasner house, 1905

plastically the composition in a fashion that suggests the abstract sculpture of a decade later in Europe (see Chapter 21).

The W. A. Glasner house of 1905 at 850 Sheridan Road in Glencoe, Ill., on the contrary was extended longitudinally and the living area for the first time not at all articulated but completely unified [265]. Something of the same longitudinal extension marks the much larger F. C. Robie house at 5757 Woodlawn Avenue in Chicago of 1909.[1a] But there the living room and dining room are separated by the chimney core and raised above the ground level. Built of fine Roman brick, this is the most monumental of these early houses. The long horizontal lines of the balcony below and the roof above dominate the composition; yet a cross element comes forward in the upper storeys to provide, less symmetrically than in his houses of cruciform plan, something of the abstract plasticity of the Gale house.

Another large house of the end of the decade, the Avery Coonley house at 300 Scottswood

Road in Riverside, Ill., of 1908, offers a quite different and much more extended plan. The square block containing the living room rises above a terrace and a reflecting pool as the main element of the design, but from this block two long wings project. That to the left includes a large dining room and also very extensive service facilities at the rear; in the one to the right are the master's suite and other bedrooms. Thus the house is, in a later phrase of Wright's, 'zoned' according to function. The upper walls are covered with a geometrical pattern produced by setting coloured tiles into the stucco, as several years earlier on the Dana house in Springfield, Ill. Wright never did quite the same thing again, but this led the way to his later use of patterned concrete blocks.

Two of Wright's non-domestic works of this period are of considerable importance. Unity Church in Oak Park has already been mentioned; the other was the Larkin Administration Building in Buffalo, N.Y., of 1904. Massive and even sculptural externally, particularly at the ends, this had a tall glass-roofed court running down the centre, around which the upper ranges of offices extended on galleries carried by somewhat Sullivanian piers. All the fittings of the offices, including the steel furniture - probably the first to be designed by an architect - were Wright's. Thus he set here a wholly new standard of elegance, consistency, and coherence in semi-industrial building.

Within the massive slab-roofed block of the Unity Temple [266], which is echoed beyond a low entrance link by the smaller block of the Sunday School, Wright achieved even more notably than inside the Larkin Building a new sort of monumental space-composition such as even his biggest houses hardly provided room for. The square auditorium with incut corners has double galleries on three sides and a pulpit platform on the fourth, behind which rises the organ. The multiple spatial elements seem to cross one another at different levels in a sort of three-dimensional plaid. Moreover, this theme is echoed in all the minor features, such as the wood stripping of the sand-finished plaster walls and the prominent lighting fixtures. Of this spatial development there had been some premonition in the auditorium block at one end of the Hillside Home School that he built for his aunts outside Spring Green, Wis., in 1902; but there the masonry of the exterior walls and piers was still rather Richardsonian and the internal gallery consisted of a square set lozenge-wise.

Wright's work down to 1910 was made available to Europeans by two publications of Wasmuth, the Berlin publisher; and the end of the first decade of the century does, coincidentally, mark a real turning point in his career.

266. Frank Lloyd Wright:
Oak Park, Ill., Unity Church, 1906

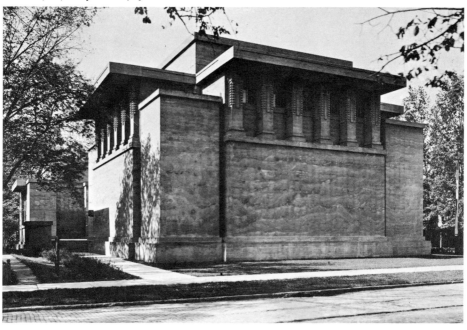

He would not be so prolific again before the forties; and henceforth, although he never ceased to build houses, these would no longer constitute the bulk of his production.

The production of the next decade, after his return from Europe in 1911, opens with two houses, however. Taliesin, which he built outside Spring Green for his mother in 1911, was soon much enlarged when he moved there himself and it always remained his principal residence. As a result of the growing needs of his family and of his school – not to speak of two major fires in 1914 and 1925 – the Taliesin[1b] of today is very different, above all in its endless ramification, from what he planned in 1911; but the vocabulary of materials and design stayed more or less constant through all the years. Where the Prairie Houses echoed in their horizontal lines the flat Illinois terrain on which most of them were set, Taliesin is wrapped around a hill-top just below the crest. The use of various levels in the interior and a landscape-like elaboration of the low-pitched roofs represent his response to this more interesting site; after that the 'Prairie' master avoided flat sites for houses whenever he could!

Taliesin, combining a house, drawing office, living accommodation for apprentices, and even farm buildings, had from almost the first a complex plan not readily definable as square, cruciform, or unilinear. But in a project of the same year 1911 in which Taliesin was originally built, that for the S. M. Booth house at Glencoe, Ill. – never executed, unfortunately, according to these plans – a new sort of organization appeared, related to the elaborated cube of the Gale house and also the the 'zoned' scheme of the Coonley house. A two-storey living-room was to provide both the spatial and the plastic core; from this wings serving different purposes would shoot out swastika-like.

The relative homogeneity of Wright's production in the first decade of the century, following after the gradual convergence of his early work during the nineties, is explained by the very similar clients and sites that he faced in designing the houses mentioned so far. This homogeneity now gave way to an increasing variety that makes it difficult to summarize the work of these years. The Coonley Playhouse, built on the Coonley estate at Riverside in 1912, bears little resemblance to the original house of four years earlier. The plan is cruciform and symmetrical; but what is new here is the way the slab roofs, set at two different levels and pierced through their wide projections in order to let light reach the windows below, were used to achieve an even more boldly sculptural quality than in the early project for the Yahara Boat Club or the Gale house of 1909. Wright's mastery of abstract decoration was wholly mature by this time. From the first he had used leaded glass in simple geometrical patterns in his windows,[2] but the windows in this playhouse are the finest of all. Moreover, these festive compositions of circles of coloured glass arranged asymmetrically resemble quite closely the abstract paintings that such artists as Kupka, Delaunay, and the Constructivists were already beginning to produce in Europe.

Northome, the F. W. Little house[2a] at Wayzata, Minn., of 1913 was also quite different from all the earlier houses, yet not at all similar to the Coonley Playhouse. Raised on a ridge above the southern shore of Lake Minnetonka, this house consisted of a series of pavilions – some open, some closed – strung along a single axis parallel to the water's edge. That containing the living room, which was of almost monumental size and scale, dominated the whole. Wright seemed able then to invent a new mode almost with every individual commission, each one with potentialities as great as those of the Prairie Houses he had so thoroughly exploited in the decade before 1910.

The major work of the immediate pre-war years, the Midway Gardens of 1913-14 on the

Midway south of Chicago, is rather hard to define precisely. Not quite a beer or *Heuriger* garden, nor yet a music-hall or cabaret in the ordinary European sense, the establishment consisted of a large outdoor dining and entertainment area with raised terraces on two sides, a stage and orchestra shed at the far end, and a closed restaurant block towards the street. Here Wright's ambitions as a decorative artist could have free play. Abstract compositions of coloured circles like those in the windows of the Coonley Playhouse appeared here as wall-high murals at the ends of the covered restaurant. Moreover, the sculptural implications of the general composition of the playhouse were carried farther in the openwork 'constructions' that he set on the tops of the towers. There is also a great deal of figurative sculpture by Alfonso Iannelli stylized in a rather Cubist way. Thus several different aspects of the abstract and near-abstract art which was just coming into independent existence in Europe were closely paralleled in the adjuncts to Wright's architecture here.

More architectonic patterns produced by simple geometrical means also ran riot at the Midway Gardens. Notable and significant was the use of extensive areas of patterned concrete blocks; these were somewhat like the patterned upper walls of the Coonley house of 1908 but all monochrome. The early demolition of the Midway Gardens makes it difficult to know whether this tremendous elaboration of the decorative aspects of Wright's architecture was symphonic or cacophonous in total effect. Whatever the degree of their success or their failure, however, they opened a sort of 'Mannerist' or 'Baroque'[3] period in his career that was destined to last for more than a decade.

In this same year 1913 Wright was first approached by emissaries of the Japanese Imperial Household to design the Imperial Hotel in Tokyo.[3a] Proceeding to Japan, Wright was largely concerned with this commission over the next nine years. Construction continued from 1916 to 1922. This was the principal production of his 'Baroque' phase. It was also a notable engineering triumph, for his ingenious use of concrete slabs carried on a multitude of concrete piles brought it safely through the earthquake of 1923. Paul Mueller, the engineer of the old Adler & Sullivan office, was his collaborator here.

Abstract ornament proliferated on the hotel; some of it, carved in greenish lava, elaborated the garden courts of the vast H-shaped plan; still more was painted in gold and colour on the ceilings of the principal interiors. Moreover, the massive proportions of the masonry walls produced an effect of castle-like solidity wholly inexpressive of the method of their support and very far removed from the light and floating character of the Prairie Houses. On the whole this hotel represented, far more than the Midway Gardens, a cul-de-sac in Wright's development. It was demolished in 1967-8.

Overlapping the period of construction of the Imperial Hotel came a series of houses in southern California in which the 'Baroque' element was gradually restrained. The earliest of these, Hollyhock House in Los Angeles and two smaller houses near by, were built for Aline Barnsdall in 1920 on a large estate bounded by Sunset and Hollywood Boulevards, Edgemont Street, and Vermont Avenue. These are of poured concrete very massively handled and carry considerable abstract sculptural ornamentation. For a slightly later series of four houses around Los Angeles, beginning with the house of 1923 for Mrs G. M. Millard at 645 Prospect Crescent in Pasadena, Wright developed a type of concrete-block construction with reinforcement in the joints that was of considerable technical interest and also offered special decorative possibilities. The idea of using concrete blocks cast with relief patterns of geometrical character goes back to the Midway Gardens, however, and walls covered with

267. Frank Lloyd Wright: Pasadena, Cal., Mrs G. M. Millard house, 1923

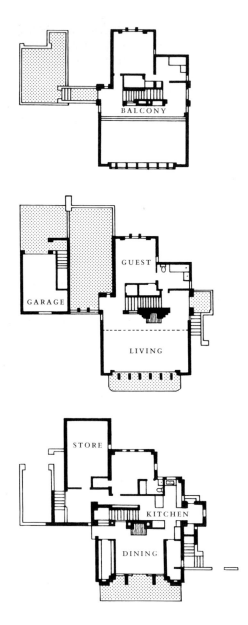

268. Frank Lloyd Wright:
Pasadena, Cal., Mrs G. M. Millard house, 1923

repeating ornamental units had first appeared on the Dana house twenty years before.

In the Millard house, particularly, the scale of the moulded blocks and the ingenious inclusion of pierced units – very similar to the pre-cast elements that Perret was using for the screen walls of his Le Raincy church at just this time – produced a masterpiece [267]. This house, however, is not solely of interest for its construction and its decoration. In contrast to the horizontal composition of almost all his earlier houses except that in Racine for the Hardys, this is a tall vertical block, entered at the middle level, with the dining room and kitchen below and the two-storey living room opening out to a balcony at the front [268]. The main bedroom is reached from a gallery overhanging the rear of the living-room. Both organizationally and visually this represents a surprising change, and the result closely resembled what a leading architect of the second generation had just then been proposing in Europe [300]. There are, for instance, no hovering eaves here; instead a parapet continues the wall plane upwards and confines a roof terrace. This is as close as Wright ever came to building a 'box-on-stilts', his term of abuse for the advanced European houses of the twenties. It was as if, after the expansiveness of his work from the Midway Gardens to Hollyhock House, Wright wished to prove here his capacity to produce a house modest in scale and compact in section as well as in plan.

In the next decade, from 1924 to 1934, Wright's actual production declined almost to zero although he was working on a series of important projects, some of which later provided the basis for executed buildings. Taliesin was rebuilt after a fire in 1925, however – it had already been rebuilt once before after an earlier fire in 1914 – and a large house of concrete blocks, with almost no use of pattern except for occasional pierced grilles, was erected for his cousin Richard Lloyd Jones in 1929 at 3700

Birmingham Road in Tulsa, Okla. That is about all.

The small M. C. Willey house of 1934 at 255 Bedford Street, S.E., in Minneapolis marked the beginning of what proved to be almost a second career for Wright. Low and L-shaped, with practically no ornament whatsoever, this modest brick house introduced a major change in domestic planning. Not only are the living room and the dining room completely unified, as was first done at the Glasner house in 1905, but the kitchen – now re-christened 'work-space' – opens into the main living area behind a range of glazed shelves [269]. Thirty years later the full implications of this development were still not quite digested in America or even fully apprehended abroad; on the contrary, a reaction from open planning was well under way.

It was not the Willey house, however, modest in size and very quiet in expression for all its

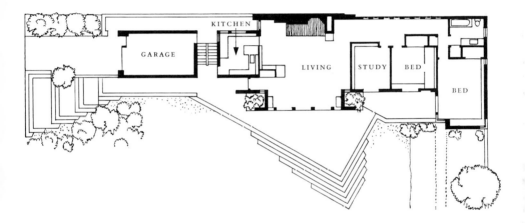

269. Frank Lloyd Wright: Minneapolis, M. C. Willey house, 1934

270 *(below and opposite)*. Frank Lloyd Wright: Falling Water, Pennsylvania, 1936-7

revolutionary plan, that signalized the renewal of Wright's activity. That he could take up his career again at the highest level of creativity became apparent to everyone with the construction of two much larger buildings both designed in 1936. Falling Water,[3b] a large house in the Pennsylvania woods, is cantilevered over a waterfall with a sense of drama even Wright had never hitherto approached. The Administration Building for the S. C. Johnson Wax Company at 1525 Howe Street in Racine, Wis., his first semi-industrial commission since the Larkin Building of 1904, was built in 1937-9. Both are as remarkable for the technical bold-

very much elaborated from, that of the Gale house of 1909 [270 A, B]. The completely unified living space is closed in by stone walls on the inner or dining side. It also extends out over the waterfall; the all-glass walls on that side, with their thin metal mullions, hardly seem to separate the interior space at all from that of the open terraces outside. A similar relationship exists between the bedrooms and their terraces on the upper floors.

Never before had Wright exploited the structural possibilities of concrete so boldly. In this amazingly plastic composition – if 'plastic' be the word for anything so light and

ness of their use of concrete – totally different in the two cases – as for their design.

Falling Water has a rear section built of rough stone which rises like a tower from the native rock on the banks of Bear Run. From this solid vertical core are cantilevered out a series of concrete slabs bounded by plain parapets at their edges. This produces a very complex horizontal composition related to, but

suspended in appearance – it seems as if he had determined to outbid the European architects of the second modern generation at their own games (see Chapter 22). His early work has, in the clarity and axial character of the organization and the serenity of its expression, a classic if hardly a Classical quality; his work of 1914-24 shows a Baroque exuberance in the proliferation of the ornament. Now that he was

271. Frank Lloyd Wright: Racine, Wisconsin,
S. C. Johnson and Sons, Administration Building
and Laboratory Tower, 1937-9 and 1946-9

approaching seventy his Romantic or anti-Classical tendencies – call them what you will – reached an intensity of purely architectonic expression comparable to the musical intensity of the late quartets of Beethoven that Wright so much admired. Falling Water, which might easily have been the swan song of Wright's career, soon to be halted again by a second World War, proved in fact but the opening *allegro* in a new period of innovation and experiment.

The Johnson Building[3c] is very different from Falling Water. In it the curve rather than the cantilever provides the principal theme, and enclosure rather than interpenetration of exterior and interior space controls both the planning and the design [271]. The main office area is tall and unified, but it is filled with a forest of inverse-tapered concrete piers rising from tiny bronze shoes to carry circular slabs of concrete whose edges all but touch. The spaces between these lilypad-like disks were filled with tubes of Pyrex glass, and bands of

similar tubes are carried around the building below the balcony and at the top of the plain red brick walls to provide additional natural light. In the more specialized adjuncts to the general office area curved and diagonal plan-elements lend a machine-like elegance to the shape of the building as a whole. Additional bands of glass tubing interrupt the smooth and continuous masonry surfaces at intervals, thus clearly indicating that these portions are of several storeys.

Falling Water and the Johnson Building were large and expensive structures; so also was Wingspread, the H. F. Johnson house that Wright built in Racine at the same time. This is zoned in the manner of the Booth project of 1911 around a tall central core. But in 1937 Wright also erected the first of what he called his 'Usonian' houses, the Herbert Jacobs house at Westmorland, near Madison, Wis. This modest L-shaped dwelling, with wooden 'sandwich' walls and a flat wooden slab roof, carried farther than the Willey house the integration of the 'work-space' or kitchen with the main living area. Here this rises in a masonry tower and is lighted by a clerestory, yet it is closely related to the space of the interior as a whole. A very considerable range of Wright's later houses are variants of the Usonian model. Some were built before the War, even more in his last decade; some are of modest dimensions like the Jacobs house, others much larger. They exist in all parts of the United States, including the East, where he had hardly worked at all before this time.

The earlier Usonian houses were designed on a square module. This is true, for example, of the version that he prepared for *Life* magazine in 1938,[4] which thereby received the same sort of national circulation that the *Ladies' Home Journal* gave to three of his projects more than a generation earlier.[5] But Wright was now interested also in developing the hexagon and the triangle as basic units. Beginning with the Hanna house of 1937 at 737 Coronado Street in Palo Alto, Cal., he continued in many others to explore the possibilities of planning based on 60-30-degree angles.

In the most extraordinary house that he built in these pre-war years, his own winter residence, Taliesin West, begun in 1938 in the desert, at Scottsdale, Ariz., 45-degree diagonals are used in the planning and almost all the structural elements are battered or canted. However, it is the materials which give this edifice – like Taliesin itself at once a house, a working place, and a school – its unique qualities. The substructure is of 'desert concrete', that is great rough blocks of tawny local stone placed in forms and loosely stuck together, so to say, with concrete; the superstructure was of dark-stained timber frames mostly filled only with canvas to allow a maximum flow of air. As at the original Taliesin in Wisconsin, Wright kept on enlarging Taliesin West, not always to its advantage.[5a] Another example of 'desert-concrete' construction, the Rose Pauson house of 1940 in near-by Phoenix, was destroyed by

fire. It was, in its sculptural way, a masterpiece of this period unlike anything else he ever built and is still an impressive ruin.

It was characteristic of Wright's activity in his 'second' career that the versatility of his invention knew no bounds. Many earlier ideas that had existed only in projects could come to fruition now that his services were in such demand. At the same time it is hard to believe that in the plain white stucco walls, extensive window bands, and thin roof slab of the E. J. Kaufmann guest house, built just above Falling Water in 1939, or in the G. D. Sturges house of the same year at 449 Skyway Road in Brentwood Heights near Los Angeles, cantilevered out from a hill-slope, Wright was not consciously rivalling the effects of the European architects of the second generation whom he professed to scorn – rivalling them, but also making very much his own such of their effects as he cared to emulate.

Wright did not drop the novel methods of construction that he had developed earlier as he tried out new ones. In his most extensive late commission, the layout of a new campus for Florida Southern College at Lakeland in Florida, begun in 1938, the plan is highly formal at the same time that it is markedly asymmetrical. It thus elaborates upon the angular themes of his project of 1927 for a desert resort at Chandler, Arizona – incidentally the point at which his interest in 60-30-degree angles began. The buildings at Florida Southern, starting with the Ann Pfeiffer Chapel of 1940 to which many more were later added, are mostly of concrete-block construction, but with much less use of patterned elements than in the executed work and projects of the twenties.

The Second World War interrupted Wright's career less than the First. Various projects initiated in the war years came to fruition soon after the war was over and gave evidence of the continuing vitality of his powers of invention. The second house for Herbert Jacobs at

Middleton in the country west of Madison, Wis., was very different from the Usonian one of 1937. Ever since an unexecuted house project of 1938 Wright had been fascinated by the possibilities of using the circle in planning. While he had tried out the form in the Florida Southern Library before the war, the Jacobs house of 1948 was the first of a series of houses that he built with curved plans. Its two-storey living area bends around a circular sunken garden court with the bedrooms opening off a balcony above [272]. On the other side the house is half buried in the hill-top, above which rise its walls of coursed rubble. A tower-like

circular core near one end of the convex side provides a strong vertical accent.

Another house of the post-war years, also based on the circle, is quite different in character. The Sol Friedman house in Pleasant-ville, N.Y., is roofed with mushroom-like concrete slabs; the two intersecting closed circles of the actual dwelling are balanced at the end of a straight terrace parapet by the open circle of the carport [273]. This was completed in 1949 with battered walls of almost Richardsonian random ashlar masonry below a strip of metal-framed windows. A still later 'house of circles' for his son David J. Wright

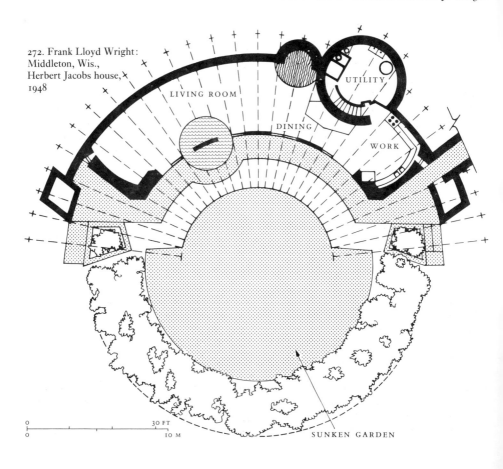

272. Frank Lloyd Wright:
Middleton, Wis.,
Herbert Jacobs house,
1948

LIVING ROOM

UTILITY

DINING

WORK

0   30 FT
0   10 M

SUNKEN GARDEN

273. Frank Lloyd Wright:
Pleasantville, N.Y., Sol Friedman house, 1948-9

was built near Phoenix, Ariz., in 1952. This is of concrete blocks and raised off the ground, with the approach up a gently sloping helical ramp to the various curved rooms on the first storey. The circle and the helix appear also in an urban building of these years, the shop for V. C. Morris in Maiden Lane, San Francisco, completed in 1949. Here the street façade is a sheer plane of yellow brick broken only by the entrance, which is a Sullivanian – or Richardsonian – arch like that of the Heurtley house of 1902. Inside, a helical ramp rises around the central circular area beneath a ceiling made of bubble-like elements executed in plastics.

A major work of these years, the extension of the Johnson Administration Building in Racine, Wis., also completed in 1949, makes much use of circles also [271]. North of the existing office building Wright surrounded a square court with open carports whose outer walls of solid brickwork shut out the surrounding city; inside these walls are ranged short concrete columns with lily-pad tops like those in the section that he built ten years earlier. In the centre of the 'piazza' thus defined rises a laboratory tower of tree-like structure. The upper floors of this, alternately square with

rounded corners and circular, are all cantilevered out from a central cylindrical core which contains the lift and the vertical canalizations. Alternate bands of brickwork and Pyrex tubing, such as were used on the original building, enclose the tower except at ground level; there the space of the court continues under the cantilevered floors above as far as the solid central core.

This relatively modest tower prepared the way for Wright's skyscraper in Bartlesville, Okla., of 1953-5, which has been mentioned earlier. Actually, however, this Price Tower,[6] which is partly occupied by offices and partly by flats, is the final realization of a project originally prepared in 1929 for a block of flats for St Mark's Church in New York. This he had elaborated in the intervening years in projects for blocks of flats in Chicago and for a hotel in Washington.

While Wright was continuing to employ in his houses of the late forties and early fifties a variety of modes of design that go back to the thirties, and also developing at Florida Southern and in Bartlesville ideas dating from his inactive period in the late twenties, he continued to strike out in other directions too. The Neils house at 2801 Burnham Boulevard on Cedar Lake in Minneapolis, Minn., completed in 1951, is all of coloured marble rubble provided by the client; the Walker house at Carmel, Cal., completed in 1952, is a glazed polygonal pavilion overhanging the sea. Where the Prairie Houses of the first decade of Wright's mature career may all seem in retrospect to have come out of the same, or nearly identical, moulds, the many houses designed in his seventies and eighties are notable for the great variety of their siting, their materials, and the geometrical themes of their planning.

Nor was the domestic field anything like the sole area of his activity. In addition to the college buildings, the shop, the skyscraper, and the laboratory that have been mentioned, Wright built during the years 1947-52 a Unitarian church in Madison, Wis., of very original character. The products of his multifarious activity in these years included, moreover, many projects for all sorts of structures, several of which were later completed – notably the Solomon R. Guggenheim Museum in New York [362, 363]. A decade and more of designing and re-designing preceded the initiation of this remarkable helical concrete building in 1956. Of three other late projects, those for an opera-house in Baghdad and for an Arizona state capitol in Phoenix, dating from 1957, will never be built; but of the county buildings for Marin County, Cal., half was finished some twenty years ago and the rest has since been completed by Wright's successors.[6a]

In spite of so much late activity, greater than that of his early maturity, in spite (or perhaps, in part, because) of its kaleidoscopic variety, Wright's actual influence was less significant than forty years before; at least it was of a very different order. He still outpaced his juniors both of the next generation and the one after; but few if any were able to follow with any success along the intensely personal paths he opened.[7] Like Perret to the end of his life,

Wright continued at ninety to offer an inspiration to all architects, but there developed no school of imitators to vulgarize his manner as there was long a group of such imitators of Perret in France.

In creative power, in productivity, and, over the half-century after 1910, in influence, Wright overshadowed all the other American architects of his generation. Inspired less by Wright than by Sullivan, there flourished for a while a sort of 'Second Chicago School'[7a] to which Purcell & Elmslie; George W. Maher (1864-1926); Schmidt, Garden & Martin,[8] and several other architects who were active in the Middle West before the First World War may be considered to belong. But this school flickered out during the twenties as most of its members succumbed to the dominant 'traditionalism' of the day or else ceased to find clients.[9] Four rather more vital and original architects appeared shortly after 1900 in California: the brothers Greene (Charles S., 1868-1957, and Henry M., 1867-1954), Irving Gill (1870-1936), and Bernard R. Maybeck (1862-1957).[10] But the productive careers of the Greenes, of Gill, and, to a lesser extent, that of Maybeck came pretty much to a close, like those of the Chicagoans, around 1915 with the resounding success of the 'traditional' buildings designed by Bertram G. Goodhue (1869-1924) for the San Diego Exhibition of that year.[11] These were in the most ornate sort of Spanish Baroque, quite archaeologically handled; and the emulation of them, which at once became endemic in California, turned most local architects away from innovation for almost twenty years.

Maybeck, who had been a graduate of the École des Beaux-Arts in the eighties, contributed to the San Francisco Exhibition of the same year the still extant Fine Arts Building in an equally 'traditional' but more Classical vein.[12] Long partly ruined, his tawny stucco columns and entablatures had the air of a

274. Bernard Maybeck:
Berkeley, Cal., Christian Science Church, 1910

painting by Pannini or Hubert Robert. For all its charm,[12a] this was a surprising work to come from a man who had earlier shown himself, in the Christian Science Church of 1910 in Berkeley, Cal., almost as bold an innovator as Wright, even though he employed for that a fantastically eclectic vocabulary of reminiscent forms [274]. Many Berkeley houses, moreover, ranging over several decades in date, also prove Maybeck to have been an architect of great originality and surprising versatility.

In Berkeley also are several houses by John Galen Howard (1864-1931) as well as his building for the University of California's School of Architecture, of which he was for long the Dean. His building at the University (which has in addition a Faculty Club and one or two other things by Maybeck), the Gregory house of about 1904, and the architect's own house of 1912 are also notable examples of free design dating from the first decades of the century. Howard's informal work is more directly related than are Wright's houses to the Shingle Style of the preceding period, though not specifically to that of Richardson, for whom, however, Howard had actually worked in the mid eighties before he came to California. Most of his work at the University, in fact, is in an Italianate vein, and the campus is dominated by his tall, campanile-like clock tower.

The production of the Greene brothers in this period, though limited and largely in Pasadena, offers a more coherent corpus than

275. Greene & Greene:
Pasadena, Cal., D. B. Gamble house, 1908-9

that of any modern American architect of their generation except Wright. Related, like the work of Howard, to the Shingle Style, which had been brought to Pasadena and Los Angeles by Eastern architects in the eighties and nineties, the Greenes' houses are most interesting for their successful assimilation of oriental influences. The best example is the Gamble house at 4 Westmorland Place in Pasadena of 1908-9 [275]. But the Pitcairn house of 1906 and the Blacker house of 1907, at 289 West State Street and at 1157 Hillcrest respectively, as well as the later Thorsen house of 1909, at 2307 Piedmont Avenue in Berkeley, now a fraternity house, are of comparable quality.

Shingled walls, low-pitched and wide-spreading gables, and extensive porte-cochères and verandas of stick-work surpassing in virtuosity those of the Stick Style, were combined by the Greenes in rather loosely organized compositions. Less formal and regular than Wright's Prairie Houses, theirs are executed throughout with a craftsmanship in wood

rivalling that of the Japanese, whom they, like Wright, so much admired. The Greenes' plans are less open than Wright's, but they made more use of verandas and balconies than he. Superb woodwork and fine stained glass combine with the specially designed furniture in the interiors to produce ensembles of a sturdy elegance hardly matched by any of Wright's. Those in the Blacker and Thorsen houses, whose clients were both in the lumber business, were especially rich.

Moreover, a 'California Bungalow' mode[13] – at worst but a parody at small scale of the Greenes' expensive mansions, at best sharing many of their virtues of directness and simplicity if not of imaginative craftsmanship – became widely popular thanks to national magazines, pattern-books, and the activities of many builders. This was true not alone in the West but throughout the country in the very years after 1910 when 'traditionalism', usually in Neo-Colonial guise, closed in most completely on American domestic architecture.

The reputation of the Greenes was long lower than that of the more articulate but less consistent Maybeck. But when modern architecture revived in California in the thirties the new men were fully aware of what the Greenes had accomplished. Thus their work provided, together with that of Maybeck and Howard, a background and a tradition for the local development of a largely autochthonous domestic architecture in the San Francisco Bay area. This was truly a living tradition[14] quite unlike the abortive revival of the architecture of the Spanish Missions, which before long it almost completely displaced. But the Mission influence was not altogether a negative one in early twentieth-century California, as the work of Irving Gill illustrates.

Gill was less consistent than the Greene brothers, and much of what he built is less striking. Like Voysey, he was at first a reformer not a revolutionary, finding his early inspiration more in the local structural tradition of the early Spanish Missions and *haciendas*. As a result some of his buildings, such as the First Church of Christ Scientist of 1904-7 in San Diego or in Los Angeles the Laughlan house of 1907 and the Banning house of 1911, at 666 West 28th Street and 503 South Commonwealth Avenue respectively, with their elliptically arched loggias and their grilles of ornamental ironwork, are almost as 'Spanish Colonial' as the work of the outright traditionalists around him.

Gill's most interesting and mature houses, thanks to their smooth stucco walls, large window areas, and avoidance of stylistic detail, can also have a deceptive air of being European rather than American and of a period some years later than that in which they were actually built. In his best work, such as the Dodge house [276] of 1915-16 once at 950 North Kings Road in Los Angeles or the Scripps house at La Jolla of 1917, now the Art Centre, the asymmetrically organized blocks, crisply cut by large

276. Irving Gill: Los Angeles,
Walter Dodge house (now demolished), 1915-16

windows of various sizes carefully sashed and disposed, with roof terraces or flat roofs above, more than rival the contemporary houses of the Austrian architect Adolf Loos [286] in the abstract distinction of the composition. They even approach rather closely the most advanced European houses of the next decade (see Chapters 21 and 22).

Gill's interiors are especially fine and also quite like Loos's. Very different from the rich orientalizing rooms designed by the Greenes, they are in fact more similar to real Japanese interiors in their severe elegance. The walls of fine smooth cabinet woods, with no mouldings at all, are warm in colour, and Voysey-like wooden grilles of plain square spindles give human scale. The whole effect, in its clarity of form and simplicity of means, is certainly more premonitory of the next stage of modern architecture than any other American work of its period.

Gill continued to practise intermittently down into the thirties, but his finest work was done in the second decade of the century. He had little influence locally and still less nationally, yet his best houses extend very notably the range of achievement of the first generation of modern architects in America, even though his later production declined sadly in quantity and even in quality. Wright alone was able to renew his career successfully after the reaction against modern architecture that dominated America from coast to coast during the twenty years from the First World War to the mid nineteen-thirties finally came to an end.

CHAPTER 20

PETER BEHRENS AND OTHER GERMAN ARCHITECTS

The pattern of architectural development in Germany in the early decades of this century was rather different from that in either France or the United States. No academy, native or foreign, no influences from the École des Beaux-Arts discouraged innovation; yet there was an early and general reaction against the whimsicality and the decorative excesses of the Art Nouveau at which most of the younger men had tried their hands before 1900. After the First World War, however, the example of Expressionism in painting and sculpture led many architects to excesses of another sort. Expressionism in architecture,[1] or something very close to it, is not restricted to Germany. The most extreme example of any consequence, and probably the earliest, is Dutch, the Scheepvaarthuis in Amsterdam of 1912–13 by van der Meij (see Chapter 21). In Germany around 1920 various architects who had earlier been predominantly 'traditional' in their approach were influenced by Expressionism, as well as others who were already programmatically modern; nor was that influence restricted to the modern architects of the first generation (see Chapter 22).

The boundary line between what, in retrospect, still seems definitely modern and what now seems very similar to the 'traditional' work of these decades in other countries is much less sharp than in America. And no German architect of their own generation had the continuously creative achievement of a Perret or a Wright to his credit. Nevertheless Peter Behrens stands out among his contemporaries because of the vigorous boldness of his industrial buildings. Moreover, the influence of his factories of around 1910 was crucial on the next genera-

tion, and several of the later leaders actually worked in his office at that relevant period. Yet all but Behrens's finest work can be matched in the production of other German architects; while his own vitality as an innovator was rather strictly limited to a few years and to what he did for one corporate client. That client was the A.E.G. (German General Electric Company), which had already employed Messel down to his death in 1909.

Messel and Ludwig Hoffmann (1851–1932) dominated the architectural scene in Berlin, where the latter was appointed City Architect in 1896 on the strength of his vast academic Imperial Law Courts of 1886–95 in Leipzig. In the early years of the century they both developed a formal mode that was more 'traditional' than modern. Parallel to Messel's and Hoffmann's usual preference for conventional sixteenth- or eighteenth-century models was Behrens's dependence on the Romantic Classicism of Schinkel, even though his positive source of inspiration was of an entirely different order. In so far as one can sort out the different architectural camps in Germany in these years, Behrens must be considered well to the artistic 'left' of Messel and Hoffmann.

Germany was certainly very receptive to new ideas in decoration when Behrens's architectural career began at the turn of the century – receptive rather than creative. There were other Germans who handled the Art Nouveau with considerable originality besides August Endell, notably Bernard Pankok (1872–1943) and Richard Riemerschmid (1868–1957); but two foreigners, neither of them very prolific builders, seem to have been the most influential figures on the German architectural scene at the opening of the new century. The Belgian Van de Velde had moved from Paris to Berlin in 1899; the Austrian Olbrich was called to Darmstadt by the Grand Duke in the same year. Olbrich stayed at Darmstadt until his early death in 1908; Van de Velde, however, left Berlin in 1902 when he was invited to Weimar to head the School of Arts and Crafts there which later became the Bauhaus. Van de Velde's finest Art Nouveau furniture dates from his Berlin years around 1900. As late as 1906,[2] the Central Hall which he designed in the Dresden Exhibition showed him still a competent if rather heavy-handed decorator in the Art Nouveau tradition.

Van de Velde's remodelling of the Folkwang Museum at Hagen of 1900-2, quite Art Nouveau in its details, his Esche house at Chemnitz of 1903, and his Leuring house at Scheveningen in Holland of the next year, both very massive and heavily mansarded, though unornamented externally like his own house of 1895-6 at Uccle, hardly require particular mention. However, for the school that he headed in Weimar he erected in 1904-11 a building even more devoid of Art Nouveau elements and notably straightforward in character. The plain white stucco walls below his usual heavy mansards were very frankly fenestrated with ranges of wide studio windows, perhaps in emulation of Mackintosh's Glasgow Art School. Indeed, the general effect is even simpler and more rectilinear than that of its possible Scottish prototype. The problem of his responsibility or lack of responsibility for the design of the Théâtre des Champs Élysées in Paris of 1911-13 has already been discussed (see Chapter 17).

Van de Velde continued to build occasionally throughout all his long life – some portions of his Kröller-Müller Museum near Otterlo in Holland were only completed in 1953 – but his last pre-war work was the theatre that he designed and executed in 1913-14 for the Werkbund Exhibition at Cologne. Some trace of the massively plastic quality of his Dresden hall of 1906 – so different from the delicacy and grace of the Art Nouveau in its best period – remained in the curved walls and roof of this edifice, but the whole effect was lighter and plainer, more abstract one might almost say.

The resemblance of Olbrich's Ernst Ludwig Haus of 1900 at the Darmstadt Artists' Colony to Mackintosh's Art School has already been noted (see Chapter 17). At Darmstadt he also continued to build houses for some years, and his work there culminated in the Wedding Tower and the Exhibition Gallery on the Matildenhöhe, erected in 1906-8. The latter is blocky and somewhat classicizing in character, at once very plain and very formal. The former, of brick, has a more Hanseatic flavour because of its arched and panelled gable; but it also includes a novel motif, bands of windows that seem to carry round a corner, that was destined to be influential everywhere in the twenties.

In what proved to be the last years of Olbrich's life – he died, it will be recalled, at the age of forty – two important commissions came to him away from Darmstadt. The Feinhals house at Cologne-Marienburg of 1908-9 repeated the blocky symmetrical composition of the Exhibition Building, the walls being articulated only with flat oblong panels. The loggia between, however, had a range of Greek Doric columns, clear evidence of the influence of Romantic Classicism that was growing stronger in Germany all through this decade. But Olbrich had little real appreciation of the subtle elegance of the work of Schinkel and his contemporaries, or so it would appear from this house.

The buildings of the East Cemetery in Munich, designed by Hans Grässel (1860-?) in 1894 and completed in 1900, are perhaps the first examples of this sort of 'Neo-Neo-Classicism'. Yet beside the contemporary Neo-

Baroque of the Munich Palace of Justice built in 1897 by Grässel's master, Friedrich von Thiersch (1852–1921), nearly as over-scaled and aggressive as Wallot's Reichstag in Berlin, the rather Schinkelesque work at the cemetery appears, in its crispness and its relative simplicity, almost as 'modern' as anything by Olbrich. As has been noted earlier, Schinkel remained a major inspiration to such a leader of the second generation of modern architects as Mies van der Rohe, so this influence had a continuing significance.

A much larger building by Olbrich than the house at Marienburg, designed in 1906 and completed after his death, the Tietz (now Kaufhof) Department Store in Düsseldorf, repeats the reiterative verticalism of those portions of Messel's Wertheim store in Berlin that were built in 1900–4, though Olbrich's detailing is not medievalizing like Messel's but rather semi-Classical. Neither of these later things maintains the promise of his Ernst Ludwig Haus; they rather illustrate that general recession from bold innovation which characterized the architecture of this decade in Germany, a recession corresponding more or less closely to the general resurgence of 'traditionalism' in England and America that came a few years later (see Chapter 24).

Peter Behrens (1868–1940), only a year younger than Olbrich, began his career as an architect at Darmstadt. From 1896 on, before being called there, he had only done decorative work of a markedly Art Nouveau sort. In his own house in the Artists' Colony of 1900–1 – the only one not built by Olbrich - the interiors still suggest the Art Nouveau, but the clumsy exterior has little interest except as a document of revolt. Yet the plan is quite like that of Wright's own house of 1889 in Oak Park, allowing a real flow of space through wide openings between entrance hall, living-room, and dining-room. By 1902 the 'Hessian' interior that he contributed to the Turin Exhibi-

tion was wholly rectilinear, presumably under the influence of Olbrich and Mackintosh. A similar severity characterized the work that he did, much of it merely open pergolas, for the Düsseldorf Garden and Art Exhibition of 1904.

By this time Behrens's personal style was maturing, although his debt to Vienna remained very evident. The Art Pavilion for the North-West German Art Exhibition held in Oldenburg in 1904 was a symmetrical composition of cubical masses, the flatness of their surfaces emphasized by linear panelling somewhat as Olbrich did at Darmstadt. The Obenauer house of 1905–6 at Sankt Johann near Saarbrücken is rather more loosely composed; indeed, its white stucco walls, slated roofs, and grouped windows distinctly recall Voysey's houses, which were by this time very well known in Germany thanks to the *Studio* and Muthesius's book. The garden front, however, is symmetrical and the plan not as open as that of his own house of four years earlier.

In Behrens's next two buildings, the small Concert Hall in the Flora Garden at Cologne of 1906 and the large Crematorium at Delstern near Hagen completed the following year, the geometrical panelling in black and white, used both inside and out, recalls a little San Miniato in Florence. But the blocky geometry of the Oldenburg pavilion and its smooth flat surfaces were also repeated, so that both these buildings have a curiously model-like look as if they were made of sheets of cardboard.

Behrens's two finest works up to this time, the Schröder house of 1908–9 – no longer extant – and the Cuno house of 1909–10 in the Hassleyerstrasse at Eppenhausen near Hagen, have a much more solid appearance, with quarry-faced masonry below and roughcast walls above [277]. The symmetrical façades, which correspond to completely symmetrical plans, are at once more tightly and more subtly composed. Here English influence seems to have been superseded by an attempt, rather

277. Peter Behrens: Hagen-Eppenhausen,
Cuno and Schröder houses, 1908-10

more successful than Olbrich's at Marienburg, to emulate Schinkel A third early house by Behrens, the Goedecke house at Oppenhausen of 1911-12, is equally formal but not symmetrical, recalling thus a little Schinkel's Schloss Glienecke near Potsdam.

Somewhat similar to Behrens's work of this period in its evident derivation from German Romantic Classicism, but more delicate in scale, was the work of Heinrich Tessenow (1876-1950),[2a] notably his Festival Theatre of 1910-13 and the other buildings he designed and erected for the Art Colony at Hellerau near Dresden. But such German work, of which a great deal was produced in the decade before the First World War, corresponds rather closely, despite the frequent stylization of detail and the serious concern with geometrical clarity in composition, to the Neo-Georgian of England and America in the early twentieth century, and also to much parallel work in the Scandinavian countries that is usually of rather higher quality (see Chapter 24).

Moreover, those Frenchmen who castigated the Théâtre des Champs Élysées as 'Boche' during the First World War because of the presumption that it was designed by Van de Velde, born a Belgian but head of a German art school, were not altogether wrong. In its scraped Classicism and rigidly geometrical *ordonnance* Perret's façade was not at all remote from one of the most characteristic German modes of the years just before 1914. Perret's industrial work was much more significant for the future.

So also with Behrens it was the challenge that his position as architect of the A.E.G. brought of working in the industrial field that made him briefly a rival of Wright, and even more particularly of Perret, as a major architectural innovator. Behrens's first work for the A.E.G., the Turbine Factory at the corner of the Hussitenstrasse and the Berlichingenstrasse in Moabit, an industrial suburb of Berlin, was erected in 1909-10 immediately after his appointment as successor to Messel. This broke new ground in several ways. It was built partly of poured concrete, partly of exposed steel, with both materials very directly expressed [278]. The side wall of glass and steel more than rivals in its openness those of the department stores designed by Art Nouveau architects [243, 247]. But Behrens's façade, in contradistinction to theirs, has no applied ornament whatsoever. Moreover, he ordered the whole composition as carefully as Schinkel might have done if either large factories or metal-and-glass construction had come within his purview.

The end façade of the Turbine Factory is slightly less frank in design. The concrete corners on either side of the central window-wall of metal and glass are battered and striated horizontally as if to suggest rusticated masonry.

The gable of the multi-faceted roof is brought forward to shelter the window-wall; this projects slightly in front of the concrete corners, almost like a Shavian bay-window raised to industrial scale. The treatment of the window-bands of the lower concrete block to the left resembles that of Schinkel's articulated walls on the Berlin Schauspielhaus, but with all the Greek mouldings omitted. Thus the functional elements of a factory executed throughout in new materials were here for the first time in Germany architectonically ordered with no dependence on decoration of any sort. Wright had done much the same five years earlier in his little-known E.-Z. Polish Factory in Chicago, but the scale of that is modest and its walls are not extensively fenestrated. Perret had come closer to it in his Garage Ponthieu in

278. Peter Behrens:
Berlin, A.E.G. Turbine Factory, 1909-10

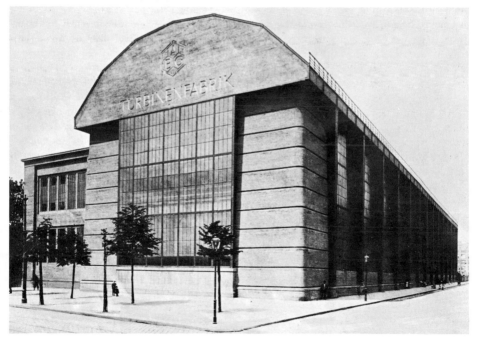

Paris, also built in 1905. There can be little question, however, that Behrens's is the finest building of the three.

In two more factories built in 1910 for the A.E.G., both much larger but neither of them quite so striking, Behrens broadened his range as an industrial architect. The High Tension Factory in the Humboldthain is of brick, not concrete or steel. Except for a few minor elements somewhat suggestive of pedimented temple-fronts translated into an industrial vocabulary, he handled the vast façades here with the same directness as the side elevation of metal and glass at the Turbine Factory. The Small Motors Factory in the Voltastrasse is similar but much finer [279]. There the brick piers have rounded corners and rise unbroken almost the full height of the building. The effect is somewhat like that portion of Messel's Wertheim Store which was built in the late

279. Peter Behrens:
Berlin, A.E.G. Small Motors Factory, 1910

nineties, but the scale is larger, and there is none of Messel's rich, half-traditional, half-Art-Nouveau detailing. Instead, the careful proportioning and the suave but extremely straightforward treatment of the structural elements again suggest Schinkel's sort of 'rationalism' yet succeed in doing so, as in the earlier Turbine Factory, with no actual reminiscence of Romantic Classical forms.

Thanks to the widening range of responsibility that German industry was now ready to give architects, Behrens not only built these big factories for the A.E.G. and also designed their retail shops all over Berlin, but he was soon asked in addition to provide some blocks of flats for the company's workmen at Hennigsdorf outside Berlin. This was a social challenge which neither Wright nor Perret had to meet. (In fact, however, Wright did in 1904 design terrace-houses that were never executed for Larkin Company workers in Buffalo; while in France low-cost housing had a very important place in Garnier's projects for a 'Cité industrielle'.) Henceforth, such housing would be a major preoccupation of most modern architects. This is true not only in Germany but all over the western world, and especially in Holland and Scandinavia. The origins of low-cost housing go back to the 1840s in England when Henry Roberts, whose Fishmongers' Hall in London has been mentioned, became the first architect to specialize in this field. But the early history of housing[3] is of more sociological than architectural interest. Moreover, what the nineteenth century esteemed to be 'model' low-cost dwellings have too often had to be demolished as 'sub-standard' in the twentieth. Worse, even the preoccupation of many modern architects with housing has not spared the twentieth century the shame of building as a public service what already must be considered slums.

Various small A.E.G. factories for making porcelain, lacquer, and other specialized products were also erected by Behrens in 1910 and

1911, none of particular interest. In 1911-12, however, there followed the Large Machine Assembly Hall at the corner of the Voltastrasse and the Hussitenstrasse near the Small Motors Factory. This rivals in quality the Turbine Factory of 1909. Once more a great rectangular volume is covered with a multi-faceted steel-framed roof, the structure below being in this instance also of steel with no use of concrete. The metal frame is largely filled with glass, but brick was introduced at the base and on the ends. The scale of this unit is less monumental than that of the Turbine Factory, though the size is much greater. The general effect, particularly that of the interior with its travelling cranes, is at once light and dramatic. A big A.E.G. plant was also built by Behrens at Riga in Russia in 1913.

Three large non-industrial commissions of 1911-12 show how this work for the A.E.G. affected Behrens's approach to design. Although it is built of stone not brick, the German Embassy opposite Monferran's St Isaac's Cathedral in Petersburg [53] is, at first sight, deceptively like the Small Motors Factory. Actually, the façade has a range of engaged Doric columns, but by their tall slim proportions and their lack of entasis these were stylized so to say 'industrially'. The great scale, the absolute regularity, and a certain coldness surely derived in part from the factories of the previous two years; but these also recall the Romantic Classical monuments of Alexander I's time in Petersburg.

Behrens's enormous office building for the Mannesmann Steel Works on the Rhine at Düsseldorf was less successful, as was also that for the Continental Rubber Company in Hanover. The latter was designed in 1911 and begun in 1913, but not completed until after the First World War, in 1920; it was destroyed in the Second World War. The heavily reiterative sort of scraped Classicism Behrens used for these overpowering masonry blocks

lacked the subtlety of composition of the Hagen houses yet retained something of the directness of expression of the A.E.G. factories. They were not untypical, however, of much large-scale German building of the second and third decades of the century. This mode developed fairly directly out of the Berlin work of Messel and Ludwig Hoffmann, although it was usually much less specifically 'traditional' in its detailing and even more aggressive in scale; a not dissimilar mode returned to official favour under Hitler in the mid thirties, usually with very coarse detailing.[3a]

With these big office buildings by Behrens and others one may compare the work of this period by various other German architects who preferred less classicizing modes. Early buildings by Fritz Schumacher (1869-1947),[3b] such as his crematorium in Dresden of 1908, also illustrate the megalomaniac tendencies of the period that seem so expressive of the expansive ambitions of William II's Second Reich. The many schools that Schumacher built in Hamburg just before the First World War are simpler, although still rather heavily scaled, and more comparable in quality to Behrens's work. One in particular, built in 1914 in the Ahrensburgerstrasse, almost echoes the elongated colonnade of Behrens's Petersburg Embassy, but the 'columns' are plain piers executed in dark red brick[4] and strung along a front that is concave not flat. The bathhouse at Eppenhausen, also of 1914, is very like the schools; while in the Kunstgewerbe Haus of the previous year on the Holstenwall in Hamburg a similar mode was employed for what is, in effect, a large office building. This seems to have initiated a local tradition of design for commercial buildings which was maintained in the twenties with little change, not only by Schumacher but by several other Hamburg architects. Schumacher's cemetery chapel, built as late as 1923, follows much the same line.

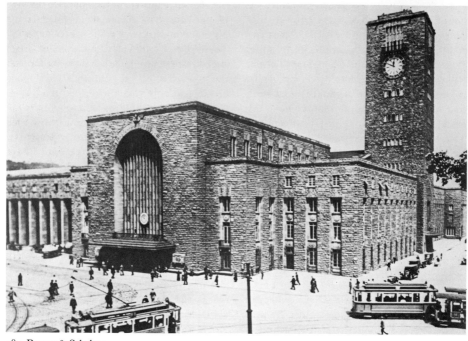

280. Bonatz & Scholer:
Stuttgart, Railway Station, 1911-14, 1919-27

In Stuttgart the railway station by Paul Bonatz (1877-1951) and F. E. Scholer (b. 1874) is the finest though not the largest of several built in Germany in these years. Designed in 1911, it was started only in 1914, just as the enormous and much less interesting one at Leipzig with its six parallel sheds, begun by Wilhelm Lossow (1852-1914) and M. H. Kühne in 1907, was reaching completion. That at Stuttgart was not finished until 1927 because of the interruption caused by the First World War. This structure has a rather Richardsonian flavour in its extensive unbroken wall surfaces of rock-faced ashlar and its plain round arches [280]. But the influence here came rather from the Munich architect Theodor Fischer (1862-1938). Fischer's Romanesquoid churches, such as that of the Redeemer in Munich of 1899-

1901 and the Garrison Church of 1908-11 in Ulm, were among the largest and most strikingly novel built in the opening years of the century in Germany; in the latter he even used ferro-concrete principals to carry the roof of the nave. Fischer's Art Gallery of 1911 in Stuttgart was both more delicate in scale and rather more archaeological in its detailing; Bonatz's Stuttgart work is bolder, simpler, and quite as handsomely expressive of the traditional materials used.

With the Stuttgart Station may be contrasted the rather earlier one at Hamburg that Heinrich Reinhardt (1868-?) and Georg Süssenguth (1862-?) built in 1903-6. There the major sections - shed, concourse, etc. - designed by the engineer Medling resemble rather closely Contamin and Dutert's Galerie des Machines at the Paris Exhibition of 1889. These great constructions of iron and glass fortunately quite overshadow the low ranges of accessory elements in masonry, with ornament still in the Meistersinger mode of the eighties, contributed by the architects. The differences between these two notable stations well illustrate that reaction towards masonry construction and a more or less traditional approach to design that was developing strength in the decade preceding the First World War. In the history of the railroad station as a type the Hamburg Hauptbahnhof represents not a new beginning but the end of a line descending from the great shed-dominated stations of the mid nineteenth century.

Intermediate in date between the Hamburg and Stuttgart stations was that at Karlsruhe built by August Stürzenacker in 1908-13. Although masonry construction and masonry forms dominate here as at Stuttgart, the simplification of mass and space composition throughout, and above all the elegant detailing,

give evidence of the continuing leadership of Olbrich at the time of his death. Olbrich never built a station himself, but he won third place in the 1903 competition for that at Basel and second place in the 1907 competition for Darmstadt.

In other specialized fields of building a forward line of development is more evident. Two big circular halls, one in Frankfurt of 1907-8 by Thiersch's son, the other in Wrocław (Breslau) built by Max Berg (1870-?) in 1910-12 [281], are more notable than the contemporary railway stations at Stuttgart and Karlsruhe. Like Behrens's industrial work for the A.E.G., these structures illustrate the vital stimulus that German architects were obtaining in these generally somewhat reactionary years from the use of engineering solutions and materials other than masonry - steel at Frankfurt, ferro-concrete at Wrocław - to cover and enclose space. In the case of Thiersch this is the more remarkable when one compares it with the traditional Louis XVI character of his

281. Max Berg:
Wrocław (Breslau), Jahrhunderthalle, 1910-12

Kurhaus at Wiesbaden completed in 1907.[4a] While Berg on the exterior of his vast hall approaches the attenuated Classicism of Perret's work of the next decade, the superb interior reminds one at once of Piranesi and of the much later structures of Pierluigi Nervi.

German architects of this generation were rarely able to carry over into the designing of more conventional structures the boldness and freshness of approach of their large-scale work. They seem to have felt no such call to regenerate architecture as Wright had imbibed from Sullivan, nor did they, like Perret, attempt to use the new materials and the new structural methods consistently for all sorts of buildings whatever their particular purpose. German production before and after the First World War, as represented in the *œuvre* of such then highly esteemed figures[5] as Oskar Kaufmann (1873-1956), German Bestelmeyer (1874-1942), and Wilhelm Kreis (1873-1955), to mention but three of the best known, shades over almost imperceptibly from industrial and semi-industrial buildings of bold and original character to a range of structures in various tasteful modes that are hardly distinguishable from the avowedly 'traditional' work of this period in other countries. This has already been noted as regards Tessenow. Characteristic examples of these men's work were Bestelmeyer's extensions of the University and the Technical High School in Munich, of 1906-10 and 1922 respectively, both in the local tradition of Theodor Fischer's work. The Museum of Prehistory in Halle that Kreis built in 1916 with K. A. Jüngst was more conservative even than Bestelmeyer's work, although Provincial-Roman rather than Romanesque in inspiration.

As in England in the late nineteenth century, individual idiosyncrasies were much cultivated, and architects tended to specialize in particular types of buildings. Kaufmann, for example, had a very personal Neo-Rococo manner, delicate and frivolous, that he employed with real appropriateness in various Berlin theatres, notably the remodelling of the Kroll Oper and the Komödie, both carried out in 1924. But Behrens remains on the whole the most interesting and accomplished architect of this generation; moreover, his opportunities for building were even greater under the Weimar Republic in the early twenties than they had been under the Kaiser.

No very great change is observable in Behrens's work after the First World War. The terrace-houses that he built in 1918 for A.E.G. workers at Hennigsdorf, and the semi-detached dwellings of a low-cost housing estate for which he was responsible at Othmarschen near Altona in 1920 are simple and solid in construction, quite like those of before the war but more conservative in design. However, at this point comes a characteristic, though brief, change of phase that illustrates his ready response to influences from the new painting and sculpture of the day. In the big complex erected for the I. G. Farben Company in 1920-4 at Höchst Behrens gave up the direct expression of new industrial building methods characteristic of his A.E.G. factories of 1909-11. The exterior was massive and almost medievalizing, even though the ranges of arches were of the unconventional parabolic form that seems to have appealed especially to Expressionist taste. In the tall glass-roofed court inside the angular forms of Expressionism are most strikingly evident; but he also introduced wholly abstract wall paintings and a few rather Constructivist lighting fixtures elsewhere in the reception rooms and offices. The result is, to say the least, ambiguous and incoherent, although the exterior is not unimpressive in general effect even today.

Expressionist influence had first appeared a little earlier than this in the work of other German architects, but it reached a peak in these years around 1920. In his pre-war industrial work Hans Poelzig (1869-1936) was not Expressionist. The Luban chemical works that he built near Poznań (Posen) in 1911-12 rivalled in size and even in directness of expression - though not in distinction - Behrens's factories for the A.E.G. After the war, however, Poelzig became a principal exponent of Expressionism in architecture. One of the earliest and most striking examples of Expressionist design on a large scale was his remodelling of the Grosses Schauspielhaus in Berlin in 1919. Here the cavernous, stalactite-ceilinged interior round the central circular stage was itself like an Expressionist stage-set and the planning encouraged a major revolution in dramatic presentation that is still controversial today. Yet his industrial work of the early twenties soon became much more straightforward again, and he later reverted to something very comparable to the stripped monumentality of Behrens's Düsseldorf and Hanover office buildings. The most prominent extant example of this is the enormous I.G. Farben headquarters that he built in 1930 in Frankfurt, occupied since the war by the U.S. Army.

One can hardly leave the subject of Expressionism in German architecture, largely confined though its more extreme manifestations were to a very short post-war period of three or four years, without mentioning two more names, those of Fritz Höger (1877-1949) and Dominikus Böhm (1880-1955).

The twenties saw a few skyscrapers erected in Germany, none of them of the great height then current in America, but sometimes as conspicuous above the existing skyline as the first skyscrapers in New York had been in the seventies. The largest, though not the tallest, and certainly the most impressive is the Chilehaus, built by Höger in Hamburg in 1923, with its Schumacher-like piers of patterned brickwork and its upper three storeys receding behind narrow terraces [282]. A large and irregular site encouraged the employment of a long double curve on the right-hand side of the

282. Fritz Höger: Hamburg, Chilehaus, 1923

hollow block, and the sharp angle at that end produces automatically a silhouette of the shrillest Expressionist order. Actually, however, Höger like other German architects was already returning by this time from earlier and wilder Expressionist adventures. To what extent he was aware of the skyscrapers of Sullivan is uncertain. The emphatically vertical scheme of design he used here, with arches linking the brick piers together below slab cornices, certainly suggests some knowledge of them, even though they were by this time all but forgotten in America.

Considerably taller than the Chilehaus, but not otherwise very distinguished, were two other German buildings of the twenties. Kreis's Wilhelm Marx Haus of 1924 in Düsseldorf, a thirteen-storey tower crowned with curious open-work tracery of interlaced brick, is still a conspicuous feature of the local skyline; but the

Planetarium and associated buildings that he erected at the Ehrenhof there two years later are better examples of the fairly restrained mode that he and others usually employed in these years. The plainer and better proportioned seventeen-storey Hochhaus am Hansaring in Cologne was built in 1925 by Jacob Koerfer (b. 1875).

Although only a few tall buildings actually rose in European cities in the twenties, the skyscraper theme fascinated the younger architects. Many bold designs for them were then projected,[5a] some of considerable significance for later developments in both the Old World and the New (see Chapter 22). The international competition for the Chicago Tribune Tower held in 1922, which many Europeans entered and the Finn Eliel Saarinen all but won, signally focused attention on a type of building hitherto considered unsuitable for the Old World, and generally accepted in Europe only in the 1950s (see Chapters 21 and 25).

The churches of Böhm, all of them Catholic, have a suavity that Höger's work lacks, but at least equal forcefulness. The Suabian War Memorial Church of 1923 at Neu-Ulm is like an imaginative film-set of the period, being a sort of free fantasia on Gothic themes with little feeling of structural reality. But his boldest church, Christ-König at Bischofsheim near Mainz of 1926, seems almost to take off from the engineer Freyssinet's hangars at Orly. The paraboloid forms are here very frankly used; yet the concrete 'barrel' vault of the nave, intersected by lower cross-vaults over the bays of the aisles, creates a strong emotional effect that is both Gothic and Expressionist in tone. The finest of his earlier churches may well be Sankt Engelbert at Cologne-Riehl of 1931-3. This is circular in plan and very ingeniously roofed, not with a dome,[6] but with lobes of paraboloid barrel-vaulting.

However, in a church built in 1929, Sankt Joseph at Hindenburg in Upper Silesia, Böhm had already turned away from the emotionalism of his earlier work towards simple rectangular forms.[7] This simplicity he maintained in his post-war churches, with the result that his last work, Maria Königin,[8] built at Marienburg outside Cologne in 1954, with its squarish plan, very slender metal supports, and side wall of glass, has very little churchly flavour left. Yet some of Böhm's very late projects indicated that many of his ambitions of thirty years ago still remained with him to the end. When a more emotional approach to church-design revived internationally in the 50s Böhm's churches could be recognized even above those of his contemporary Rudolf Schwarz as among the finest German works of the last half a century.

Compared to such a French church of the twenties as Perret's Notre-Dame at Le Raincy or such a Swiss church as Moser's Sankt Antonius in Basel, both using concrete in the rectangular and skeletal mode usually preferred at that time, Böhm's churches of the twenties once seemed semi-traditional rather than modern. One can now see, however, that there is a different and more emotive line of development in modern church architecture to which Gaudí's unfinished churches at Santa Coloma de Cervelló and Barcelona belong, as do also such later Latin American examples in ferro-concrete as the Purísima at Monterrey in Mexico by Enrique de la Mora (b. 1907) of 1939-47, São Francisco at Pampulha in Brazil, built by Oscar Niemeyer (b. 1901) in 1943, Nuestra Señora de los Milagros in Mexico City by Felix Candela (b. 1910), completed in 1955, and several completed in the mid fifties by Juvenal Moya at Bogotá in Colombia[9] (see Chapters 23 and 25). Expressionism was perhaps less of a cul de sac than its brief impingement on Behrens might lead one to suppose. Certainly it was a potent force for a few years after the First World War, and played then a significant role in breaking down the rule of 'tasteful' traditionalism inherited from the preceding decade.

As the twenties progressed, however, and extreme Expressionist influence generally receded, Behrens gave evidence of his awareness of the quite different direction that modern architecture had just taken in the hands of certain younger men, several of whom had actually been his own pupils or at least his employees. In 1925-6 he built New Ways, a house in Northampton, England, for S. J. Bassett-Lowke, earlier a client of Mackintosh's. With its smooth white stucco walls, horizontally grouped windows, and flat roof, this is of considerable historical interest, although of very little intrinsic merit.[10] No such advanced work had yet been done in England by local architects, and at this time only a very few houses of a comparably advanced character had been executed anywhere (see Chapter 22).

Despite his unusual openness of mind, which led Behrens in his fifties to attempt to rival juniors barely started on their careers – or, quite as probably, because of the lack of strong personal conviction of which this gives evidence – Behrens did not, like Frank Lloyd Wright in later life, continue to be very creative beyond this date. In Vienna, where he was called in the mid twenties to be professor of architecture at the Akademie, he settled into a sort of compromise mode. The low-cost housing blocks that he built in Vienna in 1924-5 on the Margaretengürtel, in the Stromstrasse, and in the Konstanziastrasse illustrate his characteristic uncertainty of direction in these years. If considerably sounder, they are also much less adventurous than the Bassett-Lowke house designed at almost the same time. This can be seen still more clearly at the Weissenhof in Stuttgart where many of the buildings of the German Werkbund's housing exhibition held in 1927 remain in use today.[10a] There Behrens's block of flats stands very near one designed by the director of this exhibition, his former assistant Mies van der Rohe [310], and not far from houses by such other leaders of the new generation as Gropius, Le Corbusier – who had both worked in his office also – and Oud (see Chapter 22). The contrast between his massive block and their light and open structures is the more striking because Behrens seems to have set out here to meet his juniors more than half-way.

Behrens's very latest work, the factory for the Austrian Tobacco Administration at Linz built in 1930 in association with Alexander Popp (b. 1891), was rather less conservative because of the nature of the commission. It is less mechanistic than the industrial work done so much earlier for the A.E.G., yet nonetheless impressive for its consistency of treatment and also for its human scale. The Linz factory provides a not unworthy concluding note to Behrens's ambiguous career.

The vast productivity of the German architects of Behrens's generation, both before and after the First World War, building in a boom which only came to a close around 1930 with the world-wide depression, makes it difficult to choose specific examples worth the emphasis of even brief mention. The situation is made no easier by the considerable versatility of most of the leading figures. Those few buildings that have been specifically mentioned – even most of Behrens's own work except for his A.E.G. factories – should be considered typical of the upper level of German achievement in these decades rather than monuments of unique distinction like the best things done by Perret and by Wright in the same decades. Yet, it is worth noting, for a long time neither Wright nor Perret had much effect on the general scene in their own countries, for all the seminal effect of their influence on younger architects everywhere; while the Germans achieved a tremendous volume of what can be called 'half-modern' work that notably changed the whole character of several large cities. Thus the way was prepared for a very early and wide-spread acceptance of the next stage of modern architecture, an acceptance so premature that it induced in the thirties a sharp reaction.

In 1933 a regime rose to power in Germany with doctrinaire objections to the latest phase of modern architecture, ironically castigated as *Kultur-Bolschevismus* immediately after the Bolsheviks had rejected it as unacceptably bourgeois! As a result, the leaders of the younger generation almost all emigrated (see Chapter 23); while with few exceptions those German architects who remained at home turned backwards in their tracks, though not very far backwards. Most German production in the Nazi period[10b] is all but indistinguishable, indeed, from what was often considered advanced before the First World War and even for some years thereafter. Very little of it deserves specific mention. As was the case around 1910, the more nearly the structures were of an engineering order – as for instance Bonatz's bridges for the Autobahn built over the years 1935–41 – the less they were likely to be stylized along the heavy near-Classical or semi-medieval lines the later Imperial period had established as conventional a generation before. Even the housing that Bonatz built after the War in 1945–6 at Ankara in Turkey and his Opera House there of 1947–8 are hardly as advanced as his Zeppelinbau office building of 1929–31 opposite the station in Stuttgart. Like Behrens at the same time, he had attempted there – with a certain amount of real success – to follow the ascetic principles of the younger generation that had just been so

well illustrated at Stuttgart in the Werkbund Exhibition of 1927 on the Weissenhof (see Chapter 22).

Immediately after the Second World War there was for several years some continuing use of the modes of 1910, so to call them. This was natural because of the prolonged absence of most of the leaders of the intervening generation from the country – Gropius, Mies, and Mendelsohn never returned – and the renewed activity of so many of the older generation who had made their reputation in the period 1905–25 with which this chapter has chiefly dealt. Later it was as if Germany lived through the stylistic developments of the twenties a second time, but since the 60s the newer sort of architecture has again become as ubiquitous as it was in 1930.

These tidal waves of changing taste in Germany, each representing a sharp reaction against its predecessor, make difficult such a focusing of attention on a few creative and insurgent figures as gives dramatic pungency to the history of these decades in America and France. *Jugendstil, Expressionismus, Neue Sachlichkeit*,[11] these general movements, more than even so distinguished an individual as Behrens, are the real protagonists of the German story from 1900 to 1933; but in the international frame of reference they must be subordinated to the broader currents that dominated the architecture of the western world in the period. In that frame of reference the contribution of a few Austrians more than equalled that of the more prolific Germans, down at least to the First World War.

CHAPTER 21

THE FIRST GENERATION

IN AUSTRIA, HOLLAND, AND SCANDINAVIA

The development of modern architecture in Austria between 1900 and the Nazi conquest has many connexions with that of Germany. The Austrian Olbrich had as much as anyone to do with setting off the reaction against the Art Nouveau in Germany after 1900. From the mid twenties, Behrens was active in Austria, not in Germany. Even so, and particularly for the years before the First World War, there is a separate and purely Austrian story, more limited than the German story yet at least equally notable for highly distinguished achievement. Two Austrian architects at least, Otto Wagner and Adolf Loos (1870-1933), if not

Wagner's pupil Josef Hoffmann (1870-1956), were the equals of any of the leading German architects of their day, except perhaps Behrens. Wagner, already sixty in 1901, produced his finest work after that date. The Wiener Werkstätte, founded by Hoffmann in 1903, provided a centre of activity in the field of decoration comparable to what the Century Guild and the Arts and Crafts Exhibition Society had offered earlier in England. Above all, Loos – in part possibly because he, of all Europeans of his generation, knew American architecture best – demonstrated, from his earliest executed work of 1898, a determination

283. Otto Wagner: Vienna, Postal Savings Bank, 1904-6

to renew the art of building that was as revolutionary as Wright's if less positively creative.

Soon after 1900 Wagner threw off all Art Nouveau influence. Yet the finest element in his masterpiece, the central hall of the Postal Savings Bank in the Georg Coch Platz in Vienna of 1904-6, still retains in the curvature of its glass roof and the tapering of its metal supports something of Art Nouveau grace [283]. The exteriors of this massive edifice are lightened by the very original treatment of the geometrically organized wallplanes; the thin plaques of marble which provide the sheathing suggest volume, not mass, and the delicate relief of the few and simple projections quite avoids the ponderousness of most contemporary German work. As in so much of the best German work, however, the severity of form and even the specific character of certain ornamental features reflect in a stylized way the Grecian mode of a hundred years earlier. This is somewhat surprising in Vienna, where Romantic Classicism had been on the whole both unproductive and uncreative, but doubtless Wagner knew Schinkel's work as well as did Behrens – certainly his lightness of hand is more comparable to Schinkel's.

Not least interesting technically is the consistent employment of aluminium[1] in this building. The sculptured figures by Othmar Schimkowitz which crown the façade and the visible bolts that retain the granite and marble plaques are of this new metal; so also, apparently, are the structural members that support the glazed roof of the hall; at least they are completely sheathed with it. The large rear block of the bank dates from 1912, but the original vocabulary was retained by Wagner with only some slight simplification of the detailing of the plaquage.

Sankt Leopold, the cruciform church that serves as the chapel of the Steinhof Asylum on the Gallitzinberg at Penzing outside Vienna, was built by Wagner in 1904-7 at the same time as the Postal Savings Bank. This crowns his extensive hillside layout of the whole establishment, comparable in scale to the French asylums of the mid-nineteenth century, but for the other buildings he was not directly responsible. Sankt Leopold is a large domed monument inviting comparison with Schinkel's Nikolaikirche at Potsdam. However, the linear stylization of the detailing inside and out brings to mind Olbrich's and Behrens's buildings of its own day. There is no paraphernalia of Greek orders, yet the conceptual organization of the elements is certainly in the Romantic Classical tradition, with the four arms each quite cubic and the hemispherical dome raised on a cylindrical drum. As at Schmidt's Neo-Gothic Fünfhaus church of the 1870s in Vienna, there are echoes of Fischer von Erlach's Baroque Karlskirche here also, but the spirit is not at all Baroque. All the visible metalwork here, the sheathing of the dome, the statues of angels by Schimkowitz and of saints by Richard Luksch, and even the heads of the bolts that retain the marble plaques on the exterior walls, is of gilded bronze, not aluminium. This has not worn as well, for it has lost its gilt coating, peeled off many of the bolts, and streaked the walls with verdigris. Inside the church mosaics by Rudolf Jettmar and the stained glass by Kolo Moser combine to rival the most sumptuous domestic ensembles produced by the Wiener Werkstätte, but the general effect, while light and even gay, still has a monumental dignity appropriate to a church. The walls are of plain white plaster, and narrow bands of geometrical ornament in gold and blue panel the cross vault – for, curiously enough, the central dome is not exploited internally.

Crisper in design and much simpler altogether than the Steinhof church are the blocks of low-cost flats that Wagner built in 1910-11 at 40 Neustiftgasse and next door at 4 Döblergasse. Their walls are covered with stucco lined off to suggest plaquage, and the decoration is reduced to thin bands of dark blue tiles that merely outline the surface planes. Needless to say, these blocks have not survived as well as the expensively built bank and church. Wagner's last works, a hospital not far from the Steinhof Asylum and his own house at 28 Hüttelbergstrasse, both in Penzing and of 1913, are typical but rather less interesting.[1a] The house was actually designed some seven years earlier.

Hoffmann's first architectural work of any consequence, a Convalescent Home at Purkersdorf built in 1903-4, was already simpler than Wagner's hospital of a decade later, if considerably less architectonic in effect. The plain white stucco walls are full of ample windows almost devoid of surrounding frames and very regularly disposed; cornices and other conventional elements of detail are either omitted or reduced to an absolute minimum. The result is a structure that would still look quite fresh two generations later were it not, like Wagner's flats, in shabby physical condition.

As Hoffmann's founding of the Wiener Werkstätte indicates, he was at heart less an architect than a decorator, like so many of the leading English and Scottish designers of this period and the immediately preceding one. The important commission to build a large and extremely luxurious mansion on the edge of Brussels in 1905, the Palais Stoclet at 373 Avenue de Tervueren, gave his decorative ambitions a free rein [284]. Yet the exterior of this has a good deal of the geometrical clarity of the Convalescent Home and rather more of Wagner's architectonic values. The carefully ordered asymmetrical composition is dominated by the stair-tower, somewhat as the best Italian Villas of the previous century were dominated by their off-centre belvederes. The walls appear to be no more than thin skins of marble plaques, like Wagner's, with the frequent and regularly spaced windows brought forward into the same surface plane. A decorative edging of gilded metal defines these smooth wall planes, giving the whole something of the fragile look of D'Aronco's exhibition buildings. This is especially true of such a complex accent as the tower with its tall stair-window.

The Stoclet house, as finished after six years in 1911, has some very fine interiors, cold and formal but sumptuously simple in their use of various marbles. The marble is quite undecorated on the delicate rectangular piers in the two-storey stair-hall; but in the dining-room it

284. Josef Hoffmann: Brussels, Stoclet house, 1905-11

carries inlaid patterns by Gustav Klimt of almost Art Nouveau elaboration. The effect is rather curious, somewhat resembling characteristic English interiors by Voysey and his contemporaries carried out, not in stained or painted wood, but in figured and polished marbles; yet undoubtedly this is one of the most consistent and notable great houses of the twentieth century in Europe. Seeking to provide a new sort of elegance that even the best English domestic work lacked, Hoffmann achieved here an urbane distinction only approached by Gill and the Greenes at this time in America. His houses in Vienna, such as that at 5-7 Invalidenstrasse of 1911 and the suburban one at 14-16 Gloriettegasse in Hietzing, are not in a class with the Palais Stoclet but more comparable to Olbrich's or Behrens's houses of this period in Germany. Work of similar character and equal distinction was done by Fabiani in Vienna before he settled in Gorizia in 1920. Very Hoffmann-like indeed is his building for the publisher Artaria at 9 Kohlmarkt of 1901. His Urania in the Uraniagasse of 1910 also rivals Hoffmann's best.

Successor to Wagner in general esteem, and himself a professor at the Kunstgewerbeschule, Hoffmann developed his personal style no further in the work he did after the Palais Stoclet. At the Austrian Pavilion in the Exhibition of Decorative Arts of 1925 in Paris - an exhibition organized in part to reclaim for France the primacy in the arts and crafts of decoration that had by this time passed to Vienna largely because of Hoffmann's leadership - the rather Neo-Rococo stuccoed block that he provided was much less advanced in character than the greenhouse-like portion designed by Behrens. However, his low-cost flats in the Felix-Mottlstrasse in Vienna, built like those of Behrens in the mid twenties, retain a good deal of the quality of his early sanatorium at Purkersdorf. Simple and clean, they are distinctly less blank and ponderous than

Behrens's, if also less advanced in design than those by Josef Frank (1885-1967). Frank, a somewhat younger Viennese architect of considerable ability but lesser reputation than Hoffmann, left Vienna to settle in Sweden when the Nazis took over Austria.

The international acclaim that Viennese low-cost housing of this period received when new seems rather exaggerated now. From the first its significance was more political and sociological than architectural. It happened to be built, moreover, mostly by men not of the newest generation of architects at just the time when an architectural revolution was taking place in France and Holland and Germany (see Chapters 22 and 23). Henceforth that revolution, brilliantly illustrated as regards low-cost housing in the German Werkbund's international exhibition of 1927 at Stuttgart, would affect most notably the design of such projects throughout the western world. The Viennese housing exhibition of 1930, a modest counterpart to that in Stuttgart, came too late to reform the local tradition, which largely survived well after the Second World War.

The work of Hoffmann's exact contemporary Loos 'dated' less than his and was of the greatest importance in providing inspiration to the modern architects of the second generation who brought about the revolution of the twenties. This inspiration from Loos is comparable in significance to that which the younger architects found in the work of Wright and of Perret. Loos, unlike other Austrians of his period, was primarily interested in architecture, not in decoration - indeed, he wrote in 1908 an article[2] claiming that 'ornament is crime', an attitude shared by no other architect of his generation, and least of all by his fellow Viennese. It was Loos's tragedy that a very large part of his employment before the First World War was in remodelling and redecorating flats; this constrained him so little, however, that many of these may easily be taken in photo-

285. Adolf Loos:
Vienna, Leopold Langer flat, 1901

286 and 287. Adolf Loos:
Vienna, Gustav Scheu house, 1912

graphs for completely original house interiors [285].

Although Loos began his career in the late nineties when the Art Nouveau tide ran highest, he was never at all affected by it, in part doubtless because he had spent the years 1893–6 in America beyond the range of Art Nouveau influence. The interior of the Goldman haberdashery shop in Vienna, which he designed in 1898, was entirely straight-lined and quite without any ornament; in the Café Museum of the next year the segmental ceiling and the bentwood chairs were curved, but only for structural reasons. Both are now gone, although the Knìžé men's shop in the Graben in Vienna of 1913 long gave some idea of what the former was like.

It is Loos's houses around Vienna, in Plzen, in Brno, in Montreux, and in Paris that place him as one of the four or five most important architects of his generation. His finest single extant work, however, is a small bar in Vienna. From the first he designed from the inside out, reducing his exteriors to square stucco boxes cut by many windows of different sizes and shapes. The results are very like Gill's houses in California, as has been noted already, but with no such traditional elements as Gill's arched porches. This is especially true of the Gustav Scheu house in the Larochegasse in the Vienna suburb of Hietzing [286, 287], almost

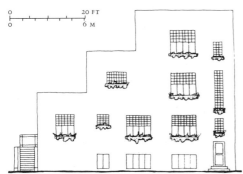

the only one left in Austria in something closely approaching its original condition. Loos was an enthusiastic admirer of English domestic architecture; this bent of his taste is curiously illustrated by his liking for English eighteenth-century furniture of the Queen Anne and Chippendale periods, which looks today so out of place in his severely rectangular rooms. But the architectural character of his interiors is never influenced by eighteenth-century modes, but only by the most advanced English work of the opening of the century which he knew well through the *Studio*. Articulated by plain wooden structural members like Voysey's interiors or, on occasion, by similar piers cladded with marble like Hoffmann's in the Stoclet house, Loos's suites of living areas are as flowing as Wright's[3] but he never provided as much interconnexion between indoors and out.

Of a succession of houses built before the First World War the much mishandled Steiner house of 1910 and the above-mentioned Scheu house of 1912, both in suburbs of Vienna, are perhaps the finest. The Villa Karma[3a] near Montreux in Switzerland, begun in 1904, has an almost Hoffmann-like sumptuousness of materials and finish within (not entirely of Loos's design); in the main he preferred, like Voysey and Wright, plainer effects.

At first his houses looked, externally, rather like quite conventional ones from which all elements of traditional detail had been scraped, as do many of the contemporary projects included in Garnier's 'Cité industrielle'. Gradually, however, Loos came to handle his simple elements of external design with more of that assurance which his domestic interiors had displayed from as early as the flat in Vienna remodelled for Leopold Langer in 1901 [285]. Both the placing and the sashing of his windows were more carefully studied; and the proportions and the juxtapositions of his rather boxy masses were abstractly ordered well before a Neoplasticist like Georges Vantongerloo in

Holland arrived at somewhat similar effects in sculpture (see Chapter 22). Compared to Wright's more complex and articulated experimentation with abstract composition in the house of 1909 for Mrs Thomas Gale or the Coonley Playhouse of 1912, there yet remains a rather negative quality about most of Loos's work. He seems to have been principally concerned to clear away inherited tradition in order to lay the foundations of an immanent new architecture. That new architecture, however, he himself was never able to bring fully into being, although others did so under his influence by the time he was in his early fifties (see Chapter 22).

In Loos's larger urban work, such as the prominent Goldman & Salatsch Building of 1910 in the Michaelerplatz in Vienna, he was ready to use marble externally and even to include classically detailed columns. But in the ground storey of this store he increased the articulated space effects characteristic of the interiors of his flats and houses to almost monumental scale. Here, in the small Kärntner Bar of 1907, and in the Café Capua of 1913, both also in Vienna, his use of fine materials with their polished surfaces uninterrupted by mouldings would eventually prove as potent an inspiration to architects of the next generation as did his more ascetic written doctrine.

The Café Capua is gone; the Goldman & Salatsch interior drastically remodelled; but the Kärntner Bar, in the Kärntner Durchgang behind 10 Kärntnerstrasse, remains a small masterpiece of modern design. During the Nazi occupation the façade lost the American flag in stained glass which ran across the top, but the exterior was never of much interest in any case. The interior is fortunately completely intact [288]. Skilful use of mirrors quite disguises its very small dimensions. Above smooth dark mahogany walls, set like screens between plain green marble piers, unframed panels of mirror that reach to the ceiling allow one to see the

288. Adolf Loos: Vienna, Kärntner Bar, 1907

strong reticulated pattern of the yellow marble ceiling extending left and right and to the rear just as if the actual area of the bar were merely an enclave in a much larger space. Because of the particular height of the mahogany wainscoting this illusion is quite perfect, for one sees only about as great a space reflected on either side as that one is actually in; if the mirrors came lower, a greater extension on either side and at the rear would be suggested than could possibly be plausible as a reflection. A continuous grille of square panels filled with translucent yellow onyx takes the place of the mirror panel across the top of the front wall. Not until Mies van der Rohe's Barcelona Pavilion of 1929 was marble used again by a modern architect with such assurance [311].

It was not these urban commissions, however, but Loos's free-standing houses that the next generation of architects studied most closely. For example, Loos's sort of domestic open planning, not Wright's, was probably the major influence on the Continent after the First World War. Moreover, the neutrality, not to say the negativity, of the exteriors of his houses provided better even than Garnier's projects the raw material from which a positive sort of architectural design could be created by younger men in the early twenties. Loos's achievement before the First World War was largely in the domestic field; after the war most of his executed work still consisted of houses and shop interiors, although he made several curious projects for larger edifices and erected a large sugar refinery for the Rohrbacher Company in Czechoslovakia in 1919. The larger projects are usually symmetrical and often decorated with columns or pilasters.

The Rufer house in Vienna of 1922 is a narrow three-storey block rather similar to Voysey's Forster house of 1891 at Bedford Park. This has a most interesting sort of open plan, with the dining room on a higher level than the living room. Loos was also working in other countries now; for his reputation, if mostly limited to advanced circles, was increasingly international. His most considerable production of this decade was the house he built in 1926 for the writer Tristan Tzara at 14 Avenue Junod in Paris, where Loos had settled four years earlier. In the Tzara house the interior is arranged somewhat like that of the Rufer house: the dining room opens into the living room but on a higher level. The tall, rather blank front, slightly concave in plan, has a more positive character than those of most of his houses, because the two-storey void sunk into its centre provides a dominating feature above the solid rubble of the ground storey.

Of still later work the Kuhner house of 1930 at Payerbach in the wooded hills near Vienna is the most original example. A two-storey hall, opening towards the view through a window-wall, occupies most of the interior, with the various other living spaces opening into it on the main floor and the bedrooms reached from a gallery above. Above the masonry base the house is externally of log-construction, chalet-like, with Tyrolean roofs of low pitch and wide-spreading eaves. This reversion to peasant materials, and even to peasant forms, was curiously premonitory of a direction modern architecture took in several countries in the thirties (see Chapter 23). Had Loos lived longer he might, like Wright, have returned to the centre of the stage. As it was, his major contribution antedated the First World War.

Perret, Wright, Behrens, and Loos: on the whole these are the four most important architects of the first modern generation, important both for their personal contribution and also for their decisive influence on later architecture. Outside the countries in which these men worked, notably in Holland and in Scandinavia, there were also architects of distinction belonging to this generation but their achievement was more limited and their influence more local, at least before the First World War. Yet

Holland, between 1910 and 1925, came closer than any other country to creating a modern style, or phase of style, that was universally accepted at home; the origins, moreover, go back to the nineties. There had not been much of a prefatory Art Nouveau episode in Holland in spite of a considerable activity in the decorative arts inspired, in part at least, by serious study of the crafts of Indonesia.

Hendrik Petrus Berlage (1856-1934), the leader of the national school, was considerably older than Perret, Wright, Behrens, or Loos, although much younger than Wagner. As in Wagner's case, his earliest work, dating from the eighties, is of a generically Renaissance character, though much less suave and academic. The influence of Cuijpers soon led him towards a medieval mode - not Gothic, however, but round-arched. Compared to *Rundbogenstil* work of the best period fifty years earlier, his round-arched buildings of the nineties are rather gawky, but not without originality in their ornamentation; above all, they are vigorously structural in their expression in a 'realistic' and, indeed, almost High Victorian way. However, the insurance company buildings in Amsterdam and The Hague that best illustrate this phase were later enlarged by him in a chaster mode, thereby losing much of their anachronistic flavour.

Berlage's major opportunity came with the competition for the design of the Amsterdam Exchange held in 1897. This competition he won with a project which seems rather Richardsonian[4] to American eyes, though he did not - apparently - know much about American work at that time. For this very extensive public edifice, built over the years 1898-1903, he used, not the stone of his insurance office across the Damrak of 1893, but the red brick of his Hague insurance office, also of 1893, varied with a modicum of stone trim still quite crudely notched and chamfered. Inside, the principal interior has exposed metal principals above

galleried walls of brick and stone. In Berlage's masculine vigour and defiant gracelessness of detailing one could hardly have a greater contrast to such another major public building, designed and built at almost precisely the same time, as Horta's Maison du Peuple in Brussels. But Horta's masterpiece climaxed rather than opened his career as an architect of international importance; certainly it did not lead to the development of a national modern school in Belgium. At least for Holland, the Exchange was more seminal, even if it lacked the revolutionary character of Wright's houses of these years or Perret's block of flats in the Rue Franklin in Paris. A fairer comparison would be with Voysey's contemporary houses, the work of an architect who was by intention rather a 'reformer' than a drastic innovator, or even with Martin Nyrop's Town Hall in Copenhagen begun five years earlier.

Berlage's near-Richardsonian mode of this period is still better illustrated in a smaller structure, that built for the Diamond Workers' Trade Union [289] in the Henri Polak Laan

289. H. P. Berlage· Amsterdam,
Diamond Workers' Union Building, 1899-1900

in Amsterdam in 1899-1900. In this, the organization of the windows into a sort of brick-mullioned screen and the less aggressive handling of the carved stone detail produces a façade not unworthy of comparison with Richardson's Sever Hall or Gaudí's Casa Güell [175]. But it is notable that it is work of the seventies and eighties in America and Spain that comes to mind, not things of this date.

The Hotel American in Amsterdam of 1898-1900 but later extended by Willem Kromhout (1864-1940) illustrates how Berlage's line was paralleled by a few local architects, and his relative originality more than outrivalled. But the lead came in Kromhout's case not from Berlage, but from Cuijpers's nephew Eduard (1859-1927), a transitional figure whose work certainly deserves more attention than it has as yet received. Kromhout's touch is lighter than Berlage's, as is also, to make a poor pun, the colour of his pale buff bricks, but his expression of structure is less 'real' and more frankly fantastic. In the detail of the exterior, and even more in the interiors, he was undoubtedly seeking to create a sort of Dutch alternative to the Art Nouveau, not curvilinear or naturalistically 'organic' but richly decorative in a semi-abstract way. The intention was worthy; the result has only lately been appreciated again.

It was not in the design of sumptuous individual buildings but in low-cost housing and in city-planning that Berlage himself was most active in the next fifteen years. In 1908, for example, he prepared a plan for the extension of The Hague, and in 1915 a more ambitious one for Amsterdam. He had built his first blocks of flats in the Linnaeusstraat in Amsterdam in 1905. These are much less Romanesquoid than his earlier work but they are equally brusque as regards the detailing. However, his architecture shortly grew much suaver. Berlage's finest work of any period, perhaps, is not in Holland but in the City of London, Holland House of 1914 at 1-4 Bury Street, E.C. This has a reticu-

290. H. P. Berlage:
London, Holland House, 1914

lated façade of moulded terracotta members more Sullivanian than Richardsonian in its verticality [290] – and by then he knew Sullivan's work from his 1911 visit to America.

The influence of Berlage in Holland was by this time very great and the esteem in which he was held – at least as much for his doctrine of direct structural expression as for his executed work – by no means restricted to his own country, since his writings were published in Germany as well as in Holland.[5] Yet, to foreign eyes, the achievement of the new school that grew up partly under his inspiration in Amsterdam is greater than his own. The work of this 'Amsterdam School' – for it was soon so called – which flourished particularly in the decade 1912–22 is at times very close to that of the German architects influenced by Expres-

represents internationally the greatest Dutch contribution to modern architecture. As the master of these men, some younger historians now judge that Cuijpers has rather more right

291. Michael de Klerk:
Amsterdam, Eigen Haard housing estate, 1917

sionism in the early twenties; but it began much earlier and has a strongly autochthonous flavour.[6] German Expressionism never inspired a building more stridently angular than the Scheepvaarthuis that J. M. van der Meij (1868–1949), a pupil of Eduard Cuijpers, built to house dock offices on the Prins Hendrik Kade in Amsterdam in 1912–15. The most extreme example of the abandon with which twentieth-century Dutch architects set out on new paths, this opened the way for the housing work of van der Meij's assistants Michael de Klerk (1884–1923) and P. L. Kramer (1881–1961), both also from Eduard Cuijpers's office, which

than Berlage to be considered the father of the Amsterdam School. Their work, moreover, has some analogies not only with German Expressionism but also with Wright's contemporary Baroque phase of 1914–24. However, the crystallization of de Klerk's personal style preceded the beginning of Wright's influence and, when that influence began during the years of the First War, it operated in fact to counter the extravagances of the Amsterdam School.

Early buildings by de Klerk, such as the housing blocks for a client named K. Hill that were designed in 1913 and erected round the Spaandammerplantsoen on the west side of

Amsterdam, have a quaintness that recalls English or American work of a generation earlier rather than van der Meij's aggressive angularity. They look almost as if they were especially fanciful projects of the Shingle Style that happened to be executed in brick instead of wood. But the elegant underscaled local brick is handled with extraordinary virtuosity, and the façades achieve a stage-set-like unreality in sharpest contrast to the often dreary matter-of-factness of low-cost housing produced in other countries in these same years. Though the Hill and the first Eigen Haard blocks near by were, in their general organization, as straightforward as Berlage's, they have a warmer human touch such as architects elsewhere – Behrens, for example, or the Scandinavians – either missed entirely or attempted to attain by a parsimonious use of more or less 'traditional' detailing.

The extension of the Eigen Haard Estate along the Zaanstraat, begun in 1917, represents perhaps the peak of de Klerk's achievement [291]. Here the many curved wall elements bring out the special qualities of Dutch brickwork; and the rather heavy wooden windowframes, brought forward as in Hoffmann's Stoclet house to the wall-plane, give continuity to the plastic modelling of the façades. Highly imaginative, even whimsical, features of detail, such as the barrel-like corner oriel, give an air of good humour, and even of the outright humorous, that is rare in any other architecture, ancient or modern; but these features are for the most part truly architectonic, not merely decorative. De Klerk's whimsy is never nightmarish, in the way Gaudí's can be, nor loud and aggressive like the Expressionists'. His highly personal style can be considered a sort of *barocchino* of the early twentieth century.

The extreme point of de Klerk's invention is seen in the post office that occupies the apex of the later portion of the Eigen Haard Estate.

This is like nothing so much as a child's toy enlarged to architectural scale in some contemporary setting for Diaghilev's Ballet Russe.[7] After this his work grew somewhat simpler and more orderly. Already the blocks he designed in 1920 for an area round the Henriette Ronnerplein in the De Dageraad Estate on the south-east side of Amsterdam are more regular and restrained; the plainest of all is the very long continuous range near by in the Amstellaan built in 1921-2, the year before his early death.

Also in the De Dageraad Estate, in the portion that runs down both sides of the P. L. Takstraat, along the Burgemeester Tellegenstraat and into the Talmastraat, Kramer showed himself even more of a virtuoso in the handling of curved wall elements of brick – here brown and buff – than de Klerk [292]. Projected in 1918 and built in 1921-3, Kramer's scheme combined tall and very plastic features at the street intersections with notably straightforward three-storey ranges in between. Thus he produced an extensive urbanistic ensemble of great homogeneity of character, yet very considerable variety of visual interest, and with a quality of craftsmanship perhaps superior to de Klerk's. But by the time this was completed Kramer had become even more chastened than de Klerk in his last work in the Amstellaan. In Kramer's Amsterdam West housing, begun in 1923, the façades are plain and flat with continuous bands of white-sashed windows. Thus these blocks are definitely related to the direction that modern architecture was taking in Holland as in France and Germany in these years at the hands of men of Kramer's own generation (see Chapter 22).

Kramer's De Bijenkorf department store of 1924-6 in the Grotemarktstraat in The Hague, however, still retains much of the plastic exuberance of his earlier housing blocks and is executed with a sumptuous range of fine materials. Kramer here employed at large scale the curved surfaces of brickwork charac-

292. Piet Kramer: Amsterdam, De Dageraad housing estate, 1918-23

teristic of De Dageraad, with notable success. Many Amsterdam canal bridges of these years illustrate also his virtuosity at elaborate semi-abstract detail carried out with excellent craftsmanship in wrought iron and carved or artificial stone. Moreover, in the mid twenties the Amsterdam City Architect's office exploited with real success in various school and police buildings a manner closely approaching that of de Klerk and Kramer.

Unfashionable even in Holland for a generation and more, the work of the Amsterdam School has been receiving the sympathetic reexamination the Art Nouveau has had for a quarter of a century. The work of de Klerk and Kramer from the mid teens to the mid twenties has survived better physically than most of the contemporary achievements of Wright and Perret, because it was so well built in the first place and has been so well maintained ever

since. Yet without being, in the proper sense of the word, Expressionist, it has closer analogies with Expressionist fantasy. It may be considered to stand in a relationship to the work of Höger and Poelzig in Germany somewhat comparable to that of Gaudí to the Art Nouveau of Brussels and Paris; for it is at once independent of outside influence and superior to the foreign work that it most closely parallels. But the Amsterdam School did not occupy the entire Dutch scene even in these, its best, years.

In no European country was the work of Frank Lloyd Wright studied earlier and with more enthusiasm than in Holland; Berlage was one of Wright's greatest admirers after his visit to America in 1911. The influence of Wright's work up to 1910, known through the Wasmuth publications, began to be evident in the later years of the First World War. Dirk Roosenburg (1887-1962), Jan Wils (b. 1891),

J. J. Van Loghem (1882-1940), and several others were notably Wrightian in the early twenties; and the magazine *Wendingen*, edited by H. T. Wijdeveld (b. 1885), continued through the mid twenties to bring Wright's later buildings and his projects of those years to European attention, notably devoting to him a magnificent series of special issues in 1925 which constitutes a document of signal importance for the study of his work of this period. The first German book on Wright after the Wasmuth publications did not appear until the next year, and the first in French only in 1928.

Wrightian ideas were readily accepted by many Dutch architects previously inspired chiefly by Berlage, not to speak of their influence on Berlage himself. Admiration for Wright's work undoubtedly played a real part in the rapid modulation of Dutch architecture towards greater severity and a more geometrical discipline in the twenties. But the major significance of the lively Dutch interest in the American[7a] lies in its effect on the development of a few younger men in these years. To the Amsterdam School there had arisen a strong opposition led by architects belonging to the De Stijl group of artists who were active in Rotterdam and Utrecht. Yet the Amsterdam School architects continued for some time to be highly productive, and the work of several prominent men, notably J. F. Staal (1879-1940) and W. M. Dudok (1884-1974), was related to both camps. But by the time Berlage was engaged on the big concrete-framed Netherlands Insurance Company Building in The Hague in 1925-6 its very Wrightian character had already been superseded in the projects and the production of Rietveld and Oud by a more ascetic mode parallel to that adumbrated by the new architects of France and Germany in the early twenties (see Chapter 22).

In the new building of the Scandinavian countries before and after the First World War admirers[7b] in other countries thought to recognize an originality and vitality comparable to that of contemporary Dutch work. As has already been remarked, it has since become evident that most of what was produced in these decades in Denmark and Sweden did not really differ very much from the work of 'traditionalists' elsewhere. Despite extremely elegant and often piquant stylization, comparable but superior to that of much German work in this period, continued maintenance of inherited principles of design and the general use of reminiscent detail sharply differentiated the characteristic production of the Scandinavians from that of the Dutch, and of course far more from that of Wright or Loos. What such men as Ragnar Östberg (1866-1945) and E. G. Asplund (1885-1940), down to his sharp change of style in the late twenties, designed and built in Sweden or P. V. Jensen Klint (1853-1930) and Kay Fisker (1893-1965) – down to his parallel change of style – in Denmark was generally still rated 'modern' in the 1920s; but almost all of it may be more properly classed with 'traditional' work in other countries. In quality, however, it often more than rivals all but the finest modern German, Austrian, and Dutch work of its day (see Chapter 24).

An exception to this statement as regards Sweden is the remarkable Engelbrekt Church of 1904-14 in Stockholm by L. I. Wahlman (1870-1952), with its great parabolic arches and its vertically massed exterior dominated by a very tall and svelte tower; there much of the experimentalism of the nineties lived on. For its influence, this is possibly as important a twentieth-century church as Perret's at Le Raincy. An even more considerable exception is a large part of the prolific production of the Finnish architect Eliel Saarinen (1873-1950) both in the Old World and in the New. Saarinen was the leading architect of Finland down to the twenties; after his removal to the United States he was Wright's chief rival of his own generation on the American scene, the careers of the early modern architects of the West Coast being by then in decline (see Chapter 19). Lars Sonck, a finer architect, was less well-known internationally.[7c]

Saarinen's earliest work in partnership with Herman Gesellius (1874–1916) and A. E. Lindgren (1874–1929) dates from the nineties. In 1900 he designed the Finnish Pavilion at the Paris Exhibition; this offered a powerful, though rather cranky, statement of Nordic originality quite opposed to the Latin elegance of the contemporary Art Nouveau and not without kinship to Berlage's Amsterdam Exchange. At home important public commissions followed rapidly: the National Museum in Helsinki in 1902 and the Helsinki railway station, for which he won the competition in 1904. This large and complex structure, built over the years 1910–14, is Saarinen's principal early work. In size and in monumentality it rivals Bonatz's Stuttgart station and also the vast stations that 'traditional' architects in America were building at much the same time (see Chapter 24). But there is much less of 'tradition' here than at the Stuttgart or, a fortiori, in the American stations. The heaviness and the grandeur are more than a little Germanic, so that the fairest comparison is with Stürzenacker's Karlsruhe station, on the whole more straightforward in design and certainly much more delicately detailed. Sonck's Tampere Cathedral[7d] of 1902–7 is more original.

Saarinen's achievement in his homeland made him well known throughout Europe; as early as 1905 one of his principal works had been a country house, Molchow, in Brandenburg in Germany. The project that he entered in the Chicago Tribune Tower competition in 1922 brought him suddenly to American attention. Although a Gothic design by John Mead Howells (1868–1959) and Raymond Hood (1881–1934) won this competition and was executed[8] on Michigan Avenue, in 1923–5, Saarinen's project (which in any case received a financially

generous second premium) had a tremendous *succès d'estime*, including the accolade of Sullivan himself. In retrospect the design appears almost as medievalizing as Howells & Hood's; but the elegance of the silhouette and the consistency of the detailing, stylized nearly to the point of absolute originality, had an enormous contemporary appeal.

By this time Americans were beginning to grow bored with the increasingly forced adaptation of familiar styles of the past to skyscraper design. Yet in 1922 they were hardly ready to recognize the positive qualities of the very plain reticulated tower, elaborated with certain minor

293. Walter Gropius with Adolf Meyer:
Project for Chigaco Tribune Tower, 1922

Constructivist touches, that was proposed by Walter Gropius (1883-1969) and Adolf Meyer (d. 1925) [293]. Today it is easy to see how close this came to reviving the Chicago tradition of the early skyscrapers,[8a] a tradition almost forgotten since the First World War, as also its great importance in the crystallization of a new architecture in the early twenties (Chapter 22).

Saarinen, after settling in the United States in 1922, designed various other skyscrapers along the lines of his Chicago project, none of them built. However, other architects at once picked up his relatively novel ideas; and undoubtedly his ideas played an important part in turning American skyscraper architects away from their long-continued dependence on the styles of the past.[8b] Hood himself was not least affected, as his black and gold American Radiator Building[9] on West 40th Street in New York, completed in 1924 even before the Chicago Tribune Tower, soon made evident. In Detroit, near which city Saarinen settled, Albert Kahn's Fisher Building is even more Saarinenesque and quite unrelated to his contemporary factories.

Called to Bloomfield Hills, Mich., by the Booth publishing family, Saarinen's first work in America was the Cranbrook School for Boys, a very extensive group of buildings begun in 1925. Here an almost Swedish elegance of craftsmanship and a profusion of semi-traditional detail were combined in a somewhat whimsical manner rather recalling English work of forty or fifty years earlier. The girls' school near by, however, Kingswood, begun in 1929, is much simpler, with an almost Wrightian horizontality and crispness of expression.

When American building activity revived in the late thirties Saarinen continued to develop. From 1937 on his American-trained son Eero (1911-61), destined later to be one of the leaders of post-war architecture in the United States, doubtless played some part in encouraging that bolder structural expression and increasing sparseness of ornamentation that characterizes his finest late works. These qualities are already very evident in the Kleinhans Music Hall in Buffalo, N.Y., of 1938; while the contrast between the straightforwardness of the Crow Island School in Winnetka, Ill., of 1939, on which the Chicago firm of Perkins, Wheeler & Will collaborated, and the quaintness and fussiness of the Cranbrook School is quite startling.

Most distinguished of all the late Saarinen works are his Tabernacle Church at Columbus, Ind., designed in 1940 and built in 1941-2, and the similar but smaller Christ Lutheran Church in Minneapolis that was built in 1949 just before his death [294]. Cool, clear, and rational, the distinguished handling of brickwork in these churches, the knowing control of light, and the careful ordering of space in the interiors remain exemplary. Their towers are more refined versions of Moser's on Sankt Antonius in Basel; yet the massing of their blocky external elements almost seems to belong to an earlier tradition, that of the English Victorian Gothic churches of the third quarter of the nineteenth century, whose reminiscent forms they abjure but which the elder Saarinen knew, at least at second-hand, from Sonck's Cathedral.

Of the first generation of modern architects there is none who survives. As long as Wright continued in active production the story that the last four chapters tried to tell could not be completed but in 1959, with his death, an architectural epoch came finally to an end. It was a rich epoch and a complex one because the men of that generation were all great individualists and proud of it. In most countries they had to fight a vigorous battle for the right to personal expression, a battle that they carried through to recognition against entrenched inertia, both professional and lay. Yet in general, the links of this generation with the later nineteenth century remained close, both in their dependence on handicraft and in their frequent tendency - least

294. Saarinen & Saarinen:
Minneapolis, Minn., Christ Lutheran Church, 1949

evident with Wright and the Dutch – to accept (up to a point) personal stylization of earlier architectural forms[10] as a substitute for that basic originality of which many were at their best truly capable.

Not since the late eighteenth century had there been any such wide international renewal of architectural aspiration. Just as then, a new generation would profit from the experiments of their elders, taking much from each, but rejecting much as well, in order to create a style – or at least a discipline – aiming at universality. By its essential principles, this discipline could not have the variety and the

intensity of personal expression which gives such colour and life to the work of the older men. Just as in the early nineteenth century, however, the architects who succeeded the great originals were far more able than they to work together. By joining their individual efforts the men of the next generation changed the character of almost all architectural production in a way that their elders were quite unable to do. Thus there came into being an architecture more completely of its own century than any style-phase of the previous hundred years – up to the Art Nouveau at least – had ever been wholly of the nineteenth century.

CHAPTER 22

THE EARLY WORK OF THE SECOND GENERATION:
WALTER GROPIUS, LE CORBUSIER,
MIES VAN DER ROHE, RIETVELD, AND OUD

The project that Gropius and Meyer offered in the competition of 1922 for the Chicago Tribune Tower, unlike Saarinen's, attracted very little contemporary attention in America [293]. Such a stripped expression of skeleton construction had, up to that time in America, been seen only in factories and warehouses. Even in Chicago, moreover, the New York ideal of the shaped tower had quite replaced the Sullivanian slab as the favourite form for pretentious skyscrapers. Ten years later, however, when the first International Exhibition of Modern Architecture was held at the new Museum of Modern Art in New York it was evident that the kind of architecture represented by Gropius's project had become widely accepted in several European countries. By that date it was even possible to deduce from

the executed work of Gropius and his chief European contemporaries, most of which was shown in the exhibition, the existence of a new style christened 'international'[1] by Alfred Barr, the Museum's director. Whether the new architecture that came into being in the twenties in Europe and later spread throughout the western world should in fact be considered a style, or even a style-phase, remains a matter of controversy; but for thirty years it was readily distinguishable from what the older generation of modern architects were still producing.

In 1922 this new architecture hardly existed except in the form of projects. Some of the most strikingly novel buildings built in the early twenties were by William Marinus Dudok in the Netherlands and by Erich Mendelsohn[2] (1887–1953) in Germany. These

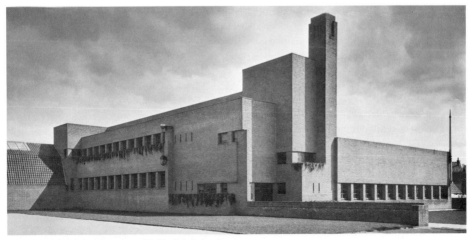

295. W. M. Dudok: Hilversum, Dr Bavink School, 1921

no longer belonged to the realm of the earlier, pre-war modern architecture. Yet the work of neither was as indicative of the direction the newer architecture was taking in these formative years as is the Gropius Chicago Tribune project. Very shortly, however, both Dudok and Mendelsohn drew closer to the main current of development of this decade, although they continued to be, in varying degree, individualists rather than whole-hearted converts to the dominant architectural mode of their generation.

Dudok's work as City Architect of Hilversum, beginning with the Public Baths and the Dr H. Bavink School in 1921, is remarkably simple and direct [295]. The volumetric clarity of his compositions is very different from the whimsically irregular organization of de Klerk's and Kramer's housing blocks [291, 292]. His rigidly geometrical arrangement of plastic elements reflects his contact with the *De Stijl*[3] group of abstract artists, notably the Dutch painters Piet Mondriaan and Theo van Doesburg and the Belgian sculptor Georges Vantongerloo. But Dudok's continued emphasis on the fine quality of his brickwork, the heaviness of his characteristically interlocking blocks, and a certain basically decorative intention still link his buildings of the twenties at Hilversum with the ideals of the older generation. Dudok's work of this period was certainly novel – and even very advanced for the date – but it remained Dutch in its idiosyncrasies, not 'international'.

The plasticity of Mendelsohn's Einstein Tower, designed in 1919 and completed in 1921, at Neubabelsberg near Berlin [296] seems at first sight not unrelated to that of Gaudí's hewn-stone Casa Milá in Barcelona of 1905-10 [253]. But it was originally intended to be executed in poured concrete – for technical reasons it is in fact mostly of brick rendered with stucco – and what one might call the 'overtones' of the forms are more mechanistic than organic. Like Dudok, Mendelsohn

had been influenced by a local school of painting. But the images he distorted according to the tenets of Expressionism came from the world of machines not, like Gaudí's, from the world of plants and animals. Mendelsohn's earlier war-time sketches[4] make this origin even more evident. The extreme point of this sort of abstract sculptural Expressionism[5] in the twenties is found in the executed work of no architect[5a] but in the cult edifice called Goetheanum at Dornach in Switzerland, designed by the creator of anthroposophy Rudolf Steiner[6] and begun in 1923.

Mendelsohn himself rejected this excessively plastic approach to architecture – an approach to which a reversion can be noted on the part of Le Corbusier in the 1940s and 50s, incidentally [324] – even before the Einstein Tower was completed. The hat factory that he built at Luckenwalde in 1920-3 was in the direct line of descent from the industrial work Behrens and Poelzig had done before the First World War. This was rightly recognized as one of the signal productions of those crucial years of the early twenties when the concepts of a new architecture were first being tentatively realized in France and in Holland, and very shortly, of course, in Germany. Dudok's buildings at Hilversum of the early twenties had a very considerable international influence;[7] Mendelsohn's Einstein Tower did not, at least not on architecture.[8] However, other work of his done in the next few years was much admired and also widely emulated, both in Germany and abroad, by the younger architects.

In spite of the importance in these years of the executed work of Dudok and of Mendelsohn, several other architects certainly had far more to do with determining the direction that architecture took from 1922 on. One was a Swiss then working in Paris, Charles-Édouard Jeanneret, known as Le Corbusier. At this time more painter than architect, Le Corbusier had earlier been an assistant of Perret's and

296. Erich Mendelsohn:
Neubabelsberg, Einstein Tower, 1921

had also worked briefly for Behrens and even for Josef Hoffmann. Two others were Dutchmen. J. J. P. Oud had practised in association with Dudok at Leiden in 1912–13, and from 1917 and 1918 he and G. T. Rietveld were in much closer contact with the artists of *De Stijl* than Dudok ever was, being actual members of that small cohesive group. Two more were Germans, Walter Gropius and Ludwig Mies van der Rohe, both of whom had been Behrens's assistants, respectively for two and for three years.

Gropius, born in 1883, was the eldest of the five and older than Mendelsohn also; Le Corbusier, Rietveld, and Mies were born in 1888; Oud in 1890.[8a] Gropius's career began as early as 1906, when he erected some plain brick workmen's houses in Pomerania even before he had finished his professional training at the Technische Hochschule in Munich. A leading professor in this school was Theodor Fischer, Bonatz's master, in whose office Oud later spent a few months in 1911. After a year of travel in Spain, Italy, and Holland Gropius entered Behrens's office in 1908, remaining there till 1910. On leaving Behrens he designed in 1911, with Adolf Meyer, the Fagus Factory at Alfeld-an-der-Leine. He

297. Walter Gropius and Adolf Meyer: Alfeld-an-der-Leine, Fagus Factory, 1911

worked once again in partnership with Adolf Meyer from after the end of the First World War until 1924-5; Meyer died in 1925.

Directly as this Alfeld factory - it made shoe-lasts - follows from Behrens's work for the A.E.G., notably the front of the Turbine Factory of 1909, its architectural expression is much more advanced [297]. There the great window remained, for all its size, but a window; here, in the main three-storey block, the slightly projecting metal chassis rise unbroken over very wide areas bounded by narrow brick piers, and the storey levels are barely indicated by solid panels identical in treatment with the glazed sash above and below them. This arrangement of transparent and opaque elements identically handled may almost - but not quite - be considered to constitute a 'curtain-wall'.[9] The omission of piers at the corners, a structural novelty here, enormously enhances the effect of transparent volume as opposed to that of solid mass. In the organization of the various industrial elements of the complete plant that are associated with the glazed block there is neither symmetry, such as Behrens was only beginning to relinquish, nor yet asymmetry of the more casual and picturesque sort; instead a modular regularity controls the whole composition. This factory has long been recognized historically as one of the most important[10] buildings of the twentieth century.

Gropius's next building, the Administration Building at the Werkbund Exhibition of 1914[10a] in Cologne, was in some ways less advanced. The main façades of this were quite symmetrical; and in the articulation of the brick piers of the ground storey, in the heavily framed central entrance and, above all, in the projecting slab roofs of the raised corners there appears to have been some direct influence from the work of Wright, notably from his hotel of 1909 in Mason City, Iowa. (This was published in the Wasmuth book of 1910, where Gropius would almost certainly have seen it.)

The glazed front of the principal storey, how-ever, and especially the rounded glass stair-towers at the ends were not at all Wrightian; they carried still further the expression of architecture as transparent volume already evident in the Fagus Factory and approached very closely indeed the mature curtain-wall concept, although at a modest scale.

Mies remained with Behrens a year longer than Gropius, after having spent three earlier years with Bruno Paul[11] (1874-1954), a more conservative architect whose best work was done as a furniture designer. His independent career began in a much less spectacular fashion than that of Gropius. The Perls house of 1911 at Zehlendorf outside Berlin was as formally symmetrical as Behrens's houses at Hagen of 1908-9 and at least as Schinkelesque. The Urbig house of 1914 at Neubabelsberg was very correctly late-eighteenth-century in its detailing. His most important work of these years, however, was the project for the H. E. L. J. Kröller house near The Hague of 1912, to contain the large and famous Kröller-Müller collection of modern paintings now at Otterlo. Of this a full-scale wood and canvas model was erected on the actual site, but it was never built.[11a] The formal though asymmetrical organization of the severe horizontal blocks, the incorporation of voids in the composition by means of loggias and pilastrades, and the cold austerity of the refined detailing of the masonry all approach very closely such things by Schinkel as the Zivilkasino at Potsdam and Schloss Glienecke, even if the characteristic belvedere tower of the latter is significantly omitted. In many ways this project was as premonitory of later modern architecture as the Fagus Factory, although the latter, as an executed building, has properly received much more notice.[12] Both Gropius and Mies were involved in the First World War from 1914 to 1918, so that the next stage in their careers opened only in 1919.

Le Corbusier, Oud, and Rietveld were neutral nationals, but their production of these early years, although less interrupted by the war, is mostly not of much intrinsic interest. After two years with Perret in Paris Le Corbusier had spent six months in Behrens's office in 1910.[13] The early house[14] he built for his parents at La Chaux de Fond in Switzerland in 1913 is more closely related to Behrens's early houses in its plain white stucco walls and fairly restricted fenestration than it is to the work of Perret or to Behrens's A.E.G. factories of 1909-11. The plan is the most interesting feature: this provides a central living area out of which other more specialized rooms open to left and right through wide glazed doors, a scheme that seems to derive from Perret's planning, or perhaps that of Loos,[15] rather than from Wright's.

Le Corbusier's next significant work was a war-time project of 1914-15 for low-cost houses called Dom-ino. These seem to derive not from anything of Perret's or Behrens's but rather directly from the ones that Tony Garnier had proposed for his 'Cité industrielle' as early as 1901-4,[16] but they are still plainer, probably because of the concurrent influence of Loos. However, Le Corbusier's only important executed building of the War years, the Villa Schwobb of 1916 at La Chaux de Fond, is closer to Perret in its elaborate formality, its much simplified academic detail, and its concrete-and-brick construction. The plan represents an advance over that of his parents' house, however, for the main living area here is carried up two storeys and lighted by a tall window-wall towards the garden. Of special significance also is the arrangement of all the flat roofs as usable terraces.

The next year, 1917, De Stijl was founded, and soon Oud and Rietveld as members of the group began to collaborate with the Dutch abstract painters and sculptors generally known as Neoplasticists.[17] In this year Oud built two villas by the seashore: Allegonda at Katwijk, designed in association with the architect M. Kamerlingh Onnes; and De Vonk at Noordwijkerhout, with interiors decorated by the De Stijl painter and critic Theo van Doesburg. The Dutch had no direct contact with Behrens, unlike the other three, but Oud was briefly with Fischer in Munich in 1911, as has been said. However, Oud's work down to this time had been essentially Berlagian: moreover, it was Berlage who evoked his interest in the work of Wright. Nevertheless, there is nothing Wrightian about these villas, but rather a Loos-like reduction of architecture to white stucco cubes. The interest of De Vonk is largely confined to the floors of bold geometric pattern executed in coloured tile by van Doesburg; Allegonda was much modified by Oud in 1927. Rietveld was primarily a furniture designer until 1921.

In 1918 Oud became City Architect of Rotterdam, where his brother occupied a prominent political position, and began work at once on the Spangen Housing Estate, Blocks I and II being of that year, Blocks VIII and IX of the next. The Tuschendijken Estate followed in 1920. These housing blocks, even more than the seaside villas, are notable for their negative rather than their positive qualities. All the elaboration of form and detail of the Amsterdam School was put aside in favour of an ascetic regularity. But various projects of these years illustrate how boldly Oud was attempting, partly under the influence of his painter and sculptor friends, partly under that of Wright, to arrive at new formal concepts. Nor was Oud alone in these years in thus attempting to translate the ideals of De Stijl into architecture. Rietveld, in a small jewellery shop in Amsterdam built in 1921, was probably the first fully to realize Neoplasticist concepts in three dimensions and at architectural scale.[18]

In Paris in the first post-war years Le Corbusier was also closely involved with painters; indeed, he himself was then as much, or more, a painter as an architect, and he never ceased painting later. With the French painter Amédée Ozenfant he had written a book on art, *Après le cubisme*, published in Paris in 1918; together they developed a post-Cubist sort of abstract painting, partly inspired by their friend Fernand Léger and partly by their interest in the simple shapes of everyday objects. This they called 'Purisme'. In support of their ideas about all the arts they began in 1920[19] to publish a review, *L'Esprit nouveau*, which continued to appear until 1925, the nursery years of the new architecture.

In succession to his Dom-ino system of multiple housing of 1914-15, Le Corbusier was developing at this time the Troyes system, using poured concrete, and also the Monol system with a reinforced-concrete skeleton deriving technically from the innovations of Perret. But the definitive formulation of his new ideals for architecture, focused as they were at this time on the sociological problem of the low-cost dwelling, lay a year or two ahead. Having no official position, he did not need, like Oud, to produce executed work in quantity before his own concepts matured. Gropius's earliest work, back in 1906, had been a low-cost housing scheme, as has been noted, and in 1911 he built another housing estate, at Wittenberg-an-der-Elbe. Economical housing was increasingly recognized as a social service for which architects ought to exploit to the utmost their technical abilities; from the first it offered a common challenge to the Dutchman, the Swiss-Parisian, and the German.

Like the Dutch and Le Corbusier, Gropius was involved with painters in the early post-war years. Appointed in 1919 head of the Art School in Weimar and also of the Applied Arts School there which Van de Velde had run before the War, he combined them and named the new school the Bauhaus.[20] Here teachers of painting and sculpture, if not architecture,

worked in closest association with teachers of the crafts in continuation and extension of the English Arts and Crafts ideals of the eighties and nineties. Soon this rather Viennese approach, brought to the Bauhaus by Adolf Itten, with its emphasis on handicraft, was revised by Gropius so that it might better fit an increasingly industrialized society.[21] To this faculty Gropius brought such advanced painters as the German-American Lyonel Feininger in 1919 and in 1922 the Russian Wassily Kandinsky and the Swiss Paul Klee. Yet it was not their advanced art but rather Expressionist painting and sculpture which still influenced the jagged War Monument that he erected in Weimar in 1921. His architectural ideals in the early post-war years before 1922, moreover, seem to have been rather closer to Poelzig's or Mendelsohn's than to those of Le Corbusier, Oud, or Rietveld.

As has been several times stated already, certain remarkable projects best displayed the direction in which several of the architects of the younger generation were moving, along nearly parallel lines, in these years preceding the general revival of building production in the mid twenties. Gropius's Chicago Tribune project of 1922, in which the line of his development shifted away from Expressionism, has already been discussed out of sequence [293]. But the most significant projects, earlier than this by several years, were by Mies and by Le Corbusier. Mies's early work had not been very adventurous up to the time when he proposed, in 1919 and in 1920-1, two revolutionary glazed skyscrapers to be built in Berlin. In both, the floors were to be cantilevered out from central supporting cores and the curtain-walls enclosing them merely light metal chasis holding great panes of glass. However, their plans, respectively jagged and curvilinear, reflected the strong influence of Expressionism, an influence that disappeared from Mies's as from Gropius's work the very next year when these Germans began to accept the architectural implications of the painting and sculpture of the most abstract Dutch and Russian artists. Van Doesburg,[22] as well as Malevitch, visited the Bauhaus in 1922, and for a short but crucial period several of the Germans seem to have drawn from Dutch sources as much inspiration as the young Dutch architects. In addition to the obvious debts of Dudok, Oud, and Rietveld to Neo-plasticism, Cornelis van Eesteren (b. 1897), later City Architect of Amsterdam, was actually collaborating with van Doesburg in these years on various house projects that were exhibited in Paris in 1923.

Less striking than Mies's skyscrapers, but more buildable, were Le Corbusier's successive Citrohan projects for houses of 1919-22 [298-300]. Brought to public attention first in *L'Esprit nouveau* and later in his extremely influential book *Vers une architecture*, published in Paris in 1923 and shortly translated into English and German, these adumbrated a new aesthetic of architecture more completely than anything that he or any other architect had yet proposed on paper, much less built. Modest in size, each Citrohan house was to consist largely of a two-storey living-room fronted like that of the La Chaux de Fond house of 1916 with a tall window-wall. This would occupy most of the façade, and it was here set within a very plain frame of rendered concrete. The dining area was to be at the rear under a balcony from which the bedroom opened. So the section is similar to Wright's Millard house of 1923.

The earlier version of the house was intended to stand on the ground [298]; in the later scheme the whole cube of the house was to be lifted up on *pilotis*, that is, free-standing piers of reinforced concrete constituting, Perret-like, essential parts of the structural skeleton [299, 300]. Like Sullivan's piers at the base of the Guaranty Building of 1894-5 [208] the effect of these *pilotis*, allowing circumambient space to pass under the enclosed building above, was to enhance very strongly the look of volume as opposed to mass. This treatment, possible only with skeleton construction in ferro-concrete, steel, or wood, soon became one of the most significant formal devices differentiating the new architecture of the twenties from what preceded it. The later Citrohan project was thus the first of the 'boxes on stilts' against which Wright continually protested, even though his own buildings themselves tended more and more frequently to be lifted off the ground by one means or another.

If the structural methods employed here by Le Corbusier came from Perret, the external

298. Le Corbusier:
First project for Citrohan house, 1919-20

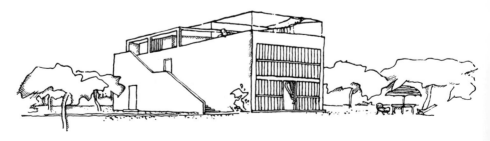

expression of his lifted box seems rather to derive from Garnier or Loos, although the rendered surfaces were evidently intended to be smoother and flatter than those of Loos's executed houses [286] and the pattern of the windows much more regularly organized in the wall-plane. With the roof terrace on top surrounded by parapets continuous with the wall-planes below, even the earlier type is apprehended as volume rather than mass, especially as there were no deep window reveals to suggest thickness in the walls such as appear in Garnier's projects and Loos's executed work. By keeping the openings absolutely in the wall-plane, as Hoffmann had done on the Stoclet house, the very exact geometrical discipline of the design of the façades could be maintained even when seen in perspective. As a result, however, the underlying structure was expressed only in the *pilotis* of the later project. Yet the wide expanse of the window-wall at the front and the characteristic shape of the other windows, oblongs extended horizontally,[23] would obviously not have been practical but for the long spans made possible by the ferro-concrete skeleton.

There was in the Citrohan projects no very close similarity to Le Corbusier's Purist pictures of these years other than the crisply geometrical ordering of the very flat façades

299 and 300. Le Corbusier: Second project for Citrohan house, 1922

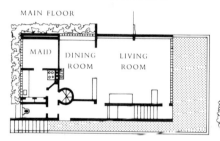

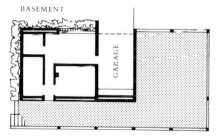

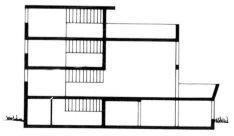

and the untextured smoothness of their surfaces. However, the extreme mechanical precision and the more-than-Loosian rejection of the inessential clearly reflected an aesthetic parallel to that adumbrated in his paintings. Certainly the effect was – as Wright and others recurrently complained – likely to prove more pictorial than architectonic when such things were executed. There was no ornament such as Oud had, in some sense, obtained at Katwijk from his painter-collaborator van Doesburg; indeed, there was hardly any detail at all, at least as architectural detail was understood by Perret and Behrens. In this respect also Le Corbusier's new architecture was closest to the personal style of Loos.

Articles in *L'Esprit nouveau* and later the illustrations in *Vers une architecture* revealed the sources of Le Corbusier's extra-architectural inspiration and made such inspiration available to others who cared to look about them with his particular vision and his clearly defined ideals for the modern world. Works of engineering, American grain-elevators and the like;[24] the forms of things that move – ocean liners, motor cars and aeroplanes:[25] such things provided some of the visual prototypes for Le Corbusier's new aesthetic of architecture.[26] But there was also the social motive of developing a method of building houses to satisfy the needs of all classes. Moreover, Le Corbusier was already – to use a term introduced later – as much a 'planner' as an architect. In 1922 he prepared a project for a city of three million inhabitants. This proposed at the core a geometrically ordered group of widely spaced cruciform skyscrapers and, round the core, ranges of blocks of flats of moderate height, not arranged along narrow streets, but distributed through a park-like terrain.

Le Corbusier had many years to wait before the world caught up with his ideas as a planner as these were promulgated in his book *Urbanisme*, published in Paris in 1925. But as

an architect[27] he was shortly building in and near Paris a series of houses, most of them of considerably greater size than his Citrohan project. Moreover, in 1927, at the Werkbund Exhibition in Stuttgart, he finally brought that to execution also, although some minor modifications were incorporated.[27a] Le Corbusier's very first post-war houses – one at Vaucresson, S.-et-O., near Paris, which has been re-

Second floor

First floor

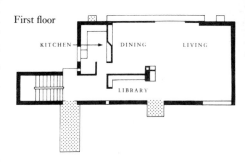

Ground floor

301. Le Corbusier:
Vaucresson, S.-et-O., house, 1923

302 and 303 *(opposite)*. Le Corbusier:
Poissy, S.-et-O., Savoye house, 1929-30

modelled quite beyond recognition, and another for Ozenfant at 53 Avenue Reille in the
Montrouge district of Paris, both designed in
1922 and built in 1923 – were naturally not
very adequate expressions of his ideals[28] [301].
But, beginning with the contiguous La Roche
and Jeanneret houses, designed originally in
1922 also and executed with many modifications
and improvements in 1924 in the Square du
Dr Blanche in the Auteuil district of Paris, and
culminating in the Savoye house at Poissy,
S.-et-O., of 1929-30 [302], the new aesthetic[29]
of the Citrohan project was exploited with
increasing virtuosity. Le Corbusier developed
much further the spatial unity of his plans,
usually keeping inside a defining rectangle but
articulating that in various ways: at the
Savoye house, for example, the main terrace is

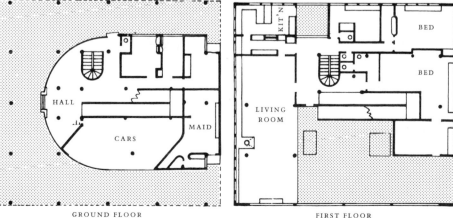

GROUND FLOOR   FIRST FLOOR

304. Le Corbusier:
Garches, S.-et-O., Les Terrasses, 1927

within the same raised box as the enclosed rooms [303]. The treatment of the exteriors likewise grew simpler and more open. Horizontal windows were grouped and extended to form continuous ribbons all the way across façades, and roofs at various levels, being completely flat, served as outdoor living-spaces. This is best seen at Les Terrasses [304], the house built in 1927 for Michael Stein at 17 Rue du Professeur Pauchet in Garches, S.-et-O.

Different colours were often used on different walls to emphasize them as individual planes, particularly in interiors. Curved elements, such as were introduced earlier in the plan of the Vaucresson house [301], appeared at the Savoye house in screens that rose around the upper roof-terrace [302]. Moreover, the geometrical discipline of his *tracés régulateurs* based on the Golden Section was used with

ever-increasing consistency.[30] At the same time the use of different colours and of curves produced, particularly at the Savoye house, a lyricism closely related to that of Purist paintings of the early twenties. This is curious, since in his paintings dating from the late twenties Le Corbusier was moving away from Purism, under the influence of Fernand Léger (and perhaps even of Surrealism), towards a looser and more connotative mode.

Le Corbusier was not the only architect of the new generation building houses in Paris in these years. Beside his, those by the Belgian Robert Mallet-Stevens (1886-1945)[31] are at once cruder and more superficial in their design. In the Rue Mallet-Stevens near Le Corbusier's La Roche and Jeanneret houses, where he built several houses close together in 1926-7, he provided a somewhat depressing glimpse of the near future, a glimpse that often proved, alas, to be only too accurate a generation later. The Cité Seurat, on the south side of Paris near Le Corbusier's Ozenfant house, offered an even larger group of new houses of the same period, several of them of much higher quality. The Chana Orloff house there is by Perret; but most of the others are by André Lurçat[32] (1894–1970), an architect of more integrity than Mallet-Stevens, if without Le Corbusier's genius. The best of Lurçat's houses, where they have been adequately maintained, possess certain common-sense virtues that Le Corbusier's lack; in the late twenties and early thirties they provided paradigms at least as popular as Le Corbusier's. His school of 1931 in Villejuif, Seine, has a special importance also, as it was in the field of school-building[33] that the new architecture first became widely accepted later in the thirties in several countries. Le Corbusier's activity was much greater than Lurçat's, however, and in one major project at least he extended the scope of the new architecture far beyond the realm of the modest private dwellings that both he and Lurçat were so largely restricted to building in the nineteen-twenties.

In 1925, in the Pavillon de l'Esprit Nouveau at the Paris Exposition des Arts Décoratifs, Le Corbusier had shown a dwelling unit of the Citrohan type arranged as a flat with a large terrace at one side, following an unexecuted project of 1922. The actual housing estate that he built at Pessac outside Bordeaux in 1925–6 was less successful, although by this time many young architects concerned with housing in other countries were finding inspiration in his work and perhaps even more in his ideas. But it was in an entirely different realm that Le Corbusier had, like Saarinen in the Chicago Tribune competition, a failure which was nonetheless a tremendous *succès d'estime*. Le Corbusier's project for the Palace of the

League of Nations[34] came very close to winning the competition of 1927. Moreover, the totally undistinguished scheme jointly produced by the elderly Frenchman P.-H. Nénot (1853–1934), who had built the new Sorbonne in Paris in 1884–9, and various other architects from several different countries eventually executed in Geneva never received the attention or the flattery of world-wide emulation and imitation which Le Corbusier's project did. This led, for example, to his selection to design the Centrosoyus in Moscow in 1928. Begun the following year, this was finally finished in 1936, but with most inadequate supervision. However, the Communist 'party line'[35] turned sharply against modern architecture in the early thirties, and no more projects by Western European architects were invited after the Palace of the Soviets competition held in 1931.

If Le Corbusier in the twenties was, by force of circumstances, almost more completely restricted to house-building than Wright had been in the preceding decades, Gropius's career in Germany developed very differently. In 1925 he was invited by the city of Dessau to come there from Weimar and re-establish the Bauhaus; in that year and the next he had a chance to build a very large and complex structure to house the school as well as his own and some other professors' houses. The houses were not notable additions to the new canon, although they were soon as much imitated as Le Corbusier's and Lurçat's. However, the Bauhaus building itself was the first major example of the new architecture to be executed, illustrating on a large scale most of its possibilities and principal themes, none of them by this date altogether novel.

The most striking element of the Bauhaus is the studio block, a four-storeyed glass box [305]. This carried to its logical limit the implications of the near-curtain-wall of the Fagus Factory, quite as Mies had already proposed for his two glass skyscraper projects, but without their

305 and 306. Walter Gropius: Dessau, Bauhaus, 1925-6

A   Auditorium
Ad Administration
C   Classroom
CS Carpentry Shop
D   Dining
E   Exhibitions
K   Kitchen
L   Laboratory
Ly Library
MS Machine Shop
PS Paint Shop
S   Store
St Stage
W   Workshops
WS Weaving Shops
X   Cloaks

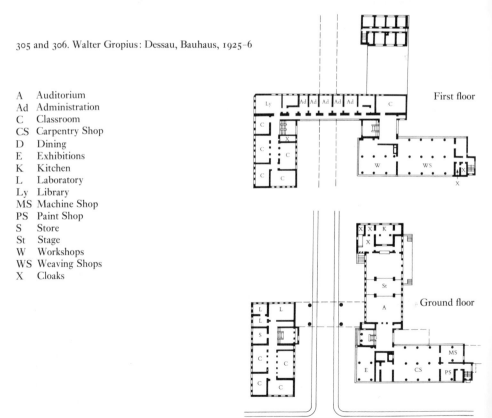

Expressionist planning. The bridge to the left of this block exploits the possibilities of great spans in ferro-concrete construction. Throughout that section and the block on the left ribbon-windows longer than Le Corbusier's at Les Terrasses open up the walls just as Mies had already proposed to do in a notable project of 1922 for a ferro-concrete office building. A lower refectory wing links the glazed block with an apartment tower at the rear; in that the grouping of the horizontal windows with the many little projecting balconies clearly expresses the fact that this portion of the building is made up of small repeated dwelling units.

The organization of this very complex structure is asymmetrical but carefully studied [306]. Where Le Corbusier had thus far composed most of his houses inside a single 'box', Gropius here combined four or more. In each

he emphasized visually the fact that the surface was but a thin shell enclosing an internal volume, but he varied the treatment according to the internal use of each portion of the building. At the same time regularity of rhythm, and often identity of measure in the parts, ordered the whole without recourse to symmetry or to the imposition of any such special system of proportion as Le Corbusier was enthusiastically developing.

⌐ Gropius did not again, until later in life in America, have such another architectural opportunity. In the following years, down to his departure from Germany with the rise of Hitler, his production was almost entirely in the field of low-cost housing. There he had the large-scale responsibilities largely denied to Le Corbusier until after the Second World War, but common enough by then in Germany.[36]

307. Walter Gropius:
Dessau, City Employment Office, 1927-8

First, in 1926–8, came the Törten Estate at Dessau consisting of terrace houses of concrete with smoothly rendered walls and horizontal windows. These were sound and economical but somewhat dull in design, the very reverse of Le Corbusier's at Pessac. At the Werkbund Exhibition of 1927, moreover, Gropius's free-standing houses did not rival Le Corbusier's in quality of design, despite their considerable technical importance as early examples of something approaching total prefabrication.

Gropius's most finished works of the twenties were all at Dessau. Besides the Bauhaus itself, there is a small block of flats rising at the end of a row of one-storey shops to form the centre of the Törten Estate of 1928. But even more notable is the Dessau City Employment Office, begun the year before. Here Gropius rejected stucco rendering,[37] hitherto almost as much the sign manual of the new architecture in Germany as in France, and surfaced his walls with brick [307]. The horizontal strips of window in the office wing, carefully related to the narrow bands of wall between and elegantly sub-divided by light metal sash, are balanced with

bold assurance against the tall vertical light of the stair tower at one end. Whether Gropius had learned from the Dutch or the Russians, by this time he had certainly become a master of abstract architectural composition in his own right.

Leaving the Bauhaus in 1928, Gropius next undertook a large housing estate, Dammerstock, at Karlsruhe. Here he combined terrace houses, somewhat ampler in size and less mechanically designed than those at Törten, with ranges of six-storey blocks of flats in the form of long, rigidly orientated slabs. Following this came the Siemensstadt Estate of 1930 outside Berlin [308]. This is the classic example of housing in tall, thin slabs, prototype of innumerable similar estates to be built throughout the western world before and after the Second World War. In Germany, however, where the form was first adumbrated, their production ceased in 1933 with the onset of the Hitler regime – it was later revived very actively, particularly by Ernst May at Hamburg and by architects of several countries in the Interbau exhibition of 1957 in Berlin.

308. Walter Gropius:
Berlin, Siemensstadt housing estate, 1930

309. Ludwig Mies van der Rohe:
Project for brick country house, 1923

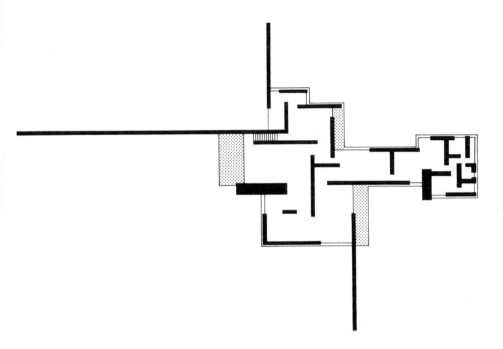

Mies in the twenties was not nearly so prolific as Gropius, nor was he so widely influential. His Wolf house of 1926 at Guben and the Lange and Esters houses at Krefeld, both of 1928, standing side by side in the Wilhelmshofallee, despite their fine dark brickwork[38] and the careful placing of the large horizontal windows, did not redeem the promise of an earlier project which he had made in 1923 for a country house; that was comparable in significance to his skyscraper schemes of the preceding years. Its plan seemed to represent the extension upward of a complex, but very rigid, geometrical pattern like those seen in Mondriaan's and van Doesburg's paintings of this period [309]. This sort of planning allowed a continuous flow of space in and around internal partitioning elements and out through wall-high glass areas to the surrounding terraces, themselves defined by the extension of the solid brick walls of the house. This openness more than rivalled, and was probably influenced by, the spatial flow in the Prairie Houses of Wright. Neoplasticist influence continued strong in Mies's work as late as his Liebknecht-Luxemburg Monument in Berlin of 1926. This was an abstract rectangular block, ingeniously composed of various brick surfaces arranged in different planes. (It was, of course, destroyed under Hitler.)

The flats that Mies built in the Afrikanische Strasse in Berlin in 1924-5 were more in line with Gropius's and Le Corbusier's contempor-

ary work than his private houses. Moreover, his block of flats [310] at the Werkbund Exhibition of 1927 on the Weissenhof at Stuttgart, of which he was the general director, with its lines of broad window-bands broken occasionally by vertical stair-windows, had an elasticity of planning and a clarity and subtlety of expression much superior to Gropius's taller and longer slabs at Dammerstock and Siemensstadt.

In 1929 came Mies's masterpiece, one of the few buildings by which the twentieth century might wish to be measured against the great ages of the past [311 A, B]. The German Pavilion at the Barcelona Exhibition, although built of permanent materials – steel, glass, marble, and travertine – was, like most exhibition buildings, only temporary. But few structures have come to be so widely known after their demolition, or so intensely admired through reproductions, except perhaps Paxton's Crystal Palace. Set on a raised travertine base almost like a Greek

stylobate, in which lies an oblong reflecting pool, the space within the pavilion was defined by no bounding walls at all but solely by the rectangle of its thin roof-slab. This was supported, almost immaterially, on a few regularly spaced metal members of delicate cruciform section sheathed in chromium. The covered area was subdivided, rather in the manner of the project of 1923 for a brick country house, by tall plate-glass panels carried in light metal chassis, some transparent, some opaque, and also by screens of highly polished marble standing apart from the metal supports. The disposition of these screens is asymmetrical but exquisitely ordered; yet it has none of that Neoplasticist complexity evident in the placing of the partitioning elements in the project of 1923. As a result, the articulated space of the pavilion has a classic serenity quite unlike the more dynamically flowing interiors of Wright's houses. At the Berlin Building Exhibition of 1931 Mies repeated the Barcelona Pavilion in

310 *(opposite)*. Ludwig Mies van der Rohe: Stuttgart, block of flats, Weissenhof, 1927

311 *(below)*. Ludwig Mies van der Rohe: Barcelona Exhibition, German Pavilion, 1929

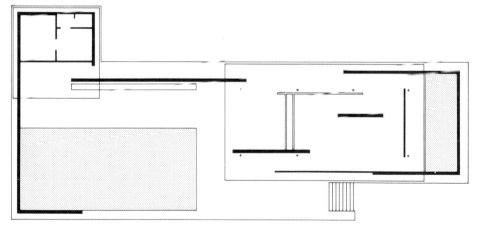

less sumptuous materials, making only slight changes in the plan so that it might provide a model for a house.

More than a little of the special quality of space-distribution in this exhibit Mies had been able to achieve already in the Tugendhat house of 1930 at Brno in Czechoslovakia. There also the screens that subdivide the unified living-space are quite separate from the delicate cruciform metal supports [312]. One of them, made of macassar ebony, partially encloses the dining-area and is semicircular in plan, thus notably enriching the general spatial effect. Externally this house is less remarkable. At the upper, or entrance, level towards the street it is quite closed in and even rather forbidding; but at the rear towards the garden there is a con-

312. Ludwig Mies van der Rohe:
Brno, Tugendhat house, 1930

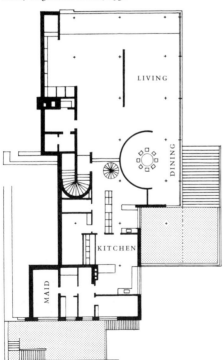

tinuous, room-high glass wall framed by stucco bands above and below. At one end an open terrace is included within the rectangle of the plan, and from this a broad flight of stone stairs descends to the ground. The contrast with the somewhat similar rear of Le Corbusier's Les Terrasses expresses well the considerable range of different effects possible within the tight limits of the new architecture even in this most rigidly doctrinaire period of the late twenties.

Within the twenties, both in France and in Germany, the new architecture received its full formulation, first in projects and shortly afterwards in executed work. At the same time Le Corbusier and Gropius provided in articles and in books the arguments in its defence.[39] Both were extremely articulate men, the one with the emotional intensity of a poet or a preacher, the other with the cool logic of a scientist or a professor. They soon found excited readers and later devoted followers all over the western world as their writings were exported, translated,[40] and paraphrased; but the significant activity of this period was by no means only French and German. Despite the continuing vitality of the Amsterdam School through the mid twenties, the new Dutch school associated with Rotterdam rose rapidly in national and international significance. Oud,[41] indeed, brought the new architecture to maturity in Holland in precisely the same years as Le Corbusier and their German contemporaries; Rietveld and several others made signal contributions also, in Rietveld's case equal in importance to Oud's.

The Oud Mathenesse housing estate at Rotterdam, which Oud undertook in 1922, is rather different from Spangen and Tuschendijken. At first sight it may appear more conservative, since it consists of small terrace houses with visible tiled roofs rather than tall blocks of flats. But rendered and painted walls replaced the brick of the earlier Rotterdam work, recalling the Loos-like treatment of his seaside villas as also the rather Wrightian projects he had designed in the intervening years. Moreover, the shapes and subdivisions of the windows were very carefully considered, so that the general effect is quite similar to the most advanced projects of Le Corbusier and of Mies designed in this same year. The influence of the De Stijl artists may not be very apparent in the façades of the houses and shops; but in the temporary building superintendent's office that Oud built here in 1923 cubical wooden elements painted in primary colours produced a composition quite like a Neoplasticist painting developed in three dimensions. It should be noted, however, that this was not, like Dudok's work of the period, at all related to the very complex Neoplasticist sculpture of Vantonger-

loo. Oud's façade of 1925 for the Café de Unie in Rotterdam, being two-dimensional, was even more like a Mondriaan painting raised to architectural scale.

It has already been mentioned that in 1923 van Doesburg was engaged in collaboration with van Eesteren on some remarkable studies, half abstract paintings, half architectural isometrics. Rietveld, in the Schröder house of 1924 in Utrecht [313], boldly carried such a hypothetical Neoplasticist architecture of discrete planes and structural lines into the world of reality even more completely than in his earlier shop in Amsterdam.

Oud early felt he had learned what Neoplasticism had to offer him. He was in any case personally closer to Mondrian than to van

313. G. T. Rietveld:
Utrecht, Schröder house, 1924

314. J. J. P. Oud:
Hook of Holland, housing estate, 1926-7

Doesburg, and Mondrian had already left
Holland for Paris in 1921. In Oud's first really
mature work, which remains also his masterpiece, two terraces with shops at their ends
built at the Hook of Holland in 1926-7 but
designed a year or two earlier, all overt emulation of contemporary painting disappeared,[41a]
except for the restriction of colour to white-

painted rendering with only small touches of
the primaries on some of the minor elements of
wood and metal [314]. The serenity of these
smooth façades with their long regular ranges
of horizontal windows, the extreme refinement
of the detailing of the fences and the doorways,
and, above all, the lyricism of the rounded
shops, their walls all of glass under a canti-

315. J. J. P. Oud: Rotterdam,
church, Kiefhoek housing estate, 1928-30

levered slab bent down at the ends, were unequalled by anything Le Corbusier or Gropius or Mies had yet built. Reputedly it was the influence of Van de Velde that led Oud to introduce curves here, much to the disgust of the Neoplasticists.

Oud's terrace-houses in the 1927 exhibition at Stuttgart were equally exemplary in their perfection of finish but slightly less interesting in their over-all design. Those by a still younger Dutch architect, Mart Stam (b. 1899), were perhaps superior. Then there followed Oud's much larger Kiefhoek housing project at Rotterdam which was built in 1928–30. Here the windows of the upper storey of each terrace became a continuous band, but something of the earlier refinement was lost as in Gropius's Siemensstadt blocks of the same period.

At Kiefhoek Oud was called on to provide a church as well as housing. Its vices as well as its virtues epitomize very well the state of the new architecture at the end of the decade [315]. Considered as elements in an abstract composition, the handling of the subordinate features of the Kiefhoek church is masterly, refining and – as it were – domesticating various adjuncts of an almost industrial order such as had earlier provided a good part of the varied visual interest of Gropius's Fagus Factory. But the main auditorium block is so box-like that it holds its place among the rows of houses only by its size, offering no expression whatsoever of its special purpose – it could as easily be a garage. A far more notable exemplar of the new architecture, still about the finest twentieth-century building in Holland, is the van Nelle Factory

316. Brinkman & van der Vlugt:
Rotterdam, van Nelle Factory, 1927

outside Rotterdam built in 1927-8 by the firm of J. A. Brinkman (1902-49) and L. C. van der Vlugt (1894-1936) but possibly designed by Stam [316]. The Dutch firm of B. Bijvoet (b. 1889) and Johannes Duiker (1890-1935) should also be mentioned for their admirable work of the twenties, starting with several Wrightian houses of 1924 at Kijkduin, but soon quite as advanced as Oud's or Rietveld's.

The conditions of the twenties – or more precisely the particular conditions under which the new architects had to work and, to a large extent, even seemed satisfied to work – restricted their scope rather considerably. In France the usual clients, often American rather than French, sought houses that were *avant-garde* and related ideologically to the painting of the Cubists and Post-Cubists. Towards the utilitarian field of low-cost housing the new architects everywhere felt a special responsibility; in Germany and Holland they readily found major opportunities for official employment at such work. Their intense concern with the aesthetic potentialities of engineering gave them a special sympathy for industrial building, but major opportunities such as the van Nelle Factory were very rare. Gropius's Bauhaus, a large and complex structure serving a cultural purpose, and the Barcelona Pavilion, an edifice with almost no other purpose than to be beautiful, were important exceptions in a range of production characterized by a surprising international consistency of type as well as of character.

Yet the hands of the various individual architects are, in fact, never difficult to distinguish and, from this time onwards, the paths of the four early leaders began definitely to diverge. It was chiefly the work of late-comers, of whom there were in the twenties large numbers only in Germany, that tended towards monotony and anonymity. Not since the early years of the nineteenth century, when Romantic

Classicism at the hands of a second generation reached a comparable clarity of stylistic definition, had there been such a rigid and humbly accepted architectural discipline. However, certain men, such as Mendelsohn and Dudok, retained in their practice of the new architecture strong traces of earlier idiosyncrasies. Much of their work lacks therefore the purity and the assured mastery of the four initiators. But Mendelsohn's Schocken Department Stores, built in several German cities in the late twenties – at Nuremberg and Stuttgart in 1926-7, at Chemnitz in 1928 – and his Petersdorf Store at Wrocław (Breslau) in 1927 are certainly superior in interest and in vitality to the new city houses and suburban villas in France; not to speak of the housing estates in Germany that were being produced in such considerable quantity by the end of the decade by architects who were literalistic adherents of the new architecture. The work of such designers showed all the naive enthusiasm, the subjection to discipline, and the doctrinaire characteristics of the activity of new converts in any field.

But when, in his Columbus Haus of 1929-31 in Berlin, Mendelsohn finally accepted a comparable discipline he was able to retain most of his earlier vitality. Here he produced a really paradigmatic commercial building – almost a small skyscraper – such as none of the four leaders ever had the opportunity of carrying to execution in the twenties. Much the same can be said for a considerably later 'baby skyscraper', Dudok's Erasmus Huis of 1939-40 in the Coolsingel in Rotterdam. This is still, after the van Nelle Factory, one of the best buildings in Rotterdam, despite all the post-war reconstruction there (see Chapter 25).

As the new architecture spread to other countries around 1930 it was naturally the lowest common denominator of its potentialities that became most widely evident. However, at just this point an international depression supervened; the building boom, with which the rise of the new architecture had been at best but coincidentally associated, soon ground to a standstill. In Germany in the early thirties, moreover, as also in Russia and considerably later and less rigidly in Italy, an authoritarian regime proscribed the new architecture. Leaders like Gropius, Mies, and Mendelsohn left the country and the new architecture was in abeyance there until after Hitler's fall.

CHAPTER 23

LATER WORK OF THE LEADERS OF THE SECOND GENERATION

Historians, whether of politics or the arts, should ideally stand at some distance from their subjects thanks to remoteness in time; in lieu of that, remoteness in space sometimes serves the same purpose. However, this historian has now reached the point at which he entered the scene; he must write, as statesmen who write history are often forced to do, of events concerning which he had first-hand knowledge – and hence, alas, first-hand prejudices. Architects, the real actors in architectural history, often write as well as build; since Vitruvius there have been many whose fame depends as much on their books as on their buildings, not least several of the men with whom Part Three of this book has dealt. But those who write about architecture as historians and critics without being active builders, who merely explain, select, and illustrate the significant work of their own day or even of the past – particularly the immediate past – are to some extent minor actors on the scene also. They cannot, therefore, be merely neutral observers, reporting without *parti pris* the ideas and the achievements of others, however hard they may try to achieve objectivity.

To have written the only monograph on Wright to appear in French, to have provided the first account in English of the new architecture, to have published a book on the work of Oud as early as 1931, modest as these contributions were, are all actions indicating a firm commitment on the part of this author. The preparation in 1931 with Philip Johnson of the first International Exhibition of Modern Architecture, held at the Museum of Modern Art in 1932, in which Le Corbusier, Gropius, Oud, and Mies were signalized as the leaders of

the new architecture, and the publication – also with Philip Johnson – of the book called *The International Style*[1] at that time were even more definite and controversial acts of participation in the dialectic of architectural development in this century.

If it seems necessary to mention these publications here and not merely to refer to them in the Notes or list them in the Bibliography, it is in no spirit of boastfulness but rather of apology. From this point on the ideal objectivity of the historian, attempting disinterestedly to piece the past together from a study of its extant monuments and from relevant contemporary documents, is inevitably coloured, if not cancelled out, by the subjectivity of the critic writing of events he knew at first hand. Concerning them, of course, his later opinions[1a] have no more real historical validity than those he held and published nearer the time when the events occurred. With this proviso the canvas may now be somewhat broadened.

By the early thirties the new architecture was by no means restricted to France, Germany, and Holland, the countries where it had originated. Yet, with the possible exception of Alvar Aalto (b. 1898) in Finland, no other leader of the calibre of the early four had appeared up to that time. The building of 1928-9 at Turku for the newspaper *Turun Sanomat* was Aalto's first mature work to be completed. In this the plastic handling of the concrete piers[2] in the interior introduced a new and personal note of architectural expression in a frankly industrial setting. His Tuberculosis Sanatorium at Paimio of 1929-33 rivalled the Bauhaus in size, if not perhaps in complexity, and was almost the first[3] major

demonstration of the special applicability of the new architecture to hospitals. The City Library at Viipuri, designed as early as 1927 but not finished until 1935, was a more original example of the new architecture. In particular, the lecture hall there, with its acoustic ceiling of irregularly wavy section made up of strips of wood, was strikingly novel. (Viipuri is now over the Russian border and hard to visit.)

In the United States the Lovell house in Los Angeles opened in 1929[3a] the American career of Richard J. Neutra (1892-1970), an Austrian who had worked briefly with Wright. In this house, with its cantilevers, its broad areas of glass, and its volumetric composition, Neutra showed the completeness with which he had already rejected the broad Wrightian road and accepted the more restricted aspirations of the newer architecture of Europe.[3b] Never, perhaps, have Wright's ideals and those of the next generation appeared so sharply opposed as at just this time, moreover. But Neutra's mature work began only considerably later than this.

In 1930-2 the tallest of all skyscrapers, the Empire State Building by Shreve, Lamb & Harmon, was rising in New York; this was a shaped tower in the local tradition although devoid of reminiscent stylistic detail. In these same years, however, a well-established 'traditional' architect, George Howe (1886-1954),[4] in association with a Swiss, William E. Lescaze (1896-1969), who had been a pupil of Karl Moser, returned to the Sullivanian slab in designing the Philadelphia Savings Fund Society Building [317]. Moreover, they treated their slab along the lines that the leading European exponents of the new architecture had adumbrated in the previous ten years. It would be a score of years before other skyscrapers of such significant and distinguished design were built in American cities (see Chapter 25).

317. Howe & Lescaze: Philadelphia, Philadelphia Savings Fund Society Building, 1932

In Sweden E. G. Asplund (1885–1940), whose architecture had hitherto been of a 'Neo-Neo-Classic' order, extremely crisp and refined but definitely reminiscent,[5] turned to the new architecture of Le Corbusier and Gropius just before he completed the Central Library of Stockholm [334], a building first projected in 1921 but not opened until 1928 (see Chapter 24). For the Stockholm Exhibition of 1930, of which he had entire charge, Asplund was soon designing an extensive and elegantly varied range of pavilions that exploited to the full the possibilities of the new architecture. In Den-

mark Kay Fisker also underwent a somewhat less drastic conversion at much the same time.

These years also saw the beginning of the English career of Berthold Lubetkin[6] (b. 1901), a Russian who had settled in England in 1930 after working for some time in France. His early Gorilla House at the Regent's Park Zoo in London was soon outshone by the smaller, but much more remarkable, Penguin Pool there of 1933, which is almost a piece of Constructivist sculpture [318]. In 1933–5 the tall block of middle-class flats, Highpoint I at Highgate outside London, was erected by the Tecton

318. Tecton: London,
Regent's Park Zoo, Penguin Pool, 1933

group, of which Lubetkin was the leading spirit. With its fine hill-top site overlooking Hampstead Heath, this cruciform tower rivalled Le Corbusier's Clarté block in Geneva of 1930-2 in interest and in quality. Almost equally impressive, and like Highpoint hardly rivalled by comparable work in London since, is the Peter Jones Department Store in Sloane Square, designed in 1935 by William Crabtree.[7] Already in 1933 Mendelsohn had settled in England, practising there for a few years in partnership with Serge Chermayeff (b. 1900) before moving on to Israel in 1936. From 1934 to 1937 Gropius was in England working with E. Maxwell Fry (b. 1899); Marcel Breuer (b. 1902), a Hungarian pupil of Gropius from the Bauhaus, was also in England working with F. R. S. Yorke (1906-62). By the mid thirties Connell, Ward & Lucas,[8] Wells Coates (1895-1958), and Frederick Gibberd (b. 1908) were also well started on their careers.[9]

In Italy, where the projects of an architect associated with Futurism,[10] Antonio Sant'Elia (1888-1916), before his death in the First World War had offered a remarkable premonition of the new architecture of the twenties, a fresh talent at least comparable in interest and individuality to Lubetkin's appeared on the scene in these years. The Casa del Fascio at Como of 1932-6 by Giuseppe Terragni (1904-43) is almost as original as Aalto's Viipuri Library but very different [319]. In its use of fine marbles and in its innate classicism it recalls Mies, yet it is as Mediterranean in spirit as his work is Northern. Unfortunately, like Sant'Elia before him, Terragni was killed in the Second World War that followed within a few years after the start of his career. However, the firm of Luigi Figini (b. 1903) and Gino Pollini (b. 1903), who developed as leaders of Italian modern architecture, also made their first mark at this time with the 'Artist's House' that they showed at the Fifth Triennale in Milan in 1933. This was

similarly calm and Latin in its handling of the 'International' vocabulary of form.

The Florence railway station, built in 1934-6 by Giovanni Michelucci (b. 1891) and five associated architects, also deserves mention. Michelucci[10a] is not to be compared with Terragni or Figini & Pollini, but his station was stylistically the most advanced in the world when it was built. Moreover, like the Casa del Fascio in Como, it offers notable evidence of the support the Fascist regime was still giving to *architettura razionale* at a time when both in Germany and in Russia other authoritarian regimes were denouncing the International Style. The Termini Station in

319. Giuseppe Terragni:
Como, Casa del Fascio, 1932-6

Rome [351] was begun even earlier from the designs of Angiolo Mazzoni. It owes its distinguished reputation as the finest station of the mid twentieth century, however, to the project of Eugenio Montuori (b. 1907) and his associates, prepared in 1947 and finally carried to effective completion in 1951 (see Chapter 25).

Yet for all the increasingly wide spread of the new architecture by the mid thirties, Le Corbusier and two Germans retained their international position of leadership despite economic depression in France and Hitlerian exile from Germany. If the amount of their executed work was much reduced – in the case of Mies for several years to nil – the geographical range of their activities was now much extended. Today, for example, Le Corbusier's work is to be found from Cambridge, Mass., in the U.S. to Tokyo in Japan; he was also a consultant on two of the largest and most striking buildings in the New World built just before and just after the Second World War, the Ministry of Education and Public Health in Rio [321] and the United Nations Secretariat[11] in New York.

Gropius and Mies, settling in America in the late thirties, became figures of crucial importance in the reform of American architectural education[12] as well as being increasingly productive as architects after the war. At Harvard University[13] and at the Illinois Institute of Technology, respectively, they set a pace for several American architects who later became leading educators, such as Howe at Yale and W. W. Wurster (1895–1974) at the Massachusetts Institute of Technology and the University of California. Mendelsohn, still very much of an individualist, but with a notable international reputation based on what he had built in England and in Israel as well as on his earlier work of the twenties in Germany, practised in America from after the war down to his death.

This extension of the field of activity and the direct influence of the European leaders further emphasized the universality of the new architecture. In the 50s American architects, such as the firm of Skidmore, Owings & Merrill,[14] working as far from home as Turkey, or Edward D. Stone (1902–78), building on three continents, provided almost the most characteristic later examples of what – and in their cases most critics would agree – was not improperly called the International Style.[14a] The American Embassies in Copenhagen and in Stockholm, and the flats for embassy personnel at Neuilly and at Boulogne outside Paris, all by Rapson[15] & Van de Gracht, were among the better examples of American work abroad of the 1950s.

But there would have been no El Panamá Hotel in Panama (1950) by Stone, no Istanbul Hilton Hotel (1954) by the Skidmore firm, and no such foreign building programme by the United States Government as was responsible for the executed embassies by Rapson & Van de Gracht of the early fifties and the ones built later by Eero Saarinen in London and Oslo, by Gropius and TAC in Athens, by Stone in New Delhi, and by Breuer in The Hague but for the pioneering of the Europeans, nor did that pioneering cease in the thirties. Only in Oud's case, because of a serious indisposition that removed him from practice for many years after 1930, was the œuvre effectively complete with the twenties; and even he later became active again. In the case of both Le Corbusier and Mies, even of Gropius, their largest commissions came only after the Second World War. Their influence in the 1950s was still as great as around 1930, in Mies's case considerably greater. The mid twentieth century for a while accepted stylistic continuity in a way that the nineteenth century was never able to do once the tradition of Romantic Classicism finally wore out. The adventurous late work of Le Corbusier, who became an elder statesman of modern architecture, counterbalanced to some extent those more rigid interpretations of the discipline his generation had founded, interpretations that threatened after the late twenties to become academic and frozen.

Many of the more characteristic demands of Le Corbusier's aesthetic canon, as it had been announced in his projects of the early twenties and adumbrated in the succession of houses that led up to the Savoye house of 1929-30 – including restrictions docilely accepted almost everywhere by advanced architects in the late twenties – were already ignored in the buildings he himself designed in the early thirties. The house that he built for Hélène de Mandrot at Le Pradet in Provence in 1930-1 is raised on no *pilotis* but sits firmly on a terrace; and its walls, where solid, are of rough, uncoursed rubble. Quiet and rectangular, with no lyrically curved

elements and little painted colour, this house accepts the surrounding landscape as Wright's had always done. Le Corbusier seemed here almost to be avowing a respect for local materials and humble village craftsmanship such as is associated with Voysey and his English contemporaries of a generation earlier that would certainly have been anathema to him in the twenties. On the other hand, the penthouse that he built in 1931 for Carlos de Beistegui on top of a block of flats on the Champs Élysées in Paris was all of plate glass and white marble. This had something of the glittering elegance of Mies's Barcelona Pavilion of two years earlier, where the polished marbles, once so brilliantly exploited by Loos, were first

320. Le Corbusier:
Paris, Swiss Hostel, Cité Universitaire, 1931-2

brought back after a decade of restriction to ascetic and impermanent surfaces of painted stucco.

The Salvation Army Building which Le Corbusier erected in 1931-2 in the Rue Cantagrel in Paris is more in line with the canon of the twenties. Unfortunately the original curtain-wall was later cut up by projecting sunbreaks added in a post-war refurbishing by Le Corbusier's former partner Pierre Jeanneret. The Maison Clarté block of flats of 1930-2 in Geneva is almost as completely glass-walled.

It was most notably the Swiss Hostel at the Cité Universitaire in Paris, designed in 1930 and built in 1931-2, which introduced various quite new elements of plan and design that Le Corbusier would develop much further after the Second World War [320]. The *pilotis* he used in the twenties were thin and round, rather like Perret's columns, though without their facets and capitals; but here a double row of heavy concrete piers of multi-curved section carries a dormitory block that is boldly cantilevered out from them both front and back. The rubble masonry of the de Mandrot house was used here once more for a tall unbroken wall of irregularly curved plan at the rear of the building; the textured and tonal surface of this wall and its effect of solidity contrasts both with the exposed concrete of the structural elements and with the smooth areas of thin stone plaquage on the upper walls. Curves in Le Corbusier's earlier work were almost always confined within a bounding rectangle and never made of massive materials; yet they lost none of their elegance in being handled in this bolder and more organic way. This is closely related to his later paintings, of which the mural in the common room here provides a major example.

The international depression closed in even more completely on France in the early thirties than it did elsewhere, and there was no subsequent revival of building activity such as other countries experienced in the years preceding the Second World War. Le Corbusier's activities were therefore more and more confined to projects, most of them for commissions outside France. However, a small block of flats, very similar to the Maison Clarté in Geneva, was built at 24 Avenue Nungesser et Coli on the western edge of Paris in 1933. The most interesting portion of this is the architect's own penthouse on top; there, like another Soane, he experimented at small scale with a variety of vault-topped spaces.

In a modest house at 49 Avenue du Chesnay in Vaucresson of 1935 there are no more curves in plan than in the Mandrot house, but segmental concrete vaults cover the rectangular bays of which the plan is made up. Moreover, as if to underline Le Corbusier's return towards nature after his earlier devotion to the abstract and the mechanistic, grass grows over their crowns to provide insulation. The exposed frame of the concrete structure, where not filled with glass brick, has panels of coursed rubble.

Le Corbusier's projects of the thirties often included new ideas that others exploited even before he was able to do so himself in executed work. For example, the Ministry of Education and Public Health in Rio de Janeiro, on which he was a consultant only, designed in 1937 and completed in 1942 by Lúcio Costa (b. 1902), Oscar Niemeyer (b. 1907), and a group of others, the great building which opened so brilliantly the story of the new architecture in Brazil [321], included on the west front the projecting sun-breaks he had first proposed in 1933 for certain tall buildings intended to be erected in Algiers. Such sun-breaks soon became characteristic of mid-century architecture in all countries where the sun's heat and glare offered a major problem – in Asia and Africa as much as in South America. By this device the all-glass wall, favourite large-scale theme of the new architecture since Mies's early skyscraper projects, received a much-needed functional

321 *(opposite)*. Lúcio Costa, Oscar Niemeyer, and others (Le Corbusier consultant):
Rio de Janeiro, Ministry of Education and Health, 1937-42

322 and 323. Le Corbusier: Marseilles, Unité d'Habitation, 1946-52

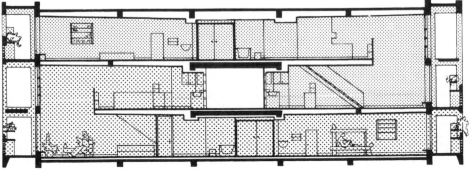

correction. As often before, a real (or supposed) practical need encouraged the satisfaction of overt or covert aesthetic aspirations; for sun-breaks very much enhanced the three-dimensional interest of large façades, substituting for the slick planar effects characteristic of the twenties a more articulated sort of surface treatment related to, but independent of, the expression of skeleton structure. Sun-breaks even came to be used where they were hardly needed, quite as has been the case with various other clichés of modern architecture.

Since the war three major works of Le Corbusier, in the estimation of many critics his masterpieces, have carried much further the sculptural tendencies of his architecture of the thirties. One of these, the block of flats called the Unité d'Habitation,[16] far out the Boulevard Michelet in Marseilles, which was first projected in 1946 and finally completed in 1952, has various other points of interest, however. The Unité realized on a large scale Le Corbusier's ideas for the mass-dwelling, providing a single tall slab large enough to house a complete community and including, half-way up, a storey intended to be entirely occupied by shops, as well as other communal facilities on the roof [322]. An ingenious section allowed two-storey living-rooms in all the flats and also permitted the use of a skip-stop lift system [323]. The framework in front of the walls provided sun protection for the tall living-room windows and also shallow balconies for each flat both front and back.

Like the Swiss Hostel, the Unité is carried on heavy supports, here arranged in a double row. These are much more massively sculptural than the earlier ones in Paris, and almost anthropomorphically expressive of weight-bearing. All the poured concrete surfaces were left rough as they came from the forms, and the prefabricated members of the outer sun-break system have an exposed pebble aggregate. Everything is bold and masculine, even coarse,

indicating a complete turnabout in Le Corbusier's understanding of the essential 'nature' – itself a rather Wrightian concept – of concrete. On the roof an abstract landscape of sculptural forms plays counterpoint to the superb backdrop of mountains. One cannot help remembering the roof of Gaudí's Casa Milá in Barcelona [253]; there are even some glazed tiles set in the concrete to provide notes of 'permanent polychrome'. Yet the window in the entrance-hall at the base of the slab is quite Neoplasticist in the pattern of its subdivisions and the use of coloured glass; while painted colour of the boldest sort, by no means restricted to the primaries, was used on the sides of the sun-breaks, though not on any of the outer surfaces. Thus was Le Corbusier's later architecture enriched by a sort of eclecticism quite remote from his Purist aesthetic of the twenties.

At Chandigarh in India, where Le Corbusier had the general responsibility for planning the entire new capital of the state of Punjab and of building the principal public monuments, he was able to complete only a few; the rest of the city is the work of other architects, principally Pierre Jeanneret and the English firm of Maxwell Fry and his wife Jane Drew. The High Courts of Justice,[17] built by Le Corbusier in 1952-6, are even more sculptural than the Unité at Marseilles. A continuous umbrella-like shell-vault of concrete rises high above the roofs of the court-rooms to allow the free passage of air. Supporting this are great rounded piers that merge into the concave surfaces over them, almost like the structural elements of the Casa Milá, but here of monumental scale. On the west side deep box-crates, with brilliant painted colours on their soffits like those on the sun-breaks of the Unité, keep the sun off the glazed walls of the court-rooms and provide that three-dimensional play first exploited on the Ministry in Rio de Janeiro.

The long slab of the Secretariat at Chandigarh, also of 1952-6, with its very varied pattern of sun-breaks, is less novel than the High Courts;[17a] but other work of the mid fifties at Ahmedabad[17b] should not be ignored (see Chapter 25). However, Le Corbusier's most extraordinary late building is in France, not in India, and therefore considerably more accessible. Architects and laymen alike continue to be strongly impressed by the intense emotionalism of his church of Notre-Dame-du-Haut at Ronchamp, Hte-Saône,[18] built in 1950-5. Whether this church has had as effective an international influence as the Unité is debatable because of its intensely personal character. But it certainly did make even more evident than the High Courts the fact that Le Corbusier in the fifties was moving in almost the opposite direction from that in which he led in the twenties.

In an exaggerated phrase Le Corbusier described his early houses as *machines à habiter*; but Notre-Dame-du-Haut is more like an enormous piece of sculpture than a 'machine for praying-in' [324]. He who once drove architecture towards the mechanistic, the precise, and the volumetric, here provided the exemplar of a new mode so plastic as almost to be naturalistic in the way of Gaudí's blocks of flats of fifty years earlier. The walls and roof are rough, indeed almost brutal, in finish, and so massive and solid that the interior of the church at certain times of the day seems positively ill-lit by the tiny deep-sunk windows that irregularly penetrate the side walls. In place of an aesthetic expression emulating the impersonal results of engineers' calculations, there is a freehand quality most comparable to the spontaneity of the sculptor. Moreover, where the overtones of his characteristic build-

324. Le Corbusier: Ronchamp,
Hte-Saône, Notre-Dame-du-Haut, 1950-5

ings of the twenties were wholly of the present, this arouses deep prehistoric atavisms – and quite intentionally. Whether the High Courts at Chandigarh and the church at Ronchamp evidenced a deep split in modern architecture or represented merely a major turning point is still not clear. Only a few have succeeded even yet in following with any real distinction the line of development they opened (see Chapter 25 and Epilogue).

The later work of the German leaders aroused no such difficult critical problems as did Le Corbusier's; yet it also ranged sometimes in directions not altogether to be expected from their best-known work of the twenties. Their careers, moreover, suffered a harsher break because of the political tribulations of their homeland than Le Corbusier suffered from the economic tribulations of France. In 1930 Mies became Director of the Bauhaus, remaining until it was closed by Hitler in 1933. Although he won a competition for the Reichsbank in Berlin as late as that year, he was allowed to do no work under the Nazis, and so he settled in the United States in 1938 after a preliminary visit the previous year.

As has been noted, Mendelsohn and Gropius, on leaving Germany in 1933, settled first in England, and both did significant work there – if not especially significant for their own careers, certainly so for the early stage of modern architecture in England. With his English partner Maxwell Fry, Gropius was responsible in 1935-7 for the Impington Village College in Cambridgeshire; this set a new pace for school design in England in the post-war years, for a while the best in the world. Mendelsohn, with Chermayeff, built in 1934-5 the De La Warr Pavilion at Bexhill on the Sussex coast. In the main this is a rather conventional example of the new architecture; but it has a semicircular glazed stair-tower that recalls the more lyrical quality of his best earlier work such as the Schocken stores.

From England Mendelsohn moved on to Israel, where a large Government Hospital by him at Haifa and the Medical Centre of the Hadassah University in Jerusalem on Mount Scopus, both of 1936-8, showed a most skilful adaptation of the international European canons to a hotter climate and a different cultural tradition, somewhat as is the case with the Ministry at Rio. Only with the onset of the war in 1941 did Mendelsohn settle in America. There his Maimonides Hospital in San Francisco of 1946-50 and synagogues and Jewish community centres in Cleveland (1946-52), St Louis (1946-50), Grand Rapids (1948-52), and St Paul (1950-4) well illustrated still his very personal command of the commonly accepted elements of the new architecture, but with the continuing inclusion of various anomalous features that seem to belong to a much earlier period of his career.

Gropius proceeded directly from England to America in 1937, having been called by Dean Joseph Hudnut of the Graduate School of Design to be Professor of Architecture at Harvard University. He became Chairman of the Architecture Department the following year, which position he retained until 1953. As has already been said, his major contribution to architecture in America was first as an educator. However, he built, in partnership with Breuer, whom he had brought to Harvard, several houses, including his own at Lincoln, Mass., and also a housing development at New Kensington, Penna., in the years 1938-41. These were, on the whole, no more successful than much of his work of the late twenties in Germany, despite an intelligent effort to adapt a European mode to American building methods, particularly as regards the use of wood, both structurally and for sheathing. This turning away, on Gropius's part, from ferroconcrete and rendered surfaces was parallel to Le Corbusier's somewhat earlier reversion to the use of local and traditional materials.

The houses that Breuer designed after he parted from Gropius had considerably more intrinsic interest; as was perhaps natural with a younger man, they soon showed a more integral adjustment to the characteristic living habits and building methods of the New World. Large-scale commissions, the first two for the Unesco Building[19] in Paris (1953–8) and for the Bijenkorf Store in Rotterdam (1953–7), not to speak of the U.S. Embassy at The Hague (1954–8), brought him back to the European scene, but as an American rather than a Hungarian or German architect, and his practice became truly international.

Gropius's principal American work was all done after the war. It included by the mid fifties two schools at Attleborough, Mass., one of 1948 and one of 1954, and the Graduate Centre of Harvard University in Cambridge, Mass., of 1949–50. These were all three designed – as also the already-mentioned Athens Embassy and other large-scale work – in association with the firm known as TAC ('The Architects' Collaborative),[19a] formed in 1946. In the double quadrangle of buildings at Harvard, forming in itself almost a complete small college, the architecture of the twenties lived on with little change. Light-coloured brick replaced stucco for the walls, however, and there was a certain rather inhibited use of plain curves in plan and of angular relationships in detail reflecting ideas that had entered

the new architecture only in the thirties. Various school and college buildings of the 50s and 60s were more successful, improving upon Gropius and Fry's Impington College of the thirties in England. After his retirement as professor, Gropius and TAC became increasingly active, and he also continued until his death in 1969 to present his well-known architectural doctrines in lectures, articles, and books[20] with little modification.

Coming to the United States a year later than Gropius, Mies also found his greatest opportunities there, and almost at once. In 1939 he was commissioned to design an entire new group of buildings for the Illinois Institute of Technology on an extensive site on the south side of Chicago. In this scheme, which is of urbanistic scale and extent, a classic, indeed an almost academic, order prevails throughout [325]. The buildings that he was able to execute, two during the war in 1942–4, many more after 1945, have a comparably classic serenity. But they also express with relentless logic the character of their predominantly steel-skeleton construction. In them Mies almost revived architectural detail by the precision and the elaboration of his handling of the elements of metal structure. As at Gropius's Graduate Centre, light-coloured brick replaced stucco for the solid wall panels. The severe patterns of the black-painted metal-work were organized with something of the purity of Mondrian's

325. Ludwig Mies van der Rohe:
Chicago, Illinois Institute of Technology, 1939–41

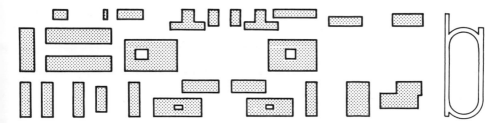

canvases of the twenties yet with a dominating symmetry. This is true also of the interior planning of the individual buildings. However, his last, Crown Hall,[20a] housing the architectural school, completed in 1956, is unsubdivided on the principal floor, and thus represented the most extreme statement of his later ideals, both structurally and in its planning.

Mies also built houses and several tall blocks of flats in and near Chicago and, with Philip Johnson (b. 1906), a New York skyscraper at 375 Park Avenue for the Seagram Company in 1956-8 [361]. His completely glazed Farnsworth house near Plano, Ill., designed in 1946 and built in 1950,[21] is a cage of white-painted welded steel raised above the river valley in which it is set and walled partly with great sheets of plate glass, partly with metal screening. The floor is a continuous plane of travertine from which broad travertine steps descend to an open travertine terrace. Planned about a central core in which are placed the fireplace, the bathrooms, and the heater, the interior

space is completely unified, the different functional areas being separated only by cupboards that do not rise to the ceiling [328]. Even more than Crown Hall, this house represented the purest and most extreme statement of aesthetic purpose in one particular direction that the new architecture had produced – a direction which was, of course, in total opposition to the increasingly complex plastic effects sought in these same years by Le Corbusier. It was, nevertheless, quite as remote from the stucco boxes characteristic of the twenties and even more remote from Mies's own brick houses of that period.

A similarly ascetic luxury is also evident in Mies's blocks of flats at 845-860 Lake Shore Drive in Chicago of 1949-51 [326, 327]. There he seemed to have arrived, not imitatively but by force of parallel logic, at something very close to the skyscrapers that Sullivan designed in the nineties [208]. Mies's structural piers, carried down to the ground as free-standing elements just as they are below the Farnsworth house,

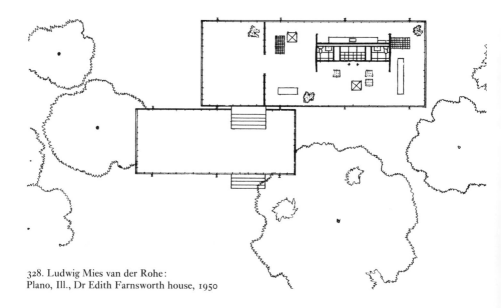

328. Ludwig Mies van der Rohe:
Plano, Ill., Dr Edith Farnsworth house, 1950

give the dominant bay rhythm, their structural steelwork being sheathed here first in protective concrete and then in black-painted metal. Between the piers continuous I-beams along the mullion lines stiffen the wall screens which are otherwise entirely of glass held in bright aluminium frames; they also provide a subsidiary rhythm, quite as Sullivan's mullions sometimes did in the eighteen eighties and nineties.

Identical in shape, rectangular slabs both, the two blocks were set close together and at right angles to one another. This placing gave a minimum of overlap as regards the lake view and a minimum of overlook as regards the privacy of the apartments. The relationship also created from these very simple shapes a notable variety of effects in perspective. The visual interest is enhanced especially by the fact that the projecting I-beams, when seen at a sharp angle, give the illusion that one wall of each block is solid; the other wall, being seen head on or nearly so, appears completely open between the structural piers and the mullions. More, nearly identical, apartment blocks[22] rose later in Chicago from Mies's designs also, including apartments beside the first two towers and two farther to the north, not to speak of those elsewhere, in Detroit, Newark, and Baltimore.

After his arrival in America Mies was not merely for fifteen years the architect of the Illinois Institute of Technology's buildings, he soon became head of its Department of Architecture also, a post he retained until he retired in 1955. Less articulate than Gropius and occupying a less important academic post, Mies's influence specifically as an educator was considerably less. On the other hand, the general influence of his work in America in the late forties and fifties was very much greater. The 'Miesian' became almost a sub-school of the new architecture not only in the United States but in several other countries: to Mies not only younger men but also many established practitioners owed for a decade and more the specific direction of much of their work (see Chapter 25).

Just before the Second World War broke out Oud, in 1938, recovered his health sufficiently to undertake a large commission, the Shell Building in The Hague, completed in the course of the next four years. In Holland there had been in the thirties a strong reaction against the new architecture led by M. J. Granpré-Molière (b. 1883) and the graduates of his school at Delft. Granpré-Molière urged a return, if not to the outright 'traditional', at least to a semi-traditionalism that was not without some similarity to what the Nazis were sponsoring in Germany. In response to this challenge Oud set out to show how the new architecture, still considered by many in Holland to be too stark and mechanistic, could be humanized. To return from stucco to brick, in this case a thin glazed white brick such as Dudok was using at this same time with great success on his quite conventionally 'International Style' Erasmus Huis office building in the Coolsingel in Rotterdam,[23] was merely to emulate the rejection of stucco in this decade by the French and German leaders in favour of more permanent, if also more traditional, walling materials, such as marble, rubble, brick, and even wood. But Oud's attempt to revive ornament and the elaborate symmetry and near-academic complications of his over-all design of the Shell building had little appeal outside Holland. In the small Esveha office building of 1952 near the station in Rotterdam and the much larger Vrijzinnige Christelijk Lyceum at 131 Goudsbloemlaan in The Hague of 1953-6 Oud returned to something much closer to the norms of the new architecture elsewhere. But the days of his international influence were over despite his belated prestige in Holland.[24] His Congress Hall in The Hague was completed in 1968 after his death.

Like several of the preceding chapters dealing with the architects of the first modern generation, this has brought some aspects of our story down to the mid century. In so doing, much of the specifically modern architecture of the twentieth century has been accounted for; the total picture is rounded out somewhat in a synoptic view of the international scene in the mid 1960s (see Chapter 25 and Epilogue). But first it is desirable to discuss briefly the architecture that was *not* modern, characteristic of earlier decades of this century. Historicism,[25] that is reminiscence of past styles, endemic throughout the nineteenth century, long lived on. It was still usual, moreover, to call such architecture 'traditional', over-favourably weighted rather than accurate though the term must be considered. Clearly a traditional architecture that produced a 'Gothic' skyscraper like Cass Gilbert's Woolworth Building [337] or vast 'Classical' railway stations like the two in New York [339] was not unduly restricted by revivalistic canons! Clearly also this sort of architecture cannot be ignored historically, since to it belong some of the largest, most prominent, and most carefully studied buildings and groups of buildings of the first third of this century. Moreover, in many countries traditionalism gave way to modern design only after the Second World War; while several of the authoritarian regimes of Europe returned for a while to its sanctions in the thirties, just as it was generally losing ground elsewhere in the western world.

There were few if any great leaders among twentieth-century traditional architects; certainly hardly more than one or two approached the calibre or the individual significance of the men whose work Part Three of this book has largely dealt with up to this point. But a conspectus can be provided, with typical examples also of work in several countries where the individual architects were less colourful, the monuments less notable, and the general level of quality less high.

CHAPTER 24

ARCHITECTURE CALLED TRADITIONAL

IN THE TWENTIETH CENTURY

Through at least the first three decades of the twentieth century most architects of the western world would have scorned the appellation 'modern' or, if they accepted it, would have defined the term very differently from the way it has been understood in the immediately preceding chapters. For twentieth-century architecture that continued the historicism[1] of the nineteenth century the usual name in English is 'traditional'. The term reflects a fond presumption that such architecture derives its sanctions from the traditions of the further past, although in fact its only real tradition is that of the preceding hundred years. Whatever one calls it, this traditional architecture includes the majority of buildings designed before 1930 in most countries of the western world and a certain, if decreasing, proportion of those erected even after the Second World War.

Statements of this sort are not very relevant when they concern the arts. In the case of every revolutionary change in architecture the same situation has obtained while the old slowly gave way to the new. Since the modern revolution may have been of the scale of the Renaissance, the student of architectural history should recall that from the early crystallization of the new Italian mode – and at first it was no more than a minor regional mode – in Florence around 1420 to the general acceptance of a new international style throughout Europe some two hundred years passed. The Baroque, in succeeding the Renaissance, came to international dominion only by gradual stages and eventually died out, not all at once

around 1750, but only gradually over the next half century in many areas in the western world.

Despite prolific production and the quite remarkable things that were occasionally achieved when historicism came to uneasy terms with new technical means – as had already happened not infrequently in the nineteenth century – the traditional architecture of the twentieth century is primarily an instance of survival; and cultural survivals are among the most difficult problems with which history has to deal. Their sluggish life, sunk in inertia and conservatism, is very different from the vitality of new developments. Yet survivals are tough and resilient, tending always to maintain themselves by their very uneventfulness. Static, not to say smug, assurance is their greatest strength; their greatest danger is the boredom resulting from excessive familiarity which they eventually induce even in their most convinced exponents.

Survivals do not generally rouse the interest of posterity. The Gothic of fifteenth-century Italy or that of seventeenth-century England has not received from historians the attention of the rising forces in the architecture of those periods. Somewhat unfairly, late and anachronistic achievements, if admired at all, are likely to be credited to the previous age. In America, for example, Grecian plantation houses built as late as the 1850s are frequently called 'Southern Colonial'. We are well enough aware today, however, that the work of the traditional architects of the last seventy or eighty years is of this century, and not of the previous one, to avoid that kind of confusion. The historian *must* attempt to give some sort of account of things like the Stockholm City Hall [330] and the Woolworth Building [337]. But the story is not an easy one to tell because it seems – at least to most scholars today – to lack plot. The rise of modern architecture, on the other hand, offers material for a dramatic narrative, for it followed the pattern of the 'success-story', just as did that of the Gothic in twelfth-century France or the beginnings of the Renaissance in fifteenth-century Italy.

In some areas a certain sort of meaningful succession can now be recognized even in the latest period of historicism. Because of the differential lags in various parts of the western world, however, it is difficult to find a scheme of organization that is at all generally applicable. All the same, those lags usually mean that certain countries were going through phases of architectural development in the early twentieth century that more advanced areas had left behind before 1900. Since those phases have been discussed in Part Two, it is unnecessary to detail here the peripheral and anachronistic 'repeats' of familiar late nineteenth-century episodes in the present century.

Without attempting to round out the picture with the citation of multiple examples, it is not impossible to suggest some of the aspects, parallel and successive, of twentieth-century historicism. There was, for example, a characteristic continuation of that reaction against the boldness and coarseness of the architecture of the third quarter of the nineteenth century which is evident in most countries, and particularly in America and England, from as early as the eighties; hence the general critical emphasis of the period on 'restraint' and on the 'tasteful'. Academically designed buildings of the 1920s were often still intended to realize aspirations that had been novel some forty years earlier; rarely, however, did they do so with a vitality comparable to that of late nineteenth-century work. So also Gothic of the

early twentieth century produced by such American architects as Ralph Adams Cram or James Gamble Rogers hardly differs in its standards from what the English Bodley and Pearson had initiated around 1870.

We have already seen in much of the work of Perret and Behrens a special kind of continuation of the Classical tradition in the twentieth century. This shades down through various degrees and kinds of simplification as represented in the personal modes of such architects as Asplund in Sweden or Marcello Piacentini in Italy to the maintenance of a Classical revivalism as absolute as that of 1800 in white marble temples like Henry Bacon's Lincoln Memorial in Washington [338].

The medievalizing currents of the nineteenth century link up with many aspects of the advanced architecture of the early twentieth century. This aftermath, often vital and creative in the fields of theory and of craftsmanship with architects as different as the English Voysey and the Spanish Gaudí, likewise shades down through various levels of decreasing stylization to a literal revivalism that is still in the Victorian tradition, but more in line with that tradition's early or Puginian phase or its late Bodleyan phase than with the Butterfieldian phase of the 1850s and 1860s.

Both on the Classical and on the Gothic side of the fence, however, there have been a few twentieth-century traditional architects whose personal stylization of borrowed forms was almost as extreme as that of the High Victorians. In their work, intense individualism and limited respect for the canons of 'taste' and 'restraint' offer real points of contact with the boldness of such modern architects of the first generation as Wright and de Klerk. This is in contrast to the other line of traditionalist integrity in the handling of materials that was solidly based on Gothic Revival standards of revived hand-craftsmanship, one of the truly positive values contributed to the next generation by such architects as Richardson in America and Webb in England. The two lines could also in some milieus combine to produce, particularly in Scandinavia, some of the most attractive works of the early twentieth century. Such an outline, blurred and overlapping in its rubrics, can do little more than suggest some of the principal later channels of the architectural currents which were carried over from the nineteenth century into the early decades of the twentieth century.

There were, even at mid century, few countries in the world where buildings of traditional design were not still being erected; but whatever life twentieth-century traditional architecture retained as late as the second and even the third decade of the century had departed by the fourth. Post-mortems on traditional architecture have been many – and often premature. The causes of death are still disputable, but the fact of dissolution is by now generally accepted. Yet the later years of traditional architecture were not completely senile. However much the youthful vitality of the newer architecture attracted sympathy and attention, as late as 1930 its impact on building production was in most countries a very limited one. It is fortunate, therefore, that not all the traditional architecture of the years 1900-30 need be dismissed with scorn, even if the standards by which it must be judged remain those of the nineteenth rather than of the twentieth century.

The nineteenth century ended, as we have seen earlier, with a surge of innovation (see Chapters 14, 15, and 16). Looking forward from the late nineties, a prophet might well have assumed that a new architecture would surely arise just beyond the turn of the century; yet within a few years a general reaction set in which took somewhat different forms in various parts of the western world. As has already been noted, there were almost everywhere strong links with the earlier Academic Reaction of the eighties against the loud and brash 'high styles'

of the mid century; indeed, it may be said that the traditional architecture of the new century was in general both a continuance and a resurgence of that reaction. In most European countries, although not in England and America, the academic architecture of the late nineteenth century seemed to represent at its best a partial resurgence or a continuance of certain aspects of earlier Romantic Classicism. Seeking a loftier pedigree, however, conservative architects often claimed that they were returning to traditions that had existed down to less than a century before their own day, quite as various reformers from Pugin to Voysey claimed they were renewing a link with one or another earlier period.

Relatively valid as this might still have been for certain aspects of the Queen Anne in England and the Colonial Revival in America, or for the parallel return to eighteenth-century modes in various Continental countries towards the end of the century, this theory had already run into serious difficulties long before 1900. A church might hope to be plausibly Gothic, but a railway station could only be Victorian Gothic; a skyscraper could not even be as Gothic as that. Moreover, the tide of retrospective eclecticism, ever rising since the mid eighteenth century, was not turned back; for both the reaction of the 1880s and the later reaction of the early 1900s represented chiefly a rejection of earlier nineteenth-century innovations, especially of novel sorts of detail, rather than positive programmes of exclusive revival.

It is possible, at least for individual countries, to make statements concerning what occurred in the field of traditional design between the 1890s and the 1930s that are not wholly without significance. Of Holland it may be said, negatively, that no reaction of consequence towards the traditional occurred before the mid thirties. In Germany the boundary line between what was traditional and what was modern was always fairly vague; yet evidence of a return to stylistic reminiscence after the earliest years of the century is to be found even in the work of leaders of the first generation of modern architects such as Olbrich and Behrens (see Chapter 20). Farther to the North in Denmark and Sweden, the Copenhagen Town Hall of

the seventies in England. It is true that Absalons Gaard, built in 1901-2 by Vilhelm Fischer (1868-1914) in the square in front of Nyrop's Town Hall, and even more notably the nearby Palace Hotel of 1907-10 by Anton Rosen (1859-1928), developed in a very much freer manner and with an almost Dutch verve.[1a] Despite some

329. Martin Nyrop:
Copenhagen, Town Hall, 1892-1902

1892-1902 [329] by Martin Nyrop (1849-1923) and the contemporary post offices and fire stations in Gävle, Stockholm, and Malmö by Ferdinand Boberg (1860-1940) resemble Berlage's Exchange in Amsterdam in their parallelism to the Richardsonian in America - which Boberg knew at first hand - or to the Shavian of

Sullivanian influence there generally followed after 1900 however, as elsewhere rather earlier, a programme of tasteful emulation of local versions of the Baroque and then, from around 1910 in Denmark and a decade later in Sweden, an even more programmatic revival of Romantic Classicism.

330. Ragnar Östberg:
Stockholm, Town Hall, 1909-23

In the Scandinavian development from 1890 to 1930 there is therefore a sort of 'plot' or recognizable sequence of phases despite their overlappings. What is usually called 'National Romanticism', rooted in the cultural climate of the eighties, had a briefer span in Denmark than in Sweden. Nyrop's Town Hall, begun in 1892, although in fact hardly more traditional than Berlage's Amsterdam Exchange, introduced the mode, and the Stockholm Town Hall [330] by Ragnar Östberg (1866–1945), completed thirty years later, brought it to a close. But its dominion in Denmark was never exclusive. Although the Custom House of 1897

331. P. V. Jensen Klint: Copenhagen, Grundvig Church, 1913, 1921-6

at Aarhus by Hack Kampmann (1856-1920) with its picturesque high roofs and corner towers belongs to the mode, his Aarhus Theatre of 1898-1900 and his City Library there of 1898-1902 do not. Externally, the theatre is in the main of Early Renaissance design, although with considerable eclecticism in the detail; on the other hand, the library is even less traditional than Nyrop's Town Hall. Both, moreover, have extremely rich plaster decoration inside that may not improperly be called Art Nouveau.

Wahlman's Engelbrekt Church of 1904-14 in Stockholm, mentioned earlier as an exception to the general dominance of tradition in Scandinavia in these decades, and the Grundvig Church in Copenhagen [331] by P. V. Jensen Klint (1853-1930), originally designed in 1913 and completed finally in 1926, are both closely related to the earlier National Romanticism of the eighties and nineties. By the time the latter was designed, however, this phase had for some years been superseded by a sort of Neo-Baroque still also very nationalistic in its choice of precedents and very romantic in their handling. Sometimes, however, this mode approached eighteenth-century revivalism of the sort that flourished in England and America. For example, the Marselisberg Slot, built by Kampmann for the Danish Crown Prince at Aarhus in 1899-1902, is the precise Danish equivalent of the best Neo-Georgian houses of the period in England and America.

Monuments such as the Masthugg Church [332] of 1910-14 in Göteborg by Sigfrid Ericsson (1879-1958) or the Högalid Church of 1916-23 in Stockholm by Ivar Tengbom (1878-1968) are hardly recognizable as traditional to non-Swedish eyes, for they are composed with a sense of visual drama quite equal to Wahlman's and very stylized in all their detailing.[1b] Ericsson's, in particular, has much in common with the American Shingle Style, although that was rarely used for churches and never for big ones of stone or brick construction.

In much secular Swedish work in the Neo-Baroque mode, such as the very typical ASEA Building of 1916-19 in Västerås by Erik Hahr (1869-1944), bold asymmetrical massing and onion-domed towers reflect the romanticism of the churches and also recall early stages of the revived Queen Anne in England of the seventies. Danish taste in the second decade of the century was much more severe than Swedish, as in fact it had long been, and the characteristic low-cost housing blocks in Copenhagen of this period, such as those of 1914 in the Amagertorv by Hansen & Hygom, are, so to say, only Neo-Baroque round the edges.

For the 1920s, however, the most significant phase was the third, that is the return to

332. Sigfrid Ericsson:
Göteborg, Masthugg Church, 1910-14

Romantic Classicism. This was initiated in Denmark by Carl Petersen (1874-1923) in his Faaborg Museum designed in 1912, and reached its climax immediately after the First World War. In Sweden the parallel phase began a bit later. By the time such men as Fisker in Denmark, Asplund in Sweden, and Aalto in Finland became 'converts' to the International Style in the late twenties, Scandinavian traditionalism had become almost as purged of stylistic detail as the architecture of Tony Garnier, or even that of Adolf Loos, had been for a generation.

On the whole the Danes and the Swedes produced the most lively and distinguished traditional architecture of the early decades of the century. Medievalizing churches in Scandinavia, such as the just-mentioned Grundvig Church in Copenhagen, where Jensen Klint followed Baltic modes that seemed strange and even Expressionist to foreign eyes, or Tengbom's Högalid Church in Stockholm, superbly sited and actually much more Baroque than Gothic in its detail, make the respectable Neo-Perpendicular and Neo-Georgian exercises of contemporary Anglo-Saxon architects look timid and unimaginative. In both cases it is the stylization of proportion – the tremendous verticality – that makes them striking and full of a sort of vitality, at once nervous and lusty, which is comparable to that of the best High Victorian Gothic churches.

The finest medievalizing work is undoubtedly Östberg's Stockholm Town Hall of 1909-23.[1c] This is an exceedingly eclectic combination of elements adapted from various periods both of the Swedish and the general European past. Superbly set at the water's edge, it is sumptuously decorated inside and out with products of craftsmanship that are of a very high order of competence [330]. Despite his eclecticism, Östberg succeeded in imposing on all his disparate elements a high degree of personal stylization at the same time that he exploited the situation with marvellous dramatic effect. There is also a witty allusiveness suggesting the art of the theatre and the exotic fantasies of the late eighteenth century. The Stockholm Town Hall provides a sort of pageant-setting for the ceremonial life of the city, recalling the splendours of town-hall architecture of many epochs of the past, even though it lacks the straightforwardness and the integrity of Nyrop's earlier Town Hall in Copenhagen.

The outside world had hardly had time to apprehend such new Scandinavian building in the years following the First World War before it became evident that architecture in these countries, hitherto on the whole in stylistic retard of developments elsewhere by almost a generation, had taken a surprisingly sharp turn. Petersen's museum at Faaborg followed the local Romantic Classical models of C. F. Hansen far more literally than any of the contemporary admirers of Schinkel in Germany were doing. Brought to completion in 1916 during the First World War, it attracted very little foreign attention at the time it was built. But the Police Headquarters in Copenhagen by Kampmann, erected after the war in 1918-22, with its great colonnaded circular court, and the Øregaard School [333] at 32 Gersonsvej in the Gentofte Kommune north of Copenhagen by Edward Thomsen (b. 1884) and G. B. Hagen (1873-1941) that followed in 1922-4 were at once noticed abroad. Both indeed are notable for their grandeur and for their simplicity, the latter realizing old Romantic Classical ideals with extraordinary success, the former coming closer to the academic work of McKim, Mead & White in America.

Still simpler, and not without a similar sort of understated grandeur surprising in such work, were the Danish low-cost housing blocks erected in the early twenties in succession to those of Hansen & Hygom. Those by Povl Baumann (1878-1963) in the Hans Tavsengade

333. Edward Thomsen and G. B. Hagen:
Gentofte Komune, Øregaard School, 1922-4

or the enormous Hornbaekhus built in 1923
by Kay Fisker, all in Copenhagen, are especially
fine. The extreme precision, the elegant craftsmanship in brick, and the ascetic detailing of
these blocks of flats, rivalling the contemporary ones by de Klerk and by Kramer in
Amsterdam in quality but subscribing to a
quite opposed aesthetic, are found also in many
Danish private houses of the twenties built by
Gotfred Tvede (1863-1947) and other architects both in the city and in the country.

Although Carl Westmann (1866-1936) in
the Röhss Museum of Handicraft at Göteborg
and Erik Lallerstedt (1864-1955) in the University of Architecture and Engineering at
Stockholm approached the simplicity and fine
craftsmanship in brick of the Danes, Swedish
work of this period was in general richer and
more robust, still reflecting the eclectic sources

of inspiration of Östberg's Town Hall. However, in 1923 Neo-Classicism of a more
attenuated and whimsical order than Petersen's
made a striking appearance in the buildings
for the Göteborg Jubilee Exhibition. Of these
the Congress Hall by Arvid Bjerke (b. 1880),
with its serried clerestories carried on arched
principals, was the boldest and least reminiscent. These Göteborg pavilions were very
influential abroad in the mid and late twenties;
detailing of Swedish inspiration then seemed
to offer to traditional designers elsewhere a
sort of Nordic spice with which to enliven
the banalities of local eighteenth-century
revivals.

Tengbom, deserting the romantic eclecticism and the emotional drama of his earlier
Högalid Church, used a highly stylized, almost
exposition-like, Neo-Classic mode for his Stock-

holm Concert Hall of 1920-6. However, the real climax in Sweden – indeed, the climax as regards all Scandinavia – came with Asplund's Central Library in Stockholm, begun in 1921 and much simplified and refined as construction proceeded through the mid twenties. Rejecting the frivolous decorative detail of his Skandia Cinema of 1922-3, Asplund rivalled the Danes in reducing architecture to geometrical simplicity [334]. Thus he might almost seem to have passed beyond C. F. Hansen and Schinkel, the Scandinavian idols of the day, to draw the inspiration for his plain cylinder rising out of a cube directly from Ledoux or Boullée[2]; while at the base he ran a continuous band of windows derived from the newest architecture of these years in France, Germany, and Holland. This juxtaposition in the same edifice of Ledoux and Le Corbusier, so to put it, is rather awkward; but it is highly symptomatic of the very slight step that the Scandina-

vians had still to take in the late twenties when they gave up revived Romantic Classicism – already pared down to basic geometry in this library and in much Danish housing – to become outright converts to the International Style.

Although Sweden and Denmark produced no modern architect of the first generation of such individual distinction as the Finns Saarinen and Sonck, and must be considered to have started out around 1900 from a position somewhat in retard of most Central Europeans, their early twentieth-century architecture largely avoided the stasis of traditionalism elsewhere, moving early through overlapping but discrete phases to a sympathetic acceptance of the new International architecture of the twenties even before that decade was over. So clear a picture is hard to discern in most other countries.

In the United States the pattern of development between the 1890s and the 1930s, in

334. E. G. Asplund:
Stockholm City Library, 1921-8

so far as one can make out any pattern at all, was quite different; nor was there in America, in the way of England in the twenties, any Swedish influence of consequence. Movements roughly equivalent to the Scandinavian National Romanticism of 1900, the Richardsonian Romanesque and the Shingle Style, had flourished in the eighties and come to an end by 1900. The Academic Reaction that early succeeded them swept on, however, for a generation or more. Despite the ruling eclecticism that permitted an archaeological sort of revived Gothic still to thrive as a mode for churches and educational institutions, the more widely favoured Classical, Renaissance, and Georgian stylisms had all been initiated by McKim, Mead & White in the eighties and early nineties. The quality of their work began to decline[2] almost as soon as their professional primacy became assured; yet their best buildings of the first decade of the new century un-

doubtedly remain among the most competent, if unexciting, examples of traditional architecture then produced anywhere. Americans, not Frenchmen, were in these decades the worthiest products of the École des Beaux-Arts, and thus heirs of the strongest academic tradition in the world.

Whether McKim, Mead & White's models be Renaissance, as in the University Club in New York [335] completed in 1900, the series of Branch Public Libraries there that were built over the next dozen years, and the Tiffany Building finished in 1906; or Classical, as in the Knickerbocker Trust in New York and the Bank of Montreal in Montreal, both completed in 1904, the very similar Girard Trust in Philadelphia of 1908, and the vast Pennsylvania Station[2a] in New York of 1906–10, this New York firm was clearly one of the truest successors to the nineteenth-century academic heritage that so many of the French were frittering

335. McKim, Mead & White:
New York, University Club, 1899–1900

336. Victor Laloux:
Paris, Gare d'Orsay, 1898–1900

away at the opening of the new century in a half-hearted flirtation with the Art Nouveau.

The Gare d'Orsay in Paris of 1898–1900 [336] by V.-A.-F. Laloux (1856–1937) is no more to be compared with the Americans' station than his Hôtel de Ville at Tours of

1904-5 with their clubs and banks – his best work, closer to the tradition of Duquesney and Hittorff, was an earlier station, that at Tours of 1895-8. Yet Laloux was often considered the most accomplished French traditional architect of the period.[3] Moreover, the McKim, Mead & White repertory of stylistic modes was wide: much wider than that of the French, although Laloux did produce in Saint-Martin at Tours, opened in 1904, a domed basilica in the line of earlier Romanesquoid churches, though not of the quality of Vaudremer's Saint-Pierre-de-Montrouge or Vaudoyer's Marseilles Cathedral, now at last completed.

McKim, Mead & White exploited a vernacular Colonial Revival, as in the E. D. Morgan house of 1900 at Wheatley Hills, Long Island, as well as a more formal Neo-Georgian, at which several others, such as Delano & Aldrich[4] and Charles A. Platt (1861-1933), were quite as competent as they. But they could also shade their Classicism towards the Byzantine, as in the Madison Avenue Presbyterian Church in New York completed in 1906, or adapt it to industrial uses, as in the I.R.T. Power Station in New York of 1903. They could even extend it upward into skyscrapers, as in the New York Municipal Building completed in 1908, concentrating all their attention on the ground floor and the crowning feature while ignoring the many-storeyed shank between; or spread it thin over large apartment houses such as that they built in 1918 at 998 Fifth Avenue, one of the best examples of the apparently solid blocks that walled one side of that thoroughfare above 57th Street facing Central Park and soon turned Park Avenue from 46th to 96th Street into a man-made canyon. The one thing they and their contemporaries seemed to be unable to do was to make their architecture live, even with the derivative vitality of the Scandinavians. Frozen ideals of stylistic 'correctness' stifled such expression of individual personality as gives real character

337. Cass Gilbert:
New York, Woolworth Building, 1913

to the work of a Tengbom or a Kampmann even when it comes closest to theirs.

In popular estimation certain buildings that made use of Gothic rather than Classical, Renaissance, or Georgian forms had a higher reputation. Cass Gilbert's already-mentioned Woolworth Building finished in 1913 [337] initiated a considerable range of Gothic sky-scrapers, including Howells & Hood's Chicago Tribune Tower of 1923–5, but it remains in the judgement of posterity the most notable example of this sort of applied medieval design. Despite the considerable acclaim it received when new, such an equally characteristic Romanesquoid example as the Shelton Hotel of 1929 by Arthur Loomis Harmon (b. 1901) rivals Gilbert's no more in interest than in height. The New York Telephone Company's Building, completed in 1926 by Ralph Walker (b. 1889) at the beginning of his career with the firm of McKenzie, Voorhees & Gmelin, is more original. Its fortress-like masses, not ineffectively relieved by ornamental touches borrowed from the Paris Exposition of 1925, and its isolated location at the Hudson River's edge, ensured that its bold silhouette should long vie, for the visitor arriving from abroad, with the so much taller and richer silhouette of the Woolworth Building. Most of the other individual big buildings of the twenties in New York and other large American cities are no more than incidental elements in the man-made mountain ranges of their skylines.

Curiously enough the 'correct' Gothic churches of this period have not lately received as favourable a response as the large-scale medievalizing secular work that is necessarily so very unlike real work of the Middle Ages. Those of Ralph Adams Cram (1863–1942), then the most esteemed Gothic practitioner, are lifeless and even crude beside Bodley's and Pearson's in England from which they largely derive. His first church, All Saints', Ashmont, outside Boston which was built in 1892 is by its early date the least anachronistic. Cram's former partner Goodhue's St Vincent Ferrer in New York completed in 1916, a competent and well-scaled example of Late Gothic that is more Continental than English in character, is rather more successful than any of their joint work or that which Cram did later with his

other partner Ferguson. Bertram Grosvenor Goodhue (1869–1924) – responsible also, as has been noted, for the Spanish Colonial revival in California – moved on in the early twenties just before his death to an eclectic sort of semi-modernism best represented by his Nebraska State Capitol in Lincoln. This is vaguely Byzantinesque, yet towered instead of being domed in what had been the tradition for state capitols ever since Bulfinch's in Boston.[4a] His contemporary Los Angeles Public Library is starker and more like a project by Tony Garnier.

There were other architects to match McKim, Mead & White directly at their own academic exercises: most notably John Russell Pope (1874–1937), with his Temple of Scottish Rite in Washington completed in 1916, a grandiose reconstruction of the Mausoleum at Halicarnassus; and Henry Bacon (1866–1924), with his Lincoln Memorial completed the following

338. Henry Bacon:
Washington, Lincoln Memorial, completed 1917

year [338]. This peripteral Greek Doric temple of white marble with a high attic might almost have been designed in Paris in the 1780s, as has been noted earlier. Equally French in spirit, but with no such evident prototypes, is the Grand Central Station in New York, built in 1903–13 by Reed & Stem and Warren &

339. Reed & Stem and Warren & Wetmore:
New York, Grand Central Station, 1903–13

Wetmore.[5] More efficiently organized than the Pennsylvania Station, its concourse is one of the grandest spaces the early twentieth century ever enclosed [339].

Compared to most work of these decades by French architects, all trained like the American leaders at the École des Beaux-Arts, the greater 'correctness' of the detailing of these buildings is notable. The boast of 'good taste' was not altogether a hollow one, although it is at best a negative rather than a positive criterion for architecture.

So extensive was American building production during the twenties that it is difficult to know how to epitomize it.[6] On the one hand, there are the later skyscrapers, essaying new stylistic garments as the older ones lost their piquancy. Even before the Romanesquoid of Harmon's Shelton Hotel had come the massive simplicity of Walker's Telephone Building.[6a] But for all the playing around with superficially novel decoration borrowed from the Paris Exposition of 1925 in the succeeding years, there was no basic renewal of form before the next decade opened. Just after the crash of 1929 terminated the boom, the second skyscraper age came to a belated close with the erection in the early thirties of Shreve, Lamb & Harmon's Empire State Building and the initiation of the Rockefeller Center project.[7] There a more urbanistic grouping, extending over a considerable area, replaced the earlier ideal of building single structures of ever greater height that had just reached its climax with the Empire State Building. This change in approach, recognized ever since as a turning point, was for a long time hardly at all followed up. However, the spaced skyscrapers of Pitts-

340. Cram & Ferguson:
Princeton, N. J., Graduate College, completed 1913

burgh's rebuilt Golden Triangle and various big later projects of renewal in large and middle-sized cities from coast to coast continued to shift the emphasis from individual structures to the wholesale reorganization of very considerable urban areas (see Chapter 25 and Epilogue).

In the terms of this chapter neither the Empire State Building nor Rockefeller Center are examples of traditional architecture, even if it is hardly proper to consider them 'modern' in the sense of the European architecture of their day. Although likewise no example of the new architecture as then understood in Europe like Howe & Lescaze's Philadelphia Savings Fund Society Building of 1932 [317], such a clean-cut skyscraper as Hood's vertically striped Daily News Building in New York marked with more distinction than its outsize rivals the end of traditional design in this field.

Almost as remarkable as the skyscrapers of the twenties in size and elaboration were the groups of new buildings in which so many academic institutions, new and old, then variously housed themselves. The mode is Classical at the Massachusetts Institute of Technology, built by Welles Bosworth (1869-1966) in 1912-15 on the Charles River in Cambridge, Mass.; 'Georgian-Colonial' in the range of 'Houses' that Coolidge, Shepley, Bulfinch & Abbott[8] built in the twenties for Harvard, also along the Charles River in Cambridge; it is Gothic at Cram & Ferguson's Graduate College at Princeton, N.J. [340] completed in 1913, in the Harkness Quadrangle, designed in 1917, and other later buildings for Yale at New Haven, Conn., by James Gamble Rogers (1867-1947), and at the Men's Campus by Horace Trumbauer (1869-1938) at Duke University in

Durham, North Carolina; it is even, by exception, Byzantinoid at Cram's Rice University at Houston, Texas, opened in 1912. The usual modes for such work were what was known as 'Collegiate' Gothic, based rather loosely on work at Oxford and Cambridge that was quite as likely to be nineteenth-century as medieval in date, and Neo-Georgian in an Anglo-American version, usually too grand to be plausibly Colonial yet too casually composed to be properly Anglo-Palladian. Curiously enough, the Gothic Cram's Neo-Georgian Sweet Briar College in Virginia of 1901-6 is more successful than much of his own medievalizing work or than comparable work by those who specialized in eighteenth-century design.

The technical competence of American architects in this period was very great, the sums of money available almost unlimited, and the avowed standards of design only the vague ones of 'taste' and 'correctness', by this time little more than a school-masterish respect for precedent in detail, though rarely in over-all composition.[9] Far less than in Scandinavia is it possible to define the particular ways in which the period expressed itself, for express itself America in these decades undoubtedly did. Yet, when Americans of this period worked abroad, what they produced is readily distinguishable from the work of local traditionalists. The American Academy on the Giannicolo in Rome, built by McKim, Mead & White in 1913, has a certain chaste precision in its High Renaissance detailing no Italian could then have achieved even if he had wanted to. In London Helmle & Corbett's[10] Bush House, rising between the Strand and Aldwych, has a clarity of form and a sense of urbanistic responsibility that few comparable buildings of its period designed by leading British architects display; up to a point, the same is true of Carrère & Hastings's[11] Devonshire House in Piccadilly of 1924-6. The Ritz Hotel of 1906 across the street by the Anglo-French firm of Mewès & Davis,[12] both of them trained at the École des Beaux-Arts as was Thomas Hastings, is bolder in scale, less priggish, but it also lacks the suavity and finish of its neighbour. Bolder also, indeed too monumental for its size, is Barclays Bank of 1926 by W. Curtis Green (1875-1960), near by in Piccadilly across Arlington Street. Of more nearly comparable quality is Green's earlier Westminster Bank of 1922-3 on the north side of Piccadilly.

Somewhere between the extreme professional competence of the traditional architects of America, a competence almost wholly anonymous in its results, and the intensely personal expression of the Scandinavians lies the pattern that the best traditional architecture, such as Green's, followed in England in the early twentieth century. But before turning to that a good deal more should first be said concerning both the competence and the anonymity of American production, since that competence and even that anonymity came to be accepted throughout the western world as desirable[13] characteristics of modern architecture by a great many architects, at least in the nineteen fifties and the nineteen sixties.

Partnerships were not unknown in the nineteenth century, although professional alliances between strong personalities rarely lasted for long. When the partner was not an equal the historian may often be excused for writing, say, of G. G. Scott and forgetting Moffatt or, with rather less justification, only of Sullivan while ignoring Adler. But architectural firms that include three or more named partners, with still other members listed only on the letterhead; others such as D. H. Burnham *and Company* and Albert Kahn *Incorporated*, or 'partnerships', such as McKim, Mead & White or Cram & Ferguson, which continued to function under the same name for decades after the death of the original partners like so many firms of lawyers: these are more or less peculiar to the twentieth century and have been thus far most common in the United States. Moreover, an architect of European background like Mies van der Rohe did not undertake large-scale operations in America, such as the group of buildings for the Illinois Institute of Technology or *a fortiori* his tall blocks of flats in Chicago and the Seagram skyscraper in New York, without associating himself with established local firms. Wright and Gropius solved the problem somewhat differently; but the Taliesin Fellowship and TAC provided them respectively with the relatively modest and idiosyncratic equivalent of the organization of the big Harrison & Abramowitz firm in New York or of one of the Skidmore, Owings & Merrill offices in Chicago, New York, San Francisco, and Portland, Oregon.

The development of the characteristic large-scale American architectural office seems to have begun in Chicago. Burnham, on the death of his designing partner Root in 1891, just after they had undertaken the primary responsibility for the general planning and building of the World's Fair of 1893, had to set up an organization of which he was no more than the executive head. But the office of McKim, his closest associate in carrying out the Fair, was certainly already far advanced along a parallel road. There is a definite connexion here also with the rise of the skyscraper, for those very large commercial buildings already required a vast amount of uninspired draughting that could be efficiently undertaken only by a large force of assistants working in what came later to be derisively called 'plan-factories'.

The same is even more true of industrial work. Here Albert Kahn took the lead around 1905 in developing a type of subdivision and flow of work in his office in Detroit comparable to the new methods of mass-production that his motor-car factories were specifically designed to facilitate. Such patterns are found at their extreme in the group[14] of firms that together produced Rockefeller Center, in the Harrison & Abramowitz office which was in effect their heir, and in the complex post-war expansion of Skidmore, Owings & Merrill. Abroad, more characteristically, such big organizations were built up in offices under a public authority such as those of the London and the Hertfordshire County Councils, the City Architects' Offices in various German cities, or the Banco Obrero housing agency in Venezuela.

'Plan-factories' are undoubtedly conducive to speed and to a certain sort of competence in the execution of large projects, but it must be evident that the architecture they produce will necessarily be anonymous. In defining the character of their competence, moreover, one must be careful not to imply too much. Only such team-work, perhaps, can organize the logistics of building production in such a way that extensive and ramified ventures are carried rapidly to completion, a desideratum of the first order in a boom period for skyscrapers that must be finished quickly in order to begin repaying their enormous cost. Efficiency is of a different sort of consequence where large-scale building schemes of a more public and social nature are being undertaken, but none the less extremely important. Le Corbusier's Unité at Marseilles, produced without an elaborate office organization, took some six years to build; as a result it was no longer 'low-cost housing' when it was finally completed.

Yet competence in the sections of a big office that deal with the plumbing, say, or the electrical system is no assurance that the quite different sort of competence required in the design department will be available. Moreover, a brilliant initial design may or may not survive intact the various modifications that other departments bring to it as the preparatory paper-work for the building moves through successive stages to ultimate execution. At best, even when a particular designer's name is associated with a particular building, as was that of Gordon Bunshaft of Skidmore, Owings & Merrill with Lever House [345], his responsibility was very different from that in Wright's for the Price Tower. Bunshaft's personal contribution was certainly greater in later work such as the Banque Lambert in Brussels.

The situation in England in the first third of the century was rather different from that in America despite a nineteenth-century inheritance which was in many aspects common to both countries. One architect, Sir Edwin Lutyens, had a personal capacity for invention along traditional lines superior to that of any American of his generation. This was not, however, of the order of individualistic intensity of an Östberg or a Jensen Klint, nor was he able, in the way of an Asplund or even a Hood, to accept around 1930 the discipline of the newer architecture of the day. Lutyens built no skyscrapers, nor did he develop the sort of office organization that carried them out in America. This was, however, occurring to some extent by the twenties and thirties in other big English offices, such as those of Sir John Burnet & Tait[15] and of W. Curtis Green.

All the same, it fell to Lutyens's lot to build some of the biggest business structures erected anywhere outside America in these years, and his career culminated in the design and construction of an imperial capital such as came the way of no American. His competence was of a more nineteenth-century order than that of the Americans, and there was certainly nothing anonymous about his work. He was, moreover, still an inspiring figure in an England where architecture, under the difficult economic conditions since the last war, tended for a decade and more to become anonymous without becoming especially competent, except for public housing and for schools (see Chapter 25).

Lutyens's beginnings were very remote from the world of business and governmental buildings with which his career wound up (see Chapter 15). Very early houses, such as Ruckmans of 1894 at Oakwood Park or Sullingstead of 1896 at Hascombe, both in Surrey, followed directly in the line of Shaw's Surrey manor-houses with their tile-hung walls, free and easy composition, and simple domesticity of tone. They are, indeed, superior to most of Shaw's – the first of which, Glen Andred, was built almost thirty years earlier and the last about this time – because of Lutyens's respect for Webb and the resultant superiority of his craftsmanship. In his finest early houses, such as Deanery Gardens at Sonning of 1901 [341], he rivalled Voysey. He was already inclined, however, like Webb in many of his later houses, to use considerable stylistic detail, usually Neo-Georgian, in his interiors, and here and there on exteriors as well.

Perhaps the revolution – or counter-revolution – in his development represented by his Heathcote of 1906 at Ilkley in Yorkshire has been somewhat exaggerated. Yet the design of this, completely symmetrical and quite elaborately Palladian in detail, did represent as great a shift in approach, taken in one jump, as that from Shaw's Glen Andred of the late sixties to his Chesters of the early nineties. It was, however, practically the same shift. Eclectic like almost all the traditional architects of his generation, Lutyens still occasionally remodelled medieval houses, but the main line of his development henceforth was certainly Neo-Georgian. Yet it was usually Neo-Georgian with an important difference from what had become by this time in England as in America a rather drearily codified mode. Nashdom at Taplow in Buckinghamshire, built in 1909, is a vast white-painted house, plain, regular, massive, and hardly at all archaeological. Yet this is so handsomely proportioned and so well built that one could well believe it to be the result of some generations-long process of accretion in the eighteenth century. Great Maytham in Kent of 1910 was Queen Anne,

341. Sir Edwin Lutyens: Sonning, Deanery Gardens, 1901 (photograph copyright *Country Life*)

but not the Queen Anne of the 1870s. Here a great mansion of the early eighteenth century was re-created with such a plausibility of craftsmanship that after only half a century it was hard to believe it was not two hundred and fifty years old. A somewhat smaller house, the Salutation at Sandwich of 1912, is similar and perhaps even more remarkable as an example of what is almost 'productive archaeology' on the part of a man who was not, in fact, at all archaeologically minded. Such houses are the twentieth-century equivalents of Devey's in the nineteenth century, but they often have a witty originality in the handling of traditional detail that has aptly been called 'naughty' and is peculiar to Lutyens.[16]

If the Georgian had to be revived in the way of the Greek and the Gothic, it could hardly have been done with more competence and more animation, certainly the Americans of Lutyens's generation rarely excelled so notably in this particular field, although many of the once highly esteemed firms mentioned earlier positively specialized in it. Beside these houses of Lutyens, the Neo-Georgian of the Shepley firm's Harvard Houses or Cram's Sweet Briar College is merely routine. Yet in such work Lutyens was still only a country-house architect.

Before discussing Lutyens's work at the Hampstead Garden Suburb, with which his association began in 1908, something should be said concerning the 'Garden City' movement[17] in general. In 1892 Ebenezer Howard[18] (1850-1928) published *Tomorrow. A Peaceful Path to Reform*, better known by the title of the edition of 1902 as *Garden Cities of Tomorrow*.

Howard's opportunity to realize his aspirations for a new sort of town began with the acquisition of land at Letchworth in 1903, but the construction of the Letchworth Garden City on the plans of Sir Raymond Unwin (1863-1940) and his partner Richard Barry Parker actually post-dates their work at the Hampstead Garden Suburb. They had, however, already laid out a 'model village' for a chocolate manufacturer at New Earswick near York in 1904.

In 1907 Dame Henrietta Barnett set out to realize some aspects of the Garden City ideal on the outskirts of London. The next year land was acquired near Golders Green on the far side of Hampstead Heath and the suburb planned as a whole by Parker & Unwin.[19] Lutyens was invited to plan and design the group of public buildings in the centre and their immediate setting [342]. This town centre was eventually largely completed, most of it from Lutyens's design, and the two churches, with the contiguous squares, provide some of

his finest work. What he did here certainly set a pace of coherence and urbanity that was unfortunately not maintained in later Garden Cities such as Welwyn, begun in 1919, that followed the rather more diffuse plan of Letchworth.

Welwyn, however, is of importance in the history of town-planning because it was not merely a residential development but included from the first an industrial estate as well. Thus it was a more complete entity and the prototype of the English 'New Towns' initiated after the Second World War. The Barnett project was originally, and has remained, an upper-middle-class suburb; yet it is unique for the orderliness and the distinction of the public buildings that Lutyens provided at the centre and the terrace-framed squares that flank them.

St Jude's, the Anglican church, begun in 1910 and not finally completed at the west end until 1933, is Lutyens's principal ecclesiastical work, his Catholic cathedral in Liverpool

342. Sir Edwin Lutyens: Hampstead Garden Suburb, London, North and South Squares, 1908

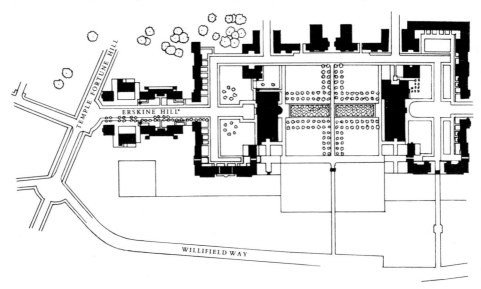

having been barely begun before his death. Lacking the emotional drama of the Scandinavian churches of its period, St Jude's has nevertheless a certain real boldness of silhouette, produced by rather eclectic means, and an elegance of craftsmanship in the brickwork that is in the finest tradition of the Gothic Revival. Yet, being by Lutyens, it is hardly at all medieval. The tall crossing tower may have slight suggestions of the Norman in its detailing and a cathedral-like scale, but in general the exterior is in a vaguely seventeenth-century vernacular descending from the later work of Shaw and Webb.

The interior, rather surprisingly, proves to be almost High Renaissance in character; there is even a barrel vault over the nave. On the other hand, the timber-work of the roofs of the aisles, which descend so low on either side, is of a structural peculiarity recalling Webb at his crankiest if not, indeed, Butterfield. Except for the highly exceptional London church of the

Holy Redeemer, Clerkenwell, built by J. D. Sedding (1837–91) in 1887–8, so truly Palladian – rather than Anglo-Palladian – internally as almost to persuade one that it is Italian, few non-Gothic churches of this quality had been built in England for two generations. Lutyens's more modest Free Church is rather similar, both inside and out, but considerably less effective.

To surround two sides of both North Square and South Square beside the churches Lutyens revived the Early Georgian terrace, varying the composition ingeniously and handling the beautifully laid bricks in two colours, reddish and greyish, with a fascinating subtlety. Unfortunately such truly urban housing stood no chance with the clientèle drawn to this and other Garden Cities as against the appeal of free-standing or semi-detached houses. No general revival of the terrace occurred. But Parker & Unwin and their emulators achieved in individual houses a standard of semi-

343. Sir Edwin Lutyens: New Delhi, Viceroy's House, 1920–31 (photograph copyright *Country Life*)

traditional suavity that represents one of the principal English achievements of the period, and something frequently imitated abroad.

Lutyens's call to lay out New Delhi as the capital of India followed in 1911, and the first plans were made before 1914. It was a commission better suited to his leaping imagination than the modest domesticity of an English Garden City. Construction of the buildings, notably the enormous Viceroy's House, began only in 1920.[20] Not since L'Enfant laid out Washington had a flat city of such amplitude and grandeur been conceived, even by Griffin in Australia. The Viceroy's House, finally finished in 1931, is official residence, centre of administration, and focus of the whole scheme – a *tour de force* for which, from the Queen Anne, the Neo-Georgian, and the Palladian, Lutyens lifted his sights to a Roman scale [343]. The result is grand and broad, adapted to the climate, and even reminiscent of the Indian architectural past in some of its forms and features. Towards the designing of such a major monument generations of Frenchmen and others who studied at the Beaux-Arts had been prepared; there is a certain irony that this opportunity came to an Englishman, trained in the most private and individualistic English way.

Nashdom and Great Maytham represent a side of Lutyens's mature talent that follows rather directly from Webb's Smeaton Manor of the seventies [187]. The work at the Hampstead Garden Suburb, and above all that at Delhi, represents another side. On the one side he had a few worthy rivals: Leonard A. S. Stokes (1858-1925)[21] was a more adventurous architect than he around 1900, with some leaning towards the Art Nouveau; Shaw's pupil Newton was almost as competent at Neo-Georgian work. Those who tried to rival him on the other side, however, Sir Reginald Blomfield (1856-1942), a pupil of Norman Shaw, and Sir Herbert Baker (1862-1946), a

pupil of Ernest George, hardly deserve mention, even though their work bulks large on the London scene and Baker's in South Africa.

Blomfield's watered-down version of Shaw's quadrant façade of the Piccadilly Hotel, carried out in the twenties, has been mentioned. Better examples of what may be called in W. S. Gilbert's terms his 'not too French, French' academicism face Piccadilly Circus. But his pretensions to cosmopolitanism, although based on a very considerable knowledge of French seventeenth- and eighteenth-century architecture, did not serve him as well as Lutyens's purely English background in continuing along the 'Monumental Queen Anne' line of Shaw's late work.

Baker's outrageous rape of Soane's masterpiece, the Bank of England, carried out over the years 1921-37, has also been mentioned; it was literally a fate worse than death. Despite a half-hearted decision to preserve a good deal of the relatively unimportant exterior, the Tivoli Corner was pointlessly stripped of its idiosyncratic crown, presumably in the name of Baker's superior 'taste'. His South Africa House of 1935, moreover, all but ruins Trafalgar Square.

Lutyens's Midland Bank of 1924, near the Bank of England in Poultry, like Baker's bank almost a skyscraper in size if not in height, at least required the destruction of no earlier work of distinction and is undoubtedly more consistently and personally designed. Yet the cliff-like massiveness of its walls, with even less evidence of the underlying structural skeleton than in office buildings of this period by American architects, is almost as anti-urbanistic as Baker's Bank of England. Because of the very narrow streets of the area, the filling up of the City of London with such structures, very few of them even of this degree of intrinsic interest, was a tragedy of the twenties that even bombing did not put right. The superiority of Corbett's Bush House, not in the rather flat detailing but in the exploitation of the fine site at the foot of Kingsway, and even in the politeness of the plain foil it offers to the Baroque elaboration of Gibbs's St Mary-le-Strand, is very notable.

Lutyens's other big Midland Bank buildings, one of 1928 in Leadenhall Street in the City and one of 1929 in King Street in Manchester, are not much of an improvement over that in Poultry. However, his elegant little Midland Bank of 1922 in Piccadilly in front of Wren's St James's is a rich and inventive exercise in the vein of Wren built of brick and stone. Anachronistic as such a design must be considered, the verve of the *pastiche* nevertheless has a distinct appeal, like a plausibly realistic setting on the stage.

Lutyens's most successful big business building is doubtless Britannic House of 1924-7. This profits from its site between Finsbury Circus and Moorgate Street, the curve of the Circus giving to the eastern front a certain major Baroque drama that is echoed in the versatile play with seventeenth-eighteenth-century motifs in the detailing. But one may well prefer the massively mock-Egyptian effect of Adelaide House by London Bridge, built by Sir John Burnet & Tait in 1924-5. This, at least, makes some approach to the new ideals of the Continent in these years. Burnet, moreover, had been for decades one of the most competent British practitioners in a local version of the international Beaux-Arts mode, as his King Edward VII wing of the British Museum of 1904 notably illustrates. Three years later Tait was the first English-born architect[22] to attempt to build in the International Style, as has been mentioned earlier. The closest Lutyens came to the Continental modes of the twenties was in his public housing.

Despite the statistical importance of its social achievement, public housing in England between the wars was generally rather routine in design, lacking either the drama of the Dutch or the restraint of the Scandinavians. On the one occasion when Lutyens turned his attention to this field, on the Grosvenor Estate in Westminster in 1928, he succeeded beyond all expectation. The bold device of chequering all the façades of his blocks of flats in alternate oblongs of brickwork, plain stucco panels, and windows is somewhat inhuman in scale but notably effective. The contrast is striking to the work of the twenties by the London County Council Architect's Office. In that a type of design not unsuited to semi-detached houses in middle-class suburbs was spread thin over vast many-storeyed masses.

Lutyens, one feels, in a different time and place - a generation earlier in England, say, or a generation later - might have been a greater architect. But even as his career actually worked out, he is not unworthy to occupy the place given him here as the 'last traditionalist'. Since his death there has not been, either in England or elsewhere, any traditional or even semi-traditional building of consequence, unless one wishes to consider Perret's work at Le Havre in the latter category.

The traditional architecture of the first third of the twentieth century in Italy and France, headquarters in so many ways of the major architectural traditions of the western world, is disappointing beside that of the countries discussed so far. In the case of France, the situation is confused by the modulation of Perret's style towards a semi-traditional Classicism which, by the thirties, official and academic taste was ready to meet half-way. In Italy Marcello Piacentini (1881-1960), the son of the architect of the Academy of Fine Arts in the Via Nazionale in Rome, always had more vitality than the French of his generation other than Perret. From the new *città bassa* of Bergamo, for which he won the competition in 1907 and which was executed in 1922-4, through his general responsibility for the *Terza Roma* (E.U.R.),[22a] Mussolini's project for a new capital between old Rome and Ostia which was to have opened with an exhibition in 1942, there is a certain assurance and amplitude of scale lacking in most contemporary work in France. Mussolini, in the middle years of Fascism, was not averse to modern architecture, as we have seen. When, under German influence, he began to turn against the International Style the choice of Piacentini to set a neo-imperial pace was as natural as the Nazis' return to the modes of twenty years earlier in Germany. Moreover, from the public buildings of Bergamo through the 'New Towns' below Rome – Littoria, Sabaudia, Pontinia, etc., partly destroyed during the Second World War – to the arcaded cube of La Padulla's Palace of Italian Civilization at E. U. R., aptly nicknamed by Italians the 'Square Colosseum', fine materials, clean if familiar proportions, and excellent craftsmanship provide certain lasting qualities not unworthy of Italian national traditions. Where Fascist work is interpolated in an earlier urbanistic scheme, as along the Via Roma in Turin between the Piazza San Carlo and the Piazza Carlo Felice, the new buildings of 1938 – here by Piacentini – fit as well with the seventeenth-century buildings of the one as with the nineteenth-century ones of the other. For all their obviousness, moreover, the colonnades of the Via Roma, all of polished granite monoliths, have a truly Roman scale and dignity. Even the Square Colosseum has a Chirico-like forcefulness suggesting something seen in a dream; while the big structures around it, only finished in the last fifteen years, are not without virtues to balance the mid century conventionality of those that have since risen beside them.

To pursue the subject of traditional architecture further would be merely to explore what can now be seen to have been not so much a cul-de-sac as a road without a goal. The standards of traditionalism – standards of 'taste', of 'literacy', of ingenious adaptation – were still on the whole nineteenth-century ones. Yet down into the thirties, traditional buildings were the big trees in the forest of twentieth-century architecture; with the rise of a new range of giants in the forest, the seedlings from which they grew seem now to have been more significant: Asplund's Stockholm Exhibition of 1930 and his Crematorium there of 1935-40 tend to obscure our vision of his earlier Library, although that is perhaps finer considered absolutely. So also the Philadelphia Savings Fund Society skyscraper of 1932, so clearly the immediate ancestor of those built in the post-war decades, draws attention away from the Woolworth Building. In England continuity was soon so completely broken that it is hard to realize how much the 'Mannerist' façade-treatment of Drake & Lasdun's tall housing slabs of 1946-56 on the Paddington Estate had in common with Lutyens's chequered Grosvenor Estate blocks of some twenty years before. However the future may judge the last traditional architects, the chapter was all but closed some twenty years ago when this book was written.

CHAPTER 25

ARCHITECTURE AT THE MID CENTURY

To describe the state of architecture in the late forties and early fifties, before and after the mid-point of this century, was far more difficult than to sketch its condition a hundred and fifty years earlier, as the first chapter of the book attempted. The western world was enormously larger in geographical extent, vastly more populous, and as a result very much more productive of buildings of all types and at all levels of quality. Many of the types most important in the twentieth century – big buildings, low-cost public housing, facilities for transportation such as bus stations and airports – did not exist in 1800. These difficulties were objective and merely implied that the sampling of executed work had to be relatively much more limited. But the very limited selection provided here was inevitably influenced by subjective criteria. The activity of two generations of historians writing on the architecture of the early nineteenth century had produced something approaching a consensus of opinion as to what is and what is not important or characteristic in that period. There remains, of course, much to be discovered concerning building in the decades around 1800, particularly as interest rises in the technical aspects of the story; yet the engineers[1] are unlikely ever to force the Soanes and the Schinkels out of the centre of the picture: moreover, men like Latrobe and Mills were themselves as much engineers as architects.

Already, in carrying the story of the production of the leading architects of the first and second generations of modern architecture down to the mid fifties, a rather uneven attempt was made to touch on their production of the last decades. The decisions as to what to include

in rounding out the picture had to be critical ones hardly comparable to the relatively objective historical process of selection that controlled in the First and Second Parts of this book. The very extent in time of what should be considered 'the present' is a subjective matter. I knew in the fifties architectural students whose present was so limited that they had never heard of Perret! To anyone under thirty the effective present will hardly extend backward more even than the twenty years since this book was originally composed. To keep this chapter more or less historical in the second edition of 1963 I saved consideration of the years since the late fifties for a new Epilogue which was also included, with modest emendations, in the third and the first integrated editions.

In most countries of the western world the Second World War occasioned a hiatus in construction that lasted nearly a full decade after the slowing down that had already begun as early as the late thirties. There was therefore a real lack of continuity between pre-war and post-war building except in those countries that remained neutral. But just as the break in the continuity of building production around 1800 resulting from the Napoleonic Wars was a limited, not an absolute, phenomenon, since the truly revolutionary developments in architecture preceded rather than followed its onset, so there was in the last post-war period very little to be recognized at first that had not had its origins well before 1939. Real changes came gradually in the fifties.

The perspective of the war seemed somehow to flatten out some of the architectural episodes that were deemed significant in the thirties, not alone the Nazi and late Fascist reaction but such minor symptoms of dissatisfaction with the general line that architectural development had taken internationally since the early twenties as the rise of the Bay Region School[2] in America and of the New Empiricism in Europe. Historians remain rather uncertain how much weight to give to these matters. Once they lost the topicality of current events they seemed no more and no less significant than the rather similar critical flurries that came later concerning the 'New Brutalism' and 'Neo-Liberty'.[3] Such flurries cannot be entirely ignored;[4] yet the general emendation of the rigid doctrines of the 'International Style' was more strikingly illustrated in the 1950s by the continued high esteem of Wright's last productions and, *a fortiori*, by the warm critical reception of Le Corbusier's remarkable church at Ronchamp than by any of the buildings that illustrated the minor reactions of the decade of the thirties. The accepted definitions of modern architecture had already become very much looser than they were a generation earlier, partly as a result of various abortive attempts at more thoroughgoing revolt. But the greatest individualists were still, paradoxically, not young men[5] in their thirties, but older masters in their seventies and eighties.

The greatest change in the post-war architectural scene, a change that began gradually during the pre-war years, was the shift in the geographical pattern. No longer did France, Germany, and Holland occupy the centre of the stage. The rise of the United States to great prominence, continuing a development already begun in the 1870s, was not surprising. Far more surprising was the rise in the importance of Italy and Japan, not only because of their actual achievements, especially in concrete construction in both cases, but as major influences. This was presaged in Italy by the work of Terragni and of Figini & Pollini in the mid thirties and was hardly inhibited there by the ambiguities of the later Fascist attitude towards

architecture just before the Second World War. The post-war British achievement was more canalized; yet it was of an autochthonous character which a long-term consideration of English architectural abilities and disabilities makes more intelligible than that flurry of new ideas, so largely of foreign origin, characterizing the mid thirties in England.

The Scandinavian countries retained their position of prominence but not pre-eminence in the international architectural scene. In contrast to their long-recognized virtues, some rather less relevant later than they once were, must be set the very different contribution of the Latin American countries, whose entry on the international scene all but post-dated the war. Production there was hardly worth mentioning a hundred and fifty years ago; by the late forties Brazil, Mexico, Colombia, and Venezuela were making a contribution on a par, in quantity and even in quality, with older and richer countries. Moreover, while the West was more and more losing political control of Africa and Asia, its cultural influence on those continents did not necessarily decline, indeed as regards architecture it probably increased. Modern architecture, originally developed to utilize to the full the most advanced technologies, was found to serve especially well also in areas where technology was least advanced. Indeed, the most characteristic building material of modern architecture, ferro-concrete, has often been exploited most ingeniously in countries where materials are dear but labour on the other hand is cheap.

Not only did many outlying parts of the world import architects along with other technicians from the West; Asia, which lay almost entirely outside the field of western culture two centuries ago, produced a vigorous modern school in Japan. Various Dominions and dependencies – South Africa, Australia, Puerto Rico, for example – likewise began to have active groups of local practitioners operating in close consort of principle with those of Europe and North America.

With so wide a range of lively activity, no continent-by-continent, much less country-by-country, survey of modern architecture was possible in a single terminal chapter.[5a] Even allowing for all the enormous climatic and cultural differences that still affect architectural production, there was still sufficient identity of principle in architecture throughout most of the world to justify an international consideration of post-war achievement in terms of various building types, moving from the macrocosm down to the microcosm – from the whole city as a planned product of architectural design to the individual dwelling-house.

Despite its vast productive capacity, the old western world in the mid twentieth century created rather fewer urban entities of distinction than did the nineteenth. Partly, this was because the building of cities has necessarily remained a slower process than the building of individual structures, even in an age when there were many fiat towns and also much concerted rebuilding of older cities partially cleared by bombing in the Second World War. Even more, perhaps, it was because it takes far longer for the 'planning' ideals of architects in any period to achieve a degree of public acceptance sufficient to ensure over decades proper control of layout and construction – or reconstruction – of whole cities than to find clients, even governmental clients, for single buildings or for extensive, but piecemeal, social projects.[5b]

Perret's Le Havre [261] was earlier characterized as the belated realization – notable even so – of ideals that dated back before the First World War. None of the post-war 'New Towns' of England were complete enough by the mid fifties to be apprehensible as urban entities; for the most part they were still only large-scale housing developments – suburbs in search of a city, so to say – exemplifying at considerably lower economic levels the ideals

of the Garden Cities of fifty years before. Better than the English examples and indicative of the widespread acceptance of Garden-City ideals was Vällingby in Sweden.[5c]

More complete urban entities of the mid century could be seen in such heavily bombed and largely rebuilt cities as Coventry in England or Hanover in Germany; yet in neither case was the architectural achievement of the highest contemporary order. They should be compared for quality with Napoleon III's Paris or Francis Joseph's Vienna rather than with Alexander I's Petersburg or Ludwig I's Munich, and even that comparison is not always very favourable to them.

In the extensive and almost explosive expansion and reconstruction of various Latin American cities it was only in Caracas that the planner Maurice Rotival was able to keep a bit ahead of the builders. But even Caracas then had only samples of the characteristic new urbanism of the mid twentieth century: two or three isolated skyscrapers and a housing development, the Cerro Piloto, differing from those in other parts of the world chiefly by its very great extent and its superb mountain-backed site. The North American cities that were growing fastest, Houston or Los Angeles or Miami Beach or Toronto in Canada, were at least as chaotic as the Latin American ones, and neither the quantity nor the quality of the individual buildings was as high. Against the eruptive growth of a city like São Paulo in Brazil could be better balanced such a North American programme of large-scale rebuilding as that which had already cleared the Golden Triangle in Pittsburgh, replacing typical nineteenth-century urban congestion with an open park and spaced cruciform skyscrapers. The new capital of Brazil, Brasilia, was not planned by Lúcio Costa even on paper until 1957.[5d]

The mid twentieth century produced no full-scale cities that properly exemplified the highest ideals of modern architects. It was necessary to wait, with fingers crossed, even to see the results of such piecemeal projects of reconstruction as that proposed by Sir William Holford for the bombed district around St Paul's Cathedral in London,[6] and still longer for such complete cities as Brasilia and Chandigarh where, however, the public buildings by Le Corbusier were in the mid fifties rapidly rising. But there were already in existence certain special entities of almost urban scale planned since the Second World War that deserved attention. Notable were the 'university cities',[6a] complete educational plants located on new terrain, planned as a whole and designed as regards their individual buildings either by a single team of architects or by several teams whose work was closely co-ordinated from start to finish. The most remarkable was that of the University of Mexico, but even here the difference in quality between such highly original structures as the Olympic Stadium of Augusto Perez Palacios (b. 1909), Raúl Salinas Moro, and Jorge Bravo Jiménez of 1951–2, with its fine relief mosaic by Diego Rivera, or the

Central Library of Juan O'Gorman, Gustavo Saavedra, and Juan Martinez de Velasco of 1951–3, with its stack tower entirely covered with mosaics designed by O'Gorman, and certain of the other equally large and prominent buildings is very notable [344]. The university city of Rio de Janeiro, for which Le Corbusier was originally called to Brazil to provide a plan in 1936, was by no means so far advanced; but the control of the design of all the buildings by a single architect, Jorge Moreira (b. 1904), who was one of the three or four ablest in Brazil, seemed then to promise a homogeneity of character and a distinction of finish unique in this field. Among several other Latin American examples begun and partly built by the mid fifties, that at Caracas by Carlos Raúl Villanueva (b. 1900) rivalled in its principal building, the Aula Magna of 1952–3 with its extraordinary acoustic ceiling by the technician Robert Newman and the sculptor Sandy Calder, the achievement of the Mexicans.

Of a very different character indeed, and initiated much earlier, is the University of

344. Carlos Lazo and others:
Mexico City, University City, begun c. 1950

Aarhus[7] in Denmark for which Kay Fisker, C. F. Møller (b. 1898), and Povl Stegmann (1888–1944) won the competition in 1931. Some of its many buildings date from before the Second World War: professors' houses of 1933, student residences of 1934, museum of natural history of 1937–8; while most of the class-room buildings were actually erected in the war years 1942–6. The work continued in the hands of Møller, and the layout of the beautiful sloping site was by C. Th. Sørenson (b. 1893). Built of buff brick with tile roofs of medium pitch, the general effect is much quieter than that of the Latin American university cities with their tall ferro-concrete buildings, crisply shaped and distinguished both by a bold use of colour and the conspicuous incorporation of work by distinguished painters and sculptors. At first sight – and to the prejudiced – the University of Aarhus might appear more conservative; but the range of new architecture is recognized by this time as wider than forty years before and Møller's *aula* in its very different way was quite as advanced as Villanueva's; or even, for that matter, as the shell-domed auditorium of 1952–5 at the Massachusetts Institute of Technology in Cambridge, Mass., by Eero Saarinen (1910–61).

One of the earliest individual building types to find wholly untraditional expression was the large block of offices. The skyscraper reached maturity early in the hands of Sullivan in Chicago; the later vagaries of the form in New York did not recommend it to European emulation, although skyscraper projects by Mies, by Gropius, and by Le Corbusier were among the most notable early evidences of the birth – on paper – of a new architecture in the years 1919–22. Howe & Lescaze's Philadelphia Savings Fund Society Building of a decade later was the first large-scale example of the acceptance in America of the new architecture of Europe; but in the thirties the building of skyscrapers languished, and many critics thought

that their day was already over. In many parts of the world that day had yet to dawn, and Europe still had very few notable examples to offer, but in the New World the fifties saw the start of a new wave of skyscraper building by no means confined to the United States. For the first time since the nineties a rather considerable number of really distinguished examples were being built in both North and South American cities. Wright's Price Tower at Bartlesville, Okla., a relatively modest one, and Mies and Johnson's Seagram Building in New York have both been mentioned already. Diagonally across Park Avenue in New York from the site of the Seagram tower stands the first epoch-making post-war skyscraper in New York, Lever House, designed by Gordon Bunshaft (b. 1909) of the Skidmore, Owings & Merrill firm and built in 1950–2 [345]. The almost completely glazed curtain-walls of the east and west sides of the United Nations Secretariat in New York – built in 1947–50 by Wallace K. Harrison (b. 1895) and his partner Max Abramowitz (b. 1908) but incorporating ideas provided by an international panel of which Le Corbusier and Niemeyer were members – are carried round three sides of Bunshaft's slab. More significant, however, was the fact that this slab, rising like the isolated United Nations building with no setbacks, covered only a portion of the available site. Thus it stands in its own envelope of space carved, as it were, out of the solid canyon of Park Avenue, just as Mies and Johnson would later set their building back 100 feet from the avenue and well in from both the side streets also. Their 'plaza' is unconfined; Bunshaft's open space is defined by a mezzanine supported on *pilotis* which is carried all round an unroofed court.

Reacting against the almost totally glazed curtain-wall of his U.N. Secretariat, a type of sheathing for large urban structures then spreading very rapidly to other countries, Harrison on the Alcoa Building of 1952 in

345. Skidmore, Owings & Merrill (Gordon Bunshaft): New York, Lever House, 1950-2

Pittsburgh used storey-high panels of aluminium cut by relatively small windows. This alternative type of sheathing was more exploited in the mid 60s than the more completely glazed sort. There was also some revival of Expressionist feeling in the complex angular design of the glazed lobby of the Alcoa Building that contrasted sharply with the paradigmatic expression of the 'International Style' seen in the Equitable Building in Portland, Ore., of 1948 by Pietro Belluschi (b. 1899), first completed of the finer post-war skyscrapers. A later Western skyscraper, the Mile-High Center in Denver, Col., built by I. M. Pei (b. 1907) in 1954–5, followed almost more closely the formula of Mies's Lake Shore Drive Apartments in Chicago than he did himself in the design of the Seagram Building the following year.

It was invidious to mention only these few North American examples, but production of similar skyscrapers was already so nationwide in the United States and in Canada that one could already hardly hope to see the single trees for the forest. Those selected for illustration or mention remained for a while conspicuous; they had not yet become lost in the crowd. But skyscrapers were no longer a prerogative of North America; some of the finest were already rising in Latin America, and these would soon be rivalled by European examples projected or even under construction by 1955.

It is a mistake to assume that North Americans housed business only in skyscrapers. More and more corporations were already moving their headquarters to the open country. Quite as significant as Lever House in the production of Skidmore, Owings & Merrill in the mid fifties was the 700-foot-square but only four-storeyed office plant of the Connecticut General Insurance Company of 1955–7, set in a park of eighteenth-century size and amenity at Bloomfield, Conn., some ten miles outside Hartford, the insurance capital. Luxury of materials, white marble and granite as well as aluminium, made up somewhat for the rigid asceticism of the standardized walls, while four interior court gardens by Noguchi and three pink granite figures by him on the slope beyond the 'artificial water' in which swans swim about below the all-glass cafeteria further balanced the expression of crisp efficiency with something warmer and more humane.

In most Latin American cities all-glass walls are impractical because of the heat and the glare of the sun. As a result, architects there developed early versions of the sun-break system introduced long before on the first tall modern building to be erected in that part of the world, the Ministry of Education in Rio; glazed curtain-walls were by no means unknown, however. The egg-crate sun-breaks of the Edificio C.B.I. of 1948–51 in São Paulo by Lucjan Korngold (b. 1897) and the horizontally patterned grid of the Retiro Odontológico of 1953–4 in Havana by Antonio Quintana Simonetti and Manuel A. Rubio gave these buildings a very different look from such examples of more North American character as the building in the Calle de Niza at the corner of the Calle de Londres in Mexico City of 1952–3 by Juan Sordo Madaleno (b. 1916), or that of the Suramericana de Seguros in the Avenida Jiménez de Quesada in Bogotá of 1954 by Cuéllar, Serrano, Gomez & Co.

The most ingenious and best designed Latin American skyscraper of the fifties, however, was the completely isolated Edificio Polar of 1953–4 at the Plaza Venezuela in Caracas. This was built by Martin Vegas Pacheco (b. 1926), a pupil of Mies at the Illinois Institute of Technology, and his partner José Miguel Galia, a pupil of the one distinguished South American architect of the first modern generation, Julio Vilamajó, at the University of Montevideo. Here the structure was reduced to four ferro-concrete piers from which the curtain-walls were cantilevered out 11 feet on all four sides. The curtain-walls have a varied infilling, part solid sandwiches of plywood and aluminium sheeting, part louvres that transmit air but not light, and part glass. These are combined in different proportions on each side according to the orientation in order to control the glare and the heat of the sun while providing direct ventilation. Since this tower was isolated, it needed no envelope of space; in fact, however, the wider mezzanine extending under the base of the tower does provide this. The two open storeys, one at ground level and one above the mezzanine, give a lightness of effect and a frank view of the essential structure that is even more striking than at Lever House, where the relation of the towering slab to the mezzanine is less boldly handled.[7a]

European skyscrapers[8] as yet rarely rivalled North American ones in height, and few large urban office buildings reached even the median level of quality of those in Latin America. In rebuilding bombed cities, however, there were opportunities that could readily be exploited for carrying certain buildings very high over a portion only of their sites, as was first done in North America at Lever House, but using the ampler spaces provided by the replanning of the cities to extend lower blocks from the main slab. One prominent example then of this treatment was the Continental Rubber Building of 1952-3 in Hanover by Werner Dierschke and Ernst Zinsser, which replaced Behrens's ponderous block of thirty years earlier that was destroyed in the war. The surface materials, mostly various stones, are serviceable and the general composition well studied, but the proportions lack the elegant lightness of the Edificio Polar. Yet the whole achieved a 'reality' of effect lacking in the C.B.I. in São Paulo, which looks, despite its great size, rather like a cardboard model; or Lever House, which too much resembles a slick cellophane-wrapped package. Some Ger-

man commercial work at smaller scale was more refined, as, for example, the Haus der Glas-Industrie of 1951 at Düsseldorf by Bernhard Pfau and Pempelfort Haus there of 1954 by Hentrich & Petschnigg,[8a] or the Burda-Moden Building of the same date in Offenburg by Egon Eiermann. Hentrich & Petschnigg were also responsible for the BASF skyscraper at Ludwigshafen, the tallest built in the Old World up to the mid fifties.

Early post-war Italian commercial work was more varied and imaginative than in other countries, but the tallest examples were not the best. Very often it was the fine marble or mosaic surfacing – echoed in the BASF – and the high quality of the craftsmanship that seemed to give them interest and an effect of luxury rarely yet found in other countries, rather than real distinction of design. Interestingly enough, since post-war Latin America then tended to follow Italian models, one of the best Italian buildings of this decade, the Olivetti offices in Milan of 1954-5 by G. A. Bernasconi, Annibale Fiocchi (b. 1915), and M. Nizzoli, has a very Latin American air because of its prominent sun-breaks. This was one of the few buildings premiated by the international jury at the São Paulo Biennal in 1957, and the only non-Brazilian one.

Industrial construction had not even then been as fully accepted into the realm of architecture as had commercial building for the past hundred years. Ever since the factories of Behrens and the warehouses of Perret, however, industrial commissions were playing an increasingly important part in modern architectural production. Probably the largest acreage of good factory-building just after the war, as earlier in the century, was in North America. With rising standards of amenity, moreover, and the substitution of road haulage for rail transportation, factories came out from behind the railway tracks and took their proper place visually as well as functionally, with well-maintained grounds as important features, in regional planning. It was hard to single out particular factories for mention, if only because their design, whether it was by engineers or by specialist architectural firms like Albert Kahn, Inc., had arrived at a largely anonymous standardization – the fate, incidentally, towards which some critics still see all twentieth-century architecture as inevitably moving.

The General Motors Technical Institute at Warren, Mich., completed by Eero Saarinen in 1955 after a decade of planning and construction, is almost more comparable in scale and complexity to a university city than to a factory; yet this group of twenty-five buildings organized round a large rectangular artificial lake is also in its use and in its character a major example of American industrial building raised at the behest of a corporate client into the realm of distinguished architecture [346, 347].

Little or no link remained between this and even the latest buildings designed by Eliel Saarinen on which his son collaborated, although the former was involved in this commission down to his death in 1950. Instead, the influence of Mies was very strong, since in the younger Saarinen's estimation at that point the Miesian discipline was most suitable to give order to such a project, in terms both of over-all planning and of the characteristic structural vocabulary of curtain-walling. Yet the necessary variety of size and shape of the buildings, determined in part by the very different activities that they house, from power-houses and engine-test cells to the Styling Centre for new motor-car models, made impossible the imposition of so classic a pattern as Mies had aimed to produce at the Illinois Institute of Technology [325]. In conscious avoidance of the monotony of the motor-car factories around Detroit, which run on without modification for

346. Eero Saarinen: Warren, Mich.,
General Motors Technical Institute, 1951–5

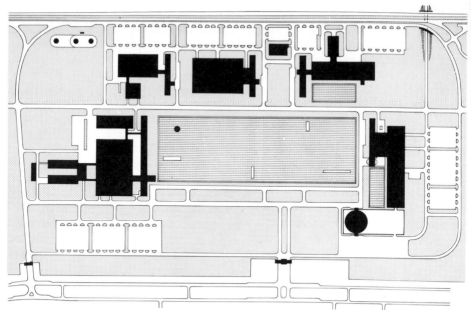

347. Saarinen & Saarinen: Warren, Mich.,
General Motors Technical Institute, 1946-55

thousands of feet, and in pursuit of ideals which most modern planners have realized only on paper, Eero Saarinen accented his long lake-front with a water-tower all of stainless steel rising out of the water and provided a special domed unit at the south end to house the display of new models beside the one section of the complex to which the outside world had some access. Moreover, he varied the characteristic metal-and-glass vocabulary of the façades – the metal in general black oxidized aluminium, the glass greenish in tone to reduce glare in the interiors – with solid walls of glazed brick in various brilliant colours, almost rivalling the Mexicans in the intensity of the reds, blues, yellows, and greens that he chose. As with the later Connecticut General plant, sculpture of distinction, here by Antoine Pevsner, provides a note of humane interest amid all the expression of mechanistic efficiency.

In Europe the Olivetti Company were more consistent patrons of distinguished design in architecture than General Motors. The main plant at Ivrea, designed by Figini & Pollini, is small by American standards, and has been in existence for some time – since 1942. It was chiefly notable because it was the heart, as it was the *raison d'etre*, of an architectural programme of almost urbanistic scope at Ivrea that was long in process of realization by Figini & Pollini, the resident architect Fiocchi, and others. Fiocchi's small foundry of 1954-5 is an exemplary industrial unit of almost Miesian elegance. Characteristic then of most Latin countries were the sun-breaks on the south-west side of the large Ivrea factory; while the north-east façade rises four storeys in sheer glass like a vast extension of Gropius's studio block at the Bauhaus. Some ten or fifteen years later, and better sited, more articulated, and more self-complete, is the Olivetti factory at Pozzuoli near Naples by Luigi Cosenza. Structurally, however, the industrial work of the engineer Nervi is more original.

Factories were still more likely to be designed by engineers than by architects; but the contribution of engineers to their design was by no means always standardized and monotonous. Particularly in those countries where the lack of steel encouraged the use of ferro-concrete, engineers were devising notably imaginative solutions to the problems of space-coverage and lighting. The Spanish-born engineer Candela in Mexico worked with ferro-concrete vaults in industrial construction with the casual ease and *ad hoc* ingenuity of a twelfth-century Frenchman building in stone; yet his church of Nuestra Señora de los Milagros of 1953–5 gave the impression of being a reversion to Expressionism, despite the unassailable mathematical and structural logic of the hyperbolic paraboloid forms of its 'ruled surfaces'. The Italian-born José Delpini, in such factories as his S.I.T. Spinning Shed of 1949–50 at Pilar in Argentina, easily rivalled the work of the leading modern architects of Argentina in the distinction as in the scale of his buildings. The Danish-born Ove Arup in England, working with the Architects Co-Partnership on the artificial rubber factory at Bryn Mawr in Wales, provided one of the first notable large-scale buildings in post-war Great Britain, and deserved much of the credit for it. To return to the work of architects, it should be noted that in England, where most post-war industrial building was rather modest in size, the power-stations of Farmer & Dark, culminating in that of 1955–7 at Marchwood, have a grandeur of scale and a logic of partially open design that ordinary factories can almost never rival.

Industrial building, still at the frontier of architecture despite the great contribution it had made to more general developments since the English mills of the 1790s, was notably international in its twentieth-century standards and its achievements. The leading industrial firms, such as Albert Kahn, Inc., and that of Frankland Dark, were asked to build in many parts of the world, for the traditions of the old-established technologies were of especial value in such work. The continued existence of cultural empires, so to call them, was still made manifest when English firms built powerhouses and factories in the Middle and Far East. James Cubitt & Partners[9] completed in Rangoon in 1955, for example, a pharmaceutical plant that was then probably the largest post-war factory of architectural interest yet built by an English firm, just as their Technical College at Kumasi in Ghana, built at the same time, was a more considerable example of a mid-twentieth-century university city than England had yet seen.[9a]

The provision of housing by organs of the State had come to be recognized almost everywhere as an essential social service, quite as modern architects always insisted that it should be. Le Corbusier's Unité at Marseilles was doubtless still the most striking example of the tall structures, slabs or 'point-blocks', which were increasingly the characteristic form of such housing, but the most notable general programmes of production were still found in England, in certain Latin American countries, and in Denmark and Sweden. The pressure of population-growth and the need for rebuilding after war-time destruction motivated such programmes almost everywhere, but in several countries notable otherwise for the high standard of their current architecture – the United States and Italy, for example – the results were disappointing indeed. A strong social tradition of public housing, moreover, as in Holland, even with the precedent there of the notably fine work of thirty and forty years ago, seemed then to be no guarantee of continued excellence in this field.[9b] Although the rising popularity of

348. London County Council Architect's Office:
London, Loughborough Road housing estate, 1954-6

housing in such tall structures was balanced in England by a continuing attachment to houses built in pairs or in terraces, such as comprised the greater part of the first New Towns, English achievement in this field on the whole exceeded that of most other countries in the ten years after the war, both in quantity and in quality. The post-war pace was set by the Churchill Gardens of A. J. Philip Powell (b. 1921) and his partner Hidalgo Moya in Pimlico, London, for which the Westminster Borough Council was the client. For over a decade the planning and building of this vast urban project went forward towards completion with rising standards of design and finish. Perhaps the finest single block is De Quincey House, with its ingenious section of duplexes approached by access galleries. But the Architect's Department of the London County Council, under the successive leadership of Robert Matthew (b. 1906) and of Sir Leslie Martin (b. 1908), within a few years had equalled and perhaps exceeded in quality, as

many times over in quantity, the achievement of Powell & Moya. Whether on urban sites, such as that at Loughborough Road in South London [348], or on more open sites, as at the Ackroydon estate in Putney or at Roehampton, by the combination of tall blocks, some square in plan, some slab-like, with ranges of lower blocks of maisonettes and terraces of houses the L.C.C. had provided - piecemeal at least - examples of mid-twentieth-century urbanism more impressive than anything the New Towns yet offered. A provincial English example of comparable excellence is the Tile Hill Estate outside Coventry by the Borough Architect's Office.[9c]

The forty-eight slabs of the Cerro Piloto development of 1955 built by the Banco Obrero, the Venezuelan public housing corporation, and designed by Guido Bermudez (b. 1925), rising against the mountains outside Caracas more than rival in extent and in scale the English examples. And in the Cerro Grande blocks of flats there, built in 1953-5, Bermudez rivalled the ingenuity of Powell & Moya and the L.C.C. in the use of duplexes. Interesting for the mixture of types – tall slabs, lower blocks of flats, and houses – is the Centro Urbano Presidente Juarez in Mexico City by Mario Pani (b. 1901); the handsome colours used here were chosen by the painter Carlos

design of tall housing blocks. In particular, the Hertfordshire County Architect's Office under C. H. Aslin (1893-1959) developed a system of construction using a light-metal skeleton and prefabricated concrete slabs that was of considerable interest. Not all the Hertfordshire schools were designed in the County Archi-

349. James Cubitt & Partners:
Langleybury, Hertfordshire, school, 1955-6

Mérida. But the most exemplary of the Latin American estates is Pedregulho outside Rio de Janeiro begun in 1948 by Affonso Eduardo Reidy (b. 1909). Here the tall serpentine block at the rear is entered at middle level from the hill slope, a scheme suggested by certain of Le Corbusier's projects of the thirties for North Africa, and various community buildings provide something of New Town character in the development, as does a range of low blocks with shops at their base[9d] in the Tile Hill Estate at Coventry. Most notable is Reidy's school at Pedregulho with its murals of *azulejos* – glazed tiles – by Cándido Portinari and its characteristic repertory of the architectural forms of the Cariocan School. Of that Reidy, a member of the original group who designed and built the Ministry of Education, was as much one of the founders as Oscar Niemeyer.

In the mid twentieth century, however, it was England that led in school design and construction even more definitely than in the

tect's office, however, and some of the best were by private architects, such as the Architects' Co-Partnership and James Cubitt & Partners[349]. The new architecture was already perhaps more widely used for schools than for most other types of buildings. Outside England those of Donald Barthelmé in Texas, such as his Elementary School at West Columbia of 1952, and by Ernest J. Kump (b. 1911) in California could be especially noted, although they represented no such concerted programme of design and construction as spread in England from Hertfordshire to other parts of the country. Outright 'traditional' schools were rare anywhere by this time.

In church architecture the post-war situation was rather different. Although Perret and Wright, Moser and Böhm, among the older generation of modern architects, all built notable new churches, till Le Corbusier's Notre-Dame-du-Haut at Ronchamp the international leaders of the next generation were rarely called on to design them; and from Oud's church of the late twenties at Oud Mathenesse through Mies's Chapel of 1952 at the Illinois Institute of Technology it seemed that the extreme rationalism of these men made it difficult if not impossible for them to provide ecclesiastical edifices which differed in any expressive way from meeting-halls. Something was said earlier of the more emotional sort of church architecture of Böhm[9e] and the line of related development in the 1930s and 40s from the semi-traditional, somewhat Gothic or Baroque, effects of the twenties to work of completely original character. Niemeyer's São Francisco at Pampulha [350], completed in 1943, was one of the buildings that early established his reputation among the most imaginative architects of his generation anywhere in the world. Soon Latin American churches as different as Candela's Nuestra Señora de los Milagros in Mexico City and the unvaulted Beato Martin Porres at Cataño

outside San Juan in Puerto Rico by Henry Klumb (b. 1905), a pupil of Wright, were illustrating a wider range of possibilities; while Juvenal Moya's Nuestra Señora de Fatimá and his chapel at the Ginnásio Moderno in Bogotá, the one of 1953–4, the other of 1954–5, followed – with considerable vulgarization – the more lyrical line of Niemeyer's São Francisco.

Less operatic, but doubtless better adapted to Protestant use, were the churches in the American Northwest by Belluschi, notably the First Presbyterian of 1951 at Cottage Grove in Oregon. Various Swiss churches, some Catholic but more of them Protestant, followed also in this line, to which such earlier-mentioned churches as Moser's Sankt Antonius in Basel of 1927 and the elder Saarinen's Christ Lutheran, Minneapolis, of 1948 belong [294]. The younger Saarinen's silo-like circular chapel of red brick at the Massachusetts Institute of Technology of 1954–5, however,

350. Oscar Niemeyer:
Pampulha, São Francisco, 1943

reverted to something much more emotional. There was great ingenuity in the handling of the lighting which streams down from above over a screen by Harry Bertoia and also penetrates more subtly round the edges of the low-arched base through the water of a surrounding moat.

Johnson in a synagogue in Port Chester, N.Y., of 1955-6, still severe in its general character, introduced coloured glass in slots between the vertical slabs with which the visible steel frame is filled and also a curved awning-like ceiling of plaster to warm and enrich the basically Miesian paradigm. Accessories by the sculptor Ibrahim Lassaw also play an important part in the interior; while the oval domed entrance vestibule is an element of almost Baroque formal interest despite its ascetic simplicity of execution. Thus, two of Mies's disciples offered in their ecclesiastical work correctives to the classroom-like coldness of his own chapel in Chicago.

Such large-scale constructions as factories and tall housing blocks, together with skyscrapers, represented the new architecture's preoccupation with building problems that the nineteenth century had already essayed, but of which the development had not as yet perhaps been carried to its logical extremes either technically or architecturally. Curiously enough, in the provision of new edifices to serve the needs of transportation, the nineteenth century in its middle decades was rather more successful in bringing the railway station to early maturity than the mid twentieth century was with the airport. One of the largest and finest post-war buildings of Italy is the Rome railway station [351], and within a few years the active campaign of modernizing and rebuilding stations in Italy was for a while reflected in other European countries. But airports had still to find so satisfactory an expression, partly because the expansion of

351. Eugenio Montuori and others:
Rome, Termini Station, completed 1951

traffic everywhere made them inadequate almost before they were completed. Too often the necessity for continual extension then destroyed such integrity of conception as the architects were able to give them in the first place. Some of the world's busiest, such as Kennedy near New York and Midway near Chicago, became already in the nineteen-fifties near-shambles beside which century-old railway stations appeared as masterpieces of up-to-date organization! Here, as in many other fields of mid-century building, there seemed to be two main lines of approach, but not properly distinguishable as 'rational' versus 'emotional', since both were almost entirely dependent on particular structural solutions. Of the first sort a relatively early example (which by then carried only local traffic and therefore did not have to be expanded), the Santos Dumont Airport by the Roberto brothers begun in 1938 and largely completed after 1944 at the bay's edge in downtown Rio de Janeiro, remained one of the best; for it was compactly planned, clear and direct in design, and elegant in the choice of materials and the use of colour. The San Juan Airport completed in 1955 by Torro, Ferrer & Torregrossa[10] in Puerto Rico was larger and somewhat less refined in detail, but an excellent example of planning in terms of circulation. Gibberd's vast London Airport was then still incomplete.

Two other airports of much the same date, the very large one at St Louis by Minoru Yamasaki (b. 1912) and Joseph W. Leinweber, and the small one by Pani and his partner Enrique del Moral at Acapulco, used concrete shell vaults with very dramatic effect. It could seem that the 'classic' stage of airport design, reached in railway stations between 1845 and 1855, was at last beginning in the late fifties, and its climax lay many years ahead, if, indeed, it has yet been reached.[10a]

From the airport to the individual dwelling, from the newest sort of structure to what is presumably the oldest, represents a considerable jump. Yet it is at least debatable whether the best houses of the mid twentieth century, continuing a line of development that has earlier been traced forward from 1800 (see Chapter 15), were not more satisfactory solutions of the problems their designing and building poses, both practically and aesthetically, than any of the airports mentioned. To a considerable extent they were as novel.[11] The dwelling may not, in the years after 1925, have developed primarily as a 'machine for living in', according to Le Corbusier's famous phrase, but it certainly became more and more a 'box for housing machinery in'. As the relative proportion of the total cost spent for mechanical equipment went up, the shell had to shrink. As the shell shrank, planning was increasingly simplified. Only rarely was the ultimate in unification of space reached, as in Mies's Farnsworth house or Philip Johnson's own house in New Canaan, Conn. [352],[11a] where only the bathroom is enclosed and the other subdivisions of the interior are but ranges of cupboards not reaching to the ceiling. Equally rare was the exclusively glass walling of these houses, clearly the extreme point of a *crescendo* that goes back at least to the window-walls of the third quarter of the nineteenth century. But if they represented the end-point of several developments, from which there was later a return even on the part of their own architects [356], the extremes that they illustrated were in many respects those towards which houses in general still seemed to be tending.

The house as a detached, individually-designed edifice was still for most people the ideal dwelling. But at no time since 1800 had such a dwelling been more of a luxury. Convenience and economy drove rich and poor alike towards more communal forms of habitation, whether they were the cabañas of the millionaires' motels at Palm Springs or the compact flats in suburban 'point-blocks'. In

352. Philip C. Johnson: New Canaan, Conn.,
the architect's own house, 1949-50

between these poles were all the varieties of
terrace-housing, 'semi-detachery', and builders'
standardized products, ranging from simplified
parodies of late traditional houses of a generation before through various vulgarizations of
more modern design to the prefabricated pack-
age-dwelling which still seemed little nearer to
receiving the general acceptance which would
make it economical than it was a hundred years
earlier. Mass housing, no matter what form it
took, whether the forty-eight tall slabs of the
Cerro Piloto or the forty-eight hundred, more
or less, semi-detached two-storey dwellings of
and English housing estate, belonged increas-

ingly to the world of bureaucratized architecture. The house, on the other hand, conceived as an individualized entity, remained
almost as much a specialized and exceptional
product as the church; yet the changes first
made in individual houses gradually affected
all housing standards. Particularly in North
and South America they still provided architectural opportunities of the greatest interest
and variety. Most Latin American houses,
for example, retained the semi-oriental ideals
of seclusion of the Iberian tradition; yet behind
the walls to cut out the world surrounding their
plots they were often opener than houses in

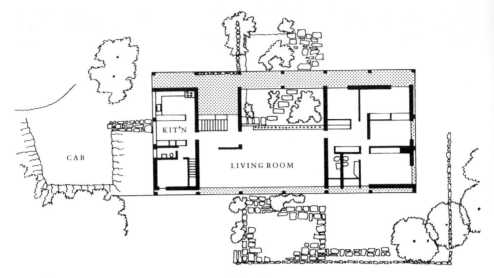

353. Osvaldo Arthur Bratke: São Paulo, Morumbí, Bratke house, 1953

354. Philip Johnson: Wayzata, Minn., Richard S. Davis house, 1954

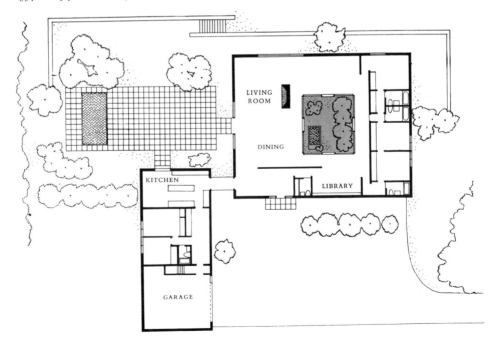

the United States, since a warm climate makes of the patio or garden the principal living area. Niemeyer's own house of 1954 at Gávea outside Rio de Janeiro is almost as much a glass box as Mies's or Johnson's, although its glass walls are set under a slab whose outline is a continuous free curve. The house of Osvaldo Arthur Bratke (b. 1907) at 3008 Avenida Morumbí outside São Paulo was also closer in plan and conception to houses in the United States, protection of various sorts being provided by grilles and movable shutters [353].

But there was much variety in mid-century house-design in Latin America, ranging all the way from such Mexican houses as those of Francisco Artigas (b. 1916) or Sordo Madaleno that present a blank wall to the street and yet open up completely to a patio or a garden, to Niemeyer's open pavilion at Gávea. In North America there was even wider diversity. Despite the equalization of climate, by that time readily provided by heating and cooling facilities, there were still great differences between one region and another in the forces of nature that must be controlled or protected against, from the insects and hurricanes of Florida to the blizzards of Minnesota, than between the various countries of Latin America. Johnson's Davis house at Wayzata in Minnesota was enclosed, however, not because of the climate, but in order to provide hanging space for an art collection, while it opened within on to a patio that can be roofed in winter [354]. Neither screening nor anchorage against high winds was conspicuous in the design of most of the Florida houses of Paul Rudolph (b. 1918). On the West Coast the aberrant casualness of the Bay Region manner of the thirties and forties became for a while increasingly disciplined. Wooden construction, pitched roofs, and a certain discursiveness of planning still contrasted, however, with more rigidly Miesian design; yet some of the houses of Joseph Esherick in and around San Francisco or of

John Yeon in Portland, Ore., to mention only two of the then West Coast architects, rivalled in distinction the later works of Johnson and Rudolph [355-7].

Whether the building of individual houses in other countries would ever again have the significance it still retained in the New World depended on many extra-architectural factors.

355. Philip C. Johnson: New Haven, Conn., Yale University, Kline Science Tower, 1962-5

The last thing a historian should pretend with regard to this or to any other aspect of the near-future is that he is capable of prophecy. The history of architecture in the second half of this century can only be written much later. The glimpses – for they are no more than that –

in the mid 1950s, no such point at which to end. From Wright, then ninety, to men two generations younger, some of whom were mentioned in this chapter, the work of the architects of the western world showed as yet no convincing evidence of a major and general

356. Philip C. Johnson:
New Canaan, Conn., Boissonnas house, 1955-6

of early post-war production given here represented a critic's and not an historian's selection, and a selection that was inevitably much influenced by what that critic then knew at first hand. It will be evident that he had lately returned from South America!

*

Despite the obligation to provide in the Introduction some sort of eighteenth-century foundation, this book had a real historical turning-point for its actual beginning; it had,

turn, however surprising in the light of his work of the twenties Le Corbusier's church at Ronchamp might seem. Perforce we stop in mid-stream and even the later Epilogue of the sixties which follows provided no true peroration. Fortunately the contemporary history of architecture was being recorded more promptly and completely than ever before in the professional press. Yet when one leaves the world of history for the world of 'current events', the time has come to turn from books to periodicals.

357. Paul Rudolph: New Haven, Conn., Yale University, Art and Architecture Building, 1959-63

In the original Bibliography there were naturally few 'monographs' – i.e. books or summary articles – devoted to the men first mentioned in this chapter, since many were then at the outset of their careers.[12]

From Papworth's 'Cottage Orné' [211] to the slabs of Loughborough Road [348] – 'model' dwellings both; from the Bank of England to Thyssen Haus [366], both housing business as it was never housed before the period with which this book deals; from Baltimore Cathedral [8] to Notre-Dame-du-Haut [324], the range of notable achievement recorded in this book is not readily outranked in variety by any other period of the same duration in the history of the western world. As to the absolute quality of that achievement, as distinguished from what may be called the 'plot'-interest of various relatively coherent developments continuing over the last two centuries, it requires a very catholic taste indeed even to pretend to pronounce. The 'revivals' of the nineteenth century and the 'traditionalism' of the twentieth century accepted the dangerous challenge of meeting the earlier past on its own ground, and this in itself was enough to reduce the absolute value of much nineteenth- and twentieth-century production. Yet there were renaissances long before there were revivals; and at almost any given moment of the past most production has been the equivalent in stylistic retardation of the traditional architecture of the twentieth century. If one must have originality, these hundred and fifty years have not lacked it, from Ledoux and Soane to Gaudí and Wright. Of the hundreds of names mentioned in these twenty-five chapters there are few doubtless equal to Bramante or to Bernini, but how many were there in the preceding hundred and fifty years? while the variety of approach represented, from a Schinkel to a Le Corbusier, from a Butterfield to a Mies, is hardly to be equalled in any comparable period of history. Above all, this is the stage of architectural history that lies between the unhallowed present and the hallowed past, between the cultural certainties – if they were so certain – of the eighteenth century and the cultural anxieties of the present. What we are we can only hope to understand by exploring the immediate ancestry of our own present. Only revivalists could afford to denigrate and ignore all that lay between them and some 'golden age' they sought to emulate. The future must build upon the foundations – so very various, so often nearly contradictory – of the architecture of the preceding two hundred years.

EPILOGUE

The years since the original edition of this book appeared in 1958 saw a building boom throughout the western world such as has never been equalled in earlier centuries; nor was this boom confined to those countries of Europe and the Americas with which this account had chiefly been concerned. These were also years of continuing – indeed even increasing – uncertainty in architectural doctrine. As might have been expected, various tendencies already touched on in the preceding chapter – both positive (although often apparently reactionary) tendencies towards greater individuality, and negative or, at least in the present context, conservative tendencies towards somewhat tired repetition of clichés of the 1930s – not only continued but became much stronger. Yet the tonality of the overall picture of current architectural production had, even by the early sixties, already changed. That relative balance between what might, at their best, be called the Miesian and the Corbusian, still maintained almost everywhere in the mid fifties, had been upset. In hindsight, for example, it already seemed that such mature and established architects as Alvar Aalto and Louis Kahn [358][1] had been inadequately treated in previous chapters – not to speak of

358. Louis I. Kahn: La Jolla, Cal., Salk Center Laboratories, 1961–5

such still older men whose activity had continued or been renewed as the Germans Hans Scharoun and Rudolf Schwarz. Various new names called for attention also: the Dutchman Aldo van Eyck, for example, the Norwegian Sverre Fehn, the Japanese Tange and Maekawa [364, 365], the Italian Viganò, and the English firm of Stirling & Gowan, to mention but a few that were all but unknown internationally in the mid fifties whose work was in the 1960s of rising consequence. Already other names might be even more apposite, but merely to list names has little interest.[1a]

For all the evidence of change, it was almost as difficult as it was ten years before to isolate the common denominator of the new tendencies except in negative terms. It was still easier to be explicit about what architects were moving away from – what they were rejecting – than whither they were headed. Any attempt in a few words to describe positively the architectural climate of around 1960 faced the difficulty that only in certain extreme works were novel architectural ideas wholly dominant; while by no means all the current building of that decade that did *not* follow in the newer directions, either by older architects such as Mies himself or by those who stayed faithful to his canons – whether intentionally or by default of any alternative allegiance – could be dismissed as merely vulgar, provincial, or *retardataire*.

The rejection of the advanced doctrines of the 1920s and 1930s has rarely yet been total.[2] The assumption of some writers, moreover, that there had been any serious and concerted return to Beaux-Arts or other pre-modern

359. Alvar Aalto: Säynatsälo, Municipal Buildings, 1951–3

360 *(opposite)*. Alvar Aalto: Muuratsälo, architect's own house, 1953

standards was, and still is, as regards the attitude of most mature architects – even those who actually have such backgrounds – something of an exaggeration. On the other hand, the particular sensibilities to which architects such as Aalto and Kahn, at least, had been successfully appealing – and in Aalto's case for some thirty years already – were certainly very different from the sensibilities that once responded to the clean geometries, the smooth surfaces, the glass walls, and the minimal detailing of the Bauhaus [305], the Savoye house [302], and the Barcelona Pavilion [311]. 'Neo-Brutalism', or *brutalismo*,[3] was as dangerous a term to use indiscriminately as any other critical catchword that had been prematurely popularized. But it did suggest, at least by a play upon words in several languages, a current climate of taste that favoured *béton brut* – naked concrete – and rough, usually rather dark-coloured, materials. Bricks, pre-cast slabs with a coarse aggregate in relief, or even stone masonry of rubble or quarry-faced granite, with rather heavy trim of raw or varnished wood and wrought iron, came to be widely preferred to the slicker, more highly finished elements that are the natural product of the increasing industrialization of the building crafts. But this was literally superficial.

Associated with the notable shift of preference as regards the texture of the skin, so to say, of buildings there was also a comparable rise of interest in broken silhouettes, uneven sky-lines, masses that were articulated rather than unified, and expressive exposure of individual structural elements, themselves often sculptural rather than mechanistic in character.

This affected in varying degree the work of almost all architects from the most Corbusian to the most Miesian. Windows, moreover, tended to be fewer and smaller, and their shapes were likely to be vertical rather than horizontal, slots instead of ribbons. So also plans often emphasized the particularity of various internal functions and over-all organization tended towards additive compilation of contiguous spatial units, in some cases equal or modular, in others disparate in both size and shape. All this would once have been disapproved by most critics as under-studied, not to say amateurish, before Aalto's mature work became a major international influence [359, 360].[3a] There was surely some reflection of the painting and the sculpture of the previous decade, even perhaps of its most advanced music, in a few architects' attempts to suggest free-hand improvisation and randomness in an art whose works, however their designing may have been initiated, are necessarily in the end products of relatively long periods of preparatory study and of complex collaborative execution.

Yet to hazard such statements as these, even though they long applied to much of the work of Aalto and were also true in varying degree of the production of architects as different in many basic ways as the Frenchman Guillaume Gillet or the Italian Franco Albini, is to be reminded of the prevalence of another kind of interest in more elaborate effects of detail – often denigrated as merely decorative – that has been exploited not only by such well-established architects as the Americans Edward Stone or Minoru Yamasaki, on the one hand, and by the German Egon Eiermann, on the other – otherwise quite opposed as a result of their very different training, experience, and personal dispositions – but by many others from Latin America to Asia and Africa.

It could, however, be said in very simple terms that what became recognized as the newest architecture had two aspects, one exaggeratedly masculine, the other almost daintily feminine. Both kinds have even been illustrated, in a curious kind of rhythmic alternation, by successive works of certain architects; both contrasted with the neutral severity of the architecture of the immediately preceding period. Yet both clearly had their half-admitted precedents in the varied and even contradictory work over many decades of Frank Lloyd Wright and that of the Expressionists half a century ago.

Even if it could be accepted in the sixties that these two tendencies represented the whole story, few are impartial enough to admit that they were *equally* characteristic of the more serious architectural production of the decade. Thanks to a revival of near-Puritanical asceticism in some quarters, sharply contrasting with the readiness in others to beguile with somewhat saccharine 'beauty', the more masculine aspect was often presented as superior morally and even as more 'advanced'; for there were still those ready, as in the 1920s and 1930s, to plead near-Hegelian necessities for one or another direction in which architecture might be moving, necessities that were often really in patent opposition to the actual pressures from the aesthetically neutral realm of technology.

But the two aspects so far noted did not, in any case, even suggest the full complexity of the situation. A third, not necessarily related to the other two yet also, possibly, subsuming both, has been more evident to historians than to most architects. Admitting the danger of pressing analogies with the morphology of earlier periods – the Gothic, say, or the Renaissance – there is at least a presumption that what we long knew as 'modern architecture' had entered (rather prematurely, it must seem) a 'late' phase. Recurrent in late phases there have usually been two distinguishable but often closely related aspects of academicism: a return towards principles that dominated the arts before the stylistic revolution with which the particular cycle began, on the one hand, and on the other the reduction to an easily applied system of formal elements of the painfully evolved features that were peculiar to the preceding 'high' phase.

But reaction, to give this aspect of the architectural scene in the sixties an unnecessarily denigratory name, was quite likely in particular instances to be more due to the special circumstances of the decade's building boom than to any hypothetical life-pattern of modern architecture. In the first half of the twentieth century economic influences were supposed, at least, to favour both technological advance in the building sciences and, concomitantly, 'advanced' design in the aesthetic sense. Not always, however, were the theoretical economies actually realized – or not, at any rate, before considerable time had passed – and 'advanced' design often proved in practice not only expensive but physically uncomfortable. Then other kinds of technological development, by setting up even more expensive new standards of amenity, notably in such things as vertical transport, glare-control, and air conditioning, often cancelled out the economies that mechanized methods of large-scale production had eventually made real. At the same time the inherent practical difficulties of such things as all-glass walls and completely open plans were increasingly realized as they were ever more generally and uncritically exploited. By the 1960s some of the technical improvements in building advocated since the 1920s, notably in the field of partial prefabrication and prefabrication of larger and larger components – whole sides of houses and flats, for example – had become widely viable, not to speak of new materials and structural methods that made certain features relatively easy and inexpensive to provide. Yet total prefabrication of dwelling units was remoter from realization – except in mobile units such as caravans[3b] – than a quarter of a century earlier, in part because the public's willingness to accept the mechanization of house-production seemed actually, in many countries, to have diminished despite the failure to catch up with the growing need for new housing.

The major building problems of the post-war world were not the occasional production of individual monuments: opera houses, churches, stadia, and the like, on which professional as well as public attention tends to focus and for which drastically new kinds of architectural expression were most readily invented. What was more significant was the large-scale reconstruction of bombed or blighted cities, the rehousing of very considerable segments of the population, and the provision of the manufacturing facilities, the offices, and the stores required by greater industrial, financial, and commercial activity. Inevitably, in a boom period, the very large volume of production over large sectors of the total range of building led, in such work, to a sort of stasis in stylistic development. A vast amount of architectural energy everywhere had to go into the mere carrying out of unprecedentedly extensive plans the major decisions for which were made as long as fifteen or twenty years before. An inertial lag was still evident wherever large urban areas, whether cleared thirty years before by bombing or in the last decade by schemes of urban renewal, were being rebuilt. Large parts of the world outside North America, moreover, had been learning how to build very tall structures and were only beginning to modify creatively what they learned.

The two decades before 1970, the fifties and the sixties, saw the production of a great part of the urban and suburban settings in which we will probably be living for the rest of this century, and doubtless well into the next. Somewhat as the post-Napoleonic period carried out at an ever lower level of quality the ambitions and aspirations of the revolutionary architects of the later eighteenth century, so the post-war years – and particularly the sixties and early seventies – saw the realization of many urbanistic ideals that seemed fantastic or Utopian when they were first proposed some fifty years ago. Inevitably there was a diminution of visual interest when certain modes of design, first adumbrated in a few unique individual structures or in relatively modest housing projects in the 1920s by architects of intense conviction and high inventive power, were applied wholesale, almost as clichés, by countless other less able and less dedicated men throughout the whole world including Communist countries. Moreover, confusions in the original ideals, only recognizable as those ideals came to large-scale actuality, were discovered and denounced. To some critics certain earlier urban conditions, against whose vices those ideals were first invoked as correctives, came to seem, by nostalgia, preferable in various human ways to the 'brave new world' of the 1920s which, to such a surprising extent, became the real world of the 1960s and early 70s.

But the reaction against the International Style, thus to describe in over-simplified form what seemed to be the consensus of many of the changes of attitude in the last twenty years, was not even yet a real counter-revolution. If the canons of the permissible and the desirable were broadened by current theory and practice towards various aspects of what may still be called the traditional – including, as by now also traditional, much that was common to various pre- or extra-International Style aspects of earlier modern architecture – certain of the presuppositions of the most advanced architects of the 1920s could still seem, though usually in revised form, quite as forward-looking as ever. For the rather limited aspects of function recognized by the Functionalists (if there ever were architects truly meriting that name), for example, far more sophisticated conceptions of function came to be accepted by most architects,

even those whose fields of work were industrial or commercial.

Yet some engineers – the Italian Nervi, whose practice became international in scope, the late Spaniard Torroja, the Mexican Candela, the Danish Arup, and the American Fuller, to mention but a few of the best known – have acquired reputations throughout the architectural profession, and even with laymen, which neither the Swiss Maillart, the Frenchman Freyssinet, nor any others had sixty years ago with architects or public. None the less, the control of architecture was not more largely in the hands of the engineers than earlier despite many prognoses, both pessimistic and optimistic, that the engineers were, or should be, taking over. Moreover the architectural quality, as distinguished from the technical ingenuity, of the works of the great engineers was often as notable as is that of those buildings by certain architects in which engineering principles were reputedly dominant such as Eero Saarinen's Chantilly airport [369].

These paragraphs are necessarily of the most general nature and critical rather than historical. Properly they should be illustrated by a considerable body of carefully described photographs, plans, and sections such as fortunately can be found in several books covering either the whole world, or single countries, individual architects, or particular types of building in this period. Some of the most useful of those that had appeared by the spring of 1967 will be found among the additions to the Bibliography. The few plates that it was possible to add in the third edition could not hope to present a conspectus of the various aspects of the situation in the sixties that were at least mentioned in this Epilogue. But the illustrations of the Seagram Building [361] and the Guggenheim

361. Ludwig Mies van der Rohe
and Philip C. Johnson:
New York, Seagram Building, 1956-8

362 and 363. Frank Lloyd Wright: New York, Guggenheim Museum, (1943-6), 1956-9

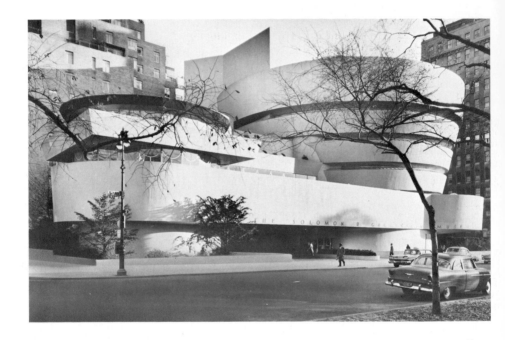

364. Kenzo Tange: Totsuka, Country Club, *c.* 1960

365 *(below)*. Kunio Maekawa:
Tokyo, Metropolitan Festival Hall, 1961

366 *(right)*. Hentrich & Petschnigg:
Düsseldorf, Thyssen Haus, 1958–60

Museum[3c] [362, 363] may underline that some of the dichotomies of the third quarter of this century in architecture could, at least by the late 1950s, be almost as well illustrated in the work of long-recognized masters of architecture as in that of men a generation or more younger. The illustrations of the work of Aalto, work actually of an earlier date, show clearly whence one of the winds of influence had for some time been blowing; while the two Japanese buildings [364, 365] in contrast to the Thyssen Haus [366] illustrate the international Corbusian and the international Miesian of the early sixties at levels that are notably high, both in the size and prominence of the structures and in intrinsic quality. Illustration 367 shows a late work of Le Corbusier.[3d]

Throughout its length this book has been less concerned with urbanism, with the architectural macrocosm, than with individual buildings; nor, for that matter, can photographs give the feeling of the newly rebuilt central and peripheral areas of our cities even as well as for the nineteenth century. The character of the Ludwigstrasse [23] or the Place de l'Opéra [121] can be fairly well apprehended from photographs; Park Avenue above the Grand Central Station, as rebuilt beginning with Lever House [345] in the last twenty years, or the cities, as distinguished from the individual public monu-

588

ments, of Chandigarh, Brasilia, and Islamabad
– or even Cumbernauld in Scotland or Reston
in the United States – cannot.

Despite all the confusion of architectural
doctrine in the 1960s, despite the vast areas of
undistinguished and even manifestly bad building, that decade did see its share of new
masterworks, or at least of structures which in
our present myopic view have already been
accepted as such. Yet, on the negative side,
many of the older leaders left us: first and
most notably Wright and Le Corbusier, more
lately Gropius and Mies, and, alas, younger
men as well: Yorke in England, in America
Eero Saarinen, and in Germany Eiermann.

Saarinen's work, since the General Motors
Technical Institute completed in 1955 and
illustrated here [346, 347] which was so very
Miesian, came by the late 1950s to epitomize
the variety, not to say the incoherence, of the
ambitions of many architects throughout the
world in those years. Happily, after a mature

career which lasted only eleven years compared
to his father Eliel's fifty, his contribution to
American, indeed to world, architecture, culminated in two works, his colleges at Yale [368]
and his airport outside Washington [369] that
in their differing, even apparently opposed,
ways expressed many of the aspirations of the
day at as high a level, perhaps, as earlier modern
architecture ever reached except in the greatest
works of Wright, Le Corbusier, and Mies. But
what made Eero Saarinen in retrospect the
typical architect of the late fifties and early
sixties had been, on the one hand, his Miesian
beginnings, in sharp reaction to his father's
half-traditional romanticism, and on the other
the fact that his *œuvre* included many works
which in their wilfulness and even, one may say,
their frivolity were well below the median
standards of serious achievement in those years.
Thus he stood, to an extent not always realized
in his brief lifetime when the kaleidoscopic
diversity of his buildings dazzled those it did

367. Le Corbusier: Eveux-sur-l'Arbresle, Rhône,
Dominican monastery of La Tourette, 1957-61

368. Eero Saarinen: New Haven, Conn., Ezra Stiles and Samuel F. B. Morse College, 1960-2

369. Eero Saarinen:
Chantilly, Va, Dulles International Airport, 1958-63

not shock, at the centre of his age. His remarkably successful career, remarkable even in
a period – so unlike several of the earlier decades
of this century – when few architects of quality,
even the most ascetic or most fanciful, were
wholly without employment, made plain one of
the central facts about the last fifteen years:
that the style or movement we call 'modern
architecture' had in many, perhaps in most,
countries achieved such total acceptance that
clients were willing, almost too willing, to trust
their architects in whatever novel direction they
wished to move, in terms of structure, of

materials, and of either asceticism or decorative
elaboration, not to speak of philosophical
content.

Remembering the extraordinary new developments in architecture that were under way
in the 1760s two hundred years ago in the
period with which the Introduction has dealt,
the historian can only end by wondering
whether in the welter of innovation of the 1950s
and 60s there lay somewhere the particular
seeds from which the architecture of the later
twentieth and twenty-first centuries will grow;
whether, to use another dubious historical

analogy, the stylistic development of the past quarter of our century corresponds to the Mannerism of the central decades of the sixteenth century in Italy. May we look forward, towards 2000 perhaps, to some such immanent movement, at once a synthesis of many preceding technical and stylistic innovations and a return to some at least of the principles of the preceding 'high' phase, yet above all a vital new creation with a life-expectancy of a hundred years and more, as was the Baroque around 1600? From the latest Baroque Western European architecture turned away two centuries ago; to the Baroque, in any revivalistic sense, it is hardly likely to return. Yet after the ever-increasing divergencies, which have been as characteristic of the years since the mid century as convergence was of twentieth-century architecture down to the 1930s, will we – perhaps before another decade has passed – begin to sense the beginnings of a new synthesis? We have certainly not been able to do so yet.

Today, the problem must be posed in world terms. So far Eastern Europe, Asia, and Africa have, on the whole, been learners and disciples of the West. Will the countries of Eastern Europe and the new countries of Asia and Africa soon be making contributions towards a new world-style, such as in the last few decades first the North Americans, next the Latin Americans, and then the Japanese made? Will the history of Western European architecture continue to be the principal story (which thanks to political conditions has been largely true up to the present) or will the Western European tradition, to which this volume has been almost completely devoted, become in the succeeding period somewhat peripheral and even alien to a situation in which underdeveloped countries will increasingly, as they come of age, tend to throw off cultural tutelage as they have mostly already thrown off political control?

The Brazilians were able to design if not to carry to completion Brasilia by themselves as well as, perhaps better than, Europeans or North Americans – above all, certainly, the architects of their own Portuguese homeland – could have done for them. The Indians, on the other hand, employed Le Corbusier and other Europeans, and the Pakistanis turned to English architects and landscape architects and also to the Americans, first Kahn, then Stone, for their new capital at Islamabad. The Japanese, who were in this respect already at the forefront, had employed Wright half a century ago for the Imperial Hotel; today it can perhaps be said that their own best work is superior to the Museum of Modern Art in Tokyo whose designs they obtained from Le Corbusier. Yet current Japanese architecture has not been, nor is it intended to be – witness the foreign-language editions of one of their architectural periodicals – outside the tradition of Western European architecture; indeed, it has represented the latest notable contribution to that architecture with which I have dealt. It is appropriate, therefore, that the roster of illustrations in this book, which began with buildings conceived – in effect at least – in Rome and built in France, in England, and even in North America, should end with buildings built in Asia following principles first adumbrated by a Swiss in France. The later eighteenth century turned inward in architecture towards the Rome and the Greece that were at the fountain-head of the Western European tradition; today we should perhaps be turning outward towards the new non-European world which seems still in the seventies, in architecture as in so much else, to be the child of Europe. Symbolically, at least, the best hope of a new architectural synthesis in the decades to come might lie in this fact; so that later histories of twentieth-century architecture will perhaps give as much attention and space to India or to some of the Arab and new African states as little Holland or vast North America have received in this account of the architecture of the last two hundred years.

NOTES

Bold numbers indicate page reference

INTRODUCTION

13. 1. Sigfried Giedion introduced this term in his *Spätbarocker und romantischer Klassizismus* in 1922 and provided an extended discussion of the concept. Fiske Kimball first used the term in English in his article 'Romantic Classicism in Architecture', *Gazette des Beaux-Arts*, XXV (1944), 95–112.
2. See Hautecœur, L., *Rome et la renaissance de l'antiquité à la fin du XVIIIᵉ siècle*, Paris, 1912. However, the deeper background of theory was French, not Roman. Unhappily the brevity with which this whole matter had to be treated here, where it is merely prefatory to an account of nineteenth- and twentieth-century architecture, made it impossible to discuss such French theorists of the early eighteenth century as J.-F. Félibien (1656–1733), A.-L. Cordemoy, and A.-F. Frézier (1682–1773); even Laugier appears somewhat out of context, since he was active not in Rome but in France. Hautecœur in *Histoire de l'architecture classique*, vols III and IV, and Kaufmann in *Architecture in the Age of Reason* – particularly in Chapter XI – elaborate this background of theory in France centring round the *Cours d'architecture . . .*, Paris, 1770–7, of J.-F. Blondel (1705–74).
2a. See Harris, J., 'Robert Mylne at the Academy of St Luke', *Architectural Review*, CXXX (1951), 341–52. Carroll Meeks in *Italian Architecture 1750–1914*, New Haven, 1966, Appendix B, 502–5, provided a long list of architect-visitors to Italy in the years 1725–1800; he also mentioned a few 'notable absentees'.
2b. On Rome in the mid-century, see also Middleton, R., 'A Very Serious Path', *Architectural Design* (April, 1967), 155–6, and Harris, J., 'Le Geay, Piranesi, and International Neo-classicism, Rome, 1740–1750', in *Essays . . . presented to R. Wittkower*, London, 1967, 189 ff.
14. 2c. Somewhat later Milizia is of considerable importance: 'The Rigorist attitude was reiterated toward the end of the century by Francesco Milizia (1725–98). His essays, which appeared from 1768 on, were reprinted in French, Spanish, Portuguese and English, some of them as late as 1820. Milizia has been variously appraised, Professor Hitchcock ignores him' (Meeks, *op. cit.*, 31–2). Meeks's note 94, p. 31, lists Milizia's writings, and he further notes the high opinion of Milizia held by many modern scholars.

3. Monographs on many architects and some men, like William Morris, who were not in fact architects will be found listed alphabetically by name in the Bibliography and are not referenced from the text. Publications devoted to individual works and articles about architects are usually referenced only in the Notes rather than in the Bibliography.
4. The changing attitudes towards the Greek Doric order provide a measure of the rise of Romantic Classicism. It is noteworthy that Soufflot was one of the first to make drawings of the very archaic Doric of Paestum, but it never occurred to him to emulate it in his own work. See Pevsner, N., and Lang, S., 'Apollo or Baboon', *Architectural Review*, CIV (1948), 271–9.
5. Winckelmann's major work is the *Geschichte der Kunst des Altertums*, 2 vols, Dresden, 1764.
16. 6. Interest in Egyptian forms can be traced all the way back through the Baroque period to the early Renaissance, but it undoubtedly increased after 1750 and lasted well into the next century. See Pevsner, N., and Lang, S., 'The Egyptian Revival', *Architectural Review*, CXIX (1956), 242–54. In the second quarter of the nineteenth century Egyptian forms were most likely to be used, especially in America, for prisons and cemetery accessories.
7. Adam studied, with the assistance of the French *pensionnaire* C.-L. Clérisseau (1722–1820), the Late Roman ruins of Diocletian's Palace at Split in 1757, and began his brilliant career in London two years later with the Admiralty Screen in Whitehall. See Adam, R., *Ruins of the Palace of the Emperor Diocletian at Spalatro*, London, 1764, and Fleming, J., *Robert Adam and his Circle*, London, 1962.
8. The present dome is a relatively late emendation; the original crowning feature was much less severe. Soufflot sent a pupil named Roche to London to make measured drawings of St Paul's in 1776, the year before he prepared this design.
In general, the Panthéon appears much more Romantic Classical today than what Soufflot actually built. The towers which once rose over the corners of the portico – in any case disapproved by Soufflot – were removed by Antoine Quatremère de Quincy (1755–1849) in 1791, and he also filled up the windows that originally cut into the plain wall surfaces. The murals are all of the nineteenth century.
9. Actually many of the spans are much too great to

be covered by single stones and the entablatures are really flat arches. There is also considerable use of iron.

9a. See Petzet, M., *Soufflot's Sainte Geneviève und der französische Kirchenbau des 18. Jahrhunderts*, Berlin, 1961.

9b. For detailed documentation, see Stroud, D., *Henry Holland*, revised ed., London [1975].

10. See Rosenau, H., 'George Dance the Younger', *Journal of the Royal Institute of British Architects*, LIV (1947), 502-7; Stroud, D., *George Dance*, London [1971]. Even more significant of developing Romantic Classical taste at this point was the character of the designs in Peyre, M.-J., *Livre sur l'architecture*, Paris, 1765.

17. 11. Vogt, A., *Boullées Newton-Denkmal*, Basel, 1969.

12. This more classical arrangement was first proposed in the 1760s by Pierre Patte (1723-1814), a theorist in the Blondel tradition, on the analogy of Palladio's theatre in Vicenza.

18. 12a. See Ledoux, C. N., *L'Architecture considérée sous le rapport de l'art . . .*, facsimile [Paris, 1962].

13. This is not true, however, of much of his executed work at Arc-Senans which has heavily plastic roofs of various shapes.

20. 14. So did Friedrich Gilly in Germany and - according to Kaufmann - Valadier in Italy.

CHAPTER 1

23. 1. See Steel, H. R., and Yerbury, F. R., *The Old Bank of England*, London, 1930, for photographic coverage of this monument of which the interiors were largely destroyed in the 1920s, and even the exterior considerably - and unnecessarily - modified (see Chapter 24).

26. 2. See Britton, J., *Illustrations of Fonthill Abbey*, London, 1823; Rutter, J., *An illustrated History and Description of Fonthill Abbey*, Shaftesbury, 1823; and Storer, J., *A Description of Fonthill Abbey, Wiltshire*, London, 1812. The most extensive modern account of the building of Fonthill Abbey is given by Brockman, H. A. N., *The Caliph of Fonthill*, London [1956].

27. 3. See also Pevsner, N., 'The Genesis of the Picturesque', *Architectural Review*, XCVI (1944), 139-46, and Pevsner, N., 'Richard Payne Knight', *Art Bulletin*, XXXI (1949), 293-320.

4. Hussey in *The Picturesque* lists many of these books and gives good examples of their illustrations. See pp. 143-4.

28. 5. First, that is, in this period. The columnar Monument in the City of London by Robert Hooke, commemorating the Great Fire, dates from the 1670s. The Nelson Pillar was demolished in 1966 by a bomb

at the time of the fiftieth anniversary of the Easter Rebellion. Unlike the Colonne Vendôme, toppled under the Paris Commune, it is unlikely to be re-erected.

6. See Telford, T., *An Account of the Improvements of the Port of London*, London, 1801. Splendid later examples also survive in Liverpool, built by the Corporation engineer Jesse Hartley (1780-1860); see Waldron, J., 'Measured Drawings of the Albert Dock Warehouses in Liverpool', *Architectural History*, IV (1961), 103-16.

29. 7. See Kimball, F., *Thomas Jefferson and the First Monument of the Classic Revival in America*, Harrisburg, 1915; Hitchcock, H. R., and Seale, W., *Temples of Democracy*, New York, 1976, chapter 11; and Pickins, B., 'Mr Jefferson as a Revolutionary Architect', *Journal of the Society of Architectural Historians*, XXXIV (1976), 257-79.

8. See Kimball, F., 'The Genesis of the White House', *Century Magazine*, February 1918.

9. See Brown, G., *History of the United States Capitol*, 2 vols, Washington, 1900-3.

10. See Kimball, F., 'Origin of the Plan of Washington, D.C.', *Architectural Review* (New York), VII (1918), 41-5; and Kite, E., *L'Enfant and Washington*, Baltimore, 1929.

30. 10a. Bishop Carroll, the client, may well have preferred the more classical design because of its resemblance to the Catholic chapel at Lulworth in Dorset, begun by John Tasker in 1785, for it was there that he was consecrated as bishop in 1790, the year of its completion. Tasker, a builder-architect, evidently based the design of his interior on James Wyatt's Pantheon in London of 1772, not on Soufflot's Panthéon: Little, B., *Catholic Churches since 1623*, London [1966], 40-1, plate 3b.

31. 11. See Alexander, R. L., 'The Public Memorial and Godefroy's Battle Monument', *Journal of the Society of Architectural Historians*, XVII (1958), 19-24.

12. See Hislop, C., and Larrabee, H. A., 'Joseph-Jacques Ramée and the Building of North and South College', *Union College Alumni Monthly*, February 1938.

12a. The foundations of the central Rotunda were laid as late as 1858 by President Eliphalet Nott, Ramée's original client. As built, however, it is a High Victorian Gothic work of the 1870s by E. T. Potter, one of Nott's two architect-grandsons (see pp. 274-5).

33. 12b. Speer, A., *Inside the Third Reich* [New York, 1970].

34. 12c. Murat, A., *La Colonne Vendôme*, Paris [1970]. 12d. Raymond, J. A., *Projet d'un arc de triomphe . . .*, Paris, 1812.

13. The idea probably originated with Soufflot, who

had earlier proposed a similar plan for the cathedral of Rennes.

36. 13a. Brongniart, A. T., *Plans du palais de la bourse de Paris . . .*, Paris, 1814.

37. 13b. See Blondel, J.-F., *Plan, coupe, et élévations du nouveau marché Saint Germain*, Paris, 1816, and Délespine, P.-J., *Marché des Blancs Manteaux*, Paris, 1827.

38. 13c. Earlier was Cagnola's trabeated Porta Ticinese of 1801–14, first of a series of city gates by various architects erected in Milan over the next fifteen years or so: Meeks, *op. cit.* (Introduction, Note 2a), 101, figures 32–7.

13d. Meeks, *op. cit.*, 121–4, note 47 (quoting the Touring Club Italiano's guide to *Napoli*, Milan, 1938, 108) makes no mention of Leconte's work of 1806, but states that the theatre was first built in 1737 by Angelo Carasale from designs by G. A. Medrano. Meeks also refers to a late reconstruction by Niccolini in 1844. Recurrent fires often make the architectural history of theatres almost impossible to disentangle.

14. See Chierici, G., *La Reggia di Caserta*, Rome, 1937; and Mongiello, G., *La Reggia di Caserta*, Caserta, 1954.

39. 15. See Hautecœur, L., *L'Architecture classique à Saint Pétersbourg à la fin du XVIIIe siècle*, Paris, 1912.

15a. Cameron in the Bibliography.

40. 16. See Thomon, T. de, *Recueil des principaux monuments construits à Saint Pétersbourg*, Petersburg, 1806; repeated in his *Traité de peinture*, Paris, 1809; and Loukomski, G., 'Thomas de Thomon', *Apollo*, XLII (1945), 297 ff.

16a. Parallel to Alexander's urbanism in Petersburg came the building up of Helsinki as capital of the then-Russian grand duchy of Finland, mostly by the German architect C. L. Engel (1778–1840) and to a plan of 1812–17 by the Swedish architect J. A. Ehrenström. Sixteen public buildings by Engel culminate in his Lutheran Cathedral high above the Senate Square. This was built in the 1830s but not consecrated until 1852. The result of Engel's activity is an exemplary Romantic Classical ensemble occupying a large part of Helsinki that is all but totally preserved.

41. 17. See Lancere, N., 'Adrien Zakharov and the Admiralty at Petersburg' (in Russian), *Starye Gody* (1911), 3–64.

17a. For the importance of primitivism as an aspect of Romantic Classicism, see Rosenblum, R., *Transformations in Late Eighteenth-Century Art*, Princeton, 1967, 140 ff.

18. Kaufmann, who illustrates the Belanger project in *Architecture in the Age of Reason*, figure 169, dates it around 1808 on the ground that slaughterhouses first began to be built in Paris in that year. It is

extremely unlikely, of course, that Hansen ever saw this project; but the similarity of his tower to Belanger's indicates how closely he was in tune with his French contemporaries. In any case similar towers are to be found in the projects published by Durand in his *Précis* of 1802–5, which Hansen must have known (see Chapter 2).

42. 18a. See Bauch, K., *Das Brandenburger Tor*, Cologne, 1966.

45. 18b. The story of the reconstruction of the interior of this theatre in the 1960s, together with many illustrations covering its complicated earlier history, is sumptuously published in *Festliche Oper*, Munich [1964].

CHAPTER 2

47. 1. Allais and others, *Projets d'architecture . . . qui ont mérités les grands prix*, Paris, 1806, and at different dates subsequently with varying authors and titles. For a collection of earlier projects, see Rosenau, H., 'The Engravings of the Grand Prix of the French Academy of Architecture', *Architectural History*, III (1960), 17–180, since the original publication is very rare.

2. Durand was already well known as the compiler of the *Recueil et parallèle des édifices en tout genre, anciens et modernes*, Paris, 1800, a curious work in which the drawings of important buildings of all periods are freely modified to bring them into conformity with the author's modular theories of proportion. This is conventionally known as 'Le grand Durand'. See also Paris, École Polytechnique, *Choix des projets d'édifices publics et particuliers . . .*, Paris, 1816.

3. Rondelet, J. B., *Traité théorique et pratique de l'art de bâtir*, 4 vols, Paris, 1802–17. There were several later editions. From 1806 Rondelet taught at the École Spéciale d'Architecture, which was shortly afterwards merged with the École Polytechnique.

48. 3a. The use of square modules is characteristic of Durand's plans and has a good deal to do with the lack in his designs of the more satisfying proportional relationships seen in the projects of the late eighteenth century.

49. 4. French designs of this period for houses were provided in profusion in the publications of J. C. Krafft. See Krafft, J. C., and Ransonette, N., *Plans, coupes, élévations des plus belles maisons et des hôtels construits à Paris et dans les environs*, Paris [c. 1802]; reprint, Paris, 1909; and Krafft, J. C., *Recueil d'architecture civile*, Paris, 1812; later ed., 1829. Krafft, J. C., and Thiollet, F., *Choix des plus jolies maisons de Paris et ses environs, édifices et monuments publics*, Paris, 1849, may also be mentioned here although very much later. It is significant of the

international availability of the earliest work listed here that it was provided with texts in French, English, and German.

52. 5. Klenze, L. von, *Walhalla in artistischer und technischer Beziehung*, Munich, 1842.

53. 6. See Hitchcock, H.-R., *Early Museum Architecture*, Hartford, 1934; and Plagemann, V., *Das deutsche Kunstmuseum, 1790–1870*, Munich, 1967.

6a. Meeks, *op. cit.* (Introduction, Note 2a), 72–8, figures 15–16, dates the Rotunda and the Sale a Croce Greca of the Vatican Museum '1776 ff.'. He notes that the Rotunda was completed by 'the Camporese' [? Giuseppe; 1763–1822] and that 'Pope Pius IX added "splendor" to it in 1861'.

7. Grandjean de Montigny, A.-H.-V., and Famin, A.-P.-Ste-M., *Architecture toscane*, Paris, 1815.

8. See Klenze, L. von, *Anweisung der Architektur des christlichen Kultus*, Munich, 1834. The Hofkirche is now being restored. The restoration of the War Ministry has been long completed, and that of parts of the Residenz round the Kaiserhof is under way.

55. 9. See Möllinger, K., *Elemente des Rundbogenstiles*, 2nd ed., Munich, 1848. It is convenient to retain the German term for this very Germanic round-arched style, even though it flourished in several countries besides Germany (see below in this chapter for Scandinavia, and Chapter 5 for America).

9a. A very detailed account for the districts along the Rhine is in Mann, A., *Die Neu-romanik, eine rheinische Komponente im Historicismus des 19. Jahrhunderts*, Cologne [1966].

57. 10. See Hübsch, H., *Die altchristlichen Kirchen nach den Baudenkmalen und älteren Beschreibungen*, 2 vols, Karlsruhe, 1862–3.

60. 10a. The Altes Museum was restored and reopened in 1966; Schinkel's Bauakademie was demolished to make way for the vast and commonplace East German Foreign Ministry completed in 1967.

62. 11. Durand, *Précis*, II, plate 13.

12. See Häberlin, C. L., *Sanssouci, Potsdam und Umgebung*, Berlin and Potsdam, 1855; Poensgen, G., *Die Bauten Friedrich Wilhelms IV in Potsdam*, Potsdam, 1930; Huth, H., *Der Park von Sanssouci*, Berlin, 1929; Kania, H., *Potsdamer Baukunst*, Berlin, 1926; *Potsdam. Staats- und Bürgerbauten*, Berlin, 1939; and Hitchcock, H.-R., 'Romantic Architecture of Potsdam', *International Studio*, 99 (1931), 46–9. Potsdam was still, in 1970, occupied by the Russian military headquarters. What the present condition of the Romantic-Classical monuments is, I do not know. The earlier Stadtpalais was demolished, as also the Garnisonkirche.

12a. See Dehio, L., *Fredrich Wilhelm IV von Preussen, ein Baukünstler der Romantik*, Munich, 1961.

13. See Sievers, J., *Das Palais des Prinzen Karl von Preussen*, Berlin, 1928.

63. 13a. Sievers, J., *Schloss Glienecke*, Berlin, 1964.

64. 14. Notably Séheult, F.-L., *Recueil d'architecture dessiné et mesuré en Italie . . . dans 1791–93*, Paris, 1821.

65. 15. See Persius, L., *Architektonische Entwürfe für den Umbau vorhandener Gebäude*, Potsdam, 1849; *Architektonische Ausführungen*, Berlin [1860?]; and Fleetwood Hesketh, R. and P., 'Ludwig Persius of Potsdam', *Architects Journal*, LXVIII (1928), 77–87, 113–20.

66. 15a. Pundt, H. G., *Schinkel's Berlin*, Cambridge, Mass., 1972.

16. Ettlinger, L., 'A German Architect's Visit to England in 1826', *Architectural Review*, XCVII (1945), 131–4.

17. See Poensgen, G., *Schloss Babelsberg*, Berlin, 1929.

67. 17a. See Frölich, M., and Sperlich, H. G., *Georg Moller, Baumeister der Romantik*, Darmstadt, 1959.

18. See Semper, G., *Das königliche Hoftheater zu Dresden*, Brunswick, 1849.

68. 19. Gärtner's design for the palace owes a good deal to a project prepared by Klenze for a palace on the Kerameikos hill which was never begun. Fortunately Schinkel's more ambitious project for a palace on the Akropolis was also not carried out. The digging away of the ground, which originally sloped up to the palace above the square, and the introduction in the 1930s of a retaining wall with the Tomb of the Unknown Soldier diminished somewhat the effectiveness of the front of the palace.

69. 19a. For the manifold building activities of this eccentric Philadelphia-born client, see Scully, V., Jr, 'Kleanthes and the Duchess of Piacenza', *Journal of the Society of Architectural Historians* (October 1963), 139–54.

20. See Amodeo, A., 'La Giovinezza di Pietro Nobile', 'La Maturità di Pietro Nobile', *L'Architettura*, I (1955), 49–52; 378–84.

70. 20a. Geist, J. F., *Passagen, ein Bautyp des 19. Jahrhunderts*, Munich, 1969.

21. See *Thorvaldsens Museum*, Copenhagen, 1953.

73. 22. See Hekker, H. C., 'De Nederlandse Bouwkunst in het Begin van de Negentiende Eeuw', *Bulletin van de Kon. Ned. Oudh. Bond*, IV (1951), 1–28.

CHAPTER 3

78. 1. The idea for the two-towered façade is probably derived from a project of 1809 by Lebas, but could also came from Gisors's Saint-Vincent in Mâcon of 1810. C. R. Cockerell's Hanover Chapel, begun in 1821, also has two towers.

2. Three pieces only of the enamelled lava decoration were put in place; owing to the ensuing outcry they were soon removed.

3. Hittorff and other architects of his generation such as Henri Labrouste and Duban, who supported his proposal to revive the external polychromy they had noted on the Classical temples of Sicily, were closer in fact to Ingres than to Delacroix. Ingres in 1828 backed Labrouste's *envoi* of the Paestum temples. Duban, one of the first to introduce polychrome decoration – the plaques of enamelled lava used in the entrance courtyard of the École des Beaux-Arts are his – was a close friend and on occasion a collaborator of Ingres. Hittorff collected paintings by Ingres and assisted him with the architectural backgrounds of his pictures, though that in the 'Stratonice', which gives perhaps the best idea of the original intentions of these architects, was supplied by Victor Baltard.

4. Actually the original paintwork on the beams and panels of the vestibules of the Gare du Nord is still there, but so dulled and begrimed that one hardly notices it. To the twentieth century the remarkable roof of Hittorff's Rotonde des Panoramas in the Champs Élysées of 1836 would be, if extant, of more interest, since it was suspended from iron cables.

5. As has been noted in Chapter 2, both de Chateauneuf and Meuron studied with Leclerc.

79. 5a. Baltard, L. P., *Projet du palais de justice . . .*, Paris, 1830.

81. 5b. Haucour, L. de, *L'Hôtel de ville de Paris à travers les siècles*, Paris, 1900.

82. 5c. Having had the privilege of reading in manuscript Neil Levine's Yale dissertation on Henri Labrouste and French architecture of the period 1830–70 and seen the École des Beaux Arts Exhibition of 1975 at the Museum of Modern Art in New York, I would now treat very differently the French material covered on pp. 82–7. It is impossible, short of almost total rewriting, to shift the emphasis in the direction I now believe to be correct. The factual information remains predominantly accurate but the critical estimates are distorted. What is now as true of France as when the book was first written is that architectural controversy still flourishes!

6. The history of this project is very complicated. As might be surmised from its character, a design was at one point prepared by Gilbert, the principal Louis Philippe architect for this sort of work. The actual construction of the Hôtel Dieu by Diet followed only after a decade of plan, yet the executed work probably incorporates something of Gilbert's design; in any case, what was built is still wholly in the spirit of Gilbert's Louis Philippe work and not at all in that of the Second Empire (see Chapter 8). Diet was Gilbert's son-in-law.

83. 7. Begun by John Harvey, continued by Thomas Hardwick, and completed by Sir Robert Smirke.

85. 7a. The Gare Montparnasse has been all but totally demolished to make way for a skyscraper.

88. 7b. Meeks, *op. cit.* (Introduction, Note 2a), 23, 163–6, figures 62–3, mentions only Poletti by name as architect of the church but does refer to the 'numerous porticoes added by various hands . . . in the long rebuilding which followed the fire of 1823'. Meeks assumes that reconstruction began at once in 1823, not two years later.

89. 7c. See Venditti, A., *Architettura neoclassica a Napoli*, Naples, 1961.

7d. 'This [the colonnades] was begun by Leopoldo Laperuta in 1808 [for Murat] and was part way along when the Bourbons returned to their throne . . .', Meeks, *op. cit.*, 181.

90. 7e. Filippis, F. de, *Le antiche residenze reali di Napoli*, Naples, 1971.

7f. Paroletti, M., *Turin . . .*, Turin, 1838.

92. 8. See Missirini, M., *Del Tempio eretto in Possagno da Antonio Canova*, Venice, 1833. Some give credit to Selva, but not Bassi his biographer. See also Meeks, C. L. V., 'Pantheon Paradigm', *Journal of the Society of Architectural Historians*, XIX (1960), 135–44.

8a. Piermarini, G., *Teatro della Scala in Milano*, reprint [Perugia, 1970].

93. 8b. 'The design was provided by Perego, a scene-designer, in 1812, and executed by the engineer Francesco Gloria and the architect Innocenzo Giusti for Gaetano Bellori', Meeks, *op. cit.*, 133.

9. See Falconetti, A., *Il Caffè Pedrocchi, dagherrotipo artistico descrittivo*, Padua, 1847; and Cimegotto, C., and others, [Centenary volume on the Caffè Pedrocchi], Padua, 1931.

95. 10. See Montferrand, A.-R. de, *L'Église cathédrale de Saint-Isaac, description architecturale, pittoresque, et historique*, Saint-Petersbourg, 1845.

CHAPTER 4

99. 1. Many additions and changes in the house were made from 1816 on; a top storey and a Picture Room of 1825–6 behind No. 14 were the most consequential. See Soane, J., *Description of the House and Museum on the North Side of Lincoln's Inn Fields*, London, 1832; enl. ed., 1835–6. No. 12 has now been added to the Museum.

2. See Note 1, Chapter 1. The new interiors were built in 1818; the front and side façades were rebuilt in 1823.

2a. Port, M. H., *Six Hundred New Churches*, London, 1961.

3. St Pancras is really based on Gibbs's St Martin's-in-the-Fields as regards the exterior; but all the fea-

tures have, so to say, been translated into the Greek of the Erechtheum. See Inwood, W. and H. W., *St Pancras New Church. Specifications . . .*, London, 1819; and Inwood, H. W., *The Erechtheion at Athens*, London, 1827.

100. 3a. Exceptional in England is C. R. Cockerell's Hanover Chapel of 1821 in Regent Street because of its two towers and the complex spatial design of the interior.

106. 4. See Smith, H. C., *Buckingham Palace*, London, 1931.

The palatial character of Cumberland Terrace is due to the fact that it faced the site of an intended summer palace in the Park planned for George IV but never even begun.

108. 5. Crook, J. M., *The British Museum*, London and New York [1972].

109. 5a. Betjeman, Sir J., *London's Historic Railway Stations* [London, 1972]; and Jackson, A. A., *London's Termini*, Newton Abbot, 1969.

110. 5b. See Rolt, L. T. C., *George and Robert Stephenson*, London, 1960; Smithson, A. M., *The Euston Arch and the Growth of the London, Midland and Scottish Railway*, London, 1968.

5c. See Fort, M., 'Francis Goodwin, 1784-1835', *Architectural History*, I (1958), 61-72.

6. See Whiffen, M., *The Architecture of Sir Charles Barry in Manchester and Neighbourhood*, Manchester, 1950.

111. 6a. See Dobson, J., *Memoir of John Dobson*, London, 1885.

6b. Oliver, T., *A New Picture of Newcastle upon Tyne*, reprint of the 1831 ed., Newcastle upon Tyne, 1970.

112. 7. In one sense the Baths of Caracalla provided Elmes's model, since the size of the great interior there was intentionally exceeded here; in another sense, this was a grandiose development of Wren's relatively modest interior of St James's, Piccadilly. Just as Gibbs was translated into Greek by the Inwoods at St Pancras', Wren was translated into Latin here, but with less precision of vocabulary.

7a. See Youngson, A. J., *The Making of Classical Edinburgh 1750-1840*, Edinburgh [1966].

116. 7b. See Taylor, J., 'Charles Fowler: Master of Markets', *Architectural Review* (March 1964), 174-82.

120. 8. See Parker, C., *Villa Rustica*, 3 vols, London, 1832, 1833, 1841; 2nd ed., London, 1848.

CHAPTER 5

121. 1. When railway stations were needed in Brazil after the mid century they were actually imported, in prefabricated iron, from England.

2. See [Haviland, J.], *A Description of Haviland's Design for the New Penitentiary . . .*, Philadelphia,

1824; Anon., *A Description of the Eastern Penitentiary . . .*, Philadelphia, 1830; Crawford, W., *Report on the Penitentiaries of the United States*, London, 1834; Demetz, F.-A., and Blouet, G.-A., *Rapport sur les penitenciers des États Unis*, Paris, 1837; and Markus, T. A., 'Pattern of the Law; Bentham's Panopticon Scheme', *Architectural Review*, CXVI (1954), 251-6.

3. See Haviland, J., *The Builder's Assistant*, 3 vols, Philadelphia, 1818-21 – the first to include plates of the Greek orders; 2nd ed., Philadelphia, 1830; Benjamin, A., *The American Builder's Companion*, Boston, 1827 (the first edition is of 1806, but Greek orders were not included until this latest edition); *The Practical House Carpenter*, Boston, 1830, with later editions to 1857; *Practice of Architecture*, New York, 1833, with later editions to 1851; *Elements of Architecture*, Boston, 1843, 2nd ed., 1849; *The Builder's Guide*, Boston, 1839, with later editions to the Civil War; Lafever, M., *The Young Builder's General Instructor*, Newark, 1829; *The Modern Builder's Guide*, New York, 1833, with later editions to 1855; *The Beauties of Modern Architecture*, New York, 1835, with later editions to 1855; *The Architectural Instructor*, New York, 1856; Shaw, E., *Civil Architecture*, Boston, 1830, with later editions to 1855; and Hills, C., *The Builder's Guide*, Hartford, 1834, with later editions to 1847.

123. 3a. Even less is visible than two decades ago, since the east front of the central section has been entirely rebuilt and the west front was also threatened by the vandalism of the late 'Architect of the U.S. Capitol' who was, in fact, no architect at all but a congressman who failed of re-election. Rebuilding of the west front is recurrently proposed.

125. 4. See Willard, S., *Plans and Sections of the Obelisk on Bunker's Hill*, Boston, 1843.

5. See Mills, R., *The American Pharos; or, Lighthouse Guide*, Washington, 1832; and *Waterworks for the Metropolitan City of Washington*, Washington, 1853.

5a. Reiff, D. D., *Washington Architecture, 1791-1861*, Washington, D.C., 1971.

6. See Thayer, R., *History, Organization and Functions of the Office of the Supervising Architect of the Treasury Department*, Washington, 1886; and Strobridge, T. R., 'Archives of the Supervising Architect - Treasury Department', *Journal of the Society of Architectural Historians*, XX (1961), 198-9. See also Overby, O., 'Ammi B. Young in the Connecticut Valley', *Journal of the Society of Architectural Historians*, XIX (1960), 119-23.

7. See O'Neal, W. B., *Jefferson's Buildings at the University of Virginia*, I, Charlottesville, 1960. Like the hill-top siting of Monticello, Jefferson's own nearby house – begun before the American Revolution

and finally completed only in 1808 – this provision of an open end towards the view illustrates his active response to the ideals of the Picturesque. For Monticello, moreover, a drawing of a Gothick garden fabrick exists. The fact that McKim, Mead & White blocked the view at the bottom of Jefferson's layout with a new building in the twentieth century is curious evidence of the lack of understanding of the essential qualities of the architecture and planning of this period on the part of even the most sophisticated 'traditional' architects – men who professed the greatest admiration for the work of such predecessors as Jefferson and yet proceeded to destroy its essence whenever the opportunity arose!

128. 8. From the time of Latrobe's Bank of 1798 the Greek temple paradigm for public buildings characteristically and quite inconsistently included vaulted interiors for protection against fire.

9. In Nicholson, Peter, *The Carpenter's Guide*, London, 1849. See also Walter, T. U., *Report[s] of the Architect of the Girard College . . .* [Philadelphia, 1834–50].

129. 10. Once more, as with Latrobe and Mills, the importance of Strickland's work as an engineer should at least be noted. The principal publications of the period in this domain are his *Reports on the Canals, Railways, Roads and other Subjects*, Philadelphia, 1826, and his *Reports, Specifications and Estimates of Public Works in the United States*, London, 1841.

130. 10a. Contrary to what the text suggests, Shryock's design for the Capitol of Kentucky preceded Town's for Connecticut. See Hitchcock, H. R., and Seale, W., *Temples of Democracy*, New York [1976]. It should be noted that at this point Davis was not yet a partner of Town, though largely responsible for designing both the Connecticut and the Indiana Capitols for which Town received the commissions.

11. The history of the building is so complex that it is difficult to know to whom the main credit should be assigned for its distinguished design. The competition held in 1838 was nominally won by Henry Walters, a Cincinnati architect, and he actually laid the foundations in 1839–40; but the executed design owes more to the competition project of the painter Thomas Cole (1801–48). See Cummings, A. L., 'The Ohio State Capitol Competition', *Journal of the Society of Architectural Historians*, XII (1953), 15–18. Modifications of the scheme initiated in 1839–40 were made in 1844, and building resumed in 1848 under the direction of William Russell West of Cincinnati. On his resignation in 1854 Nathan B. Kelly (1808–71) of Columbus succeeded, and the work was finally brought to a finish by Isaiah Rogers in 1858–61. See Hitchcock, H. R., and Seale, W., *Temples of Democracy*, New York [1976], for a more complete account.

131. 12. See Wheildon, W. W., *Memoir of Solomon Willard*, Boston, 1865.

13. Greenough is better known today as the 'herald of functionalism' than as a sculptor. See Wynne, N., and Newhall, B., 'Horatio Greenough: Herald of Functionalism', *Magazine of Art*, XXII (1939), 12–15. For his theories, see Greenough, H., *Aesthetics at Washington*, Washington, 1851; *Travels, Observations, and Experience of a Yankee Stone-cutter*, New York, 1852; and *Form and Function: Remarks on Art* (H. A. Small, ed.), Berkeley and Los Angeles, 1947.

133. 14. There are measured drawings of these commercial buildings in Hitchcock, H.-R., *Guide to Boston Architecture*, New York, 1954.

134. 15. The most thorough study of American industrial building of this period, including the housing of operatives, is Coolidge, J. P., *Mill and Mansion*, New York, 1942, which deals with Lowell, Mass. Considerable Rhode Island work is illustrated in Hitchcock, H.-R., *Rhode Island Architecture*, Providence, R.I., 1939; New York, 1969.

15a. Aromini, J. E., *Rise of the Factory Style in the U.S.A.*, [n.p.] 1956; Coolidge, J. P., *Mill and Mansion*, reprint, New York [1967]; Tann, J., *The Development of the Factory* [London, 1970]; and Zimiles, M., *Early American Mills*, New York [1973].

16. See Eliot, W. H., *A Description of the Tremont House*, Boston, 1830.

136. 17. Davis intended to include a central domed space on the model of Latrobe's Bank of 1798. This was omitted when the design of the interior was revised by Samuel Thomson or William Ross and executed by John Frazee. See Torres, L., 'Samuel Thomson and the Old Custom House', *Journal of the Society of Architectural Historians*, XX (1961), 185–90.

137. 18. See Schuyler, M., 'A Great American Architect; Leopold Eidlitz', *Architectural Record*, XXIV, 163–79, 277–92, 364–78, and, for a more general treatment, Meeks, C. L. V., 'Romanesque before Richardson in the United States', *Art Bulletin*, XXXV (1953), 17–33. See also Jordy, W., and Coe, R. (eds), *American Architecture and Other Writings*, I, Cambridge, Mass., 1961.

19. See Stone, E. M., *The Architect and Monetarian: a Brief Memoir of Thomas Alexander Tefft*, Providence, R.I., 1869, and Wriston, B., 'Architecture of Thomas Tefft', *Rhode Island School of Design Bulletin*, XVIII (1940), 37–45.

138. 20. See Meeks, C. L. V., 'Henry Austin and the Italian Villa', *Art Bulletin*, XXX (1948), 145 ff.

21. See Smith, R. C., *John Notman and the Atheneum Building*, Philadelphia, 1951.

22. See Young, A. B., *New Custom House, Boston*, Boston, 1840. The tower that now replaces the dome was built by Peabody & Stearns in 1913–15; it was the

first real skyscraper in Boston.

23. See Young, A. B., *Plans of Public Buildings in Course of Construction under the Direction of the Secretary of the Treasury*, [Washington] 1855-6.

141. 23a. Germann, G., *Gothic Revival*, London [1972].

CHAPTER 6

143. 1. Hussey devotes only a portion of his book to the Picturesque in architecture. See also Pevsner, N., 'The Picturesque in Architecture', *Journal of the Royal Institute of British Architects*, LV (1947), 55-61. C. L. V. Meeks in 'Picturesque Eclecticism', *Art Bulletin*, XXXII (1950), 226-35, extends the range of the Picturesque to include considerably more of nineteenth-century architecture than is usual. As with 'Romantic' or 'Classical', it makes a difference whether or not one uses a capital; with a capital it seems best to restrict the term Picturesque to the late eighteenth and early nineteenth centuries, although the point of view lasted down into the fifties, and it is also possible to recognize a sort of 'Neo-Picturesque' in the seventies and eighties (see Chapters 12 and 13 particularly).

2. See Note 3, Chapter 1.

3. Thomas Hopper was even more addicted to the 'Neo-Norman', as Gosford Castle in Ireland, begun in 1819, and the rather late Penrhyn Castle of 1827-37 near Bangor in Wales, all built of Mona marble and with a keep copied from that of twelfth-century Hedingham Castle in Essex, splendidly illustrate. See Fedden, R. R., 'Thomas Hopper and the Norman Revival', in *Studies in Architectural History*, II (1956).

144. 4. See Musgrave, C., *Royal Pavilion; a Study in the Romantic*, Brighton, 1951; and Roberts, H. D., *A History of the Royal Pavilion, Brighton*, London, 1939.

5. See Stroud, D., *Henry Holland*, London [1966], chapter 8.

6. See Repton, H., *Designs for the Pavilion*, London, 1808 (the drawings were made two years earlier); Musgrave, C., *Royal Pavilion*, London, 1951. Repton's scheme was much less eclectic than Nash's, being entirely based, like Sezincote, on the Daniells' book on India (see Chapter 1).

145. 7. See Dale, A., *Fashionable Brighton, 1820-1860*, London, 1947; and *History and Architecture of Brighton*, Brighton, 1950.

8. The work was begun in 1818 and continued down into the thirties. See Thompson, Francis, *A History of Chatsworth*, London, 1949; also Linstrum, D., *Sir Jeffry Wyatville, Architect to the King*, Oxford, 1972.

146. 9. See Clark, E., *The Britannia and Conway Tubular Bridges*, 2 vols and album, London, 1850.

10. This was begun only in 1837 and completed, without the elaborate Egyptian decoration that Brunel

intended, by W. H. Barlow (1812-1902) in 1864.

11. See Donner, P., 'Edensor, or Brown come True', *Architectural Review*, XCV (1944), 39-43; and Chadwick's *The Works of Sir Joseph Paxton*, 162-5, which gives primary credit to Paxton.

12. See Loudon, J. C., *Encyclopaedia of Cottage, Farm and Villa Architecture and Furniture*, London, 1833; 2nd ed. with Supplement, 1842. This is the culminating anthology of the Picturesque, summarizing and all but concluding some forty years of Cottage and Villa Book production in England.

13. In addition to the treatises of C. L. Eastlake, Kenneth Clark, Basil F. L. Clarke, and Marcus Whiffen listed in the Bibliography, see Kamphausen, A., *Gotik ohne Gott: ein Beitrag zur Deutung der Neugotik und des 19. Jahrhunderts*, Tübingen, 1952.

147. 14. See Britton, J., *The Architectural Antiquities of Great Britain*, 5 vols, London, 1804-14; *Cathedral Antiquities of Great Britain*, 14 parts, 1814-35; etc.

15. See Pugin, A. C., and Wilson, E. J., *Specimens of Gothic Architecture*, 2 vols, London [1821]; *Examples of Gothic Architecture*, London, 1831. Two more volumes of the *Examples* were published by A. W. N. Pugin after his father's death.

16. See Rickman, T., *An Attempt to Discriminate the Styles of English Architecture*, London [1817]; many later editions. The terms Rickman introduced here – Early English, Decorated, and Perpendicular – for the successive phases of the English Gothic are still in general use. For Rickman's use of iron in his early churches in Liverpool, see Chapter 7.

148. 17. See Whiffen, M., 'Rickman and Cambridge', *Architectural Review*, XCVIII (1945), 160-3.

18. Pugin's really important books concerning architecture were three: *Contrasts, or a Parallel between the Architecture of the 15th and 19th Centuries*, London, 1836; *The True Principles of Pointed or Christian Architecture*, London, 1841; and *An Apology for the Revival of Christian Architecture in England*, London, 1843. All of these have later editions which sometimes show significant omissions and additions.

18a. See Lang, S., 'The Principles of the Gothic Revival in England', *Journal of the Society of Architectural Historians* (December 1966), 240-67.

149. 19. Founded at Cambridge University in 1839 and later known as the Ecclesiological Society. The Society's periodical, *The Ecclesiologist*, which began to appear in 1841, together with their other publications, had a notable influence on architectural development in England and English-speaking countries in the forties and fifties and even later. See White, J. F., *The Cambridge Movement*, Cambridge, 1962.

20. See Bonnar, T., *Biographical Sketch of G. Meikle Kemp*, Edinburgh and London, 1892.

150. 21. The palace-planning of one Durand pupil,

Klenze, behind the regular façade of his Königsbau in Munich is actually very unsymmetrical and episodic, as Giedion points out in his *Spätbarocker und romantischer Klassizismus*.

152. 22. See Summerson, J., 'Pugin at Ramsgate', *Architectural Review*, CIII (1948), 163-6.

156. 23. An influential publication of this period was Hopkins, J., *Essay on Gothic Architecture*, Burlington, 1836. Bishop Hopkins himself designed and built several churches of the rather feeble Gothick order of the plates in this book.

157. 24. See Upjohn, R., *Upjohn's Rural Architecture*, New York, 1852.

25. See Wills, F., *Ancient English Ecclesiastical Architecture . . .*, New York, 1850, which includes designs for new churches. Similar is Hart, J., *Designs for Parish Churches in the Three Styles of English Church Architecture*, New York, 1857. Notman, however, was the most expert Neo-Gothic architect serving the American ecclesiologists; St Mark's Philadelphia, for which his plans superseded those by R. C. Carpenter, sent from England by the Ecclesiological Society, is the best evidence of his capacity as an American Camdenian. See also Stanton, P., *The Gothic Revival and American Church Architecture*, Baltimore [1968].

158. 26. Downing's major work, *A Treatise on the Theory and Practice of Landscape Gardening adapted to North America*, New York and London, 1841, with later editions to 1879 (and twentieth-century reprints), devotes only a chapter to house design. His really influential architectural books were *Cottage Residences*, New York, 1842, with later editions to 1887, and *The Architecture of Country Houses*, New York, 1850, with later editions to 1866. See *Dutchess County Department of Planning*, *Springside*, December, 1958.

27. See Scully, V. J., Jr, *The Shingle Style and the Stick Style*, New Haven, 1971.

28. See Robinson, P. F., *Rural Architecture*, London, 1822, with later editions to 1836, and also his *Designs for Ornamental Villas*, London, 1827, again with later editions to 1836.

29. The handsomest and one of the most authoritative mid-century books on chalets was by Graffenried and Sturler, *Architecture suisse*, Berne, 1844. See Landau, S. B., 'Richard Morris Hunt, the Continental Picturesque, and the "Stick Style"', *Journal of the Society of Architectural Historians*, XLII, no. 3 (1983), 272-89.

30. See Vaux, C., *Villas and Cottages*, New York, 1857, with later editions to 1874.

159. 31. See Lancaster, C., 'Oriental Forms in American Architecture', *Art Bulletin*, XXIX (1947), 183-93. For other work of Samuel Sloan, a very productive mid-century architect and architectural writer, see Coolidge, H. N., 'A Sloan Checklist, 1849-1884',

Journal of the Society of Architectural Historians, XIX (1960), 34-8; also Sloan, S., *City and Suburban Architect*, reprint of the 1859 ed., New York [1976].

32. See Owen, R. D., *Hints on Public Architecture*, New York, 1849.

32a. Turnbull, C., *The Charm of Hobart*, Sydney, 1959.

32b. Toker, F., *The Church of Notre-Dame in Montreal*, Montreal, 1970.

160. 33. Of the *Seven Lamps*, of the first volume of the *Stones of Venice*, and of the *Lectures on Architecture and Painting*, American editions appeared respectively in 1849, 1851, and 1854, the same years as the original London editions, and were succeeded by new issues and new editions at a pace far exceeding that maintained by the original publishers in England. In part this may merely mean that the American editions, all pirated, were smaller; but it is certainly evidence of an avid and extensive body of American readers from the mid century down to 1900. See Hitchcock, H. R., 'Ruskin and American Architecture . . .', in *Concerning Architecture*, 166-208, London, 1968.

33a. Pevsner, N. (ed.), *The Picturesque Garden and its Influence outside the British Isles*, Dumbarton Oaks, Washington, D.C., 1974.

34. See Chenesseau, G., *Sainte-Croix d'Orléans; histoire d'une cathédrale gothique réédifiée par les Bourbons, 1599-1829*, 3 vols, Paris, 1921.

The design of 1707 for the façade was by Robert de Cotte, J.-H. Mansart's principal lieutenant. The work was carried on more actively by A. J. Gabriel under Louis XV. With the Restoration in 1816 Louis XVIII took up the completion of the project – which Napoleon had actually ordered before Waterloo – as part of the general preoccupation of the Restoration with a strengthening of the Church, and Charles X opened the finished church in 1829. Thus the renewal of activity here in the second decade of the nineteenth century precedes the other Neo-Gothic work described below by some twenty years. But credit – or discredit – for its Rococo-Gothic character belongs to the eighteenth not to the nineteenth century.

161. 35. See Rotrou, E. de, *Dreux, ses antiquités*, *Chapelle St Louis*, Dreux, 1864.

36. The aesthetic climate of the period is presented in several books: Rosenthal, L., *L'Art et les artistes romantiques*, Paris, 1928; Robiquet, J., *L'Art et le goût sous la Restauration*, Paris, 1928; Schommer, P., *L'Art décoratif au temps du romantisme*, Paris, 1928. These were published in advance of the 'Centenaire du romantisme' of 1930.

162. 36a. Lassus, J. B. A., *Projets de restauration de Notre-Dame de Paris . . .*, Paris, 1843.

163. 37. See Thiénon, C., *Voyage pittoresque dans le Bocage de la Vendée, ou vues de Clisson et ses environs*, Paris, 1817.

38. In 1836 Viollet-le-Duc wrote to his father that every greengrocer had a small Italian Villa with a tower, but this is patently a rhetorical exaggeration.

39. See Kaufmann, E., *Three Revolutionary Architects, Boullée, Ledoux and Lequeu*, Philadelphia, 1952.

165. 39a. The intention must have been to extend the Schloss in the mode of the surviving mid-sixteenth-century portions, but the multiple cone-topped towers and the profusion of pilasters on the walls is more early French than early German Renaissance in character, thanks probably to Stüler.

166. 40. See Heideloff, K., *Nürnberg's Baudenkmale der Vorzeit*, Nuremberg, 1839; and *Die Kunst des Mittelalters in Schwaben*, Stuttgart, 1855. His *Ornaments of the Middle Ages* (to give it its English title), which began to appear in Nuremberg in 1838, had several editions with French and English text.

168. 41. This is least true in France, where the Neo-Catholic intellectuals were Gothic enthusiasts and succeeded in imposing Gothic on the architects, few of whom ever took to it with whole-hearted enthusiasm. Even Viollet-le-Duc, after the forties, was confusedly eclectic in most of his newly designed buildings as distinguished from his 'restorations' and his completions of unfinished medieval monuments (see Chapter 11).

41a. The most extended account is in Meeks, *op. cit.* (Introduction, Note 2a), chapter 3.

CHAPTER 7

169. 1. See Sheppard, R., *Cast Iron in Building*, London, 1945, and Gloag, J., and Bridgwater, D., *A History of Cast Iron in Building*, London, 1948. These accounts require considerable revision in the light of research by T. C. Bannister and by A. W. Skempton. See Note 5, *infra*, and for further illustrations, 'The Iron Pioneers', *Architectural Review*, CXXX (1961), 14–19, and Richards, J. M., *The Functional Tradition in Early Industrial Buildings*, London, 1958.

2. Problems of fire-resistance were already under discussion in England in the forties. The London Fire Department even refused to enter burning buildings with internal skeletons of iron because of the danger of their collapse; while the effectiveness of fireproofing iron columns with masonry sheathing was already being tested in 1846. I owe this information, as well as that on many other significant points in this chapter, to Turpin C. Bannister.

170. 2a. See Harris, J., 'Cast Iron Columns 1706', *Architectural Review*, CXXX (1961), 60–1.

171. 2b. See Raistrick, A., *Dynasty of Ironfounders*, London [1953].

3. See Giedion, S., *Bauen in Frankreich: Eisen, Eisen-* *beton*, Leipzig, 1928, an account which its own author and others have considerably amended since.

4. This was replaced a quarter of a century later when a new stair-hall was built by Percier and Fontaine.

4a. As far as England is concerned, such pot-vaults may have been an idea of Henry Holland's that Soane took up: Stroud, *op. cit.* (Chapter 6, Note 5).

4b. See Tann, J., *The Development of the Factory* [London, 1970].

5. See Bannister, T. C., 'The First Iron-Framed Buildings', *Architectural Review*, CVII (1950), 231–46; Skempton, A. W., and Johnson, H. R., 'The First Iron Frames', *Architectural Review*, CXXXI (1962), 175–86. In 1803–4 came two more iron-framed mills, the North Mill at Belper and one at Leeds.

6. See Fairbairn, W., *On the Application of Cast and Wrought Iron to Building Purposes*, London, 1854.

172. 7. See Buckler, J. and J. C., *Views of Eaton Hall*, London, 1826.

7a. See Hughes, Q., *Seaport, Architecture and Townscape in Liverpool*, London [1964], 136–45.

173. 8. See Mock, E., *The Architecture of Bridges*, New York, 1949; Whitney, C., *Bridges: a Study in their Art, Science and Evolution*, New York, 1929; De Maré, E., *The Bridges of Britain*, London, 1954; Andrews, C., 'Early Iron Bridges of the British Isles', *Architectural Review*, LXXX (1936), 63–8; and 'Early Victorian Bridges in Suspension in the British Isles', *Architectural Review*, LXXX (1936), 109–12; and Mehrtens, G., *Der deutsche Brückenbau im XIX Jahrhundert*, Berlin, 1900.

9. In addition to Telford's own superbly illustrated autobiography and the two modern monographs, see Sutherland, R. J. M., 'Telford', *Architectural Review*, CXIV (1953), 389–94.

10. The American James Finley built an iron-chain suspension bridge as early as 1801 and patented the system in 1808 after he had built several more. See Pope, T., *Treatise on Bridge Architecture*, New York, 1811, which was probably known to Telford.

174. 10a. Biographies of such important engineers as these are included with those of architects in the Monographs section of the Bibliography.

11. These early French bridges – and several important early English ones too – are illustrated in later editions of Rondelet's *Traité* (see Note 3, Chapter 2), and in Bruyère, L., *Études relatives à l'art des constructions*, Paris, 1823. Delon's name is also given as Dilon and Dillon.

12. See Séguin, M., *Des ponts en fil de fer*, Paris, 1824.

13. See Ellet, C., *The Wheeling Bridge* [Philadelphia, 1852]. For this bridge Roebling provided the cables but not the design.

14. See Conant, W., *The Brooklyn Bridge*, New York

[1883]; and McCullough, D., *The Great Bridge*, New York, 1972.

176. 15. Hautecœur lists nearly forty built before 1848 in Paris alone. For the Galerie d'Orléans, see Fontaine, C., *Histoire du Palais Royal*, Paris, 1834.

16. Thiollet, F., *Serrurerie de fonte et de fer récemment exécutés*, Paris, 1832, illustrates several examples.

177. 17. See Pevsner, N., 'Early Iron: Curvilinear Hothouses', *Architectural Review*, CVI (1949), 188–9.

178. 18. See Meeks, C. L. V., 'The Life of a Form: A History of the Train Shed', *Architectural Review*, CX (1951), 163–74, and his book *The Railroad Station*, New Haven, 1956; 2nd ed., 1965.

18a. See Arschavir, A. A., 'The Inception of the English Railway Station', *Architectural History*, IV (1961), 63–76, for the story before Crown Street.

179. 18b. See White, R. B., *Prefabrication, a History of its Development in Great Britain*, London, 1965, part 1.

19. See Clark, E., *The Britannia and Conway Tubular Bridges*, 2 vols and atlas, London, 1850.

180. 20. See Hitchcock, H.-R., 'The Coal Exchange', *Architectural Review*, CI (1947), 185–7. Despite valiant efforts for the preservation of this major Victorian monument and the interest of Australia in acquiring the demountable iron structure of the court for re-erection in a new National Gallery, the City Corporation demolished it in 1964. Thus key Victorian monuments were being lost just as their value began to be widely appreciated.

182. 21. See Bannister, T. C., 'The Genealogy of the Dome of the United States Capitol', *Journal of the Society of Architectural Historians*, VII (1948), 1–16.

183. 21a. See Gayle, M., *Cast Iron Architecture in New York*, New York [1974].

22. Bogardus's priority in this matter is by no means absolute. Certainly earlier in America was the Miners' Bank, built by Haviland in Pottsville, Penna., in 1829–30; but here cast iron was used only to provide a decorative sheathing of the brick walls in the absence of available stone. Also earlier was a steam flour-mill three storeys high prefabricated by Sir William Fairbairn in London in 1839 and sent to Turkey, where it was erected in Istanbul in 1840. This was more like Bogardus's building, and he had probably actually seen it when it was exhibited in London in Fairbairn's shops at Millwall before being disassembled and shipped away. Daniel D. Badger (1806–?) also claimed priority because of the many one-storey shops he had built of iron, one of which was just across Center Street in New York from Bogardus's factory. But Bogardus deserved the publicity he received at home and abroad; undoubtedly it was his activity which really started the general vogue of cast-iron fronts in the

United States. See Bogardus, J., *Cast Iron Buildings: their Construction and Advantages*, New York, 1856 (written for Bogardus by a friendly 'ghost', John W. Thomson), and Bannister, T. C., 'Bogardus Revisited, Part One: The Iron Fronts', *Journal of the Society of Architectural Historians*, XV (1956), 12–22.

184. 23. See Waite, J. G., *Iron Architecture in New York City* . . . [New York?] 1972, and Badger, D. D., and Bogardus, J., *The Origins of Cast Iron Architecture in America*, reprint, New York, 1970.

24. See Hitchcock, H.-R., 'Early Cast Iron Façades', *Architectural Review*, CIX (1951), 113–16.

25. See Hitchcock, H.-R., *The Crystal Palace* . . ., 2nd ed., Northampton, Mass., 1952; Beaver, P., *The Crystal Palace, 1851–1936; A Portrait of Victorian Enterprise*, London, 1970; and The Report of the Directors of The Crystal Palace Company, Sydenham, *The Crystal Palace Company*, London, 1953.

186. 26. See Carstensen, G., *The New York Crystal Palace*, New York, 1854; and Gayle, M., *The New York Crystal Palace, 1853–58*, New York, 1974.

26a. Roth, E., *Der Glaspalast in München* . . ., [Munich, c. 1971].

188. 27. The date of this is often given as 1855, when Labrouste took charge of the work at the Bibliothèque Nationale, and the original project for it may well be more nearly contemporaneous with the Reading Room of the British Museum.

28. Six pavilions were built first and four more before 1870, the remaining two were not erected until the 1930s. See Baltard, V., and Callet, F., *Monographie des Halles centrales de Paris construites sous le règne de Napoléon III*, Paris, 1865.

29. Technically the architect of Saint-Eugène in Paris was L.-A. Lusson, and in his monograph on the church, *Plans, coupes, élévations, et details de l'église . . . de Saint Eugène*, Paris, 1855, he does not even mention Boileau's name. However, the credit - or, to many contemporaries, the discredit - for the character of the cast-iron Gothic interior of the Paris church has always been given to Boileau.

CHAPTER 8

192. 1. A notably extreme early example is Visconti's Fontaine Molière of 1841–4 in the Rue de Richelieu.

2. Here Visconti's taste also proves to have been premonitory. His project of 1833 for a library already had a bulbous roof over the central pavilion; while that of 1849 for the Bibliothèque Nationale in the Rue de Richelieu had bold engaged orders on the central pavilion and a tall straight-sided mansard as well.

193. 3. See Hitchcock, H.-R., 'Second Empire "avant la lettre"', *Gazette des Beaux Arts*, XIII (1953), 115–30.

The existence of French analogues in the forties was insufficiently stressed there, however.

4. See Kramer, E. W., 'Detlef Lienau, an Architect of the Brown Decades', *Journal of the Society of Architectural Historians*, XIV (1955), 18–25. For an earlier mansard than Lienau's, see Dallett, J. F., 'John Notman's Mansard, 1848', *Journal of the Society of Architectural Historians*, XIX (1960), 81. The Deacon house in Boston by Lemoulnier, a French decorator, and G. J. F. Bryant also had a mansard dated 1848.

5. See Aulanier, C., *Le Nouveau Louvre de Napoléon III*, Paris [1953], and Hautecœur, L., *Histoire du Louvre*, Paris [n.d.].

195. 6. See Pinkney, D. H., *Napoleon III and the Rebuilding of Paris*, Princeton, N.J., 1958. Work began on the extension of the Rue de Rivoli in 1851; but it was only in 1853 that the Emperor found in G.-E. Haussmann (1809–91), whom he made Prefect of the Seine and later a baron, an adequate collaborator and executant for his tremendous urbanistic programme. Though he was not an architect, there is an entry for Haussmann in the Bibliography.

6a. *Les Boulevards de Paris; . . . maisons grandes et petites, hôtels, jardins, théâtres . . .*, Paris, 1877.

196. 7. A tour which can be taken vicariously is provided in a splendid set of lithographs of the period, *Paris dans sa splendeur*.

7a. Thanks to the cleaning of most of the principal buildings of Paris, largely completed in the 1960s, the prevailing tonality of Paris has become a cheerful cream-colour rather than a grimy grey. As a result many Second Empire works, both public and private, can now be seen much as they were when newly built.

8. The degree of control exercised by public authority over the façades varied. For the extension of the Rue de Rivoli, continuation of Percier and Fontaine's original design was required; and for the Place de l'Étoile and the Place de l'Opéra comprehensive designs established in advance were enforced (see below). Elsewhere only the height of the cornice line and the silhouette of the mansard were ordinarily standardized by regulation.

197. 9. Built in 1855 as the Hôtel des Chemins de Fer, but now the Hôtel du Louvre, and the work of Hittorff, Rohault de Fleury, Armand, and Pellechet. Hittorff and Rohault were also collaborating on the houses surrounding the Place de l'Étoile at this time. T. L. Donaldson, reporting on the new hotel at the Royal Institute of British Architects on 22 June 1855, remarked: 'The roof plays an important part in the design . . . much of the majesty of French buildings is derived from these lofty roofs.' Donaldson supervised the erection of the Hope house, and had thus played a personal part in the introduction of the French mansard into England six years earlier.

198. 10. It is curious that there should be uncertainty about the authorship of a complex so central to the building activity of its era. The Grand Hotel which occupies the corner of the Boulevard des Italiens to the left of the Opéra was by the team responsible for the Hôtel des Chemins de Fer at the other end of the avenue (see Note 9). Pinkney in *Napoleon III and the Rebuilding of Paris* gave credit for all the façades around the Place de l'Opéra to Rohault; Hautecœur assigned the rounded pavilions opposite the front of the Opéra to Blondel and mentioned no other architect. Whoever was responsible, Garnier felt they were much too tall and confining for his Opéra.

11. See Garnier, J.-L.-C., *Le nouvel Opéra de Paris*, 2 vols text and 6 vols plates, Paris, 1875–81; Steinhauser, M., *Die Architektur der Pariser Oper*, Munich, 1969.

200. 12. By this time Viollet-le-Duc was far more 'Victorian' than Garnier, yet his secular work had become so eclectic and even original in detail as hardly any longer to be Neo-Gothic at all (see Chapter 11). Thanks to the cleaning of the exterior of the Opéra, Garnier's polychromy is now once more visible, though the marbles he used must, when fresh, have been more striking notes of colour in a city that has always been largely monochromatic.

12a. See Hoffmann, H.-C., *Die Theaterbauten von Fellner und Helmer*, Munich, 1966, for typical opera-houses and theatres that these architects built in many cities of central and eastern Europe in the later nineteenth century.

13. See Daly, C., and Davioud, G.-J.-A., *Les Théâtres de la place du Châtelet*, Paris, 1860. Davioud, a pupil of the younger Vaudoyer, may almost be considered in international terms to have been a belated exponent of the *Rundbogenstil*. His work is relevant to the Parisian background of the American H. H. Richardson. (See Chapter 13.)

202. 14. See *Notice du Palais de Longchamps à Marseille*, Marseilles, 1872.

15. See Daly, C., *L'Architecture privée au XIXe siècle . . . sous Napoléon III; nouvelles maisons de Paris et des environs*, 3 vols, Paris, 1864; Calliat, V., *Parallèle des nouvelles maisons de Paris*, vol. II, Paris, 1864; Adam, Leveil, and LeBlanc, *Recueil des maisons les plus remarquables*, Paris, 1858; and *Maisons les plus remarquables de Paris*, Paris, 1870. César Daly, as editor of the *Revue de l'architecture*, also determined the character of the material that periodical offered in this period.

203. 15a. This is what the 1860s knew as *néo-grec*. The term is so ambiguous in its usage without detailed explanation that it has been avoided in this chapter.

204. 16. It is awkward that the long career of Viollet-le-Duc, like that of Semper, does not fall largely within any single chapter of this book. Active from the forties until the seventies, leading restorer of medieval monuments of his age in France, leading medieval archaeologist of Europe, controversial reformer of French architectural education (at least *in posse*), author of influential critical books, he was the inspirer – by his writings rather than his executed work – of a later generation of architectural innovators abroad more notably than at home. His failure to conform to the normal pattern of architectural life that usually confines a particular man's significant activity within some one phase of architectural development – such as, on the whole, each chapter of this book deals with – made it necessary to present his career in piecemeal fashion. It was partly covered in Chapter 6, with a few further mentions in this chapter, and – more significantly – in Chapter 11 in this Part and Chapter 16 at the beginning of Part Three. It is worth noting that Viollet-le-Duc is the only architect who enters this book in each of its three parts, even though it is only as an influence, not an executant, that he comes into the last part.

205. 17. And some contemporaries were ready to say Sicilian! It was started – or at least commissioned – some time before the first volume of the great treatise on Syrian architecture appeared: Vogüé, C.-J.-M. de, *Syrie Centrale*, 2 vols, Paris, 1865–77. But Vaudremer must have seen the drawings of Kalat Seman published by Duthuit in the *Gazette des architectes et du bâtiment*, 1864, No. 7, 79.

206. 18. See Daumet, H., *Notice sur M. Abadie*, Paris, 1886. It is relevant that Abadie became Diocesan Architect of Périgueux in 1874, the same year he began the Sacré-Cœur, the competition for which he had won two years earlier.

207. 18a. For characteristic French prize projects that were admired and emulated abroad, see *Les grands prix de Rome d'architecture de 1850–1900*, Paris [n.d.]. A very large number of the original drawings was shown in the École des Beaux-Arts exhibition at the Museum of Modern Art in New York in 1975. See Drexler, A. (ed.), *The Architecture of the École des Beaux Arts*, New York [1976].

19. For the Massachusetts institution, see Ware, W. R., *An Outline of a Course of Architectural Instruction*, Boston, 1866; for Columbia, see *idem*, 'The Instruction in Architecture at the School of Mines', *School of Mines Quarterly*, x (1888), 28–43.

20. Yet one of the boldest modern architects of Latin America, Carlos Raúl Villanueva (b. 1900) of Venezuela, was educated at the École des Beaux-Arts itself; and most of the other modern architects in these countries – those over fifty at least – were trained in the local Escuelas de Bellas Artes based on the Paris original.

208. 20a. Meeks, *op. cit.* (Introduction, Note 2a), 307, figures 168–71, 211: 'Later in the eighties, Poggi collaborated with Mariano Fabrini (1804–85) on the schemes for the Piazza Vittorio Emanuele, now the Piazza della Republica, and the heart of modern Florence'. The caption under Meeks's figure 171 queries the authorship of Fabrini, who died some eight years before the work began, but the megalomaniac west side of the square is certainly unworthy of Poggi.

21. The most conspicuous exception, dominating the whole city, is the Mole Antonelliana. This extraordinary edifice, begun by Alessandro Antonelli (1798–1880) in 1863, more than rivals his very tall earlier dome on San Gaudenzio in Novara, designed in 1840. Never really completed, the construction of the Mole continued intermittently down to Antonelli's death. By its great height and in some of the technicalities of its construction it rivals the Eiffel Tower and the early American skyscrapers which are posterior to it by several decades. Yet Antonelli arrived at no coherent expression of his structural innovations or, to judge from the successive purposes for which the structure has been intended to serve or has served, no real capacity to provide a functionally viable building. On the whole, as its present name implies, this is a monument chiefly to its designer's megalomania.

22. See Italy in the Bibliography.

209. 23. The third prominent edifice, surprisingly enough, is High Victorian Gothic. St Paul's, the American church, is by the English architect G. E. Street, and its curious relation to the characteristic academic blocks by Koch and his contemporaries can be appreciated in illustration 174 (see Chapter 11).

24. See Acciaresi, P., *Giuseppe Sacconi e l'opera sua massima*, Rome, 1911. Meeks, *op. cit.*, 337–47, is by reaction warm in praise of this long-scorned edifice and adds many names to the brief account given in this book. He is more convincing in his defence of the Palazzo di Giustizia, pp. 348–56.

211. 25. The best-maintained later equivalent in northern Europe is probably the Passage, as it is called, in The Hague. Built in 1882–5, this hardly rivals the Galleria Mazzini in Genoa in length and breadth, much less Mengoni's. There are many other examples, some of them considerably later, but few are in good condition today, and none have the scale of the three principal Italian examples. For earlier French examples, see Chapter 3. See Geist, J. F., *Passagen . . .*, Munich, 1969.

212. 25a. *Façaden von Palais*, Vienna, 1892, and Kapner, G., *Die Denkmäler der wiener Ringstrasse*, Vienna, 1969.

217. 25b. A rival, still well maintained, is what is now the Grandhotel Moskva-Pupp at Karlovy Vary in

Czechoslovakia, then called Karlsbad and also within the Austro-Hungarian empire. Books in English on Bohemian and Moravian architecture have little to say about nineteenth-century buildings, even those in Prague: but see Bibliography for an excellent Czech monograph and for books on Poland.

CHAPTER 9

222. 1. See Kreisel, H., *The Castles of Ludwig II of Bavaria*, Darmstadt [n.d.]; *Schloss Linderhof*, Munich, 1959; Mercanton, J., *Die Traumschlösser König Ludwigs II von Bayern*, Starnberg, c. 1964; Blunt, W., *The Dream King, Ludwig II of Bavaria*, New York, 1970, and Petzet, M., *König Ludwig II und die Kunst*, Munich, 1968.

224. 2. The design derives from the results of a competition held in 1876. Of the nine architects involved in the execution of the building, Grotjan, Lamprecht, Robertson, and Martin Haller (1835-1925) had won prizes in the competition. The tower is attributed specifically to the last and sometimes, more loosely, the whole structure.

229. 3. It should be pointed out that tall mansards allowed the addition of a full storey – sometimes even two – without increasing the height of the masonry work of the façade itself; thus there were reasons of economy as well as of fashion for their spread at this time (see Chapter 14).

232. 4. For that matter the London Ritz Hotel, built in 1905-6 by Mewès & Davis, is capped with a high mansard, although the vocabulary of their façades is a discreet and academic, if overscaled, *style Louis XVI* and the construction one of the first examples of the use of a steel skeleton of the American skyscraper type outside the United States.

234. 5. Thomas Cundy II (1790-1867) died in this year; if provided by the Estate Architect's office, the designs were either initiated before his death or else they were entirely by his assistants, perhaps directed by his surviving brother Joseph (1795-1875). .A. T. Bolton believed that the responsibility for the design lay with the builder Trollope; the Grosvenor Estate office, however, names not Trollope but the Cubitt firm as the builders. As with the Place de l'Opéra, the credit for this most notable and once conspicuous piece of Second Empire urbanism remains uncertain.

236. 5a. See the *Survey of London*, XXXVIII, *The Museums Area of South Kensington and Westminster*, [1975].

236. 5b. See, however, Castermans, A., *Parallèle des maisons de Bruxelles*, Paris, 1856, which illustrates much work that is not at all Parisian.

6. See Poelaert, J., *Le Nouveau Palais de Justice de Bruxelles*, Brussels, 1904.

238. 7. Semper was in England for several years after he left Dresden as a result of the revolution that also led to Wagner's expulsion in 1848. He did no building in England, but was closely associated with Cole and his Department of Practical Art. The catafalque of the Duke of Wellington, used at the State funeral in 1852, was of his design. His Swiss period was followed by a triumphant return to Dresden to rebuild the opera-house there and his final settlement in Vienna in 1871. Since this relatively important architect appears, like Viollet-le-Duc, in unrelated contexts in several different chapters of this book, it seems well to recall here the total range of his career to its conclusion in Vienna in the seventies, passing through Dresden, London, Zürich, and Dresden a second time.

239. 8. See Burnham, A., 'The New York Architecture of Richard M. Hunt', *Journal of the Society of Architectural Historians*, XI (1952), 9-14.

9. Of course Daly's *Revue de l'architecture* reached some American architects and also his *Architecture privée* (see Note 15, Chapter 8). See also Liénard, M., *Specimens of the Decoration and Ornamentation of the XIXth Century*, Boston, 1875, although by that date the vogue for such Second Empire detailing was all but over.

240. 10. See Walter, T. U., *Letter to the Committee on Public Buildings, in reference to an Enlargement of the Capitol* [Washington, 1850], and *Report of the Architect of the United States Capitol and the New Dome*, Washington, 1864.

11. See McKenna, R. T., 'James Renwick, Jr, and the Second Empire Style in the United States', *Magazine of Art*, XLIV (1951), 97-101.

241. 12. See Boston. Committee on Public Buildings, *The City Hall, Boston*, Boston, 1866. A considerably larger early project of 1861 emulates much more closely the New Louvre.

13. See Bunting, B., *Houses of Boston's Back Bay*, Cambridge, Mass., 1967, especially chapters 3 and 8.

245. 13a. How worthy they were is a matter of taste, but R. M. Hunt in the U.S. trained many younger architects, one of them – and most unlikely – Frank Furness (see Chapter 11).

CHAPTER 10

247. 1. See Thompson, P., 'All Saints' Church, Margaret Street, Reconsidered', *Architectural History* (1965), 73-94.

248. 1a. Despite the 'correctness' of Butterfield's detailing, an idiosyncratic coarsening can be noted at St Augustine's College in Canterbury and in other work by him done several years before All Saints'; yet, by contrast to other aspects of his mature style, his moulded detail remained conventional.

2. Since building Christ Church, Streatham, at the opening of the decade, Wild had been busy in Egypt. His curious St Mark's, Alexandria, as Saracenic as his detractors accused the Streatham church of being, was unhappily never brought to completion. Designed in 1842, work was suspended for lack of funds in 1848 and Wild then returned to England.

250. 2a. See Summerson, J., *The London Building World of the Eighteen-Sixties*, London [1973].

251. 3. Deane owed his knighthood to having been Mayor of Cork, not to his professional attainments. It would appear that Woodward did all the firm's designing and, after his death in 1861, Deane's son Thomas Newenham took over.

252. 4. See Viollet-le-Duc, E.-E., *Dictionnaire raisonné de l'architecture française du XIe au XVIe siècle*, 10 vols, Paris, 1854–68. Also Pevsner, Sir N., *Ruskin and Viollet-le-Duc*, London [1969], and Summerson, Sir J., 'Viollet-le-Duc and the Rational Point of View', *Heavenly Mansions*, New York [1963].

5. See Mackail, J. W., *The Life of William Morris*, London, 1899. Though Morris was not an architect, some of the extensive literature will be found among the monographs in the Bibliography.

254. 6. Burges designed this in 1868 in his most archaeological and articulated French Gothic manner. Construction began only in 1893, long after Burges's death, and the suave quality of the execution, so uncharacteristic of the still High Victorian date of the original design, is thereby explained; at best the design was singularly out of key with what Bodley had built.

255. 7. Since this is a Catholic church, and by a man who knew French Gothic architecture well, it provides the fairest possible comparison with Viollet-le-Duc's own new church of Saint-Denys-de-l'Estrée at St-Denis designed at almost precisely the same time [169]. Viollet-le-Duc is world-famous; Clutton is not generally considered even in England one of the leaders of his generation; yet the superiority of the Leamington church to the St-Denis church is very considerable indeed both inside and out.

256. 7a. Large Victorian country houses are more recurrently threatened with demolition even than major buildings of the period in cities. Happily Elvetham Park is maintained by a large industrial organization as a training establishment.

8. See Harbron, D., 'Thomas Harris', *Architectural Review*, XCII (1942), 63–6, and Donner, P., 'Harris Florilegium', *Architectural Review*, XCIII (1943), 51–2.

9. This is spoilt externally by an unfortunate tower added by his son A. E. Street (1855–1938) in 1884–5.

257. 10. See *The National Memorial to H.R.H. the Prince Consort*, [London] 1873.

11. Scott's aspirations for architecture, in general more sympathetic to posterity than much of what he built, will be found in his *Remarks on Secular and Domestic Architecture, Present and Future*, London, 1858.

259. 12. Although Woodward's death occurred in the same year 1861 that this club was begun, it is possible, even probable, that the original design was his.

13. See Nesfield, W. E., *Specimens of Mediaeval Architecture . . . in France and Italy*, London, 1862.

262. 14. The intentions of the church builders in this decade are well presented in Micklethwaite, J. T., *Modern Parish Churches, their Plan, Design, and Furnishing*, London, 1874.

14a. See Taylor, N., 'Wagnerian High Church: St Bartholomew's Brighton', *Architectural Review* (March 1965), 212–17.

15. An extraordinary example of the use of Victorian Gothic for a somewhat unexpected purpose was Columbia Market by H. A. Darbishire (1839–1908) set down in 1866–8 among the grim housing blocks that he built for the philanthropist Angela Burdett-Coutts. See Wilson, F. M., 'Ypres at Bethnal Green', *Architectural Review*, XCVI (1944), 131–4.

263. 16. Godwin's active and distinguished Victorian Gothic period concluded with the building of two castles in Ireland, Dromore at Pallaskenny for the Earl of Limerick in 1867–9 and Glenbegh in 1868–71. Burges was with him in Ireland when he designed Dromore, and its decorations and furnishings rivalled in elaboration and exceeded in elegance what Burges did for Lord Bute at Cardiff and Castell Coch in these years. A row with the client for Glenbegh, who complained of drastic leakage, in which Godwin's then partner Crisp deserted him, did Godwin much harm professionally. He was still a relatively important figure in the Late Victorian seventies, but more as a decorator than as an architect (see Chapter 12).

269. 16a. See Taylor, N., 'Byzantium in Brighton', *Architectural Review* (April 1966), 310–12.

CHAPTER 11

271. 1. At the Centennial Exhibition in Philadelphia the larger pavilions were all of iron and glass; and probably the most influential buildings were the British ones designed by Thomas Harris – no longer a wild 'Victorian' – in a mode closely approaching Norman Shaw's 'Manorial' mode (see Chapter 12). However, the exhibition stimulated the publication of several books on the Colonial architecture of Philadelphia which played their part in preparing the way for a 'Colonial Revival' (see Chapters 13 and 15). The Bicentennial has in 1976 focused historical attention not only on the eighteenth-century past but on the architectural situation around the centennial year.

Relevant publications, however, have in early 1976 not yet appeared.

2. Separate American editions of vols 2 and 3 did not appear promptly in 1853 in the way that of vol. 1 did in 1851. However, the three-volume American edition of 1861 was the first of the complete work.

3. See Hitchcock, H. R., 'Ruskin and American Architecture...', in *Concerning Architecture*, London, 1968, pp. 166–208.

272. 4. See Note 19, Chapter 8.

5. They had, after all, first met when they were both at R. M. Hunt's atelier in New York.

6. See Ware, W. R., *The Memorial Hall, Harvard University*, Boston, 1887.

273. 7. In the 1936 edition of my book on Richardson a later Dorsheimer plan was incorrectly associated with this Buffalo house. The house is properly identified in Hitchcock, H.-R., 'Richardson's American Express Building: A Note', *Journal of the Society of Architectural Historians*, IX (1950), 25–30 and in the 1961 and 1966 editions of the Richardson book.

274. 8. This is also missing from my 1936 Richardson book, but will be found in the article cited above and in the later editions of the book.

9. See Wight, P. B., 'Reminiscences of Russell Sturgis', *Architectural Record*, XXVI (1909), 123–31. It is perhaps worth pointing out that Farnam Hall, together with Sturgis's contiguous Battell Chapel of 1876 and his Durfee Hall at right angles to it, although neither are of at all comparable excellence, give this corner of the Old Campus at Yale a consistent High Victorian Gothic character interesting to study both in relation to the earlier Romantic Gothic of Henry Austin's library (now Dwight Chapel) of 1842–4 on the other side of the campus and the 'traditional' Collegiate Gothic of James Gamble Rogers's twentieth-century Harkness Quadrangle across High Street.

10. See Schuyler, M., 'The Work of William Appleton Potter', *Architectural Record*, XXVI (1909), 176–96.

275. 10a. See Hitchcock, H. R., *op. cit.* (Note 3), especially pp. 184–6, 200–1, and plates 23–4. Now that it has become evident this was not designed by E. T. Potter in 1858, but almost certainly a decade or more later, the High Victorian Gothic of the Union College rotunda need no longer be considered especially significant historically. See Note 12a to Chapter 1.

11. See Holly, H. H., *Church Architecture Illustrated*, Hartford, 1871. Much more extreme models can be found in general compendia of architectural design published in the late sixties and early seventies.

12. See Campbell, W., 'Frank Furness, an American Pioneer', *Architectural Review*, CX (1951), 310–15.

13. See 'Another Furness Building: Provident Life and Trust Company Building, Philadelphia', *Architectural Review*, CXII (1952), 196; 'Provident Trust

Company Banking Room, Philadelphia', *Journal of the Society of Architectural Historians*, XI (1952), 31; and Massy, J. C., 'The Provident Trust Buildings', *Journal of the Society of Architectural Historians*, XIX (1960), 79–80.

276. 14. See Withers, F. C., *Church Architecture*, New York, 1871.

15. See Upjohn, R. M., *The State Capitol, Hartford, Conn.*, Boston, 1886; and Hersey, G., 'Replication replicated, or Notes on American Bastardy', *Perspecta*, 9/10, 212–48, which is splendidly illustrated with many new photographs by John T. Hill, including various details.

16. It was the sale of the old Trinity College property to provide a site for the new Capitol that led to, and paid for, the rebuilding of the college elsewhere, for which Burges provided the designs (see Chapter 10).

277. 17. It is worth recalling that much the same could evidently be said of Fuller & Laver's San Francisco municipal group; characteristically enough for the period, this was Second Empire like their Albany Capitol, not High Victorian Gothic (see Chapter 9).

279. 18. See Viollet-le-Duc, E.-E., *Entretiens sur l'architecture*, 2 vols, Paris, 1863, 1872; and translations, *Discourses on Architecture*, 2 vols, Boston, 1875, 1881, and *Lectures on Architecture*, 2 vols, London, 1877, 1881. Originally the *Entretiens* appeared in parts, those in the first volume beginning to come out about 1860 and those in the second some six years later.

19. The two most sumptuously illustrated publications concerning Viollet-le-Duc offer very few examples of new buildings designed by him; these must be sought in periodicals and other general contemporary sources. See *Compositions et dessins de Viollet-le-Duc*, Paris, 1884, Baudot, A. de, and Roussel, J., *Dessins inédits de Viollet-le-Duc*, 3 vols, Paris [n.d.] and later items in the Bibliography.

280. 19a. *Monographie de la basilique Saint Epvre à Nancy*, [Tournai, 1890].

20. The most extravagant compilation of idiosyncratic detail in Viollet-le-Duc's work is to be seen on the tomb of Napoleon III's half-brother the Duc de Morny, erected in 1858 in Père Lachaise Cemetery in Paris. Hardly any element of the ornamentation is clearly referable to a particular stylistic source, and the whole effect is as 'Victorian' as anything the wildest High Victorians ever produced in England.

281. 20a. Henri Labrouste's work, if not that of Duban, illustrated earlier [112, 118, 126], or Duc's Palais de Justice and Garnier's Opéra [122–4], may well be considered '*non*-Renaissance'; also, they are all at least the equals in distinction of even the finest Romanesquoid churches.

282. 21. It should not be forgotten that Street's Law Courts in London were completed only a year before

Steindl began the Budapest Parliament House; but the Law Courts were, for England, extremely retardataire.

284. 22. Burges won the competition for this in 1857, but in the end Street received the commission and built the church in 1864-9.

23. See Meeks, C. L. V., 'Churches by Street on the Via Nazionale and the Via del Babuino', *Art Quarterly*, XVI (1953), 215-27.

286. 24. See Martinell, C., *La Sagrada Familia*, Barcelona, 1952, and Puig Boada, I., *El Templo de la Sagrada Familia*, Barcelona, 1952. A phenomenal number of articles have appeared concerning this church, all listed up to his date of publication (1960) by Ráfols in the late edition of his monograph on Gaudí.

290. 25. Mixing the elements of several styles in individual buildings provided the liveliest aspect of eclecticism at this time; the mere use of alternative modes had chiefly the effect of blurring the edges of all the styles of the past.

26. Compare, for example, Sigfried Giedion's presentation of the period in *Space, Time and Architecture*.

CHAPTER 12

291. 1. Many serious and conscientious English students of this period would precede such a list with the name of George Devey (1820-86). Of Devey, in whose office C. F. A. Voysey, the most original English architect of the next generation, chose to work after completing his apprenticeship with Seddon, Voysey later wrote: 'Providentially an invitation came to enter the Office of the most extensive practitioner in homes for the Nobility and Gentry. No domestic practice has equalled his in extent before or since his death.' As in the case of William Burn, whose aristocratic practice of the forties and fifties Devey's more than rivalled in the sixties and seventies, neither he nor his clients cared for publicity, and so none of his work was published, even to the slight extent that the work of Nesfield and Webb was illustrated in the professional journals. Still today his houses are known to posterity chiefly through a few articles; Godfrey, Walter, 'The Work of George Devey', *Architectural Review*, XXI (1907), 23-30, 83-8, 293-306; and 'George Devey, F.R.I.B.A., a Biographical Essay', *Journal of the Royal Institute of British Architects*, XIII (1906), 501-25.

But just as the work of Nesfield and Webb was in actuality familiar from the first to their professional friends and rivals, as also to prospective country house clients, so was that of Devey. Many of the stylistic trends so vigorously exploited by Shaw in the seventies can be traced back to Devey's houses of the preceding decade - or so such experts on the period as H. S. Goodhart-Rendel and John Brandon-Jones, who know Devey's work intimately, always insist. Foreign students of this period, from Muthesius to the Editor of this series and this author, perhaps merely because of lack of direct or even adequate indirect knowledge of Devey's houses, have never been ready to grant him so important a place in the story. Here particularly, where the story is told in an international context, the evident strength of the influence of Shaw's work abroad even more than at home justifies giving him primacy and referring only incidentally to that of Devey.

292. 2. Shaw did not immediately succeed Webb, since the latter stayed on in Street's office until the middle of 1859. There must have been close contact between them over a period of up to a year, and they remained in touch from then on. Blomfield, Shaw's biographer, being himself prejudiced against Webb, underestimates the reality and the importance of this relationship. It is only one of the many errors of fact or emphasis in his book.

To quote from a private communication from Brandon-Jones concerning Shaw and Webb: 'Each must have had a good idea of the work the other was doing. Their two offices, in Gray's Inn and Bloomsbury Square, were within a stone's-throw of one another, and Lethaby while working for Shaw was in close touch with Webb and was in his spare time assisting him with the architectural work of Morris & Co. It is quite obvious from the dates of various executed works that Lethaby was carrying over Webb's ideas and details and trying them out in work he was doing for Shaw. As for the mutual respect and friendship between Webb and Shaw, I [Brandon-Jones] have recently come across a letter written at the time of Shaw's death in which he [Webb] pays a tribute to his "old friend", and I have also seen a letter from Sydney Barnsley to Sydney Cockerell in which Barnsley says that he had called on Shaw only a few months before his death and that Shaw had been talking of Webb and saying that he still treasured some photographs given him by Webb nearly fifty years earlier.'

3. Devey's incidental work at Penshurst Place in Kent, where that notable fourteenth-century manor house was restored by him, having been done more than a decade earlier, probably prepared the way for this. It is extremely likely that Nesfield was familiar with what Devey had done there; but the line forward leads, in the late sixties, from Nesfield to Shaw, not directly from Devey to Shaw.

293. 4. See Pevsner, N., 'Art Furniture of the Seventies', *Architectural Review*, CXI (1952), 23-50; and Aslin, E., *The Aesthetic Movement*, New York [1969].

4a. The most famous instance of *japonisme* in decoration is Whistler's 'Peacock Room', now in the Freer Gallery in Washington. See Ferriday, P., 'Peacock Room', *Architectural Review*, CXXV (1959), 407–14.

5. Once again Devey had prepared the way, in this case at Betteshanger, Kent, a house built precisely ten years earlier. This will doubtless have been known both to friends of Devey's clients and to various young architects. But the Kew lodge was located where everyone could see it, even though it was not published until the nineties.

5a. One of the Kinmel Park lodges dates from 1866, so the house may have been commissioned before Shaw left Nesfield. Even so he is less likely to have been involved in the designing than at Cloverley Hall since his personal career began at this point.

294. 5b. The client was a partner of Shaw's brother in a Liverpool shipping firm.

297. 6. For this also there was precedent at Devey's Betteshanger; but Betteshanger initiated no popular mode in the way that the conspicuous London schools by Robson and Stevenson's highly touted house did at this point. For the schools, see Jones, D. G., 'Towers of Learning', *Architectural Review*, CXXIII (1958), 393–8.

299. 7. See Harbron, D., 'Queen Anne Taste and Aestheticism', *Architectural Review*, XCLV (1943), 15–18.

8. See Shaw, R. N., *Sketches for Cottages and Other Buildings . . .*, London, 1878.

301. 9. See 'The Ballad of Bedford Park', *St James's Gazette*, 17 December 1881 (reprinted by Blomfield, *Shaw*, 34–6). This is an amusing but not entirely accurate contemporary description in verse.

303. 10. The handling of this building in section is particularly ingenious, the area of the service portions at the rear of the flats being much increased by the use of lower storey heights than in the reception rooms at the front. This device has been revived since, but its earlier invention by Shaw has rarely been noted Brandon-Jones pointed out to me.

11. At least they are now so painted; it is probable they were originally of 'white' Suffolk brick, actually a very pale yellow when newly laid and unbegrimed, but more likely to be black after a few decades of exposure to the air of London!

304. 12. Hyde, H. M., 'Wilde and his Architect', *Architectural Review*, CIX (1951), 175–6.

13. It is characteristic of Shaw's prestige in America and the rapidity with which architectural ideas crossed the ocean at this time that Shaw's handsome perspective of the Alliance was published in America a few months earlier than in England.

14. White first approached Webb but, finding him too difficult to deal with, went to Shaw – a significant episode as regards both architects.

306. 15. See Brandon-Jones, J., 'Notes on the Building of Smeaton Manor', *Architectural History*, I (1958), 31–59.

CHAPTER 13

312. 1. See Webster, J. C., 'Richardson's American Express Building', *Journal of the Society of Architectural Historians*, IX (1950), 21–4, and my article cited in Note 7 to Chapter 11.

2. See Richardson, H. H., *Trinity Church, Boston*, Boston, 1888.

313. 3. For discussion of some of Richardson's sources, etc., see Hitchcock, H. R., *Richardson as a Victorian Architect*, Northampton, Mass. [1966], 5–6, 39–48, notes 22 and 44. A possible contemporary French source is Léon Vaudoyer's Cathedral of Marseilles. Begun in 1856, this was still incomplete when Vaudoyer died in 1872; but the design, if not what had been built before Richardson left France in the mid sixties, was probably known to him or, at least, other similar work and projects by Vaudoyer and his pupils Espérandieu and Davioud, such as the latter's designs prepared for the competitions at the École. Even more relevant to his stylistic formation must have been his direct contact with the Labrouste circle while working for Henri's brother Théodore.

314. 4. The source was probably the book by Vogüé of which the second volume appeared only in 1877 (see Note 17, Chapter 8). The motif first appeared in the North Easton Library, designed and begun in that year.

315. 5. See Richardson, H. H., *The Ames Memorial Building[s]*, Boston, 1886.

6. See Olmsted in the monograph section of the Bibliography. It was plausibly suggested by Larry Homolka, in a paper read at the meeting of the Society of Architectural Historians at Cleveland in January 1967, that Olmsted actually influenced the design of the Ames Gate Lodge.

7. See Richardson, H. H., *Austin Hall, Harvard Law School*, Boston, 1885.

316. 8. See Richardson, H. H., *Description of Drawings for the Proposed New County Building for Allegheny County, Penn.*, Boston, 1884.

318. 8a. The immediate model may well have been George B. Post's Produce Exchange in New York, begun in 1881, but that has Renaissance detailing.

9. See Schuyler, M., 'The Romanesque Revival in New York', *Architectural Record*, I (1891), 7–38, 151–98.

319. 10. See Bragdon, C., 'Harvey Ellis', *Architectural*

Record, XXV (1908), 173–83. The lately demolished Nash Building in Rochester, N.Y., by Harvey Ellis and his brother Charles, completed in 1884 or 1885, already resembled Richardson's later Ames Building, yet had no Richardsonian detailing. Ellis's Minneapolis buildings are the subject of an article by R. G. Kennedy, 'The Long Shadow of Harvey Ellis', in *Minnesota History*, XL (1966), 97–108. Local research on such late-nineteenth-century architects as Ellis who were active in the Middle West has lately become very productive, broadening an historical view of the period once restricted to the Eastern Seaboard and later chiefly to Chicago.

10a. *Buffington's Iron Building Company* [Minneapolis, 1893].

11. Hunt, of the older generation, was generally recognized as a leader in this camp also, although his energies in these years were principally engaged in designing and building a series of *François I* châteaux for the Vanderbilts and other millionaires that are anything but academic in their involved picturesqueness. This curious episode, which has been given exaggerated importance by some historians of American architecture, began with the designing of the two Vanderbilt houses in New York in 1879–80 (see Andrews, W., *The Vanderbilt Legend*, New York, 1941). Several architects were also briefly affected by what was hardly more than a recrudescence of a mode popular in France under Louis Philippe (see Chapter 3). A few houses by McKim, Mead & White of the early eighties are definitely *François I*, and Richardson was already using *François I* dormers in the late seventies on the Albany Capitol. Moreover, the round towers of the 'Shingle Style' undoubtedly owe something to Stanford White's sketching trips in France. This episode obviously parallels the interest in revived Northern Renaissance modes of design in Germany, Holland, and Scandinavia in these decades, and has analogies also to the contemporary work in England of George & Peto and Collcutt (see Chapters 9 and 12).

320. 12. In the designing of the Sherman house - particularly in the Shavian detailing - White had probably played an important part; he was, moreover, called on by the Shermans to enlarge the house in 1881. The library, of this date, is one of his finest pieces of interior decoration.

12a. A sketch by L. C. Tiffany, the artist-son of the family, probably provided the *parti* the architects developed. For L. C. Tiffany, see p. 389.

321. 13. One of the earliest examples of the serious study of Colonial precedent is Arthur Little's *Early New England Interiors*, Boston, 1878. However, his own work remained relatively free for some years.

14. See *Building News*, 28 April 1882.

14a. The library was cleaned when Philip Johnson built the new wing faced with the same granite in 1972.

322. 15. These tiles wore out some years ago and have now been replaced. The smooth black roof seen on illustration 194 lacks the fine scale and rich texture the pantiles now again provide.

323. 16. The conceptual organization of the exterior has seemed to most critics to have been borrowed from a much later monument, Henri Labrouste's Bibliothèque Sainte-Geneviève in Paris of the 1840s. But there is certainly none of Labrouste's exposed metalwork in the interior; all the same, the extensive use of Guastavino tile vaults, then a novel technical innovation, is very notable and was soon followed by other architects for a generation and more. Here, even more than in the Marshall Field Store, there may well have been influence from Post's Produce Exchange, if not his arcaded façades of the seventies.

17. See Burnham, D. H., *World's Columbian Exposition*, Chicago, 1894; Ives, H., *The Dream City*, St Louis, 1893; and Cameron, W., *History of the World's Columbian Exposition*, Chicago, 1893. Only Jenney & Mundie in the Horticultural Building made a positive feature of their bubble-like dome of iron and glass with a result at least as original as Sullivan's wooden-roofed Transportation Building.

18. The area round the 'Wooded Isle' was much less regular than that round the Lagoon in continuance of Olmsted's earlier and more naturalistic sort of landscaping. Into this area were shunted most of the buildings by local architects, because Burnham and McKim distrusted their capacity to conform to the academic standards they were setting.

18a. These remarkable structural feats, particularly the enormously extensive roof of the Manufactures Building, have rarely received the attention that is their due either from contemporaries or from posterity.

CHAPTER 14

328. 1. See Note 14, Chapter 5.

2. Somewhat fuller accounts of English commercial architecture in this period will be found in Hitchcock, 'Victorian Monuments of Commerce', *Architectural Review*, CV (1949), 61–74, and in Hitchcock, *Early Victorian Architecture*, Chapters XI and XII. Most of the English buildings mentioned in this chapter are illustrated either in the book or the article. See also Taylor, N., *Monuments of Commerce*, Feltham, 1968.

3. See Weisman, W., 'Commercial Palaces of New York', *Journal of the Society of Architectural Historians*, XXXVI (1954), 285–302.

330. 4. See Bogardus, J., *Cast Iron Buildings: Construction and Advantages*, New York, 1856.

5. See Hitchcock, H.-R., 'Early Cast Iron Façades',

Architectural Review, CIX (1951), 113–16. Now known as Gardner's or 'The Iron Building'. *Glasgow at a Glance*, Mack Young, A., and Doak, A. M., eds., Glasgow [1965]; figure 42, provides the name of John Baird I as architect in conjunction with McConnell, who held the structural patents. Baird's successor, James Thomson, in association with McConnell erected a less interesting iron building that also survives at 217-221 Argyle Street.

331. 6. See Weisman, W., 'Philadelphia Functionalism and Sullivan', *Journal of the Society of Architectural Historians*, XX (1961), 3-19.

7. See Sturges, W. K., 'Cast Iron in New York', *Architectural Review*, CXIV (1953), 233-8.

7a. This might well have influenced Post in designing his Produce Exchange.

333. 8. See Peterson, C., 'Ante-bellum Skyscraper', *Journal of the Society of Architectural Historians*, IX (1950), 27-9; X (1951), 25. The Jayne Building, begun by Johnston, was completed by Thomas U. Walter. It has unfortunately been demolished.

9. See Woodward, G., 'Oriel Chambers', *Architectural Review*, CXIX (1956), 268-70. Fine measured drawings by students of the University of Liverpool School of Architecture were published in *Architectural History*, II (1959), 81-94.

334. 10. See Note 1, Chapter 13.

335. 11. See Weisman, W., 'New York and the Problem of the First Skyscraper', *Journal of the Society of Architectural Historians*, XII (1953), 13-20. For a rather different opinion, see Webster, J. C., 'The Skyscraper: Logical and Historical Considerations', *Journal of the Society of Architectural Historians*, XVIII (1959), 126-39.

12. It is worth noting that neither cast-iron façades nor the vertical articulation of the Philadelphia buildings of the fifties was used in either case. Both developments of the mid century proved cul-de-sacs since the New York architects followed the established modes of the sixties for monumental buildings in these first two skyscrapers. In the same years 1873-4, however, Hunt did build the five-storey edifice at 478-482 Broadway in New York with an all cast-iron front, employing a sort of attenuated 'giant order' subsuming the three middle storeys.

336. 13. Giedion first called attention to the importance of 'balloon-frame' construction in *Space, Time and Architecture* in 1941; but see Field, W., 'A Re-examination into the Invention of the Balloon Frame', *Journal of the Society of Architectural Historians*, II (1942), 3-29.

14. See Randall, G., *The Great Fire of Chicago and its Causes*, Chicago [1871].

337. 15. See Hope, H., 'Louis Sullivan's Architectural Ornament', *Magazine of Art*, XL (1947), 110-17.

Sullivan thought of his early ornament as somehow 'Egyptian', but it is not very easy to see why. See p. 340.

15a. The ground storey has been modernized – not altogether disadvantageously, since its rusticated arches were not well related to the frank design of the rest of the façade.

16. This is not the same as the Revell Store.

338. 17. Several more storeys were added later and appear in many of the published views.

18. One must say 'metal', because structural steel was only gradually replacing cast and wrought iron at this time; all these types of ferrous material were probably used in the Home Insurance, the Rookery, and other skyscrapers of the mid eighties. Two books by W. Birkmire, *Architectural Iron and Steel*, New York, 1891, and *Skeleton Construction in Buildings*, New York, 1893, best present the technical aspects of large-scale metal construction as it matured in the eighties and early nineties.

339. 18a. The Auditorium exterior is nearly as close to that of Post's Produce Exchange as to the Field Store.

340. 19. An American edition of this book appeared in 1880. See Note 15, *supra*.

20. I owe this suggestion to Vincent Scully. An unpublished study by Etel Kramer gives the most satisfactory account of the development of Sullivan's ornament from his Paris days down to the McVickar Theatre drawings, whose importance she was the first to recognize.

342. 21. Incidentally, the signature Frank L[loyd] Wright on the drawings for a rather Richardsonian group of three masonry houses in Chicago, designed in the Adler & Sullivan office in 1888 for Victor L. Falkenau, suggests that it was Sullivan's brilliant draughtsman, as it was Jenney's assistant on the Leiter Building, who was responsible for this example of overt Richardsonian influence.

343. 22. The assumption by Carl Condit that this building was begun in 1890 seemed to lend it a special importance, until then unrecognized. But Condit in a later book, *The Chicago School of Architecture*, Chicago, *c*. 1964, 109-11, was finally able to give the true story. This need not be quoted here in full, but the name of the structural engineer, Edward C. Shankland, should be noted, as also the remarkable speed with which the ten storeys of steel-work went up between 16 July and 1 August 1895.

22a. The history of the designing of the Monadnock Building runs through many years and was very complicated. See Burnham & Root in the Bibliography.

22b. See Randall, J. D., *The Art of Office Buildings*, Springfield, Ill., 1972.

346. 23. It is so generally assumed that Sullivan's mature style is without historical antecedents that the even more definitely *quattrocento* character of the entrance here, as well as of those of the Guaranty Buildings, is rarely noted.

347. 24. The five southernmost bays are an addition made in 1906 by D. H. Burnham & Co. They follow, with some slight diminution in the bay-width, Sullivan's original design. In 1960-1 in a further southward extension of the building Holabird & Root again followed the Sullivan design fairly closely, even parodying the ornamental band around the shop windows.

349. 24a. See *Purcell and Elmslie Architects* (Walker Art Gallery Exhibition Catalogue), Minneapolis, 1953, and Gebhard, D., 'Louis Sullivan and George Grant Elmslie', *Journal of the Society of Architectural Historians*, XIX (1960), 62-8, and *A Guide to the Existing Architecture of Purcell and Elmslie*, Roswell, N. M., 1960.

350. 25. Surviving the demolished skyscraper is a smaller and earlier Singer Building, also by Flagg. Flagg was one American who retained contact with the French tradition of exposed metal construction as well as with the academic aspects of 'Beaux Arts' design as his first Singer Building illustrates.

26. See Schuyler, M., 'The Work of N. LeBrun & Sons', *Architectural Record*, XXVII (1910), 365-80. The Metropolitan Tower is, of course, the work of a firm not of a single architect; LeBrun himself had been dead for some years.

27. See Schuyler, M., '"The Towers of Manhattan" and Notes on the Woolworth Building', *Architectural Record*, XXX (1913), 98-122.

CHAPTER 15

354. 1. See Note 31, Chapter 6.

1a. For a remarkable later development of the veranda outside England, see Robertson, E. G., 'The Australian Verandah', *Architectural Review*, CXXVII (1960), 238-45.

355. 2. There are many examples in various English books of the first third of the century; characteristic are those offered by T. F. Hunt, J. B. Papworth, and P. F. Robinson. See Note 28 to Chapter 6.

356. 3. See Note 26, Chapter 6.

4. See Note 22, Chapter 6.

357. 5. See Note 27, Chapter 6.

6. See Note 13, Chapter 14.

358. 7. See Note 26, Chapter 6.

359. 8. In the *Builder* for 15 January 1859 and in the Supplement to Kerr, R., *The Gentleman's House*, 2nd ed., London, 1865.

360. 9. Contemporaries saw this house rather as a reaction towards the 'Old English' after the 'modernism' of the High Victorian Gothic and the Second Empire of the preceding decade. How conscious Shaw

himself was of the significance of his own innovations it is difficult to say.

10. The plan was first published by Muthesius in 1904; this does not mean that its character was not known to contemporary architects, however.

361. 11. By this time photo-lithographic processes made it possible for Shaw's perspectives to appear in the *Building News* practically as facsimiles of his originals. Had it been necessary, as in the fifties and sixties, to 'translate' them into wood-engravings the transmission of the Shavian influence abroad would certainly have been much less effective.

362. 12. See Note 27, Chapter 6. The term 'Eastlake' is sometimes rather inaccurately used for the Stick Style. Even for American furniture it was inaccurate, as Eastlake himself complained. See Landau, S. B., *op. cit.* (Chapter 6, Note 29).

13. See Wheeler, G., *Rural Houses*, New York, 1851, with later editions to 1868, and his *Homes for the People in Suburb and Country*, New York, 1855, with later editions to 1867.

13a. See Mason, G. C., *Newport and its Cottages*, Boston, 1875.

14. See Gardner, E. C., *Homes and How to Build Them*, Boston, 1874, and also his *Illustrated Homes*, Boston, 1875.

15. See Woodward, G. E., *Woodward's Country Houses*, New York, 1865; *Woodward's Architecture, Landscape Gardening and Rural Art*, New York, 1867; *Woodward's Cottage and Farm Houses*, New York, 1867; and *Woodward's National Architect*, New York, 1868. Of *Woodward's Country Houses* there were eight successive editions within a decade, thus rivalling in this period the popularity of Downing's *Cottage Residences* in the forties and fifties; however, it is worth noting that the latter still remained in print.

16. See Sturges, W. K., 'Long Shadow of Norman Shaw: Queen Anne Revival', *Journal of the Society of Architectural Historians*, IX (1950), 21-5.

363. 17. Scully in *The Shingle Style* provided evidence that the idea of a great hall was not unknown in America well before this, for example in the Nathan Reeves house in Newburgh, N.Y., published as 'Design No. 22' in Vaux, C., *Villas and Cottages*, New York, 1857. However, Peter Barnett has observed that an unidentified house-plan by Richardson dated 8 August 1868 – figure 12 in the 1961 and 1966 editions of my book on Richardson – is very close indeed to Waterhouse's Hinderton while the Codman plan is, in turn, an inversion of that. Thus, the missing link has at last been found, or so it seems. Hinderton was available in two publications by this date.

364. 18. The term is Vincent Scully's. Various themes touched on in this and succeeding paragraphs are discussed at length in his *The Shingle Style and the*

Stick Style, New Haven, 1971, and provided there with a full roster of illustrations.

367. 19. It is of interest that when the *Monograph of the Work of McKim, Mead & White* was prepared in 1915 almost all this early work was omitted. It has been rediscovered by critics and historians in the last thirty years, beginning with Mumford in the *Brown Decades* in 1931.

369. 20. Just how the influence reached American architects so early is not altogether clear. The first treatise in English on Japanese architecture is Morse, E. S., *Japanese Homes and Their Surroundings*, Boston, 1886; new ed., New York, 1961. See Lancaster, C., 'Japanese Buildings in the United States before 1900: Their Influence upon American Domestic Architecture', *Art Bulletin*, XXXV (1953), 217–24.

372. 20a. This house has now been taken over for preservation by the National Trust.

21. See Hitchcock, H. R., 'Frank Lloyd Wright and the "Academic Tradition" in the Nineties', *Journal of the Warburg and Courtauld Institutes*, VII (1947), 46–63.

21a. For an unsuspected but possible influence on Wright in this façade, see Gebhard, D., 'A Note on the Chicago Fair of 1893 and Frank Lloyd Wright', *Journal of the Society of Architectural Historians*, XVIII (1959), 63–5.

373. 22. Japanese influence was more evident at the Chauncey L. Williams house at 520 Edgewood Place in River Forest, Ill., of 1895, notably in the use of rough boulders at the foot of the brick wall and flanking the entrance. Wright by this time was enthusiastically interested in Japanese prints; whether he also knew Morse's book of 1886 (see Note 20 *supra*) is not clear.

374. 23. This was very much extended, but along the original lines, in 1901, as shown in illustration 231. The present River Forest Tennis Club, a much smaller structure, is not the same, though it bears some superficial resemblance to the Golf Club. The building of 1898–1901 was demolished in 1905.

377. 24. I am grateful to John Brandon-Jones for allowing me to read the manuscript of his unpublished monograph on Voysey. Without his assistance of various sorts this account of Voysey could not have been written and illustrated. See the Bibliography for more works on Voysey.

25. See Note 1, Chapter 12.

26. The 'House at Doverscourt for A. J. W. Ward', published in the *British Architect*, 11 April 1890, was apparently never executed any more than those illustrated the previous year. It is very like Perrycroft, built in 1893, the first of Voysey's important country houses, thus suggesting that on paper his style had in fact largely crystallized by this date before his Forster

house was begun. It is of interest that the plan of the Ward project is more open than those of any of his executed houses; it may well have influenced Baillie Scott (see below).

27. Brandon-Jones suggested, however, that the very plain Regency villa in which Voysey was then living in St John's Wood might have had some generic influence on the Forster house.

378. 28. At Perrycroft the mullions are of wood, originally painted green. At the Forster house they were of stone, and that is true of almost all the later houses. So also the slates here were Welsh and grey; when he began to work in the Lake District he turned to green slates, earlier used by Godwin on Whistler's house. These became standard on his later houses wherever they were built.

379. 29. For a later tribute to his influence and that of Baillie Scott abroad, see Fisker, K., 'Tre pionerer fra aarhundredskiftet', *Byggmästaren*, 1947, 221–32; the third 'pioneer', rather surprisingly, is Tessenow (see Chapter 20).

380. 29a. For a remarkable later work of Lethaby, see Pevsner, N., 'Lethaby's Last', *Architectural Review*, CXXX (1961), 354–7. This church, at Brockhampton-by-Ross in Herefordshire, was roofed with precast concrete slabs at the surprisingly early date of 1900–2; and its simplified, rather angular, Gothic design is, in effect, already proto-Expressionist.

381. 30. See Pevsner, N., 'George Walton, His Life and Work', *Journal of the Royal Institute of British Architects*, XLVI (1939), 537–48.

30a. The earliest house has been demolished as, paradoxically, only the other two were officially listed for preservation.

31. Voysey was also a notable designer of wallpapers and chintzes, perhaps the most notable of his generation in England.

CHAPTER 16

383. 1. The 'present' of the nineteen-fifties, twenty years ago when this book was written, can no longer be considered the same present as that of the mid seventies. Revisions included in the editions of 1963 and 1969 attempted in the Epilogue to update the story, but that already began to seem foolhardy, if not impossible, in the paperback edition of 1971, and would be even more presumptuous in 1976. This book, however debatable its conclusions, offers what is already history; it is necessary to turn elsewhere to various publications newly listed in the general twentieth-century section of the Bibliography and in those devoted to separate countries and individual architects – several actually by this author – for accounts of the 'current events' of the last two decades.

1a. See Madsen's *Sources of Art Nouveau*, 75–83.

2. See Schmutzler, R., 'English Origins of the Art Nouveau', *Architectural Review*, CXVII (1955), 308–16. The question is discussed further at a later point in this chapter (pp. 386–7).

384. 3. See Note 3, Chapter 7.

4. The one large structure built for this exhibition in permanent form, the Palais du Trocadéro by Davioud, a pupil of Léon Vaudoyer, has since been replaced. Not altogether unworthy in silhouette of its splendid site on the Chaillot heights, this shared none of the qualities of Eiffel's temporary pavilion. See Davioud, G., *Le Palais du Trocadéro*, Paris, 1878. As long as it lasted, however, the Trocadéro provided a sort of pendant on this side of Paris to Abadie's Sacré-Cœur atop Montmartre, begun in the same rather dreary decade of French architectural production.

5. See Note 4a, Chapter 12.

6. See Alphand, A., *L'Exposition universelle de Paris de 1889*, Paris, 1892.

7. See Eiffel, G., *La Tour de trois-cents-mètres*, Paris, 1900; Barthes, R., and Martin, A., *La Tour Eiffel* [Lausanne, 1964]; Cordat, C., *La Tour Eiffel*, Paris [1955]; and Morlaine, J., *La Tour Eiffel inconnue* [Paris, 1971].

385. 7a. However, visible diagonal bracing on the exterior of steel-framed skyscrapers returned to favour in the later 1960s. Skidmore, Owings & Merrill's John Hancock Center in Chicago, completed in 1968, the tallest new structure begun up to that date, has this feature and is markedly tapered as well.

7b. Apparently the plates referred to, which were issued separately from the two volumes of text, became available some years before the second volume, delayed by the events of 1870, was finally published in 1872.

386. 8. Bogardus's shot-towers of the fifties in New York, which were of essentially similar construction, received little contemporary or later publicity. It is still uncertain whether Jenney knew of them when he built the Home Insurance Building in Chicago in 1883–5. See Bannister, T. C., 'Bogardus Revisited, Part II', *Journal of the Society of Architectural Historians*, XVI (1957).

9. See Note 18, Chapter 11.

10. See Grady, J., 'Bibliography of the Art Nouveau', *Journal of the Society of Architectural Historians*, XIV (1955), 18–27 and *Art Nouveau* (Museum of Modern Art Exhibition Catalogue), New York [1960]. Interest in the Art Nouveau continued throughout the 1960s to be productive of handsome publications (see Bibliography). Not improperly, however, architecture received less attention than the decorative arts of the period. See Rheims, M., *L'Art 1900, ou le style Jules Verne*, Paris [1965], in which a wealth of excellent illustrations is accompanied by captions that too often offer misinformation, if any specific facts at all. Balancing the rising general interest came, unforgivably, the destruction of the most important Art Nouveau building, Horta's Maison du Peuple in Brussels, an act of vandalism comparable to the demolition of the London Coal Exchange. His Innovation department store, its façade already masked in 1958, was burned down in 1967.

11. This applies particularly to Art Nouveau decoration; the major architectural works were frequently very plastically organized, although most of the detail was linear.

387. 12. See Schmutzler, R., 'Blake and the Art Nouveau', *Architectural Review*, CXVIII (1955), 90–7.

13. See Lancaster, C., 'Oriental Contributions to Art Nouveau', *Art Bulletin*, XXXIV (1952), 297–310.

14. See Grady, J., 'Nature and the Art Nouveau', *Art Bulletin*, XXXVII (1955), 187–92.

15. See Mackmurdo, A. H., *Wren's City Churches*, Orpington, 1883.

388. 16. Not perhaps impossible: There is something a little analogous to Impressionism in the work of Shaw, though he probably had no admiration for the art of Monet and his contemporaries in the seventies even if he was at all aware of it. The same is true of the American masters of the Shingle Style. The analogy lies in the casual looseness of over-all composition and the delicacy of the touch – both tile-hanging and shingles provide a certain effect of 'broken colour' or at least 'tachiste' brushwork – even though they are usually monochrome. On the other hand, Kimball in his *American Architecture*, written forty years ago, saw an analogy to Cézanne in the return to architectural order in the mid eighties in America. There is no evidence that McKim or White then admired any French painters later than Puvis de Chavannes, however.

17. Some studio houses were certainly built in France by leading architects throughout the second half of the nineteenth century: The one that Viollet-le-Duc provided for the painter Constant Troyon in the late fifties was of notable interest – in fact, one of his best works. Moreover, the more modest *ateliers d'artiste* erected by builders provided much later, in the 1920s, precedents of value to Le Corbusier and Lurçat. See Banham, R., 'Ateliers d'artiste', *Architectural Review*, CXX (1956), 75–83.

389. 18. See Madsen, S. T., 'Horta. Works and Style of Victor Horta before 1900', *Architectural Review*, CXVIII (1955), 388–92; and Borsi, F., *Bruxelles, capitale de l'Art Nouveau* [Rome, 1971].

19. See Koch, R., *Louis C. Tiffany, Rebel in Glass*, New York [1964].

20. The wallpaper was probably one of those de-

signed by Heywood Sumner, possibly his 'Tulip' according to Elizabeth Aslin of the Victoria and Albert Museum. This was one of the considerable range of English papers shown by Jeffrey & Company at the Salon de l'Association pour l'Art d'Anvers in Antwerp in the winter of 1892–3. These papers, which included designs by most of the English leaders in the field of decorative art, had already been shown at the Paris Exposition of 1889. It is hard to believe that Horta became aware of them only when the Tassel house was nearly finished and not earlier in Antwerp or in Paris. For the Antwerp showing, see Van de Velde, H., 'Artistic Wallpapers', L'Art moderne, XIII (1893), 193–5. This article was copied in L'Emulation, XVIII (1893), 150–1, the most advanced Belgian architectural journal, where the Tassel house was published in 1895. It introduces the name of another important Belgian figure besides Horta in the story of the Art Nouveau.

21. It is of interest, although irrelevant to the inception of the Art Nouveau, that in the same year Horta became professor of architecture at the Académie like Balat before him.

391. 22. See Kaufmann, E., '224 Avenue Louise', Interiors, 116 (1957), 88–93.

393. 22a. See Note 10, supra.

395. 23. For a late tribute to Van de Velde in English, see Shand, P. M., Architectural Review, CXII (1952), 143–55. It is a major error of emphasis – and in detail an accumulation of errors of fact – that H. Lenning offers in his book The Art Nouveau (The Hague, 1951) by accepting the legend that Van de Velde was the initiator of the Art Nouveau. There is plenty of evidence that Van de Velde was aware of English innovations in decorations from the early nineties. On the other hand, despite the wallpaper in the Tassel dining-room, it should be noted that Horta's widow and his disciple Delhaye minimize, to the point of denying all but absolutely, the dependence of Horta on English sources at the time he designed the Tassel house.

24. Paul Hankar (1861–1901) was a third Belgian architectural innovator in this period. His work, however, is so crude and uneven that his name need be no more than mentioned. He is in no proper sense an exponent of the Art Nouveau. See Conrady, C., and Thibaux, R., Paul Hankar, [n.p.] 1923.

CHAPTER 17

398. 1. See Malton, J., 'Art Nouveau in Essex', Architectural Review, CXXVI (1959), 100–4. For a considerably earlier and more extraordinary example of English work approaching the Art Nouveau, see Beazley, E., 'Watts Chapel', Architectural Review, CXXX (1961), 166–72. This chapel at Compton, Surrey, was de-

signed in 1896 by Mary Watts, the widow of the painter G. F. Watts. The inspiration seems to have been predominantly Norse and Celtic.

1a. See Gout, P., L'Architecture au XXe siècle et l'Art Nouveau, Paris, 1903.

2. See Hostingue, G. d', Le Castel Béranger, œuvre de H. G., architecte, Paris, 1898.

399. 3. Both the main façade and the principal interior are essentially the work of Deglane. Louvet and Thomas were more responsible for other elements of this complex structure.

3a. Wailly, G. de, A travers l'exposition de 1900, Paris, 1899–1900.

3b. See L'architecture moderne à Paris, concours de façades, 2 vols, Paris, 1901, 1902.

402. 4. See Uhry, E., 'Agrandissements des magasins de la Samaritaine', L'Architecte, II (1907), 13–14, 20, plates X–XII.

403. 5. I owe my knowledge of this remarkable façade to Martin Kermacy. He was unable to find out by whom and when it was built; it is very probably an early work of Josef Urban, Novotny informs me.

404. 5a. Robert J. Clark, whose Princeton doctoral dissertation was devoted to the life-work of Olbrich, states that the present doors are copies of the original ones and were installed c. 1965–6.

405. 5b. The previous year the work of Toorop had been exhibited in Glasgow, so that Mackintosh's exoticism may well be Dutch-Indonesian in origin rather than Gaelic!

5c. For another rather independent Scottish architect of this period, see Walker, D. M., 'Lamond of Dundee', Architectural Review, CXXIII (1958), 269–71.

409. 5d. See Meeks, op. cit., 405–61.

5e. See Scheichenbauer, M., Alfredo Campanini, Milan, 1958.

410. 6. See Note 24, Chapter 11.

7. Among other things, it was Gaudí's use of forms inspired by primitive architecture that appealed to the taste of the 1950s and 60s. 'Primitivism' in painting and sculpture was of recurrent importance from the days of the Fauves and the Expressionists; a comparable primitivism in architecture was much rarer, except for Gaudí.

7a. See Cotton, V. E., The Book of Liverpool Cathedral, Liverpool, 1964.

411. 8. Except as regards the theories of vaulting exemplified in successive schemes for the Sagrada Familia and his church at Santa Coloma de Cervelló, Gaudí's technical innovations had been until lately little studied despite the very considerable literature devoted to his work. Research has proved that he made many important innovations in structure over and above those so evident in the crypt – the only portion executed – of the Santa Coloma church.

617

George Collins showed some of the results, still un-published, of his continuing studies in an exhibition at Columbia University in May 1962. See *Cripta de la colonia Güell de Gaudí*, Barcelona, 1968.

9. While the mosaic of broken fragments of patterned ceramic on the benches at the Park Güell suggests Cubist collages and even Dada compositions - notably the *Merzbilder* of Kurt Schwitters - the handling of the coloured glass on this façade is closer to the paint-ings of Jackson Pollock.

414. 9a. One, appropriately, is now in the collection of the Museum of Modern Art in New York, rivalling the Guimard Métro entrance in the garden there, presented by the city authorities of Paris.

416. 9b. The internal structure, as the plan indicates, is skeletal, freeing completely the disposition of the partitions between the rooms of the individual flats.

9c. A curious continuation, or more accurately revi-val, of Gaudian modes occurred in Portuguese Africa. See Beinart, J., 'Amancio Guedes, Architect of Lourenço Marques', *Architectural Review*, CXXIX (1961), 240-51.

417. 9d. The first serious attack, at least, since that of Henri Labrouste and his associates in France in the 1830s, an attack fended off by the established acade-mic forces of the École des Beaux-Arts after token acceptance of some of the rebels' principles.

10. Even Gaudí after 1910 produced little, being almost wholly occupied with the slow progress of the Sagrada Familia. Of course, in a sense Horta is another exception; but his success after 1910 was of purely local significance and dependent on his total rejection of the Art Nouveau of his youth. One can only think of the later career of Giorgio de Chirico, for so long a continuing success in Italy, but ignored by the out-side world except when he imitated his earlier work.

CHAPTER 18

421. 1. Perret intentionally avoided receiving the diploma. In France architects D.P.L.G. (*diplomé par le gouvernement*) are not allowed to become contrac-tors as well, and Perret wished to continue with the family firm.

1a. See *Concrete and Constructional Engineering*, LI (January 1956), special anniversary number reviewing the history of concrete. More important later studies are: Raafat, A. A., *Reinforced Concrete in Architecture*, New York [1958]; and Collins, P., *Concrete, The Vision of a New Architecture*, New York [1959]. See also Kramer, E. W., and Raafat, A. A., 'The Ward House, Pioneer Structure of Reinforced Concrete', *Journal of the Society of Architectural Historians*, XX (1961), 34-7.

2. See Baudot, A. de, *L'Architecture, le passé, le*

présent, Paris, 1916, and Baudot, J. de, *L'Architecture et le béton armé*, Paris, 1916.

423. 2a. Surprising as it may seem, Frank Lloyd Wright occasionally gilded even fairly rough concrete, but never major structural elements such as Perret's columns.

424. 3. See Huxtable, A. L., 'Progressive Architecture in America: Reinforced Concrete Construction. The work of Ernest L. Ransome, Engineer - 1884-1911' and 'Factory for Packard Motor Car Company - 1905, Detroit, Michigan, Albert Kahn, Architect. Ernest Wilby, Associate', *Progressive Architecture*, XXXVIII (1957), 139-42 and 121-2.

This research revealed that Albert Kahn (1869-1942) was not such a pioneer in concrete factory con-struction as had been generally supposed. However, the 'Kahn Bar' developed by his brothers' engineering firm was a major technical contribution, and un-doubtedly his motor-car factories were among the earliest major industrial works in the new material. For the alternative use of steel in American warehouse and factory construction, see Eaton, L. K., 'Frame of Steel', *Architectural Review*, CXXVI (1959), 289-90.

4. The detailed history of the concrete grain elevator cannot be given here. The prototypes for the great monuments of Buffalo, Minneapolis, and Duluth were certainly French. These monolithic cylinders are, of course, very different from the motor-car factories with their post-and-lintel construction, but the history of the elevator seems to have run nearly parallel to that of the factory. See [Torbert, D. R.], *A Century of Minnesota Architecture*, Minneapolis, 1958, unpaged.

4a. Even vaster assemblages of linked cylinders are still rising throughout the Middle West, quite as notable monumental works of 'building' if not 'archi-tecture' as the late skyscrapers of the fifties and sixties.

5. In the fifties and sixties the innovations of such engineers as Pierluigi Nervi (b. 1891) in Italy, Eduardo Torroja (1899-1961) in Spain, and Felix Candela (b. 1910) in Mexico began to revolutionize earlier con-ceptions of the possibilities of ferro-concrete (see Chapter 25). For Torroja, see *The Structures of Eduardo Torroja*, New York [1958], and Torroja, E., *The Philosophy of Structures*, Berkeley, 1958.

5a. The church was designed in 1922 on a budget of 600,000 francs. P. Collins, *Concrete*, New York [1959], 240-7, gives the best account of the commission and its execution.

426. 6. See Pfammatter, P., *Betonkirchen*, Cologne and Zurich, 1948.

428. 7. By reaction many of the same architects, not-ably Le Corbusier late in his life, consciously sought the brutality of industrial concrete finish - he called it *béton brut* - even in monumental work (see Chapter 25 and Epilogue).

429. 8. The atelier was founded in 1928.
430. 9. The team that worked with Perret on Le Havre consisted of P. Branche, P. Dubouillon, P. Feuillebois, A. Heaume, J. Imbert, M. Kaeppelin, G. Lagneau, M. Lotte, P.-E. Lambert, A. Le Donné, A. Persitz, J. Poirrier, H. Tougard, and J. Tournant, all of whom seem to have shared responsibility for the buildings flanking the Place de l'Hôtel de Ville. Poirrier, Le Donné, and Lambert were, however, joint architects-in-chief. Specific attributions are perhaps not very significant in this kind of situation, but the characteristic Hôtel Normandie (1950) is by Poirrier and the whole sea front by Lambert.
431. 10. See Garnier, T., *Une Cité industrielle*, Paris [1918]. The basic project goes back to 1901, but was much elaborated in the intervening years. Although it was unpublished, many architects were certainly familiar with its general character. See Wiebenson, D., 'Utopian Aspects of Garnier's Cité Industrielle', *Journal of the Society of Architectural Historians*, XIX (1960), 16-24.
11. See Garnier, T., *Les Grands Travaux de la ville de Lyon*, Paris, 1919.
432. 12. This applies particularly to the work of Michel Roux-Spitz (b. 1888), who became in the thirties the acknowledged leader of the profession in France.

CHAPTER 19

434. 1. See Zevi, B., *Verso un'architettura organica*, Turin, 1945; English translation, *Towards an Organic Architecture*, London, 1950.
437. 1a. Historic American Building Survey, *The Robie House*, Palos Park, Ill., 1968.
439. 1b. See Global Architecture No. 15, *Taliesin East and West*, Tokyo, n.d.
2. See Pellegrini, L., 'La decorazione funzionale del primo Wright', *L'Architettura* (1956), 198-203.
2a. When this house was demolished in the early nineteen seventies, this room and all its contents were acquired by the Metropolitan Museum of Art in New York for inclusion in its American Wing. See Heckscher, M., and Miller, E. G., *An Architect and his Client; Frank Lloyd Wright and Francis W. Little*, Metropolitan Museum of Art, New York.
440. 3. Wright's 'Baroque' period, running for approximately ten years from 1914 to 1924, parallels the Expressionist episode in European modern architecture (see Chapters 21 and 22). That may be considered to have opened with van der Meij's Scheepvaarthuis of 1912-15 in Amsterdam and to have run out in general sometime in the mid twenties. It is not apparent that there was any influence of consequence either way; indeed, the effect of studying Wright's work in the war years and the early twenties was rather adverse

to Expressionism and related tendencies, particularly in Holland where Wright's influence was strongest.
3a. James, C., *The Imperial Hotel*, Rutland, Vt., 1968.
445. 3b. Global Architecture No. 2, Frank Lloyd Wright, *The Kaufmann House*, Tokyo [1970].
446. 3c. Global Architecture No. 1, *Johnson and Son Administration Building and Research Tower*, Tokyo, 1970.
447. 4. See *Life*, V (26 Sep. 1938), 60-1.
5. See *Ladies Home Journal*, February 1901; June 1901; April 1907.
5a. Before his death Wright had already begun to glaze the voids, hirtherto protected only by canvas screens, in order to air-condition the interior. Visually, this proved an unfortunate decision. Since Wright's death the theatre burned down and has been fairly well rebuilt, but in general the condition of Taliesin West deteriorated sadly.
449. 6. Wright, F. Ll., *The Story of the Tower*, New York, 1956.
450. 6a. Of the various works completed since Wright's death, one of the most successful is the Kalita Humphreys Theatre in Dallas. As with the Guggenheim Museum, its smooth cream-painted concrete surfaces and clean, if complex, geometrical forms recall somewhat International Style buildings of the 1920s. The theatre did not suffer so much in execution from lack of Wright's supervision as the Marin County design.
7. Wright had a tendency to scoff at the work of his former junior associates and to deny the reality of their discipleship. There have been for some time in practice a good many architects who were for shorter or longer periods at Taliesin, where the Fellowship at times after the Second World War included over sixty. Those who were at Taliesin some time ago have naturally made the greater mark; many of the post-war members of the Fellowship were, even in the mid 1960s, only at the beginning of their own practice. Alden Dow (b. 1904) in Midland, Michigan, and Henry Klumb (b. 1905) in San Juan, Puerto Rico, had throughout several decades the greatest volume of work of more-or-less Wrightian inspiration to their credit. But it must not be forgotten that Richard J. Neutra (see p. 514), whose work was of a very different order, was also for a time with Wright; while there were some architects whose work was Wrightian to the point of parody who had never had any direct contact with Wright at all.
7a. The name of this regional school has varied with the years; see Brooks, A., '"Chicago School": Metamorphosis of a Term', *Journal of the Society of Architectural Historians* (May 1966), 115-18. The last decade has seen an extraordinary rise of interest in these contemporaries of Wright. Moreover Condit in his *Chicago School of Architecture* (Chicago [1964]),

otherwise a revised edition of his *Rise of the Skyscraper* (Chicago [1952]), extended his coverage to include several of them, particularly in Chapter 9, pp. 181-214, and Mark Peisch published a book at almost the same time – and confusingly enough with the same title as Condit's, though rather largely devoted to the work of Walter Burley Griffin; also a quarterly review almost exclusively devoted to the subject began to appear in 1964. Many numbers of the *Prairie School Review* have constituted modest monographs on individual architects who had been largely forgotten even though some, such as Barry Byrne, were still alive. Early volumes included I, No. 2, Guenzel & Drummond; II, No. 1, Purcell & Elmslie; III, No. 1, Hugh M. Y. Garden; III, No. 2, Marion Mahony Griffin; III, No. 4, Barry Byrne. Sullivan and Wright have not been neglected in the *Review*: I, No. 4, Prairie School Furniture; II, No. 2, The Schiller Building; III, No. 3, Wright in Japan. The publishing house responsible for the *Review* has also brought out various facsimile reprints of rare Wrightiana. See Prairie School in the monograph section of the Bibliography.

8. Richard E. Schmidt (1865-1959) and Hugh M. G. Garden (1873-1961).

9. The contribution of these men has lately received the study which it merits now the realization has come that American architecture was far less dominated by traditionalism in the first quarter of the twentieth century, particularly in the Middle West and on the Pacific Coast, than was generally supposed in the last fifty years. See Brooks, H. A., *The Prairie School* [Toronto, 1972].

10. See Thompson, E., 'The Early Domestic Architecture of the San Francisco Bay Region', *Journal of the Society of Architectural Historians*, X (1951), 15-21; Bangs, J. M., 'Bernard Ralph Maybeck, Architect, Comes into His Own', *Architectural Record*, CIII (1948), 72-9, and 'Greene and Greene', *Architectural Forum*, LXXXIX (1948), 80-9; McCoy, E., *Five California Architects*, New York, 1960; and Woodbridge, J. M. and S. B., *Buildings of the Bay Area, a Guide to the Architecture of the San Francisco Bay Region*, New York, 1960, which covers both earlier and later work.

11. See Price, C., 'Panama-California Exposition: Betram Grosvenor Goodhue and the Renaissance of Spanish-Colonial Architecture', *Architectural Record*, XXXVII (1915), 229-51.

12. See Macomber, B., *The Jewel City, its Planning and Achievement . . .*, San Francisco, 1915. Not altogether fortunately, Maybeck's Fine Arts Building, so long a ruin, has been rebuilt in solider materials. Otherwise, doubtless, it would soon have collapsed entirely; but the Hubert Robert charm of 'pleasing decay' has been lost.

451. 12a. After being rebuilt in permanent materials, this lost much of its nostalgic charm.

452. 13. See Lancaster, C., 'The American Bungalow', *Art Bulletin*, XL (1958), 239-53.

453. 14. That is, on the West Coast; considered as an alternative to the 'International Style' suitable for emulation everywhere, as it was for a few years, it had no more validity than any other regional mode.

CHAPTER 20

455. 1. Reviving interest in Expressionism led to considerable significant publication in the fifties and sixties. See, for example, Dorfles, G., *Barocco nell' architettura moderna*, Milan, 1951, especially the second part; Gregotti, G., 'L'Architettura dell' Espressionismo', *Casabella*, August 1961, [24]-48; Conrads, U., and Sperlich, H. G., *Phantastische Architektur*, Stuttgart [1960]; *The Architecture of Fantasy*, New York [1962]; and, for a particularly significant figure, Joedicke, J., 'Haering at Garkau', *Architectural Review*, CXXVII (1960), 313-18. For Expressionist publications by an architect who was very active and influential in Germany in the 1920s, see Taut, B., *Die Stadtkrone*, Jena, 1919, and *Frühlicht 1920-1922*, Berlin [1965] (a reprint). A book in English of less interest is Sharp, D., *Modern Architecture and Expressionism*, London [1966]. See also Pehnt, W., *Expressionism*, New York, 1973.

456. 2. For the development of Van de Velde's ideas in these years see *Die Renaissance im modernen Kunstgewerbe*, Berlin, 1901, and *Vom neuen Stil*, Leipzig, 1907. Van de Velde was a prolific writer; a complete list of his books and articles will be found in Madsen's *Sources of Art Nouveau*, 469.

458. 2a. See Tessenow, H., *Der Wohnhausbau*, Munich [1909].

460. 3. See Bauer, C. K., *Modern Housing*, Boston and New York, 1934; and my *Early Victorian Architecture in Britain*, Chapters XIII and XIV. See also Tarn, J. N., *Working Class Housing in 19th Century Britain*, London, 1971. For France, see Leprince, D., *Les Logements à bon marché . . .*, Paris, 1888; Levy, J., *Rapport sur les maisons d'ouvriers* [Paris, 1867]; and Madre, A. de, *Notice . . . Paris pour habitations d'ouvriers*, Paris, 1863.

461. 3a. See Germany in Bibliography.

3b. Schumacher, F., *Grundlagen der Baukunst . . .*, Munich [1916].

4. See Schumacher, F., *Das Wesen des neuzeitlichen Backsteinbaues*, Munich, 1917. The rich and decorative use of brick is as characteristic of the Hamburg School as of the Amsterdam School in these decades (see Chapter 21). See also Amsterdam School in the monograph section of the Bibliography.

464. 4a. All the same the almost Anglo-Saxon restraint evident in the designing of the Wiesbaden Kurhaus contrasts almost as much with the neo-Baroque work of the nineties by the elder Thiersch in Munich. In this respect the Kurhaus is not so remote from Berg's exterior of the Jahrhunderthalle in Silesia.

5. See Bie, O., *Der Architekt Oskar Kaufmann*, Berlin, 1928; Hegemann, W., *German Bestelmeyer*, Berlin [n.d.]; and Mayer, H., and Rehdern, G., *Wilhelm Kreis*, Essen, 1953. In the twenties a large number of such well-illustrated monographs on individual German architects were published; it is much more difficult to find adequate documentation on the work of several architects in other countries of considerably greater originality and historical importance.

466. 5a. See *Americana* (catalogue of the exhibition at the Rijksmuseum, Otterlo, 1975).

6. Paraboloid domes of ferro-concrete were used with brilliant spatial effect by Jacques Droz (b. 1882) at Sainte-Jeanne-d'Arc in Nice. This was built in 1932, just at the same time that Böhm was building Sankt Engelbert. The plan, consisting of three intersecting ellipses, is very nearly identical with that of J. B. Neumann's Baroque masterpiece Vierzehnheiligen; the result is very different, however, because of the continuity of the walls and roof here. Unfortunately Droz's church was elaborated with a tower and other features of an 'Art Déco' order.

7. Another German church-architect of the twenties whose considerable reputation survived is Otto Bartning (1883–1959). He moved much earlier in this direction than Böhm. For a statement of his intentions, see Bartning, O., *Vom neuen Kirchbau*, Berlin, 1919.

8. See *Maria Königin* [Cologne, n.d.].

9. This is not the place to discuss these churches. It may be remarked here, however, that Candela's church is considerably more Expressionist in appearance, especially the interior, than anything Böhm ever built in the twenties. Yet its strangely angular piers and vaults that *look* so much like the settings for the 'Cabinet of Dr Caligari', the most famous German Expressionist film, resulted from this engineer's consistent use of the hyperbolic paraboloid forms which he favoured primarily for technical reasons. De la Mora, Niemeyer, and Moya were content to use barrel-vault elements of plain parabolic section such as were first introduced by Böhm in 1925–6.

467. 10. The triangular bay-window lighting the stairs is still somewhat Expressionist, but the interior treatment is in general more related to geometrical abstract art. The decoration approaches the 'Art Déco' or what was known as 'Jazz-Modern' in the next ten years or so in England. The interiors that Behrens designed contrasted with the fine examples of Mackintosh's

furniture, brought from a house he had remodelled earlier for the Bassett-Lowkes.

10a. Joedicke, J., *Die Weissenhofsiedlung*, Stuttgart [1968].

468. 10b. See Lane, B., *Architecture and Politics in Germany, 1918–1945*, Cambridge, Mass., 1968; Taylor, R., *The Word in Stone*, Berkeley [1974]; and Teut, A., *Architektur im dritten Reich, 1933–45*, Berlin [1967].

11. 'New Objectivity': A generic term for some of the advanced movements that succeded Expressionism in the arts; in architecture, roughly equivalent to 'Functionalism'.

CHAPTER 21

470. 1. The use of aluminium in architecture became widespread only some forty years later, it should be noted, although it had supplied the cap of the pyramid with which T. L. Casey finally completed the Washington Monument as early as 1884 – its first use in architecture. In the nineties Thomas Harris already foresaw its great importance in building; see his *Three Periods of English Architecture*, London, 1894.

471. 1a. Graf, O. A., *Die vergessene Wagnerschule*, Vienna, 1969.

472. 2. See 'Ornament und Verbrechen' in Loos, A., *Trotzdem: Gesammelte Aufsätze 1900–1930*, Innsbruck, 1931, first published in the *Neue Freie Presse* in January 1908. A French translation of the article appeared in *L'Esprit nouveau*, I (1920), 159–68.

474. 3. Considering that Wright's open planning had by no means matured while Loos was in Chicago, American influence (if any) came probably from the houses of the Shingle Style. Because of his close *rapport* with England, however, the influence of Baillie Scott's plans was more important; while the treatment of interior trim comes closest to Voysey, as has been noted.

3a. Czech, H., *Das Looshaus*, Vienna, 1968.

477. 4. The recurrent suggestions of Richardsonian influence in Europe in the nineties are not yet adequately explained. Townsend in England knew of Richardson's work from American and English publications, and there was in England one house by Richardson, Lululund at Bushey, Herts, now largely destroyed except for the entrance. This was designed shortly before Richardson's death for Sir Hubert von Herkomer, who had painted his portrait, and executed without supervision. Boberg had been for a short while in Chicago and Bruno Schmitz (1858–1916) in Indianapolis; but there are others whose work also seems somewhat Richardsonian, such as Theodor Fischer, who certainly had not. Berlage did not visit America until 1911, when it was Wright's work that most impressed him. He and Fischer might, of course, have

known Richardson's buildings from publications. For foreign publications of Richardson's work before 1900, see pp. 333-5 in the later editions of my Richardson book. See also *Americana* (catalogue of the exhibition at the Rijksmuseum, Otterlo, 1975); Eaton, L. K., *American Architecture Comes of Age*, Cambridge, Mass. [1972]; and Hitchcock, H. R., 'American Influence Abroad', in Kaufmann, E. (ed.), *The Rise of an American Architecture*, New York [1970].

478. 5. See Berlage, H. P., *Gedanken über den Stil in der Baukunst*, Leipzig, 1905; *Grundlagen und Entwicklung der Architektur*, Berlin, 1908; and *Studies over Bouwkunst*, Rotterdam, 1910.

479. 6. The work of K. P. C. de Bazel (1869–1923), a pupil of Cuijpers who represented a rather different stream in Dutch architecture of the early twentieth century, was especially close to that of the contemporary German leaders but hardly at all related to Expressionism. His massive office building for the Nederlandsche Handel Maatschappij in Amsterdam of 1917-23 is quite similar to Behrens's nearly contemporary office blocks in Hanover and Düsseldorf, but much more intricate and inventive in its brick-and-stone detail.

480. 7. Although it is unlikely that de Klerk actually owed anything to the sets that Bakst, Benois, and others were designing for the Ballet Russe, the visual investiture of the Diaghilev productions certainly had a loosening effect on Western European taste in these years just before the First World War. For the first time Russia impinged visually on European art, but that impingement had only an oblique effect on architecture, for the art that was exported was not, of course, very architectural.

482. 7a. *Americana* (*op. cit.*, Note 4 above).

7b. Yerbury, F. R. (ed.), *Modern Danish Architecture*, New York, 1927.

483. 7c. There seems to be no monograph on this important figure in any language, but see the next Note. For material in English see the books on Finnish architecture by N. E. Wickberg (1959) and J. M. Richards (1966) listed in the Bibliography under 'Scandinavia'.

7d. See Kivinen, P., *Tamperen Tuomio-Kirkho*, Helsinki, c. 1960.

8. See *American Architect*, CXXVIII (5 October 1925).

484. 8a. Bruno Taut's brother Max's project in this competition was also remarkable, prefiguring like Mies's slightly earlier projects for glass skyscrapers the curtain-walled ones of the 1950s and 60s. Loos's entry was disappointing, an enormous Doric column with windows in the flutes. This was not, as some have supposed, intended as a joke!

8b. Robinson, C., and Bletter, R. H., *Skyscraper Style*, New York, 1975.

9. See 'The American Radiator Company Building, New York', *American Architect*, CXXVI (1924), 467–84.

485. 10. It is this that makes it so difficult to decide which architects should be discussed in Chapters 18-21 and which in Chapter 24. No two critics will agree, but most now recognize that the boundary line is not a sharp one. For this reason in *Modern Architecture*, published nearly fifty years ago, I labelled the work of this generation 'The New Tradition' and did not then reject the work of the Scandinavians as too 'traditional' to be classed, broadly at least, with that of Wright, Perret, Behrens, Wagner, and Loos, as has been done here.

CHAPTER 22

487. 1. That is, Barr proposed with our concurrence the title *The International Style* for the book prepared by myself and Philip Johnson to go with this Exhibition, drawing the word 'international' from the title of Gropius's *Internationale Architektur*. For various reasons the name 'International Style' was often castigated later; yet it has been recurrently used, with or without apology, by many critics. Since this term had for a while acquired a pejorative meaning, I avoided using it as far as possible in this book, preferring the vaguer but less controversial phrase 'modern architecture of the second generation' despite its clumsiness. In support of the claim that the original meaning of 'International Style', as used by Barr, Johnson, and myself, still retained some validity in the early fifties, there was my article 'The "International Style" Twenty Years After', *Architectural Record*, CX (1952), 89-97, which was reprinted in the new edition of *The International Style*, New York, 1966, 237-55. The 'Foreword to the 1966 Edition', pp. vii-xiii, is also relevant.

2. See Roggero, M. F., *Il Contributo di Mendelsohn alla evoluzione dell'architettura moderna*, Milan [1952].

488. 3. See Jaffé, H. L. C., *De Stijl, 1917–1931*, London [1956], and *The 'De Stijl' group*, Amsterdam [?1952]; Zevi, B., *Poetica dell'architettura neo-plastica*, Milan, 1935; and Doesburg, T. van, *Grondbegrippen der nieuwe beeldende kunst*, Haarlem, 1919.

4. See Mendelsohn, E., *Bauten und Skizzen*, Berlin, 1923; and English ed., *Buildings and Sketches*, London, 1923.

5. The question of Expressionism in architecture is a difficult one despite rising critical interest in the intentions and achievements of the architects influenced by the movement (see Note 1 to Chapter 20). As will shortly be noted, Gropius and Mies van der Rohe were both briefly affected by Expressionist con-

cepts and used forms of distinctly Expressionist character in the years 1919-21.

5a. Contemporary with Steiner's second Goetheanum came the even wilder architectural work of the German sculptor Bernhard Hoetger (1874-1949) in the Boettcherstrasse in Bremen (1926) and the artists' colony at Worpswede.

6. An earlier Goetheanum of 1913-20, which was destroyed by fire, had been largely of wood. It was not at all like Mendelsohn's Einstein Tower but still somewhat Art Nouveau. See Brunati and Mendini, *Steiner*, Milan [n.d.], for both versions. See also Steiner, R., *Wege zu einem neuen Baustil*, Dornach, 1926 (Eng. trans., London-New York, 1927), and *Der Baugedanke des Goetheanum*, Dornach, 1932; and Rosenkrantz, A., *The Goetheanum as a New Impulse in Art*, [London, n.d.].

7. For a reassessment of that influence, see Jordan, R. F., 'Dudok', *Architectural Review*, CXV (1954), 237-42.

8. It is probable that Mendelsohn's early projects and also the tower had some influence on the later development of 'streamlining' in industrial design. See Banham, R., 'Machine-aesthetic', *Architectural Review*, CXVII (1955), 224-8.

489. 8a. Oud died in 1963, Rietveld in 1964, and Le Corbusier in 1965. Of the founders of the International Style the two Germans Mies van der Rohe and Gropius, both become Americans, survived longest, dying only in 1969.

491. 9. This sort of enclosure came to be called a 'curtain-wall'. Some of the skyscrapers of the nineties in Chicago, most notably Beman's Studebaker Building of 1895 and Holabird & Roche's McClurg Building of 1899, approached it very closely, yet in them the actual supporting piers remained in the façade plane as at the Fagus Factory and thus the 'curtain' was interrupted, not continuous horizontally. The first true example of the curtain-wall applied to a large urban structure followed within a few years after the Fagus Factory, and certainly with no influence from it; this is the Hallidie Building in San Francisco, completed by Willis Polk (1867-1924) in 1918 immediately after the First World War. But see pp. 333-4 and Note 9 to Chapter 14 for Oriel Chambers of 1864-5.

10. See Weber, H., *Walter Gropius und das Faguswerk*, Munich [1961]. See also Note 12, below.

10a. *Deutscher Werkbund*, Cologne, 1914.

11. See Popp, J., *Bruno Paul*, Munich [n.d.].

11a. A large house for the Kröllers was finally built, not in The Hague but in near-by Wassenaar, by Henry Van de Velde in 1929-30. Called Groot Haesebroek, it is now the Canadian Embassy. Over the years 1937 to 1953 Van de Velde erected and extended the exhibition building for the collection in the Hogue Veluwe near Otterlo, now the Rijksmuseum Kröller-Müller. See Behrens in the Bibliography.

12. To those historians of modern architecture who found its relevant prehistory largely in the technical developments of the previous century and a half, the Fagus Factory was the more important; to those who accepted that the architecture of the mid twentieth century had aesthetic as well as technical roots, the special 'classicism' of Mies's project, like Wright's contact with the American 'Academic Tradition' of the nineties, seemed at least as important.

492. 13. Le Corbusier's first publication was an *Étude sur le mouvement d'art décoratif en Allemagne*, La Chaux de Fond, 1912, giving evidence of his closer *rapport* with Central European than with Parisian currents at this point in his life.

14. For early work of Le Corbusier, previously almost entirely unpublished, see *Perspecta*, VI (1961), 28-33. Since Le Corbusier's death scholars have been discovering and re-examining early work by him in Switzerland, as given in the first volume of the *Œuvre complète*, has yet been published. See, however, Chavanne, E., and Laville, M., 'Les Premières Constructions de Le Corbusier', *Das Werk* (December 1963), 483-8.

15. Le Corbusier's relations with Loos were very close for a year or two after Loos settled in Paris in 1923. But he undoubtedly knew of Loos's work well before the First World War, having been for a short stay in Vienna in 1908, at which time he had already begun to react against the dominant decorative emphasis in the work of Hoffmann and the Wiener Werkstätte.

16. As has been noted, Garnier's book on the 'Cité industrielle' did not appear until 1918, but his projects had long been generally known in Paris. His work attracted more attention in the early twenties, thanks to his own publication *Les Grands Travaux de la ville de Lyon*, Paris, 1919, and an article by Jean Badovici, 'L'Œuvre de Tony Garnier', in *L'Architecture vivante*, Autumn-Winter 1924.

17. See Note 3, *supra*. Also relevant is my book *Painting towards Architecture*, New York, 1948.

18. Several years earlier, possibly even before he actually joined De Stijl, Rietveld had designed and executed a remarkable 'Red-Blue' chair in which many aspects of the three-dimensional aesthetic of the group were already realized.

493. 19. The first number is not dated and may have appeared late in 1919.

20. See Bayer, H., and others, *Bauhaus 1919-28*, New York, 1938.

21. The mixed character of Bauhaus theory and production in the early years is well illustrated in Gropius,

W., *Staatliches Bauhaus, 1919-1923*, Munich [1923].

494. 22. The effect of van Doesburg's visit to Germany is controversial. Although Gropius denied, or at any rate minimized, its importance to the Bauhaus group – and, indeed, personally disliked van Doesburg – critics and historians have mostly believed the influence of Neoplasticism to have been at least as significant at this point as that of the Russians. See Zevi, B., 'L'Insegnamento critico di Theo van Doesburg', *Metron*, VII (1951), 21-37.

The most significant representative of advanced abstract art outside Germany in the Bauhaus group of resident artists was the Hungarian, Laszló Moholy-Nagy, and he was certainly much closer to the Russians than to the Dutch. Later he headed what was called the New Bauhaus in Chicago.

It is not without significance that Gropius included in 1926 Oud's *Holländische Architektur* in the series of Bauhausbücher which he edited. That indicated his special respect for the *De Stijl*-nurtured modern architecture of Holland at the time.

495. 23. Like Le Corbusier's window-walls, these horizontal strip-windows, usually called 'ribbon-windows' in English, can be traced back at least as far as Shaw's work of the sixties, though not all the intervening links can be identified. Their analogy with 'Chicago windows' is closest and, indeed, Sullivan's Carson, Pirie & Scott façades, with their wide windows crisply cut in the smooth terracotta wall-plane, were amazingly premonitory of the characteristic new window-banded façades of the twenties. Before this time window-strips were always subdivided by relatively heavy mullions in the plane of the wall, as in Voysey's houses, or set behind ranges of colonnettes or other supports, as in the clerestory of Wright's Unity Church and Doménech's Palau.

496. 24. This special vision of America was well illustrated in books of the twenties by European architectural visitors; see Mendelsohn, E., *Amerika, Bilderbuch eines Architekten*, Berlin, 1926, and Neutra, R., *Wie baut Amerika?* Stuttgart, 1927.

25. The preoccupation with the shapes of things that move – which architecture does not – seems to have reflected the motion-aesthetic of the Futurists. How well Le Corbusier knew the pre-war projects of the brilliant Italian Antonio Sant'Elia is not clear. But his own aesthetic was less related to the particular forms found in Sant'Elia's designs for buildings than to generalized Futurist dreams of speed and technical modernity. See also Note 10 to Chapter 23.

26. However, Le Corbusier's sketch books make evident that he had used his eyes to advantage on a very wide range of buildings in the Mediterranean world on his early travels, from peasant huts to the Parthenon, the Campidoglio, and Versailles. His atti-

tude towards the past was very different, evidently, from that of the Futurists, to which a somewhat closer parallel can be noted in the doctrines of Gropius.

27. Throughout this period, and indeed down to 1943, Le Corbusier practised in partnership with his cousin Pierre Jeanneret (b. 1896); technically most of his work should therefore be attributed to 'Le Corbusier & Jeanneret'. Critics and historians have not yet determined to what extent Jeanneret deserves credit for the work of the firm, nor to evaluate the late work he did independently.

27a. See Roth, A., *Zwei Wohnhäuser von Le Corbusier und Pierre Jeanneret*, Stuttgart, 1927.

497. 28. The open plan of the Vaucresson house was more significant than the treatment of the exterior; that was 'scraped' of all features in a Loos-like way, yet still quite symmetrical, at least on the garden side.

The studio-house for Ozenfant, built on a very restricted corner site, was too special in its vertical organization to be very influential. Although otherwise well maintained, the very industrial saw-toothed skylights on the roof have been removed and the terrace surrounded with a crude railing.

29. Confused by Le Corbusier's description of his houses as *machines à habiter* and the general 'machino-latry' of much of his early writing, many have mistakenly supposed that his was a machine-aesthetic. Just how to define his aesthetic other than by begging the question and merely calling it 'Corbusian' is, however, far from clear. For an early analysis stressing Le Corbusier's 'formalism', but not in the pejorative sense of Stalinist criticism, see Rowe, C., 'Mannerism and Modern Architecture', *Architectural Review*, CVII (1950), 289 300, and other later articles by Rowe in various periodicals.

498. 30. Le Corbusier's personal system of proportion, first used for the 1916 house, gradually crystallized into a very detailed mathematical scheme made generally available in his books *Le Modulor*, Boulogne-sur-Seine, 1950; English ed., London, 1954; and *Modulor II*, London, 1958.

31. See Moussinac, L., *Robert Mallet-Stevens*, Paris, 1931.

499. 32. See *André Lurçat, projets et réalisations*, Paris, 1929.

33. In this connexion Schumacher's school-building programme for Hamburg, initiated considerably earlier, was also significant.

34. See Le Corbusier, *Une maison – un palais*, Paris, 1928.

35. As building activity increased in Russia in the twenties there was considerable experimentation, mostly along Constructivist lines, and a growing acceptance of the new architecture of the western world. This continued into the early thirties. But the

competition for the Palace of the Soviets of 1931, to which Le Corbusier and Gropius as well as Poelzig and Mendelsohn were among the over two hundred architects who contributed projects, represented a major turning point. This was won by the Soviet architect B. M. Iofan (b. 1891) with a very monumental scheme designed in a variant of that megalomaniac mode of scraped classicism which had been popular for large-scale architecture in Germany under the Second Reich and which returned to favour in 1933 under the Third Reich, just after Iofan's scheme triumphed. By 1937 this relatively severe project had been elaborated by Iofan and his collaborators W. G. Helfreich and V. A. Schouko until it rose – and to the same tremendous height as the Empire State Building in New York – like a telescopic wedding-cake, terminating in a statue of Stalin a third as tall as the whole structure below.

Henceforth the 'scraping' of Classical forms ceased and Stalinist architecture in general aimed at an elaboration that was at once Baroque and Victorian in its coarse exuberance and in its illiterate use of academic clichés all but forgotten in the western world. During the later Stalinist period official Soviet criticism decried the modern architecture of the western world as a manifestation of 'bourgeois formalism'.

After the end of this period the denunciation of its characteristic architecture by Soviet leaders led to a return towards that contact with advanced western ideas evident in the twenties and early thirties. For the production of the Stalinist period, mostly very low-grade 'traditional' architecture, see *Dreissig Jahre sowjetische Architektur in der RSFSR*, Leipzig, 1950. See also the section on Russia in the Bibliography. Current achievement in Eastern Europe is chiefly in large-scale prefabricated housing. See the section on Poland in the Bibliography.

501. 36. More than rivalling Gropius's housing in its extent was that carried out by Ernst May (b. 1886) for the city of Frankfurt at this same time.

502. 37. Gropius and Meyer first used a smooth rendered surfacing on a theatre at Jena that they remodelled in 1922; this was not otherwise very significant, except that no trace of Expressionist influence, still strong in work of the year before, remained. As will appear shortly, Mies van der Rohe proposed to use brick in a design for a country house in 1923; and all the private houses he built in the twenties are of that material, though his housing blocks at Berlin and Stuttgart were rendered.

503. 38. Although Mies was not, as his second name van der Rohe might suggest, Dutch, he was always an admirer of Berlage, and his very high standards for brickwork derived from his knowledge of Dutch

building, both old and new, acquired during the year spent in Holland on the Kröller house project.

506. 39. Much of Le Corbusier's prolific writing of the twenties has already been mentioned in the text and earlier notes; for Gropius's, see Cook, R. V., *A Bibliography: Walter Gropius, 1919-1950*, Chicago [1951].

40. For example, the German translation of *Vers une architecture* appeared in 1926; the English translation in 1927 in both English and American editions. Of *Urbanisme*, the American edition is of 1927, the English of 1929, and the German of 1929 also. Mies wrote, in effect, nothing at all.

41. As has been noted, Oud, at the invitation of Gropius, wrote *Holländische Architektur* (No. 10 in the series of Bauhausbücher) in 1926 and also published many articles in Dutch, German, English, and French magazines throughout the late 20s. These and other writings by Oud down to his death in 1963 were reprinted in *Ter Wille van een levende Bouwkunst*, K. Wieckart, ed., The Hague, n.d. See also Oud in the Bibliography.

508. 41a. The most extreme example of direct emulation of Mondrian's painting has been Oud's Café de Unie of 1925.

CHAPTER 23

513. 1. See Note 1, Chapter 22.

1a. In revising this book ten years after it was first written it became very evident to me that my opinions had continued to change. Many such changes are reflected in newly added footnotes. Ten years later still, they are continuing to change, as is evident particularly in the notes, some of which are new.

2. Le Corbusier's moulded *pilotis* supporting the Swiss Hostel in Paris [320] are two years later; those under the Unité d'Habitation, which resemble Aalto's much more closely, were designed after the Second World War.

3. A hospital built in 1926-8 by Adolf Schneck and Richard Döcker (b. 1894) in Stuttgart is actually earlier but hardly comparable in quality.

514. 3a. Neutra built 'Health House' for Dr Richard Lovell in Los Angeles.

3b. Richard M. Schindler (1887-1953), another Austrian who had worked with Wright in California in the early years of the decade, had built already in 1926 an equally remarkable house for the same client, Dr Lovell, at Newport Beach, Cal. This house is rather parallel to, than derivative from, the European houses of the mid twenties by International Style architects. Little Wright influence survived and it can almost be called 'Constructivist'.

4. For Howe's earlier 'traditional' work see *Mono-*

graph of the Work of Mellor, Meigs and Howe, New York, 1923; for an assessment of his later career, see also Zevi, B., 'George Howe', *Journal of the American Institute of Architects*, XXIV (1955), 176-9. For the PFSF see Jordy, W., and Stern, R., *Journal of the Society of Architectural Historians*, XXII (1962), entire June issue. See also Stern, R., *George Howe*, New Haven, 1975.

515. 5. The same description applies roughly to Aalto's work down to the buildings mentioned above, it may be noted.

6. See Jordan, R. F., 'Lubetkin', *Architectural Review*, CXVIII (1955), 36-44.

516. 7. Technically the architects were J. Alan Slater and Arthur Hamilton Moberly (1885-1952) with Crabtree as designing associate. Professor Sir Charles Herbert Reilly (1874-1948), head of the School of Architecture at Liverpool, which he made one of the most advanced schools in the world in these years, was consultant. It is curious to recall that he had earlier been a consultant on Devonshire House in Piccadilly in London, built in 1924-6 by Carrère & Hastings (John M., 1858-1911; and Thomas, 1860-1929), when the influence of American 'traditional' architecture was strong in London (see Chapter 24).

8. Amyas Douglas Connell (b. 1901), Basil Robert Ward (b. 1902), and Colin Anderson Lucas (b. 1906); see also Note 9 to this chapter.

9. For the late twenties and early thirties, when the newer architecture first penetrated England, see Pevsner, N., 'Nine Swallows - No Summer', *Architectural Review*, XCI (1942), 109-12, and Hitchcock, H.-R., 'England and the Outside World', *Architectural Association Journal*, LXXII (1956), 96-7 (this is a special number of the *Journal* devoted to the work of Connell, Ward & Lucas, 1927-39). See also Richards, J. M., 'Wells Coates', *Architectural Review*, CXXIV (1958), 357-60.

10. If Expressionism in architecture is an episode difficult to assess despite the real achievement of several of the architects involved with it (see Chapters 20 and 22), Futurism is impossible to evaluate at all since it was only a 'might have been'. Italian modern architecture from the thirties did not derive from the projects of Sant'Elia, many of which were only then being studied for the first time. Sant'Elia and the other architects associated with Futurism wished to cut all links with the past, Terragni re-linked the 'International Style' - usually called *architettura razionale* under the Fascist regime - with Italian tradition, a line which several Italian modern architects have followed since. See Sartoris, A., *Sant'Elia e l'architettura futurista*, Rome, 1943; Tentori, F., 'Le Origini Liberty di Antonio Sant'Elia', *L'Architettura*, I (1955), 206-8; Banham, R., 'Futurism and Modern

Architecture', *Journal of the Royal Institute of British Architects*, LXIV (1957), 129-38, and 'Futurist Manifesto', *Architectural Review*, CXXVI (1959), 77-80. The greater part of Sant'Elia's drawings are now available for study at the Villa Olmo, Como. See Bibliography.

10a. A very late work executed by Michelucci in the mid sixties, the Chiesa dell'Autostrada outside Florence, is of a totally different character that may not unjustly be considered Neo-Expressionist. Rarely did the aspirations of Finsterlin around 1919 come so close to realization, except in Eero Saarinen's TWA building at Kennedy Airport completed several years earlier.

517. 11. See Le Corbusier, *UN Headquarters*, New York, 1947.

12. See Rudolph, P., 'Walter Gropius et son école', *L'Architecture d'aujourd'hui*, XX (1950), 1-116.

13. Credit for initiating the reform at Harvard must be given to the Dean of the school there, Joseph Hudnut (1886-1968), who invited Gropius to join his faculty.

14. Louis Skidmore (1897-1962), Nathaniel Owings (b. 1903), John O. Merrill (b. 1896).

14a. A decade later the production of the leading American architects when working in Europe and Asia was likely to be remote from the established International Style, except for their industrial buildings. From the Banque Lambert in Brussels by Gordon Bunshaft of Skidmore, Owings & Merrill to Louis I. Kahn's work in India, new buildings by Americans illustrate directions not very much exploited as yet by Europeans or Asiatics. Mies's Museum of Modern Art in Berlin, however, opened in the autumn of 1968, was in the late mode he had perfected nearly twenty years before. This is in sharp contrast to the Expressionism - not, in this case, Neo-Expressionism - of Hans Scharoun's Philharmonic and his National Library across the way, the one earlier, the other later. It is, however, more consonant with Hentrich & Petschnigg's Europa Centrum. The Centrum may be considered, like so much of the better German building of the fifties and sixties, to be representative of the international Miesian vein. Egon Eiermann's near-by Gedächtniskirche was much more original, though his work was more often thoroughly Miesian too. See Global Architecture No. 21, *Berlin Philharmonic Concert Hall*, Tokyo.

15. Ralph Rapson has been Dean of the School of Architecture at the University of Minnesota, it is relevant to note at this point.

522. 16. See Le Corbusier, *The Marseilles Block*, London, 1953; Global Architecture No. 18, *L'Unité d'habitation Marseille and Berlin*, Tokyo.

17. See Le Corbusier, *Œuvre complète*, [VI, 1957], 50-107.

523. 17a. Le Corbusier continued to build at Chandigarh down to his death in August 1965. The latest monumental work to be completed was the Assembly Building, included with other executed buildings and important projects for France and Italy in [Vol. VII] of the *Œuvre complète*, Zürich [1965], which covers the years 1957 to 1965. See also Global Architecture No. 30, *Chandigarh*, Tokyo.

17b. Global Architecture No. 32, *Sarabhai House and Shodhan House*, Tokyo.

18. See Stirling, J., 'Ronchamp', *Architectural Review*, CXIX (1956), 155–61. The best coverage is in Le Corbusier, *Œuvre complète*, [VI, 1957], 16–43, however. See also Le Corbusier, *The Chapel at Ronchamp*, New York, 1957; Global Architecture No. 7, *La Chapelle de Ronchamp*, Tokyo.

525. 19. In collaboration with the French architect B.-H. Zehrfuss and the Italian engineer Pierluigi Nervi.

19a. See Gropius, W., et al., eds., *The Architects Collaborative 1945–1965*, Teufen [1966].

20. For a late published statement of Gropius's principles, see *The Scope of Total Architecture*, New York, 1955, London [1956], although there is little there not to be found already in his other writings of the last fifty years. See also Note 39 to Chapter 22.

528. 20a. Global Architecture No. 14, *Crown Hall (ITT) and the New Gallery in Berlin*, Tokyo.

21. Curiously enough Philip Johnson's glass house in New Canaan, Conn., which obviously derived in several ways from the Farnsworth house, was actually erected first, in 1949; but of course Mies's plan and model of the Farnsworth house had already been published by Johnson in his book *Mies van der Rohe* in 1947. See also Global Architecture No. 27, *The Farnsworth House*, Tokyo.

529. 22. Although the design of the later towers follows closely that of the two blocks built in 1949–51, the construction is actually of ferro-concrete, not steel.

23. Thanks to the continuance in the early post-war years of the reaction of the thirties, the buildings at the south end of the Coolsingel appear to present a curious inversion of chronology. While Dudok's Bijenkorf Department Store of 1929-30, now demolished to open the view to the harbour, was characteristic of the ambiguity of much of his work, this 'baby skyscraper' of 1939-40 and also the contiguous Exchange by J. F. Staal (1879-1940), designed in 1929 and built in the thirties, appeared much more 'modern' to mid-century eyes than the first big banks and so forth rebuilt after the war – these look as if they had been designed at least a generation ago. But the wave of reaction soon ran its course; the Lijnbaan of 1953-4, a complete shopping street by van den Broek & Bakema running parallel to the Coolsingel, if not

the new Bijenkorf by Breuer of 1955-7, was among the most advanced projects carried out anywhere in the mid fifties.

24. Oud's prominent Resistance Monument on the Dam in Amsterdam opposite the Royal Palace, completed in 1956, was hardly a work of architecture but rather an enlarged pedestal and frame for sculpture. Such a commission and the honorary doctorate he received in 1955 from the University of Leiden none the less indicated the high respect he was receiving in Holland at the end of his life.

A very large building for which Oud left complete designs, a convention hall with adjuncts near Berlage's Stedelijk Museum in The Hague, reached completion in 1969. Like his other productions of the previous thirty years, it did not constitute a notable addition to the canon of his work. The late work of Rietveld down to his death in 1964 has been far more distinguished, even the posthumous Van Gogh Museum in Amsterdam. His large Art Academy at Arnhem of 1962 and the earlier pavilion of 1954-5 in the Sonsbeck Park there, rebuilt in 1965 as a tribute to his memory by the architects of Holland, in the sculpture garden of the Rijksmuseum Kröller-Müller in the Hoge Veluwe, also deserve mention, as does the somewhat earlier Zonnehof exhibition gallery at Amersfoort, his finest work since the Schröder-Schräder house of 1924 at Utrecht. More than any other architect except Mies, Rietveld continued to work in the International Style with convincing assurance down into the mid sixties.

530. 25. See Note 1 to Chapter 24.

CHAPTER 24

531. 1. 'Historicism' is a clumsy term matched by no viable adjective. It does, however, express more accurately than 'traditionalism', 'revivalism', or 'eclecticism' a certain aspect of architecture which was common throughout the last five hundred years, and not unknown in early ages. Quite simply, it means the re-use of forms borrowed from the architectural styles of the past, usually in more or less new combinations. It is late in this book to introduce a definition; but historicism is always so much taken for granted in discussing the architecture of the nineteenth century that it is only after the appearance as an alternative of exclusive modernism, rejecting all borrowed forms, that the older attitude needs to be isolated in order to discuss its continuance in this century. Characteristically, the architecture of two-thirds of the period covered by this book balanced a moderate sort of modernism with more or less of historicism. This is as true of most of the novel projects of Ledoux in the 1780s as it is of a considerable part of the work of the first generation of modern architects. However, only the 'traditional' architects remained firmly attached to the concept of historicism in the twentieth century; men like Behrens and Perret were, through the most important years of their careers at least, in highly significant revolt against it, quite as Ledoux had been in his day.

534. 1a. Historians both American and Scandinavian have begun the investigation of American inspiration – more specifically from Richardson and from Sullivan – in Finland and Sweden as well as in Denmark. See Eaton, L. K., *American Architecture Comes of Age*, Cambridge, Mass. [1972], and Marika Hausen, 'Gesellius – Lindgren – Saarinen', *Arkitekti – Arkitekten* (February 1967), 6–12.

537. 1b. In Finland Sonck's church architecture, from the Tampere Cathedral of 1902–7 to the Kallio Church in Helsinki of 1909–12, avoided the historicism of Tengbom and Ericsson, achieving all the same an autochthonous quality, particularly at Tampere, that rivalled Wahlman's Engelbrekt Church in Stockholm.

538. 1c. See Östberg, R., *The Stockholm Town Hall*, Stockholm, 1929.

541. 2. The decline is perhaps to be related at its start to the death of their associate Joseph M. Wells in 1890. Never a member of the firm, he had nevertheless been personally responsible for the design of the Villard houses [193] that had opened the academic phase of the firm's career. Later, the death of White and the retirement of McKim in the early years of the new century removed the two controlling personalities from the firm. Henceforth the office was a 'plan-factory', with high professional standards undoubtedly, but without direction other than that already established in the late eighties and nineties by the founders. In 1961 the firm finally came to an end with the death of J. K. Smith, the only surviving partner who had known the founders.

2a. When the Pennsylvania Station was demolished in 1964–5 prominent modern architects and critics led the protests. This was evidence of a much warmer attitude to the 'traditional' architecture of the early twentieth century, even in its most megalomaniac Classical aspect, than existed only a few years earlier.

542. 3. The Gare d'Orsay was scheduled for demolition in De Gaulle's time. A skyscraper on its site, if erected, would not have been a happy modification of the central Parisian city-scape.

J.-L. Pascal (1837–1920), a pupil of Gilbert who had worked with Garnier on the Opéra and succeeded Labrouste at the Bibliothèque Nationale, had at least as high a reputation, and was the teacher of several prominent English and American architects (see Chafee, R., 'The Teaching of Architecture at the École des Beaux-Arts', in Drexler, A. (ed.), *The Archi-*

tecture of the École des Beaux-Arts, New York [1976]). His severe academic style, emulated later by his Anglo-Saxon pupils, was well established by the time he designed the Faculty of Medicine at Bordeaux in the early nineties. Nénot was one of Pascal's French pupils.

4. William Adams Delano (1874–1960) was a pupil of Laloux; Chester Holmes Aldrich (1871–1940) was also trained at the École des Beaux-Arts. For an early attempt to reassess the 'traditional' houses of this period, see Lane, J., 'The Period House in the Nineteen-Twenties', *Journal of the Society of Architectural Historians*, xx (1961), 185–90.

543. 4a. The tower seems to derive from that on Sonck's Kallio Church in Helsinki, completed ten years earlier, and the portal shows the influence of that on the front of Eliel Saarinen's Helsinki Station. The 'black-versus-white' critical attitude that developed in the late twenties concerning 'traditional' architecture in America obscured many relationships that later seem historically relevant.

544. 5. The controversy as to which firm should receive credit for the design of the Grand Central Station once waxed hot. The organization of the tremendous complex was probably the work of Charles A. Reed (?–1911) and Allen H. Stem (1856–1931), who had already built other big stations in Troy, N.Y., in 1901–4 and in Tacoma in 1909–11 – as, moreover, their successors, Felheimer & Wagner, did also: Buffalo and North Station, Boston, both begun in 1927, and Cincinnati in 1929–33. Whitney Warren (1864–1943) and Charles D. Wetmore (1866–1941), who also worked with Reed & Stem on the Detroit station completed in 1913, were doubtless more responsible for the dignified and well-scaled detailing. See Marshall, D., *Grand Central*, New York, 1946.

6. Books of the period, such as *American Architecture* of 1928 by the distinguished architectural historian Fiske Kimball, or *American Architecture of Today*, also of 1928, by the then Dean of the Harvard University School of Architecture, G. H. Edgell, offer the later writer very little assistance. Kimball in the twenties was too ready to consider the continuance of the academic tradition assured – his chapter on Sullivan and Wright was entitled 'The Lost Cause' – while Edgell offers such a miscellany of buildings that no clear picture emerges. Several attempts within the period to select its major monuments fixed on much the same lot as are given prominence here; but such selections hardly help to organize the work of the day in historical terms.

6a. Even less than the Nebraska Capitol should the Telephone Building be considered traditional. Its solid forms appeal more to the latest advanced taste than the curtain-walled skyscrapers that are the direct heirs of the International Style.

7. See Weisman, W., 'Towards a New Environment: the Way of the Price Mechanism; the Rockefeller Centre', *Architectural Review*, CVIII (1950), 399-405; 'Who Designed Rockefeller Center?', *Journal of the Society of Architectural Historians*, X (1951), 11-17; and 'The First "Mature" Skyscraper', *Journal of the Society of Architectural Historians*, XVIII (1959), 54-9.

545. 8. This firm were the successors of Richardson, and Joseph Richardson is Richardson's grandson, Hugh Shepley his great-grandson. See Forbes, J. D., 'Shepley, Bulfinch, Richardson and Abbott, Architects – An Introduction', *Journal of the Society of Architectural Historians*, XVII (1958), 19-31.

546. 9. 'Compositionalism' has been suggested by Colin Rowe as a name for the style-phase with which this section deals. Composition was then conceived by many architects and theorists as an absolute to which the re-use of any sort of stylistic forms could be accommodated. It is at least open to suspicion, for example, that Rogers's Pierson College at Yale was designed originally with Gothic forms and then re-cast as Neo-Georgian. Later eyes than our own will doubtless find it possible to identify the period characteristics of traditional work of the twenties in the way many critics already feel able to do with the nineteenth-century revivals. The period-designation 'President Harding' may some day perhaps be as meaningful as 'General Grant', if hardly comparable to 'Victorian'!

10. Harvey Wiley Corbett (1873-1954), a pupil of Pascal at the École des Beaux-Arts, was probably the designer.

11. Carrère was dead by this time, but the firm name remained unchanged; as has been mentioned earlier, Professor Sir Charles Reilly was consultant, and he probably made some real contribution to the design.

12. C.-F. Mewès (1858-1947) and Arthur Joseph Davis (1878-1951), both pupils of Pascal, like Corbett.

13. Gropius was very insistent on the desirability of anonymous teamwork in architecture. His TAC, the one-time Tecton group in London, and other firms with similar names are examples of this ideal which aims, of course, at something rather different from the anonymity of the large commercial firms. Theirs is fact rather than ideal.

547. 14. See Weisman, W., 'Group Practice', *Architectural Review*, CXIV (1953), 145-51.

548. 15. Sir John J. Burnet (1857-1938), another pupil of Pascal at the École; Thomas S. Tait (1882-1954).

549. 16. See Pevsner, N., 'Building with Wit; the Architecture of Sir E. Lutyens', *Architectural Review*, CX (1951), 217-25.

17. See Purdom, C. B., *The Garden City*, London, 1913; Culpin, E. G., *The Garden City Movement Up-to-Date*, London, 1913; and Creese, W., *The Search*

for Environment, the Garden City, Before and After, New Haven, 1966.

18. See Macfadyen, D., *Sir Ebenezer Howard and the Town Planning Movement*, London, 1933.

550. 19. See Unwin, R., *Town Planning and Modern Architecture at the Hampstead Garden Suburb*, London, 1909.

552. 20. Some of the other large buildings were the work of Sir Herbert Baker, who was also responsible for another dominion capital at Pretoria in South Africa. Of his rival's intervention at New Delhi Lutyens remarked characteristically, 'It was my Bakerloo'.

21. See Drysdale, G., 'The Work of Leonard Stokes', *Journal of the Royal Institute of British Architects*, XXXIV (1927), 163-77, and Roberts, H. V. M., 'Leonard Aloysius Stokes', *Architectural Review*, C (1946), 173-7.

553. 22. The New-Zealand-born Connell's High-and-Over in Bucks of 1927 is very superior, however, to Tait's Le Chateau at Silverend in Essex, and a year earlier.

22a. *La Terza Roma. Lo sviluppo urbanistico, edilizio e tecnico di Roma capitale*, Rome, 1971.

CHAPTER 25

555. 1. No sharp distinction was made in this book between architects and engineers. Such engineers, from Telford to Candela, as have been responsible for work of architectural pretension deserve to be considered as architects, and monographic works on several of them will be found in the Bibliography.

556. 2. See San Francisco Museum of Art, *Domestic Architecture of the San Francisco Bay Region*, San Francisco, 1949.

3. See Banham, P. R., 'New Brutalism', *Architectural Review*, CXVIII (1955), 355-61. See also Banham's articles in the *Architectural Review* on 'Neo-Liberty', a term introduced by Paolo Portoghesi.

4. Consideration of such topics of once-current controversial interest more properly belongs in special critical works than in a general history, but see the Epilogue.

5. There is something symptomatic in the fact that the younger men, whether architects or critical writers, have often been content to revive early controversial attitudes of the preceding half century rather than to offer anything really new. (See Epilogue.)

557. 5a. Books covering, usually rather unselectively, the architecture of the last twenty years in various countries will be found in the Bibliography. A generously illustrated general account is provided by John Jacobus in *Twentieth-Century Architecture: The Middle Years 1940-65*, London [1966] (German language edition, Stuttgart [1966]). An Australian architect-critic's plausible attempt to analyse and even define the successive style-phases of the same years, all but unillustrated, is Robin Boyd's *The Puzzle of Architecture*, Melbourne [1965] (also London [1965]). These two books supply partially what is necessarily missing in this chapter written in 1957 and still, twenty years later, largely left as it stood: i.e., 'Mid Century' is to be interpreted rather literally as referring to the years round 1950. It should be repeated here that little attempt has been made in this chapter or the Epilogue to give references to the periodical publication of the many works of the last decades mentioned in the text or the Notes. Information concerning them and profuse illustrative coverage will be readily found in the architectural press, often that of several countries, in the case of what has been considered most notable.

5b. This is very apparent in most of the large schemes of urban renewal in various American cities undertaken in the last twenty years. Most of the buildings in these vast projects 'dated' well before they were completed so that, though erected later, they belong – at best – to the mid century stylistically.

5c. Tapiola, across the bay from Helsinki in Finland, might better be mentioned. The earlier New Towns in Great Britain were largely completed by the mid sixties. Cumbernauld in Scotland and the later sections of Peterlee were already an improvement over those near London that were built first. Reston, outside Washington, was the first notable example in the U.S.

5d. Begun later than Chandigarh but built more rapidly, Brasilia had by the late sixties most of its public buildings designed by Oscar Niemeyer and considerable areas filled up less successfully with other construction. See Stäubli, W., *Brasilia*, New York [1966]; Evenson, N., *Two Brazilian Capitals*, New Haven, 1973.

558. 6. See Holford, W., 'The Precincts of St Paul's', *Journal of the Royal Institute of British Architects*, LXIII (1956), 232–4. The rebuilding of the City went forward with rapidly increasing speed in the ten years following the publication of Lord Holford's report. The largest and most freely planned area, called the Barbican, with curtain-walled skyscrapers rather widely spaced and linked by pedestrian ways well above street level, is to the north of the district round St Paul's. Despite the clearance of much of the ground in London by bombing thirty years ago, several American cities have since carried out equally drastic projects of 'urban renewal' by demolishing existing buildings in central areas. The same is true of Stockholm.

6a. Since this was first written the remarkable increase in the numbers of students everywhere has required the building of many more complete new universities as well as a more than equivalent extension of plant at the already existing ones throughout the world. The heavy emphasis in the text on Latin America must be chiefly a reminder that this extremely significant building activity of the 1960s was well under way in the previous decade in relatively undeveloped countries.

559. 7. See Aarhus Universitet, *Hovedbygningen*, Aarhus [n.d.].

562. 7a. This Venezuelan skyscraper, carried by four concrete piers set well within the site from which the upper storeys are cantilevered out, was premonitory of one of the types of structure developed in following years for tall buildings in which ferro-concrete replaced the steel skeleton. An advanced example of this, constructed in 1967–9, is the Standard Bank in Johannesburg in South Africa by the German firm of Hentrich & Petschnigg in association with the Danish-born English engineer Ove Arup; see *Standard Bank Centre Johannesburg*, Johannesburg [1970].

8. The term skyscraper in this context is to be understood as meaning a very tall office building. Many European housing blocks, such as are discussed below, would have been considered skyscrapers a generation ago, and the same is true of much urban office building in central areas which often today rivals in height the German examples of the twenties mentioned in Chapter 20. However, the significant skyscrapers of the post-war period are much taller than this, and – perhaps equally important – they characteristically stand in their own space, rising sheer from some sort of plaza at their base. See Note 6 above.

8a. See Wurster, C., and others, *Das Hochhaus BASF*, Stuttgart, *c.* 1958. For Hentrich & Petschnigg's later and much finer Thyssen Haus in Düsseldorf, see Mittag, M., *Thyssenhaus*, Essen, 1962. There are also monographs on their less important and later, but equally conspicuous, skyscrapers for Bayer at Leverkusen and for Unilever at Hamburg. See also the previous Note and Chapter 23, Note 14a.

565. 9. James Cubitt (b. 1913), Stephen Buzas (b. 1915), Fello Atkinson (b. 1919), and Richard Maitland (b. 1917); now only Cubitt and Atkinson.

9a. By the late sixties there were several new university complexes in England more than rivalling the Ghanaian one and still others in construction, not to speak of four or five new colleges at Oxford and Cambridge.

9b. By the sixties Dutch housing was once more of good quality, superior to that in France if not to Swiss work. In France frenzied activity in the late fifties and sixties hardly caught up with a lag that had lasted for generations.

566. 9c. Better than Coventry was that which followed at Sheffield, rivalling the finest work of the L.C.C. architects.

567. 9d. The Dutch have been especially successful at incorporating shopping centres in their housing estates. The best example is perhaps that on the eastern edge of Arnhem. These contrast with American shopping centres, which are usually located in relation to highways rather than to planned residential developments.

568. 9e. The high quality of the late work of Böhm and Schwarz was not easy to maintain, yet some younger architects such as Hans Schilling, Emil Steffann, E. Burghartz, and Josef Lehmbrock have produced churches of considerable interest, especially in the Archdiocese of Cologne. Typical are various examples in the new Diocese of Essen, founded in 1958. See Kleffner, E. B., and Kuppers, L., *Neue Kirchen im Bistum Essen*, Essen [1966], especially, among work by one of the older men, Schwarz's St Andreas, Essen-Rüttenschied, 1956-7; his Holy Family, Oberhausen, 1956-8; and his St Antonius, Essen-Frohnhausen, 1958-9; and also Lehmbrock's St Joseph, Essen-Kray-Leithe, 1959-63; Schilling's St Marie, Essen-Karnap, 1961-3, and his Christ the King, Oberhausen-Buschhangen, 1961-3; and Burghartz's St Francis, Bottrop-Boy, 1960-2. Schilling's best works, however, are St Alban, Cologne, and the Benedictine abbey church at Meschede, the latter completed in 1965. Steffann's most impressive church is at Opladen and some ten years earlier. Böhm's son Gottfried's earlier churches were inferior; but his town hall at Bensberg near Cologne, completed in 1967, is a notable example of 'Brutalism', as is his church at Neviges.

570. 10. Osvaldo Luis Torro (b. 1914) and Miguel Ferrer (b. 1915).

10a. The building of airports and their rebuilding proceeded at a lively pace in the last fifteen years; it may have to begin all over again to take care of the supersonic aircraft of the 1970s. For the present stage some stabilization of design had by the late sixties been reached, mostly in a late International Style vein. See Blakenship, E. G., *The Airport*, New York [1974].

11. Architects designing for prefabrication and above all structural experimenters such as Buckminster Fuller are certainly far bolder and more revolutionary in their concepts of the house as 'controlled environment' than have been most of those who have built airports. See Fuller, R. B., *4D; Buckminster Fuller's Dymaxion House*, exhibition, Cambridge, Mass., 1930, and *What I Am Trying to Do*, London, 1968.

11a. Global Architecture No. 12, *Philip Johnson House*, Tokyo.

576. 12. The death of Eero Saarinen in 1961 brought to a premature end the career of a typical, indeed a very leading, post-war architect whose mature production dated very largely from the years since the mid fifties when this book was originally written. (See Epilogue.) Less tragic, because of their longer careers, were the deaths of Oud in 1963, Rietveld in 1964, Le Corbusier in 1965, and both Gropius and Mies in 1969. The Bibliography now includes monographs not only on Eero Saarinen, but also on Skidmore, Owings & Merrill, van den Broeck & Bakema, Gardella, Quaroni, and Villanueva, as well as on certain older modern architects not included in earlier editions, such as Griffin, Häring, the Brothers Luckhardt, May, Meyer, Östberg, and Schwarz, to mention here only those added in the editions of the sixties; seventy more have been added in this edition.

EPILOGUE

577. 1. Global Architecture No. 5, *Richards Medical Research Building and Salk Institute*, Tokyo.

578. 1a. Among Scandinavians, the Dane Jørn Utzon rose to international fame and then sank again, thanks to the controversies concerning the Sydney Opera House in Australia. Among Italians, Quaroni or Giancarlo Di Carlo might now be mentioned rather than Viganó, famous some twenty years ago as the first Italian 'Brutalist'. James Stirling's university buildings in some degree maintained the promise of his earlier work in partnership with James Gowan. See Global Architecture No. 9, *Leicester University and Cambridge University*, Tokyo.

2. The most extreme statement made in the late 1960s by an architect-critic in opposition to earlier programmes for modern architecture was Robert Venturi's *Complexity and Contradiction in Architecture*, New York, 1967. This unexpected first 'Museum of Modern Art Paper on Architecture' has been greeted – rather exaggeratedly – by Vincent Scully as 'probably the most important writing on the making of architecture since Le Corbusier's *Vers une architecture* of 1923'. There is little question that Venturi's intention was to turn the early ideas of Le Corbusier, so basic to the International Style, quite upside down.

579. 3. See Banham, R., *The New Brutalism*, London [1966].

580. 3a. Global Architecture No. 24, *Town Hall in Säynätsalo and Kansaneläkelaitos*, Tokyo.

581. 3b. By the earlier seventies the production of 'mobile homes' in the U.S. began to compare statistically with that of conventional dwelling units, and a new sort of cooperative development, the condominium, rivalled that of rented flats or free-standing houses for purchase.

587. 3c. Forma e Colore, *Wright: Il Museo Guggenheim di Carlo Cresti* [Florence, 1970?].

3d. Global Architecture No. 11, *La Couvent de la Tourette*, Tokyo.

BIBLIOGRAPHY

For the study of the architecture of the western world since about 1840 no sources are more valuable than the professional periodicals. To provide a comprehensive list with full bibliographical details would require an inordinate amount of space and many technicalities because of the complicated way such publications start and stop, initiate new series, merge, and change title. However, it may be helpful to mention, without giving any descriptive details, a few that are especially valuable to the historian. In England, the *Builder*, the *Building News*, and later the *Architectural Review* are most useful; in France the *Revue générale de l'architecture*, the *Encyclopédie d'architecture*, the *Gazette des architectes*, and later *L'architecture vivante* and *L'architecture d'aujourd'hui*. In Austria-Hungary the *Allgemeine Bauzeitung* may be cited. For the United States, the *American Architect and Building News* and later *The American Association of Architectural Bibliographers*, I–X (1965–74), the *Architectural Record*, the *Architectural Forum*, and *Progressive Architecture* cover the field from the eighteen-seventies to the present. The American *Journal of the Society of Architectural Historians* has devoted more articles to the nineteenth century than other learned journals. Particular articles in the above-mentioned and other periodicals are for the most part merely referenced in the Notes, except those that provide the equivalent of separate monographs on certain architects; such are listed here.

By 1986, several new published bibliographical tools had become available for use in this field, including the R.I.B.A. and R.I.L.A. indexes. Also of use is the new bibliographical *Macmillan Encyclopedia of Architects*, 4 vols., New York, 1982.

General Works are subdivided, necessarily with some overlap, into those covering the *Nineteenth Century* (including, in fact, the later decades of the eighteenth also) and those covering the *Twentieth Century*. There follow rubrics for separate countries or groups of countries, towns, and building types. Finally in this arrangement come the monographs on individual architects, which are quoted, regardless of country or period, alphabetically by architect.

GENERAL WORKS

NINETEENTH AND TWENTIETH CENTURIES

Great Drawings from the Collection of the R.I.B.A. New York, 1983.
LEVER, J., and RICHARDSON, M. *The Architect as Artist.* New York, 1984.
PLACZEK, A. K. (ed.). *Macmillan Encyclopedia of Architects.* 4 vols. New York, 1982.
SAINT, A. *The Image of the Architect.* New York, 1983.
SEARING, H. (ed.). *In Search of Modern Architecture: A Tribute to Henry-Russell Hitchcock.* Cambridge, Mass., 1982.
THORNTON, P. *Authentic Decor: The Domestic Interior 1620–1920.* New York, 1984.

NINETEENTH CENTURY

BENEVOLO, L. *History of Modern Architecture*, I. Cambridge, Mass. [1971].
BROADBENT, G. *Neo-Classicism.* London, 1980.
BRUNNERHAMMER, Y. *Lo stile 1925.* Milan [1966].
CASSOU, J., LANGUI, E., and PEVSNER, N. *The Sources of Modern Art.* London, 1962. (In America, *Gateway to the Twentieth Century*, New York, 1962.)
CHAMPIGNEULLE, B. *L'Art Nouveau.* Paris [1972].
COLLINS, P. *Changing Ideals in Modern Architecture.* London [1965]
FAWCETT, J. (ed.). *Seven Victorian Architects.* London, 1976.
FERGUSSON, J. *History of the Modern Styles of Architecture.* London, 1862.
FRAMPTON, K. (ed.). *Modern Architecture 1851–1919.* Tokyo, 1981.
GEIST, J. F. *Passagen, ein Bautyp des 19. Jahrhunderts.* Munich, 1969.
GERMANN, G. *Gothic Revival in Europe and Britain.* London, 1972.
GIEDION, S. *Space, Time and Architecture.* Cambridge, Mass., 1941. Later editions to 5th, 1967.
GIEDION, S. *Spätbarocker und romantischer Klassizismus.* Munich, 1922.
GRUBE, O. W. *Industrial Buildings and Factories.* New York [1971].
HARPER, R. H. *Victorian Building Regulations; Summary Tables of The Principal English Building Acts and Model By-Laws, 1840–1914.* London, 1985.
HAUTECOEUR, L. *Rome et la renaissance de l'anti-*

quité à la fin du XVIIIe siècle. Paris, 1912.

HITCHCOCK, H.-R. *Modern Architecture, Romanticism and Reintegration.* New York, 1929.

HIX, J. *The Glass House.* Cambridge, Mass. [1974].

HONOUR, H. *Neo-Classicism.* Harmondsworth, 1968.

JOSEPH, D. *Geschichte der Baukunst des XIX. Jahrhunderts.* 2 vols. Leipzig [1910].

KAUFMANN, E. *Architecture in the Age of Reason.* Cambridge, Mass., 1955.

KUBINSZKY, M. *Bahnhöfe Europas.* Stuttgart [1969].

LAVEDAN, P. *Histoire de l'urbanisme,* vol. 3. Paris, 1952.

LOYER, F. *Architecture of the Industrial Age, 1789–1914.* New York, 1983.

LUNDBERG, E. *Arkitekturens Formspråk,* IX, *Vägen till Nutiden, 1715–1850,* Stockholm, 1960; X, *Nutiden, 1850–1960,* Stockholm, 1961.

MACLEOD, R. *Style and Society.* London, 1971.

MADSEN, S. T. *Sources of Art Nouveau.* Oslo, 1956; New York, 1956.

MANZONI, P. S. *Il Razionalismo . . . (XVIII–XIX–XX secolo).* Milan, 1966.

MEEKS, C. L. V. *The Railroad Station.* New Haven, 1956.

MICHEL, A. (ed.). *Histoire de l'art depuis les premiers temps chrétiens jusqu'à nos jours,* VII, 2; VIII, 1, 2, 3. Paris, 1924–9.

MIDDLETON, R., and WATKIN, D. *Neoclassicism and Nineteenth Century Architecture.* New York, 1980.

MUTHESIUS, H. *Stilarchitektur und Baukunst: Wandlungen der Architektur im XIX. Jahrhundert.* Mülheim-Ruhr, 1902.

PAULI, G. *Die Kunst des Klassizismus und der Romantik.* Berlin, 1925.

PEVSNER, N. *An Outline of European Architecture.* Harmondsworth, 1942; later editions to 1968.

PEVSNER, N. *Pioneers of Modern Design.* London, 1936; 3rd ed., Harmondsworth, 1974.

PEVSNER, N. *Some Architectural Writers of the Nineteenth Century.* Oxford, 1972.

RÉAU, L. *Histoire de l'expansion de l'art français,* vol. I– . Paris, 1924– .

REHME, W. *Die Architektur der neuen freien Schule.* Leipzig, 1901.

STING, H. *Der Kubismus und seine Einwirkung auf die Wegbereiter der modernen Architektur.* [?Aachen], 1965.

SUMMERSON, J. (ed.). *Concerning Architecture.* London, 1968.

SUMMERSON, J. N. *Heavenly Mansions.* London, 1949.

TANN, J. *The Development of the Factory.* London [1970].

VRIEND, J. J. *Nieuwere Architectuur . . . 1800 tot Heden.* Bussum, 1957.

WIEBENSON, D. *Sources of Greek Revival Architecture.* University Park, Maryland, 1969.

TWENTIETH CENTURY

BANHAM, R. *Theory and Design in the First Machine Age.* London, 1960.

BEHRENDT, W. C. *Modern Building.* New York, 1937.

BENEVOLO, L. *History of Modern Architecture,* II. Cambridge, Mass. [1971].

Contemporary Architecture of the World 1961. Tokyo [1961].

CONRADS, U. (ed.). *Programme und Manifeste zur Architektur des 20. Jahrhunderts.* Frankfurt, c. 1964.

CONRADS, U., and SPERLICH, H.-G. *The Architecture of Fantasy,* transl. and expanded by C. C. and G. R. Collins. New York [1962].

COOK, J. W. *Conversations with Architects.* New York [1973].

CURTIS, W. J. R. *Modern Architecture since 1900.* Englewood Cliffs, N.J., 1983.

DORFLES, G. *L'Architettura moderna.* Milan, 1954.

DUNSTER, D. *Key Buildings of the Twentieth Century,* I, *Houses 1900–1944.* New York, 1985.

EATON, L. K. *American Architecture Comes of Age.* Cambridge, Mass. [1972].

Global Architecture, I–XXXII. Tokyo.

GROPIUS, W. *Internationale Architektur.* Munich, 1925.

HAMLIN, T. F. *Forms and Functions of Twentieth-Century Architecture.* 4 vols. New York, 1952.

HATJE, G., ed. *Encyclopedia of Modern Architecture.* London [1963]; New York [1964].

HILLIER, B. *The World of Art Deco.* New York, 1971.

HITCHCOCK, H. R., and JOHNSON, P. *The International Style: Architecture since 1922.* New York, 1932; 2nd ed., New York [1966].

JACOBUS, J. *Twentieth-Century Architecture: the Middle Years 1940–65.* London [1966].

JAFFÉ, H. L. C. *De Stijl, 1917–1931.* London [1956].

JENCKS, C. *Modern Movements in Architecture.* Garden City and Harmondsworth, 1973.

JOEDICKE, J. *A History of Modern Architecture.* New York, 1959.

JOEDICKE, J. *Architecture Since 1945.* New York, 1969.

PEHNT, W. *Expressionist Architecture.* New York, 1973.

PEVSNER, N., and RICHARDS, J. M. *The Anti-Rationalists.* [London] 1973.

PLATZ, G. *Die Baukunst der neuesten Zeit.* Berlin, 1927.

RICHARDS, J. M. *An Introduction to Modern Architecture.* 9th ed. Harmondsworth, 1962.

ROBINSON, C., and BLETTER, R. H. *Skyscraper Style*. New York, 1975.
SARTORIS, A. *Introduzione alla architettura moderna*. Milan, 1949.
SARTORIS, A. *Gli Elementi dell'architettura funzionale*. Milan, 1935.
SCHMUTZLER, R. *Art Nouveau-Jugendstil*. Stuttgart [1962].
SEMBACH, K.-J. *Style 1930*. New York [1972].
SFAELLOS, C. *Le Fonctionnalisme dans l'architecture contemporaine*. Paris, 1952.
SHARP, D. *Sources of Modern Architecture: A Critical Bibliography*. Westfield, N.J., 1981.
SHARPE, D. *Modern Architecture and Expressionism*. New York, 1967.
SMITH, G. E. K. *The New Architecture of Europe*. Cleveland and New York [1961]; Harmondsworth, 1962.
VRIEND, J. J. *Nieuwere Architectuur*. Bussum, 1957.
WHITTICK, A. *European Architecture in the Twentieth Century*. 2 vols. London, 1950-3.
WINGLER, H. M. *The Bauhaus*. Cambridge, Mass., 1969.
ZEVI, B. *Storia dell'architettura moderna*. Turin, 1950.

INDIVIDUAL COUNTRIES

AFRICA

KULTERMANN, U. *New Directions in African Architecture*. New York, 1969.

AUSTRALIA

Architecture in Australia (catalogue of exhibition at the R.I.B.A.). London, 1956.
BEIERS, G. *Houses of Australia*. Sydney [1948].
BOYD, R. *Australia's Home*. Carlton, 1952.
CASEY, M., and others (eds.). *Early Melbourne Architecture*. Melbourne, 1953.
COX, P. S. *The Australian Homestead*. Melbourne, 1972.
FREELAND, J. M. *Architecture in Australia*. Melbourne and Canberra [1968].
HAYES, E. *Australian Style*. Sydney [1970].
HERMAN, M. *The Architecture of Victorian Sydney*. Sydney, 1956.
HERMAN, M. *The Early Australian Architects and Their Work*. Sydney and London, 1954.
JOHNSON, D. L. *Australian Architecture 1901-1951; Sources of Modernism*. Sydney, 1980.

LEARY, F. *Colonial Heritage: Historic Buildings of New South Wales*. Sydney, 1972.
MORGAN, SIR E. J. R. *Early Adelaide Architecture 1836-1886*. Melbourne, 1969.
SHARLAND, M. *Stones of a Century*. Hobart, 1942.
SOWDEN, H. *Towards an Australian Architecture*. Sydney, 1968.

AUSTRIA-HUNGARY

DEHIO, G. *Handbuch der deutschen Kunstdenkmäler: Österreich*. Vienna, 1933.
Die Wiener Werkstätte. Vienna, 1967.
LÜTZOW, C. von, and TISCHLER, L. (eds.). *Wiener Neubauten*. 2 vols. Vienna, 1876-80.
Neubauten in Wien, Prag, Budapest. Vienna, 1904.
Neue Architektur in Österreich, 1945-1970. Vienna, 1969.
POWELL, N. *The Sacred Spring*. Greenwich, Conn., 1974.
RADOS, J. *A magyar klasszicista építészet hagyományai*. Budapest, 1953.
UHL, O. *Moderne Architektur in Wien: von Otto Wagner bis heute*. Vienna, c. 1966.
VIRGIL, B. *A magyar klasszicismus építészete*. Budapest, 1948.
Wiener Neubauten im Stil der Sezession. 6 vols. Vienna, 1908-10.

BRITISH DOMINIONS

ARCHER, M. *Indian Architecture and the British 1780-1830*. Feltham, 1968.
CLARKE, B. F. L. *Anglican Cathedrals outside the British Isles*. London, 1958.
'Commonwealth I, II', (special issues of) *Architectural Review*, October 1959; July 1960.
MCCOY, E. J. *Victorian City of New Zealand*. Dunedin, 1968.
NILSSON, S. A. *European Architecture in India, 1750-1850*. London [1968].
STACPOOLE, J. *New Zealand Art; Architecture 1820-1970*. Wellington [1972].

BULGARIA

TONER, L. *Arkhitekturala v Bulgariia, 1944-60*. Isdvo-na, 1962.

CANADA

CLERK, N. *Palladian Style in Canadian Architecture*. Ottawa, 1984.

EDE, C. M. *Canadian Architecture 1960–70*. Toronto, 1971.

GOWANS, A. *Building Canada, An Architectural History of Canadian Life*. Toronto, 1966.

GOWANS, A. *Looking at Architecture in Canada*. Toronto, 1958.

HUBBARD, R. 'Canadian Gothic', *Architectural Review*, CXVI (1954), 102–8.

KALMAN, H. D. *The Railway Hotels and the Development of the Château Style in Canada*. Victoria, B.C., 1968.

MAITLAND, L. *Neoclassical Architecture in Canada*. Ottawa, 1984.

MAYRAND, P. *Three Centuries of Architecture in Canada*. Montreal [1971].

WRIGHT, J. *Architecture of the Picturesque in Canada*. Ottawa, 1984.

CZECHOSLOVAKIA

CHYSKÝ, A., and others. *Guide to Czechoslovakia*. Prague, c. 1965.

DOSTAL, O. *Moderni Architektura w. Ceskoslovensku*. Prague, 1969.

DOSTAL, O., PECHAR, J., and POROCHÁZKA, V. *Klasicistická Architektúra na Slovensku*. Bratislava, 1955.

FOLTYN, L. *Architektúra na Slovensku do Polovice xlx Storŏcia*. Bratislava, 1958.

KAHOUN, K. *Neskorogoticka Architektúra na Slovensku a Stavilelia Uýchodného Okruhu*. Bratislava, 1973.

KNOX, B. *The Architecture of Prague and Bohemia*. London, 1965.

KNOX, B. *Bohemia and Moravia: an Architectural Companion*. London, c. 1962.

KUSY, M. *Architectura na Slovensku. 1918–1945*. Bratislava, 1971.

WIRTH, Z., and MATĚIČEK, A. *Céská Architektura, 1800–1920*. Prague, 1922.

FRANCE

AMOUROUX, D. *Guide d'architecture contemporaine en France*. [n.p.] 1972.

BARQUI, F. *L'Architecture moderne en France*. Paris [n.d.].

BAUCHAL, C. *Nouveau dictionnaire biographique et critique des architectes français*. Paris, 1887.

BIVER, M.-L. *Le Paris de Napoléon*. Paris [1963].

BRAULT, E. *Les Architectes par leurs œuvres*. 3 vols. Paris [n.d.].

CALLIAT, V. *Parallèle des maisons de Paris*. 2 vols. Paris, 1850, 1864.

CAPELLADES, J. *Guide des églises nouvelles en France*. [Paris, 1969].

DEKROM, K. *Le Style Louis-Philippe*. Verviers, 1968.

DREXLER, A. (ed.). *The Architecture of the École des Beaux-Arts*. Cambridge, Mass., 1977.

EGBERT, D. D. *The Beaux-Arts Tradition in French Architecture*. Princeton, 1980.

EMERY, M. *Un Siècle d'architecture moderne en France, 1850–1950*. [Paris, 1971].

GOURLIER, BIET, GRILLON, and TARDIEU. *Choix d'édifices publics projetés et construits en France depuis le commencement du XIX siècle*. 3 vols. Paris, 1825–36.

GROMORT, G. *L'Architecture* in *Histoire générale de l'art français de la Révolution à nos jours*, II. Paris, 1922.

HAUTECOEUR, L. *Histoire de l'architecture classique en France*, vols IV–VII. Paris, 1952–7.

KALNEIN, W. Graf, and LEVEY, M. *Art and Architecture of the Eighteenth Century in France*. Harmondsworth, 1972.

KRAFFT, J., and THIOLLET, F. *Choix des plus jolies maisons de Paris et des environs*. Paris, 1849.

MAGNE, L. *L'Architecture française du siècle*. Paris, 1889.

MIDDLETON, R. (ed.). *The Beaux-Arts and Nineteenth Century French Architecture*. Cambridge, Mass., 1982.

NORMAND, L. M. *Paris moderne ou choix de maisons*. 3 vols. Paris, 1837, 1843, 1849.

PINKNEY, D. H. *Napoleon III and the Rebuilding of Paris*. Princeton, 1958.

ROCHEGUDE, Marquis de. *Guide pratique à travers le vieux Paris*. New ed. Paris, 1923.

GERMANY

Architektur und Städtebau in der D.D.R. Leipzig, 1969.

BEENKEN, H. *Schöpferische Bauideen der deutschen Romantik*. Mainz, 1942.

Berlin, Akademie der Künste. Bauen in Berlin 1900–1964. Berlin, 1964.

Berlin und seine Bauten. Berlin, 1877.

BURCHARD, J. *The Voice of the Phoenix: Post-War Architecture in Germany*. Cambridge, Mass. [1966].

CONRADS, U., and MARSCHALL, W. *Modern Architecture in Germany*. London [1962].

DEHIO, G. *Handbuch der deutschen Kunstdenkmäler*. 5 vols. Berlin, 1905 et seq.; new ed., E. Gall, so far, 11 vols. Berlin and Munich, 1935 et seq.

DUVIGNEAU, V. *Die Potsdam-Berliner Architektur zwischen 1840–1875 . . .* Munich, 1966.

FEUERSTEIN, G. *New Directions in German Architecture*. New York, 1968.

GÜNTHER, S. *Interieurs um 1900.* Munich, 1971.
HENNIG-SCHEFOLD, M., and SCHAEFER, I. *Frühe moderne Architektur in Berlin.* [Winterthur, 1967.]
HERRMANN, W. *Deutsche Baukunst des 19. und 20. Jahrhunderts,* vol. I. Breslau, 1932.
HILBERSHEINER, L. *Berliner Architektur der 20er Jahre.* Mainz [1967].
HITCHCOCK, H.-R. *Rococo Architecture in Southern Germany.* London, 1968.
JUNGHANNS, K. *Der deutsche Werkbund: Sein erstes Jahrzehnt.* Berlin, 1982.
LANDSBERGER, F. *Die Kunst der Goethezeit.* Leipzig, 1931.
LANE, B. M. *Architecture and Politics in Germany, 1918-1945.* Cambridge, Mass., 1968.
LANG, L. *Das Bauhaus 1919-1933 Idee und Wirklichkeit.* Berlin, 1966.
LICHT, H. *Architektur Deutschlands.* 2 vols. Berlin, 1882.
MEBES, P. *Um 1800.* Munich, 1918.
MILDE, K. *Neorenaissance in der deutschen Architektur des 19. Jahrhunderts: Grundlagen, Wesen und Gültigkeit.* Dresden, 1980.
NERDINGER, W. (ed.). *Klassizismus in Bayern, Schwaben und Franken. Architekturzeichnungen 1775-1828.* Munich, 1980.
REIMANN, G. J. *Deutsche Baukunst des Klassizismus.* Leipzig, 1967.
SCHMALENBACH, F. *Jugendstil.* Würzburg, 1935.
SCHMITZ, H. *Berliner Baumeister vom Ausgang des 18. Jahrhunderts.* Berlin, 1914.
SCHUMACHER, F. *Strömungen in der deutschen Baukunst seit 1800.* Leipzig, 1935.
STEIN, R. *Klassizismus und Romantik in der Baukunst Bremens,* I. Bremen, 1964.
TAYLOR, R. R. *The Word in Stone.* Berkeley [1974].
TEUT, A. *Architektur im Dritten Reich, 1933-1945.* Berlin [1967].
VOGEL, H. *Deutsche Baukunst des Klassizismus.* Berlin, 1937.

GREAT BRITAIN

ALLSOPP, B. *Modern Architecture of Northern England.* Newcastle-upon-Tyne, 1969.
AMES, W. *Prince Albert and Victorian Taste.* London [1967].
ASLIN, E. *The Aesthetic Movement.* New York, 1969.
BOASE, T. S. R. *English Art 1800-1870.* London, 1959.
BRIGGS, A. *Victorian Cities.* London [1963].
CASSON, H. *New Sights of London.* London, 1938.
CLARK, K. *The Gothic Revival.* London, 1928; second edition 1950.
CLARKE, B. F. L. *Church Builders of the Nineteenth Century.* London, 1938.

COLVIN, H. M. *A Biographical Dictionary of English Architects, 1660-1840.* 2nd ed. London, 1978.
CROOK, J. M. *The Greek Revival.* London, 1972.
DARLEY, G. *Villages of Vision: A History of Planned Communities in England and America.* London, 1976.
DAVEY, P. *Architecture of the Arts and Crafts Movement.* New York, 1980.
DAVIS, T. *The Gothic Taste.* Newton Abbot [1974].
DERBY, M. *The Islamic Perspective: An Aspect of British Architecture and Design in the Nineteenth Century.* London, 1983.
DIXON, R., and MUTHESIUS, S. *Victorian Architecture.* New York, 1978.
EASTLAKE, C. L. *A History of the Gothic Revival.* London, 1872. Reprinted (with an introduction by J. M. Crook) Leicester University Press, 1970.
FERRIDAY, P. (ed.). *Victorian Architecture.* London, 1964.
GIROUARD, M. *Sweetness and Light. The 'Queen Anne' Movement 1860-1900.* Oxford, 1977.
GIROUARD, M. *The Victorian Country House.* Oxford, 1971.
GIROUARD, M. *Victorian Pubs.* London [1975].
GOODHART-RENDEL, H. S. *English Architecture since the Regency.* London, 1953.
GOODHART-RENDEL, H. S. 'Rogue Architects of the Victorian Era', *Journal of the Royal Institute of British Architects,* LVI (1949), 251-9.
HARBRON, D. *Amphion or the Nineteenth Century.* London and Toronto, 1930.
HARPER, R. H. *Victorian Architectural Competitions: An Index to British and Irish Architectural Competitions in The Builder, 1843-1900.* London, 1983.
HARRIS, J. *A Country House Index.* Isle of Wight, 1971.
HERSEY, G. L. *High Victorian Gothic: a Study in Associationism.* Baltimore [1972].
HITCHCOCK, H.-R. *Early Victorian Architecture in Britain.* 2 vols. New Haven and London, 1954.
HITCHCOCK, H.-R., and others. *Modern Architecture in England.* New York, 1937.
HOWELL, P. *Victorian Churches.* Feltham, 1968.
HUSSEY, C. *English Country Houses: Mid-Georgian 1760-1800.* London [1956].
HUSSEY, C. *English Country Houses: Late Georgian 1800-1840.* London [1958].
HUSSEY, C. *The Picturesque.* London, 1927.
JENKINS, F. *Architect and Patron.* London, 1961.
KAMEN, R. H. *British and Irish Architectural History: A Bibliography and Guide to the Sources of Information.* London, 1981.
KNOWLES, C. C. *The History of Building Regulation in London, 1189-1972.* London, 1972.
LANDAU, R. *New Directions in British Architecture.* New York, 1968.

LITTLE, B. *Catholic Churches since 1623*. London [1966].

MACAULAY, J. *The Gothic Revival*. Glasgow [1975].

MILLS, E. *The New Architecture in Great Britain, 1946-53*. London, 1953.

MUTHESIUS, H. *Das englische Haus*. 3 vols. Berlin, 1904-5.

MUTHESIUS, H. *Die englische Baukunst der Gegenwart*. Leipzig and Berlin, 1900.

MUTHESIUS, H. *Die neuere kirchliche Baukunst in England*. Berlin, 1902.

MUTHESIUS, S. *The English Terraced House*. New Haven, 1982.

MUTHESIUS, S. *The High Victorian Movement in Architecture, 1850-70*. London [1972].

NAYLOR, G. *The Arts and Crafts Movement*. Cambridge, Mass. [1971].

NEWMAN, J. (ed.). *Design and Practice in British Architecture: Studies in Architectural History Presented to Howard Colvin*. London, 1985.

PEVSNER, N. *The Buildings of England*. 46 vols. London, 1951-74, and later revised editions.

PILCHER, D. *The Regency Style, 1800 to 1830*. London, 1947.

POWELL, C. *An Economic History of the British Building Industry 1815-1979*. London, 1980.

RICHARDSON, A. E. 'Architecture', in G. M. Young (ed.), *Early Victorian England, 1830-1865*, II, 177-248. London, 1934.

RICHARDSON, A. E., and GILL, C. L. *Regional Architecture of the West of England*. London, 1924.

RICHARDSON, A. E. *Monumental Classic Architecture in Great Britain and Ireland*. London, 1914.

RICHARDSON, M. *The Craft Architects*. New York, 1983.

Royal Institute of British Architects. *One Hundred Years of British Architecture, 1851-1951*. London, 1951.

STAMP, G. M. (ed.). *Britain in the Thirties (Architectural Design)*. London, 1980.

STAMP, G. M. (ed.). *The English House*. London, 1986.

SUMMERSON, J. *Georgian London*. London, 1945.

SUMMERSON, J. *Ten Years of British Architecture*. London, 1956.

SUMMERSON, SIR J. N. *Victorian Architecture; Four Studies in Evaluation*. New York, 1970.

TURNOR, R. *The Smaller English House, 1500-1939*. London, 1952.

WALTON, J. K. *The English Seaside Resort: A Social History, 1750-1914*. New York, 1983.

WATKIN, D. *The English Vision: The Picturesque in Architecture, Landscape and Garden Design*. New York, 1982.

WHIFFEN, M. *Stuart and Georgian Churches outside London*. London, 1947-8.

GREECE

RUSSACK, H. H. *Deutsches Bauen in Athen*. Berlin, 1942.

HOLLAND

BEHNE, A. *Holländische Baukunst in der Gegenwart*. Berlin, 1922.

BLIJSTRA, R. *Netherlands Architecture since 1900*. Amsterdam, 1960.

BLIJSTRA, R. *Die Niederländische Architektur nach 1900*. Amsterdam, 1966.

FANELLI, G. *Architettura moderna in Olanda 1900-1940*. Florence, 1968.

JAFFÉ, H. L. C. *Mondrian and De Stijl*. Cologne, 1967.

MIERAS, J., and YERBURY, F. *Dutch Architecture of the XXth Century*. London, 1926.

MIERAS, J. P. *Na-oorlogse bouwkunst in Nederland*. Amsterdam, n.d.

Moderne Bouwkunst in Nederland. 20 vols. Rotterdam, 1932.

Nederland bouwt in Baksteen, 1800-1940. (Catalogue of exhibition at Boijmans Museum.) Rotterdam, 1941.

Nieuwe Kunst rond 1900. Exhibition. The Hague, 1960(?).

OUD, J. J. P. *Holländische Architektur*. Munich, 1926.

OUD, J. J. P. *Nieuwe Bouwkunst in Holland en Europa*. [Den Dolder, 1935.]

REBEL, B. *Het nieuwe Bouwen: Het Functionalisme in Nederland, 1918-1945*. Assen, 1983.

SZÉNASSY, I. L. *Architectuur in Nederland 1960/1967*. Amsterdam, 1969.

THIENEN, F. van. 'De bouwkunst van de laatste anderhalve eeuw', in H. van Gelder (ed.), *Kunstgeschiedenis der Nederlanden*, II. Utrecht, 1955.

TROY, N. J. *The De Stijl Environment*. Cambridge, Mass., 1983.

WATTJES, J. G. *Amsterdams Bouwkunst en Stadsschoon, 1306-1942*. Amsterdam, 1944.

WATTJES, J. G. *Nieuwe nederlandsche Bouwkunst*. 2 vols. Amsterdam, [1923]-1926.

YERBURY, F. R. *Modern Dutch Buildings*. London, 1931.

ITALY

ACCASTO, G. *L'Architettura di Roma capitale, 1870-1970*. Rome, 1971.

ALOI, R. *Nuove architetture a Milano.* Milan, 1959.
BROSIO, V. *Lo Stile Liberty in Italia.* Milan, 1967.
CARACCIOLO, E. 'Architettura dell'ottocento in Sicilia', *Metron*, VII (Oct. 1952), 29–40.
CESCHI, C. *Le Chiese di Roma dagli inizi del neoclassico al 1961.* [Rome] 1963.
FUSCO, R. DE. *Il Floreale a Napoli.* Naples [1959].
GOLFIERI, E. *Artisti neoclassici in Faenza.* Faenza, 1929.
GREGOTTI, V. *New Directions in Italian Architecture.* New York [1968].
KIDDER SMITH, G. E. *Italy Builds.* London, 1955.
KOENIG, G. K. *Architettura in Toscana, 1931–1968.* [Turin, 1968.]
KOSTOF, S. K. *The Third Rome, 1870–1950.* Exhibition. [Berkeley, 1973.]
LAVAGNINO, E. *L'Arte moderna dai neoclassici ai contemporanei.* 2 vols. Turin, 1950, enl. ed., 1961.
Lo Sviluppo urbanistico, edilizio technico di Roma capitale. Rome, 1971.
MEEKS, C. L. V. *Italian Architecture 1750–1914.* New Haven, 1966.
MUÑOZ, A. *Roma nel primo ottocento.* Rome, 1961.
NAPOLI, P. *Arte e architettura in regime fascista.* Rome [1938].
OLIVERO, E. *L'Architettura in Torino durante la prima metà dell'ottocento.* Turin [1935].
PAGANI, C. *Architettura italiana oggi.* Milan, 1955
PATETTA, L. (ed.). *L'Architettura in Italia . . .* Milan, 1972.
PICA, A. *Architettura moderna in Italia.* Milan, 1941.
REGGIORI, F. *Milano 1800–1943.* Milan, 1947.
SASSA, C. *Storia de' monumenti di Napoli e degli architetti che li edificavano,* II. Naples, 1858.
SETA, C. DE. *La Cultura architettonica in Italia tra le due guerre.* Bari, 1972.
TARCHIANO, N. *L'Architettura italiana dell'ottocento.* Florence, 1937.

JAPAN

Architettura giapponese contemporanea. Florence, 1969.
BORRAS, M. L. *Arquitectura contemporánea japonesa.* Barcelona [1970].
BOYD, R. *New Directions in Japanese Architecture.* New York, 1968.
KULTERMANN, U. *New Architecture in Japan.* London [1967].
MASUDA, T. *Living Architecture: Japanese.* New York [1970].

LATIN AMERICA

ARANGO, J., and MARTINEZ, C. *Arquitectura en Colombia.* Bogotá, 1951.

BEACHAM, H. *The Architecture of Mexico.* New York, 1969.
BULLRICH, F. *New Directions in Latin American Architecture.* New York [1969].
CETTO, M. *Modern Architecture in Mexico.* New York, 1961.
GOODWIN, P. *Brazil Builds.* New York, 1943.
HITCHCOCK, H.-R. *Latin American Architecture since 1945.* New York, 1955.
MARTINI, J. X. *La Ornamentacion en la arquitectura de Buenos Aires 1800–1900.* Buenos Aires, 1966.
MINDLIN, H. *Modern Architecture in Brazil.* New York [1956].
MYERS, I. E. *Mexico's Modern Architecture.* New York, 1952.
NEUN, H. *Album de Carácas y Venezuela.* Caracas, 1968.
SEGRE, R. *Cuba, L'Architettura della rivoluzione.* Padua, 1970.

POLAND

Architektura Polska do Poowy xix Wieku. Warsaw, 1952.
DMOCHOWSKI, Z. *The Architecture of Poland.* London, 1956.
DUMNICKI, J., and others. *Building and Architecture in Poland 1945–1966.* Warsaw, 1968.
KNOX, B. *The Architecture of Poland.* New York [1971].
OLSZEWSKI, A. *Nowa Forma w Architektwze Polskiej, 1900–1925.* Wroclav, 1967.
SZAFER, P. *Nowa Architektura Polska; Diariusz lat 1966–1970.* Warsaw, 1972.

RUSSIA

AFANASEV, K. N. *Ideen, Projekte, Bauten; Sowjetische Architektur 1917 1932.* Dresden [1973].
GRABAR, I. *Istoriya Russkagho iskusstva,* vols 3 and 4. Moscow [1912, 1915].
HAMILTON, G. H. *The Art and Architecture of Russia,* Chapters 21–23. 3rd ed. Harmondsworth, 1983.
ILYIN, M., and ALEXANDROV, A. *Moscow Monuments of Architecture.* 2 vols. Moscow, 1975.
KOPP, A. *Town and Revolution.* New York, 1970.
LISSITZKY, E. *Russland: die Rekonstruktion der Architektur in der Sowjetunion.* Vienna, 1930. Reprinted as *Russland: Architektur für eine Weltrevolution.* Frankfurt [1965].
LO GATTO, E. *Gli architetti del secolo XIX a Pietroburgo e nelle tenute imperiali.* Rome, 1943.
NEKRASOV, A. *Russki Ampir.* Moscow, 1935.

PAPERNYI, V. Kul'tura 'Dva': Sovetskaia Arkhitektura 1932–1954. Ann Arbor, c. 1985.

SENKEVITCH, A. The Evolution of the Contemporary Idiom: Soviet Architecture. [Lubboch, Texas ?] 1967.

SENKEVITCH, A. Soviet Architecture 1917–1962: A Bibliographical Guide to Source Material. Charlottesville [1974].

SHVIDKOVSKII, O. A. (comp.). Building in the U.S.S.R., 1917–1932. New York [1971].

Socialismo, città architettura U.R.S.S. 1917–1937. Rome, 1971.

Stroitel'stuo v SSSR, 1917–1967. Moscow, 1967.

VASILIEV, IU. (The Neo-Classical Architecture of Riga). Riga, 1961.

SCANDINAVIA

AHLBERG, H. Swedish Architecture of the Twentieth Century. London, 1925.

ALNAES, E., and others. Norwegian Architecture Throughout the Ages. Oslo, 1950.

CORNELL, E. Ny svensk byggnadskonst. Stockholm, 1950.

Danish Architecture of Today (catalogue of exhibition at R.I.B.A.). London, 1950.

Dansk Architektur gennem 20 Aar, 1892–1912. Copenhagen, n.d.

Denmark (special issue on Danish Architecture). Architectural Review, CIV (1948).

ELLING, C., and FISKER, K. Danish Architectural Drawings 1660–1920. Copenhagen, 1961.

FABER, T. New Danish Architecture. New York, 1968.

FINSEN, H. Ung danske arkitektur, 1930–45. Copenhagen, 1947.

FISKER, K., and YERBURY, F. R. Modern Danish Architecture. London, 1927.

HAHR, A. Architecture in Sweden. Stockholm, 1939.

HIORT, E. Nyere dansk bygningskunst. Copenhagen, 1949.

HULTEN, B. Building Modern Sweden. Harmondsworth, 1951.

Industriearkitektur i Finland. Helsinki, 1952.

JACOBSON, T. P., and SILOW, S. (eds.). Ten Lectures on Swedish Architecture. Stockholm, 1949.

JOSEPHSON, R. 'Svensk 1800-tals architektur', in Teknisk Tidskrift, LII (1922), 1–64.

KAVLI, G. Norwegian Architecture, Past and Present. Oslo, c. 1958.

LANGBERG, H. Hvem byggede hvad; Gamle og nye bygninger i Danmark. Copenhagen, 1952.

LANGBERG, H. Danmarks Bygningskultur, II. Copenhagen, 1955.

LINDBLOM, A. Sveriges Konsthistoria fran forntid till nutid, III. Stockholm, 1946.

LINDAHL, G. Högkyrkligt lågkyrkligt frikyrkligt i Svensk architektur, 1850–1950. Stockholm, 1955.

MADSEN, S. T. To Kongeslot. Oslo, 1952.

MADSEN, S. T. 'Dragestilen. Honnør til en hanet stil', Vestlandske Kunstindustrimuseums Årbok, 1949–1950, 19–62. Bergen, 1952.

MILLECH, K. Danske arkitektur stromninger, 1850–1950. Copenhagen, 1951.

New Architecture in Sweden. Stockholm, 1961.

New Swedish Architecture. Stockholm, 1940.

PAULSSON, T. Scandinavian Architecture. London, 1958.

RAY, S. Il Contributo suedese all'architettura contemporanea. Rome, 1969.

RICHARDS, J. M. A Guide to Finnish Architecture. London [1966].

SMITH, G. E. K. Sweden Builds. London, 1950.

TEMPEL, E. New Finnish Architecture. New York [1968].

WANSCHER, L. E. Danmarks arkitektur. Copenhagen, 1943.

WICKBERG, N. E. Finnish Architecture. Helsinki [1959].

SPAIN

BOHIGAS, O. Arquitectura española de la segunda republica. Barcelona, 1970.

BOHIGAS, O. Arquitectura modernista. Barcelona, 1968.

CALZADA, A. Historia de la arquitectura española. Barcelona, 1933.

CIRICI PELLICER, A. El Arte modernista catalán. Barcelona, 1951.

DOMÉNECH GIRBAU, L. Arquitectura española contemporánea. Barcelona, 1968.

FERNANDEZ ALBA, A. La Crisis de la arquitectura española (1939–1972). Madrid, 1972.

FLORES, C. Arquitectura española contemporanea. Madrid, 1961.

LOZOYA, Marqués de (CONTRAVERAS, J. de). Historia del arte hispánico, V. Barcelona, 1949.

SWITZERLAND

BACHMANN, J., and VAN MOOS, S. New Directions in Swiss Architecture. New York, 1969.

BILL, M. Moderne Schweizer Architektur, 1925–1945. Basel, 1949.

BRÖNNIMANN, R. Basler Bauten 1860–1910. Basel and Stuttgart, 1973.

CARL, B. Die Architektur der Schweiz: Klassizismus 1770–1860. Zürich, 1963.

JENNY, H. Kunstführer der Schweiz, ein Handbuch . . . der Baukunst. Bern, 1945.

Moderne Architektur in der Schweiz seit 1900. Winterthur [1970].

Moderne Schweizer Architektur, 10 vols. Basel, 1940–6.

SIVO, B. DE. *L'Architettura in Svizzera oggi.* Naples, 1968.

SMITH, G. E. K. *Switzerland Builds.* London, 1950.

UNITED STATES

ANDREWS, W. *American Gothic.* New York, 1975.

ANDREWS, W. *Architecture, Ambition and Americans.* New York, 1955.

ANDREWS, W. *Architecture in America, A Photographic History.* New York, 1960.

Architectural Record, The (Great American Architects series, reprint). New York, 1977.

Artistic Homes. New York, 1886.

CLARK, R. J. *The Arts and Crafts Movement in America.* Princeton, 1972.

CONDIT, C. W. *American Building.* Chicago, 1968.

CONDIT, C. *The Chicago School of Architecture.* Chicago [1964].

CONDIT, C. *American Building Art – The Nineteenth Century.* New York, 1960.

CONDIT, C. *American Building Art – The Twentieth Century.* New York, 1961.

CRAIG, L., *et al. The Federal Presence.* Cambridge, Mass., 1978.

CREESE, W. L. *The Crowning of the American Landscape: Eight Great Spaces and Their Buildings.* Princeton, 1985.

DENMARK, E. R. *Architecture of the Old South.* Atlanta [1926].

DOWNING, A., and SCULLY, V. J. *The Architectural Heritage of Newport, Rhode Island.* Cambridge, Mass., 1952.

EDGELL, G. H. *The American Architecture of Today.* New York and London, 1928.

FITCH, J. M. *American Building; the Forces that Shape It.* Boston, 1948; 2nd ed., 2 vols, 1967–8.

FRARY, I. T. *Early Homes of Ohio.* Richmond, 1936.

HAMLIN, T. F. *The American Spirit in Architecture.* New Haven, 1926.

HAMLIN, T. F. *Greek Revival Architecture in America.* New York, 1944.

HANDLIN, D. *The American Home: Architecture and Society, 1815–1915.* Boston, 1979.

HAYDEN, D. *Seven American Utopias: Landscapes, Dwellings and Towns, 1790–1940.* Cambridge, Mass., 1976.

HITCHCOCK, H.-R. *A Guide to Boston Architecture, 1637–1954.* New York, 1954.

HITCHCOCK, H.-R. *American Architectural Books.* 2nd ed. Minneapolis, 1962.

HITCHCOCK, H.-R. 'Art of the United States. Architecture', *Encyclopedia of World Art,* I [1959], cols. 246–77.

HITCHCOCK, H.-R. *Rhode Island Architecture.* Providence, 1939.

HITCHCOCK, H.-R., and DREXLER, A. *Built in U.S.A.: Post-War Architecture.* New York, 1952.

HOWLAND, R., and SPENCER, E. *The Architecture of Baltimore.* Baltimore, 1953.

KILHAM, W. *Boston after Bulfinch.* Cambridge, Mass., 1946.

KIMBALL, F. *American Architecture.* Indianapolis, 1928.

KIMBALL, F. *Domestic Architecture of the American Colonies and of the Early Republic.* New York, 1922.

JACKSON, H. *New York Architecture, 1650–1952.* New York, 1952.

JACKSON, K. T. *Crabgrass Frontier: The Suburbanization of the United States.* New York, 1985.

JORDY, W. H. *The Impact of European Modernism in the Mid-Twentieth Century.* Garden City, 1972.

JORDY, W. H. *Progressive and Academic Ideals at the Turn of the Twentieth Century.* Garden City, 1972.

JORDY, W. H., and MONKHOUSE, C. P. *Buildings on Paper: Rhode Island Architectural Drawings.* Providence, R.I., 1982.

KAUFMANN, E. (ed.). *The Rise of an American Architecture.* New York, 1970.

KEMPER, A. M. *Drawings by American Architects.* New York [1973].

LEWIS, A., and MORGAN, K. *American Victorian Architecture: A Survey of the 70s and 80s in Contemporary Photographs.* New York, 1975.

LONGSTRETH, R. W. *On the Edge of the World.* Cambridge, Mass., 1983.

MACCALLUM, I. *Architecture U.S.A.* London, 1959.

MCCOY, E. *Five California Architects.* New York, c. 1960.

MCCOY, E. *The Second Generation.* Salt Lake City, 1983.

MAYHEW, E. DE N., and MYERS, M. *A Documentary History of American Interiors.* New York, 1980.

MOCK, E. (ed.). *Built in U.S.A., 1932–1944.* New York, 1944.

MUMFORD, L. *The Brown Decades.* 2nd ed. New York [1955].

MUMFORD, L. *Roots of Contemporary American Architecture.* New York, 1952.

MUMFORD, L. *From the Ground Up.* New York [1957].

MUMFORD, L. *Sticks and Stones.* New York, 1924.

NEVINS, D., and STERN, R. A. M. *The Architect's Eye: American Architectural Drawings, 1799–1978.* New York, 1979.

NEWCOMB, R. *Architecture of the Old North-West Territory*. Chicago, 1950.

NEWCOMB, R. *Architecture in Old Kentucky*. Urbana, Ill., 1953.

NICHOLS, F. D., and JOHNSTON, F. B. *The Early Architecture of Georgia*. Chapel Hill, 1957.

'One Hundred Years of Significant Building', *Architectural Record*, CXIX (June 1956–June 1957) (a series of monthly features).

PIERSON, W. H. *Technology and the Picturesque, The Corporate and Early Gothic Styles*. Garden City, 1978.

RANDALL, F. *History of the Development of Building Construction in Chicago*. Urbana, Ill., 1949.

REPS, J. W. *North American Views and Viewmakers: A Union Catalogue of Lithographic Prints of Cities and Towns, 1834–1926*. Columbia, 1984.

ROOS, F. J. *Bibliography of Early American Architecture*. Urbana, 1968.

ROOS, F. J. *Writings on Early American Architecture*. Columbus, 1943.

ROTH, L. M. *A Concise History of American Architecture*. New York, 1979.

SCHUYLER, M. *American Architecture*. New York, 1892; new ed. (ed. W. Jordy and R. E. Coe), Cambridge, Mass., 1961.

SCULLY, V. J. *The Shingle and the Stick Style*. New Haven, 1971.

SCULLY, V. J. *The Shingle Style*. New Haven, 1955.

SHELDON, G. W. *Artistic Country Seats*. 2 vols. New York, 1886–[7].

SIEGEL, A. (ed.). *Chicago's Famous Buildings*. Chicago [1965].

SMITH, G. E. K. *The Architecture of the United States*. 2 vols. Garden City, 1981.

STANTON, P. B. *The Gothic Revival and American Church Architecture*. Baltimore [1968].

STERN, R. A. M. *New Directions in American Architecture*. New York, 1969.

STERN, R. A. M. *The Anglo-American Suburb. Architectural Design*. London, 1981.

TALLMADGE, T. *Architecture in Old Chicago*. Chicago, 1941.

TALLMADGE, T. *The Story of Architecture in America*. London [1928].

TSELOS, D. 'The Chicago Fair and the Myth of the "Lost Cause"', *Journal of the Society of Architectural Historians* (Dec. 1967), 259–68.

TUNNARD, C. *American Skyline*. Boston, 1955.

WHIFFEN, M., and KOEPER, F. *American Architecture*. Cambridge, Mass., 1983.

WHITE, T. (ed.). *Philadelphia Architecture in the Nineteenth Century*. Philadelphia, 1953.

WRIGHT, G. *Building the Dream: A Social History of Housing in America*. New York, 1981.

CITIES

AMSTERDAM

DE WIT, W. (ed.). *The Amsterdam School*. Cambridge, Mass., 1984.

HAAGSMA, E., et al. *Amsterdamse Gebouwen, 1880–1980*. Utrecht, 1981.

BERLIN

BORSCH-SUPON, E. *Berliner Baukunst nach Schinkel, 1840–70*. Munich, 1977.

LANGE, K.-L. *Berlin, Bauwerke der Neogothik*. Berlin, 1984.

CHICAGO

Chicago Tribune Tower Competition. New York, 1980.

KRINSKY, C. H., and VAN ZANTEN, D. *Chicago and New York: Architectural Interactions*. Chicago, 1984.

LARSON, G. R. 'Fire, Earth and Wind: Technical Sources of the Chicago Skyscraper', *Inland Architect* (September, 1981), 20–9.

See also UNITED STATES: CONDIT, RANDALL, SIEGEL, TALLMADGE.

DELHI

IRVING, R. G. *Indian Summer: Lutyens, Baker and Imperial Delhi*. New Haven, 1981.

DRESDEN

HELAS, V. *Architektur in Dresden 1800–1900*. Braunschweig, 1985.

EDINBURGH

GIFFORD, J., MCWILLIAM, C., and WALKER, D. *Edinburgh (The Buildings of Scotland)*. Harmondsworth, 1984.

KERSTING, A., and LINSAY, M. *The Buildings of Edinburgh*. London, 1981.

LENINGRAD

ALESCHINA, L. *Leningrad und Umgebung*. Berlin, 1982.

IOGANSEN, M. V., and LISOVSKIY, V. G. *Leningrad*. Leningrad, 1982.

LONDON

Greater London Council. *Survey of London.* Numerous volumes.
STAMP, G. M. *The Changing Metropolis.* Harmondsworth, 1984.
STAMP, G. M., and AMERY, C. *Victorian Buildings of London, 1837–1887.* London, 1980.

MANCHESTER

ARCHER, J. H. G. (ed.). *Art and Architecture in Victorian Manchester: Ten Illustrations of Patronage and Practice.* Manchester, 1985.

NEW YORK

CANTOR, M. (ed.). *Around the Square.* New York, 1982.
CONDIT, C. W. *The Port of New York: A History of the Railroad and Terminal System from the Beginnings to Pennsylvania Station.* Chicago, 1980.
KRINSKY, C. H. *Rockefeller Center.* New York, 1978.
STERN, R. A. M., *et al. New York 1900.* New York, 1983.

PARIS

EVENSON, N. *Paris: A Century of Change, 1878–1978.* New Haven, 1979.
GAILLARD, M. *Paris au XIXe siècle.* Paris, 1981.

POTSDAM

MIELKE, F. *Potsdamer Baukunst: das klassische Potsdam.* Berlin, 1981.

VIENNA

NEBEHAY, C. M. *Wien Speziell: Architektur und Malerei um 1900.* Vienna, 1983.

WASHINGTON, D.C.

HAFERTEPE, K. *America's Castle.* Washington, D.C., 1984.
SMALL, H. *The Library of Congress: Its Architecture and Decorations.* New York, 1982.

BUILDING TYPES

PEVSNER, N. *A History of Building Types.* London, 1976.

ARCADES AND GLASSHOUSES

FRIEMERT, C. *Die gläserne Arche: Kristallpalast London 1851–1854.* Munich, 1984.
GEIST, J. F. *Arcades: The History of a Building Type.* Cambridge, Mass., 1982.
KOPPLEKAMM, S. *Glasshouses and Wintergardens in the Nineteenth Century.* New York, 1981.

BUNGALOWS

KING, A. D. *The Bungalow: The Production of a Global Culture.* Boston, 1984.
LANCASTER, C. *The American Bungalow 1880–1920.* New York, 1985.

COLLEGE CAMPUSES

TURNER, P. V. *Campus.* Cambridge, Mass., 1984.

CONCERT HALLS, ETC.

FORSYTH, M. *Buildings for Music.* Cambridge, Mass., 1985.

COURT HOUSES

LOZE, P. *Le Palais de Justice, Monument XIXe.* Brussels, 1983.
PARE, R., *et al. Court House.* New York, 1978.

GRAND HOUSES

ASLET, C. *The Last Country Houses.* New Haven, 1982.
DENNIS, M. *Court and Garden: From the French Hotel to the City of Modern Architecture.* Cambridge, Mass., 1986.
GIROUARD, M. *Life in the English Country House.* London, 1978.

HOTELS

WATKIN, D. *Grand Hotel: The Golden Age of Palace Hotels.* New York, 1984.

HOUSING

DAUNTON, M. J. *House and Home in the Victorian City: Working Class Housing, 1850–1914.* London, 1983.
SWENARTON, M. *Homes Fit for Heroes: Politics and Architecture of Early State Housing.* London, 1981.

PUBLIC BUILDINGS

PORT, M. H. *The Houses of Parliament.* New Haven, 1976.
SMALL, H. *The Library of Congress: Its Architecture and Decorations.* New York, 1982.

RAILWAY STATIONS

BINNEY, M. *Great Railway Stations of Europe.* London, 1984.
HAMM, M., *et al. Bahnhöfe.* Berlin, 1984.
KRINGS, U. *Bahnhofsarchitektur.* Munich, 1984.
NEVINS, D. (ed.). *Grand Central Terminal: City Within the City.* New York, 1982.

ROYAL PAVILION

MORLEY, J. *The Making of the Royal Pavilion Brighton: Designs and Drawings.* Boston, 1984.

STATE CAPITOLS

HITCHCOCK, H. R., and SEALE, W. *Temples of Democracy: The State Capitols of the U.S.A.* New York, 1976.

SYNAGOGUES

BOTHE, R. (ed.). *Synagogen in Berlin.* Berlin, 1983.
KRINSKY, C. H. *Synagogues of Europe.* Cambridge, Mass., 1985.

TOWN HALLS

CUNNINGHAM, C. *Victorian and Edwardian Town Halls.* London, 1981.
Historic American Buildings Survey. *American City Halls.* Washington, D.C., 1984.
MAI, E., *et al. Das Rathaus im Kaiserreich; Kunstpolitische Aspekte einer Bauaufgabe des 19. Jahrhunderts.* Berlin, 1982.

MONOGRAPHS

AALTO
Aalto, Alvar. *Synopsis: Painting, Architecture, Sculpture . . .* Basel and Stuttgart, 1970.
Alvar Aalto. Zürich, 1970.
Fleig, K. (ed.). *Alvar Aalto.* London [1963].
Miller, W. *Alvar Aalto, An Annotated Bibliography.* New York, 1983.
Mosso, L. *L'Opera di Alvar Aalto.* Milan [1965].
Quantrill, M. *Alvar Aalto: A Critical Study.* New York, 1983.
Schildt, G. *Alvar Aalto/Sketches.* Cambridge, Mass., 1985.
ABADIE
Paul Abadie architecte 1812–1884: entre archéologie et modernité. Angoulême, 1984.
ADAM
Adam, R. and J. *The Works in Architecture.* 2 vols. London, 1778–9.
Bolton, A. T. *Robert and James Adam.* 2 vols. London, 1922.
Fleming, J. *Robert Adam and his Circle.* London, 1962.
AMSTERDAM SCHOOL
Vriend, J. J. *Amsterdamse School.* Amsterdam, 1970.
ASHBEE
Crawford, A. *C. R. Ashbee: Socialism and the Arts and Crafts Movement.* London and New Haven, 1985.
ASPLUND
Holmdahl, G., Lind, S., and Ödeen, K. (eds.). *Gunnar Asplund Architect, 1885–1940.* Stockholm [n.d.].
The Architecture of Erik Gunnar Asplund. Cambridge, Mass., 1980.
Zevi, B. *E. Gunnar Asplund.* Milan, 1948.
BADGER
Badger's Illustrated Catalogue of Cast-Iron Architecture . . . Reprint with a new introduction by Margot Gayle. New York, 1981.
BAILLIE SCOTT. *See* SCOTT (BAILLIE)
BAKER
Baker, Sir Herbert. *Architecture and Personalities.* London, 1944.
'In Memoriam Sir Herbert Baker', *South African Architectural Record,* XXXI (July 1946).
BALLU
Sédille, P. *Théodore Ballu.* Paris, 1886.
BALTARD
Decouchy, M. *Victor Baltard.* Paris, 1875.
BARRY (C.)
Barry, A. *The Life and Works of Sir C. Barry.* London, 1867.

BAZEL, DE
Reinink, A. W. *K.P.C. de Bazel.* Amsterdam, 1965.

BBPR
Bonfanti, E. *Città, museo e architettura.* Florence, 1973.

BEHRENS
Buddensieg, T., and Rogge, H. *Industrielkultur: Peter Behrens and the AEG, 1907–1914.* Cambridge, Mass., 1984.
Cremers, P. *Peter Behrens, sein Werk von 1900 bis zur Gegenwart.* Essen, 1928.
Hoeber, F. *Peter Behrens.* Munich, 1913.
Peter Behrens, 1868–1940. [Kaiserslautern, 1966.]

BELLUSCHI
Stubblebine, J. *The Northwest Architecture of Pietro Belluschi.* New York, 1953.

BENTLEY
De L'Hôpital, W. *Westminster Cathedral and its Architect.* 2 vols. London [1919].
Scott-Moncrieff, W. *John Francis Bentley.* London, 1924.

BERENGUER
Mackay, D. 'Francesc Berenguer', *Architectural Review* (Dec. 1964), 410–16.

BERLAGE
Bock, M. *Anfänge einer neuen Architektur: Berlages Beitrag zur architektonischen Kultur der Niederlande im ausgehenden 19. Jahrhundert.* Wiesbaden, 1983.
Gratama, J. *Dr H. P. Berlage Bouwmeester.* Rotterdam, 1925.
'H. P. Berlage', *Nederlands Kunsthistorisch Jaarboek,* XXV (1974).
Singelenberg, P. *H. P. Berlage.* Utrecht, 1972.

BESTELMEYER
German Bestelmeyer. Berlin, 1928.

BINDESBØLL
Bramsen, H. *Gottlieb Bindesbøll, liv og arbejder.* Copenhagen, 1959.

BLOMFIELD
Blomfield, Sir Reginald. *Memoirs of an Architect.* London, 1932.
Fellows, R. A. *Sir Reginald Blomfield; An Edwardian Architect.* London, 1985.

BÖHM
Hoff, A., Muck, H., and Thoma, R. *Dominikus Böhm.* Munich [1962].

BOITO
Grassi, L. *Camillo Boito.* Milan, 1959.

BONATZ
Tamms, F. *Paul Bonatz.* Stuttgart, 1937.

BOULLÉE
Boullée, E. L. *Architecture.* Paris [1968].
Perouse de Montclos, J. M. *Étienne-Louis Boullée...* Paris, 1969.

Rosenau, H. *Boullée's Treatise on Architecture.* London, 1953.

BOURGEOIS
Linze, G. *Victor Bourgeois.* Brussels [1959].

BREUER
Argan, G. C. *Marcel Breuer: disegno industriale e architettura.* Milan [1957].
Blake, P. *Marcel Breuer: Architect and Designer.* New York, 1949.
Izzo, A., and Guibitosi, C. *Marcel Breuer: Architettura, 1921–1980.* Florence, 1981.
Jones, C. *Marcel Breuer: 1921–1962.* Stuttgart, c. 1962.
Marcel Breuer: New Buildings and Projects. New York [1970].
Wilk, C. *Marcel Breuer: Furniture and Interiors.* New York, 1981.

BRODRICK
Wilson, T. B. *Two Leeds Architects: Cuthbert Brodrick and George Corson.* Leeds, 1937.

BRONGNIART
Silvestre de Sacy, J. *Alexandre-Théodore Brongniart.* Paris, 1940.

BRUNEL
Pugsley, A. (ed.). *The Works of Isambard Kingdom Brunel: An Engineering Appreciation.* New York, 1980.
Rolt, L. T. C. *Isambard Kingdom Brunel.* London, 1957.

BULFINCH
Kirker, H. *The Architecture of Charles Bulfinch.* Cambridge, Mass., 1969.
Place, C. *Charles Bulfinch: Architect and Citizen.* Boston, 1925.

BURGES
Crook, J. M. (ed.). *William Burges.* London, 1981.
Crook, J. M. (ed.). *The Strange Genius of William Burges: 'Art Architect', 1827–1881.* Cardiff, 1981.
Pullan, A. *Architectural Designs of William Burges.* 2 vols. London, 1883–7.

BURNHAM
Hines, T. S. *Burnham of Chicago: Architect and Planner.* New York, 1974.
Moore, C. *Daniel H. Burnham.* 2 vols. Boston and New York, 1921.
The Architectural Work of Graham, Anderson, Probst & White ... and their Predecessors D. H. Burnham & Co. and Graham, Burnham & Co. 2 vols. London, 1933.

BUTTERFIELD
Summerson, J. N. 'William Butterfield', *Architectural Review,* LXIV (Dec. 1945), 166–75. Reprinted in *Heavenly Mansions,* 159–76.
Thompson, P. *William Butterfield.* Cambridge, Mass., 1971.

BYRNE
Chappell, S. A., and Van Zanten, A. *Barry Byrne, John Lloyd Wright: Architecture and Design*. Chicago Historical Society, 1982.
See also Chapter 19, Note 7a.

CAMERON
Charles Cameron. Architectural Drawings and Photographs from the Hermitage Collection. [London, 1967?]
Loukomski, G. *Charles Cameron*. London, 1943.

CARR
York Georgian Society. *The Works in Architecture of John Carr*. [York, 1973.]

CHAMBERS
Harris, J. *Sir William Chambers, Knight of the Polar Star*. London, 1970.

DE CHATEAUNEUF
Lange, G. *Alexis de Chateauneuf*. Hamburg, 1965.

CHIATTONE
Veronesi, G. 'Disegni di Mario Chiattone 1914–1917', *Comunità* (1962).

COCKERELL
Watkin, D. *C. R. Cockerell*. London, 1974.

CRAM
Maginnis, C. *The Work of Cram and Ferguson, Architects*. New York, 1929.

CRET
White, T. B. *Paul Philippe Cret*. Philadelphia [1973].

CUBITT
Hobhouse, H. *Thomas Cubitt Master Builder*. London and New York, 1971.

CUIJPERS
Cuijpers, J. T. J. *Het Werk van Dr P. J. H. Cuijpers, 1827–1917*. Amsterdam, 1917.

DAKIN
Scully, A., Jr. *James Dakin, Architect*. Baton Rouge [1973].

DANCE
Stroud, D. *George Dance*. London, 1971.

D'ARONCO
Nicoletti, M. *Raimondo D'Aronco*. Milan, 1955.

DAVIS
Davis, A. J. *Rural Residences*. Reprint with a new introduction by Jane B. Davies. New York, 1979.
See also TOWN & DAVIS.

DEANE & WOODWARD
Blau, E. *Ruskinian Gothic: The Architecture of Deane & Woodward 1845–1861*. Princeton, 1982.

DE CARLO
Colombo, C. *Giancarlo De Carlo . . .* Milan, 1964.

DELANO & ALDRICH
Delano & Aldrich. *Portraits of Ten Country Houses*. New York, 1924.

DESPREZ
Wollin, N. *Desprez en Italie*. Malmö, 1934.

Wollin, N. *Desprez en Suède*. Stockholm, 1939.

DOMENECH Y MONTANER
Bohigas, O. 'Luis Domenech y Montaner', *Architectural Review* (Dec. 1967), 426–36.
Domenech Girbau, L. *Domènech i Montaner*. Madrid, 1981.
Domènech i Montaner, arquitecto del modernismo . . . Barcelona [1971].

DRUMMOND
See Chapter 19, Note 7a.

DUC
O'Donnell, R. 'Louis Joseph Duc in Birmingham, a "Style Latin" Church for Cardinal Newman, 1851', *Gazette des Beaux-Arts* (juillet-août, 1981), 37–44.
Sédille, P. *Joseph-Louis Duc, architecte (1802–1879)*. Paris, 1879.

DUDOK
Cramer, M., *et al. W. M. Dudok 1884–1974*. Amsterdam, 1981.
Magnee, R. M. H. *Willem M. Dudok*. [Amsterdam, 1955.]

EIDLITZ
Schuyler, M. 'A Great American Architect: Leopold Eidlitz', *Architectural Record*, XXIV (1908), 163–79, 277–92, 364–78.

EIFFEL
Bresset, M. *Gustave Eiffel, 1832–1923*. Milan [1957].
Lemaine, B. *Gustave Eiffel*. Paris, 1984.
Loyrette, H. *Gustave Eiffel*. New York, 1985.
Prevost, J. *Eiffel*. Paris, 1929.

ELMSLIE
George Grant Elmslie: Drawings for Architectural Ornament, 1902–1936. Santa Barbara [1968].
See also PURCELL & ELMSLIE.

EMERSON
Zaitzevsky, C. *The Architecture of William Ralph Emerson, 1833–1917*. Cambridge, Mass., 1969.

ENGEL
C. L. Engel. Exhibition. [Berlin, 1970.]

FIGINI E POLLINI
Tedeschi, E. G. *Figini e Pollini*. Milan, 1959.

FISCHER (K. von)
Hederer, O. *Karl von Fischer: Leben und Werk*. Munich [1960].

FISCHER (T.)
Karlinger, H. *Theodor Fischer: ein deutscher Baumeister*. Munich, 1937.
Pfister, R. *Theodor Fischer*. Munich [1968].

FISKER
Langkilde, H. E. *Arkitekten Kay Fisker*. Copenhagen, 1960.

FLAGG
Bacon, M. *Ernest Flagg*. New York and Cambridge, Mass., 1986.

FONTAINE
Biver, M.-L. *Pierre Fontaine, premier architecte de l'empereur.* Paris, *c.* 1964.
FUCHS
Kudelka, Z. *Bohuslau Fuchs.* [Prague] 1966.
FULLER
Mchale, J. *R. Buckminster Fuller.* Ravensburg [1962].
FURNESS
O'Gorman, J. F. *The Architecture of Frank Furness* . . . [Philadelphia] 1973.
GALLIER
Gallier, J. *Autobiography of James Gallier, Architect.* New York, 1973.
GANDON
Gandon, J., the Younger. *The Life of James Gandon* . . . London, 1969.
GANDY
Lukacher, B. (ed.). *Joseph Michael Gandy.* London, 1982.
GARDEN
See Chapter 19, Note 7a.
GARNIER (C.)
Moyaux, C. *Notice sur la vie et les œuvres de M. Charles Garnier.* Paris, 1899.
Steinhauser, M. *Die Architektur der Pariser Oper.* Munich, 1969.
GARNIER (T.)
Badovici, J., and Morancé, A. *L'Œuvre de Tony Garnier.* Paris, 1938.
Pawlowski, C. *Tony Garnier.* Paris, 1966.
Veronesi, G. *Tony Garnier.* Milan, 1948.
Wiebenson, D. *Tony Garnier: the Cité Industrielle.* New York, 1969.
GARDELLA
Argan, G. A. *Ignazio Gardella.* Milan, 1959.
GÄRTNER
Eggert, K. *Die Hauptwerke Friedrich von Gaertners.* Munich, 1963.
Moninger, H. *Friedrich Gärtner.* Munich, 1882.
GAUDÍ
Bergós, J. *Antoni Gaudí l'home i l'obra.* Barcelona, 1954.
Collins, G. *Antonio Gaudí.* New York, 1960.
Descharnes, R. *Gaudí; the Visionary* . . . New York [1971].
Martinell y Brunet, C. *Gaudí: su vida, su teoria, su obra.* Barcelona, 1967.
Pane, R. *Antoni Gaudí.* Milan, 1964.
Ráfols, J. F. *Gaudí, 1852–1926.* Barcelona [1960].
GENTZ
Doebber, A. *Heinrich Gentz.* Berlin, 1916.
GILBERT
Gilbert, Cass. *Reminiscences and Addresses.* New York, 1935.

GILLY
Horn-Oncken, A. *Friedrich Gilly, 1772–1800.* Berlin, 1981.
Oncken, A. *Friedrich Gilly.* Berlin, 1935.
Rietdorf, A. *Gilly.* 1940.
GINZBURG
Ginzburg, M. *Style and Epoch.* 1924 edition with introduction and translation by A. Senkevitch, Jr. Cambridge, Mass., 1982.
GODWIN
Harbron, D. *The Conscious Stone: The Life of Edward William Godwin.* London, 1949.
GOFF
Mohri, T. *Bruce Goff in Architecture.* [Tokyo, 1970.]
GOODHUE
Brown, E. *Architectural Wonder of the World: Nebraska's State Capitol Building.* Ceresco, 1965.
Whitaker, C. (ed.). *Bertram Grosvenor Goodhue – Architect and Master of Many Arts.* New York, 1925.
GREENE AND GREENE
Current, W. *Greene and Greene; Architects in the Residential Style.* Fort Worth [1974].
Makinson, R. L. *Greene & Greene: Architecture as Fine Art.* Salt Lake City, 1977.
Makinson, R. L. *A Guide to the Work of Greene & Greene.* Salt Lake City, 1974.
The Prairie School Review, v, no. 4 (1968).
GREENWAY
Ellis, M. H. *Francis Greenway: his Life and Times.* Sydney and London, 1949.
GRIFFIN
Birrell, J. *Walter Burley Griffin.* St Lucia [1964].
Johnson, D. L. *The Architecture of Walter Burley Griffen.* Melbourne, 1977.
Walter Burley Griffen, Marian Mahony Griffen; Architectural Drawings in the Burnham Library of Architecture. Chicago, 1981.
GROPIUS (M.)
Klinkoff, M. *Martin Gropius und die Berliner Schule.* Berlin, 1971.
GROPIUS (W.)
Argan, G. C. *Walter Gropius e la Bauhaus.* Turin, 1951.
Franciscono, M. *Walter Gropius and the Creation of the Bauhaus in Weimar.* Urbana [1971].
Giedion, S. *Walter Gropius.* London, 1954.
Gropius, W. *The New Architecture and the Bauhaus.* New York, 1936.
Herbert, G. *The Dream of the Factory-Made House: Walter Gropius and Konrad Wachsmann.* Cambridge, Mass., 1984.
GROSCH
Bugge, A. R. *Architekten Stadskonduktor Chr. H. Grosch* . . . Oslo, 1928.

GUIMARD
Graham, E. L. *Hector Guimard . . .* Exhibition. New York, 1970.
HAIGHT
Schuyler, M. 'Charles C. Haight', *Architectural Record Great American Artist Series*, VI (1899).
HANSEN (C. F.)
Christian Frederik Hansen, 1756–1845. Exhibition. [Hamburg, 1968.]
Hansen, C. F. *Samling af forskjellige offentlige og private Bygninger.* Copenhagen, 1847.
Langberg, H. *Omkring C. F. Hansen.* [Copenhagen] 1950.
Rubow, J. C. F. *Hansens arkitektur.* Copenhagen, 1936.
HANSEN (T.)
Jenni, U. *Theophil Hansen: Entwürfe zur Akademie der bildenden Künste Wien.* Vienna, 1985.
Niemann, J., and Feldegg, F. von. *Theophilus Hansen und seine Werke.* Vienna, 1893.
HÄRING
Lauterbach, H., and Joedicke, J. *Hugo Häring: Schriften, Entwürfe, Bauten.* Stuttgart [1965].
HASTINGS
Gray, D. *Thomas Hastings: Architect.* Boston, 1933.
HAUSSMANN
Malet, H. *Le Baron Haussmann et la renovation de Paris.* Paris [1973].
Saalman, H. *Haussmann: Paris Transformed.* New York [1971].
HENTRICH
Hitchcock, H.-R. *Hentrich-Petschnigg and Partner: Bauten und Entwürfe.* Düsseldorf [1973].
HERHOLDT
Fisker, K. *Omkring Herholdt.* Copenhagen, 1943.
HILBERSEIMER
Spaeth, D. *Ludwig Karl Hilberseimer. An Annotated Bibliography and Chronology.* New York, 1981.
HITTORFF
Hammer, K. *Jakob Ignaz Hittorff.* Stuttgart, 1968.
Normand, A. *Notice historique sur . . . J. I. Hittorff, architecte.* Paris, 1867.
HITZIG
Hitzig, F. *Ausgeführte Bauwerke.* 2 vols. Berlin [1850].
HOFFMANN
Baroni, D., and d'Auria, A. *Josef Hoffmann e la Wiener Werkstätte.* Milan, 1981.
Gresleri, G. *Josef Hoffmann.* New York, 1985.
Kleiner, L. *Josef Hoffmann.* Berlin, 1927.
Veronesi, G. *Josef Hoffmann.* Milan, 1956.
Sekler, E. F. *Josef Hoffmann: The Architectural Work.* Princeton, 1985.
Weiser, A. *Josef Hoffmann.* Geneva, 1930.

HOLABIRD & ROCHE
Bruegmann, R. 'Holabird & Roche and Holabird & Root: The First Two Generations', *Chicago History*, IX, no. 3 (1980), 130–65.
HOLLAND
Stroud, D. *Henry Holland: his Life and Architecture.* London [1966].
HOLZMEISTER
Becker, P. *Clemens Holzmeister und Salzburg.* Salzburg, 1966.
Holzmeister, C. *Bauten, Entwürfe und Handzeichnungen.* Salzburg [1937].
HOOD
North, A. T. *Raymond M. Hood.* New York, 1931.
Stern, R. A. M., and Catalano, T. P. *Raymond Hood.* New York, 1982.
HOOKER
Root, E. *Philip Hooker.* New York, 1929.
HOPE
Watkin, D. *Thomas Hope and the Neo-Classical Idea.* London, 1968.
HORTA
Borsi, F., and Portoghesi, P. *Victor Horta.* Rome, 1969.
Delevoy, R. L. *Victor Horta.* Brussels, n.d.
Madsen, S. T. 'Horta: Works and Style of Victor Horta before 1900', *Architectural Review*, CXVIII (1955), 388–92.
HOWE
Stern, R. A. M. *George Howe, Toward a Modern American Architecture.* New Haven, 1975.
HÜBSCH
Heinrich Hübsch. Exhibition Catalogue. Karlsruhe, 1883–4.
Hübsch, H. *Bauwerke.* Karlsruhe, 1842.
Valdenaire, A. *Heinrich Hübsch.* Karlsruhe, 1926.
HUNT (J. H.)
Freeland, J. M. *Architect Extraordinary; . . . John Horbury Hunt: 1838–1904.* [Melbourne, 1970.]
HUNT (R. M.)
Baker, P. R. *Richard Morris Hunt.* Cambridge, Mass., 1980.
Schuyler, M. 'The Works of the late Richard Morris Hunt', *Architectural Record*, V (Oct.–Dec., 1895), 97–180.
Stein, S. *Richard Morris Hunt.* Chicago, 1986.
HUVÉ
Le Normand. *Notice biographique sur J.-J.-M. Huvé.* Paris, 1853.
JACOBSEN
Arne Jacobsen. Exhibition. Glasgow, 1968.
Pederson, J. *Arkitekten Arne Jacobsen.* Copenhagen, 1957.
JAPPELLI
Gallimberti, N. *Giuseppe Jappelli.* Padua [1963].

JEFFERSON
Kimball, F. *Thomas Jefferson, Architect.* Boston, 1916.
JENNEY
Turak, T. *William Le Baron Jenney: A Pioneer of Modern Architecture.* Ann Arbor, 1986.
JOHNSON
Jacobus, J. M. *Philip Johnson.* New York, 1962.
Miller, N. *Johnson/Burgee: Architecture.* New York, 1979.
Miller, N. *Philip Johnson/John Burgee, Architecture 1979–1985.* New York, 1985.
Philip Johnson: Architecture 1949–1965. New York [1966].
KAHN (A.)
Albert Kahn: Architect Abroad. Exhibition. Ann Arbor [1972].
Nelson, G., *The Industrial Architecture of Albert Kahn.* New York, 1939.
KAHN (L.)
Giurgola, R. (ed.). *Louis I. Kahn.* Zürich, 1975.
Scully, V., Jr. *Louis I. Kahn.* New York, 1962.
KLENZE
Klenze, L. von. *Sammlung architektonischer Entwürfe,* 10 pts. Munich, 1830–50.
Leo von Klenze: Ein griechischer Traum. Munich, 1985.
DE KLERK
Kramer, P. M. *de Klerk. Wendingen,* VI (1924), Nos 4 and 5.
KNOWLES
Metcalf, P. *James Knowles: Victorian Editor and Architect.* New York, 1980.
KORNHÄUSEL
Thausig, P. *Joseph Kornhäusel.* Vienna, 1916.
LABROUSTE (H.)
Souvenirs d'Henri Labrouste: notes recueillies et classées par ses enfants. Paris, 1928.
LAFEVER
Landy, J. *The Architecture of Minard Lafever.* New York, 1970.
LALOUX
Cox, H. B. 'Victor Laloux; the Man and his Work', *Architects Journal,* LI (1920), 555–7.
LANGHANS
Hinrichs, W. *Karl Gotthard Langhans.* Strassburg, 1909.
LATROBE
Carter, E. C., et al. (eds.). *The Journals of Benjamin Henry Latrobe, 1799–1820: from Philadelphia to New Orleans.* New Haven, 1980.
Carter, E. C., et al. (eds.). *The Virginia Journals of Benjamin Henry Latrobe, 1795–98.* New Haven, 1977.
Hamlin, T. F. *Benjamin Henry Latrobe.* New York, 1955.

LAUGIER
Herrmann, W. *Laugier and Eighteenth-Century French Theory.* London, 1962.
LAVES
Hoeltje, G., and Weber, H. *Georg Ludwig Friedrich Laves.* Hannover [1964].
LE BAS
Vaudoyer, L. *Notice historique sur la vie et les ouvrages de M. Le Bas.* Paris, 1869.
LE CORBUSIER
Boesiger, W. *Le Corbusier & Pierre Jeanneret: Œuvre complète.* 7 vols. Zürich, 1937–65.
Boesiger, W., and Ginsberger, H. *Le Corbusier His Works 1910–1960.* New York, 1960.
Boudon, P. *Lived in Architecture: Le Corbusier's Pessac Revisited.* Cambridge, Mass., 1972.
Brady, D. *Le Corbusier: An Annotated Bibliography.* New York, 1983.
Brooks, H. A. (ed.). *The Le Corbusier Archive.* 32 vols. New York, 1982–4.
Le Corbusier Sketchbooks. 4 vols. New York and Cambridge, Mass., 1981–2.
Moos, S. von. *Le Corbusier.* Cambridge, Mass., 1979.
LEDOUX
Christ, Y. *Projets et divagations de Claude-Nicolas Ledoux, architecte du roi.* Paris [1961].
Gallet, M. *Claude-Nicolas Ledoux, 1736–1806.* Paris, 1980.
Ledoux, C.-N. *L'Architecture considérée sous le rapport de l'art, des mœurs et de la législation.* Paris, 1804. [Reprint], 2 vols. Paris, 1962.
L'Œuvre et les rêves de Claude-Nicolas Ledoux. [Paris, 1971.]
Raval, M., and Moreux, J.-Ch. *C.-N. Ledoux.* Paris, 1945.
LEFUEL
Delaborde, H. *Notice sur la vie et les ouvrages de M. Lefuel.* Paris, 1882.
LETHABY
Backemeyer, S., and Gronberg, T. (eds.). *W. R. Lethaby, 1857–1931: Architecture, Design and Education.* London, 1984.
'William Richard Lethaby, 1857–1931; a Symposium in Honour of his Centenary', *Journal of the Royal Institute of British Architects,* LXIV (1957), 218–25.
LISSITZKY
Lissitzky, El. *Russland: Architektur für eine Weltrevolution.* Berlin, 1967 (reprint of *Russland: Die Rekonstruktion der Architektur in der Sowjetunion.* Vienna, 1930).

LOOS

Adolf Loos, 1870–1933. Liège, 1983.

Altmann-Loos, E. *Mein Leben mit Adolf Loos.* Vienna, 1984.

Cucciari, M. *Das Andere: Adolf Loos e il suo Angelo.* Milan, 1981.

Kubinszky, M. *Adolf Loos.* Berlin, 1970.

Kulka, H. *Adolf Loos, das Werk des Architekten.* Vienna, 1931.

Loos, A. (ed. F. Gluck). *Sämtliche Schriften*, 1. Vienna, 1962.

Loos, A. *Spoken into the Void: Collected Essays 1897–1900.* Cambridge, Mass., 1982.

Münz, L., and Künstler, G. *Der Architekt Adolf Loos.* Vienna [1964].

Rukscheio, B., and Schachel, R. *Adolf Loos: Leben und Werk.* Salzburg, 1982.

Worbs, D. *Der Raumplan von Adolf Loos: Entwicklung der Raumbildung in Villen- und Massen- Wohnbauten.* Munich, 1981.

LOUDON

Gloag, J. *Mr Loudon's England.* Newcastle upon Tyne, 1970.

MacDougall, E. B. (ed.). *John Claudius Loudon and the Early 19th Century in Great Britain.* Washington, D.C., 1980.

LUBETKIN

Coe, P., and Reading, M. *Lubetkin and Tecton: Architecture and Social Commitment, A Critical Study.* London, 1981.

LUCKHARDT

Kulturmann, U. *Wassili und Hans Luckhardt: Bauten und Entwürfe.* Tübingen [1958].

Wassili Luckhardt. Tübingen [*c.* 1973].

LURÇAT

André Lurçat; projets et réalisations. Paris, 1929.

LUTYENS

Butler, A. S. G. *The Architecture of Sir Edwin Lutyens.* 3 vols. London, 1950.

Gradidge, R. *Edwin Lutyens, Architect Laureate.* London, 1981.

Hussey, C. *The Life of Sir Edwin Lutyens.* London, 1950.

Lutyens: The Work of the English Architect Sir Edwin Lutyens. London, 1981.

Richardson, M. *Lutyens and the Sea Captain.* London, 1981.

Richardson, M. (ed.). *Catalogue of the Drawings Collection of the Royal Institute of British Architects: Edwin Lutyens.* [Farnborough, 1973.]

Weaver, L. *Houses and Gardens by E. L. Lutyens.* London, 1913. Second edition 1921.

MCKIM, MEAD & WHITE

A Monograph of the Work of McKim, Mead and White. 4 vols. New York, 1915–25. Reprinted New York, 1973, with an essay by Leland Roth.

Roth, L. M. *The Architecture of McKim, Mead & White, 1870–1920: A Building List.* New York, 1978.

Roth, L. M. *McKim, Mead & White, Architects.* New York, 1983.

Shopsin, W. C., and Broderick, M. G. *The Villard Houses: Life Story of a Landmark.* New York, 1980.

Sturgis, R. 'The Work of McKim, Mead and White', *Architectural Record Great American Artist Series*, 1 (1895).

Wilson, R. G. *McKim, Mead & White.* New York, 1983.

MACKINTOSH

Billcliffe, R. *Charles Rennie Mackintosh: The Complete Furniture, Furniture Drawings and Interior Designs.* New York, 1979.

Howarth, T. *Charles Rennie Mackintosh and the Modern Movement.* London, 1952.

MacDonald, I. *Charles Rennie Mackintosh . . . Glasgow.* [Glasgow, 1968?]

Macleod, R. *Charles Rennie Mackintosh.* Feltham, 1968.

Macleod, R. *Charles Rennie Mackintosh.* New York, 1983.

Pevsner, N. *Charles Rennie Mackintosh.* Milan, 1950.

MACKMURDO

Catalogue of the A. H. Mackmurdo and the Century Guild Collection. Walthamstow, 1967.

Pevsner, N. 'Arthur H. Mackmurdo', *Architectural Review*, LXXXIII (1938), 141–3.

Pond, E. 'Mackmurdo Gleanings', *Architectural Review*, CXXVIII (1960), 429–31.

MAHONY

'Marion Mahony', *The Prairie School Review*, III, no. 2 (1966).

MAILLART

Bill, M. *Robert Maillart.* Zürich, 1949.

MASON

Stacpoole, J. *William Mason; The First New Zealand Architect.* Oxford, 1971.

MAY

Buekschmitt, J. *Ernst May.* Stuttgart, *c.* 1963.

MENDELSOHN

Erich Mendelsohn: das Gesamtschaffen des Architekten. Berlin, 1930.

Mendelsohn, E. *Briefe eines Architekten.* Munich [1961].

[Posener, J.] *Erich Mendelsohn, Ausstellung der Akademie der Künste . . .* [Berlin] 1968.

The Drawings of Erich Mendelsohn. Exhibition. San Francisco, 1969.

Whittick, A. *Eric Mendelsohn,* 2nd ed. London [1956].

MENGONI
Ricci, G. *La Vita e le opere dell'architetto Giuseppe Mengoni*. Bologna, 1930.
MESSEL
Behrendt, W. C. *Alfred Messel*. Berlin, 1911.
MEYER
Schnaidt, C. *Hannes Meyer: Bauten, Projekte und Schriften*. London [1965].
MICHELUCCI
Borsi, F. *Giovanni Michelucci*. Florence, c. 1966.
MIES VAN DER ROHE
Bill, M. *Ludwig Mies van der Rohe*. Milan, 1955.
Blaser, W. *Mies van der Rohe: die Kunst der Struktur*. Zürich, 1965.
Carter, P. *Mies van der Rohe at Work*. New York [1974].
Hilbersheimer, L. *Mies van der Rohe*. Chicago, 1956.
Johnson, P. *Mies van der Rohe*. 2nd ed. New York, 1953; German ed., Stuttgart [n.d.].
Mies van der Rohe. New York [1970].
Norberg-Schulz, C. *Casa Tugendhat*. Rome, 1984.
Schulze, F. *Mies van der Rohe, A Critical Biography*. Chicago, 1985.
Spaeth, D. A. *Ludwig Mies van der Rohe: An Annotated Bibliography and Chronology*. New York, 1978.
Spaeth, D. A. *Mies van der Rohe*. New York, 1983.
Speyer, A. J. *Mies van der Rohe*. Chicago, 1968.
Tegethoff, W. *Mies van der Rohe: The Villas and Country Houses*. Cambridge, Mass., 1985.
MILLS
Gallagher, H. *Robert Mills*. New York, 1935.
Liscombe, R. W. *The Church Architecture of Robert Mills*. Easley, S.C., 1985.
MITCHELL/GIURGOLA
Mitchell/Giurgola, Associates. Philadelphia [1966?].
MOLLER
Fröhlich, M., and Sperlich, H.-G. *Georg Moller, Baumeister der Romantik*. Darmstadt, 1959.
MORRIS
Clark, F. (ed.). *William Morris: Wallpapers and Chintzes*. New York [1973].
Morris Gallery, Walthamstow, England. *Catalogue of the Morris Collection*. London, 1969.
Sewter, A. C. *The Stained Glass of William Morris and his Circle*. 2 vols. New Haven, 1974-5.
Thompson, P. *The Work of William Morris*. London [1967].
Watkinson, R. *William Morris as Designer*. London [1967].
MYERS
Cotner, R. C. *The Texas State Capitol*. Austin, 1968.
NASH
Davis, T. *The Architecture of John Nash*. London, 1960.

Summerson, J. N. *John Nash, Architect to George IV*. London, 1935.
NERVI
Argan, G. C. *Pierluigi Nervi*. Milan, 1955.
Huxtable, A. L. *Pier Luigi Nervi*. New York, 1960.
Pica, A. *Pier Luigi Nervi*. Rome, 1969.
The Works of Pierluigi Nervi. [Stuttgart] and London, 1957.
NESFIELD
Brydon, J. M. 'William Eden Nesfield, 1835-1888', *Architectural Review*, I (1897), 235-7, 283-95.
Creswell, B. 'William Eden Nesfield, 1835-1888: An Impression', *Architectural Review*, II (1897), 23-32.
NEUTRA
Hines, T. S. *Richard Neutra and the Search for Modern Architecture: A Biography and History*. New York, 1982.
McCoy, E. *Richard Neutra*. New York, 1960.
Richard Neutra. New York [1971].
Richard Neutra, Buildings and Projects. Zürich, 1955.
Zevi, B. *Richard Neutra*. Milan, 1954.
NEWTON
Newton, W. G. *The Work of Ernest Newton, R.A.* London, 1923.
NIEMEYER
Oscar Niemeyer. New York [1971].
Papadaki, S. *The Work of Oscar Niemeyer*. New York, 1950.
Papadaki, S. *Oscar Niemeyer*. New York, 1960.
NOTMAN
Grieff, C. *John Notman, Architect*. Philadelphia, 1979.
OLBRICH
Architektur von Professor Joseph M. Olbrich. 3 vols. Berlin, 1901-14.
Joseph M. Olbrich und die Darmstädter Künstlerkolonie. [Darmstadt, 1967.]
Krimmel, B. (ed.). *Joseph M. Olbrich, 1867-1908*. Darmstadt, 1983.
Lux, J. A. *Joseph Maria Olbrich*. Berlin, 1919.
Schreyl, K.-H. *Joseph Maria Olbrich; die Zeichnungen in d. Kunstbibliothek Berlin*. Berlin, 1972.
Veronesi, G. *Joseph Maria Olbrich*. Milan, 1948.
OLMSTED
Beveridge, C. E. (comp.). *The Olmsted Legacy of Public Design*. New York, 1981.
Fabos, J. G. *Frederick Law Olmsted . . .* [Amherst] 1968.
Fein, A. *Frederick Law Olmsted and the American Environmental Tradition*. New York [1972].
McLaughlin, C. C. (ed.), and Beveridge, C. F. L. *Olmsted, The Formative Years 1822-1852*. Baltimore, 1977.
Olmsted, F. L., Jr and Kimball, T. *Frederick Law*

Olmsted, Landscape Architect, 1822–1903. New York, 1922–8. Reprint New York, 1970.

Roper, L. W. *Flo, A Biography of Frederick Law Olmsted.* Baltimore, 1974.

Zaitzevsky, C. *Frederick Law Olmsted and the Boston Park System.* Cambridge, Mass., 1982.

ÖSTBERG

Cornell, E. *Ragnar Östberg, svensk Arkitekt.* Stockholm, 1965.

OTTO

The Work of Frei Otto. New York [1972].

OUD

Architect J. J. P. Oud. Rotterdam, 1951.

Hitchcock, H.-R. *J. J. P. Oud.* Paris, 1931.

J. J. P. Oud: Bauten 1906–1963. Berlin, 1966.

Stamm, G. *J. J. P. Oud; Bauten und Projekte 1906–1963.* Mainz, 1984.

Veronesi, G. *J. J. Pieter Oud.* Milan, 1953.

Wiekart, K. *J. J. P. Oud.* Amsterdam, 1965.

PAXTON

Chadwick, G. F. *The Works of Sir Joseph Paxton.* London [1961].

Markham, V. *Paxton and the Bachelor Duke.* London, 1935.

Sir Joseph Paxton, 1803–65: a Centenary Exhibition. [London] 1965.

PEABODY & STERNS

Sturgis, R. 'Peabody and Sterns', *The Architectural Record Great American Artist Series*, (3) (1895–9).

PEARSON

Quiney, A. *John Loughborough Pearson.* New Haven, 1979.

PERCIER AND FONTAINE

Fouché, M. *Percier et Fontaine.* Paris, 1905.

PERRET

Architecture d'aujourd'hui, 1932 (special issue on A. Perret).

Champigneulle, B. *Auguste Perret.* Paris, 1959.

Collins, P. *Concrete – The Vision of a New Architecture*, pt III. London, 1959.

Jamot, P. *A.-G. Perret et l'architecture du béton armé.* Paris and Brussels, 1927.

Rogers, E. *Auguste Perret.* Milan, 1955.

PERSIUS

See Chapter 2, Note 15.

PEYRE

Peyre, M. J. *Œuvres d'architecture* . . . Paris, 1765. Reprint Farnborough, 1967.

PIRANESI

Focillon, H. *G. B. Piranesi.* Paris, 1918.

G. B. Piranesi, Drawings and Etchings at Columbia University. New York [1972].

PLATT

Cortissoz, R. *Monograph of the Work of Charles A. Platt.* New York, 1913.

POELZIG

Heuss, T. *Hans Poelzig.* Berlin, 1939.

Poelzig, Hans. *Gesammelte Schriften und Werke.* Berlin [1970].

POGGI

Borsi, F. *La Capitale a Firenze e l'opera di G. Poggi.* Rome, 1970.

POLLAK

Zádor, A. *Pollak Mihály, 1773–1855.* Budapest, 1960.

POST

Sturgis, R. 'A Review of the Work of George B. Post', *The Architectural Record Great American Artist Series*, no. 4 (1895–9).

Weissman, W. 'The Commercial Architecture of George B. Post', *Journal of the Society of Architectural Historians*, XXXI (1972), 176–203.

POTTER

Landau, S. B. *Edward T. and William A. Potter.* New York, 1979.

PRAIRIE SCHOOL

Brooks, H. A. *The Prairie School.* Toronto, 1972.

Hasbrouck, W. R. (ed.). *Architectural Essays from the Chicago School.* [Park Forest, Ill., 1967.]

The Prairie School Review, I (1964).

PRICE

Sturgis, R. 'Bruce Price', *The Architectural Record Great American Artist Series*, no. 5 (1895–9).

PUGIN

Ferrey, B. *Recollections of A. N. Pugin and His Father A. Pugin.* London, 1861.

Gwynn, D. *Lord Shrewsbury, Pugin and The Catholic Revival.* London, 1946.

Stanton, P. *Pugin.* New York, 1971.

Trappes-Lomax, M. *Pugin, a Mediaeval Victorian.* London, 1932.

Wedgwood, A. (ed.). *The Catalogue of the Drawings Collection of the Royal Institute of British Architects: Pugin.* Farnborough, forthcoming, 1976.

PURCELL & ELMSLIE

Purcell and Elmslie, Architects. Exhibition. Minneapolis, 1953.

The Work of Purcell and Elmslie, Architects. Park Forest, Ill., 1965.

See also ELMSLIE.

QUARONI

Tafuri, M. *Ludovico Quaroni e lo sviluppo dell' architettura moderna in Italia.* Milan [1964].

RAYMOND

Raymond, A. *Antonin Raymond: an Autobiography.* Rutland, Vt. [1973].

REIDY

Franck, K. *The Works of Affonso Eduardo Reidy.* New York, 1960.

Giedion, S. *The Works of Eduardo Affonso Reidy.* New York, 1960.

RENNIE

Boucher, C. T. G. *John Rennie 1761–1821: the Life and Work of a Great Engineer.* Manchester, *c.* 1963.

REPTON

Stroud, D. *Humphrey Repton.* London [1962].

REVELL

Alander, K. *Viljo Revell.* [New York, 1967.]

REVETT. *See* STUART.

RICHARDSON

Hitchcock, H.-R. *The Architecture of H. H. Richardson and His Times.* 2nd ed. Hamden, Conn., 1961; 3rd ed., Cambridge, Mass. [1966].

Ochsner, J. Karl. *H. H. Richardson: Complete Architectural Works.* Cambridge, Mass., 1982.

O'Gorman, J. F. *H. H. Richardson and his Office, Centennial of his Move to Boston, 1874.* Cambridge, Mass., 1974.

Van Rensselaer, M. G. *Henry Hobson Richardson and His Works.* Boston and New York, 1888.

Van Rensselaer, M. G. *Henry Hobson Richardson and His Works* (facsimile reprint). Park Forest, Ill. [1967].

RIETVELD

Brown, T. M. *The Work of G. Rietveld.* Utrecht, 1958.

Schröder Huis. Hilversum, 1963.

ROCHE

Dal Co, F. (ed.). *Kevin Roche.* New York, 1985.

Futagawa, Y. *Kevin Roche, John Dinkaloo and Associates, 1962–1975.* New York, 1976.

Hitchcock, H.-R. *Kevin Roche, John Dinkaloo and Associates, 1962–75.* Tokyo and Fribourg, 1975.

ROHAULT DE FLEURY

Rohault de Fleury, C. *Œuvre.* Paris, 1884.

ROOT

Hoffmann, D. *The Architecture of John Wellborn Root.* Baltimore [1973].

Monroe, H. *John Wellborn Root: A Study of his Life and Work.* 2nd ed. Park Forest, Ill. [1966].

Root, J. W. *Meanings of Architecture, Buildings, and Writings by John Wellborn Root.* New York [1967].

ROUX-SPITZ

Roux-Spitz, M. *Réalisations, 1924–39.* 2 vols. Paris [n.d.].

RUDOLPH

The Architecture of Paul Rudolph. New York [1970].

SAARINEN (EERO)

Eero Saarinen. New York [1971].

Saarinen, A. B. (ed.) *Eero Saarinen on his Work.* New Haven, 1962.

Temko, A. *Eero Saarinen.* New York, 1962.

SAARINEN (ELIEL)

Christ-Janer, A. *Eliel Saarinen.* Chicago, 1948.

SANT'ELIA

Caramel, L., and Longatti, R. *Antonio Sant'Elia.* Como, 1962.

Schmidt-Thomsen, J. P. *Floreale und futuristische Architektur. Das Werk von Antonio Sant'Elia.* Berlin, 1967.

SCHAROUN

Hans Scharoun. Rome, 1969.

Janofske, E. *Architektur-Räume; Idee und Gestalt bei Hans Scharoun.* Wiesbaden, 1983.

[Lauterbach, H.] *Hans Scharoun.* Ausstellung in der Akademie der Künste. [Berlin] 1967.

Sassu, A. *La Philharmonie di Hans Scharoun.* Bari, 1980.

SCHINDLER

Gebhard, D. *Schindler.* New York [1972].

SCHINKEL

Behr, A., and Hoffman, A. *Das Schauspielhaus in Berlin.* Berlin, 1984.

Griesebach, A. *Karl Friedrich Schinkel.* Leipzig, 1924.

Karl Friedrich Schinkel: Sein Werk als Architekt. Stuttgart, 1981.

Karl Friedrich Schinkel 1781–1841. Berlin, 1981.

Pevsner, N. 'Schinkel', *Journal of the Royal Institute of British Architects,* LIX (1952).

Posener, J. *Schinkel zu Ehren: Festreden 1846 bis 1980.* Berlin, 1980.

Rave, P., and others. *Karl Friedrich Schinkel Lebenswerk,* vol. [I]–[VIII]. Berlin, 1939–68.

Schinkel, K. F. *Sammlung architektonischer Entwürfe . . .* Berlin, 1819–43.

Schreiner, L. *Karl Friedrich Schinkel . . .* Münster/Westfalen, 1968.

Wolzogen, A. F. von. *Aus Schinkels Nachlass.* 3 vols. Berlin, 1862–4.

Zadow, M. *Karl Friedrich Schinkel.* Berlin, 1980.

SCHWARZ

Schwarz, R. *Denken und Bauen: Schriften und Bauwerke.* Heidelberg [1963].

SCOTT (BAILLIE)

Kornwolf, J. D. *M. H. Baillie Scott and the Arts and Crafts Movement.* Baltimore, 1972.

Scott, M. H. B. *Houses and Gardens.* London, 1906.

SCOTT FAMILY

The Catalogue of the Drawings Collection of the Royal Institute of British Architects: the Scott Family. Farnborough, 1976.

SCOTT (G. G.)

Cole, D. *The Works of Sir Gilbert Scott.* London, 1980.

Scott, G. G. *Personal and Professional Recollections by the late Sir George Gilbert Scott.* London, 1879.

Stamp, G. 'Sir Gilbert Scott's Recollections', *Architectural History,* XIX (1976).

SEDDON
Darby, M. *John Pollard Seddon*. London, 1983.
SEIDLER
Blake, P. *Architecture for the New World: the Work of Henry Seidler*. New York [1973].
SELVA
Bassi, E. *Giannantonio Selva, architetto veneziano*. Padua, 1936.
SEMPER
Dolgner, D. 'Gottfried Semper und der Rundbogenstil', *Architectura*, XI, no. 2 (1981), 157–82.
Ettlinger, L. *Gottfried Semper und die Antike*. Halle, 1937.
Hermann, W. *Gottfried Semper: In Search of Architecture*. Cambridge, Mass., 1985.
Semper, G. *Der Stil in den technischen und architektonischen Künsten*. Frankfurt, 1860.
SHAW
Blomfield, Sir R. *Richard Norman Shaw, R.A.* London, 1940.
Pevsner, N. 'Richard Norman Shaw', *Architectural Review*, LXXXIX (1941), 41–6.
Saint, A. *Richard Norman Shaw*. New Haven, 1976.
See also WEBB.
SHEPLEY, RUTAN & COOLIDGE
Sturgis, R. 'Shepley, Rutan and Coolidge', *The Architectural Record Great American Artist Series*, no. 3 (1895–9).
SKIDMORE, OWINGS, & MERRILL
Drexler, A. *The Architecture of Skidmore, Owings and Merrill, 1963–73*. New York, 1974.
Hitchcock, H. R., and Danz, E. *Architecture of Skidmore, Owings & Merrill, 1950–1962*. New York, 1963.
Skidmore, Owings and Merrill. New York, 1970.
SLOAN
Cooledge, H. N. *Samuel Sloan, Architect of Philadelphia, 1815–1884*. Philadelphia, 1986.
SOANE
Bolton, A. T. *The Works of Sir John Soane*. London, 1924.
Bolton, A. T. *The Portrait of Sir John Soane*. London, 1927.
DuPrey, P. *Sir John Soane*. London, 1986.
DuPrey, P. *John Soane, The Making of an Architect*. Chicago, 1982.
Stroud, D. *The Architecture of Sir John Soane*. London [1961].
Summerson, J. N. 'Soane: the Case-History of a Personal Style', *Journal of the Royal Institute of British Architects*, LVIII (1951), 83–9.
SOLERI
Soleri, P. *The Sketchbooks of Paolo Soleri*. [Cambridge, Mass., 1971.]

Wall, D. *Visionary Cities: the Arcology of Paolo Soleri*. New York [1971].
SOMMARUGA
L'Architettura di Giuseppe Sommaruga. Milan, 1908.
SOUFFLOT
Mondain-Monval, J. *Soufflot*. Paris, 1918.
STAM
Mart Stam, Documentation of his Work 1920–1965 . . . London, 1970.
STEINER
Zimmer, E. *Rudolf Steiner als Architekt*. [Stuttgart, 1971.]
STIRLING
James Stirling: Buildings and Projects 1950–1974. London, 1975.
STREET
Brownlee, D. *The Law Courts*. Cambridge, Mass., 1985.
Hitchcock, H. R. 'G. E. Street in the 1850s', *Journal of the Society of Architectural Historians*, XIX (1960), 145–72.
Millon, J. R. *St Paul's within the Walls, Rome: A Building History and Guide*. Dublin, N.H., 1981.
Street, A. E. *Memoir of George Edmund Street*. London, 1888.
STRICKLAND
Gilchrist, A. E. *William Strickland . . .* New York, 1969.
STUART
Lawrence, L. 'Stuart and Revett; their Literary and Architectural Careers', *Journal of the Warburg Institute*, II (1938), 128–46.
Watkin, D. *Athenian Stuart: Pioneer of the Greek Revival*. Boston, 1982.
SULLIVAN
Connely, W. *Louis Sullivan as He Lived*. New York, 1960.
Morrison, H. *Louis Sullivan*. New York, 1952.
Sprague, P. E. *The Drawings of Louis Henry Sullivan; A Catalogue of the Frank Lloyd Wright Collection at the Avery Architectural Library*. Princeton, 1979.
Sullivan, L. H. *The Autobiography of an Idea*. New York, 1953.
Sullivan, L. H. *Kindergarten Chats*. New York, 1947.
Twombly, R. *Louis Sullivan, His Life and Work*. New York, 1986.
TANGE
Boyd, R. *Kenzo Tange*. New York, 1962.
Kenzo Tange . . . Zürich, 1970.
TAUT (B.)
Junghanns, K. *Bruno Taut 1880–1938*. Berlin, 1970.
Volkmann, B. (ed.). *Bruno Taut 1880–1938*. Berlin, 1980.
Whyte, I. B. *The Crystal Chain Letters: Architectural*

Fantasies by Bruno Taut and his Circle. Cambridge, Mass., 1985.

TAUT (M.)
Max Taut . . . Berlin, 1932.

TECTON *See* LUBETKIN

TELFORD
Bracegirdle, B. *Thomas Telford.* Newton Abbot, 1973.
Life of Thomas Telford, Civil Engineer, written by himself. London, 1838.
Rolt, L. T. C. *Thomas Telford.* London, 1958.

TERRAGNI
Giuseppe Terragni e la città del razionalismo italiano. [Bari] 1969.
Labò, M. *Giuseppe Terragni.* Milan, 1947.

TESSENOW
Strey, W. (ed.). *Die Zeichnungen von Heinrich Tessenow: Der Bestand der Kunstbibliothek Berlin.* Berlin, 1981.

THOMSON
Law, G. 'Greek Thomson', *Architectural Review*, CXVI (1954), 307-16.

TOWN & DAVIS
Newton, R. H. *Town and Davis: Architects.* New York, 1942.

UPJOHN (R.)
Upjohn, E. *Richard Upjohn, Architect and Churchman.* New York, 1939.

UPJOHN (R. M.)
Upjohn, E. M. *A Brief Note on Richard Michell Upjohn* . . . [n.p.] 1971-2.

VALADIER
Marconi, P. *Giuseppe Valadier.* Rome [1964].

VAN DEN BROEK & BAKEMA
Joedicke, J. (ed.). *Architektur und Städtebau: das Werk Van den Broek und Bakema.* Stuttgart [1963].

VAN DE VELDE
Exposition: Henry Van de Velde. [Brussels, 1970.]
Hammacher, A. M. *Die Welt Henry Van de Veldes.* Antwerp, 1967.
Hüter, K.-H. *Henry Van de Velde.* Berlin, 1967.

VANVITELLI
Caroselli, M. R. *La Reggia di Caserta.* Milan, 1968.
Vanvitelli, Luigi, the younger. *Vita dell'architetto Luigi Vanvitelli.* Naples, 1825.

VILLANUEVA
Moholy-Nagy, S. *Carlos Raul Villanueva.* Caracas, 1964.

VIOLLET-LE-DUC
Eugène Viollet-le-Duc, 1814-1879. Paris [1965].
Gout, P. *Viollet-le-Duc: sa vie, son œuvre, sa doctrine.* Paris, 1914.
Les Monuments historiques de la France, XI (January-June 1965, entire number).
L'Exposition Viollet-le-Duc à Vézelay . . ., *organisée*

par l'association 'Yonne et Tourisme'. [Vézelay, 1968.]
Le Voyage d'Italie d'Eugène Viollet-le-Duc 1836-7. Paris, 1980.
Viollet-le-Duc. Galeries Nationales du Grand Palais. Paris, 1980.
Viollet-le-Duc 1814-1879 (Architectural Design Profile). New York, 1980.
Viollet-le-Duc e il restauro degli edifici in Francia. Milan, 1981.

VORONIKHIN
Panov, V. A. *Arkhitektor A. N. Voronikhin.* Moscow, 1937.
See also ZAKHAROV.

VOYSEY
Betjeman, J. 'Charles Francis Annesley Voysey; The Architect of Individualism', *Architectural Review*, LXX (1931), 93-6.
Brandon-Jones, J. *C. F. A. Vosssey: Architect and Designer, 1857-1941.* London, 1978.
Brandon-Jones, J. 'Voysey', *Journal of the Architectural Association* (1957).
Gebhard, D. *Charles F. A. Voysey.* Los Angeles, 1975.
Pevsner, N. 'Charles Francis Annesley Voysey', *Elsevier's Maandschrift*, 1940, 343-55.
Symonds, J. *Catalogue of the Drawings Collection of the Royal Institute of British Architects: Voysey.* Farnborough, 1976.

WAGNER
Geretsegger, H. *Otto Wagner, 1841-1918.* New York, 1970.
Geretsegger, H., and Peinter, M. *Otto Wagner 1841-1918: The Expanding City, the Beginning of Modern Architecture.* New York, 1979.
Lux, J. A. *Otto Wagner.* Berlin, 1919.
Pozzetto, M. *Die Schule Otto Wagners 1894-1912.* Vienna, 1980.
Wagner, O. *Einige Skizzen, Projekte und ausgeführte Bauwerke.* 4 vols. Vienna, 1890-1922.

WAHLMAN
Lind, S., and others (eds.). *Verk av L. I. Wahlman.* Stockholm, 1950.

WALLOT
Streiter, R. *Das neue Reichstagshaus in Berlin von Paul Wallot.* Berlin, 1894.

WALTER
Ennis, R. B. *Thomas Ustick Walter, Architect.* Philadelphia, 1979.
Girard College, Philadelphia. *Building Committee Annual Report.* Philadelphia, 1836-48.
Newcomb, R. 'Thomas U. Walter', *The Architect*, August, 1928.

WEBB
Brandon-Jones, J. 'The Work of Philip Webb and

Norman Shaw', *Architectural Association Journal*, LXXI (1955), 9–21.

Lethaby, W. *Philip Webb and his Work.* London, 1935.

WEINBRENNER

Valdenaire, A. *Friedrich Weinbrenner, sein Leben und seine Bauten.* Karlsruhe, 1919.

Weinbrenner, F. (ed. A. von Schneider). *Denkwürdigkeiten.* Karlsruhe [1958].

WELZENBACHER

Achleitner, F. *Lois Welzenbacher, 1889–1955.* Salzburg, 1968.

WHITE

Baldwin, C. *Stanford White.* New York, 1931.

See also MCKIM, MEAD & WHITE.

WIGHT

Landau, S. B. *P. B. Wight: Architect, Contractor and Critic, 1838–1925.* Chicago, 1981.

WILKINS

Liscombe, R. W. *William Wilkins 1778–1839.* New York, 1980.

WITHERS

Kowsky, F. R. *The Architecture of Frederick Clarke Withers and the Progress of the Gothic Revival in America after 1850.* Middletown, Conn., 1980.

WRIGHT

Ausgeführte Bauten und Entwürfe von Frank Lloyd Wright. [Berlin, 1910]; new ed., *Buildings, Plans and Designs,* New York [1963].

Brooks, H. A. (ed.). *Writings on Wright: Selected Comments on Frank Lloyd Wright.* Cambridge, Mass., 1981.

Brooks, H. A. (ed.). *Frank Lloyd Wright and the Prairie School.* New York, 1984.

Connors, J. *The Robie House of Frank Lloyd Wright.* Chicago, 1984.

Cowles, L. A. (comp.). *An Index and Guide to an Autobiography, the 1943 edition, by Frank Lloyd Wright.* Hopkins, Minn., 1977.

Doremus, T. *Frank Lloyd Wright and Le Corbusier: The Great Dialogue.* New York, 1985.

Drexler, A. *The Drawings of Frank Lloyd Wright.* New York, 1962.

Eaton, L. K. *Two Chicago Architects and their Clients: Frank Lloyd Wright and Howard Van Doren Shaw.* Cambridge, Mass., 1969.

Frank Lloyd Wright: Ausgeführte Bauten (introduction by C. R. Ashbee). Berlin, 1911.

'Frank Lloyd Wright', *Architectural Forum,* XCIV (Jan., 1951), 73–108.

Frank Lloyd Wright Drawings for a Living Architecture. New York, 1960.

Gol'dshtĕin, A. F. *Frank Lloïd Raĭt.* Moscow, 1973

Gutheim, F. (ed.) *Frank Lloyd Wright on Archi-*

tecture: Selected Writings, 1894–1940. New York, 1941.

Hanks, D. *The Decorative Designs of Frank Lloyd Wright.* New York, 1979.

Hanna, P. R. and J. S. *Frank Lloyd Wright's Hanna House: The Client's Report.* Cambridge, Mass., 1981.

Hanna, P. R. and J. S. *The Hanna House Documents.* Cambridge, Mass., 1982.

Hitchcock, H. R. *In the Nature of Materials: the Buildings of Frank Lloyd Wright, 1887–1941.* New York, 1942.

Hoffman, D. *Frank Lloyd Wright's Fallingwater.* New York, 1978.

Hoffman, D. *Frank Lloyd Wright's Robie House.* New York, 1984.

Izzo, A., and Gubitosi, C. *Frank Lloyd Wright, Three Quarters of a Century of Drawings.* New York, 1981.

Kaufmann, E. 'Frank Lloyd Wright at The Metropolitan Museum of Art', *Metropolitan Museum Bulletin* (Fall, 1982).

Kaufmann, E. *Taliesin Drawings: Recent Architecture of Frank Lloyd Wright.* New York, 1952.

Kaufmann, E., and Raeburn, B. *Frank Lloyd Wright Writings and Buildings.* New York, 1960.

Kief-Nederwöhrmeier, H. *Frank Lloyd Wright und Europa.* Stuttgart, 1983.

Lipman, J. *Frank Lloyd Wright and the Johnson Wax Buildings.* New York, 1986.

McArthur, S. de F. *Frank Lloyd Wright ... American System Built Homes in Milwaukee.* Milwaukee, 1985.

Manson, G. C. *Frank Lloyd Wright to 1910.* New York, 1958.

Meehan, P. J. *Frank Lloyd Wright: A Research Guide to Archival Sources.* New York, 1983.

Muschamp, H. *Man About Town: Frank Lloyd Wright in New York City.* Cambridge, Mass., 1983.

Pfeiffer, B. B. *Frank Lloyd Wright, Treasures of Taliesin, 76 Unbuilt Designs.* Fresno, 1985.

Starosciak, K. *Frank Lloyd Wright: a Bibliography.* [New Brighton, Minn., 1973.]

Storrer, W. A. *The Architecture of Frank Lloyd Wright: A Complete Catalogue.* 2nd ed. Cambridge, Mass., 1982.

Sweeney, R. L. *Frank Lloyd Wright: An Annotated Bibliography.* Los Angeles, 1978.

Twombly, R. C. *Frank Lloyd Wright; an Interpretive Biography.* New York, 1973.

Twombly, R. C. *Frank Lloyd Wright: His Life and Architecture.* New York, 1979.

Wijdeveld, H. T. (ed.). *The Life Work of the American Architect, Frank Lloyd Wright.* Amsterdam, 1925; 2nd ed., New York, 1965.

Wright, F. Ll. *An Autobiography.* New York, 1943.
Wright, F. Ll. *A Testament.* New York, 1957.
Wright, O. Ll. *Frank Lloyd Wright: his Life, his Work, his Words.* New York [1966].
WYATT FAMILY
Linstrum, D. The Wyatt *Catalogue of the Drawings Collection of the Royal Institute of British Architects; The Wyatt Family.* [Farnborough, 1973.]
Robinson, J. M. *The Wyatts; An Architectural Dynasty.* New York, 1979.
WYATT (J.)
Dale, A. *James Wyatt.* Oxford, 1956.

WYATT (M. D.)
Pevsner, N. *Matthew Digby Wyatt.* London, 1950.
WYATVILLE
Linstrum, D. *Sir Jeffry Wyatville, Architect to the King.* Oxford, 1972.
YBL
Ybl, E. *Ybl Miklós.* Budapest, 1956.
YORKE
The Architecture of Yorke, Rosenberg, Mardall, 1944-72. London/New York [1972].
ZAKHAROV
Arkin, D. *Zakharov i Voronikhin.* Moscow, 1953.

LIST OF ILLUSTRATIONS

Abbreviation: N.B.R. National Buildings Record

274. Bernard Maybeck: Berkeley, Cal., Christian Science Church, 1910 (W. Andrews)

275. Greene & Greene: Pasadena, Cal., D. B. Gamble house, 1908-9 (W. Andrews)

276. Irving Gill: Los Angeles, Walter Dodge house, 1915-16 (E. McCoy)

277. Peter Behrens: Hagen-Eppenhausen, Cuno and Schröder houses, 1908-10 (F. Stoedtner)

278. Peter Behrens: Berlin, A.E.G. Turbine Factory, 1909-10 (F. Stoedtner)

279. Peter Behrens: Berlin, A.E.G. Small Motors Factory, 1910 (F. Stoedtner)

280. Bonatz & Scholer: Stuttgart, Railway Station, 1911-14, 1919-27 (F. Stoedtner)

281. Max Berg: Wroclav (Breslau), Jahrhunderthalle, 1910-12 (F. Stoedtner)

282. Fritz Höger: Hamburg, Chilehaus, 1923 (Staatliche Landesbildstelle, Hamburg)

283. Otto Wagner: Vienna, Postal Savings Bank, 1904-6 (Österreichische Nationalbibliothek)

284. Josef Hoffmann: Brussels, Stoclet house, 1905-11 (Archives Centrales Iconographiques, Brussels)

285. Adolf Loos: Vienna, Leopold Langer flat, 1901 (from Glück, *Adolf Loos*)

286. Adolf Loos: Vienna, Gustav Scheu house, 1912 (from Glück, *Adolf Loos*)

287. Adolf Loos: Vienna, Gustav Scheu house, 1912, plan (Courtesy of Dr Ludwig Münz)

288. Adolf Loos: Vienna, Kärntner Bar, 1907 (Gerlach)

289. H. P. Berlage: Amsterdam, Diamond Workers' Union Building, 1899-1900 (Lichtbeelden Instituut)

290. H. P. Berlage: London, Holland House, 1914 (from Gratama, *Dr H. P. Berlage, Bouwmeester*)

291. Michael de Klerk: Amsterdam, Eigen Haard housing estate, 1917 (F. Stoedtner)

292. Piet Kramer: Amsterdam, De Dageraad housing estate, 1918-23 (Lichtbeelden Instituut)

293. Walter Gropius with Adolf Meyer: Project for Chicago Tribune Tower, 1922 (W. Gropius)

294. Saarinen & Saarinen: Minneapolis, Minn., Christ Lutheran Church, 1949 (G. M. Ryan)

295. W. M. Dudok: Hilversum, Dr Bavink School, 1921 (C. A. Deul)

296. Erich Mendelsohn: Neubabelsberg, Einstein Tower, 1921 (Landbildstelle, Berlin)

297. Walter Gropius and Adolf Meyer: Alfeld-an-der-Leine, Fagus Factory, 1911 (Museum of Modern Art)

298. Le Corbusier: First project for Citrohan house, 1919-20, perspective (from Le Corbusier, *Œuvre complète*, 1)

299. Le Corbusier: Second project for Citrohan house, 1922 (from Le Corbusier, *Œuvre complète*, 1)

300. Le Corbusier: Second project for Citrohan house, 1922, plans and section (from Le Corbusier, *Œuvre complète*, 1; redrawn by Paul White)

301. Le Corbusier: Vaucresson, S.-et-O., house, 1923, plans (from Le Corbusier, *Œuvre complète*, 1)

302. Le Corbusier: Poissy, S.-et-O., Savoye house, 1929-30 (L. Hervé)

303. Le Corbusier: Poissy, S.-et-O., Savoye house, 1929-30, plan (from Hitchcock, *Modern Architecture*, p. 67)

304. Le Corbusier: Garches, S.-et-O., Les Terrasses, 1927 (Museum of Modern Art)

305. Walter Gropius: Dessau, Bauhaus, 1925-6 (Museum of Modern Art)

306. Walter Gropius: Dessau, Bauhaus, 1925-6, plans (from Hitchcock, *Modern Architecture*, p. 67; redrawn by Paul White)

307. Walter Gropius: Dessau, City Employment Office, 1927-8 (Museum of Modern Art)

308. Walter Gropius: Berlin, Siemensstadt housing estate, 1930 (Museum of Modern Art)

309. Ludwig Mies van der Rohe: Project for brick country house, 1923, plan (from Johnson, *Mies van der Rohe*, p. 32)

310. Ludwig Mies van der Rohe: Stuttgart, block of flats, Weissenhof, 1927 (Museum of Modern Art)

311. Ludwig Mies van der Rohe: Barcelona Exhibition, German Pavilion, 1929 (photo, F. Stoedtner; plan from C. Philip Johnson, *Mies van der Rohe* (Stuttgart, 1947), redrawn by Paul White)

312. Ludwig Mies van der Rohe: Brno, Tugendhat house, 1930, plan (from Hitchcock, *Modern Architecture*, p. 127)

313. G. T. Rietveld: Utrecht, Schröder house, 1924 (F. Stoedtner)

314. J. J. P. Oud: Hook of Holland, housing estate, 1926-7 (Museum of Modern Art)

315. J. J. P. Oud: Rotterdam, church, Kiefhoek housing estate, 1928-30 (Museum of Modern Art)

316. Brinkman & van der Vlugt: Rotterdam, van Nelle Factory, 1927 (E. M. van Ojen)

317. Howe & Lescaze: Philadelphia, Philadelphia Savings Fund Society Building, 1932 (Museum of Modern Art)

318. Tecton: London, Regent's Park Zoo, Penguin Pool, 1933 (Museum of Modern Art)

319. Giuseppe Terragni: Como, Casa del Fascio, 1932-6 (G. E. Kidder Smith)

320. Le Corbusier: Paris, Swiss Hostel, Cité Universitaire, 1931-2 (L. Hervé)

321. Lúcio Costa, Oscar Niemeyer, and others (Le Corbusier consultant): Rio de Janeiro, Ministry of Education and Health, 1937-42 (G. E. Kidder-Smith)

INDEX

References to the notes are given only where they indicate matters of special interest or importance: such references are given to the page on which the note occurs, followed by the number of the chapter to which it belongs, and the number of the note. Thus $611(13)^{11}$ indicates page 611, chapter 13, note 11. The system followed in towns and cities is to print the name of the building first, followed where applicable by the name of the street in which it is located and by the district or suburb. Thus the White House,

Tite Street, Chelsea, will be found in the main London entry under White House, and Saint-Jean-Baptiste, Neuilly, in the main Paris entry under Saint-Jean-Baptiste; each, however, is cross-referenced in the main index, as Chelsea, see London (White House). More remote suburbs generally have separate entries. Country houses are entered under their own names rather than under nearby towns and villages. Individual architects are not cross-referenced to firms if theirs is the first name in the firm's title.